Youth Activism

An International Encyclopedia

Volume 2: K–Z

Lonnie R. Sherrod
Editor

Constance A. Flanagan and Ron Kassimir
Associate Editors

Amy K. Syvertsen
Assistant Editor

GREENWOOD PRESS
Westport, Connecticut • London

Library of Congress Cataloging-in-Publication Data

Youth activism : an international encyclopedia /
  Lonnie R. Sherrod, editor.
    p. cm.
  Includes bibliographical references and index.
  ISBN 0–313–32811–0 (set : alk. paper)—ISBN 0–313–32812–9
(v. 1 : alk. paper)—ISBN 0–313–32813–7 (v. 2 : alk. paper)
    1. Youth—Political activity—Encyclopedias.   2. Social action—Encyclopedias.
3. Political participation—Encyclopedias.   4. Social advocacy—Encyclopedias.
5. Student movements—Encyclopedias.   6. Youth development—
Encyclopedias.   I. Sherrod, Lonnie R.
  HQ799.2.P6Y65   2006
  320'.0835'03—dc22   2005019216

British Library Cataloguing in Publication Data is available.

Library of Congress Catalog Card Number: 2005019216
ISBN: 0–313–32811–0 (set)
      0–313–32812–9 (v.1)
      0–313–32813–7 (v.2)

First published in 2006

Greenwood Press, 88 Post Road West, Westport, CT 06881
An imprint of Greenwood Publishing Group, Inc.
www.greenwood.com

Printed in the United States of America

The paper used in this book complies with the
Permanent Paper Standard issued by the National
Information Standards Organization (Z39.48–1984).

10 9 8 7 6 5 4 3 2 1

We dedicate this encyclopedia to all those young people throughout history who have risked their own well-being, comfort, and safety to make the world a better place for their fellow men and women. They are our youth activists.

Contents

List of Entries

Guide to Related Topics

Adolescent and Youth Development

Acculturation
Adult Partners in Youth Activism
Adult Roles in Youth Activism
Child Labor
Civic Engagement in Diverse Youth
Civic Identity
Civic Virtue
Communication and Youth Socialization
Community Collaboration
Community Justice
Community Service
Developmental Assets
Emerging Adulthood
Empathy
Empowerment
Ethnic Identity
Flow: Youth Motivation and Engagement
Identity and Activism
Moral Development
Moral Exemplars

Peer Influences on Political Development
Personality and Youth Political Involvement
Positive Development
Prosocial Behaviors
Pubertal Timing
Rights of Participation of Children
    and Youth
Rights, Youth Perceptions of
School Engagement
School Influences and Civic Engagement
Service Learning
Service Learning and Citizenship Education
Social-Emotional Learning Programs
    for Youth
Social Justice
Social Responsibility
Social Trust
Spirituality
Voice
Volunteerism

Adult Involvement with Youth

Adult Partners in Youth Activism
Adult Roles in Youth Activism
Adultism
Athletic-Square Model of Youth Sport
Character Education
Civil Society and Positive Youth Development
Communication and Youth Socialization
Community Collaborations
Empowerment
Environmental Education (EE)
Ethnic Identity
4-H
Generational Conflict
Generational Replacement

Identity and Organizing in Older Youth
Intergenerational Programs and Practices
Juvenile Justice
Moral Exemplars
Parental Influences on Youth Activism
Political Participation and Youth Councils
Positive Youth Development, Programs
    Promoting
Racial Socialization
Urban Communities, Youth
    Programming in
Youth Commissions
Youth-Led Action Research, Evaluation,
    and Planning

Advocacy for Social Causes

Advocacy
Advocacy Day
American Indian Movement (AIM)
Animal Rights
Anti-Nazi Youth Resistance
Anti-Tobacco Youth Activism
Antiwar Activism
Campus Compact
Campus Crusade for Christ International
  (CCC)
Child Labor
Child Soldiers
Civic Environmentalism
Civil Rights Movement
Community Justice
Earth Force
Environmental Education (EE)
Feminism
Gay-Straight Alliances in Schools (GSAs)

Global Justice Activism
Grassroots Youth Movements
High-School Students' Rights Movement
  of the 1960s
Juvenile Justice
Labor Movement
Mental-Health Advocacy in Youth
Political Consumerism
Rights of Participation of Children
  and Youth
Social Justice
Social Movements
Student Action with Farmworkers (SAF)
Student Political Activism
Sustainability
Terrorism, Youth Activism
  Responses to
United Students Against Sweatshops
  (USAS)

Education

Acculturation
Adult Partners in Youth Activism
AmeriCorps
Athletic-Square Model of Youth Sport
Campus Compact
Campus Crusade for Christ International
  (CCC)
Catholic Education and the Ethic of Social
  Justice
Character Education
Citizenship Education Policies in the States
Deliberative Democracy
Democratic Education
Digital Divide
Diversity Education
Earth Force
Environmental Education (EE)
Gay-Straight Alliances in Schools (GSAs)
Global Citizenship Education (GCE) in the
  United States

High-School Students' Rights Movement
  of the 1960s
IEA Civic Education Study
Just Community High Schools and Youth
  Activism
Kids Voting USA (KVUSA)
National Alliance for Civic Education
  (NACE)
National and Community Service
Public Scholarship
School Engagement
School Influences and Civic Engagement
Service Learning
Service Learning and Citizenship Education
Social-Emotional Learning Programs
  for Youth
Student Political Activism
Student Voices Project
*Tinker v. Des Moines Independent School
  District* (1969)

Gender and Sexuality

AIDS Advocacy in South Africa
Chat Rooms, Girls' Empowerment and

Empowerment
Feminism

Global and Transnational Issues

Historical Examples, Causes, and Movements

International Examples of Activism and Social Movements

Indonesia, Youth Activism in
National Identity and Youth
Nigeria, Youth Activism in
Palestinian *Intifada*
Russia, Youth Activism in
Serbia, Youth Activism in (1990–2000)
Soweto Youth Activism (South Africa)

Statute of the Child and Adolescent
   (Brazil)
Tiananmen Square Massacre (1989)
Turkey, Youth Activism in
United Nations, Youth Activism and
Zapatista Rebellion (Mexico)
Zionist Youth Organizations

Law and Justice

Catholic Education and the Ethic of
   Social Justice
Community Justice
Democracy
Democratic Education
Gangs
Gangs and Politics
Homies Unidos
Juvenile Justice
Mental-Health Advocacy and Youth

Racial and Ethnic Inequality
Rights of Participation of Children
   and Youth
Rights, Youth Perceptions of
Social Justice
Social Responsibility
State and Youth, the
Statute of the Child and Adolescent (Brazil)
Tinker v. Des Moines Independent
   School District (1969)

Media and Internet Influences and Uses

Advocacy Day
Chat Rooms, Girls' Empowerment and
Communication and Youth Socialization
Digital Divide
Empowerment
Film/Video as Tool for Youth Activism
Global Justice Activism
Hip-Hop Generation

Mental-Health Advocacy in Youth
MTV's Choose or Lose Campaign (1992–)
New Media
Participatory Action Research (PAR) by Youth
Political Consumerism
Public Art
Punk Rock Youth Subculture
Terrorism, Youth Activism Responses to

Organizations and Programs

Advocacy Day
American Indian Movement (AIM)
AmeriCorps
Campus Compact
Campus Crusade for Christ International
   (CCC)
Civilian Conservation Corps (CCC)
Earth Force
4-H
Global Youth Action Network (GYAN)
Homies Unidos
Innovations in Civic Participation (ICP)
Intergenerational Programs and Practices
Jesuit Volunteer Corps (JVC)
KidSpeak

Kids Voting USA (KVUSA)
MTV's Choose or Lose Campaign (1992–)
National Alliance for Civic Education
   (NACE)
Participatory Action Research (PAR)
   by Youth
Student Action with Farmworkers (SAF)
Student Voices Project
United Nations, Youth Activism and
United Students Against Sweatshops
   (USAS)
Youth Commissions
Youth Leadership for Development
   Initiative (YLDI)
Zionist Youth Organizations

Political Context

Positive Youth Development

Social Justice
Social Responsibility
Social Trust
Spirituality

Urban Communities, Youth Programming in
Volunteerism
Youth Leadership for Development
    Initiative (YLDI)

Religion

Campus Crusade for Christ International
    (CCC)
Catholic Education and the Ethic of
    Social Justice
Civic Virtue
Community Justice
Community Service
Empathy
Identity and Activism
Jesuit Volunteer Corps (JVC)

Moral Cognition and Youth Activism
Moral Development
Moral Exemplars
Prosocial Behaviors
Religiosity and American Youth
Religiosity and Civic Engagement in African
    American Youth
Social Justice
Spirituality
Zionist Youth Organizations

Social Background Factors

Acculturation
Arab Americans
Australia, Youth Activism in
Civic Engagement in Diverse Youth
Civil Rights Movement
Demographic Trends Affecting the
    World's Youth
Diversity Education
Emerging Adulthood
Ethnic Identity
Gender Differences in the Political
    Attitudes of Youth
Generational Replacement
Homies Unidos
Identity and Activism
Identity and Organizing in Older Youth
Immigrant Youth in the United States
Juvenile Justice

Minority Youth Voter Turnout
Native American Youth
Nigeria, Youth Activism in
Parental Influences on Youth Activism
Peer Influences on Political Development
Personality and Youth Political Involvement
Poverty, Welfare Reform, and Adolescents
Pubertal Timing
Queer, Sexuality, and Gender Activism
Racial and Ethnic Inequality
Racial Socialization
Religiosity and American Youth
Religiosity and Civic Engagement in
    African American Youth
Serbia, Youth Activism in (1990–2000)
Soweto Youth Activism (South Africa)
Spirituality
Transnational Identity

Social Relationships and Networks

Adult Partners in Youth Activism
Adult Roles in Youth Activism
Animal Rights
Anti-Nazi Youth Resistance
Anti-Tobacco Youth Activism
Antiwar Activism
Community Collaboration
Community Service

Developmental Assets
Gangs
Gangs and Politics
Gay-Straight Alliances in Schools (GSAs)
Global Youth Action Network (GYAN)
Grassroots Youth Movements
High-School Students' Rights Movement
    of the 1960s

Voices of Activism

Youth Culture

K

KidSpeak. KidSpeak is a youth public forum that empowers young people to advocate on their own behalf. Operating on a statewide and local basis, KidSpeak brings youth before listening panels comprised of legislators, other public officials, and community leaders to speak out on issues important to them. KidSpeak forums are typically held in policymaking settings such as the state capitol and city halls to provide young people with an authentic civic engagement experience and to provide policymakers the rare opportunity to hear the voices of young people. Given the opportunity, in ways both poignant and powerful, youth can change the way adults make decisions.

Critical elements to help meet the objectives of KidSpeak events include identifying a diverse group, providing a structured program, and providing an authentic civic engagement for young people to experience in the public-policy space. Targeted recruitment has proven essential to incorporating young people who can provide authentic stories that relate to various issues facing other youth, their communities, and the state. To ensure diversity in perspective, young people are recruited from a range of ethnic, economic, and geographic backgrounds. Young people who possess leadership potential but are not always identified as traditional youth leaders are also identified. Middle-school and high-school-age youth are recruited from across the state from youth-focused direct-service organizations such as schools, child-welfare providers, and after-school programs. During the youth recruitment process, Michigan's Children also recruits a listening panel of twenty to twenty-five people. Invitations are sent to legislators, government administrators, the state board of education, representatives of major private funders, major business interests, and other opinion leaders from Michigan's Children's board and elsewhere. During campaign cycles, candidates for office and office holders are invited.

A structured process and agenda is planned to help engage policymakers and to provide the safe space for young people to share their stories. KidSpeak is generally held in the state capitol and sometimes at city halls for local events—the same places adults go to testify before the legislature and other government leaders. Young people are asked not only to share the problems they face in their communities but also to share solutions. Written testimony is requested prior to the event from each speaker, to simulate the experience of testifying in a government hearing. Typically, there is no topic identified for a statewide KidSpeak, but, at times, pressing policy requires a theme. At the event, Michigan's Children's president and CEO provides an overview of the KidSpeak concept, introduces the listening panel, and calls up the youth speakers one at a time to testify. Michigan's Children schedules a half hour at the end of the proceedings to allow the listening panel to ask questions or clarify a speaker's point.

Today there are a lot of programs which allow youth to speak out on issues. What makes KidSpeak unique is that it provides an authentic experience where young people testify in the same manner as adults—in the same place, to the same people, and in the same format. Feedback from youth participants have shown that young people feel empowered by the experience, which enables them to express their thoughts on issues affecting them. Many young people have also shown improvement in their self-esteem. The KidSpeak program also promotes future civic involvement. As a statewide advocacy group, KidSpeak allows Michigan's Children to "put a face" on the important issues members of government address in policies affecting young people. Officials appreciate hearing from their youngest constituency, something atypical in their busy schedules. The program keeps Michigan's Children, an organization that does not provide direct services to youth, in tune with what is occurring in the lives of youth in the state. Michigan's Children records and uses the testimony shared at KidSpeak in materials sent to supporters and to government officials.

KidSpeak is a part of Michigan's Children's Youth Policy Leadership Program (YPLP) that is designed to empower young people by providing them with opportunities for meaningful participation in civic life. YPLP is a chance for young people to learn how to become effective citizens and to take active roles in their communities, thus laying the foundation from which future leaders may emerge. YPLP connects youth to policymaking through KidSpeak and Youth Legislative Day activities. In addition, Michigan's Children alerts communities to public-policy issues affecting youth and provides technical assistance to communities to build capacity for youth-led policy forums. Through YPLP the organization also provides advocacy training and facilitates opportunities for young people to interact with state-level policymakers, including opportunities to testify at legislative hearings.

Michigan's Children is a statewide, multi-issue, independent, broad-based advocacy group that acts as a policy voice for children and youth. The organization works with policymakers, other organizations, businesses, communities, and the public to improve the quality of life for children and their families and to ensure that every young person in Michigan has an opportunity to become a healthy, productive, and responsible adult. Michigan's Children is a member of Voices for America's Children, a national organization based in Washington, D.C., committed to working at the state and local levels to improve the well-being of children.

See also Advocacy; Communication and Youth Socialization; Empowerment; Student Voices Project.

Recommended Reading

Irby, M., Ferber, T., Pittman, K., with Tolman, J., and Yohalem, N., (2001). *Youth Action: Youth Contributing to Communities, Communities Supporting Youth.* Community and Youth Development Series, Vol. 6. Takoma Park, MD: Forum for Youth Investment, International Youth Foundation.

Zeldin, S., McDaniel, A. K., Topitzes, D., and Calvert, M. (2000). *Youth in Decision-Making: A Study of the Impacts of Youth on Adults and Organizations.* Madison: University of Wisconsin Press.

Shanetta Martin

Kids Voting USA (KVUSA). Kids Voting USA (KVUSA), a curriculum taught during election campaigns, seeks to create a microcosm of deliberative democracy as students analyze candidate messages, monitor news coverage, and prepare for classroom discussions and debates. The energy and excitement created by KVUSA has produced some surprising and unintended effects. When cultivated by interactive lesson plans, youth discussion triggers a flow of political contagion that extends beyond the school itself, into families and adolescent peer groups. Exchanges of opinions, knowledge, and perspectives create an expanding field of political discussion that connects otherwise separate settings, such as the classroom and the living room. As the drama of Election Day builds, students bounce ideas back and forth among themselves and between teachers and parents. Even parents who had never shown any interest in politics get caught up in this web of adolescent enthusiasm.

The interactive approach of KVUSA contrasts with the passive learning of many standard curricula in which students acquire

Children participate in the Kids Voting Program. *Courtesy of Kids Voting Massachusetts.*

textbook knowledge of government but not a passion for political expression. Kids Voting students themselves seem to defy the expectations of a pessimistic cadre of scholars, who have for decades dismissed schools as ineffective agents of political socialization and who have complained about the supposed apathy of American youth.

While unique in several respects, Kids Voting USA is part of a larger movement in the United States to reassert the civic mission of schools in preparing young people for citizenship. A confluence of factors has inspired an era of curriculum experimentation. Studies show a widening gap between youth and adults in political engagement, generating widespread concern among educators and political scientists. And institutions that historically worked to mobilize youth, most notably the two major parties, have largely given up on youth outreach, according to critics. Consequently,

schools have been described as perhaps the last and the best opportunity to revitalize a youth culture of political engagement. Promising initiatives include the extension of service learning to political participation and the use of new technology to create simulations such as online diplomatic negotiations (see also Intergenerational Programs and Practices, School Influences and Civic Engagement, Service Learning, Service Learning and Citizenship Education, and Student Voices Project).

KVUSA stands out in this flurry of innovation by virtue of a holistic strategy that integrates the influences of classrooms, peer groups, families, news media, and elections. This synergistic approach provides a hopeful view of the potential for youth activism in light of much research showing that when schools, families, and news media act in isolation to each other, they are often ineffective as agents of political socialization. Kids Voting works through lesson plans that encourage students to obtain information about candidates and ballot issues during the final months of an election campaign, to coincide with the initial months of the school year. By preparing for and participating in peer-centered discussions in school, students acquire confidence and motivation for initiating political conversations at home. Sometimes homework assignments incorporate family discussion, as when adolescents interview parents about their voting histories and candidate preferences. But research on Kids Voting's effects suggests that many of these conversations at home are initiated *spontaneously* by students. A teenager with a head full of opinions and the confidence to express partisan views for the first time can be a formidable force indeed. And while parents might not always appreciate a politically precocious child, the discussions that follow benefit both children and parents in terms of increased political involvement.

The family-inclusive approach of Kids Voting began with a hunch and in an unlikely setting for rethinking the role of schools in civic education. On a fishing trip to Costa Rica, three businessmen from Arizona learned that that country enjoyed a voter turnout rate of about 80 percent. A tradition of children accompanying parents to the polls helped to account for the high turnout. Thus began Kids Voting USA as the three men returned to Arizona and supported a pilot program involving forty schools in metropolitan Phoenix. The nonpartisan, nonprofit program went statewide in 1990 with 750,000 students and 17,000 teachers. KVUSA branched out to eleven states in 1992 and in 2004 encompassed 4.3 million students and 200,000 teachers in 10,600 schools, 17,000 voter precincts in more than thirty states, and 50,000 volunteers.

As a strategy for student-centered learning, KVUSA creates incentives and opportunities for deliberation. In political philosophy, deliberative democracy refers to a participatory system in which citizens voluntarily engage in discussion to share knowledge, to express and to refine opinions, and to understand the perspectives of others (see also Deliberative Democracy). Research has shown that KVUSA students become more skilled at holding political conversations by embracing many of the ideals for discourse espoused by theorists of deliberative democracy. For instance, the curriculum promotes dispositions such as the confidence to challenge others, the courage to express unpopular opinions, and the willingness to listen to opponents. Students learn to participate in spirited but respectful discourse. Also evident is a desire that is at the heart of deliberative democracy—motivation to validate opinions by testing them out in conversations and seeing if they are persuasive in various settings outside the classroom.

Kids Voting embodies a multipronged approach through experiential learning, cooperative activities, and group problem solving. Lesson plans are designed for each grade level (K–12). For example, teachers might ask K–2 students to decorate a "wish tree" with stars that declare their hopes for the future of their schools and neighborhoods. This exercise promotes civic-mindedness and community awareness. Students in grades 6–8 might evaluate information on a candidate by processing the information through a decision-making chart that asks questions about the credibility and reliability of sources. Students not only learn about candidates and issues, they achieve higher levels of media literacy as they think critically about news coverage and political advertisements.

The overall program includes three domains. Within the classroom, Civics Alive! promotes the rights and responsibilities of voting and the principle that citizens should study and discuss electoral issues. The program reaches out to new communities with a bilingual "Family Guide/*Guía Familiar*." Students use the guide for activities such as creating a family election album and acting as political reporters to interview family members about their views on voting.

Second, KVUSA offers service-learning opportunities for high-school students in its Destination Democracy program. Activities provide meaningful civic engagement through registering voters, mentoring younger students, researching and debating public-policy issues, and working for candidates. Teenagers become involved in political processes rather than merely learning about them from a textbook.

The final aspect of the program is the actual voting of students on Election Day; students cast ballots alongside parents in a concurrent election. The youngest students vote on at least one candidate race and proposition while the high-school students vote on as many state and federal ballot questions as possible. Community volunteers help to coordinate the mock voting exercise at polling sites and local news media often publicize the results, documenting the extent to which students agree or disagree with parents on key issues.

The innovative aspects of Kids Voting have drawn a great deal of interest from scholars of political socialization. Evaluations in various regions of the country and in numerous election cycles have made KVUSA the most intensely studied curriculum aimed at electoral activism. Bruce Merrill and James Simon conducted the first studies of Kids Voting's effects in the early 1990s and documented positive assessments from students and teachers, along with increased voting turnout among parents. Their studies confirmed that Kids Voting boosts adult turnout in the range of 3–5 percent. In 1996 Diana Carlin found that in Kansas communities with a KVUSA program, the voting rate for registered eighteen-year-olds was 14 percent higher than for peers not exposed to the curriculum.

Perhaps the most remarkable characteristic of KVUSA is the way it interacts with families even though such connections are often inadvertent. By interaction we mean that Kids Voting's influences are often magnified by family background or by the way in which family members respond collectively. These interactions involve *closing gaps* in political involvement, a second chance at citizenship for parents, the stimulation of *civic parenting*, the transformation of the family into a *domestic sphere* for deliberation, and the genesis of political identity.

Research in San Jose, California, in 1994 showed that the curriculum was particularly effective for students of low socioeconomic status (SES). A research team led by the late Steven Chaffee at Stanford University reported that the curriculum narrowed or completely closed gaps between high- and low-SES students for indicators of news-media use, political discussion, and the formation of partisan opinions. In a separate evaluation of the same program, Jack McLeod at the University of Wisconsin–Madison showed that the curriculum reduced the gender gap for election knowledge. While boys benefited as well, girls increased substantially their frequency of political discussion with parents and peers.

KVUSA also appears to promote equality of political interest with respect to ethnicity. An evaluation of the program in El Paso County, Colorado, in 2002 revealed that Hispanic students benefited the most from the curriculum. These students apparently became concerned about a proposed state amendment to enforce English-only instruction. Kids Voting interacted with family ethnic background to narrow or completely close gaps in attention to news, attention to the amendment campaign, knowledge, integration of new information, willingness to listen to opposing views, willingness to disagree, and support for political participation.

The curriculum's promotion of civic equality reveals a pleasant irony. While low-SES parents were typically not socialized to politics as children themselves, family discussion prompted by Kids Voting provides them with a second chance at civic involvement. This occurs through "trickle-up influence." Students in many of these homes—not parents—take the lead in initiating conversations about an election campaign. In anticipation of future conversations, parents pay more attention to news, acquire knowledge, and adopt partisan opinions.

Kids Voting, in fact, has helped to resolve a dilemma that stymied social scientists for decades. The problem of political disengagement is intertwined with socioeconomic status, so that household income and parents' educational background strongly predict the likelihood that parents and their children will be interested in politics. Well-meaning efforts to promote equality in civic participation often backfire because only the higher SES families usually pay attention to news media and information campaigns. Despite the historic increase in literacy and the expansion of mass media, low-SES adults have often been dismissed as "chronic know-nothings." Their offspring seemed destined to the same fate of disengagement because politics and news are rarely discussed in these homes. The same problem of household civic deficits occurs in many communities of ethnic minorities. And these barriers to active citizenship are exacerbated by what one author calls the "savage inequalities" of public funding for disadvantaged school districts. Schools possess the capability of reaching children from all backgrounds, but the potential of instruction to reach parents with political messages was scarcely imagined by theorists until the emergence of Kids Voting. By experimenting with lesson plans that motivate students to talk with parents about elections, Kids Voting illustrates how schools can engage parents indirectly.

The phenomenon of trickle-up influence is connected to recent evidence that Kids Voting makes adults more aware of their responsibilities in the realm of civic parenting. When students initiate political conversations at home, parents become more interested in what is being taught in the classroom. One consequence is that parents encourage students to express political opinions at school. A boomerang dynamic occurs as schools stimulate student discussion at home, which prompts parents to motivate their children to contribute more actively in classroom discussions and debates. In the long term, adult interest in civics instruction might lead to other positive outcomes such as parents volunteering for school activities or otherwise becoming more involved in communities. The promotion of civic parenting could be particularly beneficial for immigrant or politically disengaged parents.

We can think of the family's response to Kids Voting in the way that aspen leaves shimmer in the wind. Family members are connected in reciprocal interaction, just as leaves from the same branch respond jointly to air currents. The flow of discussion originates from KVUSA students during campaigns, but the family as a social system adapts to the need for increased political competence. When children and parents encourage each other to express opinions and to pay attention to news, the family can be viewed as a domestic sphere for informal conversations about public affairs. This "ordinary political talk," as some scholars describe it, is significant because formal discourse in public settings is intimidating to many citizens. After all, politics is about the expression of conflicting values. The family as a domestic sphere provides a relatively safe setting for practicing political expression, such as testing out tentative opinions and validating whether personal hunches are persuasive. This is not to say that all parents embrace a teenager's partisan opinions. But this tension is often resolved by parents arming themselves with increased political knowledge. Recent research shows that when the family operates this way—as a domestic sphere—students and parents are more willing to express themselves in public settings such as city council meetings.

Finally, Kids Voting interacts with families in the formation of political identification. We no longer live in an era in which many adolescents simply adopt the partisan views of their parents (see also Civic Identity and Parental Influences on Youth Activism). The direct inheritance of partisan identification seems implausible given evidence that compelling issues, not party loyalty, mobilize youth activism. Often young people are interested in participation that bypasses the two major parties, as reflected in the street theater of protests and the creative use of the Internet to confront corporations (see also Political Consumerism). But the family is still important in political socialization because adolescents are curious as to how their opinions stack up with those of parents. KVUSA seems to nudge adolescents down a path of identity exploration as they compare alternative perspectives from peers, teachers, media, parents, and siblings.

The documented effects of Kids Voting help us to imagine a new role for the school in preparing youth for citizenship. Schools are often described as "laboratories of democracy." But metaphors can limit insights as well as inspire. In science, labs allow researchers to isolate factors in the identification of causal processes, but often experiments are by necessity artificial in the creation of controlled conditions. Schools work best in civic education not as controlled environments, separated from other venues for political expression. Instead of viewing schools as labs for democracy, we can envision them as *staging grounds*. Schools provide the initial resources and structure for civic learning, but as Kids Voting demonstrates, students benefit the most when they trek outside the classroom to express democratic dispositions.

See also Democracy; Democratic Education; Film/Video as a Tool for Youth Activism; Minority Youth Voter Turnout; MTV's Choose or Lose Campaign (1992–); Peer Influences on Political Development; Personality and Youth Political Involvement; Political Consumerism; Political Participation and Youth Councils; Rights of Participation of Children and Youth; Student Political Activism.

Recommended Reading

Carnegie Corporation of New York and CIRCLE: Center for Information and Research on Civic Learning and Engagement (2003). *The Civic Mission of School*. New York: Carnegie Corporation of New York.

Jennings, M. K., and Niemi, R. G. (1974). *The Political Character of Adolescence: The Influence of Families and Schools*. Princeton, NJ: Princeton University Press.

Kids Voting USA (2004). *Kids Voting USA Research Summary*. See http://www.kidsvotingusa.org/.

Kim, J., Wyatt, R. O., and Katz, E. (1999). "News, Talk, Opinion, Participation: The Part Played by Conversation in Deliberative Democracy." *Political Communication*, 16: 359–360.

Kozol, J. (1991). *Savage Inequalities: Children in America's Schools*. New York: Crown Publishing.

McDevitt, M. (2002). *What Works in Civics Education? An Evaluation of the Kids Voting USA Curriculum*. John S. and James L. Knight Foundation. See http://www.knightfdn.org/default.asp?story=research/civic/kids_voting/index.html.

McDevitt, M., and Chaffee, S. H. (1998). "Second Chance Political Socialization: 'Trickle-Up' Effects of Children on Parents." In *Engaging the Public: How Government and the Media Can Reinvigorate American Democracy*, edited by T. J. Johnson, C. E. Hays, and S. P. Hays. Lanham, MD: Rowman and Littlefield, pp. 57–66.

McDevitt, M., and Chaffee, S. H. (2000). "Closing Gaps in Political Communication and Knowledge: Effects of a School Intervention." *Communication Research*, 27: 259–292.

McLeod, J. M., Eveland, W. P., Jr., and Horowitz, E. M. (1998). "Going Beyond Adults and Voter Turnout: Evaluating a Socialization Program Involving Schools, Family and Media." In *Engaging the Public: How Government and the Media Can Reinvigorate American Democracy*, edited by T. J. Johnson, C. E. Hays, and S. P. Hays. Lanham, MD: Rowman and Littlefield, pp. 217–234.

Merrill, B. D., Simon, J., and Adrian, E. (1994). "Boosting Voter Turnout: The Kids Voting Program." *Journal of Social Studies Research*, 18: 2–7.

Niemi, R. G., and Jennings, M. K. (1991). "Issues and Inheritance in the Formation of Party Identification." *American Journal of Political Science*, 35: 970–988.

Niemi, R. G., and Junn, J. (1998). *Civic Education: What Makes Students Learn*. New Haven, CT: Yale University Press.

Shermis, S. S., and Barth, J. L. (1982). "Teaching for Passive Citizenship: A Critique of Philosophical Assumptions." *Theory and Research in Social Education*, 10: 17–37.

Michael McDevitt

KVUSA. *See* Kids Voting USA (KVUSA).

L

Labor Movement. The activism of young people in the United States around labor and workplace issues can be traced back to the early twentieth century. As mass-circulation magazines and newspapers publicized the appalling conditions found in the nation's tenement houses, sweatshops, and company towns, a segment of middle- and upper-middle-class youth reacted strongly to industrial capitalism's harsh treatment of the working class. Rebelling against their genteel backgrounds and often inspired by liberal and radical ideologies, some youth went to work in factories, fields, and mines to observe conditions firsthand, while others wrote articles about their experiences, joined picket lines, or became union organizers and activists. In the working class and the labor movement, they often found the values of service, sacrifice, and solidarity that they believed were lacking in the middle class and also discovered a vehicle through which they could attempt to promote broader social change. Harvard graduate John Reed, who was active in labor struggles as both a journalist and participant, became perhaps the most visible symbol for this generation's activism and was joined by other young people who were attracted to the drama of labor conflict and the struggle to make the American workplace more just and humane.

In addition to middle-class youth who supported working-class struggles, young workers themselves were active in turn-of-the-century efforts to change conditions in their workplaces. Most notably, the epic struggles of garment workers rebelling against sweatshop conditions included many young women who not only looked to improve their lives on the job but also sought greater personal independence and the opportunity to become part of a stirring social crusade. These women were instrumental in helping to establish the International Ladies Garment Workers Union and initiating a process that began to reform the garment industry. Although the union did offer educational programs for these young activists, its ultimate commitment was ambivalent, given its view that young women would eventually marry and leave the labor force rather than remain as long-term workers. Indeed, the notion that age, in contrast to ethnicity, race, or gender, was not a fixed identity has historically limited labor's outreach to young workers and led unions to focus on older members whose commitment to the job appeared to be more enduring.

With the profound shock that accompanied the Great Depression and the upsurge of industrial unionism engineered by the Congress of Industrial Organizations (CIO), the labor movement fully emerged as a social force during the 1930s. In addition to empathizing with dispossessed workers, many young people drew closer to the labor movement as a result of their own economic hardship and the sense that corporate America had irresponsibly plunged the nation into crisis. The Socialist and especially the Communist parties attracted newly radicalized youth, directing many of them into factory work, union organizing, and support for labor struggles. The Marxian belief that the working class could act as an agent of radical social transformation seemed plausible to these young reformers and radicals, especially during the heady days of sit-down strikes, capitulation to labor by some of the nation's largest corporations, and the willingness of government to exercise greater control over corporate behavior and the conduct of labor relations. This was also a period when young working-class activists could vault into positions of labor leadership, as did James Carey of the United Electrical Workers, who at age twenty-five assumed the presidency of his union, and Harold Gibbons, who became a vice president of the American Federation of Teachers at age twenty-six.

Ironically, by the 1960s, when young activists poured their energy into the civil rights, women's, and anti–Vietnam War movements, they largely ignored the labor movement. As the founders of Students for a Democratic Society observed in their classic political manifesto, "The Port Huron Statement": "In some measure, labor has succumbed to institutionalization, its social idealism waning under the tendencies of bureaucracy, materialism, [and] business ethics" (1962). The generation gap between labor and youth grew even more pronounced as the New Left began to sharply question American foreign policy, leading to disturbing images of construction workers attacking antiwar protestors in the streets of New York in 1970. Reflecting the insurgent spirit of the decade and aligning themselves with the counterculture, many young workers joined student activists in protest, rebelling against incumbent union leadership and attacking it as unresponsive to such issues as racism, the speedup of work, and the erosion of living standards by spiraling inflation. For many student activists and young workers, the labor movement now appeared, in the parlance of the 1960s, "to be part of the problem rather than part of the solution."

Yet there was one workers' movement in the 1960s and early 1970s that did capture the imagination of young people and introduced a new generation to labor struggles: the United Farm Workers (UFW). The effort to bring justice to one of America's most marginalized and oppressed groups of workers galvanized many young people to support the union's nationwide consumer boycotts of nonunion grapes and lettuce. Finding in the UFW the kind of idealism and militancy not manifested elsewhere in the house of labor, many young activists became committed supporters and in some instances union organizers. At a time when unions were dismissed by much of the New Left, the UFW offered these young people a rare sense of connection to the labor movement. Later, many of these UFW-trained activists entered more mainstream unions, bringing with them concrete organizing skills and an expansive vision of labor's social mission.

The distance between youth and the labor movement widened, however, during the 1970s and the first half of the 1980s. Facing serious membership decline as a result of deindustrialization and the relocation of manufacturing operations overseas, unions sought to stem these job losses via protectionist legislation and support for expanded construction and real-estate development, nuclear power, and heightened defense spending. This strategy clashed with the nascent environmental, antinuclear, and smart-growth movements and also with efforts to curb military spending that were attracting the support of young activists. For many young people new to political involvement and unaware of the labor movement's history of social commitment, these conflicts reinforced labor's image as a special interest indifferent to broader notions of the common good.

It was not until the mid-1980s that the labor movement began to renew its connection with young people. Seeking to reinvigorate its declining ranks by attracting a new generation of organizers, the American Federation of Labor–Congress of Industrial Organizations (AFL-CIO) launched the Organizing Institute in 1985. The Organizing Institute has recruited and trained hundreds of young people to become union organizers over the last eighteen years, drawing heavily from student activists in an attempt to tap their energy and idealism. Although the daunting task of union organizing has led to considerable turnover among recruits, the Organizing Institute has made acquiring jobs in the labor movement much more accessible to young people and helped to revive labor's image as a place where youth can work effectively for social change.

The election of John Sweeney as AFL-CIO president in 1995 and the accession to labor leadership of many former 1960s activists has led to further efforts aimed at attracting youth to the labor movement. In addition to increasing support for the Organizing Institute, the AFL-CIO launched the Union Summer program in 1996. Modeled after the civil rights movement's Freedom Summer initiative, Union Summer offers internships to students that allow them to participate in union activities and evaluate the possibility of a career in the labor movement. The AFL-CIO and especially the Union of Needle, Industrial, and Textile Employees (UNITE) have also supported another important effort that has generated considerable activism on college campuses: the student antisweatshop movement. Coinciding with youthful concern that globalization is enriching multinational corporations and the developed world at the expense of developing nations and their workers, the antisweatshop movement has focused national attention on the conditions under which popular youth-oriented items such as sneakers and sportswear are produced. Under the aegis of United Students Against Sweatshops, this movement has pressured universities and companies to accept codes of conduct ensuring that goods are produced under humane conditions where workers' rights are respected. The student movement against sweatshops echoes similar efforts that touched the nation's conscience one hundred years earlier. The current movement features a sophisticated use of new technology to mobilize students quickly and a savvy media awareness that has garnered antisweatshop campaigns much favorable publicity.

In addition to antisweatshop activity, the last fifteen years have seen another campus-based movement that has forged new ties between youth and labor: the emergence of graduate-student unionism. Driven by sharp reductions in public funding and the tilt of research toward commercial applications, universities have increasingly employed graduate students and adjunct instructors as a cheap alternative to more expensive tenured faculty. Given these circumstances, graduate students have increasingly come to regard themselves as workers in an employment relationship who need bargaining power. In spite of fierce resistance from university administrations, graduate students are increasingly gaining legal recognition of their employee status. Nearly thirty graduate-student unions are currently recognized by public universities, although the National Labor Relations Board recently overturned a regional labor board ruling granting employee status to graduate students at a major private university. Unions are devoting considerable resources to graduate-student organizing, and these efforts can be expected to accelerate as tight higher-education budgets dictate continued reliance on graduate-student labor. This burgeoning connection between graduate students and the labor movement is creating a cohort of young professionals sympathetic to unions who will doubtless carry this awareness into subsequent workplace environments and civic engagements.

More recently, there has been a renewed interest in the relationship between youth and the world of work. According to a 1999 report from the National Research Council nearly 80 percent of high-school-age youth work at after-school jobs, and these young workers suffer job-related injuries at nearly double the rates for older workers. There is growing concern that youth have been the age-group most adversely affected by the current recession, experiencing much greater unemployment than other segments of the labor force. A 2002 survey conducted by Hart Associates for the AFL-CIO found that while young workers between the ages of eighteen and thirty-four believe deeply in the American dream, they fear their future prospects for finding secure employment and fair treatment at work are limited. Finally, new research on youth employed in service industries suggests that unions need to make special efforts to help young workers balance the competing demands of work and school and demonstrate that involvement in the labor movement can help them fulfill their aspirations. In Canada outreach to youth has advanced much more quickly than in the United States, and through youth committees, youth-oriented conferences, and projects to advance on-the-job safety, unions have begun the process of attempting to incorporate young workers' concerns into the agenda of the labor movement.

The relationship between young people and the labor movement has historically contained inherent tensions. For youth, unions have often appeared less a vibrant social movement than a distant bureaucracy mired in legalism, prone to compromise, and in the words of one critic, "pale, male, and stale." Unions are themselves conflicted about the role of youth. On the one hand, they welcome the energy and enthusiasm of the young, yet know that the romantic imagery young people often attach to the labor movement fails to appreciate the very real constraints under which unions are forced to operate. Nonetheless, the labor movement's core values of solidarity, collective action, and respect for the dignity of work should prove attractive to young people uncertain about their futures and seeking alternatives to an individualistic, market-driven culture. The rise of new opportunities for youth to become involved in unions and the growing public attention being paid to youth as workers suggest that the evolving relationship between youth and labor will become the subject of more concerted scholarly analysis and greater institutional support from the labor movement.

See also Child Labor; Child Soldiers; Civilian Conservation Corps (CCC); Empowerment; Social Movements; Social Networks; Voice.

Recommended Reading

Bussel, R. (1999). *From Harvard to the Ranks of Labor: Powers Hapgood and the American Working Class*. University Park, PA: Penn State University Press.

Foerster, A. (2001). "Confronting the Dilemmas of Organizing: Obstacles and Innovations at the AFL-CIO Organizing Institute." In *Rekindling the Movement: Labor's Quest for Relevance in the Twenty-first Century*, edited by L. Turner, H. Katz, and R. Hurd. Ithaca, NY: Cornell University Press.

Glenn, S. (1990). *Daughters of the Shtetl: Life and Labor in the Immigrant Generation*. Ithaca, NY: Cornell University Press.

Hart, P. D. Associates (2002). *High Hopes, Little Trust: A Study of Young Workers and Their Ups and Downs in the New Economy*. Washington, D.C.: AFL-CIO.

Howe, I. (1982). *A Margin of Hope: An Intellectual Autobiography*. San Diego: Harcourt Brace Jovanovich.

Lafer, G. (Summer 2003). "Graduate Student Unions: Organizing in a Changed Academic Economy." *Labor Studies Journal*, 28 (2): 1–19.

Miller, J. (1987). *"Democracy Is in the Streets": From Port Huron to the Siege of Chicago*. New York: Simon and Schuster.

National Research Council (1998). *Protecting Youth at Work: Health, Safety, and Development of Working Children and Adolescents in the United States*. Washington, D.C.: National Academy Press.

Sum, A., and Taggert, R., with Palma, S., and McLaughlin, J. (2002). *The National Economic Recession and Its Impacts on Employment among the Nation's Young Adults (Sixteen- to Twenty-four-Years-Old): The Untold Story of Rising Youth Joblessness*. Boston: Center for Labor Market Studies, Northeastern University.

Tannock, S. (2001). *Youth at Work: The Unionized Fast-Food and Grocery Workplace*. Philadelphia: Temple University Press.

Robert Bussel

M

Mental-Health Advocacy in Youth. Mental-health advocacy is a movement that involves people who have experienced mental-health services working together to help and support one another and to improve the quality of care provided. This is done by participating in treatment planning, policymaking, and program development. Youth's role in advocacy involves insuring that their voices and their needs are equally considered in the process. "Nothing about us without us" is the call to action resounded in the youth mental-health advocacy movement. This means simply that no decision should be considered nor action taken involving the mental health of youth without their participation.

The foundation for this movement is based on youth-development principles that state that in order for young people to be successful they need a combination of resources. These include opportunities to feel competent and useful, have a sense of belonging, and feel powerful (Benson 2003). Central to these principles and specific to mental-health advocacy are the core concepts of shared power, taking a strength-based approach to mental health, and thinking about "engaging" youth as opposed to "involving" them in their care and within youth-serving systems.

Shared power refers to the type of partnership that is held between youth and adults. It promotes the difference between "power with" youth in contrast to traditionally held "power over" youth. "Power with" youth focuses on common interest, cooperation, shared access to valued resources, nonhierarchical thinking and structure, and open participation. This type of relationship creates the opportunity for youth voices to be heard and youth opinions to be acted upon.

Taking a strength-based approach to mental health involves looking for solutions instead of problems. Solutions are created based on what youth do well and how they identify their own needs. This type of thinking prevents stigma and avoids blame. It allows youth to feel competent and empowered.

The way that language is used in the youth advocacy movement is very important. One example is the way in which adults and systems of care are encouraged to try to engage youth and accept their participation instead of trying to involve and consult with them. Young people are already involved in matters that are important to their lives. They know what it is like to struggle with their mental-health problems, and they know what can be helpful. Focusing on engagement puts an emphasis on equal responsibility in developing the relationship between youth and those who traditionally hold power over them. It recognizes the value of a young person's experience and opinions, and it encourages shared power.

Youth use many different approaches to influence the way in which mental-health services are used and delivered. One way of understanding this is by looking at three areas: contact with the political, economic, and social spheres of society; participation and planning in the community; and decision-making in areas that will influence ones' well-being (Youth Council for Northern Ireland 1993).

There are many points of opportunity to influence and participate in political, economic, and social arenas. The youth advocacy movement insists that youth should have a voice in all policymaking and governing bodies.

An example of powerful youth advocacy on a national policy level occurred at the U.S. Surgeon General's Conference on Children's Mental Health (2000). At this pioneering meeting young people were invited to sit at the tables with families and professionals to discuss the Surgeon General's Report on Mental Health. However, due to what they felt was a lack of respect, they unanimously decided not to participate in the conference on the second day. The youth only rejoined the group after writing a manifesto asking the parents and professionals to treat them with respect and dignity. Among the requests were to not use acronyms to describe youth in meetings, to fund and support youth organizations with the same intensity family organizations were being supported, and to make room for meaningful participation when youth are asked to sit at policy tables. After this presentation the entire conference became more youth-friendly.

Federal government policymakers have responded enthusiastically to this call to action and have made advances that have enabled youth participation to flourish nationwide. Much of the leadership in this area has come from the System of Care Communities under the guidance of the United States Substance Abuse and Mental Health Services Administration (SAMHSA) Center for Mental Health Services (CMHS). The Systems of Care Communities have the goal of creating reform within the child and adolescent mental-health system. System of Care Communities that have received federal fiscal support since 2002 have been required to involve young people in the policy and planning of the system of care development through to service delivery and evaluation. These communities are mandated to hire a youth coordinator as a key staff member in the development of the system of care. Furthermore, in partnership with youth and System of Care Community members, the Technical Assistance Partnership for Child and Family Mental Health has set forth principles in youth engagement and involvement and has produced a definitive resource manual (Matarese, McGinnis, and Mora in press) to assist mental-health communities in accomplishing this goal.

Young people also have influence on local, regional, and state policy levels. They provide input to local mental-health boards, commissions, and task forces in the child-serving systems. Youth can influence the types of services that are offered and the amount of money that is spent on resources and services by participating in committees and serving on boards of directors in the private and nonprofit sectors as well. In addition to board and committee participation, young people have taken part in social marketing campaigns and evaluation.

Social marketing is the perfect venue for youth to implement their knowledge and experience. This involves creating messages and campaigns that transmit important information about mental health to the public. Young people are ideally positioned to know how to communicate what is important, what works, and what does not to their peers.

Participation in research provides young people with knowledge about the depths of various social concerns, and they can mobilize their experience as researchers to disseminate this information to others. This requires youth to take part in identifying the questions, contributing to the research design, collecting and evaluating the data, interpreting the results, and disseminating the findings.

An example of a youth-driven and designed evaluation project is the Metropolitan Child and Adolescent Network Teen Advisory Council (TAC) in Chicago. A group of ten young people who were consumers of mental-health services designed and administered a survey addressing the incidence of violence within the teen mental-health population. The second phase of this project involved the production of a film discussion on teen violence, "Letz Talk about Violence." In September of 2002 the president's Bush's New Freedom Commission on Children's Mental Health invited the TAC young people to present this project to the commission when it was in Chicago. The presentation is now posted on the New Freedom Commission's Web site.

Youth engage the community by establishing support groups and peer-mentoring programs; reaching out to local mental-health administrators; and by providing education for professionals and peers regarding mental-health issues. Young people feel more able to control their own lives in a positive way while avoiding riskier behaviors and strengthening their connection to the community and their education when they are able to improve the lives of others.

One example of youth engaging the community through educating others is the You-n-Me Project (Youth and Mental Health Education) being developed by the Mental Health Association of New York City. The You-n-Me Project is a peer-mentoring and youth-development program that is designed to train teams of youth, comprised of consumers of mental-health services and those who are not, as mental-health peer educators. The peer-mentoring teams fight stigma through modeled acceptance of each other and by the inability of their audiences to distinguish who has suffered from mental-health problems and who has not. Audiences will then leave with a greater sense that people with mental illness are no different than you or me and that more people struggle with these difficulties than one realizes. Youth are engaged in all phases of the project including developing the curriculum, selecting and training the peer educators, teaching the curriculum, and researching the outcomes.

Another example of youth participation in the community is Youth Forum in West-chester County, New York. Youth Forum is a peer-run, peer-to-peer support group for adolescents and young adults transitioning from children's services to adult services. It was developed with the support of Westchester County's Department of Community Mental Health and Westchester's family support organization, Family Ties. Youth Forum members acknowledged that for many youth who have a mental illness or who are involved in the child-serving systems, stigma silences them. Youth Forum works to stop the silence and to provide opportunities for young people to communicate their system-related experiences as well as their strengths and abilities. It creates opportunities for young people to be successfully heard, to bond and create friendships, and to assume leadership positions. Youth Forum members developed "What Helps–What Harms," a document outlining what helped and what hurt them in inpatient psychiatric hospitalization, residential treatment facilities, school settings, individual and family therapy, and in their home communities. They have presented it at local and national conferences. This was an empowering process for the young people as families, professionals, and providers listened to their experiences and recommendations and took the document seriously.

Participating in advocacy activities can play a tremendous role in promoting a young person's well-being. Youth advocates share personal stories of how their lives have transformed: sometimes coming from a place of desperation and despair and having frequent thoughts of self-harm to a sense of importance and personal accomplishment. Learning to become a youth mental-health advocate can enhance a young person's interpersonal skills. It can improve his or her abilities to listen to others and to voice concerns in ways that can be heard and acted upon. Practicing advocacy can lead to improvement of self-esteem, grades in school, and attitudes toward parents, teachers, and health-care providers.

Young people who use their personal struggles with mental health as a means of helping others are also constantly faced with the reality of their own recovery. This means that it is important for them to keep their own health needs in mind. Personal health and continuing recovery are important concepts to be mindful of in and out of advocacy efforts. Successful advocates have practices to maintain well-being in their own lives and strategies to stay healthy in their work.

One way that youth influence their own well-being is through partnering with their health-care providers in their own care. Traditionally, youth are not voluntary consumers of mental-health services and can often be forced to receive treatment unwillingly. When youth are educated about treatment choices and options and are engaged in decision-making it promotes responsibility and leads to better outcomes. Youth who are given autonomy and are engaged in treatment drop out less, have better adjustment into treatment, and have improved relationships with the adults involved in the decision-making.

Youth advocates find it essential to keep a balance between their own personal needs and those of the young people they are trying to help. Establishing personal and professional boundaries is important. It requires young people to have sense of how much they can take on and what is too much. Healthy advocacy practice also includes the need to understand limitations about revealing personal information in order to prevent youth from feeling too vulnerable or exposed. Youth mental-health advocates model healthy practices to their peers by taking advantage of the supports in their environments and by taking care of themselves.

The youth mental-health advocacy movement is young but is gaining great momentum. Youth can make powerful changes when the opportunity is created. They can often voice concerns and point out needed changes that adults are unable or afraid to voice. Youth are forcing adults, organizations, systems, and governments to hear them, engage them, and partner with them. Young people are changing the ways that mental-health services are provided and the ways in which services are utilized. They are changing the ways in which policy is created and money is spent. They are changing the ways people think about them, the ways people think about mental health, and the ways people think about themselves. They are indeed insuring that there is "Nothing about them without them!"

See also Advocacy; Voice.

Recommended Reading

Adelman, H. S., MacDonald, V. M., Nelson, P., Smith, D. C., and Taylor, L. (1990). "Motivational Readiness and the Participation of Children with Learning and Behavior Problems in Psychoeducational Decision Making." *Journal-of-Learning-Disabilities*, 23 (3): 171–176.

Benson, P. L. (2003). "Developmental Assets and Asset-Building Community: Conceptual and Empirical Foundations." In *Developmental Assets and Asset-Building Communities: Implications for Research, Policy, and Practice*, edited by R. M. Lerner, and P. L. Benson New York: Kluwer Academic/Plenum Publishers.

Lewis, A., ed. (2003). *Shaping the Future of American Youth: Youth Policy in the Twenty-first Century*. Washington, D.C.: American Youth Policy Forum.

Matarese, McGinnis, and Mora (2005). *Youth Involvement for Systems of Care: A Guide to Empowerment*. Washington, D.C.: Technical Assistance Partnership for Child and Family Mental Health.

Youth Council for Northern Ireland (1993). *Participation: Youth Work Curriculum Guidelines*. Belfast: Youth Counsel for Northern Ireland.

Adam G. Stein, Marlene Matarese, and Kristina Hebner

Mexico. *See* Zapatista Rebellion (Mexico).

Minority Youth Voter Turnout. Electoral participation in the United States consists of two steps. First, individuals must register to vote. Second, once registered, they are then able to cast a vote. In order to measure participation in the electoral process, political scientists and other researchers use three major measures of

Growing racial and ethnic composition of young people aged eighteen to twenty-four, 1972–2004

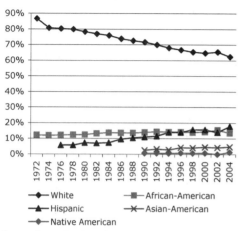

Source: Current Population Survey, November Supplements, 1972-2002, and March 2004 Current Population Annual Demographic File.

participation. These include voter registration rates (the percent of an eligible population that has registered to vote), voter turnout rates (percent of the eligible population that voted), and the composition of voters in a given election (the percent of all voters who are young, for example). The most common measure of participation, and that presented in the above figure, is voter turnout.

Regarding electoral participation, young people are less likely both to be registered to vote and to cast a vote. Furthermore, the trend in youth voter turnout has been a decline over the past thirty years. There is no single best measure of voter turnout available. Even with the same dataset, many researchers will produce different estimates. However, no matter how we measure voter turnout, the declining trend in youth voter participation is consistent. Across racial and ethnic groups, voter participation by minority youth has generally trailed the participation of non-Hispanic whites since 1972, when young people aged eighteen to twenty were first given the right to vote. However, as shown in Lopez (2003a), this overall declining trend masks several underlying trends, including a surge in African American youth voter turnout since 1984 and large differences across ethnicities for Latinos where Cuban American youth participate at rates similar to non-Hispanic whites.

Growing Diversity of American Youth

Youth between the ages of eighteen and twenty-four number approximately 27.8 million, of whom 24.8 million were U.S. citizens in 2004. This represents a slight increase in the size of the youth population relative to 2000 but also is smaller than the size of the youth population in the 1970s. However, in coming years, it is expected that the number of young people between ages eighteen and twenty-four will grow. Currently, there are 72 million citizens younger than eighteen, almost as large a cohort as the baby-boomer generation currently in its forties to sixties which numbers 77 million.

In conjunction with the general decline in youth voter turnout since 1972 has been

Population estimates in millions, 2004

Race/Ethnicity	Ages 18–24	Ages 18–25	Ages 18–29	Ages 30+
White, NH	17.3	19.6	28.6	122.4
African American, NH	3.8	4.3	6.2	17.8
Latino	5.0	5.7	8.8	17.7
Asian American, NH	1.3	1.5	2.4	7.4
Native American, NH	0.4	0.4	0.6	1.9
Mixed Race/Other, NH	0.04	0.05	0.06	0.08
All Races/Ethnicities	27.8	31.5	46.6	167.4

Note: Estimates are calculated using the March 2004 Current Population Survey Demographic File and represent estimates of citizens and non-citizens. NH, non-Hispanic.

a growing diversity among young people. Since 1972 the proportion of young people between eighteen and twenty-four from minority groups has grown to represent over 35 percent of all young people, with the share of young people who are Latino rising faster than any other group. In recent years, the share of youth who are African American and Latino have been almost equal. However, while the share of young people who are Latino have been almost equal, not all young Latinos are eligible to vote since many are not citizens of the United States. Without citizenship, they cannot participate in federal elections such as presidential elections. When this is taken into account, in 2004 Latinos represented 12 percent of the citizen population, while African Americans represented 15 percent of all young citizens (see the table titled "Population estimates in millions, 2004").

2004 Election

While the general trend since 1972 has been a decline in youth voter turnout, 2004 was a stand-out year in youth electoral participation. Estimates of voter turnout suggest that in 2004, voter turnout among young people was 47 percent among eighteen- to twenty-four-year-olds, up 11 percentage points over 2000, and 49 percent among eighteen- to twenty-nine-year-olds, up nine percentage points over 2000. In both cases, turnout in 2004 was as high as turnout in the mid-1970s. However, while young people appeared to turnout at higher rates in 2004 than in 2000, there continue to

be substantial differences in voter turnout across racial/ethnic groups, continuing trends that have been in place since the mid-1980s. Specifically, voter turnout was up for all groups, with the greatest percentage point increases occurring among non-Hispanic White and non-Hispanic African American youth.

However, there is more than one way to assess voter participation among voters. Besides voter turnout, one can consider the demographic composition of voters on Election Day as suggested by exit polls. Measuring voter turnout for a group is not as easy a task as might be expected. There are two measures of voter turnout that are commonly used. First, one can measure what is called "voter turnout." This is calculated by taking the number of votes cast in a city or state or nation and dividing it by the number of people eligible to vote. For the graphs in this document, all voter turnout rates are calculated by taking the number of votes cast and dividing it by the number of U.S. citizens. A second measure of voter participation is the composition of voters. This measure is typically obtained from national exit polls and only reflects the composition of voters on the day the exit poll was conducted. In this case, we can talk about the share of voters who are young, Latino, or female. Any changes in this share will be an indication of changes in participation by that group. (See the CIRCLE working paper by Lopez, Kirby, Sagoff, and Herbst 2005b entitled "The Youth Vote 2004, with a Historical Look

Demographic composition of eighteen- to twenty-nine-year-old voters

Race/Ethnicity	Presidential Election Year				
	2004	2000	1996	1992	1988
African American, NH	17%	11.7%	13.0%	9.8%	8.6%
Latino	8%	9.9%	8.1%	3.4%	***
Asian American	2%	2.5%	1.4%	1.5%	***
White, NH	71%	74.1%	75.4%	83.9%	85.3%
Other	2%	1.9%	2.0%	1.5%	6.1%

Source: National exit polls from the National Election Pool (2004), the Voter News Service (1992–2000), and the ABC News Secret Ballot poll from 1988. Note that for 1988, Latinos are counted in multiple categories, and Asian Americans are counted as "other". NH, non-Hispanic.

at Voting Patterns, 1972–2004," July 2005.) Young African American voters comprised a greater share of all young voters in 2004 than in any other year since 1988. Furthermore, their representation in the 2004 youth electorate was beyond their representation in the citizen population, which in 2004 stood at 15 percent. For Latinos, Asian Americans, and others, there was a one to two percentage point decline in their representation in the youth electorate (see the table titled "Demographic composition of eighteen- to twenty-nine-year-old voters.")

Trends in Voter Turnout

As shown in Levine, Kirby, and Sagoff (2005a), voter turnout in presidential years among young people has been on decline since 1972 and on a slight decline in years without a presidential election. However, while the general trend in voter turnout among young people is downward, since 1984 African Americans have matched the voter turnout rates of their white counterparts, with the exception of 1992. For young Latinos, Asian Americans, and white non-Hispanics, in contrast, the trend in voter

turnout has been steady and generally 10 to 20 percentage points below that of African American and white non-Hispanic youth. This difference has also been present for all Latino and Asian American adults (see figures titled "Voter turnout in presidential years among eighteen- to twenty-four-year-old citizens, by race and ethnicity," "Voter turnout in midterm election years among eighteen- to twenty-four-year-old citizens," and "Voter turnout in presidential years among adult citizens eighteen and older.")

Compared to adults, young people generally vote at lower rates, and this pattern of participation is present in all ethnic groups. However, this pattern is more pronounced for Latinos, Asian Americans, and Native Americans than for African Americans or Native Americans. As shown in the table titled "Voter turnout among citizens in 2004," according to data from the November Supplement of the Bureau of Labor Statistics' monthly Current Population Survey, young Latinos turned out to vote in 2004 at the rate of 34.9 percent, while Latinos over the age of fifty-five turned out to vote at the rate of 63.2 percent in 2000. Similarly, for Asian Americans, young Asian Americans turned out to vote at a rate of 40.0 percent, while those over fifty-five turned out at a rate of

Voter turnout in presidential years among eighteen- to twenty-four-year-old citizens, by race and ethnicity

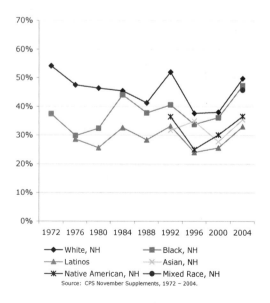

Source: CPS November Supplements, 1972 – 2004.

Voter turnout in midterm election years among eighteen- to twenty-four-year-old citizens

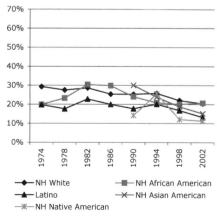

Source: Current Population Survey, November Supplements, 1974–2002.

Voter turnout in presidential years among adult citizens eighteen and older

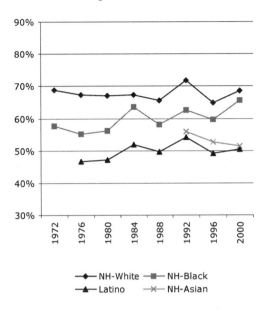

Source: Current Population Survey, November Supplements, 1972-2000.

57.2 percent. While these gaps of 30 and 17 percentage points, respectively, are large, they are not all that different from patterns observed among non-Hispanic white and non-Hispanic African American citizens.

Part of the observed differences between older and younger Latinos, and Latinos and non-Hispanics more generally, may be driven by factors reflected in young Latinos' view of their efficacy and role in the political process. (Unfortunately, similar reliable information is not available for Asian American youth.) With regards to casting a vote, Lopez (2003a) reports that while a large majority of young people say it is not difficult to cast a vote, young Latinos are more likely to say that it is difficult compared to young non-Hispanic whites and African Americans. Similarly, as shown in Lopez (2004), young Latinos are less likely than their non-Hispanic white counterparts to say that they can make a difference in solving the problems of their communities. Furthermore, young Latinos are less likely than their non-Hispanic white counterparts to say that they talked about politics with their parents. Finally, young Latinos are more likely than their non-Hispanic white or non-Hispanic African American counterparts to say that "candidates do not take young people seriously," that candidates never come to their communities, and that candidates "would rather talk to older/wealthier voters." All of this suggests that young Latinos generally feel that they can have less impact on the results of elections than other young people and also that the political process pays relatively less attention to the needs of young Latinos.

See also Deliberative Democracy; Democracy; Democratic Education; Hip-Hop Generation; Kids Voting USA (KVUSA); MTV's Choose or Lose Campaign (1992–); New Media; Peer Influences on Political Development; Personality and Youth Political Development; Rights of Participation of Children and Youth; Rights, Youth Perceptions of; State and Youth, The; Student Political Activism; Student Voices Project.

Voter turnout among citizens in 2004

Age Group	Latino	White, NH	African American, NH	Asian American, NH	Native American, NH	Mixed Race, NH
18–24	33.0%	49.8%	47.3%	35.5%	36.6%	45.8%
25–29	39.5%	56.2%	52.9%	28.4%	33.5%	47.6%
30–55	49.6%	68.4%	63.1%	47.3%	49.9%	62.7%
56+	59.1%	74.0%	66.3%	49.9%	60.7%	70.9%
All	*47.2%*	*67.2%*	*60.3%*	*44.6%*	*48.7%*	*59.1%*

Note: All results are for citizens only. All results are based on author's tabulation from the Current Population Survey, November Supplement 2004. NH, non-Hispanic.

Recommended Reading

Lopez, M. H. (December 2003a). "Electoral Engagement among Latinos." *Latino Research at Notre Dame*, 1 (2).

Lopez, M. H. (March 2003b). *Electoral Engagement among Latino Youth*. College Park, MD: Center for Information and Research on Civic Learning and Engagement.

Lopez, M. H. (December 2004). *Civic Engagement among Minority Youth*. College Park, MD: Center for Information and Research on Civic Learning and Engagement.

Lopez, M. H., Kirby, E., and Sagoff, J. (July 2005a). *The Youth Vote 2004*. College Park, MD: Center for Information and Research on Civic Learning and Engagement.

Lopez, M. H., Kirby, E., Sagoff, J., and Herbst, C. (July 2005b). *The Youth Vote 2004 with a Historical Look at Youth Voting Patterns 1972–2004*. College Park, MD: Center for Information and Research on Civic Learning and Engagement.

Mark Hugo Lopez

Moral Cognition and Youth Activism. Kohlberg's theory of the development of moral reasoning has been successfully applied to many kinds of social and moral issues, making it appropriate for the study of youth activism. In fact, it is ideal for the study of youth activism because it recognizes that moral problems are problems precisely because each side or perspective can bring moral values to support it, and adolescence and youth is the time of life when young people are eager to use their more sophisticated hypothetical and deductive reasoning skills to propose solutions for the problems of all kinds, whether in their families, schools, nations, or the world. It is a time of urgent idealism.

Kohlberg's continuing influence on moral psychology lies in (1) relating psychological research to philosophical ideas, such as justice; (2) understanding that children actively think about moral problems and social relationships; (3) documenting that the way children think about moral issues is not primarily influenced by adults but follows a developmental sequence of stages; and (4) acknowledging that the positive emotions of empathy and sympathy are related to the processes of perspective taking that are key to moral-reasoning development.

Research on the development of moral reasoning in children and youth began in the late 1950s. The study of its relationship with youth activism began soon after in the late 1960s with the Vietnam War, the American civil rights movement, and the Berkeley free-speech movement. Lawrence Kohlberg, who is generally considered the "father" of moral-development research, launched this area with a study of boys ten to sixteen years old whom he interviewed every three years into their early forties in the 1980s. The major results are Kohlberg's well-known six-stage theory of moral-reasoning development and a democratic community approach to education called the Just Community. The creation and practice of several Just Community programs in high schools led to the development of the idea that institutions possess a moral culture which can be developed by the group decisions of its members. The Just Community approach creates the conditions for moral action and youth activism by creating a positive school culture and strong sense of community, fostering the moral understanding and reasoning of students and teachers, and promoting a sense of responsibility and empathy in students and teachers for the welfare and well-being of individual members and the group as a whole.

Kohlberg challenged the existing view in the 1950s that morality should be studied *only* as virtues (e.g., honesty) that children and adults either do or do not possess. Instead he posed moral dilemmas in which two values conflict (e.g., saving a life or obeying a law) and a person's moral development is measured by the reasons and arguments he gives to support his choice. The moral-judgment interview (MJI) is a valid and reliable measure that asks for oral or written responses to three moral dilemmas. The most famous is the Heinz dilemma: should Heinz steal a drug developed by a local druggist in an imaginary European town to save his wife from dying of a rare form of cancer? Although Kohlberg analyzed the modes of thinking of only ninety-eight boys living in the Chicago area, the effects have been far-reaching.

Kohlberg's goal was to understand why people act morally and activism can be one example of moral action. He maintained that the key to moral action or functioning is people's understanding (both intellectually and emotionally) of morality as they live it in their everyday life. The following five aspects that link moral development to youth activism are highlighted in this entry, which ends with a description of the Just Community approach as an example of how schools can promote positive youth activism:

1. That people reason about moral problems differently as they grow older;
2. That contexts or situations in which a moral problem occurs influence how it is seen and solved;
3. That people's emotions influence their moral decisions and actions;
4. That higher-stage reasoning leads to more consistency between people's moral judgments and what they do; and
5. That people's sense of identity and sense of responsibility are important in their decisions to act morally.

How people reason about moral problems develops as they grow older. They can see a moral problem from several different perspectives. They can take the roles of more individuals and groups involved in a social or moral problem, even those they disagree with or their enemies. They can better evaluate the moral and values-based reasons they and others give. They are more able to understand why certain values are more primary than others when moral values conflict (i.e., life is more important than property). Moreover, they do not confuse moral reasons with those based on personality and/or personal preferences.

Research supports the assumptions that (1) moral reasoning develops through stages; (2) each stage is a coherent pattern of thinking; (3) development through the stages is orderly, moving from less to more complex reasoning with no falling back to earlier stages of thinking; (4) the pattern of reasoning at each stage is integrated into the next higher stage; and (5) the same stages or patterns of thinking are universal.

There are six stages, two in each of three levels, as follows:

1. Preconventional level (stages one and two)
2. Conventional level (stages three and four)
3. Postconventional level (stages five and six)

At stage one, right or moral is defined as literal obedience to rules and authority and avoiding punishment; reasoning that is typical of young children. At stage two, right is defined by making fair exchanges in concrete, immediate terms. School-age children define justice as each person getting the same amount or being treated the same as the other. The move into the conventional level denotes a shift to being able to take the perspective of others, of groups, and society. At stage three, adolescents and adults define right from an interpersonal perspective. They are aware of shared feelings and expectations and put themselves in the other person's shoes as a means to come to a moral decision. At stage four, young adults and adults take a normative perspective. Right or morality is defined by the relationships of individuals to society and its institutions, such as the law, marriage, and so forth. There is a focus on obligations, roles, and rules. At stage five, a person takes a prior-to-society perspective; that is, he recognizes that rights, such as the rights to life and liberty, exist regardless of whether they are recognized by society. More generalizable ideas, such as tolerance, equity, due process, and impartiality, are used to make moral decisions. Stage five reasoning makes clear distinctions between a legal and moral point of view but sometimes finds it hard to integrate them. At stage six, a person takes the perspective of a moral point of view, a point of view that ideally all human beings should take toward one another as equal autonomous persons. This means he or she makes moral decisions by considering the points of view of all affected, even future generations, using a procedure of prescriptive role-taking. The unique aspect of stage six is the *deliberate* use of universal principles of justice, equity, equality of human rights, and respect for the dignity of human beings as individuals. "These characteristics of stage six reasoning require that stage six raise dialogue to a principle, a principle of procedure or 'moral musical chairs'" (Kohlberg 1984, 638).

The context or situation in which a moral problem occurs influences moral reasoning. Since the 1960s researchers have conducted hundreds of studies in over sixty countries. The large majority of these studies support the developmental and universal nature of moral reasoning and explore its relationship to family functioning, educational and occupational attainment, and how social, cultural, and personality differences are reflected in the reasons people give to support their moral decisions.

It is important to point out two areas of criticism and briefly summarize what the research has found. First, during the 1980s criticisms arose from Carol Gilligan and others that Kohlberg's theory could not account for the moral reasoning of women. Subsequent research and a meta-analysis by Lawrence Walker demonstrated that the method is not biased against females when similar groups in terms of age and education are compared. Second, criticisms and debates about the universal nature of moral-reasoning development arose and continue today. These debates center on the higher stages (five and six) and raise a fundamental question; that is, whether the underlying reasoning used by people in Eastern and African cultures can be understood and assessed from a Kohlbergian perspective. Summarizing this area, it can be said that most researchers agree that children's reasoning about social and moral issues develops in the same ways regardless of their ethnicity, country, culture, religion, or social class; that there are universal values shared by all cultures and groups (e.g., the values of life and life quality, truthfulness, freedom or autonomy, law, property, and

religious and spiritual beliefs); but that different cultures may emphasize some of these values over others. Both across cultures and within a single culture there exists a limited range of moral ideas, specifically justice, rights, community, and welfare, supporting the universality of morality. However, many studies simultaneously support individual, situational, and cultural differences when specific moral ideas, values, norms, and principles are used. The last important finding is that some cultures have strong values not widely shared by other cultures; for instance, filial piety or complete deference to the parent's wishes is an important value in many Asian cultures but is not important in Western cultures. Although the universality of specific aspects of morality will continue to be debated, cross-cultural research in both psychology and sociology suggests that the morality of different cultures and nations has more in common than differences, and specifically, that there are universal values embodied in the ethics of all cultures.

In addition, individuals see situations differently; what may be a moral problem for one may be a personal or pragmatic decision for another. Lawrence Walker and his colleagues' research on moral action demonstrates that personality traits, especially agreeableness and meeting life's challenges with a sense of agency or effectiveness in addition to identity development and moral reasoning, distinguish moral exemplars from comparison individuals.

There is substantial research that shows our roles as child or adult, teacher or student, or secretary or boss affect the moral meanings we see in both the ordinary and unique and difficult events of our lives. James Rest developed a paper-and-pencil measure of preferences for different stage arguments related to the Heinz and other moral dilemmas, the defining-issues test (DIT). The DIT and the MJI correlate similarly across age-groups. Results from several hundred studies over twenty-five years show that moral development on the DIT is related to education, especially college, to the kinds of professions/careers people have, and to their work experiences. In addition Rest and his colleagues, Darcia Narvaez, Stephen Thoma, and Muriel Bebeau, have shown that people's sensitivity to moral issues, their political beliefs, and their sense of responsibility as well as their moral reasoning are involved in predicting moral action.

Elliot Turiel developed a theory that focuses on what children think are right and wrong actions in three large contexts or domains—moral (e.g., eat only your fair share of the food served), conventional (e.g., don't sing at the dining table), and personal (e.g., preferring to eat five small meals a day). In the last twenty years, Turiel and his colleagues, Larry Nucci and Judith Smetana, have assessed children's understanding of parental as well as other adult (e.g., teacher) and peer authority using structured interviews and systematic observations. These studies show that by the ages of nine or ten (1) children distinguish between the three domains when discussing social issues; (2) younger children first distinguish between the moral and conventional domains; (3) even fairly young children know it is wrong to commit a moral transgression (e.g., stealing or lying) even if told to do so by a parent or adult; and (4) these three domains are cross-culturally valid.

In 1980 Robert Selman laid out a sequence of perspective-taking abilities, the ability that underlies moral reasoning. He and his colleagues' primary research methods are semi-structured interviews and analysis of transcripts of peer and adult-child interactions. Their research has led to a new practice in clinical psychology called "pair therapy" in which a therapist helps an internalizing (i.e., often depressed or anxious) child and an externalizing (i.e., often bullying or violent) child relate to each other and becomes friends. As the therapy continues, the children and adolescents moderate their extreme styles and achieve better interpersonal understanding. Pair therapy not only develops interpersonal skills and friendships, it also decreases children's and adolescents'

emotional problems. Selman and his colleagues have gone on to create school intervention programs that foster friendships and diminish bullying. Selman theorized that being able to take the perspective of others is key to healthy interpersonal functioning just as Kohlberg had theorized that it is key to moral-reasoning development. Selman's focus on interpersonal relationships links research in the Kohlbergian tradition to theories of moral emotion, especially empathy.

People's emotions and their sense of identity also influence their moral decisions and actions. Martin Hoffman and Nancy Eisenberg have each argued that the development of empathy is primary and underlies perspective taking and the ability to make moral judgments. Research suggests that empathic arousal may be a "hardwired" tendency in infants. Newborns show distress when exposed to the distress of other infants, and they often initiate exchanges of emotional cues with adults. In young children it seems that empathy is developed through interchanges with adults. Prosocial behaviors such as sharing toys and expressing sympathy are displayed by very young children. Prosocial behavior can be motivated either by self-oriented egoistic desires, especially in children, or by other-oriented moral feelings, values, and/or principles. In other words, children and even adults may be helpful to another in order to gain something (e.g., praise, gratitude, money) or because they feel empathic and sympathetic toward another and want to help him or her. Prosocial behavior toward peers increases with age, with the greatest increase occurring between childhood and early adolescence followed by a decrease from age fifteen through the college years. Eisenberg argues that adolescents realize that there is competition for help from teachers, to get into college, and so forth and become less willing to help when they see that helping their peers may actually or potentially interfere with their own legitimate self-interest.

Both Hoffman and Eisenberg have written on the relationship of empathy development to Kohlbergian moral-reasoning development, agreeing with Kohlberg and Selman that the increasing ability to take another's perspective links the fields of emotional and cognitive development.

People also act to avoid feeling guilty, ashamed, and disgusted with themselves—these are the negative emotions of moral evaluation. Some psychologists have argued that the negative emotions are the core of moral action. They say that evaluative moral emotions are essential for moral learning, the development of conscience, and for society to maintain its values. Their research has focused mostly on the emotions of guilt and shame. Guilt and shame are regarded as "self-conscious" emotions. These feelings arise because people evaluate their actions after having done them. Adults often feel guilt at the same time as they feel empathy, especially if they are thinking they will not help out in a specific situation. In contrast, people feel shame when they feel personally distressed by a situation, similar to a young child's crying in mimicry of another's distress. Kochanska has found that how mothers socialized their toddlers and the toddlers' guilty expressions were related to their sense of conscience when measured six years later, as eight- to ten-year-olds. On the other hand, instead of seeing moral feelings of guilt and shame as aiding the development of conscience, Nunner-Winkler's research suggests that moral feelings are not motivators but rather are expressions of a person's commitment to do what is right and not what is wrong in any given situation. Her longitudinal research found that children under six or seven believe that someone who does something wrong will feel good about himself if he succeeds but that they changed their views as they grew older, believing that wrongdoers feel guilt and shame.

While cultural values, social roles, personality, and certain emotions may encourage moral action, *higher stage reasoning itself leads to more consistency between people's moral judgments and how they choose to act.* Kohlberg hypothesized that acting consistently with one's judgment when one thinks that there is a right action in a situation should be truer for people using higher stages of moral reasoning. In such situations the judgments of people reasoning at higher stages should be less clouded by pragmatic considerations and what Kohlberg termed quasi-obligations—reasons or excuses for not acting which may be legitimate in other situations but not in one in which the person has decided there is a right action available to him. There are studies that show people who reason at higher stages do fewer acts they feel are morally wrong and more frequently do what they believe is right. Whether keeping a promise to mail back questionnaires to a researcher, helping a college-student peer who pretended to be sick from using an illicit drug, or participating in the Berkeley free-speech movement in the late 1960s, about 25 percent of stage-three reasoners, 35–65 percent of stage-four reasoners, and at least 75 percent of stage-five reasoners did what they decided was right. Looking at the relationship between moral judgment and action in one of psychology's most famous experiments, the Milgram experiment, the same outcome was found. The Milgram experiments conducted in the 1950s sought to understand why lower-level Nazi soldiers followed orders to exterminate Jews, gypsies, Polish Catholics, and others. Participants were ordered by a researcher to "shock" an unseen person for errors made on a memory task. Although participants pushed buttons when ordered, shocks were not actually administered, but realistic cries, moans, and pleas came from behind a screen. Twenty-six undergraduate participants were also given the moral-judgment interview. Results showed that 50 percent of those who reasoned at stage three versus 87 percent of those who reasoned at stage four quit the experiment and refused to shock the imaginary victim after the first few moans. Studies of cheating by college and high-school students show parallel results. At least 75 percent of those reasoning at stages one or two, 65–75 percent of those reasoning at stage three, 45–55 percent of those reasoning at stage four, and only 20 percent of those reasoning at stage five cheated.

These series of studies demonstrate two important ideas for understanding youth activism: (1) an individual adolescent's or youth's moral reasoning influences how he or she acts in the real world in both common and unusual situations; and (2) to understand why many adolescents and youth who reason at stages three, four, or five do not act consistently with what they think is right, we must bring in the ideas of identity and responsibility.

People's sense of identity and sense of responsibility are important in their decisions to act morally. Currently several psychologists suggest that the motivation to act morally, to do altruistic acts, and to become engaged in positive activism is seated in one's sense of identity. Augusto Blasi argues that intentionality is the essence of moral functioning or action and that intentions originate from and express a unified self, that is, the self-as-agent, the acting self. As people grow from infancy through adolescence and into young adulthood, the extent to which they develop a sense of control, mastery, and ownership influences their conscious identity. To the extent that they are exposed to moral values and principles and express their own moral feelings and ideas, they develop a moral identity. For some people their identity may be defined by their moral stances; for others, morality plays a more minor role and other ideals such as truth, beauty, or even negative ideals—for example, winning at all costs—may more clearly define their sense of identity.

Being responsible and taking responsibility links one's actions to oneself. Responsibility says that "I" have done something, and "I" will take credit or blame for having done it. We are given responsibility in our families, at work, by our religious institutions, and so forth. Like-

wise, we take responsibility in those settings and others. Sometimes people take responsibility *upon* themselves; these are cases of prosocial and altruistic actions when done to help individuals; they are cases of positive activism when done for the betterment of society.

Daniel Hart and his colleagues used two different national datasets, each with over 20,000 participants, to study high-school students' community service as an important form of youth activism. They found that participating in school clubs or teams, feeling attached to school—especially for black youth, higher parental education, being in a family headed by two parents, being female, being white, and having higher school grades are related to voluntary community service. Importantly, living in an urban area decreases adolescents' feelings of attachment toward their schools and decreases their community service. This research mirrors other educational research that suggests that American schools fail to engage minority youth in opportunities for service as well as for learning. When schools can create cultures that engage black youth, young men, and academically marginal youth, then more of them will engage in community service, indicating that they feel responsible as citizens in a society of which they feel a part.

Higgins-D'Alessandro analyzed how teachers in a Kohlbergian Just Community program expanded their teaching responsibilities to include explicit respect for the students, efforts to engage all students by knowing their personal interests and strengths, and by supporting and challenging students in and outside classes. These teachers reported that the school culture supported and changed them as well as their students. The study verifies this change; the teachers' moral reasoning developed to stage five (the highest level found in any longitudinal study) over their time in the school.

The Just Community program is described to demonstrate some key aspects of schooling that foster youth development and activism. American psychologist-philosophers George Herbert Mead and James Mark Baldwin, the American pragmatist John Dewey, and European social scientists Jean Piaget and Emile Durkheim inspired Kohlberg, his colleagues, and teachers. They took Durkheim's suggestion to invest routine classroom discipline with moral meaning by treating the intervention classrooms as small societies with their own rules, obligations, and senses of social cohesion. They democratized that view with Dewey's progressive-education ideas and through the creation of democratic governance. In addition, they adapted the idea of a *madrich*, the mentor of a group of same-aged children who stays with them throughout their education on Israeli kibbutzim, and incorporated it into the teacher's role, empowering teachers to be counselors and advocates both for individual students and for the good of the community as a whole. The cognitive-developmental perspective from Piaget informed the structures of the intervention most appropriate to adolescents: face-to-face meetings of various sizes, from personal small groups to a large, more formal town forum with open discussions. The result is the Just Community approach to civic, moral, and character education.

The goals of the Just Community intervention are as follows:

1. To foster the cognitive, perspective taking, moral, and empathic development of community members, both students and teachers;
2. To deepen individuals' sense of justice and mutual respect;
3. To create a community with a moral culture, that is, a community that extends the empathy and personal dialog common in adolescent friendship groups or cliques to a broader range of peers and teachers, thus developing shared norms of mutual respect, solidarity, and integration; and
4. To be a model for school change.

The Just Community approach is usually realized as a school-within-a-school intervention that includes about one hundred students and four to five teachers in high schools. (For younger students this approach is usually taken within single classrooms.) High school Just Communities are democratically governed; each member, teacher and student alike, have one vote on issues of governance, school functioning, and classroom management, including such issues as waiting lists, criteria for entry, mandatory community service, and discipline. Teachers maintain their authority as experts of curriculum and teaching. Weekly community meetings for all are proceeded by small group meetings (advisor groups); in each, one teacher and a group of fifteen students discuss and formulate ideas and positions on negative issues of governance and community—such as rules and consequences for cheating, disruptions, and so forth—and on positive ones—such as creating a student bill of rights, mandating community service, and deciding on school trips and their rules, and so forth. The fairness or discipline committee (two teachers and six to eight students) also meets weekly, hearing cases of rules violations and interpersonal problems that community members choose to bring to the committee. The focus is on solving problems and increasing understanding; therefore, many sanctions involve helping, such as one student volunteering to call and wake a constant latecomer to ensure he will be able to get to school on time. Service on this committee is mandatory and rotates; it is not just the privilege of the "good kids." The other necessary committee is the agenda committee, a teacher and rotating group of students who gather information from the community in order to set agendas for discussion and decisions.

Evaluations of Just Community programs show that they promote the development of students' and teachers' moral reasoning and enhance school culture, that is, foster the development of school communities in which members hold themselves accountable to agreed upon standards of fairness and for acting responsibly and prosocially in their programs and in the larger schools as well (Power, Higgins, and Kohlberg 1989). Analysis of videotapes of one Just Community program's weekly community meetings over three years showed democratic decision-making created a reciprocal process of building a sense of cohesion or community and establishing norms, for instance, against cheating, vandalism, and drug use and for helping each other and doing community service.

A four-year longitudinal study of three democratically run alternative programs, two of which were Just Communities, and three comparison groups from the larger high schools in which they were housed showed several important results. First, the moral cultures (norms and sense of community) of the three large high schools were the same even though they differed by neighborhood, social class, and academic reputation. Essentially all were authoritarian and fostered individualistic and self-protectionist attitudes among the students—not unlike most American high schools. The students described their schools' cultures using stage two reasoning, seeing the school as a place with limited supplies, often unfair competition, and teacher favoritism. In contrast, the democratic-school students described their schools' cultures using stage three and four reasoning, grounded in valuing their relationships as a family or community. Thus, the intervention creates a different and more positive moral culture than exists in a regular high school. By and large, Just Community students believe that their communities are special, educationally and socially. When discussing preferentially admitting more recent black applicants into the Cambridge Just Community over white students on the waiting list, both black and white students argued that because "this school is really something and (even though) everyone should get into it, more black people should be able to get

into it because it is really good" (Power, Higgins, and Kohlberg 1989, 170).

Second, students in the three democratic programs showed significantly higher stage moral reasoning and development when asked to solve school dilemmas over three years compared to the comparison high-school students, who reasoned at stage two and showed no development on the same dilemmas. Additionally, students in the two Just Community programs showed higher-stage moral thinking first when solving school dilemmas and then later on the moral-judgment interview dilemmas (i.e., Heinz, etc.). School experiences represented the leading edge of their problem solving. This indicates that the moral culture of a school can influence students' individual growth or stagnation.

Third, the consistency of democratic-school students' reasoning between school and hypothetical dilemmas serves as an impetus for activism. The Scarsdale Just Community voted on mandatory community service for a number of years; currently, it is voluntary but widespread throughout the group. Another example of activism was the vote to achieve racial integration in the Cambridge Just Community, discussed above. Practicing democracy and struggling with issues of fairness is an important form of youth activism if it is understood correctly as the training ground for actively engaged adult citizenship and activism.

Fourth, students in the democratic schools expected their peers and themselves to act responsibly and prosocially toward each other and toward others in the high school and larger community. Comparison students, in contrast, did not expect their peers either to be responsible or to help others in any way. One student in the Scarsdale Just Community expressed the shared norm of helping, "I guess it's an unwritten law.... There is an agreement of, that's just, that's coming out of working together and helping people" (Power, Higgins, and Kohlberg 1989, 260).

Another study of two Just Community programs in a low socioeconomic status

(SES) neighborhood high school in the Bronx, New York, showed that over two years the students reported a stronger moral culture, more fairness, less vandalism and fighting, and better teacher-student and student-student relationships than reported by comparison students.

All these findings indicate a very important idea about adolescent behavior—their actions are determined in large part by the norms and values of the groups to which they belong. Schools can either be one of these groups or leave the students alone to develop their own peer groups. Students who feel attached or engaged with their schools are less truant, perform better academically, and are more likely to engage in community service, one of the predominant forms of youth activism. In addition, students who have the opportunity to attend schools that foster open discussion and democratic decision-making learn firsthand to become engaged and active citizens. Community service and civic engagement in schools provide opportunities for students to use—in concert—their moral reasoning, empathy, and sense of responsibility for themselves and others, and thus, they are important forums for youth development and vital forms of youth activism.

See also Civic Virtue; Democratic Education; 4-H; Just Community High Schools and Youth Activism; Moral Development; Moral Exemplars; School Influences and Civic Engagement.

Recommended Reading

Eisenberg, N. (2000). "Emotion, Regulation and Moral Development." *Annual Review of Psychology*, 51: 665–697.
Higgins-D'Alessandro, A. (2002)."The Necessity of Teacher Development." In *Influential Lives*, edited by A. Higgins-D'Alessandro and K. B. Jankowski. Chicago: Monographs of SRCD, University of Chicago Press.
Kohlberg, L. (1984). *Essays on Moral Development*, vol. 2, *The Psychology of Moral Development*. San Francisco: Harper & Row.
Lapsley, Daniel K., and Narvaez, Darcia, eds. (2004). *Moral Development, Self, and Identity*. Mahwah, NJ: Lawrence Erlbaum Associates.
Power, F. C., Higgins, A., and Kohlberg, L. (1989). *Lawrence Kohlberg's Approach to Moral Education*. New York: Columbia University Press.
Turiel, E. (1997). "The Development of Morality." In *Social, Emotional, and Personality Development*, Vol. 3, edited by Nancy Eisenberg. *Handbook of Child Psychology*. 5th ed. New York: Wiley Publishers, pp. 863–932.

Ann Higgins-D'Alessandro

Moral Development. Moral development involves learning and expressing standards of right and wrong and gaining a sense of duty and obligation. What is considered good and bad, proper and improper, is grounded in values (e.g., caring, personal achievement, fairness) and ideals (e.g., virtues, ethical principles, civil rights) and reflected in cultural tradition, law, and social institutions, especially the family, education, and religion. How moral values are formed, what motivates moral behavior, and why people may or may not act on their moral beliefs are questions that have been debated throughout history.

While scholars and theologians continue the discussion today, this examination of moral development and its relation to youth activism is based on contemporary theory and research in psychology and the social sciences. After briefly identifying some of the central dimensions of morality, the principal social and psychological explanations for moral development are reviewed. These explanations or theories describe moral learning and a variety of influences on people's beliefs and behavior. Next, the relationship between morality and youth activism is explored by examining young people's development and the various forms of their activism as well as what the research indicates about moral development and youth activism.

Youth activism is considered here in its broadest sense as referring to the participation of young people in activities intended to improve the community and in youth movements to change society. Schools, religious groups, political organizations, and local and national institutions encourage youngsters to volunteer in their communities, which is generally considered an excellent way to foster young people's moral values, character, and citizenship.

Youth movements are another form of activism and may be defined as the organized, conscious attempt of young people to bring about or resist social change. Youth movements may be initiated by young people or sponsored by adults and adult organizations. A survey of modern history indicates that from 1815 onward, youth movements erupted periodically, resulting in at least five identifiable waves or clusters of youth movement activity. What began as a few youth movements in the early nineteenth century became global in scope by the 1960s and 1980s (see Braungart and Braungart 1990). Youth movements are especially threatening to adult authorities, often creating societal turmoil and sometimes toppling governments and revolutionizing societies. Not surprisingly, the morality of youth movements has been hotly contested, with some people depicting youthful protesters as psychologically disturbed, rebellious hooligans, whereas others view young activists as highly principled citizens attempting to correct society's failings in the struggle for democracy.

It is important to understand that morality has several dimensions and operates on many levels. There is social morality, which concerns the norms, expectations, and ideals promoted by society and groups, and there is personal morality, which is a person's own thoughts and feelings about what is good and bad, right and wrong. Social and personal morality may correspond, or there may be tension and strain between what society considers moral and what the individual thinks is acceptable.

At a psychological level, morality includes several more dimensions—a cognitive or knowledge dimension, involving a person's thoughts and beliefs about morality; an affective dimension, concerning a person's emotional reactions and intensity of feelings about moral situations and issues; and a behavioral dimension, involving a person's moral actions. The extent to which these three dimensions correspond

is not always clear. For example, although people's morality is often inferred from their behavior, some individuals may act in moral ways without truly supporting underlying moral beliefs, whereas others may hold dearly to some ideal or principle but are unwilling or unable to express their morality by taking action. The fit, or lack of it, between moral thought and action is sometimes referred to as "belief-behavior consistency."

It also should be noted that there are different types of social morality, such as conventional morality, which reflects widely agreed-upon social norms; prosocial behavior, which is oriented to helping and promoting the social good; and altruism, which is not only prosocial but involves self-sacrifice on the part of the actor. Another type of social morality is civil disobedience, which occurs when social norms and laws are considered unacceptable or unethical and are violated in the name of forging a better society. Best known is Mahatma Gandhi's campaign of passive resistance and nonviolent civil disobedience in India during the era of British colonialism. Gandhi's philosophy and strategy provided the model for Martin Luther King Jr. and the civil rights movement in the American South during the 1960s as well as numerous other social movements throughout the world.

Another significant dimension involves the developmental nature of morality. Essentially, morality is learned, which depends heavily on the changes and advancements in children's ability to reason, their emotional growth, and their experiences. Over the course of childhood, youngsters are taught normative standards, virtues, and responsibilities by the adult generation. How children are taught moral attitudes and behavior partially depends on an understanding of children's ability to think and reason at different ages and on the assumptions made about children's fundamental human nature. A centuries-old controversy concerns whether children are born naturally bad and sinful and thus require discipline and punishment to curb their immoral impulses, or whether most children are basically good and primarily need loving guidance for their innate decency to unfold. However children are taught, once moral standards have been learned and internalized, violations of morality typically produce emotional reactions such as guilt, shame, and distress. As Kingsley Davis described, "'Morality' . . . lays stress upon the inner sense of obligation, the feeling of right and wrong." By adolescence, young people are expected to have developed a conscience, which enables them to make independent judgments about the "rightness" and "wrongness" of their own and others' behaviors, intentions, rights, and obligations.

There is as yet no all-encompassing theory of moral development. Rather, there are a number of perspectives in psychology and the social sciences that attempt to explain the formation, motivations, and influences on moral behavior. Each perspective focuses on a particular dimension of morality and has implications for understanding youth activism.

A long-standing and widely accepted explanation for moral development is based on socialization theory in sociology and social-learning theory in psychology. Socialization theory focuses on the interplay between the social and personal dimensions of morality with the emphasis on the impact of society and significant others on the individual's moral learning. According to this perspective, morality is acquired through social interaction with other people, groups, and institutions—sometimes referred to as "agents" of socialization. Socialization promotes societal stability; it begins early in life and largely involves the generational transmission of cultural tradition, social norms, and orientations to right and wrong, duty, and responsibility.

The assumption is that the various agents of socialization are the sources of children's moral development. The family exerts the primary influence on the formation of children's attitudes and behavior—recognizing that the family's notions of morality are affected by its socialization experiences and status in society (e.g., social class, education, ethnicity). Religious organizations are especially concerned with moral education and attempt to socialize youngsters through sacred teachings and rituals as well as ethical codes, principles, and rules for behavior. Schools are also expected to educate youngsters about moral behavior in a variety of ways, such as enforcing rules of civility, teaching society's traditions and virtues, and fostering character development and good citizenship. While there is general agreement that character and citizenship are promoted by having students contribute to their communities as part of their civics-education experience, parents, teachers, and politicians debate whether social activism should be taught and advocated as a significant dimension of good citizenship. Many historians, political scientists, and educators believe that in democracies, civic morality includes the obligation to take individual and collective action against wrongdoing and injustice and to work to improve and reform society as responsible citizens. Others, however, maintain that teaching social activism and civil disobedience has no business being taught in the schools.

Behaviorists and social-learning theorists in psychology explain how morality is learned. Essentially, children learn right from wrong and their duties and obligations by observing role models and by receiving rewards, incentives, and punishment for their acceptable or unacceptable actions. As they mature, youngsters gradually internalize the morality that they have been taught, although some additional socialization agents (e.g., peers, media, organizations, groups) may alter their attitudes and behavior. According to this view, the formation of young people's values and whether they become activists depend largely on their moral learning, socialization experiences, and the positive reinforcement and support they receive for their activism.

In contrast to socialization theory, Sigmund Freud focused deep within the individual's personality and psyche to account for the formation and expression of moral values and behavior. According to Freud, the process of moral development is riddled with conscious and unconscious emotional tensions and conflicts. Arguing that moral development is at odds with basic human nature, Freud maintained that the bulk of moral learning occurs during childhood as youngsters struggle with curbing their impulses (the id) under pressure from parents and authorities to develop socially acceptable attitudes and behavior (the superego). This tension-filled process is mediated by the ego as part of personality development and problem solving. A healthy ego enhances the ability to manage conflicts and strains between the id and the superego. In general, the very process of learning morality generates anxieties between youngsters and adults as well as psychological conflicts within the young person about making the proper choices.

By adolescence, Freud said, young people should have formed a conscience—although some people never really develop an internal sense of right and wrong, which sets the stage for immoral and pathological behavior. Generational discord may become pronounced during adolescence as youngsters struggle against parents and authority to become their own persons and to replace or surpass the adult generation. Adolescents' rebellious behavior is one sign of the generational tension. According to this explanation, youth activism is motivated largely by the youngster's moral psyche (the interplay among the id, ego, and superego) and the extent of intergenerational conflict between youth and adults. Hence, youth activism in the community would be viewed as promoting superego development, whereas participation in youth movements is often attributed to generational animosity and the rebellious inclinations of youth.

Cognitive theory in psychology emphasizes the developmental dimension of morality and the interplay between the individual and the social environment. The critical factor in learning and expressing morality is a person's stage in life and how he or she thinks and reasons. As Jean Piaget demonstrated, cognitive skills (perception, thought, memory) develop slowly over the course of childhood and adolescence. Young children regard the world only from their perspective and do not understand the views or feelings of others. It is not until adolescence that youngsters are able to think abstractly and can comprehend the various dimensions of morality.

Building on Piaget's cognitive-development theory, Lawrence Kohlberg (1981) formulated one of the most influential explanations of moral development. Kohlberg's three-level, six-stage theory describes fundamental changes in moral reasoning from early childhood through adolescence. More specifically, young children operate at what Kohlberg calls a *preconventional* level of moral development and view morality from a self-centered (egocentric) punishment and reward perspective. School-age children typically exhibit a *conventional* level of morality as they come to grips with society's norms and the need to conform. During adolescence or young adulthood, some youngsters move beyond conventional moral reasoning to a *postconventional* level of morality, characterized by increasingly sophisticated thinking about justice, a greater consideration of issues beyond the self, and more independent moral judgments. Research indicates that not everyone reaches an advanced level of moral thought, with many adults functioning at a conventional level of morality and some at a preconventional level. Education and social experiences, said Kohlberg, promote moral development and more sophisticated moral reasoning.

According to this perspective, youngsters engaging in community service would likely reflect conventional moral reasoning, although the experience of community service might advance a young person's moral thinking and judgment. Kohlberg's theory was proposed and widely discussed in the 1960s during the heyday of the civil rights movement, student movement, and the anti–Vietnam War protests in the United States. Some argued that young people who protested and joined social movements reflected postconventional moral reasoning, as evidenced by their rhetoric and determination to take a personal stand and work for a more just and equitable society. People opposed to the youthful protests and movements contended that many of the young activists functioned at a preconventional level of moral reasoning and were merely foisting their self-centered views on society.

Kohlberg's theory was criticized for being overly principled, rational, and biased and for neglecting the importance of emotional considerations in moral learning and behavior. Superior abstract reasoning, it was argued, is not necessarily indicative of stellar moral behavior. Since the 1980s, some psychologists have stressed the importance of caring relationships, emotions, empathy, and a prosocial dimension of behavior in moral development and decision-making. For example, finding that young women and young men often evaluate moral situations in different ways, Carol Gilligan concluded that caring and concerns for human relationships are as important or more important in moral judgments than abstract moral reasoning, justice, and the ability to justify actions based on *a priori* principles. Psychologists Nancy Eisenberg (1989) and Martin Hoffman (2000) argued that empathy and the moral emotions of guilt, shame, sympathy, distress, and moral outrage are expressed very early in childhood (contrary to Piaget) and play a primary role in learning morality and provide a significant source of motivation for taking action on the basis of one's convictions. As Jonathan Haidt remarked, "moral emotions and intuitions drive moral reasoning, just as surely as a dog wags its tail."

According to this view, emotions cannot be neglected in moral development, and recent neuropsychological research supports this perspective. For example, brain-imaging studies of subjects evaluating moral dilemmas disclosed that both reason and emotions were involved in judgments about hypothetical and personal ethical situations. Moreover, the more difficult and personal the moral dilemma, the more the emotional centers of the brain were active in decision. This explanation suggests that moral learning is more than cognitive; it is emotional and relational. Young people are largely moved to engage in either community activism or youth movements because of their empathy for the plight of others and feelings of guilt, sympathy, and moral outrage at the injustices and inequities of society.

No matter how thorough someone's moral socialization, well-developed their conscience and ability to reason, or finely tuned their empathy or emotions, moral action may not be taken in ethically challenging situations, which raises the question, why do some people react in morally courageous ways whereas others do not? To some psychologists the answer lies more fundamentally in the character and identity of the person. According to this view, moral action springs largely from people's feelings of commitment to humanity and sense of self as a moral person. From an Eriksonian perspective, Aquino and Reed explained, "identity is rooted in the very core of one's being, involves being true to oneself in action, and is associated with respect for one's understanding of reality." Moral goals are integrated into the self, which is far more important in motivating behavior than is principled reasoning.

Moral-identity theory has often been used to explain altruistic behavior, with one's identity as a moral person serving as a strong motivator for social action. For example, studies of moral exemplars, such as people who rescued Jews during World War II, indicated that they did not necessarily reason at highly abstract levels. To them, it was essential to act. Although putting themselves at great risk, not to have helped would have gone against their standards and core identity. As one rescuer explained, when someone comes to the door "what are you supposed to tell them—'Sorry, we are full already?' ... When someone comes and says, 'I escaped from the camp,' what is the alternative? One alternative is to push him out and close the door—the other is to pull him into the house and say, 'Sit down, relax, wash up. You'll be as hungry as we are because we have only this bread.'" Prosocial and altruistic activists are committed to a sense of self that acts to promote and protect the welfare of others.

Moral-identity theory provides a rationale for having young people volunteer in the community, which is intended to build a stronger sense of self as ethical and caring people. It also suggests that young people involved in movements for social change participate because they view themselves as moral individuals who feel a deep sense of obligation to act on their convictions. One question is how lasting is the effect of youthful activism on moral identity as people mature?

Most of the explanations discussed thus far focus on factors within the individual to explain moral development and behavior—their learning, psychological conflicts, reasoning, emotions, and identity. Many social psychologists and social scientists emphasize the impact of the immediate situation and the influence of the larger social and historical context on moral learning and behavior. For example, Hartshorne's and May's (1928) classic experiment demonstrated that children's personality trait of honesty did not correspond well with whether they behaved in honest or dishonest ways when presented with specific situations involving temptation. And, from the 1930s onward, much of the research in social psychology has confirmed the importance of the situation in influencing an individual's behavior. For example, whether people help others in distress (altruism research) or report ethical violations is affected less by personality characteristics than by situational factors, such as how many other people are available to help, time pressures, organizational culture, and support for aiding others. Social psychology research also indicates that the expression of moral attitudes may be more strongly affected by group dynamics, leadership, and inter- and intragroup conflict than by individual beliefs and personality.

Beyond the situational and group level, sociologists, anthropologists, and historians have long maintained that societal trends and events—the social context—have a decided impact on moral learning and behavior. Several forces are at work. One way the social context influences moral and social development involves cohort or generational effects. A cohort is an age group born around the same time in history that experiences societal events together during the same stages of life. It is the impact of these shared experiences that helps shape the collective moral and social attitudes of an age group while growing up in society. When societies change rapidly, the youth generation may reject the morality and values of the adult generation as being old-fashioned and outmoded. Moreover, young people's social attitudes crystallize during the stage of youth and do not change much with age. Another dimension of the social context involves societal trends and events, which have an effect on people's reactions and responses to the current situation during any period in history. Thus, consideration needs to be given to the social climate, conditions, and influences that promote youth activism in all its forms during a historical era and affect the success or failure of activists' efforts. From this perspective, youth activism is seen largely as a function of cohort-generational experiences in conjunction with the societal and global trends that promote or inhibit activism, the availability of resources and social support for activism, and the reactions and responses of the adult generation and authorities to youth activism.

The next question is what is the relationship between moral development and youth activism? As Youniss and Yates observed, "The rich literature on youth activism has not been adequately integrated into the study of moral development" (1999, 363). In piecing together the research literature, several questions are addressed. First, what is it about the stage of youth that draws young people to activism, what form does their activism take, and to what extent is morality connected to their activism? Second, what does the research indicate about the various explanations for moral development in relation to youth activism? As these questions are addressed, the interplay among the various explanations for moral development becomes evident.

Young children are not expected to engage in community activism in any significant way, and rarely have they been involved in social movements. Why is it that beginning in early adolescence through the college years, schools, religious and local groups, and communities often make a concerted effort to expose young people to community service as a way of promoting their moral character and civic responsibility? Moreover, why are most social movements comprised of young people in their late adolescence and early adulthood? To understand youth activism, it is necessary to appreciate the significant developmental advancements that occur over the course of adolescence, which partially explain adults' concern with young people's morality and some young people's interest in becoming active in improving or changing society.

From a developmental perspective, puberty triggers nervous-system changes that foster more elaborate cognitive skills. Over the course of adolescence, the young person becomes better able to think abstractly, engage in critical thinking, and imagine alternatives and the future. These advancements in thinking, in turn, allow youth to better understand and evaluate the complex world of society, politics, and morality. With their newfound critical skills, adolescents become more aware of gaps between the "ideal" and the "real" and, as a result, are more critical of themselves, their parents, authority, and how society functions. Education and social experiences are important influences on this process.

One consequence of these developments is that morality comes to the forefront during adolescence. Erik Erikson (1968) describes adolescents as being on a "search for fidelity"—looking for someone or something to be "true." Adult hypocrisy, society's shortcomings and failed promises may become glaring disappointments to adolescents in search of an ideal world— all the more so, says Adelson, because young people think in black-and-white terms and cannot yet appreciate the "shades of gray" characteristic of more complex adult thinking, which comes with experience. By late adolescence and early adulthood, these cognitive accomplishments make it possible for some youth to move beyond conventional moral reasoning to postconventional moral judgments and concerns with abstract ethical issues such as justice and human rights.

Puberty also signals that the youngster is no longer a child and is about to enter the world of adulthood. Gaining independence becomes a principal goal for young people, accompanied by the tensions and difficulties that ensue in the parent-child relationship and between the youth generation and adult generation, especially when social change is rapid. As part of the struggle for independence, young people gravitate toward their peers and become concerned with finding their own identity and place in society as future adults.

Given these developments, it is not surprising that young people may be drawn to social activism. Youth activism itself is a moral statement, as young people make a commitment to act on their beliefs about right and wrong to correct or improve society in some way. Taking action is an attempt to bring closure to perceived gaps between the ideal and the real and between one's belief and behavior; it authorizes the young person to be a moral agent of change, and it helps establish or confirm the youngster's identity as a moral person. As an illustration, adult recruiters and youth movement leaders often make appeals to young people's inclinations to correct society's failings (search for fidelity) and join with like-minded others (affiliate with peers) to benefit other people and society in some way (forge an identity and a connection between the self and society). Consider this slogan from the pre–World War I *Mlada Bosna* youth movement: "Youth will bring a new empire of liberty and man, and save the Serbian soul from vice and decay."

To understand youth activism it is important to appreciate the different forms it may take. Following Enlightenment values and the Age of Revolution, youth activism reflects moderate-extreme, left-right visions of change. Moderate left or liberal youth favor a progressive democratic society, whereas moderate right or conservative youth endorse tradition or a romanticized past. Moderate groups are generally willing to compromise and are concerned with using conventional means to achieve their goals. Many of the efforts to promote young people's service to the community reflect moderate forms of activism, as do youth activist groups sponsored by mainstream adult organizations.

During most eras of youth movement activity, there is a range of activist groups— what Mannheim referred to as "generation units"—that support a variety of moderate-extreme and left-right ideologies. Typically, youth groups on the extreme left break with the present in favor of radical or revolutionary change and are quickly challenged by youth on the extreme right who are staunch traditionalists or reactionary. Extremists, whether far left or far right, express distain for the status quo; they reject compromise in their quest for an ideal or utopian-like society and may well endorse unconventional or unethical means to achieve their idealized goals. Fearful of extremist ideologies and tactics, moderate

youth groups are likely to rally to support conventional beliefs and morally acceptable tactics. As an illustration, youth activism took many forms during the 1960s in the United States, which included extremist left- and right-wing youth activist groups, moderate civil rights groups and extremist black power groups, the mainstream Young Democrats and Young Republicans, culturally oriented hippie groups, moderate youthful religious organizations, a variety of newly formed feminist groups, and a budding gay rights movement. Each of these youth factions or generation units justified their beliefs and actions on the basis of deeply held moral values.

If there is any question whether morality is associated with youth movements in general, it is put to rest when examining the issues that galvanized young people to organize for social change ever since the first youth movement in Germany in 1815. Reflecting the values of the Enlightenment, the principal issue around which youth movements have mobilized for nearly two centuries has been citizenship, with young people organizing against repression, corruption, and injustice in the struggle for democratic civic values, such as individual rights, freedom, equality, and self-determination. At times, religious morality fuels political activism, such as the 1960s civil rights movement. Characterizing civil rights activists as "ideal citizens," Fendrich found that students in the civil rights movement were deeply committed to social responsibility and worked earnestly to change inequitable adult institutions.

The struggle for citizenship, however, takes various forms in different societies (capitalist, socialist), often involving imbalances between freedom and equality. It also should be noted that not all youth movements are constructive or democratic, such as the fascist and totalitarian youth movements during the 1930s Great Depression in Europe and the United States and the many youthful terrorist groups in history and throughout the world today. Yet, even the most destructive youth movements and terrorist groups maintain that their actions are driven by some higher moral mission. As a leader of the terrorist Weathermen group in the late 1960s told his audience, "Violence, when directed at the oppressor, is human as well as necessary."

The various explanations for moral development raise a number of questions about the relationship between morality and youth activism. One long-standing question is whether youth activism reflects young people's family socialization experiences or youthful rebellion and deep-seated emotional conflicts with their parents? In his review of the research, Gross concluded that study after study of youth activists supports socialization theory. Thus, rather than rebelling against their parents, most youth activists are attempting to put into practice the moral, social, and political values learned in the home. In short, young radical-left activists tend to come from homes where parents favor a far-left position; conservative youth activists are from homes where the parents endorse conservatism; and youth favoring moderate politics and evolutionary social change typically have parents who are moderates. Moreover, youth who take action on their convictions are more apt to have their family's support, compared to youth who are sympathetic to a cause but do not act on their beliefs.

Another question concerns whether young people who engage in activism operate at a higher level of moral reasoning than their nonactivist peers. Studies using standard measures of cognitive moral development based on Kohlberg's theory found that college students reasoning at a postconventional level were more likely to become involved in liberal or left-wing activism, and a few left-wing activists reasoned at a preconventional level of morality. Conservative activists and nonactivist youth most often reasoned at a conventional level. Supporting socialization theory, the various levels of moral reasoning reflected different styles of family upbringing. Haan,

Smith, and Block reported that young people at a conventional level of morality tended to come from more traditional and harmonious family backgrounds, whereas activists at a postconventional level came from families that valued individuality and expressiveness and did not shy away from disagreement and conflict. The activists who exhibited preconventional moral reasoning reported more discrepant attitudes from their parents and were more rebellious.

However, to assume that young people active in social causes are highly moral is an error. One problem in emphasizing abstract reasoning as the highest level of moral development concerns activists who are zealots and believe themselves to be totally dedicated to their cause and morally superior in their beliefs and commitment. As Keniston commented, "Many crimes have been committed in the name of the highest principles, sincerely held" (1970, 591). Social activism, Keniston cautioned, must be tempered by compassion and caring; otherwise, the result may be destruction and violence in the name of a social cause. According to Hoffman (2000), empathy and moral emotions play a positive role in youthful activism that is directed toward improving another person or group, such as civil rights and human rights. A significant dynamic involves feelings of guilt over one's advantaged position relative to the injustices suffered by others. However, some young activists' guilt may become convoluted, as evidenced by upper-middle-class youth who join nihilistic and terrorist groups because they feel guilty and engage in destructive and outrageous actions to demonstrate a rejection of their privileged backgrounds.

The questions of why youth movements arise during certain eras in history and why they may become violent are best answered from a social context and situational perspective. According to a survey of youth movements in history, the principal societal conditions associated with the rise of youth movement activity included a relatively large-size youth cohort, increased educational opportunities for young people, societal breakdowns (e.g., economic depressions, wars, discrimination, corruption) and discontinuities (e.g., rapid technological change, new cultural and nationalist movements), coupled with the opportunity and resources to mobilize young people for social action. Supporting a social-psychology perspective, research also suggests that once a young person enters an activist organization, the dynamics of inter- and intragroup conflict serve as a major force for sustaining young people's participation in social activism. Moreover, intense intergroup competition and conflict increase the likelihood of distorted perceptions and thinking and a misrepresentation of reality that may fuel a spiral of escalating violence—partially explaining why youth movements may sometimes move from a positive or prosocial effort to reform society to a phase of aggressive conflict, unethical behavior, and destructive acts.

Two final questions are what effect does youth activism have on young people's moral values and identity, and how lasting is the effect? Confirming moral-identity theory, Teske reported that activists' identities did, in fact, develop through their activism, which one activist described as becoming "the kind of person I want to be" (1997, 132). Hart and Fegley found that there was a closer correspondence and greater integration between the ideal and real self for adolescent moral exemplars when compared to their peers. Youniss and Yates (1999) reviewed a number of longitudinal studies and concluded that participation in community service while in high school had lasting effects, which included academic performance, continued community service after high school, more memberships in voluntary associations, and greater likelihood of voting and holding leadership positions. Similarly, college students who participated in the 1960s civil rights movement frequently remained active in social causes and community activities from ten to twenty-five years after

their youth movement experiences. Follow-up studies of former activists in political youth movements, whether left or right, found little change in their social, moral, and political values as they aged, with many remaining socially and politically active throughout their adult years in a variety of ways.

As this entry suggests, the moral development of young people cannot be explained by any single social or psychological theory—largely because morality is multidimensional, with a host of social, psychological, and developmental influences coming into play. Socialization and social-learning theories explain how moral values and orientations are formed during the childhood years, most strongly influenced by the family. Cognitive theory identifies the various ways in which children, adolescents, and adults may think and reason when presented with ethical dilemmas. Yet, moral development involves more than social learning and cognitive functioning. Caring, emotions, and empathy are intertwined with moral learning and reasoning and are a significant source of motivation for behavior from early childhood onward.

During adolescence, developmental changes are paramount in explaining the importance of morality in young people's lives, their independence in exercising moral judgments, and the interest of some in improving or changing their communities or societies in small and large ways. It is during the stage of youth that social activism first becomes an issue. For those who participate, there appears to be a notable influence on young people's moral identity, which lasts into adulthood. Historical research indicates that the issues generating youth activism are frequently moral in substance, with generational relations, group dynamics, and societal trends and events having considerable bearing on the forms that young people's activism may take.

See also Civic Virtue; Empathy; Moral Cognition and Youth Activism; Moral Exemplars.

Recommended Reading

Braungart, M. M., and Braungart, R. G. (1990). "The Life-Course Development of Left- and Right-Wing Youth Activist Leaders from the 1960s." *Political Psychology*, 11: 243–282.

Eisenberg, N. (1989). "The Development of Prosocial Values." In *Social and Moral Values*, edited by N. Eisenberg, J. Reykowski, and E. Staub. *Individual and Societal Perspectives*. Hillsdale, NJ: Lawrence Erlbaum Associates, Publishers, pp. 87–103.

Erikson, E. H. (1968). *Identity: Youth and Crisis*. New York: Norton.

Gilligan, C. (1982). *In a Different Voice: Psychological Theory and Women's Development*. Cambridge, MA: Harvard University Press.

Hartshorne, H., and May, M. A. (1928). *Studies in the Nature of Character*, vol. 1, *Studies in Deceit*. New York: Macmillan.

Hoffman, M. L. (2000). *Empathy and Moral Development: Implications for Caring and Justice*. New York: Cambridge University Press.

Keniston, K. (1970). "Student Activism, Moral Development, and Morality." *American Journal of Orthopsychiatry*, 40: 577–592.

Kohlberg, L. (1981). *Essays on Moral Development*. San Francisco: Harper and Row.

Teske, N. (1997). *Political Activists in America: The Identity Construction Model of Political Participation*. New York: Cambridge University Press.

Youniss, J., and Yates, M. (1999). "Youth Service and Moral-Civic Identity: A Case for Everyday Morality." *Educational Psychology Review*, 11: 361–376.

Margaret M. Braungart and Richard G. Braungart

Moral Exemplars. Media coverage on youth activities in recent years has been dominated by national attention to dramatic and tragic acts of antisocial behaviors. However, as many scholars and professionals point out, most youth are engaged in normative and positive social activities. Although much national attention has been drawn by antisocial behaviors of some youth, there are many examples of youth who engage in compelling and dramatic acts of heroism, charity, and self-sacrifice. Those acts are the cornerstone of positive and beneficial changes to our communities and societies. Those remarkable youth have been the focus of investigators who study moral or care exemplars. What motivates those exceptional individuals? What are the antecedent conditions and personal characteristics of people who exhibit those behaviors? Given the multiple and significant benefits of individuals who exhibit those characteristics, how can we foster and promote those behaviors in our society?

"Moral exemplars" (sometimes referred to as care exemplars) is the term used to describe individuals who chronically exhibit positive social behaviors that are acknowledged by peers as providing great benefits for the majority of people in their communities and societies. Thus, moral exemplars are considered model citizens whose actions in their communities are valued by the majority of their peers and have positively impacted their surroundings. Historically, Susan B. Anthony, Cesar Chavez, Mahatma Gandhi, Martin Luther King Jr., Abraham Lincoln, Nelson Mandela, Mother Theresa, and George Washington are individuals who we might typically think of when we think of moral exemplars. Although most times we think of people who are historically famous, there are many moral exemplars who never attained fame and recognition by the broader society. Indeed, many youth activists are engaged in morally exemplar activities.

In recent decades, the opportunities for youth to engage in activities with a positive impact have increased through government-sponsored programs (e.g., AmeriCorps), nonprofit agencies, hospitals, schools, church-sponsored programs, social-service agencies, and private organizations. Furthermore, the availability of resources to promote moral ideals and activities has increased because of easier accessibility to the Internet (e.g., Web sites, chat rooms). The range of activities includes exemplary programs in the arts and humanities, environmental issues, health care, crime, poverty, animal- and human-rights issues, education, and social inequality, among many others. According to an annual national survey, the number of youth engaged in charitable, volunteer activities in the United States has increased tremendously in the last decade. The trend is expected to continue to grow as youth become more aware of social issues and as the social capital of youth and activism opportunities increase.

Several different approaches have been used to understand moral exemplars and each approach has furthered our understanding of these remarkable people. Because moral exemplars are defined by the selfless behaviors that they often engage in, social scientists have had to define morally exemplar behaviors. According to many scholars, the types of behaviors or actions that moral exemplars often exhibit can be considered altruistically motivated actions. Altruistically motivated behaviors are a subset of prosocial behaviors that specifically refers to actions intended primarily for the benefit of others with little or no consideration of possible consequences (including rewards) to the self. Often these actions incur a cost or risk to oneself. In other words, these are individuals whose primary motivation is to assist or help others while possibly incurring a cost to themselves. Therefore, it is possible that a person might assist someone and receive recognition or a reward for doing so—the key is whether the person assisted with the intention to receive the reward or recognition or whether the person assisted with the intention to benefit the other and the reward or recognition was a minimal consideration. If it was the latter, then the behavior is considered to be altruistically motivated. The challenge for social scientists has always been whether one can accurately determine the underlying primary intention of any behavior.

Some scholars are skeptical of the existence of altruistically motivated behaviors and suggest that all human behaviors have underlying selfish motives. However, many other scholars have provided evidence of the existence of altruistically motivated behaviors. In some cases, the behaviors are exhibited under special circumstances. For example, acts of heroism under extreme circumstances (e.g., war, threat of starvation, protecting your child) usually fall under this category. In other cases, some researchers have shown that there are individuals who frequently engage in prosocial behaviors that appear to be motivated to benefit others. Social scientists have suggested that those latter individuals might have prosocial or altruistic personalities. That is not to say that people with altruistic personalities do not ever engage in behaviors to benefit themselves; however, in general, these individuals are often considerate of others in their actions. Furthermore, their actions often are consistent with promoting the welfare of others rather than at the cost of others. In addition, altruistically motivated individuals often exemplify moral courage—they enact benevolent behaviors in the face of adversity.

Despite the debate surrounding altruism, the study of prosocial behaviors (and moral exemplars) is useful because society clearly desires such beneficial behaviors. The fact that we can identify individuals as moral exemplars reflects the fact that our society makes moral judgments of people's behaviors. Some scholars point out that the debate between selfishly motivated and selflessly motivated behaviors reflects our Western, individualistic orientation. In many collectivist-oriented societies, morally exemplar behaviors are valued for their positive impact on their societies with minimal regard for the underlying motive. Still other scientists have attempted to develop methodologies to assess the underlying motive of people's prosocial behaviors or they focus on understanding prosocial behaviors with little concern for the true underlying motive. The debate among scholars as to whether true altruism exists still continues but the acknowledgment that there are some individuals who are regarded as moral exemplars by our society is never in doubt.

The adaptive and functional benefits of morally exemplar behaviors have long been acknowledged by people who study the evolutionary history of behaviors.

There are many examples of altruism and self-sacrificial behaviors in the animal kingdom. In humans, altruism and prosocial behaviors are the benchmark of cooperative societies. Sociobiologists have proposed several theories to explain the evolutionary significance of prosocial behaviors and altruism. The kin selection or genetic similarity hypothesis posits that individuals might assist others to increase the reproductive success and fitness of their genetic pool, particularly helping those people who are genetically related (and who possibly possess similar personal characteristics). For example, altruistically motivated behaviors can enhance the all-important emotional and attachment ties that bind parent and offspring. Without a biological basis for altruistic behaviors, the reproductive success of one's own gene pool would be at high risk. Another hypothesis, reciprocal altruism, states that individuals are most likely to help those who might help them in the future, thus enhancing their own reproductive success. Imagine a world where people are motivated solely by their own interests. It would be difficult, if not impossible, to imagine how such a world would have much social progress or even how such a world could survive.

Although those hypotheses might provide the big reasons why altruism and prosocial behaviors exist, most scholars agree that evolutionary-theory-based explanations are little use in understanding these behaviors in our day-to-day lives. To social scientists, the more pertinent questions include: What are the biological processes responsible for morally exemplar behaviors? What are the socialization experiences of individuals who have these characteristics? And what are the personal characteristics of moral exemplars?

Characteristics of Moral Exemplars

Are individuals who exhibit extraordinary moral commitment and behavior dramatically different from other people? Research suggests that this is generally not the case. Rather, scholars think that most people are capable of extraordinary moral commitments and behaviors. Researchers have shown that moral exemplars transcend demographic boundaries. That is, morally exemplar behavior is observed across different ages, races, genders, ethnic groups, and socioeconomic levels. Moral exemplars just seem to act on personal characteristics conducive to morality more than other people.

One unique approach for understanding characteristics of moral exemplars has been to ask people what they think makes moral individuals different. In one classic study of adolescent moral exemplars, Hart and his colleagues asked youth from a poor, inner-city community to nominate other youth whom they admired and respected as care exemplars. It is noteworthy that, despite inherent difficulties associated with growing up in an impoverished community, there were still a number of adolescents who "demonstrated unusually admirable commitment to care for others" (Hart, Atkins, and Ford 1995, 322). One such adolescent was David Street, a seventeen-year-old African American male. He was not only an excellent student but also served in leadership positions at school, participated as a youth representative on boards for several community organizations, and was heavily involved in volunteer activities working through a local public-service agency to help younger adolescents in need. When fifteen moral exemplars like David were asked, "What kind of a person are you?" they were more likely than a group of nonexemplars to use moral or caring traits (e.g., "honest"), activities (e.g., "helping others"), and goals (e.g., "community involvement") to describe themselves. For example, David Street mentioned that one of his important characteristics was that he "wasn't a bad influence," and a primary goal of his was "being involved in the community." Their findings suggested that care exemplar youth were more likely to have a strong moral sense of self than nonexemplar youth.

Interestingly, the two groups did not differ on moral-reasoning abilities—suggesting that both groups are equally capable of thinking in cognitively sophisticated ways about moral-dilemma situations.

Other studies have focused on examining adolescent (and adult) conceptions of moral identity. In one study Walker and Pitts surveyed youth and adults, asking them to identify terms that reflect a "moral person." The researchers found that youth defined a moral person as having strongly held moral principles and high moral standards. Furthermore, moral individuals were thought of as being self-confident with a sense of integrity such that they were committed to living their lives in ways consistent with their values and standards. Moreover, moral individuals were seen as being caring and compassionate of others as well as loyal and dependable. Another recent study conducted by Dan Lapsley found similar results. The studies suggest that youth do have clear expectations about individuals whom they consider to embody a strong moral character. Morally exemplar individuals have a combination of strong moral values, and they are compassionate and caring.

In one of the early studies of moral exemplars, Colby and Damon conducted in-depth interviews with twenty-three people nominated as moral exemplars by a panel of moral philosophers, theologians, and other professionals. One such moral exemplar, Virginia Foster Durr, grew up in a white family that was racist against black people, yet she went on to be a key figure in fighting for African American civil rights. She spent over thirty years struggling to change laws in Alabama to afford more equal rights to blacks, and she and her husband provided legal services primarily to poor black clients who were victims of discrimination. Because of their beliefs and commitments, she and her husband lived much of their lives with very little money.

Colby and Damon found that Virginia and the other exemplars had several things in common. For example, they had strongly held values, in particular caring, justice, and integrity. They seemed to feel more empathy toward others and were more motivated to act on those feelings. Their moral acts were often automatic or habitual. They frequently acted with certainty and seemed compelled to do what they knew was right, regardless of consequences to themselves. Exemplars tended to seek experiences and associations with others that would help them develop morally. They were less self-focused and had positive attitudes toward their life, work, and other people. Additionally, many drew inspiration through faith in a higher power (e.g., God). The researchers concluded that one of the key features of moral exemplars is a strong sense of moral identity, which means that they define themselves largely in moral terms and that there is congruency between what they most want to do and what they know is right. This leads them to feel a strong sense of responsibility and obligation to do what they see as moral.

Scholars in social and personality psychology have often sought to understand personality differences between people who help and those who choose not to help in situations where there are great personal risks involved. In one of the early studies of moral exemplars, Oliner and Oliner sought to understand the motives behind individuals who risked their lives to rescue Jews during World War II. During the Nazi occupation of Europe, approximately 6 million Jews were murdered (60 percent of those in Europe). However, the numbers could have been a lot worse had it not been for the heroic efforts of a small minority of non-Jewish people who helped rescue Jews at great risk to themselves and their families. Furthermore, the majority of the rescuers actually helped over a period of several years. Rescue activities typically included things such as helping keep Jews alive by getting them food and water, helping them escape from prisons, smuggling them out of the country, or helping them stay hidden if they stayed in the country.

Rescuers who were discovered were often tortured or executed.

The researchers examined differences between those who helped rescue Jews and those who chose not to. Participants responded to a lengthy questionnaire, and analyses compared results of 231 rescuers and 126 nonrescuers. Rescuers tended to have greater access to opportunities to help and resources that would aid them in helping. However, these were often a result of their own choices and characteristics (e.g., since they were friendlier toward Jews, they were more likely to be asked for help). Rescuers also had strongly internalized moral values, particularly caring, justice, and social responsibility, and they felt more motivated to act on these values. Furthermore, the rescuers believed that those values should apply to all humanity (e.g., regardless of race or religion). The rescuers also reported relatively high levels of empathy and were more motivated to act on these feelings. In addition, rescuers of Jews had a stronger sense of self-confidence in, control over, and responsibility for their own behavior.

In a recent review of the literature, Staub concluded that highly moral individuals tend to act based on certain types of motivational orientations. First, some act on an empathic orientation, meaning that they are motivated to moral action based on feelings of empathy toward others. Second, others are motivated by a prosocial-values orientation, which means they have internalized caring values and feel responsible for the welfare of others. And third, those motivated by a moral-principles orientation act out of a desire to live up to certain moral principles. Furthermore, Staub suggests that moral exemplars are individuals who possess *moral courage*—the ability to persist and apply their moral principles and desires in the face of adversity.

In recent years, some scholars have begun to think of moral exemplars as experts in the moral domain, just like scientists, musicians, athletes, and others can be experts in their areas. This approach does not see moral exemplarity as the possession of moral personality traits or virtues. Rather, highly moral individuals are higher on certain skills than others, which allows them to more effectively perceive, interpret, and respond to moral situations. Thus, individuals with *moral expertise* are better able to sense when another person is in need of help, determine how best to help them, feel a sense of responsibility for helping, and then are likely to succeed in doing what is necessary to help. Furthermore, individuals who acquire moral expertise are capable of responding quickly to moral situations so that their moral decision-making and actions are often highly efficient.

Programs Designed to Promote Morally Exemplar Behaviors

Many scholars who study moral exemplars have embraced the notion of *application* and have attempted to develop programs to foster and promote morally exemplar behaviors in our everyday lives. The programs are quite varied and focus on different aspects of our society. Some programs emphasize changing the individual directly; other programs focus on change through social institutions such as families, schools, or workplaces.

In 1968, under the supervision of Larry Kohlberg, a prominent moral-developmental psychologist, a moral-development curriculum was implemented in the high schools in several communities within the boroughs of New York City. The initial goal of the Just Community approach to moral character education was to encourage students to develop more sophisticated ways of thinking in moral-dilemma situations. Kohlberg believed that fostering children's moral-reasoning abilities would result in more positive moral behaviors. The Just Community approach included the goals of establishing a community based on democracy and fairness, maintaining a climate of trust, and encouraging the use of higher levels of moral reasoning. To meet these goals, students were encouraged to develop school rules and disciplining policies. Furthermore, students conducted regular meetings to assess the weekly progress of their policy system and to discuss moral-dilemma situations to foster their moral-reasoning abilities. Overall, the findings of the program evaluations were promising, though limited.

Another moral-development program proved to be quite ambitious. The Child Development Project discussed by Battistich and his colleagues has five major components that focus on moral development from an individual-centered approach. They are as follows: (1) cooperative learning, (2) developmental discipline, (3) helping activities, (4) highlighting prosocial values, and (5) promoting social understanding. Research designed to evaluate this school-based program indicates that there are strong positive effects of the program (especially long-term effects). Among the findings, students who participate in the program engage in more prosocial behavior and exhibit more empathy. Also, students in the program choose more positive social and cooperative strategies in resolving group conflicts.

Another innovative type of program focuses on instituting change through sports activities. Youth sport development programs promote moral development while allowing the youth to engage in sports activity. One model program is the STARR (Sports Teaching Adolescents Responsibility and Resiliency) program based in Camden, New Jersey, and run by Daniel Hart and his colleagues. It uses sports activities as a medium for teaching moral responsibility and modeling positive conduct, good decision-making, and coping skills. The goals of the program are to encourage community service, to train adult coaches to be moral exemplars, and to promote adolescent-to-adolescent responsibility and healthy development.

Other programs focus on fostering the positive characteristics of individuals. Empathy-training programs primarily concentrate on fostering empathy skills. The two main goals in an empathy-training program are to promote understanding of other people's situations and to nurture emotional sensitivity to others. Prior research has shown that both components are associated positively with prosocial behaviors and negatively with aggression. One prime example is the Roots of Empathy (ROE) program. The ROE program is based in Canada (offered to over 10,000 students across the country) and is designed to build parenting skills and to raise the levels of empathy. A recent evaluation showed that children in the ROE program evidenced increases in social understanding and prosocial behaviors and decreases in aggressive behaviors when compared to a matched sample of children who were not in the program. In general, evaluation studies from various empathy-training programs have shown that children who participate in such programs tend to exhibit more prosocial behaviors than children who do not participate in the programs.

Other common moral-development programs include service learning and volunteering programs. An example of a service-learning program is the *Learn and Serve America* program. This national initiative seeks to implement service-learning programs around the country. Preliminary research findings indicate that students who participate in this program have a positive experience. Students also report that they become connected with members of their community, they are committed to their experience, and they find pleasure in helping other. Other research suggests that students truly benefited from service learning. The benefits can include a gain of positive self-esteem, a sense that they make meaningful contribution to their respective communities, and an increased desire to acquire more knowledge through their experiences.

It is strongly advised by many researchers that service learning and volunteering programs must include two important dimensions: the programs must emphasize that learning is the main goal of the program and there should be some evaluation mechanism. Moreover, scholars have noted in recent studies that requiring students to participate in volunteer activities can create adverse reactions and undermine future volunteerism. One possible manner to address this concern is to provide service-learning students volunteer placement choices. Evaluation of service learning programs is strongly recommended due to the fact that there is a paucity of information about the positive short- and long-term effects of such programs. Scholars also note that volunteer facilitators must monitor closely students' social and academic development. Finally, it is important to monitor the impact of the program on the community to ensure positive connections between the program, the student and the community agencies.

We have briefly reviewed what is known regarding moral exemplars and programs designed to promote and foster moral exemplary behaviors. However, there are many gaps in our understanding of moral exemplars. For example, there is virtually no research that examines moral exemplars across different cultures or even within ethnic minority groups in the United States Moreover, as mentioned earlier, we have limited understanding of the development of moral exemplars. In addition, although numerous programs have been developed to foster and promote moral exemplary behaviors, there is a need for rigorous evaluations of those programs.

Summary and Conclusions

Although there is a clear need for more research on moral exemplars and moral-development programs, there is remarkable consistency regarding the characteristics of moral exemplars. First, moral exemplars tend to be strongly motivated by compassion and internalized moral values. Second, moral exemplars have high moral standards and expectations of themselves and they endorse moral values such as caring, justice, equality, integrity and social responsibility. Third, they have a strong sense of themselves as moral individuals with a desire to do what is right and a sense of responsibility to do so regardless of possible personal consequences. Fourth, moral exemplars often act with certainty, confidence, and control. Fifth, many moral exemplars are religious or spiritual. And sixth, they may have certain abilities that allow them to more effectively and often automatically perceive of, interpret, and respond to moral situations. Researchers also suggest that moral and care exemplars might be more common than we are led to believe – that would certainly be promising.

Note: Funding support to one of the authors of this entry, Gustavo Carlo, was provided by a grant from the National Science Foundation (NSF 01-32302). Correspondence may be addressed to Gustavo Carlo, Department of Psychology, University of Nebraska–Lincoln, Lincoln, NE 68588, e-mail: gcarlo@unl.edu.

See also Adult Roles in Youth Activism; Empathy; Just Community High Schools and Youth Activism; Moral Congition and Youth Activism; Moral Development; Parental Influences on Youth Activism; Prosocial Behaviors; Service-Learning.

Recommended Reading

Battistich, V., Watson, M., Solomon, D., Schaps, E., and Solomon, J. (1991). "The Child Development Project: A Comprehensive Program for the Development of Prosocial Character." In W. M. Kurtines, and J. L. Gewirtz, eds. *Handbook of Moral Behavior and Development*. Volume 3: *Application*. Mahwah, NJ: Lawrence Erlbaum Associates, pp. 1–33.

Colby, A., and Damon, W. (1992). *Some Do Care: Contemporary Lives of Moral Commitment*. New York: The Free Press.

Eisenberg, N., and Fabes, R. A. (1998). "Prosocial Development." In W. Damon, seriesed., and & N. Eisenberg, vol. ed. *Handbook of Child Psychology*. Volume 3: *Social, Emotional, and Personality Development*. 5th ed. New York: John Wiley, pp. 701–778.

Feshbach, N. D. (1989). "Empathy Training and Prosocial Behavior." In Hinde, eds *Aggression and War*, edited by J. Grobel and R. A. Hinde New York: Cambridge University Press, pp. 101–111.

Hart, D., Atkins, R., and Ford, D. (1998). "Urban America as a Context for the Development of Moral Identity in Adolescence." *Journal of Social Issues, 54*: 513–530.

Oliner, S. P., and Oliner, P. M. (1988). *The Altruistic Personality: Rescuers of Jews in Nazi Europe.* New York: The Free Press.

Gustavo Carlo, Sam Hardy, and Myesha Alberts

Motivation of Youth. *See* Flow: Youth Motivation and Engagement.

MTV's Choose or Lose Campaign (1992–). Since the launch of MTV's Choose or Lose campaign in 1992, MTV has emerged as the channel of choice for candidates seeking to reach and empower young people. Commanding the attention of more eighteen- to thirty-four-year-old viewers than CNN, MSNBC, Headline News, CNBC, and the Fox News channel combined, MTV is unrivaled in its ability to bridge the gap between candidates and young voters. In recent years, the parties and candidates have caught on. An article in the June 30, 2004, issue of the *Wall Street Journal* described "high-level party operatives" as "busy seeking coverage by key television channels—MTV, for example."

Choose or Lose is MTV's comprehensive prosocial campaign to inform young adults about the political process and mobilize young adults aged eighteen to thirty to register and vote. The award-winning campaign consists of news programming, public service announcements (PSAs), concerts, and grassroots events focusing on the issues pertaining to and affecting young people during each presidential election year. Choose or Lose has been uniquely successful because it goes beyond informing young adults about the political process and urging them to show up at the polls on Election Day. Choose or Lose seeks to voice the most urgent political concerns of young viewers and actively encourages the leading presidential candidates to address those concerns. Moreover, Choose or Lose covers campaigns as only MTV can. Choose or Lose subverts the Washington punditry, which tends to turn off young voters with historical references, blatant partisanship, and an emphasis on the process, rather than the ends, of politics. Choose or Lose opts to bring the questions and concerns of real young people directly to the candidates, oftentimes in their own words.

In 1992 MTV News went on the road with the candidates, covering the primaries and explaining the political process to the MTV audience. That year MTV was able to obtain exclusive interviews with all three of the presidential candidates and established itself as the leading political voice for young people nationwide as well as their most trusted source for political news. In the aftermath of the election MTV was often credited for having generated widespread excitement among young people and with drawing the highest number of eighteen- to twenty-four-year-olds to the polls since eighteen-year-olds were given the right to vote in 1972.

In 1996 MTV took the Choose or Lose campaign cross-country with the Choose or Lose bus tour. The Choose or Lose bus traveled 80,000 miles, reaching young people in forty-eight states. In addition, MTV devoted over one hundred hours of airtime to election coverage and issues. For a second time, all three presidential candidates and two vice-presidential candidates came on MTV to reach out to young voters. With their efforts in 1992 and 1996, MTV, in conjunction with its affiliate Rock the Vote, had registered nearly 1 million young voters.

In 2000 MTV renewed its commitment to informing young people about the political process with weekly Choose or Lose news segments, issue-oriented news specials, interviews with the candidates, concerts with top artists, and unprecedented online outreach. Once again, MTV successfully convinced candidates to speak directly to young people through interviews and forums. Choose or Lose's team of young reporters interviewed George W. Bush on the campaign trail, and in a televised town-hall forum with Al Gore 150 young people had their questions answered on topics ranging from Napster to student loans. MTV's coverage of the primary season, party conventions, and general election culminated with an election night wrap-up special.

On-air programming in 2000 also included a news special entitled "Where Were You at 22?," which profiled the prepolitical lives of six of the presidential candidates, giving audiences a unique glimpse into the candidates when they were young people and allowing them to see the candidates at an age and place in their lives that they could relate to. For another news special, "The Gun Fight," MTV and TIME magazine teamed up to explore the controversial issue of guns and their impact on young people.

In addition, MTV aired seventy different public-service announcements with a frequency as high as two or three each hour throughout the year, urging young people to vote and affirming that their vote mattered. A series of "I Will Vote Because . . ." public-service announcements featured celebrities like Eddie Vedder, Cameron Diaz, Master P, Al Gore, George W. Bush, and President Bill Clinton sharing why they planned to vote in 2000.

Off the air, Choose or Lose teamed up with the Youth Vote Coalition, which in 2000 was made up of over fifty organizations, including the League of Women Voters, Leadership Conference on Civil Rights, and Rock the Vote, for an outdoor Get Out the Vote advertising campaign. For thirty-eight days leading up to the election, public-service ads on buses and subways in ten major cities across the country reminded people to go to the polls and vote. Over a million celebrity, grassroots, and automated Get Out the Vote phone messages were delivered to young people right before Election Day. In 2000, in conjunction with the Youth Vote 2000 Coalition and Rock the Vote, MTV registered over a million young voters—more than in the previous two elections combined.

Online, the Choose or Lose Web site (ChooseorLose.com) reached young people where they were, that is, at their desktops. The site offered voter registration, bipartisan information about issues and the campaign, and a forum for discussion and debate. Over 8 million young people received an interactive, electronic PSA enabling them to register to vote and to apply for an absentee ballot. The number of voters registered online quadrupled from 1996 to 2000—surging from 40,000 in 1996 to some 170,000 in 2000—in part because of the success of ChooseorLose.com.

The impact of Choose or Lose's efforts was apparent: 700,000 more eighteen- to twenty-four-year-olds voted in 2000 than in 1996. Moreover, a national survey conducted by Penn Schoen and Berland just before the election revealed that 61 percent of likely voters between the ages of eighteen and twenty-four had seen or heard about the Choose or Lose campaign, and 81 percent of those who had seen Choose or Lose programming said it made them more likely to register and vote in the 2000 election (U.S. Census Bureau; CNN exit polling data; Penn Schoen and Berland National Survey 2000).

For the first time ever, in 2004 MTV's Choose or Lose set an ambitious goal focused on youth voter turnout. The goal was to help mobilize 20 million young adults aged eighteen to thirty to vote on Election Day, a substantial increase over the just more than 17 million who voted in 2000. Dubbed "20 Million Loud," this call to action was adopted as an achievable goal by a diverse coalition of innovative youth organizations, including Citizen Change, Rock the Vote, Hip-Hop Team Vote, WWE's Smackdown Your Vote!, New Voters Project, Declare Yourself, Meetup.com, Project Vote Smart, National Council of La Raza, Youth Venture, CIRCLE, the NAACP, Harvard University Institute of Politics, and more than one hundred organizations in the Youth Vote Coalition.

Throughout 2004, Choose or Lose 2004 and its partners conducted a series of high-profile, high-impact events on the air, online, and off the air kicking off with two MTV News specials, "Diary: Gideon in Iraq" airing in January and "Louder Now!" in February, and culminating in the fall with MTV's first-ever national, online "PRE-Lection," in which young adults cast their vote in a mock election and declared their choice for president of the United States.

In addition, the channel aired a series of celebrity "Choose" PSAs featuring celebrities such as Jennifer Lopez, Tom Cruise, Tony Hawk, Beyoncé, Chris Rock, Elijah Wood, and Julia Roberts sharing their proactive "choose" statements, such as "choose to get involved" or "choose to care," with the audience. In all, MTV aired twelve long-form Choose or Lose documentaries, covering issues ranging from the war in Iraq to jobs to drugs to sexual health and hip-hop and politics. More than 30 million viewers watched Choose or Lose's programming in 2004, including two consecutive programs, which were the most watched in the history of Choose or Lose.

The 2004 Choose or Lose Web site allowed users to register to vote in their home states, get information on the candidates and a number of issues, join online forums to actively discuss those issues, get involved on a local level, reach out to candidates, and connect with MTV's partner organizations. MTV.com, in partnership with Meetup.com and Rock the Vote, helped to organize monthly local "meetups" on the first Tuesday of every month at seven p.m., which enabled young people to get involved in their local political process, discuss the issues, and help register voters.

Choose or Lose continues to battle the common misperception that young people are not involved in the political process and will not turn out to vote. And in 2004, after an unprecedented investment in Choose or Lose, young people did it. According to estimates, 21 million eighteen- to twenty-nine-year-olds voted, meaning we far exceeded the "20 Million Loud" goal for eighteen- to thirty-year-olds.

See also Deliberative Democracy; Democracy; Democratic Education; Hip-Hop Generation; Kids Voting USA (KVUSA); Minority Youth Voter Turnout; New Media; Peer Influences on Political Development; Personality and Youth Political Development; Punk Rock Youth Subculture; Rights of Participation of Children and Youth; Rights, Youth Perceptions of; State and Youth, The; Student Political Activism; Student Voices Project; Voice.

Recommended Reading

Eisner, J. (2004). *Taking Back the Vote: Getting American Youth Involved in Our Democracy.* Boston, MA: Beacon Press.

Additional Web Sites

MTV Choose or Lose: http://www.mtv.com/chooseorlose/

Youth Vote Coalition: http://www.youthvote.org/

Rock the Vote: http://www.rockthevote.com/home.php

Public Interest Research Group: http://www.uspirg.org/

Voto Latino: http://www.votolatino.org/

Project Vote Smart: http://www.vote-smart.org/

Leslie Pope and Ian V. Rowe

N

NACE. *See* National Alliance for Civic Education (NACE).

National Alliance for Civic Education (NACE). The National Alliance for Civic Education (NACE) was founded in 2000 to unite many individuals and groups who have worked to promote civic knowledge and engagement among citizens, especially youth. A catalyzing event for the organization of NACE was the release of the National Assessment of Educational Progress (NAEP) Report's 1998 civic assessment (U.S. Department of Education 1999), which pointed to inadequacies in civic knowledge among students across the country. Although young people are participating in alternative forms of civic engagement in record numbers, through activities such as service learning and other forms of volunteering to benefit community, those who came together to form NACE are deeply concerned that youth also are less involved in traditional forms of civic engagement than in the past (U.S. Census Bureau; The Tarrance Group; and Lake, Snell, Perry and Associates 1999) and have less command of civic knowledge, skills, and dispositions necessary to the health of our democracy.

Mission and Goals

The mission of NACE is to help young people across the nation to "better understand the significance of effective civic education for a well-functioning democracy" (NACE 2000). To achieve this mission the alliance's central focus is to increase the civic knowledge and engagement of youth, including youth political activism. The belief in the capacity of young people as core determinants in the process of democracy is a driving force of NACE. As such, the alliance has adopted several key goals to strengthen the civic education of youth and ultimately, their role in democracy:

- Work with states and localities to strengthen their commitment to civic education and engagement
- Seek expansion of civic education in state curriculum guidelines
- Improve the preparation and professional development of teachers engaged in civic education
- Ensure the accessibility of up-to-date civic teaching materials and techniques
- Strengthen the links between elementary and secondary education and colleges and universities around civic education and engagement
- Work with the federal government to improve the collection and assessment of data in civic education
- Expand opportunities for young people to participate meaningfully in the civic life of their communities

NACE has both national and international individual and group members committed to its goals. The growing membership includes educators, practitioners, policymakers, funders, researchers, and others representing a range of organizations who have come together to present a collective voice for civic education to inspire youth engagement and activism.

NACE Web Site

The NACE Web site, http://www.cived. net, serves as the primary communication mechanism for the alliance while also engaging its membership more actively in the organization. Through the "What's New" section, located on the Web site's homepage, daily updates of civic-education policy, practice, and research inform members and the general public about current civic-education issues. These announcements are archived on a regular basis.

Also featured on the homepage is a "Special Focus Section." Constructed as a way to provide in-depth views on key issues that impact youth civic education and engagement, this section has recently highlighted two important documents that are illustrative of NACE's commitment to insuring youth political activism.

"The Civic Mission of Schools" report (Gibson and Levine 2003), released in 2003 by the Carnegie Corporation of New York and the Center for Information and Research on Civic Learning and Engagement, summarizes the evidence in support of civic education in K–12 schools; analyzes trends in political and civic engagement; identifies promising approaches to civic education; and offers recommendations to educators, policymakers, funders, researchers, and others. "The Civic Mission of Schools" identifies schools as an important venue for civic education. It states that "schools are the only institution with the capacity and mandate to reach virtually every young person in the country; they are best equipped to address the cognitive aspects of good citizenship; and they are communities in which young people learn to interact, argue, and work together with others, an important condition for future citizenship" (12). Moreover, the report indicates that school-based civic-education programs can successfully increase young people's knowledge, skills, interest, and commitment. "The Civic Mission of Schools" asserts that now is an important time to focus on civic education because school-based civic education is in decline; schools need to address disturbing trends related to youth civic engagement; and schools can capitalize on several positive trends related to youth civic engagement.

The 1999 IEA Civic Education Study

The 1999 International Association for the Evaluation of Educational Achievement's civic education study is the largest and most rigorous study of civic education ever conducted internationally. Researchers surveyed nearly 90,000 fourteen-year-old students in twenty-eight countries (including the United States) and 50,000 seventeen- to nineteen-year-olds in sixteen countries during the second phase of the study. At least two important aspects of the IEA study reveal its impact on youth political activism—the importance of developing a broad range of youth civic competencies and the role of learning both in and out of school. Several additional reports have resulted from this comprehensive study. All of these reports provide cross-national analyses that illustrate what fourteen-year-old students and seventeen- to nineteen-year-old students know and believe about democratic institutions and processes. They also give a snapshot of the civic activities young people engage in, what their intentions are for future participation.

NACE Organizational Structure

NACE has no bylaws and has an interim set of individuals voluntarily serving on the steering committee and the three task forces working to advance the mission of the alliance. The steering committee periodically meets to discuss organizational aspects such as how best to approach new work and distribution of information to the membership. Steering committee members have agreed to provide for (1) rotating terms for members of the steering committee and task forces, (2) establishing new task forces as needed, and (3) seeking funding to sustain the organization.

The three NACE task forces are: liaison to group members; public support and advocacy; and research and outcomes evaluation. Each of the task forces consists of about ten members who exchange information about civic education and civic engagement. Pertinent to youth activism is the role of NACE in disseminating "The Civic Mission of Schools" report. There is agreement that the report is an important and useful document confirming the need for civic education and suggested ways for effective civic education and that NACE should strongly support its widespread dissemination. The members also agree that NACE is a portal for dissemination and discussed how to encourage NACE member organizations to call their own members' attention to the report and suggest how it can be used at as many local, state, and federal levels as possible. NACE supports the process by encouraging its members to provide suggestions for strategies including linking on the NACE Web site, highlighting information from the report, strongly encouraging members and nonmembers to utilize and disseminate the report, and providing ongoing feedback to NACE or CIRCLE about its use.

The research and outcomes evaluation task force discusses activities that contribute to the goals of the membership. Of special interest to youth activism, participants exchange information about the projects on civic education and engagement that they are undertaking. A few examples include work on the National Student Voices Project that adopts the Annenberg curriculum and is being implemented in New Jersey by the New Jersey Civic Education Consortium.

The National Alliance for Civic Education recognizes the potential of service learning to address a wide range of student competencies, including civic engagement. And, it supports the view of "The Civic Mission of Schools" that service-learning programs that are most effective for civic education address a variety of common concerns such as ways to engage students and faculty in meaningful public issues that pursue civic outcomes, to connect service with the broader curriculum beyond academics, to provide opportunities for reflection, and to ensure a fit with a broader philosophy of education. NACE is supportive of the impact of quality service learning on areas such as students' social responsibility, commitment to volunteering, tolerance, and issues of diversity. Furco and Billig (2002) agree, suggesting that service-learning research needs to examine a host of questions related to civic engagement, citizenship, and democracy.

NACE is working hard to bring recognition to increased opportunities for youth to engage in civic education. As its work expands, the alliance will continue to advocate for civic education policies, promote quality research, provide information on the activities of its members (and others) across the country, and serve as a portal for civic education, civic engagement, and youth political activism both nationally and internationally.

See also Character Education; Citizenship Education Policies in the States; Civic Virtue; Democratic Education; Diversity Education; Environmental Education (EE); Global Citizenship Education (GCE) in the United States; IEA Civic Education Study; Just Community High Schools and Youth Activism; Prosocial Behaviors; School Engagement; School Influences and Civic Engagement; Service Learning and Citizenship Education.

Recommended Reading

Amadeo, J., Torney-Purta, J., Lehmann, R., Husfeldt, V., and Nikolava, R. (2002). *Civic Knowledge and Engagement: An IEA Study of Uppersecondary Students in Sixteen Countries.* Amsterdam, the Netherlands: International Association for the Evaluation of Educational Achievement.

Boys and Girls Clubs of America (May 2000). "Youth Today: What Teens Tell Teens, Bridge to Next Century Survey." Atlanta, GA: Boys and Girls Clubs of America. In *A Time to Serve, A Time to Learn: Service-Learning and The Promise of Democracy*, edited by J. C. Kielsmeier. *Phi Delta Kappan*, 652–657.

Furco, A., and Billig, S. H., eds. (2002). *Service-Learning: The Essence of the Pedagogy.* Greenwich: Information Age Publishing.

Gibson, C., and Levine, P., eds. (2003). *The Civic Mission of Schools.* New York and College Park, MD: Carnegie Corporation of New York and Center for Information and Researh on Civic Learning and Engagement.

National Alliance for Civic Education. See http://www.cived.net.

The Tarrance Group, Inc., and Lake, Snell, Perry and Associates (1999). *New Millennium Project—Phase 1: A Nationwide Study of Fifteen- to Twenty-four-Year-Old Youth.* National Association of Secretaries of State.

Torney-Purta, J., and Amadeo, J. A. (2004). *Strengthening Democracy in the Americas through Civic Education: An Empirical Analysis Highlighting the Views of Students and Teachers.* Washington, D.C.: Organization of American States.

Torney-Purta, J., Lehmann, R., Oswald, H., and Schulz, W. (2001). *Citizenship and Education in Twenty-eight Countries: Civic Knowledge and Engagement at Age Fourteen.* Amsterdam, the Netherlands: International Association for the Evaluation of Educational Achievement.

U.S. Census Bureau (November 2000). "Voting and Registration in the Election 2000." *U.S. Census Current Population Surveys 2000.* See http://www.census.gov/prod/2002pubs/p20-542.pdf.

U.S. Department of Education. Office of Educational Research and Improvement. National Center for Education Statistics (1999). *The NAEP 1998 Civics Report Card Highlights*, NCES 2000–460. Washington, D.C.

Gary A. Homana

National and Community Service. National and community service is a strategy designed to promote youth civic participation and responsibility by providing opportunities for individuals to serve their country and fellow citizens. Youth participating in national and community-service programs are provided modest levels of compensation, including assistance for educational expenses, in exchange for time working for or with a nonprofit, charitable organization, or community organization. These organizations are independent of government; focus their efforts on local as well as national social and economic problems, and utilize the resources of youth to enhance the organization's ability to meet its mission. Together, these efforts are designed to build an ethic of citizenship, while providing nonprofit and community organizations a means to expand their efforts.

National and community-service programs are based on the American tradition of assisting individuals, families, and communities that either have not fully shared in America's prosperity or have short-term needs created by changes in life circumstances. Paired with a process of civic reflection, service also connects youth who serve with basic American ideals such as freedom and liberty; helps to bridge ethnic, racial, religious, and economic divides; and strengthens our understanding of the responsibilities of American citizenship.

Youth participating in national- and community-service programs engage in a host of activities designed to address pressing social problems, such as homelessness, hunger, joblessness, and urban decline. Other activities include efforts designed to strengthen natural-resource management, promote private voluntary action, and support and expand the efforts of nongovernmental charitable organizations.

History

In a 1910 essay titled "The Moral Equivalent to War," the noted philosopher and psychologist William James originated the concept of national service in the United States. Wishing to promote an alternative to military service, James outlined national service as an activity available to all and benefiting the entire nation. As part of his efforts to combat the Great Depression of the 1930s, President Franklin D. Roosevelt created the first national service program in 1933. Called the Civilian Conservation Corps (CCC), the CCC represented an early New Deal program geared toward relieving unemployment by offering young, unemployed men the opportunity to engage in conservation work that ranged from reforestation to historic preservation.

Building on scientific philanthropy, particularly its belief that welfare policies should offer a chance instead of charity, Secretary of Labor Frances Perkins promoted the CCC concept with similar language: "The man gets a chance to keep healthfully occupied in return for the relief funds, and ... the government gets something valuable in return" ("Miss Perkins" 1933). Thus, CCC members signed on for a service term of six to eighteen months, lived in work camps, earned $30 in cash a month, and received benefits including food and health care. From 1933 to 1942, 3 million Americans subsequently improved

Children help with the remodeling of a house for a low-income family in the local community.

their lives and the United States through the CCC.

Although media reports and others continually lauded the CCC for offering men an improved outlook and for developing improved citizenship, the CCC ended during World War II, and national service did not reemerge until the 1960s. In 1961 President John F. Kennedy established the Peace Corps as one measure to arrest the growth of communism in underdeveloped countries. After providing extensive training, this program placed American volunteers in foreign countries for two-year tours.

Three years later, President Lyndon B. Johnson's "war on poverty" developed a domestic volunteer program more akin to the CCC. Authorized in 1964, Volunteers in Service to America (VISTA) provides opportunities and subsistence support for volunteers to serve one-year terms in nonprofit community organizations and public agencies. VISTA volunteers create and expand the capacity of programs designed to ameliorate the wide variety of social problems experienced by poor Americans and ultimately bring low-income individuals and communities out of poverty. By leveraging human, financial, and material resources, VISTA volunteers have increased the capacity of thousands of low-income communities across the country to solve community problems. In this same decade, the federal government also created episodic, part-time volunteer opportunities for older Americans. In what later became known as Senior Corps, these programs encompassed the Retired and Senior Volunteering Program (RSVP), Foster Grandparents, and Senior Companions. In the early 1970s, President Richard M. Nixon and the U.S. Congress created the Action Agency (inspired by the war on poverty phrase "community action") to house all volunteer programs, including the Peace Corps.

When military conscription ended in 1973, some individuals promoted compulsory national service for youth as an inexpensive way to tackle unmet social needs, but that idea never gained traction among policymakers. Two decades later, however, President George H. W. Bush demonstrated a greater interest in supporting volunteering at the federal level. In his administration, Bush created a White House Office of National Service and signed the National and Community Service Act of 1990, which supported service-learning programs in educational institutions and demonstration grants for national service programs.

Three years later, President Bill Clinton built on this foundation by establishing AmeriCorps through the National and Community Service Trust Act (1993). As the marquee part of this legislation, AmeriCorps represented a major effort to encourage young Americans to serve their communities and their country by participating in national- and community-service programs. AmeriCorps engages Americans aged seventeen and older in full- and part-time service to meet community needs in education, the environment, public safety, homeland security, and other areas. In exchange for their service, AmeriCorps members earn a modest living stipend and health benefits as well as an education award that could be used for paying for future higher education or repaying student loans. The majority of AmeriCorps participants are youth under age twenty-four and serve with local and national nonprofit organizations to tutor and mentor youth, build affordable housing, teach computer skills, clean parks and streams, and help communities respond to disasters. Harkening back to its predecessor, the CCC, AmeriCorps also includes a smaller program called the National Civilian Community Corps (NCCC), which places young Americans in teams for ten months to work on natural disasters and other community needs. NCCC is a residential youth-service program designed to provide opportunities for young Americans eighteen to twenty-

four years of age to serve together in teams to respond to the needs of communities across the country. While also encompassing VISTA, the entire AmeriCorps initiative dwarfed that program while offering long-term volunteering opportunities, usually full-time for one year in nonprofit organizations and addressing a myriad of community problems. By adding the education voucher as an incentive for service, Clinton argued that AmeriCorps would go further in "rewarding responsibility."

The 1993 legislation also created the Corporation for National and Community Service, an independent federal agency in charge of overseeing and implementing AmeriCorps, Senior Corps, and Learn and Serve America (promoting service in primary and secondary schools and in higher education). Administratively, the corporation inherited the war-on-poverty programs housed in the Action Agency, while expanding its size and scope via AmeriCorps and Learn and Serve. Within a decade, the agency supported over 2 million service participants annually.

Contemporary Policy Debates

After the creation of AmeriCorps, Clinton and other national service program adherents received a torrent of criticism from conservatives. In fact, Republican congressional members routinely attempted to eliminate AmeriCorps and youth-service programs during the 1990s. These national service critics distrusted using the federal government to connect young Americans to volunteer opportunities and argued that "paid volunteering" sullied the purity of volunteering and the importance of self-government while ultimately weakening the fabric of the voluntary sector. Along different lines, numerous liberals also expressed concern with the idea of national service. They viewed the federal government's promotion of youth volunteering as an implicit effort to remove the government's social-welfare responsibilities and preferred supporting more traditional welfare programs.

In response, national service supporters routinely assert that American youth civic engagement needs to be spurred and supported by the government because such activities ultimately benefit individual communities in many ways. Proponents also argue that national youth-service programs operate on the local level, are guided by community needs, and do not instill the entitlement attitude perpetuated by government welfare programs. These supporters emphasize that programs such as AmeriCorps generate additional volunteers in their respective communities, offer the opportunity for race and class integration, and promote social responsibility.

When the Republican presidency of George W. Bush began in 2001, national service programs gained more bipartisan appeal. Despite persistent criticism by some members of his party, President Bush viewed national service as an integral part of community life and tied its programs to homeland security after the terrorist attacks of September 11, 2001. Besides advocating an expansion of national service, he also wished to revise national service initiatives so they connect more closely with grassroots efforts, build on the preexisting community attachments of volunteers, and expand the capacity of community associations.

Comparative Perspective

Throughout the world, national youth-service programs—compulsory or voluntary—may be categorized into four conceptual models and four organizational models. Among conceptual models, the national-development or nation-building model was designed to overcome ethnic, geographic, and cultural differences, while delivering health, education, and agricultural services. The experimental model was designed to assist young people in making the transition from student to fully contributing adult. The third model, national youth service as an alternative to military service, was once the most common form of national service. Finally, in the popular intervention model, youth service plays a significant role in overcoming failed educational systems and youth unemployment and dissatisfaction. Through service, the intervention model provides young people with learning and experience to enable them to access the otherwise unattainable.

Four organizational models describe how youth service is mobilized, administered, and supported to achieve national goals. In Nigeria, for example, the central government has established a number of bureaucracies to run the state national service program. This is the federal-bureaucrat model. Botswana uses the secretariat model, in which a small, independent government body takes responsibility for the state's programs, which are in turn run by other government departments or nongovernmental organizations. The education-provider-driven model, as used in Mexico, ties access to higher education to compulsory service. Finally, in the United States, a public-private model has emerged with the Corporation for National and Community Service's selecting programs and providing resources and oversight. These programs are managed locally through public-private partnerships.

Empirical Studies

A recent meta-analysis of the service research field indicates that the number of studies and evaluations on youth service have increased steadily throughout the 1990s. Much of the work completed to date is interdisciplinary. That is, it is found in a wide variety of academic disciplines and professional fields, but it is less likely to be the focus of traditional social-science disciplines such as economics, sociology, political science, and anthropology. The interdisciplinary nature of this research has created terminological problems and fragmentation, making it difficult to aggregate the literature's findings and stipulate general findings that are universal for national- and community-service programs.

Until recently, many studies on national- and community-service programs have typically taken the form of implementation studies or process evaluations, where a small number of programs are studied, and the outcomes measured are perceptions of a program's success as seen by national- and community-service members, non-profit host organizations, recipients of service, or all three. As one might expect, these inquiries have generally found a high level of satisfaction among all actors who participate in publicly sponsored community service.

However, more recent studies have used research designs associated with the more rigorous social-science methods. These studies are designed to assess whether national- and community-service programs actually produce the intended effects (or social value) on service participants, non-profit organizations, local communities, and beneficiaries, or society at large. Typically, these studies rely on a pre- and post-test design to capture the effects of a program, using statistical controls to capture observed variation among variables thought to influence the dependent variable under analysis. This research indicates that national and community service—specifically the AmeriCorps programs—has a significant impact on volunteers' civic engagement and level of community participation, and these effects exist regardless of an AmeriCorps member's demographic characteristics or political orientation. Research also suggests national- and community-service programs may provide a foundation for youth to pursue careers in public service.

See also AmeriCorps; ·Civilian Conservation Corps (CCC); Community Service; Service Learning; Service Learning and Citizenship Education; Volunteerism.

Recommended Reading

Corporation for National and Community Service (2004). *Serving Country and Community: A Study of Service in AmeriCorps*. Washington, D.C.: Corporation for National and Community Service.

Eberly, D., and Sherraden, M., eds. (1990). *The Moral Equivalent of War?* New York: Greenwood.

Evers, W. M., ed. (1990). *National Service, Pro and Con.* Stanford, CA: Hoover Institution Press.

Ford Foundation (2000). *Worldwide Workshop on Youth Involvement as a Strategy for Social, Economic and Democratic Development.* New York: Ford Foundation.

Grantmaker Forum on National and Community Service (May 2000). *The State of Service-Related Research: Opportunities to Build a Field.* Berkeley, CA: Grantmaker Forum on National and Community Service.

"Miss Perkins Firm in Job Bill Defense" (March 24, 1933). *The New York Times,* p. 10.

Moskos, C. (1988). *A Call to Civic Service: National Service for Country and Community.* New York: Free Press.

Perry, J., Thompson, A., Tschirhart, M., Mesch, D., and Geunjoo, L. (1999). "Inside a Swiss Army Knife: An Assessment of AmeriCorps." *Journal of Public Administration Research and Theory,* 9 (2): 225–250.

Simon, C. (November-December 2002). "Testing for Bias in the Impact of AmeriCorps Service on Volunteer Participation: Evidence of Success in Achieving a Neutrality Program Objective." *Public Administration Review,* 62 (6): 670–678.

Simon, C., and Wang, C. (1999). *Impact of AmeriCorps on Members' Political and Social Efficacy, Social Trust, Institutional Confidence, and Values in Idaho, Montana, Oregon, and Washington.* Portland, OR: Northwest Regional Educational Laboratory.

Waldman, S. (1995). *The Bill: How Legislation Really Becomes Law: A Case Study of the National Service Bill.* New York: Viking.

Wofford, H., Waldman, S., and Bandow, D. (1996). "AmeriCorps the Beautiful?" *Policy Review,* 79: 28–36.

Kevin S. Cramer, David A. Reingold,
Robert T. Grimm Jr., and Kristin A. Goss

National Identity and Youth. A sense of belonging is a key social need that human beings strive to fulfill. Historically, people created a sense of belonging to others who were part of the same families, tribes, or clans. In modern times, however, since the development of the nation-state, individuals have also sought a sense of belonging in a broader collective—the nation. National identity, then, is a term for the emotional attachment and connection that individuals feel toward the nation with which individuals identify through elements such as a common language, customs, cultural or religious traditions, residence within particular geographic borders, or a shared conception of an ethnic origin.

One of the unique aspects of national identity, as Benedict Anderson argues, is that people share a sense of emotional attachment and loyalty toward millions of strangers whom they do not know and will likely never meet. This attachment helps create a sense of "us" and "them," defining who is included in and excluded from the nation. Even when there is a clear consensus on who "belongs" to the nation, however, national identity may not mean the same thing to everyone living in the same nation. Although there is often one dominant understanding of national identity and how it should be expressed, there are also alternative expressions of national identity from groups and individuals who may not agree with the dominant version.

A distinction can be made between two expressions of national identity: *patriotism*, or a positive attachment to the nation, and *nationalism*, in which other groups are excluded in the process of developing a positive attachment to the nation. It is also important to note that national identity is different from citizenship status, although many nation-states do not differentiate between the two concepts.

In the United States the metaphor of the "melting pot" has been used to explain how one national identity could unite the millions of immigrants from diverse backgrounds. According to this metaphor, an American national identity emerges from many diverse cultures and backgrounds blending together. The melting pot also refers to the process through which immigrants were molded into one common identity by assimilating to an American way of life, adopting the nation's values and ideals, and shedding their prior national attachments. Today, the idea of the melting pot has been criticized, as the notion that one must reject one's own identity in order to take on a new American iden-

tity is called into question. A growing number of recent citizens define themselves as "hyphenated Americans," such as "Asian-Americans" or "Latino-Americans," instead of or in addition to being simply Americans. Some have argued that instead of the melting pot, a more appropriate metaphor for American national identity is a tossed salad—in which each of the ingredients (lettuce, cucumbers, carrots, tomatoes, etc.) keep their unique characteristics, yet come together to form a whole. What this change in metaphor implies is that it is increasingly possible to have hybrid identities in which an American national identity does not replace other cultural identities but rather complements them. We see this among young Americans on college campuses, where second-and third-generation immigrants are increasingly exploring their roots and cultural heritage through coursework, college majors, and study-abroad programs.

Young people learn to identify with the nation through direct efforts on the part of states, national governments, civic groups, or schools. These institutions have an interest in shaping a sense of national identity among citizens in order to inspire the kinds of loyalty to the nation that motivates individuals to be civically engaged. Much of this happens through socialization, which is the process through which individuals learn the values, norms, skills, and behaviors deemed necessary to function effectively in any given society. Schools play a particularly important role in the process of socialization to a national identity. John Dewey, an American philosopher of education, argued that the school should be a miniature community, a first society, in which children learn to be citizens. There are at least three ways in which schools work to strengthen young people's national identity: through teaching the national language; through the curriculum and textbooks, particularly in history and civics; and through everyday school practices and interactions with peer groups.

First, the ability to communicate through a shared language is essential for the development of a national identity. Basic literacy and spoken language skills facilitate this communication and create access to media, textbooks, and newspapers, which convey common messages to citizens. National forms of media and texts, argues Benedict Anderson, allow people to feel connected, despite the fact that they do not know each other personally. Through listening to national evening news broadcasts or presidential speeches and debates, or through reading government reports, such as the report of the 9/11 Commission in the United States, Americans communicate with one another and develop their national identity through the shared use of language.

A second way in which schools create and strengthen national identity is through the educational curriculum. In schools, children learn about their nation's history, traditions, literary figures, and national heroes. Textbooks, curriculum, school projects, and events all help to convey national myths and stories, wars, historical events, and other cultural aspects of nations. Such aspects of schooling help to shape students' values and ideals and establish national heroes as role models. Moreover, the educational curriculum includes classes such as civic education, which aims to affect young people's involvement and participation in national civic life.

Finally, a third way in which schools reinforce national identity and pride is through daily school practices. Starting each school day by raising or pledging allegiance to the flag is one clear example. In addition, school ceremonies celebrating and commemorating national holidays and events, such as elementary school Thanksgiving plays in the United States, stimulate an emotional connection to the abstract concept of the nation and create a shared sense of history. National spelling bees, the Presidential Physical Fitness awards, and other national artistic or academic competitions all help to reinforce the idea of and

orient young people toward identification with one another and with the nation.

In addition to experiencing socialization in schools, young people are socialized toward a national identity through relationships in their families and peer groups, as well as in the media (through music, art, sports, and pop and consumer culture). Listening to the national anthem before the start of sporting events, learning how to fold and hang the American flag at summer camp, or listening to music with song titles that use the word "American," all help to reinforce national identity and a sense of connection to the nation. During interactions with peer groups, individuals across generations develop different ways of relating to the nation as they experience national and international events in formative ways. This was the case for many young people during the civil rights movement when youth social protests created critiques of the government and the nation in ways that were very different from prior generations'. In the post–9/11 era in the United States, many young people have expressed strongly patriotic views. In the spring of 2003, for example, some young Americans actively sanctioned what they felt to be an inappropriate expression of national identity by the Dixie Chicks, after the singers criticized President Bush at a concert. The fans' critiques, combined with radio-station boycotts, led to an apology from the singers. Not all young people agreed with this critique of the Dixie Chicks, of course—which illustrates that there are differences in conceptions and expressions of national identity *within* generations as well as *between* them.

The emergence of distinctly national artistic forms, such as Andy Warhol's pop-art usage of familiar American products and icons like Campbell's soup cans and photographs of Marilyn Monroe, or Elvis Presley's American-bred rock 'n' roll music, also help to define how Americans perceive themselves and how they are seen by the world. Today, rap music, portraying tough, rebellious street culture, is a dominant feature of the American music scene and is gaining popularity in the rest of the world as well.

In Hollywood, films and television programs draw heavily on American culture for themes and plots, which helps to shape everyday conceptions of what it means to be an American. National sports, such as baseball and football, reinforce national identity during such acts as the singing of the national anthem before the start of games. And in the business world, national identity plays a role in marketing product quality and in trying to create customer loyalty. Marking a product as American or "made in America," for example, has proved to be a successful marketing strategy for businesses that wish to attract customers or purchasers based on emotional ties—such as solidarity or loyalty—to the nation and to national companies. The U.S. Patent and Trade Office claims that more than 16,000 products and services have used the word "America" in some way to describe or label their items.

National identities are fluid and dynamic concepts, changing over time and in response to different events. Even single events or occurrences have the power to affect national identities. The events of September 11, 2001, for example, significantly influenced American national identity and the way it is discussed and mediated in schools, the media, and among individuals. Public displays of American patriotic sentiments and solidarity with Americans who lost their lives on 9/11 were evidenced by the waving of flags and the use of flag motifs on bumper stickers, lapel pins, ribbons, or on paper signs in merchant shop windows in the weeks and months after September 11. During times of war, national identity and patriotic sentiments also become more pronounced. Car stickers and magnets with flag motifs and the statement, "Support Our Troops," yellow ribbons tied around trees in suburban and rural front yards, and the broadcasting of photos and names of fallen American soldiers at the end of national news broadcasts are all ways in which national identity is expressed and reinforced during times of conflict or perceived international threat.

The role of wars and international conflict is also important in revealing the ways in which national identity can be gendered, meaning that it affects men and women differently. Men's relationships to the state and nation, historically, have been linked to military service and to the ultimate sacrifice of dying for the nation in warfare. But for women, who have been restricted from military service in much of the world, loyalty in some cases was considered to be to their husbands or to their families rather than to the state, as Kerber points out. Their relationships to the state and nation were mediated not by sacrificing their own lives in warfare but as mothers by giving birth to and raising future citizens. Additionally, for centuries, even in democratic countries, women were not permitted to vote, which further weakened their relationship with the nation. This is still the case in some countries today, where women are denied the right to full and equal participation as citizens. These kinds of restrictions have an impact on national identities.

Examples of cases outside of the United States also illustrate how national identity differs in various settings. In Europe national identities have been significantly affected by European integration into the European Union. Although the integration of Europe began as mainly a regional-economical union, it has developed into a more complex collaborative that transcends economic concerns, as the notion of a unified sense of European ethics, values, and ways of life begins to develop. Whether and how a separate European identity that is distinct from the national identities of its member states can be formulated remains unknown. Individual European countries each have long histories of national and regional identifications that are closely tied to national languages and regional dialects, cultures, traditions, and a shared history. Some scholars like Cederman and Delanty who are studying the idea of a European national identity agree, therefore, that it is unlikely that individual member states' identities would be replaced by a newly formed European identity. Rather, since identities are typically multilayered and dynamic, a European identity could be a supplemental transnational identity to be combined with individuals' attachments and identifications with national, local, and regional entities.

Nevertheless, attempts to consolidate a European identity have clearly been made. The creation of a flag, an anthem, and the development of large-scale cultural projects that include student exchanges are evidence of this. The new common European currency and the right of European citizens to travel, work, and live across national borders have contributed to a growing sense of connectedness across Europe. Educational programs and curricula have been developed and implemented to foster the process of socialization to new roles as Europeans, so that European citizens are prepared to participate in elections and decision-making processes. As a result, although regional and national identities will remain important, young people in Germany, France, and other European countries will gradually identify much more as "Europeans" than was the case for their parents and grandparents.

While the European case illustrates the complexities inherent in the relationships between national and transnational identities, the examples of Palestine and Israel reveal how a powerful sense of national identification can be fostered through a complex combination of ethnic and religious bonds and territory. Territory and religion play a central role in both Israeli and Palestinian national identities. In Israeli schools, for example, young people study the Jewish people's biblical connection to the land and study biblical texts, which tell the story of God assigning the land of Israel to the Jewish people. On field trips and archeological digs, youth reenact their ancestors' experiences and dig up remnants of ancient Jewish life. Through national holidays dedicated to celebrating Israel's independence, to commemorating Israel's fallen soldiers, or to remembering the horrors of the Holocaust, young Israelis internalize the notion that the state of Israel is essential for the existence of the Jewish people. The bond between the people and the land is also emphasized through military service. All young Israelis, both men and women, are required to serve in the Israeli Defense Force (IDF). Military service encapsulates the ultimate form of national identification because an individual is expected to risk his or her life for the nation.

As in Israel, territory plays a critical role in national identity for Palestinians, where a large community defines itself through its attachment to a territory and is identified as a nation—although at present, a Palestinian state does not exist. Socialization processes in Palestinian families, schools, and in the media help to construct Palestinian national identity based on the community's historical existence on the land called Palestine. As in the Israeli case, historical, religious, and ethnic elements are combined with modern experiences to create the myths and symbols that construct national identity. Likewise, the predicament of Palestinian existence as, in Eriksen's phrase, a "nation without a state" has been a powerful force in defining the Palestinian national identity and galvanizing Palestinians in their struggle for recognition and for a state.

In the context of conflict over land, Israeli and Palestinian national identities, both grounded in claims to the same historical territory, oppose each other, making the conflict difficult to resolve to the complete satisfaction of either nation. Each people created its national narrative and national identity in absolute opposition to the other group, ultimately perceiving its own opportunity for development and growth to be in conflict with the other's hopes for development. The educational systems of each nation became a place where national narratives were absorbed and reproduced, as each society focused its socialization agents on preparing their young to take part in the national struggle. Young people will have an important role to play in the coming years, as each generation of Israelis and Palestinians will re-create the nation(s), perhaps in ways quite different from the nations imagined by older generations. Israeli and Palestinian young people may take an active role in imagining a national future based on peaceful coexistence rather than conflict. Organizations and programs intended to help young people do just that—the Seeds of Peace summer camps, for example, bring Israeli, Palestinian, and American youth together, along with youth from other regions in conflict. Indeed, there is still hope that the Palestinian/Israeli conflict can be resolved peacefully, especially when compared to other national conflicts that once seemed intractable. There are examples of nations that have undergone tremendous transformations in their national identities and their interactions with neighboring countries, even within relatively short periods of time. Germany is one of the clearest examples.

Just two generations ago, Germany was one of the most virulently nationalistic nations on earth, as the National Socialist Party's nationalistic fervor ultimately culminated in the attempted extermination of millions of Germans and non-Germans who were deemed unworthy of membership in the national community for reason of race, religion, sexual orientation, physical or mental handicap, or political persuasion. This intertwining of nationalistic sentiments with racist and xenophobic beliefs during World War II leaves many Germans today with a deep sense of discomfort with and suspicion of national identity or patriotic sentiments. National pride, in fact, has been a taboo in Germany, and today, the phrase "I am proud to be a German" implicitly identifies individuals as right-wing extremists.

However, many people in the younger generation in Germany today express resistance to the taboo on national pride, at least in part because national pride signifies something different for their generation than it does for their parents. Pride, for many of these young people, is not equated automatically with fascism or racism but is rather perceived to be a normal reflection of one's identification with the nation's collective accomplishments. Many young people in Germany argue that they should be allowed to be proud of the things that Germany has accomplished since World War II. They argue against the unfairness of living with a taboo that resulted from the actions of their grandparents' generation, even while acknowledging the importance of teaching about the Holocaust so that nothing like it ever happens again. In short, they argue for a transformed view of and relationship with their nation and thus reflect a changing national conception of what it means to be German.

As these cases illustrate, nationalism and national identity are extraordinarily powerful forces. Although they are abstract notions, they are also concepts for which people are willing to kill and be killed. Scholars differ about what makes nationalism and national identity so powerful. Anderson argues that nationalism derives its force from its combination of political legitimation and emotional power, while Eriksen emphasizes the role of symbols in creating loyalty and a feeling of belonging. As we have seen, the United States has constructed a shared identity through the development of founding myths, the establishment of heroic founding fathers, and the emphasis on a common set of values and ideals: liberty, freedom, and the pursuit of happiness. Generations of immigrants have come to identify with their places of origin, the birthplaces of their parent or grandparents, as well as with the United States, as the emergence of hyphenated American identities illustrates.

The examples of the European Union, Palestine, Israel, and Germany reveal the importance of regional change, territory, religion, and generational transformations for the development of national identities. Taken together, all of these examples demonstrate that national identity is not fixed or stable but is always deeply intertwined with the historical and cultural contexts of any given nation. National identities are not formed only at one time for all time. Rather, they develop and change over time in reaction to national and international events and long-term social change. Likewise, the continuities and changes in national identity do not simply happen. National identity is made and remade, especially by young people as they encounter experiences that shape them as members of a nation.

See also Civic Identity; Ethnic Identity; European Identity and Citizenship; Identity and Activism; Identity and Organizing in Older Youth; Serbia, Youth Activism in (1990–2000); Transnational Identity.

Recommended Reading

Anderson, Benedict (1991). *Imagined Communities: Reflections on the Origin and Spread of Nationalism.* Revised Edition. New York: Verso.

Anderson, James, Wilson, Liam, and Wilson, Thomas, eds. (2003). *European Studies: An Interdisciplinary Series in European Culture, History, and Politics,* vol. 19, *Culture and Cooperation in Europe's Borderlands.* New York: Rodopi.

Berezin, Mabel (1999). "Political Belonging: Emotion, Nation and Identity in Fascist Italy." In *State/Culture: State-Formation after the Cultural Turn,* edited by George Steinmetz. Ithaca: Cornell University Press, pp. 355–377.

Cederman, Lars-Erik, ed. (2001). *Constructing Europe's Identity: The External Dimension.* Boulder: Lynne Rienner Publishers.

Delanty, Gerard (2000). *Citizenship in a Global Age: Society, Culture, Politics.* Buckingham and Philadelphia: Open University Press.

Dewey, John (2001). *The School and Society and the Child and the Curriculum.* Mineola, NY: Dover Publications.

Eriksen, Thomas H. (1993). *Ethnicity and Nationalism: Anthropological Perspectives.* London: Pluto Press.

Gellner, Ernest (1983). *Nations and Nationalism.* London: Oxford University Press.

Göçek, Fatma M., ed. (2002). *Social Constructions of Nationalism in the Middle East.* Albany: State University of New York Press.

Jackson, David (2002). *Entertainment and Politics: The Influence of Pop Culture on Young Adult Political Socialization.* New York: Peter Lang.

Jacoby, Tamar (2004). *Reinventing the Melting Pot: The New Immigrants and What It Means to Be American.* New York: Basic Books.

Kerber, Linda K. (1998). *No Constitutional Right to Be Ladies: Women and the Obligations of Citizenship.* New York: Hill and Wang.

Newman, David (2001). "From National to Post-National Territorial Identities in Israel-Palestine." *GeoJournal,* 53 (3): 235–246.

Phillips, Donald G. (2000). *Post-National Patriotism and the Feasibility of Post-National Community in United Germany.* Westport, CT: Praeger Publishers.

Rabinowitz, Dan, Anderson, James, Liam O'Dowd, Liam, and Wilson, Thomas, eds. (2003). "Borders and Their Discontents: Israel's Green Line, Arabness and Unilateral Separation." *European Studies: An Interdisciplinary Series in European Culture, History, and Politics 19: Culture and Cooperation in Europe's Borderlands.* Amsterdam: Rodopi, pp. 217–231.

Worchel, Stephen, and Coutant, Dawna (1997). "The Tangled Web of Loyalty: Nationalism, Patriotism, and Ethnocentrism." In *Patriotism in the Lives of Individuals and Nations,* edited by Daniel Bar-tal and Ervin Staub. Chicago: Nelson Hall Publishing, pp. 190–210.

Cynthia Miller-Idriss and Merav Ben-Nun

Native American Youth. For the Kootenai and Salish people in Montana and the Hopi in Arizona their languages are taproots to all of the traditions of spirituality, ceremony, craft, and history that bind each tribe together. Those original languages, and therefore much of the culture that defines each tribe, were largely lost to several generations—people who are now parents and grandparents to young adults and children—during the time the U.S. government imposed boarding schools that forbade the use of original native languages. Starting in 1999, young people in each tribe, along with their elders, have created language- and culture-revitalization projects through the Charting Community Connections (CCC) initiative as a means to mobilize their communities around the goal of preventing another "lost generation," believing that their languages are pathways to the survival of culture, and culture is a path to strong community. Strong community leads to increased

A five-year-old Native American boy wears ceremonial dress at a traditional pow wow. *Courtesy of Skjold Photographs.*

opportunity for livelihoods, education, and creativity—opportunities for native people to move beyond survival and build strong places based in deep culture in which their families can thrive.

Dr. Johnel Barcus is a member of the Blackfeet tribe in another part of Montana and an evaluator for the Charting Community Connections project, led by the Innovation Center for Community and Youth Development in partnership with the National 4-H Council and supported by the resources of the Ford Foundation. Barcus points to a growing awareness and desire to grab at the last strings of language before they disappear. "Parents and Grandparents feel the loss [of language] deeply," she says, pointing to the Hopi *Pu'tavi*, Salish *Nkwusm*, and Kootenai *Ksanka* projects as responses to this loss.

Mainstream cultural shifts have paved the way for young Hopi, Salish, and Kootenai people to develop an interest in cultural revitalization. In the late 1970s the American community-college system began to create spin-off campuses on native reservations. This helped to keep more young native people closer to home and provided some opportunities in that context to begin to celebrate specific native cultures. In the mid-1980s, says Barcus, it became, in some mainstream circles, "good to be Indian again." An understanding began to develop in both mainstream and native consciousnesses that there are profound differences between the tribes of North America, that to be "native" means little more than sharing a history of being the first people on this soil, and an understanding of oppression and poverty. Unique identities—cultural identities—were to be found in the answers to the question, "What does it mean to be a member of your clan, tribe, or village, in particular?" Language was the first thread to pull toward finding that answer.

Young people, the children and grandchildren of the "lost generation," have stepped in as part of the Charting Community Connections projects to pull this thread. As they do this work, they have learned valuable lessons around youth activism in cultures such as theirs, indigenous cultures based in a deep respect for age and the leadership of elders. As young people and elders have collaborated in the cultural revitalization projects, they have discovered ways to encourage and sustain youth activism in the context of the old ways they seek to renew.

Since each tribe has a culture of its own, each requires strategies for community development that are unique from others. The Salish and Kootenai people share land, for example, but not history or traditions, the Salish having been forced out of their native Bitterroot Valley to live with the Kootenai. The Salish *Nkwusm* project is led by a group of young adults who worked with Salish elders to learn the language and have created an immersion language preschool. *Nkwusm* leaders understood that to gain the support of the tribal council for the preschool project, they would need the support, in fact the up-front voices, of elder community members. They set about engaging with the elders in the traditional way, offering to help with tasks such as gathering and cutting wood, asking for instruction in traditional crafts and other activities. They developed relationships with elders that were right with traditional ways and from within those relationships could ask for the help of elders in supporting their community organizing. Many in the community remember a particular council meeting in which children, young adults, and elders stood together before the council in a successful bid for support. Had the young organizers insisted from the outset on "being heard" or "questioning authority," their efforts would likely have been not only ineffective but inconsistent with their goals.

The Kootenai *Ksanka* language preservation project is creating a bilingual preschool program and an after-school language and culture program for five- to eighteen-year-olds. *Ksanka* is led exclusively by elders; no young people appear to be leading in the ways one might expect in a mainstream organization. But at one Kootenai community event, a Kootenai language cakewalk in which eighty or so young people, mostly young children, participated, teenage community members played a crucial role. No meetings were held beforehand with the young people to solicit or direct their involvement in these activities, but they showed up nonetheless and then began to teach and mentor the younger children. In very real ways the teenagers "took charge," instructing younger children on appropriate behavior, teaching them words, and directing their activities.

Among the Hopi, where the people identify primarily with their particular village and then with the tribe, the people of the village of Mishongnovi, where *Pu'Tavi* began, have broadened their reach throughout Hopi villages with young activists involved at both grassroots and staff levels. The *Pu'Tavi* office is staffed by at least one young person, and young people throughout the community have engaged in activities such as the rebuilding of one village center. But as they worked, they accepted the advice and teaching of the elders who watched, even learning how to make a traditional drink to keep themselves going in the heat. *Pu'Tavi* organizes silversmithing courses in which young people participate, and computer-education classes in which whole families participate in support of small, local businesses. Each person, including young people, who takes time away from the business of survival to learn these new skills takes an active stance, one might even argue an *activist* stance in the revitalization of his or her culture and community.

In each of the communities involved in the Charting Community Connections project, the notion of youth development, certainly youth activism, as it has evolved in mainstream culture may in fact be "maladaptive," in the words of Beth Tucker, an advisor to the project and extension director in Cococino County, Arizona. In mainstream culture, adults are often asked to "partner" with young people in social change. The notion of youth "partnering" with elders in the Salish, Kootenai, and Hopi communities is antithetical to the goal of their work, which is to revitalize their traditional culture, a culture that rests heavily on the primacy of elder leadership. Tucker and her colleagues have wondered why "on three different sites, we don't see youth taking charge" in the ways that have evolved in the United States during the past several decades—questioning authority, leading discussions and rallies, and demanding attention. One young Salish organizer responds with the suggestion that that the whole notion of "youth leadership" doesn't fit for him in the context of his culture, preferring instead to be considered "engaged" in the collective work of the community.

According to Tucker, there is a "desperate, overwhelming expression" at all three sites of the desire for youth to be active in the effort to understand and revitalize native cultures, but mainstream supporters of the Charting Community Connections projects originally kept pushing youth involvement. Tucker says, "But to our way of thinking—which may be a white way of thinking—if they are not up in front of the room and on boards, they are not leaders." But in each of the examples cited above, youth were indeed leading, acting on their own initiative, generating ideas, even taking charge—usually with no adult *supervision*, certainly not in equal *partnership* with elders, but in community with them, engaged with them.

To an outsider some of these young people may not be considered activists, but "we're not looking deep enough," says Tucker, "we're not looking for the right indicators yet," of youth activism in these settings. The Kootenai cakewalk events and Hopi computer classes are examples of the ways whole families get involved with events at these sites. This is one of the lessons of the CCC projects around youth activism, says Johnel Barcus, the project evaluator. "You've got to look at the whole family [not just teenagers]. Offer everything to mom, dad, and all the kids," she says. Tucker speaks with similar conviction, "Events aren't just for kids—everybody comes. The children have free reign. Nobody is saying do this, don't do that. There has to be teaching and learning going on, but it's happening in different ways." In the Kootenai example, even though elders are in the culturally sanctioned role as leaders, the teaching and learning of the younger children depended on the self-initiated, culturally appropriate *engagement* of the older children acting to effect change in their community. These young people are youth activists, certainly, even if not in the mainstream sense of the word.

In just three years, people of all ages in the three Charting Community Connections project communities have become more fluent speakers of their native languages and more active in community events. In many cases this has led to an increase in economic and educational gains; certainly it has led to more consistent support for each other as these communities struggle to gain ground in the face of continuing injustice, poverty, isolation, and challenges to their cultural identities. Young people have played a primary role in each of these projects, rarely looking like typical youth activists, yet always engaged and always bringing their particular energy and perspectives as young people to the process.

Note: Special thanks to Dr. Johnel Barcus and Beth Tucker, as well as to the members of the *Pu'Tavi*, *Ksanka*, and *Nkwusm* organizations.

See also American Indian Movement.

Recommended Reading

Innovation Center: http://www.theinnovation-center.org

Lucinda J. Garthwaite

New Media. The Internet is a huge and miscellaneous collection of text, pictures, data, software, sound, and video, all stored as digital code and linked together into a network. The phrase "new media" refers to these interconnected digital products, which include items as disparate as interactive maps and downloadable music; library catalogs and personal diaries; massive multiplayer fantasy games and scientific datasets.

Until the mid-1990s, the most obvious feature of the Internet was widespread, collaborative creativity. Many people who had Internet connections also *contributed* (for no fee) software, comments on discussion boards, e-mail messages, or early Web sites. Commerce was forbidden, and it was very difficult (as well as uncommon) to protect intellectual property. One could get free access to virtually all sites on the nascent World Wide Web and easily borrow formats and ideas for one's own purposes. The essential software that ran the network was "open source"; large numbers of people had contributed lines of computer code

The Internet is one of the most powerful new media available to modern youth, particularly in the West. *Courtesy of Skjold Photographs.*

to programs that were free for anyone to use at no cost. According to Manuel Castells, a "hacker" ethic of creativity and sharing had originated in California college towns in the 1960s, but it was now influential among programmers in government and in such corporations as AT&T, IBM, and Xerox. The whole Internet, seen as a collection of digitized public goods, has been called a "commons" because information, ideas, and resources were shared, just as medieval peasants once shared land for grazing and collecting firewood.

The medieval commons was lost when lords asserted private property rights over the land that peasants had historically shared and put up walls or hedgerows to block access. This was the "enclosure movement," and something similar is happening online. Software and Web site designs are increasingly protected by copyrights or patents. Many Web sites require passwords and charge fees. The ones that attract the most traffic are commercial, technically sophisticated, and both illegal and impossible for ordinary people to emulate. Cable companies that provide home access charge customers extra for contributing ("uploading") material, because they prefer people to consume ("download") material.

Therefore, most of the millions of people who have "gone online" since the mid-1990s have experienced the Internet as a relatively passive medium. Only a relative few can create software or Web sites, usually for purposes set by their corporate or governmental employers. Nevertheless, individuals and nonprofit groups are still innovating and creating free public goods in parts of the Internet. This creativity is an alternative to consumerism; it may strengthen psychological connections among participants, and it often has civic or political purposes.

Young people have consistently led the development of the Internet commons. A 2003 survey by the Pew Internet and American Life Project found that only 19 percent of Internet users (or 21 million Americans) had created content for the Internet. However, those under thirty were most likely to be creative (27 percent). The youngest Americans surveyed in this poll were eighteen, so we know nothing about those under eighteen, but children and adolescents clearly contribute content as well.

There is little statistical information about who is creating or using each type of creative material for the Internet, nor do we know the amount of each type that is extant on the Web. Further, we lack any systematic studies of the political or civic *impact* of such work. The following, then, is a rather impressionistic, subjective, and necessarily incomplete list of the current forms:

Online organizations: Political, ideological, and civic organizations have been formed largely or entirely online, representing virtually all ideologies, identities, and agendas. Their organizational structures also vary greatly, but compared to offline groups, they are more likely to have anonymous or pseudonymous members. Anonymity has the advantage of allowing candor, which is especially beneficial for members of stigmatized groups (such as the only gay adolescent in a small community). It also allows people to experiment with novel identities. However, anonymity may have the disadvantage of making relationships relatively superficial. If members can adopt fictitious identities then they can *change* their identities as soon as anyone threatens to expel or socially ostracize them. Online interaction can therefore permit behavior that is disruptive to the group itself. In a recent focus group, college students complained about incivility in online discussions; one said that face-to-face dialogs were better because "you're forced to remember your manners, to remember that the people you're talking to *are* people."

Compared to offline groups, online ones tend to be easier to "exit" but harder to change by exercising "voice" (to use Albert Hirschman's terminology), because there is no method of democratic decision-making that one can influence. Because exit is easy, groups tend not to discipline their own members by demanding contributions or particular forms of behavior in return for membership. Again, compared to offline groups, online ones tend to be "thin" rather than "thick." Bruce Bimber explains that in a "thick" group, such as a family or ethnic group, members are committed to the survival and flourishing of the collectivity, but they debate its purposes. In a "thin" group, they enter having some purpose in mind; they view membership as instrumental to that goal.

Although many online groups are "thin," unstructured, and easy to exit, this is not true of massive, multiplayer games, whose participants invest considerable time in developing fictional characters. Often, they become highly committed to the flourishing of the game community as an end in itself.

However, online political or civic groups more typically allow members to visit a Web site, contribute money, and/or elect to receive e-mail messages. A prominent example is MoveOn.org, a liberal organization in the United States that claims 2 million members as of January 2005. MoveOn.org was formed to oppose the impeachment of President Clinton but now tackles issues that its members choose by voting. It has raised and spent millions of dollars to influence U.S. policy. No information is available about the median age of MoveOn.org members or staff, but Danny Schecter describes it as an "an intergenerational grouping heavily peopled by young voters, something that most political constituencies lack."

Web logs or "*blogs*": A "blog" is a frequently updated Web site. Conventionally, it is updated every day, with the latest entries appearing at the top. Another convention is to list the author's other favorite blogs (with links). As a result, blogs are heavily connected, and participants increasingly speak of a single "blogosphere." Since the number and prominence of links to a Web site determines how highly it is rated by search engines, bestowing a link on another site is a gift; the whole "blogosphere" operates as a kind of gift economy.

Usually one person maintains each blog, which gives it the flavor of a diary. However, there are "group blogs" to which multiple people contribute. Many blogs allow visitors to post comments, either on the same Web site with the original entries or elsewhere on the Internet (connected with an automatic link). A blog can be built using the same techniques used to construct other Web sites. However, free software is now available that automates the process of making sophisticated-looking interactive blogs.

The first blogs developed before 1997. Many were simply lists of links to news stories that their authors feared would be overlooked. These blogs were "alternative filters"—ways to accentuate news stories that went against the grain of mainstream reporting. Increasingly, bloggers added commentary and even original reporting or set-piece interviews. The number of blogs increased rapidly, starting in 2001. For example, the libertarian law professor Glenn Reynolds started his "Instapundit" blog on September 9, 2001, but achieved global renown with his criticism of the mainstream press for being, in his view, too defensive about America and too quick to sanction restrictions on civil liberties. "Instapundit" now draws between 50,000 and 100,000 daily visitors (estimates are imprecise).

There are blogs on practically every subject, including many about efforts to lose weight and tips on computer programming. But many are political. According to one list of the most popular blogs (called "Truth Laid Bare"), nine out of the top ten are political. Political bloggers see themselves as an alternative political press.

During the Iraq War, popular blogs by Iraqis inside Baghdad added a new aspect to war correspondence. One of the most influential Iraqi bloggers is a young man with the pseudonym Salam Pax. During the 2004 U.S. election, candidates widely experimented with campaign blogs that were more or less open to visitors to post comments and ask questions.

Although the world's most popular blogs are written by journalists and lawyers over age thirty, blogging is popular among the young, including those under fifteen. There is no current way to measure the number of youth blogs or their share of the total, but unsystematic exploration of the "blogosphere" suggests that it is tilted toward people under thirty. The most popular liberal political blog on the Web (and an impressively researched publication), is the Daily Kos, which includes weekly comments by Stephen Yellin, who was fifteen at the time this was written.

WIKIs: A WIKI is a document that is placed online with software that allows anyone to edit or expand it. The document thus evolves as a result of many people's contributions. The "Wikipedia" is a collection of roughly 200,000 heavily interlinked WIKI articles. Although one might predict that allowing anyone to add or subtract any material to a document would cause it to lose value and be vandalized, WIKI texts often evolve in impressive ways. Again, there is no statistical evidence about the age distribution of WIKI users and contributors, but casual observation suggests that many are young.

Youth journalism: The Internet is often praised for permitting "free" speech, since publishing text online costs virtually nothing. Thus, computer networks circumvent one traditional economic barrier to publishing. However, there is an oversupply of such "free" writing, much of which attracts few readers and is of fairly low quality. More interesting are the possibilities of "low-cost speech," such as (for example) online news stories that involve original reporting, fact-checking, editing, and layout. Such work takes time and specialized skills, so it is not literally "free." However, the extremely low cost of publishing the final product on a Web site allows many more people to become news producers than was hitherto possible. Youth, in particular, have more opportunities to generate news than ever before. Many adult-led programs offer training and technical assistance to youth journalists.

An example is Harlem Live, billed as an "Internet publication by the youth of New York." Its Web site (http://www. harlemlive.org) resembles the multipage sites or "portals" commonly created by large metropolitan daily newspapers. However, Harlem Live is managed entirely by youth, who draw on the skills of professional mentors.

Video and audio production: Not all low-cost speech takes the form of text. Using digital cameras (for still or moving pictures), audio recorders, and animation software, people can cheaply generate short audio and/or video files to post on the Internet. There are now numerous projects in which young people receive training to create and edit short documentaries and public-service announcements, often with political or social messages (see Film/ Video as a Tool for Youth Activism).

Community mapping: Many people believe that youth benefit from mapping local assets (e.g., nonprofits or work opportunities), problems (e.g., the locations of environmental or crime "hot spots"), and hypothetical future plans for their communities. While youth can make maps using paper and pencil, computers are powerful and accessible tools. GIS (an acronym that stands variously for Geographical Information System or Global Indexing System) is a process by which geographical features are given standardized "geocodes" to mark their location on the earth's surface. Newly collected data can be merged with public GIS datasets provided by governments. Thus, for example, youth mappers can identify all the local educational opportunities, give them "geocodes," and merge them with data about local streets and buildings. Such a database can then automatically generate a professional-looking map, which can either be posted online as a static image or else set up so that visitors to a Web site can manipulate it. (For example, visitors can choose to see only certain features of an area.)

Hacktivism: "Hackers" are people with specialized computer skills and an anti-authoritarian, sometimes anarchist, ideology. "Hacktivists" are hackers who use their skills in pursuit of political goals. For example, if they oppose legal censorship of Web sites, then they may find ways to disseminate banned material anonymously so that no one can be prosecuted. If they dislike wiretaps and other forms of surveillance, then they may invent encryption techniques that can defeat current surveillance technology. If they oppose copyrights or patents, then they appropriate and distribute corporate intellectual property free of charge. And if they strongly dislike the point of view expressed on a Web site, they may post unauthorized messages, edit it for subversive purposes, or even shut it down.

Although some people conduct similar activities for personal enrichment, "hack-tivists" are committed to a kind of electronic civil disobedience; their objectives are political. Most people would probably agree that Chinese dissidents who publish a Web site for free political debate are acting creatively, even though their behavior may be illegal in China. If they design and use software to evade state censorship, that seems an especially creative use of the Internet. However, a project like Floodnet (which tries to "flood" the White House's Web site "in response to violations made by the U.S. government against the U.S. people") could be seen as destructive rather than creative, depending on one's core beliefs about the American government.

There is no aggregate data about the age distribution of hacktivists, who are necessarily secretive. However, anecdotal evidence suggests that most are young—and many younger than eighteen.

See also Chat Rooms, Girls' Empowerment and; Digital Divide; Film/Video as a Tool for Youth Activism; Global Justice Activism; MTV's Choose or Lose Campaign (1992–); Student Voices Project.

Recommended Reading

Bimber, B. (1998). "The Internet and Political Transformation: Populism, Community, and Accelerated Pluralism." *Polity*, 31: 148.

Blood, R. (September 7, 2001). "Weblogs: A History and Perspective." See http://www. rebeccablood.net/essays/weblog_history.html.

Castells, M. (2000). *The Rise of the Network Society*. Oxford: Blackwell.

Hirschman, A. O. (1971). *Exit, Voice, and Loyalty*. Cambridge, MA: Harvard University Press.

Lessig, L. (2001). *The Future of Ideas: The Fate of the Commons in a Networked World*. New York: Random House.

Schecter, D. (January 13, 2004). "MoveOn Meets Up to Unveil Winning Ad." See http://www. mediachannel.org.

Singel, R. (January 27, 2004). "Teen Blogger Turns Heads Online." *Wired News*.

Truth Laid Bear (2005). "Weblogs by Average Daily Traffic." See http://www.truthlaidbear. com/TrafficRanking.php.

Peter Levine

Nigeria, Youth Activism in. Young people have always been central to political dynamics in Nigeria, but the ways in which they have responded to their consistent disconnection from dominant social, political, and economic processes and the limits on their status as citizens has changed dramatically over time. Young people, in organizational terms, have tended to be among the most militant collective actors in Nigeria from the colonial period onward, but their goals and the means to achieve them have shifted. However, at all key moments in Nigeria's recent political history, young people have both reflected and shaped its sociopolitical and economic realities.

In the colonial era young people, some of whom were educated in England and the United States, were responsible for galvanizing the people to demand self-rule and ultimately independence from British colonial rule. Since that time, the intervention of youth in public processes has created a bifurcation between young and old people in debates over the proper response to social, political, and economic realities, which have tended to exclude large portions of the population. The Nigerian Youth Movement (NYM) was the first major pivotal youth organization that was responsible for the radicalization of the anticolonial movement in the late 1930s and early 1940s. The movement represented the first national expression of youth political militancy in Nigeria. Its militant posture on the issue of self-government was given impetus by the return to colonial Nigeria of young men who had been trained in England and United States. Two of these returnees, Nnamdi Azikiwe (popularly called Zik), an American-trained political scientist and journalist, and H. O. Davies, who was a student of Harold Laski at the London School of Economics, were particularly influential in the movement. The NYM supplanted the old-guard politicians organized around the National Democratic Party (NDP) and even fielded candidates who beat the NDP candidates in colonial elections with their trenchant calls for Nigerians to take over the leadership of the country.

In 1938, the NYM published the Nigerian Youth Charter which emphasized the "unification" of all ethnic groups in the country toward the creation of a "common ideal" and the cultivation of public opinion buoyed by higher moral and intellectual duty to building national consciousness. However, the NYM was soon sundered along ethnic lines as its leaders clashed, with Azikiwe, the Igbos, and some Ijebu (Yoruba) leaving the movement. From this crisis emerged another major nationalist youth movement dedicated to spreading and entrenching the powerful vision and ideas of Azikiwe, who had become the most prominent radical nationalist.

The Zikist movement, inaugurated in 1946 as a reaction to the factionalism of the NYM, picked up and rearticulated Zik's idea of a "New Africa" addressed to "youth in mind and age," whom he described as "renascent Africans" in the vanguard of African liberation. In contrast were the old guard, "traditional" chiefs and conservative pro-colonial politicians who constituted "old Africa." Zik had called on the latter to yield to the leadership of youth in African politics. Zikism was therefore a critique by youth of not only colonial rule but also the social conditions and structures produced by the colonial order. As a "new philosophy of New Africa," Zikism emphasized the "redemption of Africa from social wreckage, political servitude and economic impotency, [and] extricating Africa from ideological confusion, psychological immaturity, spiritual complacency, and mental stagnation." The movement, like the NYM, was eventually destroyed by internal wrangling as Zik, the "patron saint" of the movement, disassociated himself from the group.

As members of this generation of nationalists aged and took over the reigns of power, first during the experiments in self-rule in the regions in the late 1950s and later after independence was won in 1960, a new crop of young activists entered the national scene. Generally, apart from the youth wing of political parties created during the decade before independence, the most visible youth organizations that emerged in these years embraced socialist ideas and ideals in ways that rearticulated the rhetoric of the struggle against "imperialists" and their local collaborators that was ascendant in the late colonial era. In March 1957, three years before independence, students of the University College, Ibadan, the only university in Nigeria at the time, held a mass meeting where they passed a resolution demanding the immediate withdrawal of Great Britain from Nigerian territory. The political movement in the country seized this initiative to strengthen the campaign for independence. Building on this momentum after independence, the socialist Nigerian Youth Congress (NYC) worked with the student movement in 1960 to protest against the defense pact that the government of Nigeria signed with the departing colonial power, Great Britain. A mass rally against the defense pact was staged on November 28, 1960. Azikiwe, who had become the governor-general of independent Nigeria (and president in 1963 when republic status was granted), granted audience to the students in his official residence in Lagos. The ultimate abandoning of the pact by the Nigerian government demonstrated that the "revolutionary" student movement had become a powerful instrument of public and national articulation of dissent for Nigerian youth. Consequently, the history of the student movement became entwined with the political history of Nigeria.

But by the mid-1960s, the student movement, represented in the National Union of Nigerian Students (NUNS) became enmeshed in internal crisis along ethnic lines as students in the University of Nigeria, Nsukka (UNN), located in the eastern (Igbo) part of the country challenged the leadership of the national association by the students of the University of Ibadan, located in the western (Yoruba) part. The president of the UNN student body, Isaac Adaka Boro, was later to lead the first armed secessionist group in Nigeria when he declared an "independent republic of Yenagoa," a province in the present River State, shortly after graduating from Nsukka. The rebellion was quashed and Boro was sentenced to death by the military regime.

In the post–Civil War years of the early 1970s, Nigerian youth were accused of retreating from nationalism and activism. Interestingly, this was the oil-boom era in which the head of the military government announced that the problem with Nigeria was not money but what to do with it. As part of developing national consciousness and patriotic zeal in Nigerian youth, a National Youth Service Program (NYSC) was created in 1973. The compulsory one-year service program in which graduates of higher institutions are posted to parts of Nigeria other than their place of origin, has continued up until now. Initially, students organized a protest against this program, but they were eventually compelled to participate in it after graduation.

The student movement resumed as the core of youth activism and citizenship struggles in the late 1970s and 1980s. When the military banned NUNS, the students created a new association called the National Association of Nigerian Students (NANS), which carried on the struggle to protect Nigerian students and the fight against injustice and national political, economic, and social paralysis. A crucial point in the history of youth activism in Nigeria was the response to national economic hardship occasioned by the adoption of Structural Adjustment Program (SAP) by the military regime in 1989. Organized by NANS, the widespread anti–SAP riots thoroughly embarrassed the military government and are believed to have emboldened the coup plotters who attempted to seize power from General Ibrahim Babangida the following April. In response, the regime and its security apparatus devised ways to counter and divide the student movement and to prevent radical elements from taking it over. The group was banned many times, but the students ignored the ban.

After similar anti–SAP riots organized by NANS in 1992, these measures against the radical student movement were accentuated in ways that have prevented it from regaining the national political leverage it once had. This included the creation of "peace movements" that fought against the mainstream student body, a systematic process of compromising student-union leaders and using university authorities to circumscribe the activities of the students. These measures coincided and connected with the growing militancy of religious movements on campuses, which now claim greater membership and loyalty than the student union. The participation of NANS in the pro-democracy movement of the early 1990s, therefore, was secondary to other civic organizations such as human-rights groups. However, marginalized urban youth constituted the foot soldiers of the widespread protests that were organized to press for democratic rule.

The breakdown in the military-supervised democratic transition program in the early 1990s was to mark another turning point in the political history of Nigeria with significant consequences for youth politics. The elaborate and laborious transition to civilian rule instituted by the General Ibrahim Babangida regime ended with the presidential election on June 12, 1993, one that was judged by both local and international observers as the freest and fairest election in Nigeria. The elections were held against the backdrop of several twists and turns designed by the military regime to subvert the process. However, in spite of the fact that the elections were free and fair and that they produced the first southerner to be popularly elected as president of Nigeria, Babangida annulled the elections. This threw Nigeria into a deep crisis with ethno-regional and religious dimensions, which threatened the continued existence of Nigeria as a united country.

This was the context in which the new phenomenon of ethnic militias dramatically emerged. The factors that predispose some Nigerian youth to activism and ultimately violence in the 1990s are not only related to their age. Most significantly, they concern young people's insertion in and/or exclusion from social, economic, and political processes and their membership in ethnic and religious groups which overdetermine political action. This situation and their identity-based and at times violent responses to it are shaped both by immediate events such as the 1993 annulment and long-term processes within the Nigerian state.

One could argue that the failure of the Nigerian youth, despite the history of their struggles, to radically transform the organization of the Nigerian state, produced the frustrations that led to the present attempt at ensuring this transformation from an ethno-political basis, sometimes by violent means. Reflecting the economic and political crisis and social anomie, the disillusionment of the youth generates the current challenge of ethnic militia groups and quasi-guerrilla movements. The most prominent of these ethnic militia groups are the Oodua People's Congress (OPC) in the Yoruba West; the Arewa People's Congress (APC) in the Hausa-Fulani North; the Ijaw Youth Council (IYC) and the Egbesu Boys, both in the oil-bearing Niger Delta region; and the National Youth Council of Ogoni People (NYCOP), whose activities have since become muted after the hanging of Ogoni leaders, including the writer and environmental-rights activist Ken Saro-Wiwa in November 1995 by the late General Sani Abacha's regime. Apart from the APC, which was formed specifically to challenge the OPC and preserve the existing distribution of power, all the groups were formed to challenge the status quo in Nigeria.

The OPC was formed in 1994 in the wake of the annulment of the presidential elections won by billionaire businessman and publisher Moshood Abiola, a Yoruba, and his subsequent unjust detention and trial. It explicitly states that its mission is to defend the interests of more than 30 million Yoruba. The group itself was soon to split—with a faction that describes itself as the "militant" faction, led by the then twenty-nine-year-old artisan Gani Adams, precipitating violent clashes with constituents of other ethnic groups in the Yoruba areas, particularly the Hausa-Fulani. Adams' faction lists factors that necessitated the formation of the group to include imbalances in power and wealth among different groups, military rule and repressive decrees, debasement of ethnic nationalities, ethnic cleansing, insecurity of life and property, and the collapse of the educational system. The OPC regards all of these as manifestations of the "domination and hegemony" of the Nigerian state by the Hausa-Fulani ethnic coalition. It therefore resolved to use any means necessary to fight this domination while insisting on complete restructuring of Nigeria into a truly federal state, the right to self-determination by all nationalities, regional autonomy, and free and high-quality education for all Nigerians, among other requirements. Even though the urban violence in which the group has been involved is deplored by the government, the police, and prominent people, the group enjoyed the confidence of urban dwellers in terms of its vigilante activities, which reportedly led to a significant decrease in armed robbery.

The IYC, made up mostly of university-educated activists, is the youth group that claims to defend the interests of the Ijaw ethnic group in the Niger Delta of Nigeria. The Ijaw constitute the fourth-largest ethnic group in Nigeria, but they are classified as a "minority" group. The IYC, like other Niger Delta youth groups including the now muted NYCOP, argue that since the discovery of crude oil in commercial quantity in Ijawland in 1958, oil companies such as Shell, AGIP, Elf, Chevron, and Mobil have colluded with the military and successive governments of Nigeria in what they regard as "a war of economic exploitation, environmental degradation, and of internal colonialism." The IYC sees itself as involved in the struggle to ensure justice and uphold the right of the Ijaw to share in the oil wealth derived from their soil. The youth took the course of activism and vio-

lence, the council argues, as a result of the failure of many years of dialog with the Nigerian state to end "decades of environmental pollution, corporate violence, unjust socioeconomic structure, and political oppression."

In 1998 the IYC demanded the immediate withdrawal from Ijawland of all "military forces of occupation and repression by the Nigerian state," declaring that "any oil company that employs the services of the armed forces of the Nigerian state to 'protect' its operations will be viewed as an enemy of the Ijaw people." Following this declaration, the spate of violence in the Niger Delta heightened, as the IYC and other militant youth groups were accused of killings, sabotaging oil installations, and taking foreign oil workers hostage. This has led to the remilitarization of the Niger Delta by the civilian government. Despite this, armed youth gangs have stepped up their campaign.

The new phase of armed quasi-insurgency against the Nigerian state is being waged by the 2,000-man Niger Delta's People Volunteer Force (NDPVF), led by Alhaji Muhahid Dokubu Asari, former leader of the IYC and former law student who dropped out of the university to lead the campaign against the environmental devastation and intense economic deprivation which are contrasted with the 2.5 million barrels of oil produced daily from their doorstep. Asari, son of a former high-court judge, seeks the independence of the Niger Delta area from Nigeria. As a first step, he joins his voice with those calling for the convocation of a Sovereign National Conference to determine whether the ethnic groups wish to continue within a united Nigeria. Asari's militia youth and rival groups, who all serve different political interests, roam the swamps and creeks of the Niger Delta, indulging in the lucrative business of oil bunkering. For these young people, oil bunkering does not constitute theft because the oil is "ours"; rather, it is the Nigerian state that they consider as a "thief."

There is a tendency to glamorize the victimhood of the Nigerian youth and gloss over the participation of some young people and youthful organizations in creating the social and political conditions of most youth. From the Youth Earnestly Ask for Abacha (YEEA), which was formed by a young man, Daniel Kanu, to "popularly" urge General Sani Abacha (1993–1998), Nigeria's most tyrannical and murderous head of state, to *civilianize* himself and run for the presidency, to the young men all over the country who take traditional titles and even ascend traditional stools in the Niger Delta, it is clear that Nigerian youth's actions are differentiated and related to their diverse social situations and life chances.

Still, it must be admitted that the phenomenon of youth militia groups in Nigeria is clearly the product of the failure to engage the critical issues of national unity in Nigeria, a country of about more than 250 ethnic groups and several faiths. It is also the consequence of many decades of official irresponsibility and the failure to squarely address the bleak future faced by so many Nigerian youth in the context of the deepening national economic crisis. Young people appear to be the most devastated by the dysfunctional nature of the Nigerian state and so youth activism can be seen as a response to the challenges that this reality poses to their status as citizens. The ways in which the youth negotiate the material conditions of their lives and how they subjectively encounter and interpret these conditions is deeply connected to the crisis of citizenship in Nigeria. It has been argued that while there are citizens *of* Nigeria, there are no citizens *in* Nigeria. This helps to explain why some contemporary Nigerian youth, in asking what can be done to ameliorate and change the conditions that marginalize and oppress them, have decided on violence as one of the means of confronting these conditions.

See also Australia, Youth Activism in; Demographic Trends Affecting the World's Youth; Eastern Europe, Youth and Citizenship in; Europe, Comparing Youth Activism in; European Identity and Citizenship; Immigrant Youth in Europe—Turks in Germany; Immigrant Youth in the United States; India, Youth Activism in; Indonesia, Youth Activism in; Palestinian *Intifada*; Russia, Youth Activism in; Serbia, Youth Activism in (1990–2000); Soweto Youth Activism (South Africa); State and Youth, The; Statute of the Child and Adolescent (Brazil); Tiananmen Square Massacre; Transnational Identity; Transnational Youth Activism; Turkey, Youth Activism in; United Nations, Youth Activism and; Xenophobia; Zapatista Rebellion (Mexico); Zionist Youth Organizations.

Recommended Reading

Adejumobi, Said. "Structural Adjustment, Students' Movement and Popular Struggles in Nigeria, 1986–1996." In *Identity Transformation and Identity Politics Under Structural Adjustment in Nigeria*, edited by Attahiru Jega. Uppsala: Nordiska Afrikainstitutet.

Akinyele, R. T. (2001). "Ethnic Militancy and National Stability in Nigeria: A Case Study of the Oodua People's Congress." *African Affairs*, 100: 623–640.

Coleman, James S. (1958). *Nigeria: Background to Nationalism*. Berkeley: University of California Press.

Diouf, Mamadou (September 2003). "Engaging Postcolonial Cultures: African Youth and Public Space." *African Studies Review*, 46 (2): 1–12.

Nolte, Insa (2004). "Identity and Violence: The Politics of Youth in Ijebu-Remo, Nigeria." *Journal of Modern African Studies*, 42 (1): 61–89.

Obadare, Ebenezer (2003). "White Collar Fundamentalism: Youth, Religiosity and Uncivil Society in Nigeria." *AAPS Occasional Paper Series*, 7 (3): 1–41.

Sesay, Amodu, Ukeje, Charles, Aina, Olabisi, and Adetanwa, eds. (2003). *Ethnic Militias and the Future of Democracy in Nigeria*. Ile-Ife, Nigeria: Obafemi Awolowo University Press, 2003.

Ukeje, Charles (2001). "Youth, Violence and the Collapse of Public Order in the Niger Delta of Nigeria." *Africa Development*, XXVI (1–2): 1–27.

Wale Adebanwi

P

Palestinian *Intifada*. The 1987–1993 Palestinian uprising against Israel, known as the *Intifada* (Arabic for uprising or shaking off), was a unique and, therefore, significantly instructive political movement. One of its most distinctive characteristics was the exceptionally high rate of adolescent participation in the conflict. Historically, up to 25 percent of youth of a given population have been activists in social or political movements, but greater than 80 percent of Palestinian adolescents participated in the *Intifada*. When considering that the movement lasted for a full six years and that it involved extensive, often daily, violence, the *Intifada* serves both as an illustration of the degree to which youth can commit themselves to a political cause (in the face of substantial risk) and as a case study of how and why adolescents can understand, engage in, process, and respond to substantial and severe violence.

In addition to the extraordinarily high participation rate, adolescents—commonly referred to as *shebab* (Arabic for youth)— were the primary, frontline force in the conflict against the Israeli Defense Force (IDF). They were sometimes nicknamed the "stone throwers" or "children of the stone" because their most visible form of activism was throwing rocks at the IDF tanks and jeeps that patrolled the refugee camps, villages, or towns of the West Bank, East Jerusalem, or the Gaza Strip, the three areas where Palestinians under the control of the state of Israel live. Television crews flocked to the region to record these frequent, often dramatic, "David versus Goliath" scenes, something that clearly emboldened the youth to continue their activist commitment as they saw themselves become key players in the sudden world attention to the difficulties of their lives and to their struggle for liberation. Other than stone throwing, *shebab* were active in many ways, including marching and demonstrating to protest against the occupation in general, in response to specific incursions of the IDF into their neighborhoods or against collective punishments such as curfews, closures of the territories, school closures, and so forth. *Shebab* often erected barricades of various materials or ignited tires to impede the movement of the IDF, particularly within the narrow refugee camp streets and alleys. They were vital couriers of strategic details of the struggle through delivering leaflets of instruction to residents or by writing slogans of directives or admonitions on the walls of buildings. They served also as decoys or sentinels warning of approaching IDF forces. They carried reserves of stones, food, or medical supplies to other *shebab* and adults on the front lines. They visited the families of fallen companions. And some made and threw Molotov cocktails at the IDF tanks.

The costs of such activism were high. Failing to quell the uprising, the IDF strategies became increasingly severe. Since the *shebab* were the front-liners, they received the brunt of the attempts to quash the rebellion, a strategy labeled by Israel as the "iron fist" policy for dealing with the insurrection. These tactics included firing tear gas into groups of demonstrators and into school yards, firing at demonstrators or stone throwers with rubber or live bullets, intentionally breaking the arms of the *shebab*, detentions, arrests, imprisonments,

In this 1988 photo, Palestinian boys throw rocks at Israeli soldiers. *Copyright Peter Turnley/ Corbis.*

torture, and the ubiquitous house raids during which *shebab* suspected of throwing stones were rousted out of their beds in the early morning hours and beaten. The trauma of the *Intifada* also included serious internal conflict, particularly as the movement evolved over time. The unity within the Palestinian struggle that characterized the first two or three years of the conflict eventually fragmented into conflict among the various factions of Palestinians who grew to hold different political assessments of how the conflict should be conducted and won. In those later years there was also substantial internal violence that *shebab* either witnessed or participated in, particularly in the form of the killing of Palestinians who were found or suspected to be informants (i.e., collaborators) with the IDF.

It is important here to distinguish the 1987–1993 *Intifada* from the current conflict between Palestinians and Israelis that, at this writing, is still very much alive. In 2000 seven years after the end of the first

Intifada, this "second" *Intifada* erupted. Although it is clearly related to the first uprising in that it is yet another substantial episode in the historical conflict, it is so different in operation from the original *Intifada* that it does not warrant simultaneous coverage here. Much of the distinction rests on the radically different modes of conflict used by Palestinians in the two movements and also in the severity of the tactics used by the IDF. The first *Intifada* was a classic, popular movement with virtually all segments of the society (young/ old, male/female) resisting the occupation forces, often collectively. Their methods were relatively crude, with virtually no real weapons until the later years of the movement when some rudimentary firearms were introduced.

In contrast, the current conflict is better understood in terms of guerilla warfare, with a more selective group of combatants— mostly young adults—equipped with much more sophisticated armaments such as semi-automatic rifles, grenades, small missiles, and so forth. Importantly, suicide bombing, one of the core tactics of the current conflict, was not part of the original *Intifada*. The first suicide bombing by a Palestinian did not occur until 1993, after the formal end of the first *Intifada*. Furthermore, although there is no shortage of adolescents (or younger children) who have engaged in first *Intifada*-type activism during the current conflict, the role of these youth is clearly incidental relative to the *shebab* of the first *Intifada*, both in terms of the reduced media attention they receive and in terms of the lesser effectiveness of their contributions. Thus, although the second *Intifada* is in some ways a more significant movement due to the ferocity of the fighting, which itself represents the advanced levels of frustration and desperation of both sides with the intractability of the overall conflict, the attention and study it certainly deserves would not, however, be focused on adolescents and their activism.

Two fundamental lessons are being learned by researchers studying the activist experiences of Palestinian *shebab* of the first *Intifada*. One is a profound awareness of just how complex life can be, even for adolescents. For them, the *Intifada* was not an isolated insurrection; rather, it was another in a long series of regular conflicts between Palestinians and Israeli Jews over the primary political issues of territory and nationalism. These conflicts began early in the twentieth century when the initially harmonious relations between Eastern European and Russian Jews, who had begun migrating at the turn of the century to Palestine to establish a homeland under the political banner of Zionism, and the indigenous Arabs, who at the time represented 90 percent of the population of Palestine, evolved into mutual suspicion and nationalistic aspirations. There were many small and large conflicts over the ensuing decades. In virtually all of these, the Arab Palestinians were defeated. The largest of these conflicts was the War of 1948, which resulted in the creation of the state of Israel on approximately two-thirds of the territory of Palestine. Hundreds of thousands of Palestinians were displaced to neighboring regions, most importantly Egypt and Jordan. These territories then came under Israeli control and were designated occupied territories as the result of the Israeli victory in the 1967 Six-Day War.

The reason this history is critical to understanding Palestinian *shebab* is because it thoroughly informed their own understanding of the meaning of the conflict and their potential role in it. Unlike adolescents in many parts of the world, the *shebab* were extremely well-versed in political history, due primarily to the oral accounts continually expressed to them directly by their parents and grandparents. This transmission was facilitated by the fact that all three generations were living together in the refugee camps established by the United Nations after these wars. To add to the complexity, the enduring and seemingly intractable conflict occurred in the context of substantial poverty, overcrowding, inadequate water quantity and quality, and restricted access to satisfactory education. All of these are conditions that are thoroughly taxing even without the concomitant political violence. Critically, they were markers for an overall sense of inequity and injustice felt by the residents of the territories. The Gaza Strip is the clearest example of this where, on its scant 125 square miles (five miles wide, twenty-five miles long on average), approximately 1.25 million Palestinians live in its eight refugee camps and surrounding towns and villages and approximately 6,000 Israeli Jews live in nineteen settlements covering fully 35 percent of Gaza's land. Unlike the relatively modern and well-equipped settlements that dot the strip, at the time of the *Intifada* none of the camps had sewer systems, and Palestinians in and outside of the camps had irregular (Israeli-controlled) access to electricity and water. Schools operated often on triple shifts and access to quality higher education was limited.

Although recollections of the *shebab* include occasional anecdotes expressed with the bravado and thrill that recall Western stereotypes of risk-seeking adolescents, their narratives are dominated by recitations that reveal a demanding complexity of psychological experiences. This internal experience often involved substantial wrestling between competing emotions (e.g., excitement and fear, defiance and deference, pride and shame, hope and frustration, etc.) and challenges to choose among a strategic variety of activist behaviors (e. g., spontaneous response to IDF intrusions, enticements to draw in IDF forces to be met either with quickly organized or carefully planned ambushes of stones, etc.). The most remarkable feature of their retrospective narratives, however, is the relative absence of complaint about the substantial economic inequities they endured or even of the often, very harsh treatment they received at the hands of the IDF, particularly during imprisonments (approximately 25 percent of *shebab* had some experience with imprisonment). They appeared to perceive the latter as one of the costs of their activism.

Their narratives, instead, reflected a unanimous passion for what they considered to be the grander values of social and political justice, that is, their right to have a cultural and ethnic identity (e.g., at times during the occupation, even the word "Palestine" was expunged from their textbooks) and to live in a defined political entity with real autonomy for self-government. *Shebab*, themselves, recognized that their preoccupation with this broad level of political and human rights essentially "cost them their childhood," but, characteristic of their lack of concern for their individual well-being in favor of the good of the people as a whole, their assessment of this cost was that it was outweighed by the maturity they gained in "becoming men" playing a significant historical role in the struggle. Not surprisingly, the majority of them claimed an immediate willingness to repeat their engagement should another struggle ensue.

This level of sophistication of reasoning and prioritization and this degree of commitment to activism in the face of real personal harm does not fit well with the popular stereotypes of adolescents who have been described, particularly by professionals, as erratic and excessively preoccupied with self-focused, internal conflicts about their identity and meeting their personal and social needs. The reason for this incompatibility in profiles of adolescents has largely to do with the reality that the information driving the less favorable view of adolescents has stemmed mostly from research on the relatively well-off adolescents of the developed world who are not particularly challenged to display competence of the type demanded of Palestinian adolescents (or of the majority of adolescents in the world who share with their families the responsibilities of survival in difficult economic and political circumstances). While real progress is being made in the West trying to promote and harness adolescent competence, the lingering negative appraisal of adolescents is evident in the scores of books filling bookstore shelves that describe either the social and mental difficulties some adolescents have or offer themselves as guides to help parents and educators (and adolescents) "survive" the purportedly vexing period of adolescence.

The second key lesson to be learned from this generation of activists flows directly from this unusual complexity of day-to-day psychological, social, economic, cultural, and political experiences. It has to do with understanding the long-term consequences to children of exposure and/or involvement in substantial violence. Contrary to what one might expect intuitively or from reading the research on violence, the Palestinian *shebab* functioned quite well and normally, despite sustained involvement in serious violence. Relative to other cultures, they continued to have very low rates of antisocial behavior, low rates of interpersonal violence, and high values for education, family, religion, and culture.

Indeed, the activist experiences of many *shebab* lead to increased (not decreased) levels of self-respect, identity formation, and civic involvement. This is not to say, of course, that there are not many youth who did suffer and continue to suffer substantially from the trauma of their experiences in the *Intifada*. But just as in populations of youth not exposed to political violence, the proportion of Palestinian adolescents who faced substantial psychological, emotional, or social difficulty is very small, and it is likely comprised largely of those who had a preconflict history of difficulty.

On the other hand, there are examples of populations exposed to substantial political violence in which large portions of youth suffer significantly. One recent example is Bosnia, where during virtually the same time period as the *Intifada*, Bosnians faced menacing aggression from Serbia. The capital city, Sarajevo, was, for example, under a literal siege for four consecutive years with its population fully constrained and exposed to frequent, unpredictable attacks from surrounding Serbian troops. Narratives of adolescents from Sarajevo are dominated, in direct contrast to those of Palestinian adolescents, by despair, bitterness, confusion, apathy, and by self-reports of widespread antisocial behavior.

What could account for such stark differences in these two populations of adolescents exposed to severe and sustained violence? One key factor is activism itself. Unlike Palestinian adolescents who played a significant role in resisting the control of the opposition, Bosnian adolescents had no opportunity to resist. Beyond this important issue of participation, the meaning that youth were able to attach to the conflict itself—in terms of its purpose, origin, and legitimacy as a means in pursing valued goals—appear also to be critical. As noted earlier, Palestinian adolescent activists had a clear and detailed understanding of the roots of the *Intifada*, and they were able to harness social, cultural, religious, and human-rights justifications for the goals of the uprising. In contrast, Bosnian adolescents were surprised by the onset of the war, and they were not (and still are not) able to set the conflict in any logical, coherent understanding of their history or their future. Growing research is highlighting the power of this meaning-making in equipping adolescents to cope effectively with their experiences with political violence (another example is the South African adolescents who were activists in the struggles against apartheid), even, notably, among groups of "child soldiers" (e.g., in many current conflicts in Africa) who are coerced to participate in horrible acts of violence.

The continuing and worsening conflict between Israel and Palestinians demands concern for the well-being of all segments of both populations. How *shebab* of the first *Intifada*, now young adults, ultimately fare in life is necessarily contingent in part on the degree to which the dispute will be resolved or, at least, minimized. This would seem to be particularly critical for them because of how much and how authentically they sacrificed for it. In any case, their activism during the first *Intifada* will remain a compelling illustration of the capacity of adolescents to forego concerns with personal issues and safety, to be moved to activism by awareness of historical and political realities, and to process its attendant difficulties and violence with competence.

See also Australia, Youth Activism in; Demographic Trends Affecting the World's Youth; Eastern Europe, Youth and Citizenship in; Europe, Comparing Youth Activism in; European Identity and Citizenship; Immigrant Youth in Europe—Turks in Germany; Immigrant Youth in the United States; India, Youth Activism in; Indonesia, Youth Activism in; National Identity and Youth; Nigeria, Youth Activism in; Russia, Youth Activism in; Serbia, Youth Activism in (1990–2000); Soweto Youth Activism (South Africa); State and Youth, The; Statute of the Child and Adolescent (Brazil); Tiananmen Square Massacre (1989);

Transnational Identity; Transnational Youth Activism; Turkey, Youth Activism in; United Nations, Youth Activism and; Xenophobia; Zapatista Rebellion (Mexico); Zionist Youth Organizations.

Recommended Reading

Barber, B. K. (2005). *One Heart, So Many Stones: The Story of the Palestinian Youth.* New York: Palgrave Macmillan.

Barber, B. K., ed. (2005). *Adolescents and War: How Youth Deal with Political Violence.* New York: Oxford University Press.

Bucaille, L. (2004). *Growing up Palestinian: Israeli Occupation and the* Intifada *Generation.* Newark, NJ: Princeton University Press.

Doughty, D., and El Aydi, M. (1995). *Gaza: Legacy of Occupation: A Photographer's Journey.* Bloomfield, CT: Kumarian Press.

Khalidi, R. (1997). *Palestinian Identity.* New York: Columbia University Press.

Tessler, M. (1994). *A History of the Israeli-Palestinian Conflict.* Bloomington: Indiana University Press.

Brian K. Barber

PAR. *See* Participatory Action Research (PAR) by Youth.

Parental Influences on Youth Activism. Parents influence youth activism along five main paths. First, children model their parents' political behavior, and parents inculcate their attitudes in their children. Second, parents' child-rearing strategies can shape their children's future activism by providing a safe environment for moral development and self-discovery. Third, parents influence the social networks in which their children become involved, and these networks are sources of recruitment into activism. Fourth, parents' social class affects children's educational attainment, which in turn is strongly linked to political achievement. Fifth, parents can provide a home environment with materials and open discussion that encourages political maturity and interest, which can lead to activism. Each of these five ways in which parental influence on youth activism has been discovered through empirical research is discussed below.

Parents are influential role models for their children in all domains, especially early in life, so it is not surprising that children of politically active parents are more likely to be politically active than children of nonpolitically active parents. For example, one survey found that students whose parents had protested the Vietnam War were more likely to protest the 1991 Gulf War than were students whose parents had not protested the Vietnam War. Also, students whose parents supported the Vietnam War were more likely to support the Gulf War efforts than were students whose parents had opposed U.S. involvement in the Vietnam War.

Parents need not be activists to influence their children; research suggests ordinary political participation increases the likelihood that children will become activists. For example, in one longitudinal survey from 1965 to 1997, ninety-four respondents reported significant protest activities in young adulthood ("activists"), and 222 had no activism experience. In this study, there was evidence across three generations (i.e., the activists, the activists' parents, and the activists' children) that politically active parents were more likely to have politically active children. First, the activists had higher rates of political participation (e.g., writing a letter to the editor, attending rallies, demonstrating) compared to nonactivists. Second, parents of activists were more likely to be politically involved than parents of nonactivists. By 1997, the activists were in their fifties, and many had children. The activists' offspring participated politically at a higher rate than did nonactivists' offspring. In addition, children whose parents were politically active were more likely to become protestors than children whose parents were not politically active. There is some evidence that suggests that politically active parents increase the likelihood of their children becoming politically active.

Parents shape the type as well as the level of youth activism. Parents transmit values that mold children's political activity. Interviews of 1960s activist leaders were done to chart the life-course development of activists. One group consisted of thirteen left-wing leaders of Students for a Democratic Society (SDS), who were concerned with civil rights, race relations, and opposing the Vietnam War. The second group was comprised of eleven right-wing leaders of Young Americans for Freedom (YAF), who opposed Communism, supported economic freedom, and advocated limits on government powers. Most of the activist leaders reported the same political attitudes as their parents and family members; for example, left-wing leaders had left-wing parents.

Parents' child-rearing strategies influence youth activism. For example, kindergarten children whose parents used a child-centered parenting style (e.g., the mother's relationship with the child was rated as warm, the mother thinks the child is wonderful, cute, bright, etc.) were more likely to become activists in the 1960s social movements than children whose parents did not use this parenting style. While an interaction of many factors influences moral development, child-centered parenting styles provide a safe environment for children to explore their identity and morals and teach children how to treat and judge others, which encourages cooperation and empathy.

From music lessons, little-league baseball, ballet, club membership, and student government to volunteering and protesting, parents are often the driving force behind what activities a child becomes involved in, or not involved in, and the intensity of involvement. Membership in organizations is one of the main pathways for recruitment into activist groups and activities. Therefore, parents influence their children's activism by encouraging and supporting participation in organizations. For example, children's involvement in a service club and parents (of college students) being involved in labor unions are associated with children becoming activists.

In addition to parents influencing their children's activism by encouraging their children to be members of certain organizations, parents can also dissuade or even prevent their children from becoming activists. One study examined responses of those who applied for and were accepted to volunteer for the Freedom Summer 1964 (involving the registration of black voters and the operation of Freedom Schools where public schools had been closed in Mississippi). The most frequent reason that no-shows gave for not participating was their parents' opposition to their volunteering (25 percent of the respondents).

Parents have a tremendous influence on their children's educational aspirations and final level of educational attainment. People who attend college are more likely to become activists for many reasons: recruitment for causes often occurs at college, at least in the twentieth and twenty-first centuries; college education can increase political knowledge; college friends can influence students' activism; and the status quo is often challenged in the classroom. Some research has found that protesters were more common on college campuses than in other locations, and the people who attended college were more likely to protest than those who did not go to college. Other studies have found that attending college was a significant predictor of activism.

Youth activism is influenced by the materials available in the home, such as books, newspapers, magazines, and access to television and computers, as well as an environment of open discussion about current events and politics. Also, parents' socioeconomic status may influence what social networks and opportunities are available to their children. Most studies find that higher levels of socioeconomic status lead to more activism, or they acknowledge the influence of socioeconomic status by controlling for it in their analyses.

While there is a long history of youth activism in social movements, such as the Children's Crusade in France in 1212, the Harvard protest in America in 1768, and the civil rights movement of the 1960s, most research is Western and is recent, focusing particularly on the sixties student movement and Vietnam protests. Thus, conclusions drawn from this body of research may or may not apply to other cultures and other historical times.

What causes an adolescent or a young adult to become enmeshed in a social movement, participating in protests, marches, sit-ins, lockouts, boycotts, and petitions? We have reviewed a number of studies that demonstrate that parents influence activism in their children by serving as role models, through their child-rearing practices, by directing their children's involvement in organizations and shaping their children's educational attainment, and by creating a home environment rich with resources and discussions supporting political activity.

See also Adult Partners in Youth Activism; Adult Roles in Youth Activism; Generational Conflict; Generational Replacement; Moral Exemplars; Peer Influences on Political Development; Prosocial Behaviors; School Influences and Civic Engagement.

Recommended Reading

Adams, R. (1991). *Protests by Pupils: Empowerment, Schooling, and the State.* New York: Falmer Press.

Braungart, M. M., and Braungart, R. G. (1990a). "The Life-Course Development of Left- and Right-Wing Youth Activist Leaders from the 1960s." *Political Psychology*, 11: 243–282.

Braungart, M. M., and Braungart, R. G. (1990b). "Studying Youth Politics: A Reply to Flack." *Political Psychology*, 11: 293–307.

Duncan, L. E., and Stewart, A. J. (1995). "Still Bringing the Vietnam War Home: Sources of Contemporary Student Activism." *Personality and Social Psychology Bulletin*, 21: 914–924.

Franz, C. E., and McClelland, D. C. (1994). "Lives of Women and Men Active in the Social Protests of the 1960s: A Longitudinal Study." *Journal of Personality and Social Psychology*, 66: 196–205.

Hart, D., Atkins, R., and Donnelly, T. M. (In Press). "Community Service and Moral Development." In *Handbook of Moral Development*, edited by M. Killen and J. Smetana. Hillsdale, NJ: Lawrence Erlbaum Associates.

Illick, J. E. (1979). "Perspectives on American Student Activism." *Journal of Psychohistory*, 7: 175–187.

Jennings, M. K. (2002). "Generation Units and the Student Protest Movement in the United States: An Intra- and Intergenerational Analysis." *Political Psychology*, 23: 303–323.

McAdam, D. (1988). *Freedom Summer.* New York: Oxford University Press.

Nassi, A. J. (1981). "Survivors of the Sixties: Comparative Psychosocial and Political Development of Former Berkeley Student Activists." *American Psychologist*, 36: 653–761.

Paulsen, R. (1994). "Status and Action: How Stratification Affects the Protest Participation of Young Adults." *Sociological Perspectives*, 37: 635–649.

Sherkat, D. E., and Blocker, T. J. (1994). "The Political Development of Sixties' Activists: Identifying the Influence of Class, Gender, and Socialization on Protest Participation." *Social Forces*, 72: 821–842.

Teachman, J. D., and Paasch, K. (1998). "The Family and Educational Aspirations." *Journal of Marriage and the Family*, 60: 704–714.

Thomas M. Donnelly, Robert Atkins, and Daniel Hart

Participatory Action Research (PAR) by Youth. Across the nation there is a small but growing movement of youth participatory action research (PAR). Young people are redefining the very nature of research—from what it means to be a social scientist, to what the research enterprise should look like. As Sati Singleton, a youth researcher from the community-based organization Mothers on the Move in New York City, says, gone are the days when "researchers" are assumed to be lab coat-wearing, older, white men with pocket protectors.

"Investigating how it is that schools in the suburbs have more resources and more money to spend on their students than city schools—learning firsthand how politicians think about students like me—has changed me permanently," says Kouri, a youth researcher with the Educational Opportunity Gap Project. "Being a researcher, I see the world differently ... now I see it beyond the flat."

Young people across the nation, and indeed the world, are setting off on their own as well as joining up with adults in universities, schools, community organizations, nonprofits, and foundations to research questions relevant to their lives, families, communities, and the nation. From New York to California young people are asking why their schools are both separate and

unequal (e.g., Educational Opportunity Gap Project, Youth Organizing Communities), why they are not allowed access to sex education (e.g., Sex Etc.), why prisons have larger budgets than schools (e.g., Youth Justice Coalition/Free LA), why the media misrepresents their peers (e.g., Youth Media Council), and why it feels that police are harassing rather than protecting them (e.g., Street Surveillance Project). In this entry we will briefly introduce the theory, method, and ethics of PAR and provide snapshots of how it is being practiced by and with youth across the United States.

Participatory action research is a methodological stance rooted in the belief that knowledge is produced in collaboration and in action: that those "studied" have knowledge and must be repositioned as subjects, architects, of research. Repositioning youth as researchers rather than the "researched" in youth PAR shifts the practice of researching *on* youth to *with* youth—a position that stands in sharp contrast to the current neo-liberal constructions of youth as dangerous, apathetic, empty receptacles, lacking connection, in need of product "branding," blind consum-

ers, and so on. Participatory action research is based largely on the theory and practice of Latin American activist scholars and has been typically practiced within community-based social-action projects, with a commitment to understanding, documenting, and/or evaluating the impact that social programs, social problems, and/or social movements bear on individuals and communities. In the United States action research was pioneered by Kurt Lewin who dared to assert in 1951 that participant knowledge was as foundational to validity and democratic and participatory research as it was foundational to social change. Lewin challenged the artificial borders separating theory, research, and action, insisting "no action without research; no research without action" (quoted in Adelman 1997). In his refusal to separate thought from action and his insistence on the integration of science and practice, he argued that social processes could be understood only when they were changed (see Cherry and Borshuk 1998).

Across history and current texts PAR scholars, drawing from feminist and critical race theorists, have worked to articulate a set of methods and ethics of PAR, the heart of which lies in the understanding that people—especially those who have experienced historic oppression—hold deep knowledge about their lives and experiences and should help shape the questions, frame the interpretations, and style the research products that ultimately effect them most intimately. As Paulo Freire (1993) eloquently described, "the silenced are not just incidental to the curiosity of the researcher but are the masters of inquiry into the underlying causes of the events in their world. In this context research becomes a means of moving them beyond silence into a quest to proclaim the world." This recognition presents a fundamental challenge to what Habermas called "scientism" or what John Gaventa called "official knowledge" as the sole legitimate claim to truth. It is what Sati illustrates in the cartoon introducing this entry. While there is no "official" set of PAR guidelines, as participatory work is by nature a process that grows and evolves out of the concerns of the research collective and their communities, there are some fundamental principles, which include the following:

- Commitment to research as a tool of social struggle designed toward revealing radical possibilities—a perspective critical of "what is" and demanding "what must be" (see Greene 1988)
- Understanding of the importance of participation *with*, not only *for*, community; and refusal to research *on* communities (see Lykes 2001)
- Acknowledgment that intellectually powerful and searing social commentary is very often developed at the bottom of social hierarchies (see Ladson-Billings 2000; Matsuda 1995)
- Recognition that local customs and practices are profound sites for possible learning, shared engagement, and long-term social change and therefore must be incorporated into the praxis of participatory research (see Smith 1999)
- Insistence on analyzing power dynamics and social-positionality within the

research collective and analyzing *dissonance* and *dissent* as potential sites of knowledge rather than silencing them (see Torre 2003)
- Commitment to collectively addressing questions of audience, product, and what is left behind once the research is complete. In this spirit, creating a legacy of inquiry, a process of change, and material resources to enable transformation are commonly understood to be crucial to the PAR project (see Russell and Bohan 1999)

While there are a growing number of youth PAR projects that are located within colleges and universities (see the Educational Opportunity Gap Project at the Graduate Center of the City University of New York; the Youth Action Research Group at Georgetown University; and Education, Access, and Democracy in Los Angeles of Teaching to Change LA at the University of California at Los Angeles), youth PAR is most commonly seeded within organizing campaigns run by young people in community organizations, nonprofits, and, in some instances, foundations. The focus of the vast majority of youth research centers on educational justice, access to quality health care, the criminalization of youth, gang violence, police brutality, race/gender/sexuality oppression, gentrification, and environmental issues. The result is a fervent sense of purpose and urgency in youth PAR as young people are using research not only to produce new knowledge and challenge dominant representations but to produce, organize for, and practice change. The goal of much of the work is to not only to expose injustice but to advocate for local and national policy reform. Examples include the following ten groups and projects:

Educational Opportunity Gap Project (Greater New York/New Jersey; see http://www.gse.harvard.edu/hfrp/eval/issue22/pp2.html). A participatory action research collaborative of youth from urban and suburban schools in New York and New Jersey and researchers from the Graduate Center of the City University of New York investigate why educational-opportunity gaps persist in racially integrated public high schools. Youth researchers were trained in research methods, co-created a survey on youth perspectives on schooling and social justice (n = 7,049 students across fifteen schools districts), and assisted in analysis and interpretation. Focus groups and individual interviews were conducted with a variety of young people (n = 196 youth in focus groups), schools were cross-visited, and original research was generated by youth on questions of statewide finance inequity, tracking, and differential suspension rates by race/ethnicity. Youth are creating *Echoes*, a performance of the research through spoken word and movement in order to commemorate the fiftieth anniversary of *Brown v. Board of Education*.

Youth Organizing Communities (Greater Los Angeles, CA; see http://www.innercitystruggle.org). Youth-initiated group with branches in Los Angeles, East Los Angeles, and San Diego that organizes students around the demand that "education is a human right." YOC utilizes research and activism to fight for educational justice and to call for schools not jails. Youth define strategies and agendas, create and conduct surveys, train and organize peers, meet with school administrators and media representatives, and mobilize community support.

Youth Action Research Institute (Hartford, CT; see http://www.incommunityresearch.org/research/yari.htm). Formerly the National Teen Action Research Center of the Institute for Community Research, YARI promotes the use of action research for personal, group, and community development. Youth PAR projects have investigated questions around the availability of and access to support systems for urban lesbian, gay, bisexual, transgender, or questioning youth; relationships between young women and their mothers; drug, alcohol, and tobacco prevention; and community and family development. YARI trains teams of community youth researchers to conduct and use research as a tool for addressing issues of concern and importance to them, their communities, and schools.

Sistas and Brothas United (Bronx, NY; see http://www.nwbccc.org/). A youth founded spin-off of the Northwest Bronx Community and Clergy Coalition, SBU involves local young people in documenting conditions in the northwest Bronx and then launching community action. Their recent initiatives include the following: school-facilities campaigns that brought about substantial improvements in facilities and resources at several neighborhood high schools; teacher and student surveys and youth-initiated professional development aimed at improving teacher quality in area high schools; and a proposal (with Fordham University) for a new small school with a community-action theme called the Leadership Institute for Social Justice.

Youth Justice Coalition/Free LA (Los Angeles, CA). The coalition provides an established response to what it describes as California's "undeclared war on youth"— legislation that increases the criminalization of vulnerable youth in a state that already sets records for youth incarceration. The coalition is led by youth ages eight to twenty-four who have been arrested, detained, incarcerated, on probation, or on parole. Engaged as researchers, teachers, journalists, and policymakers, youth work to help others to understand the critical links between community conditions and larger issues of race, gender, income, and immigration.

Philadelphia Student Union (Philadelphia, PA; see http://www.phillystudentunion.org/). Through community organizing and leadership development, the PSU organizes and trains students at five public high schools across the city to work with teachers to fight declining school budgets, improve inadequate facilities, challenge privatization in the Philadelphia public schools, and plan the creation of create smaller, specialized high schools. PSU surveyed 1,042 students and found that the three top issues that students wanted addressed were creation of a multicultural and engaging curriculum, greater student involvement in school governance, and more guidance counselors. They also called for multiservice centers in schools that could provide services such as peer mediation and help with various other school-based and personal problems.

Fed Up Honeys (New York, NY; see http://www.fed-up-honeys.org). Young women of color from the Lower East Side of New York City launched a participatory action research project in collaboration with a researcher from the Graduate Center of the City University of New York to investigate the impact of gentrification and the restructuring of the public sector on the lived experiences of young urban women of color on the Lower East Side. Their research led to the creation of a report titled "Makes Me Mad: Stereotypes of Young Women of Color," a Web site, and a sticker campaign addressing the impact of stereotypes on the daily lives of young urban women of color.

Students 4 Justice/Colorado Progressive Coalition (Denver, CO; see http://www.progressivecoalition.org/body.htm). This youth-led youth organizing arm of the Colorado Progressive Coalition fights for greater public school accountability and student participation in Denver's public high schools. In August 2001 the group released a special report, "On the Outside Looking In: Racial Tracking at Denver's East High School," that documented the uneven access to accelerated and advanced placement (AP) classes and college counseling at this large, racially mixed high school.

Youth Action Research Group (Washington, D.C.; see http://socialjustice.georgetown.edu/research/yarg/index.html). YARG trains youth in participatory action research methods and ethnographic techniques to better understand the surrounding community for the purpose of addressing pressing social issues. Believing that in order to confront the challenges our communities face, people—not just their advocates—need to define issues and develop strategies for action, YARG works with community residents to define, research, and critically analyze the challenges facing their neighborhoods. Georgetown University faculty and students work with the YARG staff and youth participants to engage in collaborative research in the community with the hope of developing new leaders and engaging more people in community organizing and local citizenship.

Committee Against Anti-Asian Violence Youth Leadership Project (New York, NY; see http://www.caaav.org/projects/ylp.php). The Youth Leadership Project of CAAAV trains youth in basic organizing skills and research with a focus on building solidarity between Southeast Asians of the Bronx and all communities facing injustice and systemic oppression. Youth run their own community-based summer projects in an overall attempt to increase self-determination in their communities and organize against racism, sexism, classism, homophobia, colonialism, and other systems of oppression. In 2001 they researched and surveyed Southeast Asian tenement residents about how workfare affects their lives and produced the documentary *Eating Welfare*.

Across research settings youth engaged in PAR are active collaborators in every aspect of the research. Alone or together with adults they name the "problems"; frame the inquiry; create the measures, surveys, interview schedules, and focus-group protocols; conduct participant observation and archival searches; analyze and interpret the data; create the research products; write up reports; and present to audiences of community members, academics, and policymakers. Adult collaborators in these research projects carry responsibilities to create environments where all researchers (whether they be students, community members, Spanish-speaking, teachers, clerks, gang-involved, white, Asian, rich, or poor, etc.) come to the research table simultaneously bearing intellectual and experiential gifts and in need of further education on the tools of research. This underscores a respect for the knowledge embedded in the diversity within the group and the need for a common language of research so that all can participate as equally as possible. When PAR collectives are organized as "contact zones," as purposely diverse communities that explicitly acknowledge power and privilege within the group (see Pratt 1992) and *use* these differences as resources to further the social justice agenda of the research, there is the potential to produce research that is optically and ethically layered, that addresses issues that otherwise might be left uninterrogated, that pushes boundaries considered comfortable, and that explodes categories once thought to be "normal."

As with all social movements and all research projects, participatory work with youth carries questions of ethics, vulnerabilities, and negotiations of power. The dynamics vary based on the nature of the work, the "situatedness" of the struggle, and launching site for the research. Methods and strategic moves differ when PAR emerges from within community organizing where allies and targets are clear, in contrast to PAR launched centrally from within inequitable (e.g., schools) or oppressive (e.g., prisons) social institutions. Depending on the project, youth may decide to work alone or with adults. They may design research that seeks to change local conditions or simply expose injustice; they may seek to collaborate with representatives within the institution under scrutiny or reveal the systemic inequities brewing within. As a result, research products may vary—from performance to scholarly documents, from Web sites to organizing campaigns, from 1-800 tell-all phone numbers to presentations at professional conferences. Regardless of settings, context, politics, and players, PAR enables research to stretch toward radical social

change. With youth at the center PAR builds skills, communities, organizing, and scholarship.

We leave you with the following scene from one of the "feedback sessions" from the Educational Opportunity Gap Project—when one of the youth researchers was trying to detail the racialized patterns of school suspensions to his largely white teaching faculty.

The youth researcher Nozier said, "Now I'd like you to look at the suspension data and notice that black males in high schools were twice as likely as white males to be suspended, and there are almost no differences between black males and black females. But for whites, males are three times more likely to be suspended than females: 22 percent of black males, 19 percent of black females, 11 percent of white males, and 4 percent of white females." The educators, arms crossed, challenged the data. Nozier continued, "You know me, I spend a lot of time in the discipline room. It's really almost all black males." More denial came from the educators. Nozier turns to the charts projected on the screen, "You don't have to believe me, but I speak for the hundreds of black males who filled out this survey. We have to do something about it."

While the session within the school was, perhaps predictably, filled with resistance, Nozier has continued his efforts and is now working with a cross-school coalition of youth researchers who were scheduled to perform "Echoes: Racial Struggles for Justice Fifty Years after Brown" on May 15, 2004, for the fiftieth anniversary of *Brown v. Board of Education.*

Youth PAR, like all PAR, takes theory, practice, politics, and action seriously. The research community is diverse and, by definition, grounded in local politics. The investigation is rigorous. The analysis promises to be kaleidoscopic, oscillating, and bold. Counterexplanations will percolate, and dominant discourses may stutter or at least share the dias with competing explanations. But PAR insists on action in the form of policy, practice, organizational change, and/or social movements. Toward this end PAR is designed to reveal the rhythms of injustice and those spots of possibility, extraordinary spaces where democratic practice could or does take place.

We end with a sense of urgency because that is where PAR begins—it is a defining motivation for youth engaged in action research for social justice. Participatory action research projects are radical strategies rooted in the "soil of discontent," generated in response to oppressive conditions of struggle. While we don't believe for a moment that social injustice is a "cognitive" problem, we have witnessed participatory research by, for, or with youth in collaboration with social movements within and beyond public institutions prick the "psychic amnesia" that has infected America.

See also Voice; Youth Commissions; Youth-Led Action Research, Evaluation, and Planning.

Recommended Reading

Cahill, C., Arenas, E., Jiang, N., Rios-Moore, I., and Threatts, T. (2004). "Speaking Back: Listening to the Voices of Young Urban Women of Color." In *All About the Girl*, edited by A. Harris. New York: Routledge.

Fine, M., and Torre, M. E. (2004). "Re-membering Exclusions: Participatory Action Research in Public Institutions." *Qualitative Research in Psychology*, 1 (1): 15–37.

Fine, M., Torre, M. E., Boudin, K., Bowen, I., Clark, J., Hylton, D., Martinez, M., "Missy," Rivera, M., Roberts, R. A., Smart, P., and Upegui, D. (2003). "Participatory Action Research: Within and beyond Bars." In *Qualitative Research in Psychology: Expanding Perspectives in Methodology and Design*, edited by P. Camic, J. E. Rhodes, and L. Yardley. Washington, D.C.: American Psychological Association.

Fine, M., and Weis, L. (2003). *Silenced Voices, Extraordinary Conversations*. New York: Teachers College Press.

Kemmis, S., and McTaggart, R. (2000). "Participatory Action Research." In *Handbook of Qualitative Research*, 2nd ed., edited by N. K. Denzin and Y. S. Lincoln. Thousand Oaks, CA: Sage, pp. 567–605.

Lewin, K. (1951). *Field Theory in Social Science: Selected Theoretical Papers*. New York: Harper.

Torre, M. E. (2004). "The Alchemy of Integrated Spaces: Youth Participation in Collectives of Difference." In *Beyond Silenced Voices*, edited by L. Weis and M. Fine. Albany: NY: State University of New York Press.

Torre, M. E., and Fine, M. (2003). "Youth Researchers Critically Reframe Questions of Educational Justice." *Evaluation Exchange*, 9 (2): 6, 22.

María Elena Torre and Michelle Fine

Peace Corps. *See* AmeriCorps.

Peer Influences on Political Development. Peers mutually influence one another's decisions, values, and behaviors. The popular press tends to portray this influence as entirely negative despite myriad counterexamples of the positive influence of young people on their peers. In fact, this volume is replete with examples of young people influencing other young people to enact powerful change. This influence extends to political development. As peers join together in their mutual pursuit of a common good (whether that good be widely accepted or highly contested), they influence one another's political development.

In the United States it is not the norm to hear teenagers talking about electoral politics between classes or late at night on the telephone. In reality, the majority of teens have probably never asked a classmate for their thoughts about candidates running for Congress or whether they support welfare reform or if they're planning to attend the upcoming city-council meeting. This does not, however, diminish the influence that peers have on their age-mates' political development.

Narrowly defined, the word *political* describes all things related to the government. However, a broader definition of political development encompasses not only how youth come to understand and hold the government accountable but also how they develop the capacities (e.g., communication, sense of solidarity, conflict-resolution skills, tolerance) that undergird their civic engagement.

Peers influence one another's political development in three ways:

First, peers influence each other's values and decisions. During adolescence young people experience a normative developmental shift in allegiance and emotional ties from their parents to their peers. The increased value put on peer relationships during this time period places peers in a position where they can directly influence the values and decisions of their age-mates.

Second, young people tend to take on the political themes that dominate their generation and characterize youth culture. Youth culture and generational values underpin young people's political attitudes and actions.

And third, the affective bonds and identities that result from participation in peer-oriented school and community organizations empower youth with the skills, courage, and support necessary to stand up for their political convictions.

Values and Decisions

Adolescence is marked by a shift in young people's relationships with and allegiance to their peers. In order to accommodate the increased autonomy of this developmental period, adolescents recast their relationships with family members as peer relationships increase in importance. As a result, for many things peers become the normative reference group to whom they look for approval and support. This is especially the case for domains such as style or culture. This normative shift from parents to peers allows young people to stretch beyond the family—itself an incubator of civic values—and explore fresh ideas and forge new relationships. Experimentation with new roles and exploration of new ideas helps adolescents define their unique identities and establish their roles as members of the community.

Adolescents' political development is grounded in their cumulative social experiences. Daily interactions with peers, family members, school, and the larger community provide young people with opportunities to define their roles as citizens

and develop the skills necessary to be active members of the polity. Everyday activities that occur between peers, such as being able to articulate their thoughts when friends ask their opinions, resolve conflicts with teammates, or come to understand peers' different perspectives, help adolescents to develop the civic capacities necessary to participate in their communities. Because adolescents spend increasing amounts of time in each other's presence, the experiences they share become very important to one another's individual development.

The experiences that young people have with their peers directly influence their ideas, values, and the opportunities to which they are exposed. For instance, suppose sixteen-year-old Jamal and his classmate Owen are assigned to be partners for an upcoming science project. Owen and Jamal would neither consider themselves friends nor even acquaintances, since they have been in few classes together. The objective of the project is to use green construction (i.e., using only naturally occurring materials such as leaves and twigs) to fabricate a kite that functions. Throughout the design phase of the project, Owen and Jamal offer innovative ideas to enhance the appearance and decrease the weight of the kite. By listening to and building upon one another's ideas they agree on a design that incorporates both of their ideas and that maximizes the functionality of their kite. As the project comes to a close, Jamal asks Owen if he'd be interested in enlisting their kite in an upcoming regional science fair that he'd read about in the school newspaper. In this simple example of peer interaction, Jamal and Owen benefited from the experience of working together. Both young men had the opportunity to practice and hone important civic skills—active listening, collaboration, organization, and the art of compromise—and used their relationship as a means to open doors to new opportunities (i.e., participating in the regional science fair). This example illustrates the personal and collective possibilities that arise when people connect with others: they expand their social networks, develop their individual capacities, and allow for other opportunities to arise including the possibility of being recruited into other activities or organizations. Ultimately, such recruitment opportunities are venues for civic engagement.

As important as this shift toward greater peer influence is in adolescence, peer influence does not become the only or overriding influence. That is, the influence of peers does not necessarily trump that of parents. Rather, because of the homogeneity that often exists between an adolescent's family and peer group, it can be argued that the peer group becomes more of a *political reinforcer* rather than a *political resocializer* of a young person's values. In other words, during adolescence peers would tend to reinforce rather than replace values learned in the family. Nevertheless, peers directly influence their age-mates' political development by introducing new ideas, challenging one another's values, and creating new opportunities to become engaged.

Adolescence brings about new opportunities of choice in how free time is spent—participating in extracurricular activities and attending social functions without adult supervision, not to mention the freedom that often comes with getting a driver's license. Interaction among peers provides a frame of reference for adolescents' actions. It makes logical sense that students who have friends are more likely to be exposed to or involved in a more diverse array of activities. That is, the larger the social network, the more people there are to encourage membership in a club, the more invitations there are to attend various types of activities, and the more likely young people are to do these things because there is comfort (and courage) in numbers.

Beyond close friendships and classrooms, peers interact in extracurricular activities and organizations. Participation in community and school-based organiza-

tions offers youth a multitude of opportunities to develop civic capacities, cultivate a sense of group unity, and organize around shared interests. Extracurricular activities and organizations provide youth with a safe, nonthreatening forum to find their voice, test ideas, negotiate differences, and work collectively to solve problems—all skills that apply to civic work. Unlike other institutions of socialization (e.g., family, schools), youth organizations tend to be more egalitarian. Whereas parents and teachers often have the final say in matters at home and school, adolescents who are involved in youth-centered groups or organizations often have equal say in the decision-making process. Such active contributions to the organization often bolster feelings of ownership and loyalty to the group. The experience of being part of an ongoing organization or group and of identifying with its values and goals gives young people a sense of what it means to be part of a "public" or an interest group. Thus organizational experiences in one's youth are early precursors of civic engagement in adulthood.

Youth Culture

The company young people keep and the prevailing youth culture influence the types of activities in which they choose to engage. Being accepted by peers is very important to adolescents. Often, peer acceptance is contingent upon a teen's willingness to conform to group norms which are heavily influenced by the prevailing youth culture. For example, if, in the heat of the 2004 presidential election campaign, the other young people in a teen's peer group—as well as their celebrity idols on MTV—are sporting T-shirts with political messages (e.g., Vote or Die), the teen becomes more inclined to wear a similar shirt because it is the "in" thing to do. Another contemporary medium of peer influence is hip-hop, which has been used throughout the world not only to reach and teach young people about social injustice but also to agitate them to action. Young people's friends and the broader youth culture dictate what is "in" and "out" as well as what is accepted behavior and what is not. Such social pressures have a direct influence on the activities, behaviors, and ideologies that young people choose to adopt.

Affective Bonds and Identity

When people join forces with their peers and contribute equally to a common cause—whether it is to win a soccer match or boycott a business that manufactures products in sweatshops—members of the group begin to feel a sense of unity called *group solidarity*. When members of the group function as *one* to successfully complete a task they begin to feel efficacious. This is called *collective efficacy*. To the extent that adolescents feel a sense of solidarity with their peers, they become committed to serving the common good (e.g., protecting the environment because it is "OUR" environment).

The foundation of collective efficacy is trust; members of the group trust that their peers will do their part. Peers hold one another accountable for the tasks they are assigned and expect everyone to contribute. Unlike families, membership in the group or organization has to be earned by adequately fulfilling responsibilities. If a teen habitually forgets to take out the trash at home, it is unlikely that his or her family will disown him or her. However, membership in groups and organizations is less static, and such displays of irresponsibility will likely earn little trust from other group members. In terms of political development, responsibility is a fundamental lesson. A democracy—*government by the people*—thrives only if its citizens fully embrace their rights and responsibilities. Maintaining a democracy requires that citizens actively participate by doing things such as voting in elections, protesting injustice, and volunteering with the elderly. In other words, the existence and sustainability of a democracy is contingent upon the citizenry's ability to uphold its responsibilities. To the extent that adolescents learn to be responsible to something larger than themselves, they are learning a fundamental civic value—responsibility to the common good. Young people learn responsibility to the greater good by being held accountable by peers.

Young people often join community and school-based organizations because they are interested in the mission or experience upon which the group is organized. For example, youth may be drawn to an organization and its membership because they share a common identity (e.g., student, women, Asian American, GLBT) or ideology (e.g., Jewish, tolerance). For many—young and old—who feel excluded from the mainstream, finding membership in an organization of people who feel the way they do or with whom they can identify serves as a viable pathway to civic engagement. Such organizations often become powerful sources of activism. Building on their shared identity, these groups foster a sense of solidarity and efficacy that allows them to join together, to be included, and to voice their convictions.

Although clearly beneficial, it is important to acknowledge the potential limitations of group solidarity. Friendship can be a positive force in creating affective ties with the polity. However, friendship can also be a form of social exclusion that limits youth's exposure to those outside of the friendship circle. Like friendship, the bonds of group solidarity are a double-edged sword: they can unite the group, making it stronger than the sum of its parts, or they can serve as a barrier that prevents them from bridging to other individuals or groups. Similar to social cliques, the latter undermines the most rudimentary principle of democracy—inclusion. Solidarity that precludes inclusion can be curbed by encouraging members of groups to diversify their involvements and the types of people with whom they interact. Furthermore, young people who engage with people who are different from themselves have higher levels of social trust, that is, a general belief that most people are trustworthy.

Learning to organize is an important skill in a democracy where it is rare for an individual to execute radical change alone. History does, however, offer myriad examples of the political potential of small groups of committed citizens organizing and successfully effecting widespread social change (e.g., see Youth Commissions). In addition to being more influential, collective efficacy provides the group with a sense of worth and the motivation necessary to overcome any bulwark of opposition and continue to push its agenda forward (for examples, see Keniston 1968; McAdam 1988).

See also Deliberative Democracy; Democracy; MTV's Choose or Lose Campaign (1992–); New Media; Personality and Youth Political Development; Punk Rock Youth Subculture; Rights of Participation of Children and Youth; Rights, Youth Perceptions of; Riot Grrrl; Student Political Activism.

Recommended Reading

Keniston, K. (1968). *Young Radicals: Notes on Committed Youth*. New York: Harcourt, Brace and World.

McAdam, D. (1988). *Freedom Summer*. New York: Oxford University Press.

Sigel, R. S. (1970). *Learning about Politics*. New York: Random House.

Amy K. Syvertsen and Constance A. Flanagan

Personality and Youth Political Involvement. Personality plays an important role in determining whether adolescents and young adults will become politically active. However, relatively little of the research on political activism has focused on aspects of personality that influence youth political behavior. In the 1960s and 1970s psychologists studied how personality related to college students' involvement in the social movements of their time, such as the civil rights movement, women's movement, and Vietnam War protests. Since this period, research on the relationship between personality and activism has decreased, possibly because there have not been social movements that have as strongly captured the attention and interest of American youth. Regardless, the literature suggests that two types of personality characteristics, traits and cognitions, influence whether a young individual will choose to participate in civic and political activities.

Personality is an individual's characteristic pattern of thinking, feeling, and being that is thought to influence behavior across situations. Personality is considered an "individual difference" dimension because it defines individuals as unique entities and explains differences between them. Some personality characteristics (e.g., temperament) and some traits (e.g., extraversion) are thought to be heritable or have a genetic component. However, many aspects of personality (e.g., beliefs and attitudes) develop over the life course, often being learned through interactions with parents, peers, and other significant people (e.g., teachers, clergy). Two types of personality characteristics are particularly relevant to youth activism: traits and cognitions. *Traits* are basic categories of personality that describe how an individual generally behaves, such as a tendency to be sociable or trusting. *Cognitive* aspects of personality, such as self-efficacy, relate to information processing, including what individuals believe, how they make judgments, and how they think.

Many aspects of personality that are especially relevant for activism are thought to develop during adolescence and young adulthood. Personality traits have been shown to become increasingly more stable across the life span. Personality changes in adolescence and young adulthood are thought to result from biological, emotional, and social developments that take place at this time. Furthermore, during this period individuals develop an identity or an understanding of who they are. Part of identity development is a search for ideas and ideologies to believe in—the development of morals and values, including those about politics. Identity development involves becoming committed to these beliefs as well as to group, and taking action on their behalf. Adolescence is also a time to try out different roles, such as activist and leader, before committing to more permanent adult roles. Additionally, late adolescence and young adulthood are times in which individuals often leave their families, exposing them to new people and experiences that cause them to develop new perspectives on a wide range of issues, including social and political ones. As such, adolescence and young adulthood is a time in which aspects of personality that are important to political involvement develop, strengthen, and mature.

Three types of personality traits have been related to youth activism: extroversion, authoritarianism, and trust. *Extroversion* is the tendency to be sociable, active, and assertive. Many forms of political activity are done in groups, such as working on campaigns, participating in rallies or protests, or being involved in school-based political organizations (e.g., student council or Model United Nations). As a result, those individuals who are more outgoing and sociable are thought to be more interested in and comfortable engaging in such activities. In terms of political interest, a study examined black college students' intent to participate in the Black College Day March on Washington in 1980, a rally in protest of the U.S. Department of Education's desegregation plans to close black colleges and universities or merge them with white institutions. They found that those black students who were more extroverted planned to attend the march. Another study focused on actual political behaviors found that high-school students who were more sociable were more politically active in four areas: voting in a local or national election, working on a political campaign, attending rallies, and contributing money or buying tickets to political events. Thus, youth who are more extroverted do appear to be more politically involved.

Another personality trait related to youth activism is *authoritarianism*. Individuals with an authoritarian personality tend to value and support traditional, legal authority (such as the government) and believe that the rules of this authority should be followed. This aspect of personality reflects individuals' beliefs about the current system of government and power and has been shown to influence their attitudes about political engagement. For example, college students were asked about their activism, both for and against the first Gulf War that occurred in 1991. Those students low on authoritarianism held more negative attitudes about the war and were more likely to have participated in demonstrations protesting the war. In contrast, those students high on authoritarianism held more positive attitudes about the war, and these attitudes predicted their engagement in pro-war demonstrations. In addition, a study of Dutch adolescents found that less authoritarian attitudes were related to higher moral reasoning which itself has been related to more political activism as will be discussed later in this chapter.

Thus, attitudes toward authority seem to influence whether youth are politically active in ways that are consistent with their beliefs. Specifically, those who hold beliefs and attitudes that reflect relatively little support for authority are more likely to protest government actions whereas those with relatively high support for authority are more likely to support government action. However, this relationship is indirect; that is, authoritarian attitudes seem to influence other attitudes and beliefs (e.g., about specific wars), and it is these beliefs that directly influence political activism.

Trust, belief in the good intentions of others, is another personality trait that is thought to influence youth civic participation. Because participation in organizations, at rallies, and so forth often takes place with relatively unknown strangers (or for their benefit), trust is needed for individuals to invest themselves in such causes without feeling that they are doing so at a personal cost. Consistent with this idea, a study of high-school students found that those who trusted others more felt they were more effective in their community-service activities and were more likely to have run for office in their student government. While trust may lead individuals to become involved civically, it can also be developed as a result of civic engagement. That is, working with other individuals toward a common goal and seeing the effect of one's involvement may serve to strengthen trust in other people as well as in the political and social system.

Three types of personality cognitions have been examined in relation to youth political involvement: sense of control, moral reasoning, and social values. Concerning one's sense of control, two related cognitive-personality concepts, *locus of control* and *self-efficacy*, have received the greatest amount of attention as correlates of youth political involvement. Both of these concepts have to do with whether individuals feel that they have control over outcomes in their lives. Locus of control is an individual's belief about the causes of what happens. Those with an internal locus of control believe that what happens to them depends on their own behavior (e.g., their own skill, effort, or ability). In contrast, those with an external locus of control believe that their outcomes are determined by outside forces beyond their control (e.g., powerful other people, the government, God, luck), rather than through their behavior. Self-efficacy is similar to internal locus of control; those individuals with a greater sense of self-efficacy believe that they can achieve the outcome that they desire (e.g., working hard to get good grades).

Many studies looking at these concepts have found that those youth with a sense of control are more likely to be politically engaged. Two studies of black southern college students in the 1960s found that students who were more actively involved in issues around civil rights and integration had a more internal locus of control than those students who were not involved in these causes. In terms of voting behavior, an American study found that youth with an internal locus of control were more likely to vote in a local or national election, while a study of British youth found that those with a more external locus of control were more cynical and, in turn, voted less. Finally, a study of private high-school (and younger) students found that those with an internal locus of control felt that they were effective and made a contribution through their community service.

Researchers have also examined whether individuals' sense of control specifically in political areas relates to youth activism. Several studies of high-school and college students in Canada and the United States found that those individuals who believed that they had more control over social and political issues and could make a difference through politics were more politically active for a variety of causes including pro-choice, antiabortion, and antiwar protests. Thus, those who believe that their behaviors can successfully effect a change, particularly in the domain of politics, are more likely to attempt to do so through their political activism.

A few other studies have examined *individual-system blame*, an aspect of personality that is similar to the control dimensions discussed above. This characteristic reflects the extent to which individuals assign blame for negative or undesirable circumstances (i.e., social inequalities) to individuals (individual blame) or to the social and political system (system blame). Studies in this area have found that those individuals who placed more blame on the system, rather than the individual, for racial injustice were more politically active in social movements as college students. Thus, youth activism may be more likely not only when individuals feel that they can make a difference within politics, but also when they believe that some of the existing social problems can be remedied if the political and social systems are changed.

As was mentioned previously, another aspect of personality that is related to youth political activity is *moral reasoning*. Moral reasoning is the way that an individual thinks about whether a behavior is right or wrong. At earlier stages of moral reasoning (i.e., premoral reasoning), the individual is self-focused and behaviors that satisfy the individual's needs are considered to be moral. At middle stages the individual is thought to have conventional reasoning in which something is considered to be moral if it follows the rules put forth by society. At the highest stages of moral reasoning (i.e., principled reasoning), the individual considers the welfare of others and uses her or his own principles and conscience to judge whether something is moral. The development of more complex moral reasoning often occurs during adolescence because it requires a greater cognitive ability (e.g., intelligence and abstract thinking), which also develops during this period.

Moral reasoning appears to be most relevant to understanding young people's attitudes about societal issues (e.g., alternative lifestyles, abortion, freedom of expression) rather than other types of political issues (e.g., economics), as suggested by a study of Dutch adolescents that found that those with higher levels of moral reasoning held more "progressive" political attitudes about cultural matters. Other studies have found that youth with higher levels of moral reasoning are more likely to engage in political activism for both liberal and conservative causes. This may be because those individuals who think about moral issues at a higher level are more interested in participating in moral activities that represent their beliefs, such as sit-ins or protests. On the other hand, the discussion of moral and political issues that takes place through participation in politics may be a way for youth to develop and increase the sophistication of their moral reasoning.

Certain *values* may also be related to youth politics. Values are beliefs about what, generally, is considered to be good or important. Having values that place importance on notions such as making a contribution to society or helping others lay the groundwork for activism, as individuals

become active in support of their beliefs. One study of adolescents in seven countries found that those who reported that their parents had instilled in them the value of social responsibility thought it was more important to contribute to and improve their society. In some countries, those adolescents who believed it was important to contribute to their country did more volunteer work. Thus, believing that it is good to get involved in one's community or society may lead young people to do so, given the right context.

Together, the research suggests that there are several aspects of personality that relate to youth political involvement. Many of these studies used college students as their sample, a convenient but also decidedly relevant group for studies related to participation and activism. College introduces youth to new people with different ideas and beliefs that may lead them to question, change, or refine their previous beliefs and cognitions. College is a time of learning and growth with the continued development of cognitive ability and personality. It also provides new opportunities, including those for political involvement permitting the expression of personality traits and cognitions through political action. However, more research on younger groups such as high-school-aged youth is needed in order to capture some of the dynamic changes in personality that take place during early adolescence and may influence youth activism.

In sum, research has shown that the personality traits of extroversion, authoritarianism, and trust, and personality cognitions related to control, moral responsibility, and social values are significant in our understanding of youth civic and political participation. Certainly, there are likely to be other traits and cognitions relevant to understanding youth political involvement, such as openness to new experiences and a sense of self that includes concerns with social matters. However, the current research suggests that there are important, stable, internal characteristics—certain traits and cognitions—that engender political participation in youth. These traits and cognitions seem to place youth in a condition of readiness for activism. That is, they create certain ways of being, thinking, and perceiving others and one's place in the world that encourage youth to get involved in making social change happen.

See also Deliberative Democracy; Democracy; Democratic Education; Minority Youth Voter Turnout; Moral Development; MTV's Choose or Lose Campaign (1992–); New Media; Peer Influences on Political Development; Rights of Participation of Children and Youth; Rights, Youth Perceptions of; Social Trust; State and Youth, The; Student Political Activism.

Recommended Reading

Crystal, D. S., and DeBell, M. (2002). "Sources of Civic Orientation among American Youth: Trust, Religious Valuation, and Attributes of Responsibility." *Political Psychology*, 23: 113–132.

Duncan, L. E., and Stewart, A. J. (1995). "Still Bringing the Vietnam War Home: Sources of Contemporary Student Activism." *Personality and Social Psychology Bulletin*, 21: 914–924.

Flanagan, C. A., Bowes, J. M., Jonsson, B., Csapo, B., and Sheblanova, E. (1998). "Ties That Bind: Correlates of Adolescents' Civic Commitments in Seven Countries." *Journal of Social Issues*, 54: 457–475.

Glanville, J. L. (1999). "Political Socialization or Selection? Adolescent Extracurricular Participation and Political Activity in Early Adulthood." *Social Science Quarterly*, 80: 279–290.

Laird, P. G. (2003). "Bridging the Divide: The Role of Perceived Control in Mediating Reasoning and Activism." *Journal of Moral Education*, 32: 35–49.

Raaijmakers, Q. A. W., Verbogt, T. F. M. A., and Vollebergh, W. A. M. (1998). "Moral Reasoning and Political Beliefs of Dutch Adolescents and Young Adults." *Journal of Social Issues*, 54: 531–546.

Isis H. Settles and Jennifer S. Pratt-Hyatt

Political Consumerism. Formally defined, political consumerism is the choice of producers and products with the aim of changing ethically or politically objectionable institutional or market practices. These consumer choices are informed by attitudes and values regarding issues of justice and fairness, noneconomic issues that concern personal and family well-being.

December is the season of giving. Streets and shopping windows are decorated in holiday colors, and Christmas music and spirit fill shopping malls. For retail stores it is a most lucrative time of year. Newspaper, television, radio, and now even Internet advertisements try to convince people that they truly can show their loved ones how much they really care by giving them special gifts at Christmastime. A particular focus of marketing attention is the younger generation, a group seen as easy prey for marketing strategists because of their concern over personal appearance and the social status accompanying brand-name clothing, shoes, and other consumer-oriented material goods. But this characterization does not apply to all young people. Christmas season is also when the political consumerism movement gears up for focused action to question the basis of consumer society. Many young people are involved in this reevaluation of Western consumer-driven society.

A few holiday seasons ago, BehindTheLabel.com, an online advocacy network, put out an urgent appeal against the Gap, a large clothing chain with stores in several nations that markets its clothes to young people. It urged consumers not to patronize Gap stores, claiming on its online slideshow: "The Gap uses sweatshop labor, if you buy Gap you do too. Make a difference. Be the generation that stops sweatshops. Tell your family and friends: Don't buy me Gap this holiday season." In Canada advocates wearing Santa outfits appeared in shopping malls to call attention to the effects of our commercial society in other parts of the world. Elsewhere, activists against sweatshops have taken to the streets. In the Netherlands, for example, Dutch protesters dressed themselves as angels to attract consumer attention on a busy public street lined with clothing stores and asked shoppers to send the company of their choice a Christmas card asking about its offshore production practices and codes of conduct.

These examples tell the stories of many young people who are conscientious consumers. They use the marketplace to challenge how we live, work, and do politics in the world today. These young activists urge us to think about consumer society in new ways by confronting what they consider to be an ethically blind and consumption-crazed society. They encourage individual consumers to fight for the rights of workers and animals and against unbridled free trade, the power of transnational corporations, and the use of pesticides and genetically modified organisms in our food. This type of engagement stands in seeming contrast to the common critique of today's young people as materialistically oriented. Although the numbers indicate that, for example, college freshmen have an increased interest in becoming financially well-off, the trend lines also show that they attach more importance to contributing to society. People who use the market in this fashion are political consumers.

Although the concept is fairly new, political consumerism is an old phenomenon. Historical studies of the United States and Europe have shown how the market has frequently been used as an arena for political activism. Women, marginalized groups, and young people have, for instance, employed their purchasing power to help put an end to domestic American sweatshop labor in the early 1900s by buying "white label" goods, to combat various kinds of discrimination through boycotts, and to fight for peace by encouraging their parents to be socially responsible when they invest in the stock market. Citizens both young and old from different nations have even joined together in international boycotts to protest governmental or corporate policy. Well-known examples include those against Nestlé, South Africa, and grape producers. Recently France and the United States have been the focus of grassroots international boycotts because of their positions on the Iraq War in the spring of 2003.

Political consumerism comes in different forms. Citizens *boycott* to express po-

litical sentiment and they "*buycott*" or use labeling schemes to support corporations that represent values—environmentalism, fair trade, and sustainable development, for example—that they support. Political consumerism can also have an uglier face, as when boycotts and buycotts are used in struggles against particular ethnic, religious, or racial groups and for the advancement of nationalistic goals. The "Don't Buy Jewish" boycotts that began in Europe at the end of the nineteenth century are the clearest and best-known example of this ugly face of political consumerism. Even current boycott campaigns against corporations seen as "gay friendly" and "pro-abortion" can be put in this category. Sometimes a political consumerist campaign has both a pretty and ugly face, as shown in the African American "Don't Buy Where You Can't Work" campaign in the in the early 1900s, around 1930, that was used both by citizens struggling to improve the plight of African Americans and also black nationalist groups who used boycotts to promote antiwhite and anti-Semitic attitudes.

Young people are engaged in all forms of political consumerism. Survey research from different countries shows that they are more interested in grassroots engagements and in using the market than other channels for political participation. When asked in 2002 if they had ever "not bought something because of the conditions under which it was made," 52 percent of young Americans between the ages of fifteen and twenty-five said "yes," and a majority stated that they had done so in the last year. The same survey reports that 44 percent of young Americans said they *had* bought a certain product because they liked the values of the company that made it (Orlander 2004). Political consumerism ranked by far the highest for young people out of a range of political activities including contacting a public official, writing a letter to a newspaper editor, and participating in protests and rallies. About two-thirds of the respondents said that they were not involved in any kind of conventional political engagement.

Clearly, the high percentage of political consumers among young people is caused partially by the fact that those below eighteen years of age are not yet allowed to vote. However, political consumerism might still be considered a new and important tool for political engagement for young people.

European surveys also point to the importance of the marketplace as an arena for young people to engage in politics. People aged twenty to twenty-nine who said that they bought a product for ethical or political reasons ranged from about 6 percent in Italy to over 50 percent in Scandinavia. Political consumerism is most widespread in Sweden with 65 percent of this age category having boycotted for political reasons. Swedish national surveys confirm this picture and show that many young people claim that they have used political consumerism more than just once, with youngsters who have extensive education as the most involved. A study conducted by the Swedish National Board for Youth Affairs shows that almost everyone in this age group has at some time boycotted or would consider boycotting for a political reason. What is particularly interesting is that this high level of appeal (just under 100 percent) can be compared with a bit fewer than 70 percent who stated that they were generally interested in party and legislative politics. In other words, political consumerism has the potential to evolve into a widespread phenomenon of participation that may be particularly suitable for young citizens.

Young citizens' market-based political strategies go beyond boycotting and buycotting, which are commonly targeted in survey research. Young people are also activists in Internet campaigns and use the Internet to voice their individual opinions on consumer society and transnational corporations; mobilize their schools, universities, or fellow students to take actions regarding consumer issues; and engage in culture jamming. Most frequently, young people use these means of involvement in their fight for workers' rights in developing and Western countries and for the treatment of animals. This engagement is channeled through a variety of opportunities for activism that are offered by the "no sweat" and animal rights movements, two global advocacy movements that developed strongly in the 1990s and 2000s. The "no sweat" movement, represented by North American antisweatshop advocacy networks and the European Clean Clothes Campaign, fights for good working conditions in the global garment industry. The crusade for proper animal welfare, including bans on animal testing and fur trading as well as the promotion of vegetarianism and veganism, are the key motivators of the animal rights movement.

A fairly new tool for these advocacy movements and even individual young citizens who support them is culture jamming/adbusting. Culture jamming is directed against corporate power and involves activities that generally fall under the categories of media hacking, information warfare, terror-art, and guerrilla semiotics. They are individualized types of actions that can be performed alone but that help a common cause. The most famous case of culture jamming was initiated by former MIT graduate student Jonah Peretti, who ordered a pair of customizable Nike shoes with the word "sweatshop" on them. This request turned him into a global celebrity. The e-mails—completely independent of his control or encouragement—reached an estimated 11.4 million people around the globe. This is an example of culture jamming in the classical sense, in that he utilized Nike's own marketing strategy to argue for his request. Peretti's story shows that the Internet is an important tool for global social-activist network building, and it illustrates how individualized lifestyle choices can dovetail with responsibility taking for global social justice.

Postcard campaigns are another important form of culture jamming used frequently by the antisweatshop movement. Typically, activists pass out postcards in front of targeted clothing stores and at music concerts, movement events, and other public happenings that draw crowds of young people. They urge those they encounter to send postcard messages to clothing companies. Postcards depicting sweatshop labor and making fun of corporate advertisements are available online from the Clean Clothes Campaign Web site. Young people find this form of activism enjoyable because they appreciate direct political messages that poke fun at authority and because they can choose the card, write a message in the appropriate text box, choose the addressee, and then send it off. Examples of culture-jamming postcards include the following: "Income GAP. An American Classic," a play on the Gap's logo; a card portraying Mickey Mouse with fangs and reading "BOM!!! Beware of Mickey. Disney Sweatshops in South China," which provides information on the salary level of the Disney CEO and the wages paid to Disney workers in China; another showing a picture of a man with money stuffed in his mouth and the words "the true colors of Benetton" written across his shirt; and a rewording of the Levi's jeans patch as "Evil Strauss and Co. $$$."

The animal rights movement has its own culture jamming campaigns that offer supporters personal items for sale over the Internet so they can wear their values. Students have come to class with T-shirts depicting the Burger King logotype but with the words "Murder King." Many young people find these activities appealing because they provide a way of expressing concerns about global justice by offering immediate, countercultural involvement with causes that research shows interest youth. These kinds of involvements have also been called lifestyle politics because the sharing of political messages and the engagements in political acts are embedded in everyday life. For younger generations, politics is enmeshed with their daily life choices about how they dress, what they eat, what they buy, and what music they listen to in their free time.

Political consumerist strategies interest young people because they allow them wiggle room to live, design, and build their own involvements. "Modding" is a term from the computer-game world that characterizes this kind of youthful involvement. Political consumerist networks allow people to "mod" (i.e., to modify) political activism. Educational meetings organized by the Clean Clothes Campaign can end with participants planning their own public-action days to be implemented without central supervision in their hometowns. Other advocacy campaigns encourage do-it-yourself involvement by providing people with a toolbox or action package to build their own activism. The Canadian antisweatshop network, Maquila Solidarity Network, even distributes a Sweatshop Fashion Show toolkit, which has been used by young people across the country to raise awareness about sweatshop abuses in a fun and educational way. These tools help young people plan alternative shows whose purpose is the creation of public spectacles that question the politics of fashion products. Because of their alternative nature, these activities are often picked up by the media in various countries.

Political consumerist activists like the Maquila Solidarity Network also target school environments, particularly high schools. Its "No Sweat Schools" campaigns rally students together to declare their school free of sweatshop products. Their goal is to negotiate an agreement with their school stipulating that it will not purchase uniforms for students, staff, teams, and others that are made under sweatshop conditions. These campaigns are almost always initiated by students themselves, even though they are based on the mobilization and facts provided by the Maquila Solidarity Network. The process of a campaign often involves raising student awareness, lobbying principals and teachers, developing a plan for change or a code of conduct, and lobbying the board of education or a local municipal council. For many pupils this is the first time that they have engaged with the social and political institutions in their communities. During the campaign, students learn that they are more than just individualized consumers and that their actions are part of a political and economic machine with the potential for real power in the corporate and political worlds. The pupils move from the consumer-to-producer relationship to a relationship of institutional purchaser-to-supplier. Young people easily feel that their power has been increased through this shift. University students in the United States have undertaken similar efforts and have even established the organization United Students Against Sweatshops (USAS), an effort considered by some to be the new student movement for the 1990s and 2000s.

Youth involvement with the global garment industry has mobilized other people, both young and old, into action and even led to institution-building efforts to follow up agreements made together with student political consumerist activists. The Workers' Rights Consortium, a nonprofit organization, was, for example, created by college students, university administrators, and labor rights experts to make sure that university-adopted codes of conduct are effectively enforced. The "disclosure campaign" lobbied the Canadian federal government in 2002 for a change in its labeling regulations governing manufactured goods sold in Canada. It all started when a student in British Columbia, outraged about not being able to find sufficient information about how her clothes had been produced, cut a label out of one of her purchases and sent it to the government along with a demand for more consumer information. The physical defacement of her clothes made a powerful statement that resonated with other concerned young people across the country, who subsequently decided to send in their labels as well. With the help of the Maquila Solidarity Network's Web site, which advertised the campaign, tens of thousands of clothing labels and petitions signed by over 20,000 Canadians were delivered to the office of the Ministry of Industry, thus demonstrating that support for product transparency had gained broad public support.

Networks and campaigns from the animal rights movement also understand the importance of youth involvement in their campaigns. They encourage young people to act on their values, do their own thing, and "mod" their involvements by offering toolkits and proposals for how to get involved. An entire Web site of People for the Ethical Treatment of Animals, PETA-Kids, is devoted to enticing young people into this kind of activism. It premieres a short animated film called *The Meatrix*. With music from *The Matrix* in the background, young people are told about problems with agricultural animal welfare and that it is "you the consumer that has the real power ... click here and I will show you how to escape the Meatrix." Following the link brings one to the "get active" page, which includes tips about grassroots, everyday, social and food, consumer, armchair, and Web activism.

Most available research tends to show that young people do not dominate the ranks of people who buy organic food and eco-labeled household products. Most likely this is because of financial restrictions in choosing products that can be more expensive at times than nonlabeled ones and because very young people do not shop for food supplies and household goods as frequently as the older generations. Yet other forms of political consumerism like boycotts, culture jamming, creation of public spectacles, and attempts to influence the consumer choices made by older generations interest them greatly. Why is this?

The phenomenon of political consumerism is embedded in the ongoing debate about how and why young citizens have been turning their backs on electoral politics in unprecedented numbers. Indeed, much of the decline in voter turnout over the past decade can be explained by the increasing numbers of young citizens not turning up to vote at election time. In the 2000 U.S. presidential election, only 36 percent of young voters between the ages of eighteen and twenty-four actually used their right to vote. Scattered evidence also suggests that the membership base of youth organizations is in decline, even more so than party membership in general.

Large-scale societal transformation explains young peoples' dissatisfaction with conventional forms of political involvement. They tend to dislike participation in bureaucratic and time-consuming organizations, and they typically prefer more spontaneous, informal, and egalitarian networks and organizations. This has been called the postmaterialist value shift, entailing heightened interest by younger generations in Western societies for values outside of the material world of physical safety and economic security. The phenomenon of political consumerism fits squarely into this new development. Not only does it offer new ways of political engagement outside of mainstream institutions, it also seeks to spread postmaterialist values and ideas of justice, equality, and fairness in all parts of the world.

Young citizens have also been found to distrust traditional or mainstream forms of political involvement (e.g., political parties, parliaments, Congress, labor unions), and they have made conscious choices to avoid them. Instead, they confront societal problems directly, as exemplified by political consumerism. This desire for new forms of activism helps to explain youth involvement in antisweatshop campaigns. North American young people who join the campaign and who become active are often at first very disaffected from the political process. They do not believe that voting or joining a party makes a difference. Yet during a given campaign when pupils or students come into contact with government officials, they get drawn into the conventional political process.

Through political consumerism, young people can directly confront transnational corporations and consumer society. They can work with their concerns about the quality of our environment and animal and human rights. Political consumerism allows them to "mod" their involvement to suit their own needs and consciousnesses. The toolkits and activity packages offer them ideas for individual and collective ways to force a variety of actors to take notice of the problems caused by our consumption patterns and corporate efforts to make us consume at an ever faster rate. Young people can decide for themselves which actors and problems to target. They can use political consumerism to call attention to the need for institutions at the global political level, the growing importance of transnational corporations, or consumer society itself.

With the help of political consumerist toolkits, young people are increasingly demanding more transparency in and control over commodity chains that seem far removed from their everyday lives. Through public performances, jokes, political messages on their clothing, and with the help of the Internet, they demand that corporations reveal the hidden politics and economic, human, ecological, and animal costs of common consumer goods and services. Young people are increasingly crying out to take responsibility for the ecological and ethical "footprints" that we all leave behind after purchasing goods at shopping malls, school cafeterias, and fast-food hamburger and chicken chains. They are demanding that corporate actors share in this responsibility taking with them.

See also Animal Rights; Deliberative Democracy; Democracy; Democratic Education; Global Justice Activism; Minority Youth Voter Turnout; MTV's Choose or Lose Campaign (1992–); New Media; Peer Influences on Political Development; Personality and Youth Political Development; Political Participation and Youth Councils; Rights of Participation of Children and Youth; Rights, Youth Perceptions of; Social Movements; Student Political Activism; Transnational Youth Activism; United Students Against Sweatshops (USAS).

Recommended Reading

Au, W. J. (April 16, 2002). *Triumph of the Mod: Player-Created Additions to Computer Games Aren't a Hobby Anymore—They're*

the Lifeblood of the Industry. See http://
archive.salon.com/tech/feature/2002/04/
16/modding/print.html.

Bennett, W. L. (1998). "The UnCivic Culture:
Communication, Identity, and the Rise of
Lifestyle Politics." PS, Political Science and
Politics, 31 (4): 41–61.

Dery, M. (1993). Culture Jamming: Hacking, Slash-
ing and Sniping in the Empire of Signs. See
http://www.levity.com/markdery/jam.html.

Featherstone, L., and United Students Against
Sweatshops. (2002). Students Against Sweatshops. London: Verso.

Friedman, M. (1999). Consumer Boycotts: Effecting Change through the Marketplace and
the Media. New York: Routledge.

Higher Education Research Institute (2004). The
American Freshman: National Norms for Fall
2003—Charts and Graphs. See http://www.
gseis.ucla.edu/heri/03_norms_charts.pdf.

Inglehart, R. (1997). Modernization and Post-
modernization. Princeton, NJ: Princeton University Press.

Micheletti, M. (2003). Political Virtue and Shopping: Individuals, Consumerism, and Collective Action. New York: Palgrave Macmillan.

Micheletti, M., Follesdal, A., and Stolle, D.
(2003). Politics, Products, and Markets: Exploring Political Consumerism Past and
Present. New Brunswick, NJ: Transaction
Publishers.

Micheletti, M., and Stolle, D. (2004). Politiska
konsumenter: marknaden som arena för politiska val. In Ju mer vi är tillsammans, edited
by S. Holmberg and L. Weibull. Gothenburg:
SOM-institutet.

Olander, M. (July 2003). How Young People
Express Their Political Views. From the
CIRCLE (Center for Information and Re-
search for Civic Learning and Engagement)
Web site, see http://www.civicyouth.org/
PopUps/expressviews.pdf.

Peretti, J., and Micheletti, M. (2003). "The Nike
Sweatshop E-mail: Political Consumerism,
Internet, and Culture Jamming." In Politics,
Products, and Markets: Exploring Political
Consumerism Past and Present, edited by
M. Micheletti, A. Follesdal, and D. Stolle.
New Brunswick, NJ: Transaction Press.

Stolle, D., and Hooghe, M. (2004). "Inaccurate,
Exceptional, One-Sided or Irrelevant? The
Debate about the Alleged Decline of Social
Capital and Civic Engagement in Western So-
cieties." British Journal of Political Science,
34 (4): 703–721.

Workers' Rights Organization (2004). See http://
www.workersrights.org/.

Michele Micheletti and Dietlind Stolle

**Political Participation and Youth Coun-
cils.** Young people's involvement in the
public world of politics, particularly for
those under the voting age, has always attracted conflicting commentary and publicity. Young people are seen to embody
democratic ideals in their enthusiasm for
justice and fairness. At the same time they
are seen as naïve and unworldly, unsuited
to the murky reality of party politics. Young
people's ambiguous place in the political
world is due, in part, to conflicting social
ideas about young people as political participants. Young people's experiences in
youth and school councils reflect this
ambiguity.

In one sense young people's participation in politics has always been important
as it is often taken as a measure of the vi-
brancy and health of a community or society. There has been a healthy tension
between those young people working
within conventional political structures
and those with a critical and idealistic
view of social change within social movements outside the political establishment.
Young people's enthusiasm for change and
their commitment to justice and fairness
acts as a catalyst inside and outside political systems.

However, the desire to tap into the enthusiasm and commitments of young people has become more difficult in recent
years because of what political commentators call the "democratic deficit." Concerns
are expressed in the United Kingdom and
the United States about the extent to which
young people are committed to existing
liberal democratic systems. Over the past
two decades young people between ages
eighteen and twenty-four have become
much less likely to vote in elections, and
recent research has suggested that young
people express a degree of cynicism toward
conventional party politics. The Economic
and Social Research Council in the United
Kingdom recently reported that the low
turnout at the 2001 general election in the
United Kingdom, particularly by young
people, seems to confirm the view that
there is a widening gulf between the citizen, disengaged from traditional forms of

democratic involvement and government with its commitment to a more inclusive and participatory democracy and citizenship education.

Arguably, the delicate balance between the need to incorporate young people within "adult" political structures and the rebellious instincts of the young to find alternative solutions has tipped too far in favor of the latter. Thus politicians and educators in the United Kingdom are devising methods for the inclusion of young people within the political system. National and local youth parliaments have been set up in which members represent the interests of young people on a range of local and national issues. Towns and cities across the United Kingdom are consulting with young people, bringing the United Kingdom in line with other European countries with more established youth agendas through youth councils.

To further this commitment to young people's political inclusion, schools in England and Wales are emphasizing concepts such as democracy and rights as citizenship education is introduced to the national curriculum. More attention is being paid to the importance of participation in the political process in relation to voting and greater involvement in civic and community activities. Citizenship education also encourages young people to get involved in politics in "micro" terms within schools, with school councils being taken more seriously by both teachers and students. Thus, young people are being encouraged to express their views and represent their interests in a number of ways at national and local levels.

While politicians and educators are starting to take young people's views more seriously, young people's lack of enthusiasm for conventional politics may be due to ideas perpetuated through the media that undermine young people's capacity to participate in decision-making processes in schools and local communities. Two sets of powerful images serve to compromise the status of young people as political activists

and bring into question the extent to which adults trust young people. First, there is the recurring idea of young people as troublemakers, particularly where youngsters meet and congregate in public spaces, such as the street and the shopping mall. Topics such as gang culture and child crime and associations between school absence and delinquency are frequently referred to by social commentators and journalists in creating stereotypical images of youngsters causing widespread disruption in public spaces. Parents, families, and teachers are blamed, demands are made on adults to take more control, and in general, young people are said to need firmer guidance and be given fewer opportunities to express their sometimes uncompromising views.

A second negative stereotype is the vulnerable teenager, at risk from crime, abuse, and exploitation. Today's young people often make more demands on society and tend to have far more opportunities to explore their social environments than in the past. Some commentators have interpreted these opportunities as risks to which youngsters are increasingly exposed, both inside and outside their families. The emphasis is on a level of safety and protection that provides the basis for youngsters to explore and be innovative in adolescence, giving them the confidence to make stands and express their independent views in later life. However, powerful images generated by the media of street violence, "deviant families," and violence in schools may actually produce more fearful young people and extend the protective structures within families well into the young person's adolescence, past the point when young people are expected to have a strong sense of their independence. This ultimately restricts the kinds of opportunities that youngsters have to innovate in their own terms and take the kind of "healthy" risks that provide society with vibrant and socially committed young citizens.

This emphasis on protection and control among the adult population leads to a lack of trust between young people and adults.

Consequently adults err on the side of dictating what is in young people's best interests. This takes young people further away from centers of power and influence within society and works against any moves toward recognizing and including young people as political participants. In effect, we have contrary views and trends: young people are both a potential social problem and a potent source of social change. One recent example of this ambiguity was the recent antiwar demonstrations in the United Kingdom. Young people left their classrooms temporarily to express their views on the war against Iraq on the street with their adult counterparts. Some saw this positively as young people engaging with important current global and political issues, supporting popular opinion against the involvement of the United Kingdom in the Iraq War. Others were more critical, with the young protesters seen as troublemakers and truants using the demonstrations as an excuse to "bunk off" school.

Recent examples from the United Kingdom of young people's political participation in civic and school councils illustrate some of these conflicting ideas about young people as political participants. Much evidence exists of powerful commitments among the young participants to ensure that young people have a voice. In addition, there was plenty of enthusiasm among teachers and adult civic leaders for more youthful participation. There was a clear recognition that institutions that ignore young people's opinions and fail to provide structures for the expression of these opinions are out of date.

Regarding civic youth councils, councilors were elected by their peers to represent their interests within their towns and local communities. Crime prevention, leisure facilities for young people, and transportation were key topics on their agendas. In some cases councilors used their influence to challenge the lack of trust among the older population. Through links with adult community groups they were committed to changing the pessimistic view of teenagers'

capabilities and social positions. The young participants were challenging negative media stereotypes of "troublesome youth" through their good works.

Trust was more ambiguously expressed by school staff in relation to the school councils. On the one hand, school councilors were supported by their teachers when trying to create channels through which students expressed their views on school affairs. Staff provided students with the time and opportunity to hold elections, often set up council meetings, and in some cases offered financial support when it was needed. However, there were constant battles by staff and students over control of the student agenda. Student interests among other things revolved around food—the cost and quality of school lunches and fairness—the questioning of rules that only applied to young people—and student access to prohibited areas of the school. Staff, on the other hand, tended to see these issues as trivial and unrealistic, a reflection of the partial and limited horizons of young people. School staff members were trying to shape the school council agenda in terms of what they thought were "big" educational issues such as the curriculum, student behavior, and moral responsibility. While the teachers might be suggesting that students ought to get involved in more serious "adult" issues in school, the agenda is being determined by adults irrespective of the wishes of students. This illustrates the ambiguous commitment of school staff to democracy in school. Students have their own space within which they can have their interests represented, but whether these interests are taken seriously depends on the extent to which they coincide with the interests of the teaching staff.

In concluding, two recent global developments may strengthen the idea of young people as political participants and make it more likely that young people's views are listened to and respected: global commitments to children's rights and the rise of the Internet. The United Nations Conventions on the Rights of the Child, passed in 1989, encourages governments across the world to take seriously the rights of children and young people to participate and have a voice. The United States is one of two remaining countries to sign up to the convention, and the United Kingdom has been heavily criticized for not taking these new rights seriously. Nevertheless, pressure can be brought to bear on countries and organizations worldwide to commit to the idea that children and young people are full members of society and governments should find ways of providing young people with more effective ways of expressing their opinions and interests.

A second and more radical trend is the widening of sources for political criticism among young people. Kenway and Bullen refer to the youthful "cyber flaneur" as "the child who transgresses the spatial, physical, and temporal boundaries of the corporate world through technology." The youthful cyber flaneur uses his or her Internet skills to make global connections with a range of ideas and movements, giving him or her more space to observe and cast a critical eye over the "branded Web" (i.e., the Web sites dominated by the corporate consumer culture). There is also the search for other online activists as well as other alternative sites. The Internet thus allows young people to take a far more political stance by, for example, challenging the powerful influence of multinational corporations. Young people gather more information and get more involved with a range of activist sites such as McSpotlight, NikeWatch, and Adbusters, which seek to identify corporate practices and uncover abuses of economic power. Young people can thus become part of a global civil society of pamphleteers and political activists, their membership conditional on Internet access rather than age-related political rights.

See also Deliberative Democracy; Democracy; Democratic Education; Kids Voting USA (KVUSA); Minority Youth Voter Turnout; MTV's Choose or Lose Campaign (1992–); New Media; Peer Influences on Political Development; Personality and Youth Political Involvement; Political Consumerism; Rights of Participation of Children and Youth; Rights, Youth Perceptions of; State and Youth, The; Student Political Activism; Youth Commissions.

Recommended Reading

Casman, P. (1996). "Children's Participation: Children's City Councils." In *Understanding Children's Rights*, edited by E. Verhellen. Ghent: Children Rights Centre.

Craig, S., and Earl Bennett, S., eds. (1997). *After the Boom: The Politics of Generation X*. Maryland: Rowman and Littlefield.

Economic and Social Research Council (ESRC) (2001). *Mind the Gap: The Democratic Deficit*. ESRC's Fifth National Social Science Conference. See http:www.esrc.ac.uk/esrccontent/connect.

Furedi, F. (2002). *Culture of Fear: Risk-Taking and the Morality of Low Expectation*. London: Continuum.

Hart, R. (1997). *Children's Participation: The Theory and Practice of Involving Young Citizens*. London: Earth Scan.

Kenway, J., and Bullen, E. (2001). *Consuming Children: Education-Entertainment-Advertising*. Buckingham: Open University Press.

Matthews, H., Taylor, M., Percy-Smith, B., and Limb, M. (2000). "The Unacceptable *Flaneur*: The Shopping Mall as a Teenage Hangout." *Childhood*, 7, 3: 279–294.

National Centre for Social Research (2000). *Young People's Politics: Political Interest and Engagement Amongst Fourteen- to Twenty-four-Year-Olds*. York: YPS.

Wyness, M. (2003). "Children's Space and Interests: Constructing an Agenda for Student Voice." *Children's Geographies*, 1.2: 223–239.

Michael Wyness

Politics. *See* Gangs and Politics.

Positive Development. Participation in activism, of course, develops youth's capabilities as activists. They are likely to learn organizing skills, gain a sense of political empowerment, and build social networks that make them more effective activists in the future. But participation may also encourage young people's development in broader ways. Youth may acquire critical-thinking skills, become more responsible, and develop a clearer sense of identity. Some youth have the experience of "waking up" or coming alive, which leads to general transformations in who they are. As a result of these broader transformations, they may change their approaches to school and career or alter how they relate to people. We are concerned here with understanding these general processes of development. What broader developmental changes occur in youth activists, and how do these changes occur? First, we need to provide some background.

What Is Positive Development?

There is a field of social science concerned specifically with the question of "adolescent development." This field includes thousands of university professors and others who do research, develop theories, and teach about the age period of youth. Much of the research in this field, however, has focused on young people's problem behaviors from conflicts with parents to drug use, delinquency, and suicide. Like the rest of society, many of these researchers have bought into a negative image of youth: that they represent a host of problems that need to be prevented.

The term "positive youth development" has been introduced to bring together scholars and practitioners concerned with young people's development as an affirmative process. Those who identify with this new label do not deny that many youth have problems (as do many adults). But, in the words of Karen Pittman, they recognize that "problem free is not fully prepared" (see Pittman, Irby, and Ferber 2000). The core issue is not solving youth's problems but facilitating their growth as contributing members of society.

A key tenet of the positive-development perspective is that people are *agents* of their own development. This means that development is not something that other people do to you. In fact, this does not work very well; people cannot be easily changed from the outside. Rather development is something you do to and for yourself. It is a process of self-change. Sometimes this happens as part of a group: people

change and grow as a collective. The driving force behind the types of positive development we will talk about is people being actively motivated and engaged (see Larson 2000). They take charge of who they are, who they want to be, and how to get there.

Of course, changing oneself, like changing society, is not easy. There are obstacles and constraints within ourselves and in the world around us that stand in the way. Inertia is strong; many youth are apathetic or easily discouraged. Parents, schools, and peers are often invested in the status quo and encourage conformity. Another tenet of this perspective is that human behavior and development need to be understood in terms of the relationship between people and their environment. A person's future is shaped within the constraints and realities of the environment. Taking command of one's future, therefore, requires knowing and navigating these constraints. It has been argued, for example, that the development of urban youth requires their coming to recognize the forces of social, economic, and political oppression that shape and constrain their lives, and parallel statements can be made about other groups of youth. But as Gandhi said, "constraints make possibilities." Understanding the constraints in a situation allows you to conceptualize them as challenges that can be overcome. Positive development is a process in which youth act as agents within the reality of these constraints to learn and develop themselves.

Youth Activism Programs as a Context for Positive Development

Youth activism can often provide favorable conditions for this process of self-change. When people are engaged in critical examination of society, it is almost inevitable that they turn some of that critical examination on themselves. When they are engaged in trying to change institutions, they are likely to have experiences, learn skills, and become motivated to change their ways of thinking and acting.

To illustrate this process we are going to focus on one effective youth activism program that we studied in depth. We focus on a youth activism program because such programs often incorporate an agenda of youth development into their mission of community development (see Sullivan 2000). Of course, much youth activism occurs outside youth programs, and self-change can certainly occur in any activism context.

The program we studied, Generation Y, is devoted to educational justice and equal rights. Urban high-school-aged youth in this program work to improve their schools and, as their brochure says, "fight for our rights." Many of the characteristics of Generation Y resemble those in other youth activism programs. It is youth-led and focuses on issues that are directly relevant to its Hispanic, African American, and Arab membership. It combines working for social change with educational activities aimed at raising members' political consciousness and skills. Most youth join the program to fulfill a service requirement for high school, but many stay on as they become invested in social change. The program is coordinated by a highly effective Arab American young man, Jason Massad (names of people in this entry are pseudonyms), who works side by side with the youth as a partner in their work.

We followed members of Generation Y for a period of four months. During this time, the youth organized a citywide youth summit and worked on several action campaigns, including trying to reduce the capricious use of suspensions by their schools. Our information came from participant observations and ongoing interviews with the youth and with Jason. This information showed that, as youth worked toward social change, they also grew personally in many different ways. We will describe four of these ways.

Types of Positive Development

Action skills. One thing the young people in Generation Y learned was how to get things done. Many adolescents (and adults for that matter) live in the present moment and have limited abilities to organize there efforts to work toward a goal. Yet many jobs in the modern world require skills to formulate and carry out a plan; often this requires using information and being able to influence people and human systems. The young people in Generation Y developed these kinds of action skills. We will illustrate this by describing what they learned through their campaign to change the school's capricious use of suspensions.

The idea that you could actually change a big school system may sound naïve. What is harder to change than a huge bureaucracy? First, the young people in Generation Y realized that they had to gather information on the problem they were addressing. They surveyed students about suspensions at their schools. They even used the U.S. Freedom of Information Act to access the school system's own records on suspensions. The data showed that the majority of suspensions were for reasons that the school board's policies defined as "minor," like being late for class or bringing a cell phone to school. Second, they learned how to use this information strategically. They figured out that good information was key to influencing the board of education. They prepared charts and testimonials that documented how many students were being suspended for minor reasons. Third, they developed a deliberate plan of action. One youth, Leon, described how many board members were initially indifferent to their presentations. "But after we kept doing it and doing it, you know, getting more and more concrete facts and solid figures, after a while it was too obvious to ignore," he said. "If you have research and analysis, then you can't ignore it." Persuaded by the evidence, the school CEO and board directed principals to limit suspensions to "major" offenses, like substance use and violence.

The action skills the youth learned through this and other campaigns were many. In the contemporary world information is power, and they had learned how to use this power to achieve their ends. They had also learned important teamwork, communication, and planning skills, and they had learned to view constraints and obstacles as challenges to be solved. These action skills were valuable to the youth's future campaigns for social change, but they were also useful in these young people's personal lives. They described using them in their schoolwork, career planning, and in other contexts.

Personal empowerment. Acquiring these action skills led youth to feel more confident in their ability to take on challenges. To create social change it is often necessary to do things that you have never done before. This might range from speaking at rallies to learning a new computer system or knocking on doors in your neighborhood and sometimes getting the door slammed in your face. What we noticed in our interviews was a transition from a point where members of Generation Y were anxious about their abilities to handle such challenges to becoming more self-assured.

After taking part in several campaigns to improve public schools, many youth had developed the ability to carry out imposing tasks with confidence. Some members spoke in small, closed-door meetings with school board members, while others volunteered to speak at rallies or on panel discussions with audiences in the hundreds. Youth took this self-confidence with them outside of the program as well as into other areas of their lives by being more outspoken in class or by feeling that difficult career goals were now attainable. One youth, Rosa, described how she had changed: "I didn't think I could be a lawyer. I'm like, it's got a lot of schooling, but I think it [Generation Y] has really made me say, yes, it's a possibility." The sense of empowerment that youth gained from successful political actions thus led to a more general sense of empowerment in other areas of their lives as well.

Transcending the self. Another developmental change that we witnessed at Generation Y involved learning to understand others. Humans are by nature egocentric and ethnocentric. We are born seeing things from our own personal point of view. These youth made strides in transcending this egocentrism and learning to see things from others' points of view. We were particularly struck by the growth they reported in being able to interact with people who were different from them in ethnicity, religion, and sexual orientation. We call this "bridging difference," and it is a form of development that is crucial in the global and mobile world of the twenty-first century. Adult life requires that you be able to interact with diverse people at work, in your community, and even within your own family.

Generation Y was a context in which youth developed this ability for bridging difference. First, it provided young people safe chances to interact with people from different groups. Hispanic youth, African Americans, and Arab youth all worked together on equal footing and began to learn about each others' ways of life. As a result of these interactions, they reported overcoming stereotypes and breaking through barriers defined by race and sexual orientation. They discovered the humanity in these others: in the language of youth, they learned that people from these groups were "cool." They also learned to be sensitive. One said, "Instead of, like before, listening and actually not paying attention, now I really pay attention. I've learned to hear people out more."

As a result of this ability to transcend the self, youth reported developing many friendships through Generation Y, friendships that bridged diverse worlds. In the language of sociology, they developed connections that provided valuable social capital (Jarrett, Sullivan, and Watkins in press). Other research shows that youth in civicaction programs form more meaningful relationships with youth and adults than occur in other types of youth programs.

Formation of an identity and life goals. A central task of development for adolescents and early adults is finding one's place in the world by determining one's identity (see Erikson 1968). This includes choosing one's values, developing a worldview, and deciding what one desires to do with one's life. Establishing an identity in turn allows individuals to begin committing to the steps that are necessary to achieve those outcomes. Research suggests that youth activism programs are particularly rich contexts for young people to explore and work on identity issues. We saw this happening at Generation Y, partly as a product of some of the changes we have already described.

Since Generation Y's campaigns dealt largely with improving education, it is not surprising that many youth involved with the program become more committed to academic pursuits than they were before beginning the program. Rosa, mentioned above, reported a newfound desire to become a lawyer and was beginning to take classes that would help her on that path. Another member said, "I really wasn't into school, and now since I'm talking to people [in Generation Y], they got me more interested in school, and now it's just like, it's really changed me a lot.... I used to really want a car, and now it's like, 'Bleah, screw that, I could use that [money] for school!' It's made me really focus on school."

In several of our interviews, members of Generation Y told us the program helped them find what it was that they wanted to do in the future and to commit to these life goals.

Research by McAdam (1988) documents how youth activism can affect a person's identity well into their adult lives. He followed eighty college-aged applicants to the Freedom Summer program of 1964, a highly influential program in which young people assisted with the registration of black voters in Mississippi as part of the civil rights movement. Half of these college applicants ended up participating, while the other half did not. Twenty years later, the group that went to Mississippi was clearly distinguishable from the applicants who did not participate in the program. Several Freedom Summer volunteers had moved on to become key figures in the women's movement, the free-speech movement, and the antiwar movement of the late 1960s and 1970s. It is also interesting to note that many of the activists from this period delayed establishing families and careers, and some never did fit themselves into these traditional roles. They carved out unique life trajectories that did not always conform to the accepted societal paths. Although some endured strain and bore personal costs from these decisions, the important point is that their youth activism experiences clearly had an impact on their development of identity and life goals.

Ingredients for Positive Development

What is it about youth activism programs that foster these different types of human development? As we said, positive development is a process in which people are agents of transformations in themselves. They do not develop these qualities simply by showing up. Youth learn from engaging in social change, becoming invested, and from an active process of learning from their experiences. What is important about youth activism programs (and perhaps activist pursuits more generally) is that they provide ingredients that support this process.

Community and culture of change. First, youth activism programs bring you into contact with people and a way of doing things that facilitate development. They provide a community of social and personal change. You start spending time with peers and adults who genuinely care about broader social issues. The teens at Generation Y reported that their friends outside the program were not focused on the future. "They are just living for today," said one young woman. By becoming involved with this program, members encountered others who shared their concern with problems in the community and were working to change them. These new friends became collaborators and sources of support. They learned together and reinforced each other's political and personal growth.

This community also shared a culture of change—a way of thinking and acting—that supported development. People at Generation Y were conversant with other social-change movements and the struggles of the individuals who participated in those movements. They talked about Martin Luther King Jr., Malcolm X, Che Guevara, and others, and they internalized lessons from their lives. Their culture included encouragement of self-expression, for example, through reciting poetry at rallies. It also included the practice of self-examination, such as thinking about how one's own behavior toward gay, lesbian, bisexual, and transgendered (GLBT) people might resemble acts of discrimination they had experienced as a Latino, Latina, or African American (Watkins, Larson, and Sullivan 2005). A powerful aspect of being a member of a community is that one comes to understand and internalize the norms of thinking and acting that make the group function. The culture of Generation Y, then, provided models and norms, which youth absorbed.

Adult scaffolding. Another important ingredient of youth activism programs is the participation of adults who are committed to facilitating young people's development. At Generation Y, Jason was committed to supporting members' growth. One thing he did was to periodically organize educational sessions for the youth on different political movements and techniques of social action. In these sessions, he did not try to impose his own ideas onto the youth but rather encouraged student-centered learning. These educational sessions often involved hands-on learning experiences or discussions in which youth were supported for developing their own ideas. He said, "I think that the first most important thing is giving them the opportunity and, like, pushing them out of their safety zone, and they can test out their skills and see, 'Oh, this wasn't that hard,' or 'This is what I have a problem with.'" He was providing

conditions for the youth to be active learners: to build new skills and confidence in these skills.

Most importantly Jason helped the youth learn through their social-action campaigns. He did this, first, by making sure that the youth held leadership of the campaigns. The target of these campaigns and other significant decisions were made by the youth. This ownership meant youth were invested in learning to be effective. But at the same time, he contributed his expertise to help the youth navigate obstacles and keep these campaigns on track. Youth-development research indicates that adults in effective youth programs do not stand back from the work but share their expertise and provide strategic support. For example, one young man reported that if he didn't understand how to do something, Jason broke it down for him. Our research suggests that the most effective conditions for development occur when adult leaders balance these two things: they support youth ownership and at the same time help keep the work on track.

Cycles of learning. Perhaps the most important ingredient is that these programs provide chances for the youth to learn through cycles of real-life experience. At Generation Y the development of action skills, confidence, bridging difference, and identity occurred through real-life encounters. They were often developed through youth finding themselves in situations in which they had to demonstrate these qualities and then learned from their successes and mistakes. This is consistent with theories of experiential learning, which emphasize that people learn best from engaging in real-world actions and then reflecting on what they have done. They learn through a cycle of self-initiated action followed by self-monitoring, obtaining feedback, and evaluating how things turned out.

A supportive community and leaders are important to this process. At Generation Y the group went through the cycle together and learned together. Jason's efforts to keep the work on track were helpful to insuring that the cycle was completed. It was the practice at Generation Y, as in other youth activism programs (Sullivan 2000), to always debrief after the culmination of an action or campaign. They asked: What had gone right? What could have been done better? How did events and constraints influence what happened? Development for the young people in Generation Y appeared to have occurred through their engagement in these cycles of acting and learning.

Much more research is needed to understand these processes, but the important message we want to impart is that human development (or "youth development") and effective activism are not two separate things. They are closely interrelated with each other. Working to promote change in the community often results in changes that are positive both for oneself and the community.

See also Civil Society and Positive Youth Development; Positive Psychology; Positive Youth Development, Programs Promoting; Prosocial Behaviors.

Recommended Reading

Fendrich, J. (1993). *Ideal Citizens: The Legacy of the Civil Rights Movement.* Albany: State University of New York Press.

Ginwright, S., and James, T. (Winter 2002). "From Assets to Agents of Change." *New Directions for Youth Development,* 96: 27–46.

Larson, R. (2000). "Toward a Psychology of Positive Youth Development." *American Psychologist,* 55: 170–183.

Larson, R., Jarrett, R., Hansen, D., Pearce, N., Sullivan, P., Walker, K., Watkins, N., and Wood, D. (In Press). "Youth Programs as Contexts of Positive Development." In *International Handbook of Positive Psychology in Practice: From Research to Application,* edited by A. Linley and S. Joseph. New York: Wiley.

McAdam, D. (1988). *Freedom Summer.* New York: Oxford University Press.

Pittman, K., Irby, M., and Ferber, T. (2000). "Unfinished Business: Further Reflections on a Decade of Promoting Youth Development." In *Youth Development: Issues, Challenges, and Directions,* edited by Public/Private Ventures. Philadelphia: Public/Private Ventures.

Sullivan, L. (2000). *An Emerging Model for Working with Youth: Community Organizing + Youth = Youth Organizing.* Funders' Collaborative on Youth Organizing. See http://www.fcyo.org.

Watkins, N., Larson, R., and Sullivan, P. (Submitted). "Bridging Intergroup Differences in a Community Youth Program."

Wheeler, W. (2003). *Lessons in Leadership: How Young People Change Their Communities and Themselves.* Takoma Park, MD: Innovation Center for Community and Youth Development.

Youniss, J., McLellan, J. A., and Yates, M. (1997). "What We Know about Engendering Civic Identity." *American Behavioral Scientist,* 40 (5): 620–631.

Yu, H. C., and Lewis-Charp, H. (2003). "Sneak Peek on Research: Intersection of Civic Activism and Youth Development." *Insight,* 5 (1): 7–8.

Reed Larson and Dustin Wood

Positive Psychology. *Positive psychology* is an umbrella term introduced by Martin Seligman as one of his initiatives as 1998 president of the American Psychological Association (Seligman 2002). The trigger for positive psychology was a desire to counter the fact that psychology since World War II has directed much of its efforts toward human problems and how to remedy them.

In the past fifty years psychologists have focused on psychopathology: conceptualizing, treating, and preventing psychological disorders in order to improve the human condition. However, these approaches embrace a disease model where well-being is viewed only as the absence of disorder or distress. Positive psychology challenges this assumption. Although a pathology-focused psychology has yielded much, it has neglected what makes life most worth living and what can go right with people. Thus, calls have been made for balanced attention to be given to the positive aspects of human life.

The emerging field of positive psychology focuses as much on strength as on weakness, has as much interest in building the best things in life as in repairing the worst, and attends as much to fulfilling the lives of healthy people as to healing the wounds of the distressed (Seligman and Csikszentmihalyi 2000). Positive psychology tries to study scientifically how people flourish and thrive, not just how they survive distress and tragedy. The *Handbook of*

Positive Psychology consists of more than fifty chapters describing such representative positive psychology topics as resilience, flow, creativity, optimism, wisdom, authenticity, compassion, altruism, meaningfulness, and humor. The positive among us exists if we only look for it.

Positive psychology nonetheless demands a sea change in perspective. Psychologists interested in promoting human potential need to start with different assumptions. For example, Frisch (1999) has shown that long after their depressive symptoms have abated, people may continue to be dissatisfied with their lives. Positive psychology is concerned with such people and how their lives can be made happier and more productive as opposed to simply symptom-free. One fruitful avenue for nurturing the psychological good life lies in the scientific study of character and virtues.

Strengths of character like hope, kindness, social intelligence, perseverance, and perspective buffer against the negative consequences of stress and trauma, preventing or mitigating disorders in their wake; they also contribute to a satisfying life. Even if disorder occurs, character strengths often co-exist with symptoms and can provide a sturdy foundation on which to base therapeutic interventions.

Character strengths also help youth to thrive. Children and adolescents who love learning, who endorse positive values, who are socially competent, and who have a sense of purpose are more likely to succeed at school, to assume positions of leadership, to value diversity, to delay gratification, and to help others.

The most basic assumption that positive psychology urges is that human goodness and excellence are as authentic as disease, disorder, and distress. We can divide the concerns of positive psychology into three related topics: the study of positive subjective experiences (happiness, pleasure, gratification, fulfillment), the study of positive individual traits (character, talents, interests, values) that enable positive experiences, and the study of institutions that enable the good life, from deliberately-created programs like Big Brothers/Big Sisters to naturally occurring agents of socialization like the family or school. From the perspective of positive psychology, none of these topics is secondary, derivative, illusory, or epiphenomenal.

As Seligman (2002) implied, positive development may be facilitated when institutions, traits (e.g., character strengths), and subjective experiences (e.g., happiness) are in alignment. Positive institutions enable positive traits, which in turn enable positive subjective experiences. Indeed, the good life probably represents a coming together of these three domains.

Positive psychology is a science, which means that its goal is to provide empirical evidence for understanding and eventually cultivating the good life. The task for positive psychology is to provide the most objective facts possible about the phenomena it studies so that everyday people and society as a whole can make an informed decision about what goals to pursue in what circumstances. Not all of the news will be upbeat, but it will be of value precisely because it provides an appropriately nuanced view of the good life.

The goals of positive psychology are description and explanation as opposed to prescription. For example, in our own studies of optimism, we have documented many beneficial consequences of optimism: perseverance, achievement, popularity, even good health and longer life. But we have also found a notable downside: optimistic people consistently underestimate risks. Should someone be an optimist or a pessimist? The answer informed by data is that it depends on the situation and what we value in that situation.

Positive psychology implies that the study of people who are happy, healthy, and talented will allow psychologists to help all people, troubled or not. Indeed, the field of positive psychology reclaims one of the traditional missions of psychology: making the lives of *all* people fulfilling by identifying and building human strengths and virtues and nurturing them beyond the absence of disease.

Within the framework of positive psychology, one can find a comprehensive scheme for understanding and promoting positive youth development. "Problem-free is not fully prepared" (Pittman 2000). We know little about the mechanisms of positive youth development. Positive psychology suggests that we have to identify and study human strengths and other components of the good life in order to promote and maintain positive youth development.

The positive perspective applied to youth development challenges prevailing notions that young people are fragile and flawed and that all are at risk. It recognizes what is good and resilient in young people and focuses on each and every child's unique talents, strengths, interests, and future potential. Positive youth development assumes that no child has been left behind, at least if we take an appropriately broad view of young people.

The positive perspective in youth development avoids labeling troubled youth as across-the-board failures. Instead, it urges that their problems be placed in the context of the whole person. Calling someone a depressive, a bulimic, a drug user, or a high-school dropout overlooks what else may be true about that individual.

Positive psychology provides a useful vantage on social activism. First, social activism—especially among youth—is not surprising. It provides a way to fulfill basic social needs and concerns. It lays the foundation for a life of civic engagement. Positive psychology regards the civic virtues and social responsibilities that undergird activism as essential components of a thriving community. Activism is a way for people to form an identity that coalesces around a cause. Social scientists should not treat activism as the peculiar case, and they should not assume that apathy among youth is a more important topic.

Second, social activism should be regarded as genuine and certainly not secondary to or derivative from "selfish" concerns. When theorists and researchers characterize and study activism, they might consider borrowing some of the constructs that have been productively used by positive psychologists, like flow, meaning, and virtue.

Third, social activism can take many forms, and social scientists should be willing to recognize its plurality. In contrast to Tolstoy's familiar adage that all happy families are the same, we believe that unhappy families (as well as unhappy individuals and unhappy groups) have a numbing sameness—it is happiness that can take infinite forms. The same is true for social activism, which can and does exist at all points along the political spectrum.

Fourth, social activism is usually undertaken by individuals working together in a group. Some groups are more effective in accomplishing goals and completing tasks than are other groups, and the perspective of positive psychology might provide a way of understanding successful versus unsuccessful social movements.

Fifth, the evidence should tell us which forms of social activism have desirable consequences and which do not. Research is clear that participation in civil rights activities during the 1960s had long-term benefits; youthful activists became civically engaged adults (e.g., Franz and McClelland 1994). In contrast, history is just as clear that the Fifth Crusade of 1212—the so-called "Children's Crusade"—was a disaster for all involved. Thousands of young people from Europe meandered no further than Italy, where they were captured and sold into slavery.

Finally, attention to social activism among young people can expand positive psychology, which sometimes focuses on the individual taken out of a social context. In contrast, social activists are those who deliberately create or remake a variety of social institutions according to an articulated vision of the good life. There is much to be learned here.

See also Civil Society and Positive Youth Development; Positive Development;

Positive Youth Development, Programs Promoting.

Recommended Reading

Frisch, M. B. (1999). "Quality of Life Assessment/ Intervention and the Quality of Life Inventory." In *The Use of Psychological Testing for Treatment Planning and Outcome Assessment*, 2nd ed., edited by M. R. Maruish. Hillsdale, NJ: Lawrence Erlbaum, pp. 1227–1331.

Peterson, C., and Seligman, M. E. P. (2004). *Character Strengths and Virtues: A Classification and Handbook*. New York: Oxford University Press/Washington, D.C.: American Psychological Association.

Pittman, K. J. (May 2, 2000). "What Youth Need: Services, Supports, and Opportunities, the Ingredients for Youth." Paper prepared for presentation at the White House Conference on Teenagers, Washington, D.C.

Scales, P. C., Benson, P. L., Leffert, N., and Blyth, D. A. (2000). "Contributions of Developmental Assets to the Prediction of Thriving among Adolescents." *Applied Developmental Science*, 4: 27–46.

Seligman, M. E. P. (2002). *Authentic Happiness*. New York: Free Press.

Seligman, M. E. P., and Csikszentmihalyi, M. (2000). "Positive Psychology: An Introduction." *American Psychologist*, 55: 5–14.

Nansook Park and Christopher Peterson

Positive Youth Development, Programs Promoting. Generally speaking, positive youth development or well-being encompasses all our hopes and aspirations for a nation of healthy, happy, and competent adolescents on their way to productive and satisfying adulthoods. Differences arise, however, when we look at what specifically constitutes "healthy, happy, and competent" adolescents as well as "productive and satisfying" adulthoods.

The meaning of the endpoint of successful adolescent development, adulthood well-being, fluctuates depending on the purpose and audience. From an economic perspective, self-sufficiency is the primary requirement: an individual gainfully employed or living in a family with an income above the poverty threshold with adequate housing and not reliant on public funds or services is considered a "successful" adult. To others, psychological stability and well-being are critical. Regardless of which criteria for adult well-being one chooses, the foundation for these behaviors begin during childhood and adolescence.

Opinions on what to include on lists of successful adolescent development vary as well. The differences, however, are mostly in the organization and terminology. Typically, successful adolescent development is discussed in term of skills and competence in the physical, intellectual, psychological, emotional, and social arenas (see National Research Council and Institute of Medicine 2002). Sometimes these areas are extended to emphasize other qualities such as the moral and spiritual, civic, and cultural. In other cases, these domains are shortened to succinctly express desired outcomes for our nation's youth: the ability to be productive, connect, and navigate. Others categorize the desired outcomes for youth into five Cs: (1) *competence* in academic, social, and vocational areas; (2) *confidence* or a positive self-identity; (3) *connections* to community, family, and peers; (4) *character* or positive values, integrity, and moral commitment; and (5) *contribution*.

Researchers produce similar lists when discussing the inputs, ingredients, or assets necessary to help youth develop into successful adolescents on their way to successful adulthoods. These lists typically include people, experiences, and opportunities in the varying contexts that influence development, including the family, school, peers, neighborhood, and larger social context. Theory, empirical research, and practical wisdom converge to suggest important personal and social assets for positive development (see National Research Council and Institute of Medicine 2002; Roth and Brooks-Gunn 2000). For example, the Search Institute describes forty internal and external assets believed to be the universal building blocks of positive development. The twenty external assets envelop youth with familial and extra-familial networks that provide support, empowerment, boundaries and expectation, and constructive use of time. These external assets describe the necessary ingredients in youth's environment (home, school, community) for positive development. The twenty internal assets serve to nurture within individuals positive commitments, values and identities, as well as social competencies. The internal assets illustrate personal qualities that facilitate positive development (see Benson 1997).

Put another way, youth need access to safe places, challenging experiences, and caring people on a daily basis. In their extensive review of developmental theory and empirical research, the Committee on Community-Level Programs for Youth suggests a provisional list of eight features of positive developmental settings. Whether at home, school, among friends, in an after-school program, or in the community, positive developmental settings provide (1) physical and psychological safety; (2) appropriate structure; (3) supportive relationships; (4) opportunities to belong; (5) positive social norms; (6) support for efficacy and mattering; (7) opportunities for skill building; and (8) integration of family, school, and community efforts.

Adolescence, a time of bodily changes, expanding independence, and growing self-discovery, is sometimes characterized as a series of challenges. Each challenge carries the possibility of risk, opportunity, or both. Scholars of adolescent development refer to these challenges as developmental transitions or critical junctures along the path that connects children to their transformed physical, mental, and social adult selves. Each transition requires some change in adolescents' roles, how they make sense of themselves and their world, and how others view them. Despite the multiple physical changes and social challenges facing adolescents, it would be misleading to view adolescence as a time of total upheaval.

Contrary to popular opinion, the vast majority of youth emerge from the second decade of life without lasting problems. Most individuals navigate transitions equipped with the competencies needed to meet new challenges and take on new roles while further developing the skills necessary for these new roles. However, many do not enter adulthood with all of the competencies they will need. The numerous changes during adolescence appear to be overwhelming only for some adolescents—those with less optimal peer and family relationships, poorer coping skills, and academic difficulties during middle childhood. Thus, circumstances from different environments—the family, peers, and school—impact adolescents' preparation for, and success at, navigating the transitions inherent in their development. Much research literature exists documenting the influence of some contexts, such as the family and school, but less empirical research has focused on the more distal contexts, such as the neighborhood or country, and even less research addresses the interactions among contexts.

Studies of the role of the family in promoting positive development typically focus on characteristics of the family context (e.g., income, structure) or relationships within the family (e.g., quality of the marital or parent-child relationship or parenting styles) or some combination of the two. The litany of family characteristics that negatively influence adolescent development is well-known—poverty, single parenthood, and low parental education. Growing evidence demonstrates that such risks can be offset by adequate parent-adolescent relationships. For example, frequently unsupervised adolescents with warm and accepting parents who provide consistent and firm control and monitoring, even from a distance, engage in fewer problem behaviors than their unsupervised peers without such relationships. Parental support and monitoring also predict positive outcomes for youth, such as stable identity and goals for the future. Reviews of the research on family relationships consistently describe the dimensions of parent-adolescent relationships that promote healthy development—closeness, communication, supervision/monitoring, and engagement in youth's lives.

Demographic changes in American families, such as increased maternal employment and single parenthood, have led to a decrease in the amount of time youth spend with their parents, particularly in the after-school hours. In addition, increased autonomy, including more unsupervised time alone and with peers, is viewed as developmentally appropriate in American society. This time fosters independence, provides opportunities for self-sufficiency, and develops a sense of efficacy. In one study the percentage of their waking hours that white adolescents spent with families fell from 33 percent to 14 percent between the fifth and twelfth grades.

The effects for adolescents of spending less time with their families depend on what they are doing during that time. The negative effects of unsupervised time, particularly with peers, has been emphasized by the widely publicized FBI statistics that show violent juvenile crime peaks on weekdays between the hours of two and eight p.m. Time away from parents provides increased opportunity for experimentation in other health-compromising behaviors as well. Data from the National Longitudinal Study on Adolescent Health, a study of a nationally representative (cross-sectional) sample of over 12,000 seventh through twelfth graders, presented at the White House Conference on Teenagers, used the frequency of family meals as a proxy for time with parents. Youth who did not eat dinner with a parent five or more days a week showed dramatically higher rates of smoking, drinking, marijuana use, getting into fights, and initiation of sexual activity.

Increased autonomy for adolescents does not necessarily mean the need for less supervision than in the childhood years. Supervision and limit setting remain critical. Parental regulation of adolescents, especially via structuring and monitoring behavior compared to setting rules, is associated with greater influence on how adolescents use their free time and is inversely associated with adolescent problem behaviors. Higher levels of parental monitoring are associated with lower rates of adolescent delinquency, sexual activity, and depression, as well as higher academic grades. Parental monitoring has also been associated with influencing adolescent relationships with peers. For example, adolescents with less parental supervision show greater susceptibility to peer influences encouraging health-compromising behaviors. Consistent and firm control and monitoring can be provided from a distance. Monitoring can take the form of telephone calls to youth or conversations with the parents of the youth's friends. Caring and monitoring together seem to result in the least risk-taking in youth. These effects may be, in part, the result of youth feeling more comfortable talking to their parents. Thus, monitoring through communication is important, not merely strict control.

The level of supervision or parental monitoring necessary for healthy development may differ as a function of adolescents' peer and neighborhood environments. A higher degree of limit setting may be necessary for youth living in dangerous neighborhoods with low community control and higher levels of problem behavior among peers.

As children enter and progress through adolescence, they spend increasing amounts of time with peers and place increasing value on these relationships. The peer group, which includes both friends of varying closeness and others in their age group with whom they interact, influences adolescent development in many positive and negative ways.

Ample research has documented the role of peers in instigating engagement in such health-compromising behaviors as cigarette smoking, substance use, early sexual activity and pregnancy, and violence. Friendships also promote moral development, coping strategies, increased self-esteem, and assistance in dealing with stressful situations. Peer relationships allow adolescents to recognize societal norms, practice defining and sharing leadership roles, and initiate and maintain social bonds. Regardless of whether positive or negative, close and best friends have the greatest influence and are also the most important to adolescents.

Peer influence does not operate as a single force in adolescents' worlds. Rather, the susceptibility of adolescents to peer influence is determined by several factors. Adolescents with poorer relationships with adults are more influenced by peers. In particular, adolescents are influenced more by friends when they experience neglecting or rejecting parental relationships. Adolescent research also suggests that youth who are alienated from conventional groups (e.g., school and family) often establish strong social bonds with antisocial peer groups to establish a sense of belonging.

Adolescents consistently spend large periods of time in school, so it is not surprising that what occurs in school has an impact. Researchers investigate the school context in a variety of ways. One line of research brings together characteristics of the school environment and the developmental needs of adolescents to explain the decline in academic achievement and increase in social, emotional, and behavioral problems that begin to appear during early adolescence.

Eccles and her colleagues (1993) document fewer such changes among students in K–8 schools compared to students attending K–6 schools. They ascribe the detrimental changes to the timing of the switch to a new middle or junior-high school. At the same time most adolescents are experiencing the physical, psychological, and social changes of puberty, they must also begin at a new school. This transition requires young adolescents to adjust to the different demands of a new peer group, new teachers, and new class structure.

Further compounding the problem, students' elementary schools are more aligned with their psychological needs than their new middle- or junior-high-school environments. Middle and junior-high schools are characterized by increased school size, bureaucratic organization, departmentalization, and decreased individual attention and opportunities for close relationships with teachers compared to elementary schools. In the classroom middle- and junior-high-school teachers tend to place greater emphasis on teacher control and discipline; provide fewer opportunities for student decision-making, choice, and self-management; and employ more competitive standards for grading and judging competence than teachers in elementary-school classes. They also feel less effective as teachers, especially for low-ability students. Thus, at a time when young adolescents need careful monitoring by caring adults and challenging, but safe, opportunities to explore different behaviors and identities, schools offer less personal, more restrictive, and more competitive environments.

As in families, the quality of student-teacher relationships also contributes to healthy adolescent behavior. In their longitudinal study of high-risk children, Werner and Smith (1992) found that disadvantaged youth who "beat the odds" found emotional support outside their own families, often in a favorite teacher who became a role model, friend, and confidant. Among participants in the Adolescent Health Study, youth who reported strong emotional attachments to their teachers were less likely to use drugs and alcohol, attempt suicide, engage in violence, or become sexually active at an early age. In fact, positive relationships with teachers exerted a stronger influence on adolescents' health-related behaviors than the school-structure variables (classroom size, attendance and dropout rates, school type, and amount of teacher training). As with parental relationships, the specifics of fostering a supportive teacher-student relationship may vary for different youth. DuBois, Felner, Meares, and Krier (1994) found an association between high levels of school support and student outcomes (better grades and lower alcohol use) only for youth with multiple disadvantages, such as living in poverty and experiencing family breakup, not for youth without disadvantages.

Adolescents' relationships to school also appear to influence their behavior. Academic achievement and involvement in school-related activities are two ways of measuring adolescents' engagement with school. Research consistently finds that adolescents with poor academic skills and low grades are more likely to engage in health-compromising behaviors. In a sixteen-year longitudinal study of school adaptation and social development, Cairns and Cairns (1994) found that engagement in extracurricular activities reduced health-compromising behaviors, particularly for students at greatest risk for dropping out. However, involvement in activities did not lower the rates of binge drinking, and involvement in varsity sports actually increased such behavior (see also Eccles and Barber 1999).

Today, almost all youth work at some point during their high-school years. Over 70 percent of the participants in the Monitoring the Future study reported working for pay, and almost half the males and one-third of the females worked more than twenty hours per week. Despite the public's favorable attitudes toward employment during adolescence, the influence of the workplace on adolescent development remains controversial. The ideal adolescent workplace would offer youth the chance to widen their horizons, particularly in terms of future careers, develop organizational skills, learn about responsibility, and gain valuable knowledge. As the research summarized below suggests, however, the reality of youth employment presents risks as well as opportunities for adolescent development.

Recent efforts at bridging the school-to-work transition suggest increasing adolescent involvement in the workplace as a way to teach youth the practical tasks necessary for later success as adult workers and to expose them to a wide range of occupational options. Similarly, most parents approve of their adolescents' employment, believing it offers increasing autonomy and independence, opportunities for responsibility, and practice in time management. Empirical research shows some positive consequences from adolescent employment, including self-reported punctuality, dependability, and personal responsibility, and, specifically for girls, increased self-reliance and decreased high-school dropout for employment of fewer than twenty hours per week and increased employment and earnings in the years following high school. Among poor, urban African American youth, adolescent employment is linked to completion of high school and, for males, increased likelihood of college attendance. This is consistent with ethnographic work with low-income youth, which finds the adult monitoring and economic gains from employment can result in increased school engagement and decreased criminal and delinquent behavior.

Working during adolescence also carries risks. Health risks include increased exposure to dangerous machinery, noxious fumes, excessive heat and cold, and chronic fatigue from long hours or working at night, which results in injury serious enough to require emergency-room treatment each year for approximately 64,000 youth aged fourteen to seventeen. Psychological risks include stress from taking on adult responsibilities without adequate support or coping skills, disruptions in social relationships, and distress from the overload caused by school and work activities. Findings from prominent studies describe negative consequences of adolescent employment, such as emotional distress, increased cigarette, alcohol and illicit-drug use, and higher rates of school tardiness and misconduct.

The discrepancy in findings about the consequences of adolescent employment stems from the lack of distinction between informal work, such as babysitting or summer jobs, and formal part-time work, as well as the failure to consider the quality of the work environment. Long hours spent working in poor-quality formal jobs during the school year appear to be the most detrimental to adolescents' grades and health, particularly regarding alcohol use and smoking. Restaurant work, the archetypical teenage job, can be characterized as a poor quality job—it requires few skills, offers little adult supervision, is unconnected to anticipated future jobs, and is done only for money. Alternatively, the same research found many direct benefits of high-quality work experiences, including reduced substance use and better mental health.

It is difficult to define an adolescents' neighborhood. School districts, census tracts, and town lines can often result in different neighborhood boundaries. Trying to identify one's community is further complicated when social relations are included, particularly with the increased use of technology. Viewing community as shared relationships and social supports, however, puts a human face on the traditional research approach to neighborhoods. Also referred to as social capital, these relationships can make a difference in the lives of youth. In a study of nearly 350 Chicago neighborhoods, the level of involvement of community residents, termed collective efficacy, significantly reduced both the perceived and actual levels of violence, even in the poorest neighborhoods.

The lack of "face" within a community explains the concentration of adolescent problem behaviors in some communities. For example, the behavior of adults in the community can influence adolescent behavior through the presence of adult role models and monitoring (collective socialization) or by the concentration of problem behaviors influencing adolescents through peer influences. Still, family characteristics are more prominent than neighborhood characteristics in predicting youth outcomes. Neighborhood characteristics do affect family characteristics, particularly parenting behavior. In neighborhoods with few economic or social resources, rates of parental warmth and appropriate and consistent discipline of youth are lower than in nondisadvantaged neighborhoods. At-risk urban youth living in neighborhoods with less cohesion and social control experience lower rates of parental monitoring than adolescents residing in areas with greater collective efficacy. To the extent that neighborhood characteristics have a negative effect on parenting behavior, where one lives influences adolescent vulnerability to negative influences and limits exposure to experiences that promote positive development. For example, the association between parental monitoring and decreased externalizing behavior problems is stronger for youth living in neighborhoods characterized by high levels of residential instability than for youth living in more stable communities.

The lessons learned from the research on positive adolescent development provide lessons for those interested in improving programs for youth. Based on the review of the contexts impacting adolescent development, we suggested some factors that can increase program benefits for youth. The research on the familial context leads to the following implications for programs. To create a developmentally appropriate setting for adolescents, programs should include the following: caring adults who provide appropriate levels of supervision, age-appropriate levels of adolescent autonomy within the program, and continued (i.e., long term) contact with program leaders and participants.

The research on the peer-group context for adolescent development suggests that programs should include the following: structures and activities that foster positive peer relationships, a choice in activities that allows participants new opportunities for friendships with peers with similar interests, and program designs that incorporate adolescents' desire to interact with peers.

The research on the school setting as a context for adolescent development indicates that programs that include the following will best meet the developmental needs of adolescents: close, personal, and continued contact with program adults; adults who are role models for prosocial behavior and attitudes; opportunities for ownership, voice, and choice in designing and implementing activities; and developmentally appropriate program structure (e.g., group size) and activities.

The research on the importance of the quality of the workplace as a context for adolescent development draws parallels to quality of activities. To maximize benefits to adolescents, this line of research advises that the activities include real responsibility and accountability, the chance for adolescents' to make meaningful contributions, and opportunities for skill development through activities that require students to take an active and appropriately challenging role.

The research on neighborhoods as contexts for adolescent development brings to mind the following program implications: program components or activities should incorporate features of the local community (e.g., history, politics, etc.) and opportunities for students to change local communities for the better.

See also Civil Society and Positive Youth Development; Positive Development; Positive Psychology.

Recommended Reading

Mahoney, J. L., Larson, R. W., and Eccles, J. S. (2005). *Organized Activities as Contexts of Development: Extracurricular Activities, After-School and Community Programs.* Mahwah, NJ: Lawrence Erlbaum Associates.

McLaughlin, M. W. (2000). *Community Counts: How Youth Organizations Matter for Youth Development.* Washington, D.C.: Public Education Network.

National Research Council and Institute of Medicine (2002). "Community Programs to Promote Youth Development." In *Committee on Community-Level Programs for Youth*, edited by J. S. Eccles and J. A. Gootman. Washington, D.C.: National Academy Press.

Roth, J., Brooks-Gunn, J., Murray, L., and Foster, W. (1998). "Promoting Healthy Adolescents: Synthesis of Youth Development Program Evaluations." *Journal of Research on Adolescence,* 8 (4), 423–459.

Roth, J. L., and Brooks-Gunn, J. (2003). "What Is a Youth Development Program? Identifying Defining Principles." In *Promoting Positive*

Child, Adolescent, and Family Development: A Handbook of Program and Policy Innovations, Vol. 2, edited by R. M. Lerner, F. Jacobs, and D. Wertlieb. Thousand Oaks, CA: Sage Publications.

Additional Web Sites

The Forum for Youth Investment: http://www.forumforyouthinvestment.org. The forum is a leader in the youth-development field. The Web site has many briefs and reports on the issues.

After-School Alliance:http://www.afterschoolalliance.org. This is a general Web site geared to parents and teachers on activities in the after-school hours.

National Youth Development Information Center: http://www.nydic.org/nydic. The center is a more general site with information and links to all things pertaining to programs and positive youth development.

Harvard Family Research Project: http://www.gse.harvard.edu/~hfrp/. The project compiles descriptions of effective programs. It also provides briefs and reports related to the latest findings and evaluations of programs.

Jodie Roth and Jeanne Brooks-Gunn

Poverty, Welfare Reform, and Adolescents. In 1996 President Bill Clinton signed a new welfare policy into law, resulting in dramatic changes in the employment choices facing poor families. The Personal Responsibility and Work Opportunity Reconciliation Act (PRWORA) ended the federal guarantee of cash assistance and replaced the Aid to Families with Dependent Children (AFDC) program with the Temporary Assistance for Needy Families (TANF) program. TANF requires recipients to participate in work or work-based activities in order to receive cash assistance. Under AFDC the federal government automatically provided cash assistance to every qualified family. Now Congress provides a block grant to each state, and states have more flexibility in determining how that money is spent. However, the federal law places new restrictions on welfare; for example, most recipients are subject to a five-year lifetime limit on the receipt of cash benefits, and most adults can receive welfare for no more than two consecutive years without engaging in work.

At the same time the booming economy of the mid- to late-1990s helped single mothers reach unprecedented employment levels. In addition to the forces of economic growth, single mothers' employment rates rose in response to policy levers, including expansion of the Earned Income Tax Credit and state and federal welfare-program changes. Together, these forces dramatically increased the employment of single mothers.

Any major life transition, such as moving from welfare to work, could affect mothers' well-being, their relationships with their children, and their children's adjustment. Developmental theory suggests that increased employment for welfare mothers could improve their self-esteem, motivation, and sense of personal control. These improvements could lead to better parenting and concomitant improvements in the social, academic, or emotional adjustment of their children. Increased economic resources from earnings could also benefit children. On the other hand, reform might increase psychological stresses or exposure to ecological stresses, which can be harmful to children. And, if employment is unstable or erratic, material hardships could ensue and family routines could be disrupted, thus diminishing child well-being.

Whereas research to date has found neutral or slightly positive effects of low-income single mothers' transitions into work on the well-being of younger children, some studies have identified more negative effects for some subgroups of teenage children. Negative effects for teenage children seem to be concentrated among those who have a younger sibling at home, suggesting that some teens might take on increased (and possibly stressful) household responsibilities in the face of their mothers' transitions to work. Low-income mothers' employment might also negatively affect adolescents specifically (versus young children) for reasons related to the role of the environment outside of the home, which adolescents are more likely to be exposed to. For example, peer- or neighborhood-influences perspectives recognize that adolescents, unlike younger children, spend less time with parents in their proximal home environments and spend more time with others. Moreover, when mothers are working, adolescents may be more likely to be in self-care. Thus, mothers at work may have fewer opportunities to monitor and supervise adolescents, and this may be correlated with negative developmental outcomes.

See also Parental Influences on Youth Activism.

Recommended Reading

Chase-Lansdale, L., Moffit, P., Lohman, B., Cherlin, A., Coley, R., and Pittman, L., et al. (2003). "Mothers' Transitions from Welfare to Work and the Well-Being of Preschoolers and Adolescents." *Science*, 299: 1548–1552.

Ariel Kalil

Prosocial Behaviors. Youth engage in many behaviors that benefit others and society. Many teens share valuable resources with others—they donate or lend money to a needy peer, they comfort a distressed friend, they volunteer their services to a neighbor or a community organization, they protect or defend a bully victim, or they might provide assistance during an emergency. When youth's actions are designed with the primary intention of benefiting others in need, scholars refer to those behaviors as prosocial behaviors. Understanding prosocial behaviors is closely linked to understanding positive forms of youth activism.

There is a long intellectual history in the study of prosocial behaviors. Many of the early writings in major religions depict stories of bravery, heroism, kindness, and generosity, and the major figures in those religions (i.e., Buddha, Jesus, Muhammad) are often endowed with prosocial characteristics. In philosophy prosocial behavior is the topic of many major essays that discuss the inherent moral nature of humans. However, somewhat surprisingly, the study of prosocial behaviors is relatively new in the social sciences. Although there were sporadic studies of prosocial behaviors in the early twentieth century, most systematic and focused studies did not begin until the 1970s.

In 1964 Catherine "Kitty" Genovese was walking home to her apartment in Queens, New York, when she was suddenly approached by a man and attacked. The man stabbed her repeatedly, and Kitty, bleeding profusely, ran to the open street screaming for help. The event was witnessed by thirty-eight people who saw the man stabbing her repeatedly while she cried for help. However, no one called the police or tried to intervene on her behalf. By the time an anonymous bystander finally called the police, approximately thirty minutes after the initial attack, the murderer had fled, and Kitty was dead. One witness stated later, "So many, many times in the night, I heard screaming. I'm not the police, and my English speaking is not perfect." The Genovese murder captured national media attention and the attention of social scientists. How can humans be so insensitive to the needs of others?

Bibb Latané and John Darley, two social psychologists, designed a series of studies to examine why people do not assist distressed others in those types of situations. The studies focused on situational variables that might influence people's decision to assist. The researchers who conducted these classic "bystander intervention" studies discovered that, in general, the more people who observe such events, the less likely people are to assist (see Latané and Darley 1970). Latané and Darley labeled this phenomenon "diffusion of responsibility." Often, people assume that others will help, that others are more capable of helping, or that it might not be a real emergency. The researchers found that there are many situational factors that might influence people's assessment of an emergency situation.

The bystander intervention studies showed that situational factors can affect people's willingness to help others. However, a number of other researchers became interested in personal variables that influence people's willingness to help others. Sociobiologists and ethologists (people who study the evolutionary history and adaptive functions of behaviors) have long noted the biological basis for prosocial and altruistic behaviors. Altruistic behaviors refer to a subset of prosocial behaviors that are motivated by selfless desires—often at a cost to oneself. Scholars have observed prosocial and altruistic behaviors in many different animal species as well as in humans (see Moral Exemplars for additional information on altruism). One source that has been identified as a personal motivator of prosocial behaviors is empathy (Batson 1991; Hoffman 2000). Empathy is referred to as a feeling similar to that of another. There are two major components of empathy, the cognitive and the affective. The cognitive component, called affective perspective taking, refers to understanding another's emotional state. The affective component, called affective empathy, refers to the emotional reaction of the observer. It is important to be able to understand another's emotions in order to react emotionally to that person's distress.

Empathy is believed to lead to several possible additional observer reactions. Two, in particular, are relevant to understanding prosocial behaviors. The first possibility is that empathy could lead to sympathy. Sympathy is a feeling of concern or sorrow for another. It is an other-oriented response that can lead to prosocial behavior with the purpose of relieving another person's suffering or distress. The second possible reaction is personal distress. Personal distress is defined as a self-focused, aversive emotional reaction to another's suffering. This latter reaction does not usually lead to prosocial behaviors (e.g., they might avoid more exposure to the distress), or it can lead to selfishly motivated prosocial behaviors (e.g., helping behavior to make oneself feel better).

In addition to empathy and sympathy, there are other emotional reactions that are associated with prosocial behaviors. For example, guilt (i.e., an aversive reaction that results from not living up to one's standards) and shame (i.e., failing to live up to other people's expectations) can lead someone to act kindly toward others. Similarly, one could assist another person when one is in a good mood or when one is sad (this latter response often induces selfishly motivated prosocial behaviors). When a person is in a good mood, the person might feel generous toward others. In contrast, when a person is in a bad mood, the person might help others to make himself or herself feel better.

One area that has been the focus of many researchers is the study of social cognitions associated with prosocial behaviors. Scholars have long noted that there are age-related differences in prosocial behaviors and that those differences might be accounted for by age-related differences in social cognitions. Perspective taking and moral reasoning are two social cognitions that have been identified as central to explaining age-related differences in prosocial behaviors. There are three types of perspective taking (affective, social or cognitive, and perceptual). Of those types of perspective taking, affective and social perspective taking have been closely associated with prosocial behaviors. Understanding a person's thoughts, intentions, or situation might facilitate helping that person; for example, when you see a person on the ground has fallen off a bicycle, inferring that he or she might want help from someone to get up or might need someone to get medical assistance. Similarly, understanding another person's emotional state (i.e., affective perspective taking) can lead to prosocial action. For example, seeing someone crying, often an expression of sadness, shows us that the person might need help or assistance. In general, researchers have shown reliable, though modest, relations between perspective taking and prosocial behaviors in studies with children and adolescents. Furthermore, investigators have shown that children's perspective taking becomes more sophisticated with age such that there is a shift from

self-centeredness to considering and thinking about others and the broader society.

Another social cognition frequently associated with prosocial behaviors is moral reasoning. Moral reasoning is defined as thinking about a social situation when one's desires, needs, or motives are in conflict with another's (this could be conflict between individuals or with social institutions). We are often faced with moral dilemmas in our everyday lives, although most of the time we do not think about them much. Other times we are faced with moral dilemmas that we cannot avoid thinking about. One such situation is when our own needs are in conflict with the needs of another. For example, we might be driving to work late along a road and see someone whose car is stopped by the side of the road. Do we stop and ask whether the person needs help? Or do we continue because we are going to be late for an important meeting at work? Many times we might continue to work and justify doing so by assuming that someone else is going to help that person. Other times we might not want to stop and help because we think it is too dangerous. Still other times we might stop and ask if they need help. Our thinking about what we might do under those circumstances (and if we changed the circumstances) reflects our moral reasoning about prosocial situations. Scholars have found reliable differences in the way people reason about such situations. For example, investigators have found that children's thinking about such situations becomes more complex as they grow older, such that their thinking shifts from external concerns (e.g., concern with physical needs, concern with gaining authority figures' approval) to internalized, value-based thinking. Perhaps more importantly, researchers have found that people who think about other people's needs or who express empathic and prosocial value-based thinking are most likely to engage in prosocial behaviors.

Given the potential benefits of prosocial behaviors, there is great interest in how parents can foster these behaviors in their children. Scholars have found several ways that parents can promote prosocial behaviors. One way is through parental disciplining actions or practices. For example, parents who explain to their children the consequences of their behaviors and who praise and reward them for positive behaviors are more likely to have children who behave prosocially (Eisenberg and Fabes 1998). Parents can also promote prosocial behaviors by serving as role models of charity and kindness. Instruction alone has not been found to be effective in promoting prosocial behaviors, but parents who display consistency between their exhortations and actions (i.e., practice what they preach) are more likely to have children who act prosocially. Prosocial behaviors can also be fostered by providing children with meaningful opportunities for service. Parents need to allow their children to participate and enjoy the positive benefits of helping others so children can more fully understand the emotional rewards inherent in helping. Moreover, affectionate and nurturing parents can promote and model the expression of empathy and emotional sensitivity to others. Finally, parents can guide youth to be prosocial by encouraging and supporting activities with positive peer models.

Siblings also play a role in the development of prosocial behaviors, primarily because sibling relationships are ripe with opportunities for children to learn perspective taking and emotional understanding. Researchers have found that as early as two years of age, children display prosocial behaviors toward their siblings and that preschool-aged children are more likely to be responsive toward younger siblings than unfamiliar children (Eisenberg and Fabes 1998). As sibling relationships are rooted in the family context, the ways in which parents encourage prosocial behaviors are related to how effective sibling relationships can be in fostering prosocial behaviors. In other words, if the parent is sensitive and encourages the older child to act pro-

socially toward her younger sibling by explaining the younger sibling's feelings, the older child will be more caring toward the younger sibling. Perhaps for this reason, and as a result of gender roles encouraging girls to be helpful and caring, older sisters in general show higher rates of prosocial behavior in the context of the sibling relationship.

Peer relationships and friendships exert considerable influence on the normative development of children, including their prosocial development. These relationships influence a variety of factors from school adjustment to learning practical information, development of cognitive capabilities, and psychosocial adjustment and well-being. These factors in turn can have significant influences on the development of prosocial behaviors, as children who are more socially adjusted also tend to be more prosocial toward others. In addition, peer relationships can also be important venues through which children learn principles of reciprocity, and children are more likely to show prosocial behaviors toward peers with whom they have positive relationships.

The significant role that peers play in prosocial behaviors and other aspects of development becomes even more salient as children enter into adolescence. Adolescence is a period in which peer relationships and friendships become more intense, increase in complexity and perceived significance, and become more salient. And while their relationships with their parents continue to hold significance, adolescents rely more and more on their friends. There is research that suggests that peers who frequently express prosocial behaviors are deemed more popular by their peer group. Furthermore, those youth who have close supportive relationships with their peers express more prosocial behaviors.

Prosocial development and the factors that promote it are likely influenced by the sociocultural milieu in which the child is embedded. Indeed, researchers have shown that children of various societies differ in their levels of prosocial behaviors, as well as the factors that predict their development. Early comparative research has shown, for example, that children from subsistence-based economies, in which the whole family participates in productive labor, have relatively high levels of prosocial behaviors and responsibility (Whiting and Edwards 1988). Similarly, research on cooperative behaviors among children within the United States suggests that some ethnic minority children, such as Latinos, display relatively high levels of cooperative behaviors with their peers.

What factors might contribute to such cross-societal and cross-ethnic differences in prosocial development? As with most other behaviors, it is likely a collection of factors working together that will help us understand prosocial development. Some scholars believe that cultural belief systems and the values that societies and groups emphasize contribute to this divergence. For example, some societies tend toward collectivism—wherein group members rely on each other in multiple ways and encourage group-oriented rather than self-oriented behaviors. Children who grow up in those societies might be socialized in ways that promote cooperation and positive behaviors toward others, or at least toward their friends and families. In contrast, children who grow up in individualist societies are socialized for more competitive behaviors, self-sufficiency, and independence. Children who are raised in individualist societies might then be expected to exhibit fewer prosocial and cooperative behaviors. Some research exists to support these ideas, although studies remain sparse.

In addition to broad cultural tendencies and value systems, the specific societal beliefs and expectations regarding behaviors can also impact the prosocial development of children. For example, societal beliefs about the roles of children and the opportunities afforded to them have been shown to vary widely. In some societies, children are seen as members of the workforce, and are expected to participate responsibly in household work and even wage labor. In such instances, children are placed in contexts and situations wherein they are afforded opportunities to be prosocial and socially responsible, and those contexts can contribute much to their prosocial development. In others, young children are expected to tend to their younger siblings, an experience that has been found to contribute to prosocial responding. Cultures vary in the extent to which they expect children to participate in these contexts, which is reflected in the varying amounts of time children spend in such settings. This is not to say, however, that children benefit most from laboring like adults in workforces and on house chores. Extreme workloads and overwhelming work demands and responsibilities can also impede healthy development.

The correlates of prosocial behaviors also might differ across societies. For example, some correlates that might be predictive of prosocial development in one society might not necessarily show the same paths of influence in others. As mentioned earlier, a variety of parenting practices have been found to contribute to the development of prosocial behaviors. At least in the United States, research suggests that children raised by parents who are warm and emotionally close to them show higher levels of prosocial behaviors. In some culture groups these factors appear to be less essential than other factors, such as parental flexibility. Correlates of prosocial behaviors are embedded in socioecological contexts, which can modify these patterns of influence—making some factors more significant in some contexts than in others. Among some immigrant families, for example, there are additional challenges faced, such as adjustment to a new community and new family economic challenges. In such cases, it is sometimes familial flexibility and adaptability that best contribute to healthy development, rather than closeness.

In summary, the need to further study prosocial behaviors and youth activism is clear given the potential positive impact of these types of behaviors on our communities (Carlo and Randall 2001). Scholars have directed much of their attention to understanding the origins and development of prosocial behaviors. Our knowledge about those behaviors has provided us with a window of understanding how to best foster and promote positive forms of youth activism. Social scientists have shown that an understanding of prosocial behaviors requires an understanding of the sociocultural milieu in which the behaviors are embedded. Furthermore, prosocial behaviors are multiply determined by biological factors, familial and peer relationships, situational factors, and by cognitive and emotional processes. Clearly, however, there is much more to be learned regarding the interplay of those multiple determinants.

Note: Funding support for Gustavo Carlo was provided by a grant from the National Science Foundation (NSF 01-32302). Correspondence may be addressed to Gustavo Carlo, Department of Psychology, University of Nebraska–Lincoln, Lincoln, NE 68588, e-mail: gcarlo@unl.edu.

See also Character Education; Citizenship Education Policies in the States; Civic Virtue; Democratic Education; Diversity Education; Environmental Education (EE); IEA Civic Education Study; Just Community High Schools and Youth Activism; National Alliance for Civic Education (NACE); Positive Development; School Engagement; School Influences and Civic Engagement.

Recommended Reading

Batson, C. D. (1991). *The Altruism Question: Toward a Social Psychological Answer.* Hillsdale, NJ: Lawrence Erlbaum Associates.

Carlo, G., and Randall, B. (2001). "Are All Prosocial Behaviors Equal? A Socioecological Developmental Conception of Prosocial Behavior." In *Advances in Psychology Research*, Vol. 2, edited by F. Columbus. Huntington, NY: Nova Science Publishers, pp. 151–170.

Eisenberg, N., and Fabes, R. A. (1998). "Prosocial Development." In *Handbook of Child Psychology, Social, Emotional, and Personality Development*, Vol. 3, 5th ed., edited by W. Damon (series) and N. Eisenberg (vol.). New York: John Wiley, pp. 701–778.

Hoffman, M. L. (2000). *Empathy and Moral Development: Implications for Caring and Justice.* Cambridge: Cambridge University Press.

Latané, B., and Darley, J. M. (1970). *The Unresponsive Bystander: Why Doesn't He Help?* New York: Appleton-Crofts.

Whiting, B. B., and Edwards, C. P. (1988). *Children of Different Worlds.* Cambridge, MA: Harvard University Press.

Gustavo Carlo, Maria R. T. de Guzman, and Laura M. Padilla-Walker

Pubertal Timing. Puberty is generally considered the first transition that marks the entry into adolescence. With puberty, individuals change in physical appearance from child to adult and gain the capacity for reproduction. However, these changes do not appear overnight; for most youth, it will take four to five years from the time that initial physical signs of puberty begin until development is complete. Moreover, hormonal changes of puberty begin prior to initial external signs of development, and final growth in height and bone structure will continue into young adulthood for many youth. The length of pubertal development and the dramatic changes in form and function that ensue from it are no doubt part of the reason that puberty is frequently perceived by the individual, family members, and adults, in general, as such a salient part of the transition into adolescence.

Notably, these changes do not occur at the same time for all children and adolescents. In the first systematic studies by Tanner and his colleagues of pubertal development, Tanner observed that there was substantial variation among children in the ages when they first began and subsequently progressed through pubertal development. Although such variations are completely normal, it means that among any group of young adolescents, for example those in middle school, some may not have begun puberty, looking much younger than their peers, others may have noticeable signs of development typical of their peers, and still others may have nearly reached their adult height and look much older than their peers. Most adolescents will go through puberty at about the same time as peers of the same gender; however, some will be earlier and some will be later than same gender peers.

The focus of this entry is on the impact of the timing of pubertal development on adolescent development and behavioral changes during adolescence. A brief review of the biological changes of puberty is provided as background for this discussion. For a detailed discussion of pubertal processes, see Grumbach and Styne (1998).

Physical Changes of Puberty

Tanner and his colleagues identified five areas of internal and external changes at puberty: (1) growth spurt; (2) increases in and redistribution of body fat and muscle tissue; (3) development of the circulatory and respiratory systems, resulting in increased strength and endurance; (4) maturation of secondary sexual characteristics and reproductive organs; and (5) changes in hormonal-endocrine systems which regulate and coordinate pubertal development and reproduction. Most children begin pubertal development during the middle-childhood years with the first increases in adrenal androgens beginning around six- to eight-years-old. About two years later, gonadal hormones begin to increase; most often girls enter this stage earlier than do boys.

For girls the first observable sign of puberty is breast budding which usually occurs between eight and thirteen years old with a mean age of 9.96 for white girls and a mean age of 8.87 for black girls. The first growth of pubic hair often appears shortly after breast budding. Girls begin growth in height about this time with the most rapid growth occurring around mid-puberty. The first menstrual cycle, menarche, follows the peak in height velocity with a mean age of 12.88 for white girls and a mean age of 12.16 for black girls. As can be seen, recent studies have found that African American girls mature earlier on average than their Caucasian counterparts. Other race or ethnic group differences have not been established (see Archibald, Graber, and Brooks-Gunn 2003 and Hayward 2003 for recent reviews.)

As indicated, boys typically begin to show physical signs of puberty about one to two years later than girls. The initial sign of sexual development in boys is the beginning of growth of the testicles around ages eleven to 11.5 years. Pubic hair begins to appear shortly after this. Boys begin to grow in height around this time and experience their most rapid growth in height between thirteen and fourteen years of age on average; this is also about the time that maturation of reproductive function of the testicles occurs as indicated by the first ejaculation. Other pubertal changes in boys include voice change and the appearance of facial hair, both of which occur in the later stages of puberty (see Archibald, Graber, and Brooks-Gunn 2003 and Hayward 2003 for recent reviews.)

As indicated, both girls and boys experience changes in their distribution of fat and muscle during pubertal development with boys having greater increases in muscle mass and girls having greater increases in fat along with greater distribution of fat to the hips and breast areas. The emergence of acne along with changes in sweat glands, while not linked to the reproductive aspects of puberty, often results in many behavioral changes in the areas of personal hygiene. Overall, the physical changes that occur with puberty have psychological significance in connection with feelings of body consciousness as young adolescents adapt to their changing bodies.

The Psychological Experience of Pubertal Timing

Adults and youth themselves frequently attribute behavioral change—moodiness, the need for greater independence from parents, sexual interest—to puberty, or more often "raging hormones." Some evidence does indicate that hormonal changes at puberty are linked to increases in sexual interest and changes in emotions; at the same time, such behavioral changes are experienced in a social context, which also influences how young adolescents express their new or changing emotions. In fact, much of the influence of pubertal development on the behaviors of young adolescents does not appear to be directly the result of hormonal changes but instead is more closely linked to the social experience of puberty. That is, the physical changes of pubertal development—growth in breasts in girls, growth in height and weight in both boys and girls—are clearly observable to the adolescents themselves and to their peers, parents, and others. As such, these changes serve as cues that the individual is becoming more adult-like and may expect to engage in behaviors that more closely fit with an adult role.

In particular, whereas puberty may serve as an indicator for all adolescents that they are growing up, some youth may feel more out of sync with their peers or atypical because of the timing of their pubertal development. As indicated, timing of puberty refers to going through puberty earlier, at about the same time, or later than one's peers. In general, it is off-time development that has been thought to be more challenging. It has been suggested that how individuals cope with and are influenced by puberty depends upon their emotional and cognitive skills when the transition occurs; hence, early maturation may result in poorer adjustment as these young adolescents start puberty and experience successive stages of it prior to developing cognitive or coping skills that may be needed to deal with this challenge. For example, young adolescents who are early maturers are likely to look older than their same-age peers; as such, adults or older peers may think they are older. These youth may then be more likely to find themselves in social situations and facing social challenges that are more common for older adolescents—for example, being at a party where drugs or alcohol are being used.

In contrast, it has also been suggested that adolescents may be likely to evaluate themselves in comparison to social norms, placing value on "normative" versus "nonnormative" development; in this case, early or late maturation is "deviant" from one's peers and perceiving oneself as different may result in negative emotions. For girls who mature early, the experience of gaining weight and being larger than other girls and often same-age boys leads to poor self-evaluations, subsequent problems in body image, and sometimes eating problems for these girls. At the same time, late-maturing boys are smaller and shorter than all their same-age peers; again, gender norms for physical appearance would place these boys at risk for negative self-evaluations and possibly the need to compensate via other behaviors.

Over the past five to ten years, several studies have found that pubertal timing is linked with adolescent adjustment and problem behaviors as had been hypothesized. In particular, early-maturing girls appear to be at greatest risk for problems during adolescence and even into adulthood. Early-maturing girls have been found to have higher prevalence of major depressive disorder, conduct disorder, eating disorders, and suicide attempts in comparison to on-time and late-maturing girls by the time they are in high school. Studies have also found that these girls have higher rates and earlier initiation of alcohol and substance use than other girls, as early as the middle-school years, and earlier ages of initiation of sexual intercourse (see Graber chapter in Hayward 2003 for a more detailed review). Most recently, my colleagues and I have also shown that pubertal timing has longer-term consequences on psychopathology into young adulthood. Thus, what has been most striking in the literature are the consistent associations of early maturation with serious disorders rather than just a few elevated symptoms. And, early maturation in girls is linked to a broad range of problems rather than just one type of problem. Although many studies have been conducted with Caucasian, middle-class samples, recent studies have found that early maturation may also be a risk for internalizing and externalizing problems among African American girls.

Interestingly, among girls and young women only early maturation has been pervasively linked to problems. Late maturation appears to have few negative consequences in girls. In one study, late maturation was associated with higher prevalence of depression during the high-school years, but this association disappeared by young adulthood. Other studies have, in fact, found that late maturation was associated with positive academic achievement. For example, late-maturing girls were more likely to do homework and have higher school achievement during the high-school years and in another study had higher rates of college completion in young adulthood. It has been suggested that because these girls may look younger than their age-mates they may be perceived as less mature or less appropriate for social activities such as dating. Hence, late-maturing girls may focus their energies on academic rather than social pursuits, a choice that clearly pays off in the long run.

Studies that have examined pubertal timing in boys have not found the same associations as those seen for girls. For boys, early maturation has been linked with elevated depressive symptoms, alcohol use and abuse, and delinquent and externalizing behaviors during the middle- and high-school years (see Graber chapter in Hayward 2003 for a more detailed review). Only a few studies have examined timing in non-Caucasian boys but there is some evidence that early maturation is a risk for delinquent behaviors and other externalizing behaviors among African American and possibly Latino boys as well as Caucasian boys. No studies to date have found higher rates of serious disorders among early-maturing boys as was seen for early-maturing girls. However, one lasting effect of early maturation has been demonstrated as a problem into adulthood. In one of the only

studies to look at timing effects into adulthood, my colleagues and I found that among young men who were early maturers daily tobacco-use rates were nearly twice as high as the national average for men ages twenty-five to thirty-four (40 percent versus 26.6 percent, respectively). Clearly, daily tobacco use is a serious health-compromising behavior. It may be that because these young men looked older when they were adolescents it was easier for them to purchase and smoke cigarettes with fewer adult objections or intervention, resulting in eventual nicotine addiction.

In contrast to the pattern seen for early maturation in boys, late maturation seems to have its most serious impact on boys during late adolescence and young adulthood. During the high-school years, late maturation has been linked to elevated psychological distress. However, in young adulthood men who were late maturers had higher rates of disruptive behavior disorder and higher rates of substance use than their on-time counterparts.

That serious effects of pubertal timing can be seen among young adults and in particular for early-maturing girls and late-maturing boys indicates that there may be important evaluations of the self as "deviant" or out of sync from others. Given the gender differences in when adolescents are likely to progress through the physical changes of puberty, early-maturing girls are the first of any cohort of children to begin puberty, and late-maturing boys are the last of that cohort to begin puberty. As such, they are the most socially out of sync with peers and hence may be experiencing the most negative consequences.

Despite the pervasiveness of the problems with being off-time, especially for early-maturing girls, there is less conclusive information on why this occurs. It has often been suggested that one risk for early-maturing girls is associating with older peers, especially older boys. Early-maturing girls who are dating or who associate with older peers are more likely to have adjustment problems (e.g., eating problems) and greater substance use and delinquent behaviors than early-maturing girls who do not spend time with older peers. As noted, looking older may be particularly risky for girls as it exposes them to pressures they are not ready to deal with.

Other researchers have found that puberty in combination with other challenges places early-maturing girls at risk. For example, girls with prior behavior problems in childhood who also went through puberty early have been shown to have greater increases in behavior problems during adolescence than girls who had prior problems but didn't mature early; that is, early maturation accentuated or exacerbated prior difficulties. In other studies, it has been shown that early-maturing girls may also be more likely to experience a school change from elementary to middle school while they are at the peak of pubertal changes. Presumably, simultaneous changes of puberty and school change resulted in poorer adjustment as these girls did not have time to adapt to or cope with either transition before having to deal with the other one.

Finally, early-maturing girls also appear to have greater difficulties in their relationships with family members and possibly peers. Whereas conflict with parents is often thought to be part of the normative process of asserting one's independence from parents, early-maturing girls appear to have more sustained conflictual interactions with parents and report less family and peer support in the high-school years and young adulthood. As such, early maturation may be a risk for social deficits and unhealthy patterns of asserting one's independence.

In conclusion, it is clear that how puberty is experienced in a social context has important implications for adolescent development. In terms of the broader themes of this volume, puberty has rarely, if ever, been directly linked to the development of activism during adolescence. At the same time, it is no doubt a part of beginning to see oneself as an adult and a part of taking on the roles that one thinks are those of an adult; a part of adult roles is clearly that of citizen and participant in society. In fact, it might be argued that the disparity that emerges during adolescence between one's physical appearance as an adult and one's role in society as an adult is one reason that some youth seek out disruptive or unhealthy behaviors (e.g., alcohol use, conflict with authority figures, or criminal behaviors such as theft) as they test out independence and different roles perceived to be adult- or less child-like. It may be that some of the difficulties that off-time pubertal development imposes are in part the result of difficulties in finding healthy adult roles and being able to assume these roles.

See also Acculturation; Parental Influences on Youth Activism.

Recommended Reading

Archibald, A. B., Graber, J. A., and Brooks-Gunn, J. (2003). "Pubertal Processes and Physiological Growth in Adolescence." In *Handbook on Adolescence*, edited by G. R. Adams and M. Berzonsky. Oxford: Blackwell Publishers, pp. 24–47.

Graber, J. A., Seeley, J. R., Brooks-Gunn, J., and Lewinsohn, P. M. (2004). "Is Pubertal Timing Associated with Psychopathology in Young Adulthood?" *Journal of the American Academy of Child and Adolescent Psychiatry*, 43 (6): 718–726.

Grumbach, M. M., and Styne, D. M. (1998). "Puberty: Ontogeny, neuroendocrinology, physiology and disorders" In *Williams Textbook of Endrocrinology*, edited by J. D. Wilsom, D. W. Foster, and H. M. Kronenberg. Philadelphia, PA: WW Saunders, pp. 1509–1625.

Hayward, C., ed. (2003). *Gender Differences at Puberty*. New York: Cambridge University Press.

Julia A. Graber

Public Art. Public art is the practice of involving an artist or artists in the conception, development, and transformation of public space. Youth become involved in these practices through participation in public art projects and interaction with the art form. Public art can instill in young people a sense of belonging in their community, expose them to different cultures, and help them become aware of spacial relationships in the context of their surroundings. Various studies have shown that public art programs designed for youth participation enhance young people's attitudes about themselves and their futures, enhance thinking and problem-solving skills, and decrease delinquent behavior. Through the arts, youth can help to change and improve their immediate environments.

Successful public art resonates with the site in context; engages the community; meets the clients', artists', and community's intentions; and provides a sense of civic and community pride. Young people involved in the art process become cultural workers, stimulating new ideas and contributing to environmental and cultural renewal. Youth participation can help create a new heritage that reflects thoughts and ideas of modern issues that young people are facing today. Involvement with the conception of the art allows the youth to teach community and family members about subject matter that may be unfamiliar to those community members.

We must distinguish between "plop art" and public art. Often in the planning of major construction sites the corporation or business will add an extension of some sculptural piece in the overall building plan as a "contribution to society." This art often does not reflect the community in any way and is made only with the business' best interest in mind. To some, these contributions are considered worthy of praise. Art for art's sake and strictly as a form of aesthetic pleasure will always exist. Beautifying our communities with traditional art forms that are pleasing to the eye plays a significant role in the appreciation and understanding of the importance of art. From ancient cave paintings to computer-animated billboards the public is forced to interact with their surroundings and in doing so learns about ancient history and modern trends.

However, public art is different in several important ways. Public art does not exist without collaboration and integration of different ideas. This collaboration can include artists, architects, landscape architects, urban designers, engineers, planners, state and local councils, and legislators. Public art can be done in traditional art forms such as painting and sculpture but can also incorporate media, music, text, performance, computer technology, environmental and found objects, installations, and any other medium used for expression in this period of the postmodern artistic movement. It can reflect heritage, social change, a specific area, or an issue. It can also commemorate an individual's or group's contribution to the community or can point to the future of the community. Public art attracts residential and commercial occupiers, stimulates tourism, contributes to local distinctiveness through the use of open spaces, reduces levels of crime by giving a sense of personal ownership to one's community, creates a cultural legacy for the future, introduces innovation and experimentation in shared spaces, and plays a key role in urban and rural regeneration.

In the twenty-first century new definitions of public art are emerging. The world is always changing and many artists, critics, and community members now view public art as a form of activism. Feminist and ethnic issues, gay rights, political injustice, homelessness, foreign affairs, sexual awareness, crime, environmental hazards, child abuse, rape, cultural diversity, and other social issues are addressed. Art that *does* and not just *is* opens the viewers' eyes to the relevance and importance of issues that might directly or indirectly affect their way of life.

Pubic art as a form of activism can be part of a community's cultural development, bringing a conscious awareness to the values and choices made within a particular area. Youth involved in public art programs exercise their social imagination and learn how to combine personal interests with the interests of the community. Motivation and collaboration go hand in hand as youth learn how to work together and make significant contributions to their society. There are many youth public art programs where mural painting, theater and dance performances, filmmaking, and sculpture installations play a huge role in teaching young adults skills and values of citizenship and public scholarship. Being involved in community cultural development provides youth with opportunities for self and social empowerment.

Many public art programs across the globe are designed specifically for at-risk youth. In the United States programs such as Youth arts Public art in Portland, Oregon, Urban smARTSs in San Antonio, Philadelphia mural arts, and many others share common goals: to divert at-risk youth from the juvenile justice system, to improve their social behavior and social skills, to improve their academic performance and commitment to school, to develop their art skills, to provide them with opportunities to perform and exhibit their art, and to provide an after-school safe haven. Research has been done by an organization called Arts for America on the effect of programs such as these and has proven that incorporation of youth art programs into the community does indeed lower teen crime and enhance the academic abilities of the participating youth.

Chicana muralist Judy Baca is a great example of an artist who has worked with youth on public art projects for social change. With support from the city of Los Angeles and her association, Social and Public Art Resource Center (SPARC), she founded the citywide mural project in 1974 in which artists of all ages produced interactive community murals. In 1976 she started her work on *The Great Wall of Los Angeles*, a 2,400-foot long mural located in a flood control channel of the Los Angeles River. It was painted over the course of several summers by hundreds of teenagers, including parolees from the juvenile justice system, and remains a work in progress to this day. *The Great Wall of Los Angeles* portrays the struggles and contributions of immigrant minorities, indigenous peoples, and women who, up until that time, were not publicly recognized as a part *of* California's history. This mural is an excellent model for political activism and education through the arts.

The future lies in the hands of the youth of today, and with their hands positive change with productive outcomes can be generated and communicated. Through the arts young people can help shape and mold positive attitudes and responses within their communities and create an awareness of issues that may be common to other young adults but misunderstood by their peers. Participation and engagement in public art sites allow young adults to question their surroundings, express new ideas, and open their eyes to the endless possibilities of community cultural development.

See also Film/Video as a Tool for Youth Activism; Hip-Hop Generation; MTV's Choose or Lose Campaign (1992–); New Media; Public Scholarship.

Recommended Reading

Adams, D., and Goldberg, A. (2002). *Community, Culture, and Globalization*. New York: Rockefeller Foundation.

Adams, D, and Goldberg, A. (2002). "Creative Community." In *The Art of Cultural Development*. New York: Rockefeller Foundation.

Gablik, S. (1991). *The Reenchantment of Art*. New York: Thames and Hudson.

Lacy, S. (1995). *Mapping the Terrain, New Genre Public Art*. Seattle: Bay Press.

Lippard, L. R. (1997). *The Lure of the Local*. New York: New Press.

Mirzoeff, N. (1998). *The Visual Culture Reader*. New York: Routledge.

Weintraub, L. (1996). *Art on the Edge and Over*. Litchfield, CT: Art Insights.

Additional Web Sites

Arts for America: http://www.artsforamerica.org

Mural Arts Program, Philadelphia: http://www.muralarts.org

The Social and Public Art Resource Center (SPARC): http://www.sparcmurals.org

Youth Arts: http://www.youtharts.org

Natalia Pilato

Public Scholarship. Public scholarship is the conduct of scholarly and creative work, including teaching, research, artistic performance, and service, in ways that contribute to informed engagement in the democratic process. Public scholarship places an emphasis on the public nature of the work, an idea meant to capture the democratic obligation of schools and citizens, and the ideal of knowledge as a public good. At colleges and universities, public scholarship recognizes the importance of learning to be scholarly and to use scholarship for public purposes, as well as the value of learning for personal growth and to prepare for a meaningful career.

The idea of public scholarship is based upon two pillars. The first is the recognition of an obligation, which some scholars believe to be implicit in the American Constitution, to engage in the collective political welfare of the community—that is, to take an active role in democracy. Some of these scholars suggest that the democratic engagement obligation goes beyond even the individual's personally rooted duties to care for family, friends, and self. The second pillar is the idea of knowledge as a public good. And because knowledge is the primary business of colleges and universities, this has particular relevance for what faculty and student scholars do, both on and off campus.

Public scholarship in the twenty-first century has origins in many realms in addition to the U.S. Constitution. These include: the seventeenth-century Enlightenment belief in reasoning and the value of scientific discovery; the eighteenth-century ideals of democratic governance and individual liberty expressed by the European writers, artists, and journalists known as the *philosophes*; in the nineteenth century in the United States the creation of the 1862 Morrill Act of Land Grant colleges, which established universities as public trusts for learning and the application of discovery; and the twentieth-century view of colleges and universities as habitats for the integration of undergraduate and graduate education, research, and service.

To understand why public scholarship is viewed as an important idea and a rewarding practice, it is useful to look carefully at the idea that the U.S. Constitution includes an obligation to participate in the democracy and then at the claim that public scholarship provides an important means of doing so.

The American Constitution, including the Bill of Rights and the amendments that followed, were unique. They created a popular government of "WE the People" in order to "secure the blessings of liberty," not for monarchs or rulers, but for "ourselves and our posterity." The idea that people could, as citizens, simultaneously govern and be governed was revolutionary. It was made the more so by the recognition in the Declaration of Independence of an expectation of public political participation that soon after found voice in the new checks and balances of constitutional tripart government.

Many of the constitutional framers understood that people could make decisions based upon knowledge and reason. As a result, the framers designed a government comprised of, elected by, and responsible to citizens. "WE the People" were, and *are*, expected to take part in the political discourse of the nation and to act politically through voting, public speech, the media, petition, and peaceful assembly.

Philosopher and college president Alexander Meiklejohn made one of the primary connections between democracy and education explicit in 1948 when he wrote, "The primary task of American education is to arouse and to cultivate, in all the members of the body politic, a desire to understand what our plan of national government is" (Meickjohn 1948, 3). He believed that democracy is based upon informed participation and that informed participation is based upon education.

The Constitution's familiar first amendment command that "Congress shall make no law ... abridging the freedom of speech, or of the press, or the right of the people peaceably to assemble, and to petition the government for a redress of grievances" suggests more, however, than the need to understand democracy. As a cornerstone of democratic governance, the first amendment is also a lynchpin for viewing public scholarship as a powerful means of providing the kind of public political activism democracy requires. The claim that the first amendment is a foundation of public scholarship activism is fashioned upon a building-block construct that recognizes the value of enlightened public participation.

"The critical dimension of individual liberty," historian Eric Foner wrote, "is the right to participate in public affairs" (Foner 1998, xvii). And to participate in public affairs? "Freedom to think as you will and to speak as you think are means indispensable to the discovery and spread of political truth," Supreme Court Justice Louis Brandeis wrote in 1927. Brandeis viewed unfettered communication as more than a right. He saw public discussion as a political duty. "This should be a fundamental principle of American government," Brandeis said (Brandeis 1927, 375). Justice William Brennan echoed Brandeis' conclusion in *New York Times v. Sullivan,* a landmark Supreme Court case that arose in 1964 from the heat of protest during the civil rights movement in the South. "The principle of the freedom of speech springs," Brennan wrote, "from the necessities of ... self-governance."

The principles of democracy embedded in this view of participatory democracy have four elements. First, the purpose of the state is to enable individual freedom, rather than state sovereignty for its own sake. Second, to achieve individual freedom, citizens must enjoy a right to participate in civic affairs. Third, productive participation in civic affairs is grounded upon free trade in discovery and ideas, which serves as the intellectual roadmap of political, social, and personal discovery. And fourth, the preservation of individual liberty in a democracy requires the coupled political duties of active participation and acquisition of the knowledge necessary to generate beneficial, productive engagement.

The roots of this inspiration lie deep in America's historical soil. Thomas Jefferson described the value of intellectual and civic education in 1787 when he wrote, "Were it left to me to decide whether we should have a government without newspapers, or newspapers without government, I should not hesitate a moment to prefer the latter. But I should mean that every man should receive those papers, and be capable of reading them" (Brennan 1964, 270). Jefferson recognized that individual liberty requires an unfettered press and a literate community.

The growth of a community capable of reading Jefferson's papers—virtual as well as ink—has been nourished by the contemporary recognition that education is no less an element of democratic governance than is the newspaper. Like the press, education conveys social, political, and cultural expectations and provides the underpinnings of reasoned democratic engagement. And like other media, including art, music, the Internet, and journalism, it is a function of the schools to prepare citizens to read Jefferson's papers critically and to use the knowledge gained to participate effectively in the arena of democratic activism.

If the scholarship of discovery and learning are the basis for wise citizenship, scholarship also provides the tools for direct democratic activism. There are many examples. At Stanford University, the Public Service Scholars Program enables undergraduates to develop senior theses that bring their scholarship to bear on local community issues such as poverty, hunger, and health. The explicit application of their discoveries and the readiness to test their assumptions in communities beyond the classroom deeply roots their activism in public scholarship. Penn State University, founded in the land grant and extension traditions, offers a public scholarship interdisciplinary minor in civic and community engagement in which students combine coursework focused on democracy, community involvement, and topics related to their academic interests with applied fieldwork and an integrative capstone thesis or project.

These are not examples of volunteerism in which community organizations rely on individuals who offer to lend a hand in whatever manner best suits the agency, such as manning phone banks for fundraising, clearing park trails, or delivering meals. Nor are they examples, strictly speaking, of public service for its own sake since, like volunteerism, service does not require explicit attention to using scholarship as a means of democratic participation.

What makes these examples of public scholarship? Psychology students have combined coursework and understanding of youth development with fieldwork to intervene in middle-school adolescent bullying. They are using their academic skills to contribute to public ends, and they are confronting the implications and consequences of their chosen fields for the public's well-being. Likewise, students in engineering and materials sciences have developed environmentally and economically sound housing contributions in the Midwest. Geography and business students have studied and raised new policy questions about inner-city transportation practices in an urban Northeast city. West Coast students have focused on literacy and other needs among the children of migrant laborers. In each case scholarship provides the basis for involvement. At the University of Minnesota, Penn State, and elsewhere, administrators, faculty, and students are, through grassroots discussion, new pedagogies, and new standards of peer review, redefining what it means to engage in the public's scholarship.

In each case, discovery and its applications explicitly incorporate three elements: a recognition of the obligation to develop democratic engagement among students; a responsibility to focus discovery and creative performance on the social, civic, economic, educational, artistic, scientific, and cultural well-being of the neighborhoods beyond the academy, as well as on basic research and disciplinary teaching; and the development of a curriculum of consequence in which the conduct of teaching, learning, discovery, and performance provide a means through which students and faculty can view their work, not as

segregated from society, but as the contributions of activist scholar-citizens with membership in a larger community.

See also Deliberative Democracy; Democracy; Democratic Education.

Recommended Reading

Antonio, A., Astin, H., and Cress, C. (2000). "Community Service and Higher Education: A Look at the Nation's Faculty." *Review of Higher Education*, 22 (4): 373–398.

Astin, A., Sax, L. J., and Avalos, J. (1999). "Long Term Effects of Volunteerism during the Undergraduate Years." *Review of Higher Education*, 22 (2): 187–202.

Barber, B. (1992). *An Aristocracy of Everyone: The Politics of Education and the Future of America.* New York: Ballantine Books.

Boyte, H. C. (2004). *Going Public: Academics and Public Life.* Dayton, OH: Kettering Foundation.

Brandeis, L. (1927). *Whitney v. California* 247 U.S. 357, 375–377.

Brennan, W. (1964). *New York Times v Sullivan* 376 U.S. 254, 270.

Cohen, J. (1989). *Congress Shall Make No Law: Oliver Wendell Holmes, the First Amendment, and Judicial Decision Making.* Ames: Iowa State University Press.

Cohen, J. (2001). "Shouting Fire in a Crowded Classroom: From Holmes to Homeroom." In *Communication, a Different Kind of Horse Race: Essays Honoring Richard F. Carter*, edited by B. Dervin and S. Chaffee. Peekskill, NJ: Hampton Press.

Foner, E. (1998). *The Story of American Freedom.* New York: W. W. Norton.

Jefferson, T. (January 16, 1787). Letter to Edward Carrington. In *The Writings of Thomas Jefferson*, edited by P. L. Ford. New York: Putnam, pp. 357–361.

Meiklejohn, A. (1948). *Political Freedom: The Constitutional Powers of the People.* New York: Oxford University Press.

New York Times v. Sullivan, 376 U.S. 254 (1964).

Shulman, L. (1997). "Professing the Liberal Arts." In *Education and Democracy: Re-imagining Liberal Arts in America*, edited by R. Orrill. New York: College Board, pp. 151–173.

Jeremy Cohen

Punk Rock Youth Subculture. Rick, the bassist for a punk rock band called the Casualties, recently had this to say about the change in lifestyle for him and his bandmates: "Initially we weren't politically oriented at all, but now the state of the world is so bad, it's stuff we can't just get drunk and be blind to.... we've got to stand up and pay attention to what's going on, and be a part of something." The punk rock youth want to be a part of something. Like Rick, many of them define punk as more than just a way to have fun and play music. Teenagers wearing patches of their favorite bands on their jean jackets form identities and find a place to fit in within the punk subculture. Punk rockers have always been known as the outsiders—in school, in their families, and in society as a whole.

The image of the punk rocker since the days of the United Kingdom's earliest up-starts, the Sex Pistols, has always been one associated with disorder, both in appearance and in lifestyle. Many punks still believe in growing their Mohawks and wearing combat boots as a way to represent their taste in fashion, as well as a way to make a statement about how they view society. Punks believe the world is wrought with corrupt authority figures and exploit-ative employment conditions. They believe that the majority of people are blind to grim realities that exist in our society, and show little imperative to engage in civil or political matters. They sympathize with other social outcasts, the lower classes, and victims of wars that they view as pointless. For the youth involved, the punk subculture has proven to be a positive space for artistic expression, the means for political involvement, and a place where individuals develop ideas on matters concerning topics such as ethics and social justice.

Although many punks believe in beginning a dialog and a plan to address how specifically to influence governmental policy, punk has clearly been more successful in establishing its own civil society of sorts, which focuses more on a grassroots ethic of participation and a colorful social scene. A major tenet of the punk philosophy is that there should be an emphasis on a "do-it-yourself" (DIY) attitude, in which the creation and distribution of music and other works of art is done without relying on large, profit-driven enterprises. At punk rock shows the bands emphasize that the

entire crowd needs to be involved—in the dancing, in the formation of new bands, and in creating other forms of expression such as homemade magazines. By building a subculture of cooperation and trust, their aim is to create a feeling of collectivity at the shows while stressing the autonomy and worth of every individual. Punk rock offers youth an alternative community, where the main ethos driving the movement can be encapsulated in the mottos "think for yourself" and "question everything." For any alienated and bored teenager with a penchant for loud, fast music, the message of punk rock is enticing indeed.

Many bands are overtly political, making bold critiques against governmental abuse of power. A cause for division within punk is that, although the movement sympathizes with victims of war, economic inequality, and marginalized groups in general, its followers have been divided as to whether a punk rocker's aim is to focus on fortifying the strength of its subculture or to represent itself as a populist movement striving for political and social change. Brett Gurewitz, member of the band Bad Religion, states: "I don't think rock 'n' roll was meant to be elitist, not any genre of it, and punk rock most of all. Punk rock claims to be a populist movement, and if it's a populist movement, then let's put it on every radio station."

Immediately following a punk rock explosion in the year 1977, bands like the Clash became household names. Many bands changed musically but remained committed to lyrics raising a political and working-class consciousness. The dramatic success of these bands compromised the early subcultural development that a few fans and bands built in the formative years. Punks began to sneer at the success of the bigger bands, dubbing them as "sell-outs." Indeed, although punk music has seen its share of rise and decline in the fickle tastes of the masses, the real opportunity for a more grassroots movement occurred when bands played a local legion-hall show rather than a full-fledged concert to thousands.

Although there always have been and always will be casual musical fans of the punk rock genre, legions of youth throughout punk's existence have identified themselves and punk in a much more comprehensive way. To retain the integrity and freedom of their expression, these fans have classified the subcultural underground of punk as different from the mainstream representation some bands have enjoyed. They believe that marketing music for mass appeal compromises the efforts of the committed fan base, which views punk as a musical genre as well as a community.

The idea of having a high self-esteem, being proud in one's punk identity, originates in the punk belief that in society authority figures and the media constantly define what we should all strive to become and what we should dare not attempt. In the process, individuals who do not conform to the values and aspirations of everyone else are shunned, feared, and rejected by the majority. Punk rock provides a means of expression that allows youth to feel less anxious to express themselves however they please in an environment that stresses racial, ethnic, and gender tolerance.

As in any other social movement, punks have divided themselves into various subcategories based on everything from differences in the style of punk played to the use of or abstinence from alcohol and drugs. In reaction to this, punk bands of today stress the need for punks to see what unites them rather than what divides them. The means for serious, planned, collective political activism, however, has been mired because punks have always insisted on living without rules or leaders within their own subculture. This has led many punks to have only the music show as the one-time meeting ground for the community at large, while living in relative isolation and disconnect the rest of the time. Although life-committed punks still wear "Punk's not Dead" patches on their jackets, one must question what exactly being alive means. Because there are no clear expectations in the unpredictable periods of local involvement or disengagement, the devoted punk, much like the devoted Christian, always has a thousand worries about the purity, power, and authentic participation of others in his community. And yet the victories of a popular protest or the merits of one idea versus another are less important than what the journalist Gina Arnold sees as punk's purpose. According to Arnold, "Punk rock's purpose is to engender communities in this soulless and spiritless age. Punk rock's minions build their own churches, where the faithful gather and sing, and within those sullen edifices, its rituals are as primitive, and yet as personally uplifting, as any caveman's conclave or medieval religious rite."

Punk rock began in the United Kingdom as a mainstream musical success that eventually went "underground" as a result of both popular disinterest in the genre and efforts by committed individuals who believed in continuing punk's legacy as a form of rebellion. By the early 1980s punk was well recognized in the United States. Bands like the Dead Kennedys on the West Coast and Minor Threat on the East Coast had a committed fan base and created independent labels to ensure the survival of their rebellious expression. Today, punk also has a following in almost every Western and Eastern European country, as well as a significant one in Japan and Canada.

See also Hip-Hop Generation; MTV's Choose or Lose Campaign (1992–); New Media; Riot Grrrl.

Recommended Reading

Arnold, Gina (1997). *Kiss This: Punk in the Present Tense.* New York: St. Martin's Griffin.
Levine, Noah (2004). *Dharma Punx.* New York: Harper Collins.
Savage, Jon (1992). *England's Dreaming: Anarchy, Sex Pistols, Punk Rock, and Beyond.* New York: St. Martin's Press.
Taylor, Stephen (2003). *False Prophet: Fieldnotes from the Punk Underground.* Middletown, CT: Wesleyan University Press.
Warner, Brad (2003). *Hardcore Zen: Punk Rock, Monster Movies and the Truth about Reality.* Somerville, MA: Wisedom Publications.

Gokhan Balaban

Q

Queer, Sexuality, and Gender Activism. Queer, sexuality, and gender issues have recently emerged as particularly salient focal points of contemporary social justice activism for young people. That is, these issues are central to the social justice issues that motivate many of today's youth. We argue that this is an historically recent phenomenon but one that grows out of the civil rights, women's rights, sexual rights, and gay rights movements of the last fifty years. Specifically, contemporary youth are growing up during the first period in history in which queer, sexuality, and gender issues have each become prominent in the public consciousness—and specifically in consciousness among young people. Little public discourse on these issues existed prior to early attention to "women's liberation" and "gay rights" in the 1960s and 1970s, and since that time adults have created and dominated the discourse. However, in recent years young people have pursued activism and helped generate a discourse to support it; their efforts are fundamentally grounded in the conceptual and experiential links among queer, sexuality, and gender issues. In some communities and instances, adults have initiated youth activism; in others, adults support it. Finally, there are several examples in which young people have initiated and sustained the queer, sexuality, and gender activism.

Contemporary youth activism around queer, sexuality, and gender issues has grown out of prior civil rights and social justice movements. In the 1960s and 1970s sexuality and gender issues were prominent in social justice activism, and young people, particularly college students, were central to those movements. In the mid-1980s, attention to HIV/AIDS brought a significant shift in public awareness of queer and lesbian, gay, bisexual, and transgender (LGBT) issues and their implications for people's lives. Then in the 1990s the banning of self-acknowledged LGB persons from military service and bans on same-sex marriage and civil unions for same-sex couples (McGarry and Wasserman 1998) moved LGBT and queer issues into a mainstream public discourse, which has persisted ever since. In this discourse LGBT and queer issues are distinct but inseparable from larger issues of sexuality and gender social change and activism.

These historic developments provide the context for queer, sexuality, and gender activism by young people. In the 1990s several key events in the United States galvanized youth consciousness around these issues, including the death of University of Wyoming student Matthew Shepard, the school shootings at Columbine High School, the high-profile legal battles in Salt Lake City, Utah, and Orange County, California, to prohibit gay-straight alliances (GSAs) in public schools, and the U.S. Supreme Court decision that affirmed the right of the Boy Scouts of America to discriminate in their membership policies against gay and atheist men and boys (Russell 2002). Thus, while past generations grew up in a society that was often silent about LGBT lives, contemporary youth are growing up in a time of increased public awareness of—and at times public hostility toward—queer, sexuality, and gender issues.

Ironically, while popular media increasingly focus on these issues and their

A nineteen-year-old woman marches in a local gay pride parade. *Courtesy of Skjold Photographs.*

relevance for young people, other key institutions that influence youth—for example, families, schools, and religious institutions—remain generally silent. This is true for many controversial gender and sexual issues in the United States, even for those issues that are directly relevant to young people. Rarely do schools or families afford young people opportunities to discuss sexism, homophobia, shifting gender identities, or coming out, for example, although media images and messages on all of these issues are ever-present. To develop spaces in which they can acknowledge these concerns and challenge conventional ideas, many young people turn to existing community organizations for youth or, sometimes with adults' assistance, form new community organizations or school-based groups such as GSAs (Russell 2002).

Much of the youth activism related to queer, sexuality, and gender issues has taken place in high schools. While schools are the primary spaces in which young people learn from peers about cultural expectations, stereotypes, and regulation regarding sexuality and gender, schools may also be sites for youth resistance. High-school GSAs reflect the significance of sexuality as a justice issue for contemporary youth. In these groups, heterosexually identified youth, typically girls, often make up the leadership and membership. For these heterosexual youth sexual freedom is a justice issue; for some straight young women, their own experiences of the regulation of gender have made them acutely aware of the gender and sexual regulation with which LGB youth contend. GSAs represent some young people's efforts to create new social organizations; other young people focus their activism on remaking existing high-school institutions. LGBT young people are increasingly resisting the heterosexual scripting of the high-school proms, complete with their crowned kings and queens and informally enforced norms around dating. LGBT and queer proms offer young people access to experiences routinely denied them and represent an effort to "expose the [heterosexual society's] tyranny, to challenge its hegemony" (Best 2000).

Young people have also pursued queer, sexuality, and gender activism at the college level. University and college campuses across the country feature LGBT and queer student organizations that offer safe spaces for students questioning their sexual identities, social outlets for LGBTQ students, and institutional sites from which to advocate for curricular and policy changes. The Gender Public Advocacy Coalition (GenderPAC) is a national gender rights organization that has seen a recent explosion of interest among college students in their advocacy work (GenderPAC 2004). Transgender students and their allies are remaking the gender culture on university and college campuses as they successfully lobby administrators to establish all-gender bathrooms, housing for transgender students, and health-care forms that ask students to report their "gender identity history" and not whether they are female or male (Bernstein 2004). In all of these efforts young people's campus activism builds on precedents that people of color and feminist women set when they established ethnic and women's studies programs in the late twentieth century as part of intellectual and political movements for racial and gender justice.

Youth activism is not confined to school and campus settings. Rather, social services and community-based organizations are important contemporary sites of activism around queer, sexuality, and gender issues by young people. Youth concerned with sexual and gender justice are increasingly turning to community-based peer sexuality education programs. For some, peer education offers an opportunity to combat the abstinence-until-marriage lessons that dominate most contemporary school-based sexuality education; in youth-led instruction many young people feel freer to explore sexual issues, including curiosities about practices and pleasure, experiences of sexual intimacy, and challenges for youth with nonconforming gender and sexual identities. Peer education allows other young people a chance to create and to claim instructional spaces outside of school and away from the sometimes oppressive presence of adults. And in the field of social services, youth living in foster care have begun to be advocates for rights and freedom for queer, sexuality, and gender expression.

These brief examples highlight the growing numbers of young people who feel entitled to sexual and gender self-determination. Many recognize a basic human right to romantic love, intimacy, and sexual fulfillment. Ironically, these individualistic notions of rights and self-determination appear to motivate a significant youth movement *against* sexual and gender inequalities in young people's schools and communities and *for* broad sexual and gender social justice. Many of today's youth activists are acting on a collective awareness of sexual and gender injustices. Some, like straight young women who belong to GSAs or peer educa-

tors working in communities considered "at-risk," work with people who seem at first glance to be quite unlike them—for example, gay and lesbian youth or youth with limited strategies for negotiating sexual risk. However, their notions of sexual rights and the history of gender and sexuality activism that precedes them allow these youth activists to achieve significant empathy and to fight for a sexual-and-gender just world.

Individualist and essentialist thinking dominate contemporary views of sexuality and gender. The majority of adults and young people alike consider sexuality and gender as fundamentally personal and individual experiences and not products of historic and cultural norms and attitudes. However, for some recent cohorts of young people, contemporary activism related to queer, sexuality, and gender issues has been opportunities to thinking about larger social and cultural issues. These issues are central to the most contested public debates, and while structural barriers typically exclude young people from the discourse, many youth have taken on these issues for themselves and their communities. The inherent links among young people's individual experiences, larger questions of human (and thus youth) rights and citizenship, and a historical moment in which youth, gender, and sexuality are at the fore compel many youth to engage in larger social justice issues—issues that have been beyond the exposure and experience of previous generations of young people.

See also Gay-Straight Alliances in Schools (GSAs).

Recommended Reading

Best, A. L. (2000). *Prom Night: Youth, Schools, and Popular Culture.* New York: Routledge.

GenderPAC (February 2004). "Student Interest in GenderYOUTH Exploding." See News@GPAC.

McGarry, M., and Wasserman, F. (1998). *Becoming Visible: An Illustrated History of Lesbian and Gay Life in Twentieth-Century America.* New York: Penguin Studio.

Russell, S. T. (2002). "Queer in America: Sexual Minority Youth and Citizenship." *Applied Developmental Science,* 6: 258–263

Jessica Fields and Stephen T. Russell

R

Racial and Ethnic Inequality. Race relations constitute a complex and dynamic topic. The definition of race itself has been in flux with early conceptions of biological race replaced by recognition that race is a social construction.

One consistent theme dominates the history of race relations. White privilege in its many variations and manifestations is a common thread throughout. A racial hierarchy with whites on top and nonwhites below has existed since the beginning of U.S. history. However, there have been shifts in the positions of various nonwhite groups, and the rapid influx of new immigrants makes the future uncertain.

Minorities have endured harsh, dehumanizing treatment and overt discrimination at many points in U.S. history. The enslavement of blacks is one of the most powerful instances of such treatment. Slavery dramatically influenced American race relations, leaving social, psychological, and economic legacies. Even after the liberation of slaves, formal policies and informal practices ensured that blacks were treated as second-class citizens. Blacks' rights to integrated schooling and equal access to public accommodations were secured less than half a century ago. Another instance is the mistreatment of Native Americans. Hundreds of thousands died at the hands of whites, and survivors were forced from their homelands onto reservations. During World War II, Japanese Americans were forced to leave their homes and live in remote internment camps, despite the fact that most of the internees were American citizens and there was no evidence of disloyalty. The internees re-gained their freedom after the war, but their financial loss in homes, businesses, and forgone income is estimated at $4 billion.

Discrimination and inequality have continued into the latter half of the twentieth century. The case of residential segregation is a clear example of this. Segregation exists at alarmingly high levels, particularly for blacks. Residential segregation is not due to blacks' preferences to live in black neighborhoods; survey research demonstrates that most blacks prefer areas that are racially mixed. Nor do socioeconomic differences between blacks and whites explain residential segregation. If the socioeconomic explanation were true, rich blacks would live with rich whites and poor blacks with poor whites. This is not the case. In fact, segregation is mostly due to discriminatory policies and practices. Blacks and other minorities continue to receive inferior treatment from real estate and financial agencies. Minorities are still discouraged from buying or renting homes in mostly white neighborhoods and are more often denied mortgages than whites of comparable financial status. This is true despite legislation such as the Fair Housing Law of 1968, which prohibits discrimination in the sale, rental, and financing of housing, and the Home Mortgage Disclosure Act of 1975, which requires financial institutions to disclose all records to ensure that discrimination is not occurring.

Other tactics that maintain segregation fall outside the realm of the law. Intimidation has often been used to ensure that blacks feel uneasy in white neighborhoods. Although such strategies have become less common, their effect is pervasive: a substantial portion of blacks —60 percent— indicate they would not want to be the first to move in to an all-white neighborhood. Blacks' perceptions that white residents would be unwelcoming are not inaccurate. Although whites are gradually becoming more tolerant of living alongside blacks, there is a steady drop in whites' willingness to enter or stay in a neighborhood as the size of the black population increases, with less than half of whites willing to move into a neighborhood that is one-third black.

Why are high levels of housing segregation so detrimental? According to Myrdal (1944), segregation is a key factor accounting for blacks' subordinate status. Segregation ensures that blacks will not attend schools or share community-based facilities with whites and allows prejudiced white officials to provide poor services to blacks without harming whites. The isolation of blacks, particularly those in poor neighborhoods, may also encourage the development of an oppositional culture. That is, sometimes the intense frustration and rejection felt by blacks may foster norms and behaviors that directly oppose those of the middle-class white culture, further limiting blacks' mainstream success. Segregation also limits blacks' social networks, reducing the ability to obtain jobs and other resources. Overall then, segregation is a powerful detriment to blacks' success and happiness. Although blacks are more likely than other groups to experience segregation, segregated housing afflicts other groups as well. Hispanics are increasingly likely to be isolated in Hispanic and black neighborhoods, while Native Americans continue to be segregated on reservations.

Persistent racial disparities in education are another cause for concern, especially because education is a powerful determinant of other outcomes, such as occupation, income, and wealth. Whites and certain Asian subgroups tend to finish more years of schooling than most minorities. The black high-school dropout rate is approximately twice the rate for whites.

Blacks' rate of college attendance is relatively low and their attrition rate high, leaving blacks only half as likely as whites to complete a bachelor's degree. There are also telling differences in school quality. Minorities are more likely to attend schools with inadequate funding, underqualified teachers, and sub-par classrooms and teaching tools. Some of the differences in school quality are attributable to school segregation, which has recently been on the rise, for Hispanic as well as black children. In 2001 more than one-third of Hispanic children attended "intensely segregated" schools, where 90 percent or more of their classmates were minorities. An even larger proportion of black children attended schools where the minority enrollment was between 90 and 100 percent.

In light of the stark disparities in educational outcomes across racial groups, it is not surprising that income and wealth levels also vary dramatically across groups. First, sizeable income differences continue to exist, with whites on top. An apparent exception is Japanese Americans, who have similar levels of income to that of whites. However, closer examination shows that given their unparalleled educational achievement, Japanese Americans should have *higher* incomes than whites. The fact that their economic status is approximately equal to that of whites suggests that racial discrimination is at work, depressing Japanese American income from the very high levels their superior education should bring.

Also, there are vast racial differences in wealth—in assets such as homes, cars, land, and stocks. The discrepancy between the wealth of college-educated blacks and whites is alarming, college-educated blacks having an average of $15,250 in assets and college-educated whites an average of $44,069. Income and wealth are the "twin pillars" that help maintain a satisfactory quality of life, and a deficiency in wealth jeopardizes economic stability. In the absence of wealth, living standards become dependent on an uninterrupted source of earnings. Given that the unemployment rate for black men is approximately double that of white men, blacks' wealth deficiencies are particularly disadvantageous.

The wealth gap is significant not only for present inequality but for future inequality as well. First, research demonstrates that parents' wealth is a powerful predictor in determining whether their children attend and graduate from college. Given the enormous cost of college tuition, parents cannot afford to pay for college solely using income; thus, wealth becomes especially important in financing children's education. White parents' greater ability to assist their children's educational advancement ensures white children's economic advantage, maintaining race differences in socioeconomic status in the next generation. The unequal wealth distribution also maintains inequality by giving whites a greater ability to pass down valued assets across generations, reinforcing whites' position at the top of the economic ladder. Overall then, it is important to pay attention to trends in income *and* wealth. Even if the income gap were to close, differences in wealth would guarantee that an economic hierarchy would be maintained.

Minority status also costs people their health. Black Americans' life expectancies are far below those of whites, particularly among men. The life expectancy for black males born in 2000 is approximately 68.2 years, compared with 74.8 years for white men. Much of this gap is attributable to the racial disparity in mortality rates before age sixty. Large gaps in infant mortality also exist, as fourteen out of one thousand black babies born in 2001 died before they reached one year, compared with 5.7 out of one thousand white babies. Although this gap has closed slightly in the past few decades, it is not likely to disappear in the near future. In addition to living fewer years, blacks are more likely to live with chronic health problems. While earlier research suggested that genetic differences were responsible for such differences, recent literature indicates that health disparities are primarily attributable to other factors. First, whites' greater socioeconomic and racial status allows for better health care, resources to maintain a healthy diet, residence in areas with better air quality and sanitation, and increased exposure to health-related information. Racism is another factor that may depress minorities' health. The psychological distress associated with racism can take a toll on physical and mental health and may increase the likelihood of engaging in violence and substance abuse.

Improved health status among minorities might be seen if a universal health-care policy were to be enacted, reducing the "cost of being black." Such a policy would ensure that blacks would have access to health care in spite of their economic disadvantage, thus improving the overall health of the black population. However, it is likely that race differences in health will linger because blacks' inferior health is due not only to an inability to afford health coverage but also to features of black neighborhoods like overcrowded and underfunded hospitals, poor air quality, and the emotional stress of being black.

Overall, what accounts for the racial disparities discussed earlier? One factor is prejudice on the part of teachers, real-estate agents, employers, politicians, and health-care providers. *Prejudice* is a preconceived notion about a group that is often based on limited information. Prejudice may be the result of a number of processes. It may result when people classify others into "ingroups" and "outgroups" and, in service of self-esteem, favor ingroup members while assigning negative traits to outgroup members. Once at the top of the ladder, dominant group members may have developed strong feelings about the material entitlements of their group. This may result in feelings of threat when other groups demand or achieve equality.

Prejudice may also be learned from family members, peers, teachers, political figures, and media. Some suggest that prejudice is so deeply rooted in our culture that most people simply can't help but internalize it to varying degrees. As Beverly Tatum (1997) states, "Cultural racism ... is like smog in the air. Sometimes it is so thick it is visible, other times less apparent, but always, day in and day out, we are breathing it in. None of us would introduce ourselves as 'smog-breathers' (and most of us don't want to be described as prejudiced), but if we live in a smoggy place, how can we avoid breathing the air?" While many people fight to control these subconscious feelings of prejudice, they may nonetheless emerge.

It is important to note, however, that prejudice, which is a feeling, does not necessarily go hand in hand with *discrimination*, which is the differential treatment of people based on their group membership. Some people may be prejudiced and yet fail to act on their feelings, particularly when the norms or context don't encourage it. For example, a restaurant owner may have negative feelings toward blacks and therefore wish not to serve them but may in fact serve blacks in order to avoid confrontation or bad publicity. On the other hand, some may feel relatively open-minded toward other groups and yet will discriminate if the circumstances encourage it. For example, unprejudiced people may laugh at a racist joke or ignore a racist remark in order to avoid tension.

Discrimination may also occur in the absence of prejudice when policies that are driven by nonracial motives ultimately harm members of certain racial groups. The recruitment methods used by colleges and universities demonstrate this. Colleges often focus their recruitment efforts in communities that have traditionally sent them many students. These communities are more likely to be white and middle class, thereby ensuring that most recruits will be white and middle class as well. Such discrimination may be unintentional, but it has powerful, far-reaching consequences nonetheless. Of course there are cases in which institutional procedures

may be motivated by racial prejudice on the part of individuals with power. An alliance of prejudice and power is particularly insidious, as ill motives on the part of one or a few influential individuals can ultimately impair the lives of many.

While our discussion of past and current race relations may assist speculation about the future, a host of unprecedented factors make predictions rather tenuous. First, the "browning of America," which refers to the dramatic shift from European to Asian and Hispanic immigration since the 1960s, raises fresh questions regarding the trajectory of American race relations. It is unclear how fully new immigrants will assimilate into American culture, given the fact that many find permanent residence in ethnic neighborhoods. Some face barriers, such as housing discrimination, strong enough to ensure that residence outside ethnic enclaves is nearly impossible. Others choose to settle in these ethnic neighborhoods to benefit from the economic, social, and emotional support of their co-ethnics and to preserve ethnic identity and values.

This growth of the Hispanic and Asian populations, accompanied by residential clustering and cultural retention, may heighten whites' sense of threat. As a result, Asians and Hispanics may lose some of their status advantages relative to blacks. On the other hand, whites may adapt to the presence of a larger and possibly more culturally distinct immigrant population. And what would this mean for African Americans? White Anglo adaptation to the presence of larger and more distinct Hispanic and Asian populations might benefit blacks by reinforcing the value of racial and ethnic diversity. Conversely, it might preserve blacks' inferior status and carve a path toward a new racial hierarchy in which blackness, as opposed to whiteness, is a key grouping factor.

Immigration may affect race relations in other ways. Americans have grown increasingly wary of the potential effects of immigrants on national and local economies. Fears of the displacement of American workers, depression of wages, and drains on social services are potent and may potentially heighten interracial tensions. Also, susceptibility of the United States to illegal immigration plants fears about terrorist attacks similar to that of September 11, 2001. New measures to tighten security may depress the immigrant flow. Ironically, such exclusionary measures could ease racial tensions, by allowing the kind of breathing period that benefited earlier immigrants' assimilation, limiting immigrants' ties to their native culture and diminishing white threat.

A second unprecedented factor is the expanded black middle class. Middle-class status, whether based on income or self-employment, has been attained by a growing proportion of blacks. This development represents progress, but it also introduces complications. Middle-class blacks hold only a small fraction of the assets held by their typical white counterparts. Remembering the earlier discussion highlighting the importance of both income and wealth in maintaining economic stability, we must conclude that blacks' middle-class status is fragile. Also, the structure of the black community is becoming more and more unbalanced. The growing middle class has left behind an inner-city "underclass" facing dire poverty and acute social disorganization. In short, with a comfortable working class and a significant upper class missing, the black population is essentially bifurcated into two groups—one at significant economic disadvantage and the other only tenuously managing middle-class status. Predictions for the future are difficult.

A third source of uncertainly lies in equivocal evidence about trends in white racial attitudes. There are some indications that whites' attitudes toward minorities have become more liberal. For example, surveys show that Americans are generally more approving now of interracial marriage and electing a black president. However, several caveats are needed. First, attitudes do not necessarily translate into behavior. That is, whites may be increasingly likely to support racial equality in *principle*, but they may in fact be less supportive of the *implementation* of policies to correct racial inequality. For example, while white people are increasingly likely to say that they believe black and white children should attend the same schools, far fewer support government policies that would actually ensure school integration. This suggests that along with some positive shift in valuing racial equality, white survey respondents may feel increasing pressure to give the politically correct answers that they believe interviewers wish to hear. This makes valid assessment of white attitudes difficult.

Attenuation of prejudice since the 1950s is presumably part of the reason for deterioration of racial boundaries through higher rates of interracial marriage. Interracial marriages still make up a very small fraction of the total, but that fraction has grown from .7 percent in 1970 to 2.2 percent in 1992. Rates differ across racial groups with intermarriage most common between whites and Asian Americans, followed by whites and Hispanics. Unions between white and blacks are also on the rise, but they are the least common type of interracial marriage. The continued growth in interracial marriages, and the consequent rising number of interracial children, may eventually blur group boundaries in such a way that "race" becomes a meaningless construct. However, the intermarriage rate will have to increase dramatically in order for this to happen. Such an increase may or may not be in the cards.

A final factor that may influence intergroup boundaries is potential coalitions among have-nots of all racial groups. Minorities and poor whites may recognize that the most efficient way to undermine white privilege is to join collectively. Perhaps the future holds an alliance of various races and ethnicities in order to powerfully confront practices and processes that maintain racial and class inequality.

In sum, the coming decades carry the potential for far-reaching change in race and ethnic relations within the United States, but nothing is certain.

See also Civil Rights Movement; Ethnic Identity; Hip-Hop Generation; Racial Socialization; Religiosity and Civic Engagement in African American Youth; Social Justice.

Recommended Reading

Conley, D. (1999). *Being Black, Living in the Red: Race, Wealth, and Social Policy in America*. Berkeley: University of California Press.

Farley, R., Steeh, C., Krysan, M., Jackson, T., and Reeves, K. (1994). "Stereotypes and Segregation: Neighborhoods in the Detroit Area." *American Journal of Sociology*, 100: 750–780.

Myrdal, G. (1944). *An American Dilemma: The Negro Problem and Modern Democracy*. New York: Harper and Row.

Schuman, H., Steeh, C., Bobo, L., and Krysan, M. (1997). *Racial Attitudes in America: Trends and Interpretations*. Cambridge: Harvard University Press.

Tatum, B. (1997). *Why Are All the Black Kids Sitting Together in the Cafeteria? and Other Conversations about Race*. New York: Basic Books.

Yinger, J. (1995). *Closed Doors, Opportunities Lost: The Continuing Costs of Housing Discrimination*. New York: Russell Sage Foundation.

Meredith J. Greif and Marylee C. Taylor

Racial Socialization. The term racial socialization has been defined as the ability for adults to communicate messages about race to children who are primarily black in a society in which being black has negative connotations. This task shared by all parents involves the responsibility of teaching young black children to be physically and emotionally sound individuals in a predominately majority culture. Not all black parents believe in socializing their children to deal with race, but those who do find that their children are better able to handle unreceptive and unfriendly settings across America.

Parents who do subscribe to the role of racial socialization use a variety of messages and techniques. Several types of messages, images, and activities around race and cultural pride are typically used by parents. For example, a young couple may organize a family trip to the Martin Luther King Museum in Atlanta, Georgia. Along the route, planned stops include houses, businesses, and other establishments that were of importance during the civil rights movement. Another family may choose to keep a number of books and other literature in the home that demonstrate the positive contributions of black Americans in society. Despite the method used, black parents have found that teaching young black children how to cope with the reality of race and discrimination will stunt the blow later in life.

Families are critical to the racial socialization process. They provide the foundation of attitudes, norms, values, and behaviors. Black children who have a foundation set in positive images and beliefs are in a better position to become resilient to the potential challenges of life. In addition to this, they are aware of historical, political, and social struggles of their race. Black families who engage in the racial socialization process are priming their children to be strong, independent individuals who are able to become productive citizens in a society.

In addition to having a direct impact on the behaviors and beliefs of young people, racial socialization has also had a direct influence on group identity and collective behaviors. Young people who are cognizant of themselves are more aware of their identity group and in essence are more likely to identify with people who reflect their beliefs, attitudes, and cultural heritage. Racial identity allows children to share a common racial heritage with a particular group. For young black children this can be seen in neighborhood playgroups and classrooms. In adolescents group identity is found among school lunchrooms and social cliques in mixed cultural settings. It is even prevalent on college campuses, such as the black Greek organizations of fraternities and sororities and other campus groups. Cultural identity becomes an integral part of self-identity especially in situations where black youth are in predominately white schools or institutions. Take for instance the lunchroom where one can find segmented populations. Blacks, whites, Asians, and Hispanics are all sitting in their respective groups throughout the lunchroom. While racial identity tends to create segmented pockets of individuals, it does create a natural buffer for young people to defend against psychological insults and disappointments. Racial identity supports young people's abilities to feel confident about themselves, to feel positive about their race, and to behave in an optimistic manner when faced with negativity about their race or ethnic group.

Racial socialization has a profound effect on young black children and activism. Since they have been exposed to a positive perspective about themselves and their culture, they are in prime positions to engage in activities that will lead to an improved world. Young black children who understand the cultural, social, and political history of their race are more likely to engage in activities that will continue to promote the legacy of their race. As they grow and develop into young adults, they are likely to carry the message of the Freedom Riders, the Student Nonviolent Coordinating Committee (SNCC), and other young activists groups created during the civil rights era. Black children who have been a part of the racial socialization process have the ability to provide a different perspective to community engagement and activism.

The developmental period of racial socialization provides young black youth with a positive exposure and understanding of their culture. Activism for black youth may take the form of connectedness with community, church, social groups, or political organizations. Salient topics for racially socialized youth may appear in the form of issues that impact their race and cultural identity. While black youth may become involved in activities, they may find themselves much more likely to volunteer for groups that have a direct impact on their culture or racial identity. For example, engaged black youth may find it important to focus on issues relevant to black communities such as access to quality goods and services, affordable heath care, quality education for all ages, safety, and adequate jobs and services in communities.

Activism within racially socialized black youth will inherently influence group interaction, group identity, racial group interaction, and the ability to see themselves as change agents in their communities.

See also Ethnic Identity; Racial and Ethnic Inequality; Religiosity and Civic Engagement in African American Youth.

Recommended Reading

Allen, R., and Bagozzi, R. (2001). "Cohort Differences in the Structure and Outcomes of an African American Belief." *Journal of Black Psychology*, 27: 367–400.

Cheatham, H. E., and Stewart, J. B. (1990). *Black Families Interdisciplinary Perspective*. New Brunswick, NJ: Transaction Publishers.

Tatum, B. D. (1997). *Why Are All the Black Kids Sitting Together in the Cafeteria? and Other Conversations about Race*. New York: Basic Books.

Thomas, A. J., and Speight, S. L. (1999). "Racial Identity and Racial Socialization Attitudes of African American Parents. *Journal of Black Psychology*, 25 (2): 152–170.

Nicole Webster

Religiosity and American Youth. Overall, religious involvement remains relatively high in the United States among adolescents by contrast with trends for many other Western countries. While weekly church attendance by adolescents has decreased by about 8 percent between 1976 and 1999, religious beliefs remain an important aspect of adolescents' lives in the United States, and religion has a powerful impact on adolescents and their development.

This entry will seek to clarify the following: (1) the important influences on the development and maintenance of religious beliefs and practices among youth, (2) the relationship between juvenile religiosity and indicators of adjustment, including

Teenagers pass the offering basket at church. *Courtesy of Skjold Photographs.*

mood, substance use, and expressions of sexuality, and, perhaps most importantly, (3) the components of religious beliefs and practices that may account for its tonic influence on adolescent adjustment.

Religious socialization literature has generally focused on three agents that influence religiosity among youth: parents, peers, and educational systems (including church). Overall, it appears that parental religiousness, with mothers being more influential than fathers, exercises the most important influence in the developing religious attitudes and practices of children and adolescents, both directly through modeling overt religiosity (e.g., church attendance) and indirectly through the management of other influences (e.g., the selection of primary and secondary schools), which in turn may have some influence on young people's religion. Perhaps not surprisingly, the research literature indicates that parental influence becomes weaker as adolescents grow into adulthood.

Beyond parental influence, church is most often found to be a significant contributor to religious socialization, especially in middle adolescence at roughly the time when young people may be less susceptible to parental influence. While there are certainly explanatory hypotheses for this influence of church, which will be discussed below, research is needed to identify how exposure to regular church attendance, church teachings, and religious rituals may influence adolescent religiosity.

While relatively few studies have isolated the effect of peer influence on religiousness, it appears that peer influence may exercise a supplementary reinforcing effect, augmenting the more direct influence of parental religiousness. That is, when parents and peers are articulating and practicing the same religious beliefs and traditions, the adolescent is all the more likely to endorse that brand of religiosity. Concerning the effect of educational systems, the bulk of evidence suggests that church-related school attendance has little direct influence on adolescent religiousness but, like peer influence, may exercise a supplementary reinforcing effect to parental religiousness. More specifically, if parents and the church emphasize the same religious perspective, the resulting combined religious socialization effects may be especially strong. On the other hand, if parents rely entirely on religious educational systems to promote religious attitudes and practices among their children, they will likely be disappointed by the end results.

Overall, it appears that religiosity is associated with a host of positive values and behaviors and may function as a protector against threats to normal adjustment, such as drug and alcohol use, promiscuous sexuality, and depression and suicide.

A large body of literature indicates that two key indicators of religiosity, namely church attendance and the self-reported importance of religious faith, are associated with reduced rates of drug, alcohol, and tobacco use, as well as with fewer reports of delinquency and suicide (actual and attempted) among American teenagers. Religiosity also appears associated with lower reported levels of depression and hopelessness, which may explain its negative association with suicidality. Finally, research indicates that religiosity is associated with a fewer number of sexual partners, reduced frequency of sexual intercourse, and reduced teenage pregnancy.

Religiosity has also been associated with a range of positive health promoting behaviors, including better diet, exercise, sleep, dental hygiene, and seatbelt use. Church attendance and positive perceptions of religion have also been associated with positive school attitudes and behaviors, as well as with greater political involvement and community service.

In sum, it appears that religiosity represents a body of overwhelmingly positive, healthy attitudes and practices that promote well-being and protect against impulsivity and its negative consequences. While research is in progress to explore the reasons for these positive benefits of religiosity, some preliminary explanations are explored below.

One of the most important functions of religion is to pass on a set of values or universal moral standards according to which adherents may make personal and professional choices. As such, American religions can provide adolescents with substantive normative directives by which to conduct their lives, and these directives are particularly useful to youth who are asking critical questions about their own identities, values, and places in the world. Not surprisingly, religious youth are more involved in political and civic engagements and are less prone to activities that are associated with a more diffuse identity (e.g., substance abuse, promiscuity, depression). By eliminating or substantially reducing the experiences of confusion about matters of morality, meaning of life, and purposes of work and love, religious moral codes are likely to enhance security among adolescents and liberate their energies for investment in positive contributions to peers, family, and to their larger social networks.

Another key contribution of religion is to ensure that spiritual experiences are transmitted to church constituents, giving confidence to believers in their exercise of moral virtues and confirming the presence of a benevolent and loving divine presence. The awareness of a transcendent presence in daily life, that is, an awareness of something larger than all that one can objectively contain or measure, has been associated with lower alcohol and drug use and with more positive effects among freshmen college students, and this association bears replication with younger adolescents. It is likely that spiritual transcendence affords a larger perspective on the purpose and direction of one's life by reassuring the believer that some divine presence is looking after them and guiding their paths and that they are not alone in their quest for meaning. As such, spiritual transcendence may mitigate the sense of isolation that frequently accompanies the adolescent preoccupation with separation from parents and may facilitate the transition to a healthy exercise of autonomy.

American religions likewise provide youth with adult and peer-group role models, who demonstrate by their enactment of values that the church's moral directives are feasible, although perhaps not immediately gratifying (e.g., sexual abstinence). These coping models likely provide support and encouragement to youth, reminding them of the purpose of living a moral life. These role models may also motivate youth to sustain their commitment to the enactment of moral virtues, by linking adolescent compliance with the maintenance of their company, the approval of a respected body of elders, and the blessing of God. These are apt to serve as powerful motivational forces to account for the commitment of youth to living a moral life.

Besides exposure to moral guidelines, spiritual experiences, and role models, religious participation may contribute to certain learned competencies that are associated with better adjustment. Among these competencies are religious coping skills, community and leadership skills, and a broader cultural awareness that may be associated with increased tolerance for complexity.

Confronted by a host of stressors in adolescence, many are at a loss for how to cope with diverse demands on their time and attention. Religiosity offers youth ways to use their beliefs and practices to cope with these stressors and to find peace. For example, youth may be encouraged to collaborate with God in getting through a difficult time and to turn to God's strength and direction as a partner in managing stress and finding solutions to their problems. They might likewise be encouraged to put their problems in God's hands and to let God take control of their lives, thereby relieving them of the burden of finding solutions on their own. These patterns of collaborative and deferring religious coping have been studied extensively among various age groups facing diverse life challenges, and they are associated with successful coping, more positive mood, and more satisfying emotional well-being overall. Having a secure relationship with God and allowing God to assist in times of trial is associated with positive outcomes whereas having an insecure, unstable relationship with God, in which the individual may perceive that God is punitive or that the devil is in control is, not surprisingly, associated with more negative outcomes in terms of emotional and even physical well-being.

Beyond an overall positive religious coping style, religiosity may also direct youth to engage in certain practices that are associated with good mental hygiene. For example, research has supported the association of prayer and meditation with physical and mental health benefits across the life cycle. In addition, the practice of forgiveness may be an especially useful practice for youth, who in their process of self-identification and shifting allegiances may especially benefit from strategies to repair relationships, instead of holding grudges and suffering the unhealthy consequences of unexpressed anger or unbridled aggression.

Because religious beliefs and practices are perpetuated in the context of community settings (i.e., church, mosque, or synagogue), religious participation often initiates youth, directly or indirectly, into the practice of organizational and leadership skills. As churches are organizations that rely largely on the volunteer efforts of the members, youth are frequently included in the organization of various tasks and outreach efforts, and they are charged with responsibilities under the mentorship of more senior peers or adults. These experiences of guided exposure to initiating projects and seeing them through to completion, as well as of receiving the feedback and appreciation of members who are being served by their efforts, will likely serve to develop skills that will be useful to the young adult throughout his or her lifetime and that will afford adaptive outlets to creative energies in adolescence. This aspect of religiosity may thereby serve the twofold purpose of distracting the youth from boredom and frustration—frequent adolescent complaints—and at the same time directing the youth to engage in purposeful activity that has very tangible results in which he or she may take pride.

Cultural exposure is yet another benefit of religiosity that may influence positive attitudes and more adaptive behaviors in adolescence. Through Bible study and familiarity with sacred scriptures, church participation affords opportunities to learn about a different culture, its traditions, its history, and in some cases to learn its language. These experiences have the potential to expand the worldview of the adolescent and to foster a broader tolerance for diverse viewpoints. This is not always the case, however, with certain religious traditions that may emphasize intolerance and rigid conformity with one's own tradition as superior to others, but it is more often the case that religious organizations defend the values of tolerance and mutual respect. Exposure to other cultures that were the first bearers of one's religious tradition will likely increase such tolerance and promote more healthy attitudes toward other cultures and traditions.

In a similar vein, participation in church life regularly exposes youth to a range of age groups, enabling young people to interact with other peers, younger and older, as well as with adults who may range in age across several generations. Particularly in an age of the breakdown of the nuclear family, in which routine expressions of affection and support between siblings and across generations are often sacrificed in the name of efficiency (i.e., to facilitate maximum participation in employment or sport), this unique forum for interpersonal and transgenerational expression may afford a unique opportunity to develop skills at communicating with younger and older people. The challenge of these encounters is to put one's needs and interests in language that can be understood and appreciated by various age groups, and these communication skills may account for the success of religious youth in verbalizing their needs more effectively, rather than acting them out in destructive ways.

By all accounts, religiosity appears to serve a positive function in the adjustment and well-being of youth, and while the specific mechanisms by which it achieves this success are not yet definitively substantiated by empirical research, this entry has explored some plausible explanations for its tonic effects. Future inquiry would

profitably include measures of the constructs discussed above in longitudinal study designs to detect how well religiosity and its various correlates do indeed protect youth and promote emotional and behavioral adjustment.

See also Campus Crusade for Christ International (CCC); Catholic Education and the Ethic of Social Justice; Religiosity and Civic Engagement in African American Youth; Spirituality.

Recommended Reading

Cobb, N. J. (2001). *Adolescence: Continuity, Change, and Diversity*, 4th ed. Mountain View, CA: Mayfield.

Hyde, K.E. (1990). *Religion in Childhood and Adolescence: A Comprehensive Review of the Research*. Birmingham, AL: Religious Education Press.

Spilka, B., Hood, R., Hunsberger, B., and Gorsuch, R., eds. (2003). *The Psychology of Religion*. New York: Guilford Press.

John Cecero

Religiosity and Civic Engagement in African American Youth. Religion is defined as an organized system of beliefs, practices, and rituals that help people connect to the sacred or transcendent (i.e., God, higher power, ultimate truth) and that encourage people to understand their relationship responsibility to others. Civic engagement offers opportunities for people to express their religious beliefs and values through activities such as volunteer work and political activism. It is not surprising that African American religiosity and civic engagement share a long history given the social and historical context surrounding African American religiosity.

The roots of African American religion can be traced back hundreds of years to the time of slavery. In the early 1600s the first African slaves arrived at the English colonies. Along with them came African spiritual beliefs. Traditional African religions made no distinction between the sacred and secular or between this life and life after death. All of life was part of a continuum in which the living, as well as dead ancestors, participated. Although most

A thirteen-year-old African American girl prays while kneeling in the pew of her church. *Courtesy of Skjold Photographs.*

African tribes believed in a supreme being, they also believed many other spirits existed in the trees, the rivers, the sun, and other places in nature. Thus, the slaves were pagans in the eyes of their predominately Christian slave owners and efforts to convert them to Christianity began.

Large numbers of African Americans converted to evangelical Christianity during the religious revival periods known as the Great Awakenings from the 1740s through the 1780s. The type of evangelical Christianity encouraged by slave owners in the South was aimed at preserving the southern way of life. The slave owners did not want African Americans to read biblical scriptures for themselves for fear they would begin to see themselves as equal to whites. State legislatures were pressured to pass laws inhibiting African Americans from assembling to worship on their own and from becoming literate. Religion was

meant to offer solace for pain and sorrow and provide reason for joy, praise, and hope through focus on otherworldly goals rather than on the struggles of this life. If the slaves learned to turn the other cheek and focus on their rewards in the next life, they might be more willing to accept their current fate in life.

Despite the best efforts of the slave owners, some African Americans learned to read and began to study the Bible for themselves. The desire to practice their religion in their own way, including interpretation of religious scriptures, inspired the formation of "invisible" churches where African Americans gathered in secret to practice their faith. They would meet in secluded locations late at night to sing, pray, and preach. They learned speaking skills, received food and clothing when needed, and were given encouragement to survive the harsh realities of slavery. The religious community provided a sense of family to slaves, who were often denied even basic associations with their families, and encouraged commitment to the well-being of others.

Their religion also fostered a belief in "freedom to be as God had intended all men and women to be. Free to belong to God." Slave narratives reveal images of themselves as soldiers in a war against oppression. African American leaders emerged from the invisible churches, and rebellion against slavery began. Thus, the intertwining of African American religion with civic engagement grew strong hidden in the invisible churches of the African American slaves.

After the Civil War the civic involvement of the African American churches continued by providing slaves with economic education, encouraging them to be educated, helping keep families together, and training leaders of the black community. The civic role of the church, no longer the invisible institution it was during slavery, remained much the same after emancipation as before. Freedom from slavery was followed by one hundred years of segregation and racism that prohibited African Americans from participating in mainstream society. The African American churches continued to provide for those in need and to call for social change. The struggle for freedom from slavery was replaced by the struggle for freedom to be educated, employed, and to move freely in white society.

The civil rights movement grew out of and was inspired by African American religious institutions. Prior to the Voting Rights Act of 1965, African Americans did not have equal access to politics as a means for social change. The black church was the only institution controlled by African Americans and as such became a focal point for leaders of the civil rights movement.

Even today, social justice and community involvement are the primary roles served by African American churches. Churches are central to African American communities. They provide social and economic support by providing health and medical care, food and education services, attending to families with special needs, and providing a network of friends. Churches also foster African American cultural identity and encourage social-justice projects. Study of civic life in an African American community in Chicago revealed that cultural practices within the African American church strengthen group identity and serve as a resource for political organizing and activism. The cultural practices included holding hands during prayer, call-and-response interaction, singing, clapping, and swaying to music. In addition to encouraging solidarity through cultural practices, African American religiosity also provides a sacred higher purpose that justifies involvement in political action.

While African American religious beliefs, values, and practices encourage civic involvement in many forms, there continues to be tension between an "other worldly" and "this worldly" focus in African American religiosity. Some people

believe African American religiosity encourages too much of an "other worldly" focus that offers escape from and avoidance of the injustices in life rather than trying to change them. These people believe the African American church should be a force for change and resistance to the current social structures as well as providing for those who are disadvantaged. Regardless of an "other worldly" or "this worldly" orientation, African American religious ideology encourages civic engagement in a variety of ways.

In addition to the dual role of the African American church in providing for needs in the community and empowering the black community to seek social change, church civic-engagement activities can also promote healthy development for African American youth. Whether it is through activism, such as the Million Man March in Washington in the mid-1990s or service activities in the local community, religion-based civic activities related to caring for those in need, creating better neighborhoods, and working for social change also benefit future generations of African Americans. Involvement of youth in religious civic activities encourages development of prosocial and moral values, a sense of a larger purpose in life, good coping skills, a sense of being connected and valued by the religious community, and many other assets that facilitate and promote healthy development. African American churches are in a unique position to promote healthy physical, psychological, intellectual, emotional, and social development for African American youth through civic-engagement activities.

In 2002 the National Research Council issued a report that identified personal and social assets and characteristics of contexts that facilitate positive youth development (see Eccles and Gootman 2002). For example, safety is a basic need to support positive development. Safety includes physical safety from violence and unsafe health conditions, as well as psychological safety. As influential institutions in African

American communities, churches can influence the social norms that promote safety in local communities. Also, churches are most likely one of the safest places in the neighborhood where youth are less likely to be the victims of violence or to witness violence.

In addition to providing safety, churches can provide youth with developmentally appropriate levels of structure. Children need to experience stability and predictability in their environments. Adolescents also benefit from clear rules, expectations, and consistently enforced limits on their behavior. The structure needs to match the age of the youth with younger children needing more structure than older youth, who need more autonomy. Church civic activities that monitor and enforce rules and expectations encourage engagement and connection to the church.

Connection is another important feature of environments that promote healthy development. Given their social and historical development, African American churches should also excel in providing opportunities for youth to experience feelings of belonging to the religious community. Youth who have a strong sense of membership and belonging to a group are less antisocial and more committed to social responsibility. African American churches also encourage a strong ethnic identity, feelings of belonging to one's ethnic group, which corresponds with more positive self-esteem, stronger ego identity, and greater involvement in school.

Supportive social networks are also a cornerstone of African American churches and meet another need of youth. Social support means relationships with adults that offer secure attachments, warmth, support, and good communication. Support includes emotional support as well as guidance that helps young people with problems and decisions in life. Supportive relationships with adults provide youth with good role modeling and constructive feedback to benefit their physical, intellectual, psychological, and social growth.

African American religious institutions may serve as a major conveyer of prosocial norms to youth. Religious groups, like other groups, develop a group "culture" that includes not only beliefs, values, and attitudes but also behavioral norms. When youth participate in religious services that encourage prosocial values and in activities that demonstrate positive behaviors, these group norms can have lasting effects on their behavior. Religious youth are less likely to be involved in problem behaviors such as substance abuse, premature sexual involvement, and delinquency. African American youth who participate in religious services and civic-engagement activities may internalize prosocial norms that shape their future community service and social justice activism behaviors.

African American religious institutions that provide opportunities to be of service in their communities and participate in social activism activities can contribute to youth's sense of efficacy and feelings that they can make a difference. African American religious institutions emphasize the importance of being involved and making a difference, and they offer options for youth to participate in these activities. In addition to fostering a sense of mattering, civic-engagement opportunities also provide opportunities to build life skills, including social skills.

The dire circumstances of slavery gave birth to African American religiosity. Through continued economic, social, and political exclusion, African American churches became more communal and more encompassing of community needs than most European American religious institutions. African American churches not only played a crucial role in social-justice movements, such as the civil rights movement, but they continue to be important in organizing a variety of civic activities that benefit the African American community at local and global levels.

See also Campus Crusade for Christ International (CCC); Catholic Education and the Ethic of Social Justice; Ethnic

Identity; Minority Youth Voter Turnout; Racial and Ethnic Inequality; Racial Socialization; Religiosity and American Youth; Spirituality.

Recommended Reading

Eccles, J. S., and Gootman, J. A., eds. (2002). *Community Programs to Promote Youth Development*. Washington, D.C.: National Academy Press.

Frazier, E. F. (1964). *The Negro Church in America*. New York: Schocken.

Harris, F. (1994). "Something Within: Religion as a Mobilize of African American Political Activism." *Journal of Politics*, 56: 42–68.

Lincoln, E. C., and Mamiya, L. (1990). *The Black Church in the African American Experience*. Durham, NC: Duke University Press.

Patillo-McCoy, M. (December 1998). "Church Culture as a Strategy of Action in the Black Community." *American Sociological Review*, 63: 767–784.

Janice Templeton and Jacquelynne Eccles

Rights of Participation of Children and Youth.

In 1989 the United Nations (UN) adopted the Convention on the Rights of the Child (CRC), a set of universal standards for the protection and development of children that has been ratified by all member nations of the United Nations except the United States. This document has extraordinary implications for how children and youth should be perceived and treated. Because many countries have extended childhood by keeping children in school, the *child* in the CRC refers to "every human being under the age of eighteen years unless, under the law applicable to the child, majority is attained earlier." For this reason, the term "child" is used in this essay to cover this age range. In many countries the CRC has stimulated the growth of a new vision of childhood. In addition to articles of the CRC that guarantee children's rights to survival, proper development, and protection from abuse and exploitation, the CRC takes the remarkable step of stressing that children should be thought of as active citizens with the kinds of civil rights that most people had previously not associated with children, including the right to be heard on all matters that

concern them, according to their capacity. The so-called "participation articles" are designed in part to further guarantee children's protection as individuals with rights rather than possessions by stating that children should know about their rights and be able to voice them, but they are also visionary articles which recognize children as developing citizens. They are a challenge to every nation.

The CRC is meant to serve as a standard for the establishment of national legal and moral codes concerning children. The extent to which they successfully do that is reviewed regularly by the UN Committee on the Rights of the Child. It will take a long time before we see broad changes in attitudes toward children's participation in civic life in most countries, but the CRC is a very well written document that can serve as a most valuable instrument of persuasion for those persons wishing to promote the idea of children and youth as independent, thinking subjects capable and deserving of a greater degree of participation. Even in the United States, where it has not been ratified, it can be used in support of youth activism because it has universal recognition and is increasingly treated by nations as a set of universal norms, even without the United States' recognition.

Children's Participation As Recognized in the UN Convention

Those sections of the CRC that are most relevant to the issue of child and youth participation are reproduced below. The first four articles listed focus most exclusively on the right to participate. An additional four are added because they are also explicit in their recognition of the importance of maximizing children's involvement according to their capacities. (The italicized headings are *by the author*.)

Freedom of Expression

Article 12

1. States Parties shall assure to the child who is capable of forming his or her own views the right to express those

views freely in all matters affecting the child, the views of the child being given due weight in accordance with the age and maturity of the child.

2. For this purpose, the child shall in particular be provided the opportunity to be heard in any judicial and administrative proceedings affecting the child, either directly, or though a representative or an appropriate body, in a manner consistent with the procedural rules of national law.

Article 13

1. The child shall have the right to freedom of expression; this right shall include freedom to seek, receive, and impart information and ideas of all kinds, regardless of frontiers, either orally, in writing or in print, in the form of art, or through other media of the child's choice.

2. The exercise of this right may be subject to certain restriction, but these shall only be such as are provided by law and are necessary:
   a. For respect of the rights and reputations of others; or
   b. For the protection of national security or of public order (ordure public), or of public health and morals.

Freedom of Thought, Conscience, and Religion

Article 14

1. States Parties shall respect the right of the child to freedom of thought, conscience, and religion.

2. States Parties shall respect the rights and duties of the parents and, when applicable, legal guardians, to provide direction to the child in the exercise of his or her right in a manner consistent with the evolving capacities of the child.

3. Freedom to manifest one's religion or beliefs may be subject only to such implications as are prescribed by law and are necessary to protect public safety, order, health or morals, or the fundamental right and freedoms of others.

Freedom of Assembly

Article 15

1. States Parties recognize the rights of the child to freedom of association and freedom of peaceful assembly.

2. No restrictions may be placed on the exercise of these rights other than those imposed in conformity with the law and which are necessary in a democratic society in the interests of national security or public safety, public order (order public), the protection of public health or morals, or the protection of the rights and freedoms of others.

Access to Information

Article 17

States Parties recognize the important function performed by the mass media and shall ensure that the child has access to information and material from a diversity of national and international sources, especially those aimed at the promotion of his or her social, spiritual, and moral well-being and physical and mental health. To this end, States Parties shall:

   a. Encourage the mass media to disseminate information and material of social and cultural benefit to the child and in accordance with the spirit of article 29;
   b. Encourage international cooperation in the production, exchange, and dissemination of such information and material from a diversity of cultural, national, and international sources;
   c. Encourage the production and dissemination of children's books;
   d. Encourage the mass media to have particular regard to the linguistic needs of the child who belongs to a minority group or who is indigenous;
   e. Encourage the development of appropriate guidelines for the protection of the child from information and material injurious to his or her well-being, bearing in mind the provisions of articles 13 and 18.

Special Support for Disabled Children

Article 23

1. States Parties recognize that a mentally or physically disabled child

should enjoy a full and decent life in conditions which ensure dignity, promote self-reliance, and facilitate the child's active participation in the community.

Education for Personal Fulfillment and Responsible Citizenship

Article 29

1. States Parties agree that the education of the child shall be directed to:
   a. The development of the child's personality, talents, and mental and physical abilities to their fullest potential;
   b. The development of respect for human rights and fundamental freedoms, and for the principles enshrined in the Charter of the United Nations;
   c. The development of respect for the child's parents, his or her own cultural identity, language, and values, for the national values of the country in which the child is living, the country from which he or she may originate, and for civilizations different from his or her own;
   d. The preparation of the child for responsible life in a free society, in the spirit of understanding, peace, tolerance, equality of sexes, and friendship among all peoples, ethnic, national, and religious groups and persons of indigenous origin;
   e. The development of respect for the natural environment.
2. No part of the present article or article 28 shall be construed so as to interfere with the liberty of individuals and bodies to establish and direct educational institutions, subject always to the observance of the principles set forth in paragraph 1 of the present article and to the requirements that the education given in such institutions shall conform to such minimum standards as may be laid down by the State.

Play and Participation in Cultural and Artistic Life

Article 31

1. States Parties recognize the right of the child to rest and leisure, to engage in play and recreational activities appropriate to the age of the child, and to participate freely in cultural life and the arts.
2. States Parties shall respect and promote the right of the child to participate fully in cultural and artistic life and shall encourage the provision of appropriate and equal opportunities for cultural, artistic, recreational, and leisure activity.

Why Young People Need to Be Allowed to Participate

There are at least three ways that the CRC specifically emphasizes children's right to participate: for children to be enabled to protect themselves, for their needs to be met, and, more generally, because participation is fundamental to their development. Most crucially, it is believed that giving children more of a voice in their own self-determination will improve the protective aspects of the CRC. It is probably this theme more than any other that has convinced the UN Committee on the Rights of the Child since they began reviewing the compliance of nations to the CRC that the participation articles are critical to its success in any country—more like a primary principle that runs through the CRC than just a set of articles. Equally important is the right for a child to know about his or her rights. The most documented violations to date have concerned street children and working children, commercially sexually exploited children, and children denied the care of their families in abusive kinds of institutional care, but the process is gradually expanding to other, more hidden, domains like domestic child abuse. The second reason the CRC gives for involving children in decisions is for their needs to be better met. The simple point here is that if children's services and programs are to be appropriate to them, then to the maximal degree possible children should have a voice in expressing their needs. Finally, the CRC builds from the well-established theories of child development which state that children develop to their fullest and as more flexible individuals when they're participating maximally in their own development and learning.

While the CRC calls for children to be allowed to participate in the cultural life of their communities, it does not specify community development. But this is a natural extension from many of the other articles, particularly article 12 on the right to participate in decisions that affect the child. Furthermore, genuine participation in the community fosters a sense of local responsibility and the development of citizenship. Many international nongovernmental organizations (NGOs) working for children—most notably the largest one, the International Save the Children Alliance—now emphasize citizenship in children and see participation as an integral aspect of that. But in spite of the clear implications of the CRC for children's participation in so many aspects of their everyday lives, there's still a great emphasis of many NGOs and international development agencies concerned with children on emphasizing children's formal participation in the political arena. Regrettably, this is almost always in single, high-profile events like conferences and forums. This seems to be a misguided emphasis for a variety of reasons. First of all, to pull select children together for occasional meetings where they have a voice about political affairs without knowing anything about their everyday participation seems delusional at best and may even be deceptive. More specifically, if we do not have everyday structures for children's participation, it's difficult to know how any government agency could responsibly invite children's participation in a way that would be representative of all children. It's true that such nonrepresentative structures are common in the adult world, but if we're talking about children's participation as part of a new and improved vision of democracy, then surely we need to do it in a

way which is more authentic. There is a need for fewer trite examples of children speaking or singing about how they are the future or how they alone best understand global environmental problems and more models that genuinely recognize the untapped competencies of children to play a significant role in community-based sustainable development, particularly when collaborating with adults.

There is by no means a common understanding of citizenship in the increasing international discourse of children as citizens. Some international children's agencies argue that the participatory language of the CRC relates to new theories of citizenship and to more direct or participatory democracy. Some critics, however, fear that this is an extension of the naïveté of liberal democratic theory: that children are individual citizens with a voice but not recognizing the enormous material differences in the abilities of families to lay the foundations for their children to compete equally in an ever more aggressive global marketplace. A more extreme position is posed by those who see children as an underprivileged class, in opposition to adult culture. Some of the clearest statements describing children as an underclass that needs to be empowered have come from some members of the movement for street and working children in Latin America. The term *"protaganismo"* is used by this movement to refer to the idea that children must be the protagonists of their own rights and see themselves as conscious agents of social change. The movement is concerned with achieving a redefinition of power in society, based in a direct questioning of the nature of adult power. This new social movement emerged because of the conclusion of many children's rights promoters that "protectionism" still dominates the conception of work with children throughout the world, and that is still ineffective in helping the masses of children who work at a very young age or are abused, neglected, or even involved in warfare. The best protection and guarantee for the development of childhood, they believe, is self-protection.

The NGOs that work with street and working children in many countries have helped children read and interpret the CRC as a way of empowering them in the struggle to improve their lives. These street workers, or "promoters," as they are often called in Latin America, see themselves as offering a supportive role for the children who must learn to be protagonists. It is ironic that in many countries the principles of the CRC are better known by children who are illiterate and who live primarily on the streets, beyond the influence of their families, than by those who are well-off and live within the homes of intact families. Sadly, this is not also true of the millions of working children who are hidden even from the street workers, trapped inside factories or in domestic slavery inside homes. It is also particularly difficult to promote children's right to education and participation in those very poor families that rely on the income of their children's labor in the short term and themselves lack basic human rights.

Whichever orientation one has toward citizenship in childhood it is clear that there has been a great change in the way many organizations see children's political agency in dozens of countries. As the movement for children's rights as citizens expands, it is increasingly being recognized that there is a need to evaluate the impact of their participatory experiences. Is the international promotion of children's participation leading children to think more about issues of the public good, about the rights of all to have a voice regardless of age or special characteristics? Already some agencies are trying to measure the import of participatory programs on local social capital where civic community is something that is made up of more horizontal relationships. There are already some exciting signs in many countries that new forms of highly inclusive children's organizations based on the principles of children's rights are emerging that move us forward from the models of youth participation in the twentieth century with their emphasis on "leadership" training. These new organizations bring the values of human rights and the skills of building more horizontal relationships and patterns of power.

Children on the Cultural Front Line

Giving children a voice to speak out about their rights without regard to its cultural appropriateness might be thought of as just another example of the inappropriate universalizing of the norms of the dominant cultures of "the North" or "minority world." The question of with whom and how a child may speak in any culture goes to the core of that culture's ideas of child rearing. Yet most observers of children's lives across cultures would argue that the CRC has already been a valuable instrument for improving the lives of many children, particularly those who are abused and neglected. Many would also argue that having children know their rights and being able to speak out about them has often been crucial to their protection. There is a need for an ongoing critical debate on this topic in all nations in order to successfully navigate the difficult territory that lies between the danger of universalizing norms of acceptable behavior for children and the danger of a cultural relativity that holds the naïve believe that children in some cultures may never need to know that they have rights. Many authors have struggled with the question of how to achieve some international norms for children without imposing them through a universalization of the norms, yet without completely eroding them through arguments of cultural relativity. One route is to achieve normative consensus through a principle of "procedural universality." This involves the establishment of procedures and processes within each culture to ensure a diversity of perspectives before establishing new procedures, such as children speaking out in public, and opportunities for contestation, revision, and change of such new procedures. For the possibility of transformation to occur within the culture this must involve the establishment of the conditions that will enable alternative interpretations of cultural norms to emerge and to compete with the dominant ones. This kind of dialog happened at a national level, for example, in Brazil in the early days after the adoption of the CRC. In helping to establish this kind of dialog, whether at the national or local level, a strategy is needed that is cognizant of the power relationships in how it involves children in demonstrations of their capacities to be engaged in dialog. The street children who spoke out in Brasília at a crucial time in the establishment of the new democratic constitution for the nation of Brazil had long been involved in relatively democratic local groups and also had the advice and support of trained street workers.

The CRC goes some ways toward resolving the dilemmas of changing views of childhood and children's agency by stressing the role of the family in the child's exercise of his or her rights. How and at what age children are socialized by their families and communities to participate fully in society varies enormously according to the culture and is not something that can be universally mandated. It is therefore fitting that the role of the family is stressed in the following preamble to the CRC: "States parties shall respect the responsibilities, rights, and duties of parents or, where applicable, the members of the extended family or community as provided for by local custom, legal guardians, or other persons legally responsible for the child, to provide, in a manner consistent with the evolving capabilities of the child, appropriate direction and guidance in the exercise by the child of the rights recognized in the present Convention."

But many would argue that on the question of protection of children this is too strong a statement because in many cases children need to be protected from their families. This issue is now being fought out through the establishment of new legal statutes in many countries. This essay however focuses on the civic participation of children and youth, not their defense and participation in legal proceedings. Nevertheless, it is more generally true that if children are to be encouraged to participate, we need to work also with their parents, who themselves may not have had opportunities to participate in society and may not know of their own human rights. The view of children as citizens with rights, including the right to an independent voice, is a great challenge for most cultures. To hear of children's rights for the first time from children's own mouths sometimes leads to violence against them. It can also be argued that the strategy of primarily promoting children's rights awareness through children themselves is not sufficiently respectful of parents and can undermine families.

There is a great need for more research on the complex changing landscape of cultural views regarding children and child rearing in an attempt to improve the dialog on children's participation and the promotion of children's rights in different cultures. This involves addressing a number of important theoretical issues in the contemporary debates about childhood, including the concept of "rights" and the emphasis on the "individual." Unfortunately, most theory on children's development has been generated in the industrialized countries of the "minority world," particularly the United States. These theories have often become universal standards that are applied internationally to institutional settings such as schools, child care, youth programs, and parenting classes. These can undermine parents and become threats to cultural continuity and local self-determination. The same has been happening with the promotion of children's participation. The models of child development that have been constructed in the field of developmental psychology and that are reproduced in the CRC stress individual autonomy and independence versus the collective acculturation of children that is strong in many cultures but about which much less is written.

A common cry of resistance by parents to the CRC is that children need to be protected so that they can have a childhood. Precisely how to balance children's needs for physical and psychological protection with their participatory rights remains a complex issue that many nations have begun to face since they ratified the CRC. If this process is done in an informed and sensitive way, children's participation in each culture will look different. It remains to be seen how successful those who work with children can be in promoting the concept of children's rights within families, both rich and poor. Families are often highly authoritarian structures. Many parents fear that "children's rights" implies a loss of control over children, who, they think, already have too much freedom. In fact, this is probably the primary reason why politicians in the United States have not brought the CRC into Congress for ratification. This is a misreading of the CRC, for it does not call for a collapse in discipline or in the teaching of responsibility to others. Neither does it seek to remove the rights of parents, but it calls for a transparency of action and an openness to listen and to communicate with children according to their maximum capacity. The debate about children's rights can be expected to rage for many years because it involves a fundamental change in any culture and how that culture reproduces itself. As the debate rages, inevitably arguments become simplified and polarized. Confusion commonly seems to revolve around the meaning of authority. The granting of children's rights should not undermine the legitimate authority of parents and other children's caregivers; the purpose is to challenge arbitrary authority. This relates to a substantial body of theory on parenting style in the field of child development. According to progressive writers on the subject, adults must be able to justify their exercise of authority to their children as soon as children are capable of understanding. But this is a Western perspective on child rearing and a recent one at that, one which still is not shared by a large proportion of parents. There are enormous differences in cultural understandings around the world as to what kinds of authority are acceptable to exercise with children, and these will not change quickly. It surely cannot be questioned, however, that in all cultures there is a need for serious reflection on this issue, and in spite of some cultural bias, the CRC is a superb base document from which to begin this reflection.

See also Deliberative Democracy; Democracy; Democratic Education; Kids Voting USA (KVUSA); Minority Youth Voter Turnout; MTV's Choose or Lose Campaign (1992–); New Media; Rights, Youth Perceptions of; State and Youth, The; Student Political Activism; Student Voices Project; United Nations, Youth Activism and; Voice.

Recommended Reading

CRIN (Child Rights Information Network). See the Web site at http://www.CRIN.org for a great deal of valuable information on children's rights, to see the UN Convention on the Rights of the Child (CRC), and to see a recent international summary of the state of children's participation in relation to the CRC.

Cussianovich, Alejandro (1997). *Algunas premisas para la reflexión y las prácticas sociales con niños y adolescentes trabajadores.* Lima: Radda Barnen.

Hart, R. A. (1992). *Children's Participation: from Tokenism to Citizenship.* UNICEF Innocenti Essays, No. 4, UNICEF/International Child Development Centre, Florence, Italy. It is also available at http://www.cerg1.org.

NATs. *Revista internacional desde los niños y adolescentes trabajadores.* Published twice per year. Available from NATs, Av. Tomas Guido No. 257, Lima 14, Peru.

Swift, Anthony (1997). *Children for Social Change: Education for Citizenship of Street and Working Children in Brazil.* Nottingham, UK: Educational Heretics Press.

UNICEF (2003). Special issue of *The State of the World's Children* on children's participation. See http://www.unicef.org/sowc2003.

Roger A. Hart

Rights, Youth Perceptions of. The notion of children as individuals possessing specific rights is considered to be of relatively recent origin. The children's rights movement formed during the nineteenth century initially focused on providing children with rights of protection and welfare or what has now come to be known as nurturance rights. More recently, however, society has come to believe that not only do children need to be cared for and protected but that to some extent children have the right to participate in decisions about their own lives. This growing concern with children's participation or self-determination rights is evident in the manner in which the medical and mental-health professions, as well as the social services, educational, and legal systems, are working toward extending additional decision-making rights to young people.

Internationally, the emphasis on children's nurturance and self-expression rights is reflected in the UN Convention on the Rights of the Child (CRC), which includes children's educational, political, civic, social, and cultural rights. The CRC ratified by all countries in the world with the exception of the United States and Somalia, attempts to strike a balance between children's nurturance and self-determination or participation rights. This balance is reflected in two fundamental tenets which underpin the CRC: "the best interests of the child" and the "evolving capacities of the child." By establishing children as individuals with their own rights and freedoms the CRC challenges the dependent status of children.

A major concern in extending additional decision-making rights to children is whether young people understand their rights in a reasonable and meaningful way. How children and adolescents think about their rights has important implications for advocacy, young people's legal and political socialization, and their ability to exercise their rights effectively. However, most attempts to delineate an adequate framework for balancing children's nurturance and self-determination rights have failed to take into account available empirical evidence of young people's abilities to understand their rights.

A number of research studies conducted primarily in the United States and Canada have examined children's perceptions and views regarding their rights. Some of the first work on this topic was conducted at the University of Nebraska by Gary Melton. Employing a global-stage approach he reported that the development of children's perceptions of their rights (such as the right to privacy) progresses from an egocentric stage where rights are viewed as privileges that can be given or taken away by the whims of those in authority, characteristic of young children, to seeing rights in terms of abstract universal principles, a stage of thinking not typically seen before early adolescence.

However, it was not clear whether hard-stage theories adequately captured either the subtleties or complexities of children's thinking about rights. In contrast, to the global-stage approach, several recent studies have examined children's perceptions of rights from a domain-specific perspective. For instance, Charles Helwig of the University of the Toronto found that even young adolescents exhibit abstract thinking about rights and civil liberties such as freedom of speech and religion. In addition, Martin Ruck and colleagues comparing Canadian children's perceptions of self-determination and nurturance rights in a variety of social contexts reported that children and young adolescents tend to perceive nurturance rights as more important in their lives than self-determination rights, while by mid-adolescence both types of rights are viewed as meaningful. By middle childhood most children were aware of the universal nature of rights.

The results of these recent studies suggest that how young people view nurturance and self-determination rights appears to be related to how they construct their social knowledge of the world. For instance, children's and adolescents' thinking about situations dealing with nurturance rights is related to their understanding of familial roles and relationships. On the other hand, how young people think about self-determination rights corresponds to their understanding of moral rules and their growing sociolegal knowledge. The findings of the recent work in this area indicate that how children and adolescents think about their rights depends not only on maturational factors but also on the specific context or situation in which the right is embedded (home, school, or greater society) as well as the type of right (nurturance or self-determination) under consideration.

As primary agents of children's socialization, parents are undoubtedly an important influence in terms of how children and youth think about rights. However, empirical research addressing the relationship between parents' and children's views about children's rights is sparse. In one of the few published studies on this topic Ruck, Peterson-Badali, and Day examined mothers' and adolescents' perspectives about children's nurturance and self-determination rights in the home. They found that pre- and early adolescents were more likely than their mothers to perceive self-determination rights as important for young people, while mothers were more likely than these adolescents to favor nurturance and protection rights for their children. In contrast, by mid-adolescence mothers and adolescents showed equal support for both types of children's rights. It appears that by mid-adolescence mothers perceive their children as being capable of autonomous decision-making, a view consistent with this group of adolescents' own perceptions. The similarity of the oldest adolescents' and mothers' views in this regard suggests that by mid-adolescence parents and children have most likely already negotiated a number of important rights-related issues.

Also of interest is the question of whether there are cultural differences in young people's perceptions of rights. For example, Gary Melton and Susan Limber found differences between American and Norwegian youth in terms of perceptions of self-determination and nurturance rights. Compared to their Norwegian counterparts, American youth viewed self-determination and autonomy as more salient than nurturance rights. For example, issues such as self-expression and being able to make their own choices were important for American children. In contrast, Norwegian children placed more emphasis on children's protection and nurturance rights than American youngsters. We can also compare this finding to the work of Ruck and colleagues, which found that Canadian children tend to have extremely positive views toward both types of children's rights. Researchers have suggested that such cultural differences may be linked to variation in sociopolitical attitudes and this contention has received some empirical support.

Differences pertaining to the cultural constructs of individualism and collectivism also offer an interesting perspective regarding children's views of nurturance and self-determination rights. Cultures which are characterized as individualistic value individual rights and autonomy, while those characterized as collectivistic are orientated to interdependence and group cooperation. Consequently, one might expect that children in traditional or collectivistic societies would favor the protection and provision of rights that are seen as relating to the welfare or well-being of children (nurturance orientation), while children in more individualistic societies would favor autonomy and independence (self-determination orientation).

Available work examining the influence of cultural values on children's reasoning about and conceptions of their rights suggests that children's views of rights do not follow a strictly cultural orientation such that children from diverse cultures do not necessarily support one type of right over the other. In addition, as in Western or individualistic societies, concepts of autonomy, individual rights, and freedom are also important considerations for young people living in more traditional or collectivistic cultural orientations (e.g., China, Malaysia). The results of recent work indicates that individuals of different cultures take into account various features of the situations they are asked to consider when making judgments about rights, and in some instances they may reject existing cultural practices.

Although we know considerably more about young people's perceptions of rights than we did just a decade ago, there are still a number of important questions that need to be addressed. Research is needed to examine the degree to which there are possible gender differences in young people's conceptions of rights. Although consistent gender differences have typically not been reported in the majority of studies investigating young people's conceptions of rights, it is possible that differences in how boys and girls experience various aspects of their social world may also lead to differences in their perceptions of nurturance and self-determination rights. For example, in families with traditional gender roles boys are often granted considerably more autonomy and decision-making opportunities than girls. Research is also needed that examines how disadvantaged or marginalized children and youth conceive of and experience rights. For instance, in a recent survey of New Zealand high-school students Karen Nairn and Anne Smith found that most students believed that sexual-minority youth would not feel safe or protected at their schools. In addition, a number of the heterosexual students they surveyed at times employed rights discourse to argue for their right to be safe from "homosexuals" and/or to hold religious beliefs that oppose the rights of gay, lesbian, bisexual, and transgender students. However, we know relatively little about how lesbian, gay, bisexual, and transgender youth perceive or actually experience their rights in schools or other contexts. Yet, perhaps not surprisingly, recent work by Stacey Horn of the University of Illinois at Chicago indicates that sexual-minority youth often experience rights violations in school contexts, par-

ticularly around issues of safety. Further research on this topic is clearly needed.

In addition, studies need to continue to examine the influence of various cultural contexts on young people's thinking about their rights and rights-related situations. Finally, the issue of children's rights is a complex and at times controversial one, both in terms of children's entitlement to nurturance and protection (e.g., in the areas of health care, child protection, and youth justice) and their rights to self-determination or participation (e.g., access to civil liberties such as freedom of speech and religion and the debate regarding young people's right to independently consent to health care). Research continuing to address how young people perceive and experience their rights will play an important role in determining the appropriate balance between children's nurturance and self-determination rights.

See also Deliberative Democracy; Democracy; Democratic Education; Rights of Participation of Children and Youth; State and Youth, The; Student Political Activism; United Nations, Youth Activism and.

Recommended Reading

Flekkoy, M. R., and Kaufman, N. H. (1997). *The Participation Rights of the Child: Rights and Responsibility in Family and Society*. Bristol, PA: Jessica Kingsley.

Hart, S. N. (1991). "From Property to Person Status: Historical Perspectives on Children's Rights." *American Psychologist*, 46 (1): 53–59.

Helwig, C. C. (1995). "Adolescents' and Young Adults' Conceptions of Civil Liberties: Freedom of Speech and Religion." *Child Development*, 66: 152–166.

Melton, G. B. (1983). *Child Advocacy: Psychological Issues and Interventions*. New York: Plenum Press.

Nairn, K., and Smith, A. B. (2003). "Taking Students Seriously: Their Rights to Be Safe at School." *Gender and Education*, 15 (2): 133–149.

Ruck, M. D., Abramovitch, R., and Keating, D. P. (1998). "Children's and Adolescents' Understanding of Rights: Balancing Nurturance and Self-Determination." *Child Development*, 64 (2): 404–417.

Ruck, M. D., Peterson-Badali, M., and Day, D. (2002). "Adolescents' and Mothers' Understanding of Children's Rights in the Home."

Journal of Research on Adolescence, 12 (3): 373–398.

Takanishi, R. (1978). "Childhood as a Social Issue: Historical Roots of Contemporary Child Advocacy Movements." *Journal of Social Issues*, 34 (2): 8–28.

Walker, N. E., Brooks, C. M., and Wrightsman, L. S. (1999). *Children's Rights in the United States: In Search of a National Policy*. Thousand Oaks, CA: Sage.

Martin D. Ruck and Michele Peterson-Badali

Riot Grrrl. The origin of the Riot Grrrl movement is usually traced to the early 1990s to a loosely formed movement of young, mainly white and middle-class, women, a large proportion of whom identified as queer, who gathered in Washington, D.C., and in Olympia, Washington. With their roots in punk rock music and their motto "Grrrls need guitars," the Riot Grrrls rendered the civil rights movement slogan "Black Power" into "Girl Power" and used it to strategically distance themselves from the adult patriarchal worlds of status, hierarchies, and standards. The reclaiming of the word girl or "grrrl" (standing for growl) marks a celebration of both the fierce and aggressive potential of girls as well as reconstitution of girl culture as a positive force embracing self-expression through fashion, attitude, and a do-it-yourself (DIY) approach to cultural production.

Bands such as Bikini Kill, Bratmobile, and Heavens to Betsy exemplify this combination with their mixing of a girlish aesthetic with all that is most threatening in a female adult: rage, bitterness, and political acuity. Many grrrls used their bodies to convey this ironic melding of style with political expression by, for example, the juxtaposition of gendered signs such as "1950s dresses with combat boots, shaved hair with lipstick, studded belts with platform heels" (Klein 1997, 222) and by writing politically loaded words such as "rape," "shame," and "slut" on their arms and stomachs. By most accounts the movement was a response to the sexism, elitism, and violence of local masculinist punk scenes where exclusionary practices meant that girls were considered less than full members of the scene. In contrast, the "girl power" of the Riot Grrrl encouraged young women to see themselves not as the passive consumers of culture, including that of the punk scene, but as producers and creators of knowledge, as verbal and expressive dissenters. Their critiques address their own and others' experiences as women as well as their experiences of race, sexuality, class, and other forms of embodiedness. As a result, Riot Grrrl is viewed by many who study U.S. girls'/young women's cultures as exemplary of what's being called "youth feminism."

The movement's inauguration was in August 1991 during the week-long International Pop Underground Convention in Washington, D.C., where Girl Day opened the gathering. Writing in Girl Germs #4, Rebecca B, one girl who was there, describes the significance of the event: "Girl's night will always be precious to me because, believe it or not, it was the first time I saw women stand on a stage as though they truly belonged there. The first time I had ever heard the voice of a sister proudly singing the rage so shamefully locked in my own heart. Until girls' night, I never knew that punk rock was anything but a phallic extension of the white middle class male's frustrations" (1991).

A year later a three-day national Riot Grrrl convention was held in Washington, D.C., comprising a number of educational workshops on topics such as violence against women, fat oppression, and unlearning racism (Jacques 2001, 47). The Washington, D.C., Riot Grrrl Manifesto emerged from the conference with a clear articulation of a rationale for the movement and what it was about. It reads in part: "RIOT GRRRL IS ... BECAUSE we need to accept and support each other as girls; acknowledge our different approaches to life and accepting all of them as valid.... BECAUSE we seek to create revolution in our own lives every single day by envisioning and creating alternatives to the status quo."

In addition to weekly meetings, the Riot Grrrls network through fanzines (zines), which are self-written and designed, photocopied publications that they hand out and mail to other girls. The writings take up a full range of themes and styles—angry, supportive, advice giving, on issues like relationships, harassment, rape, and mental, physical, and verbal abuse. Cartoons, photographs, collages, and text, which are often autobiographical, are typical zine content. Zines, according to many engaged in writing them, originate from a need for expression, a need girls have to discover the truth about themselves and their lives. Through zines, they claim, young women are uncensored and free to discuss their realities. Zines may be considered "paradoxical feminist writing spaces" because of the way writers negotiate with and appropriate the discourses of dominant culture and liberal feminism. These feminist autobiographical writings are critical sites for the construction of social identities, noting how they may be marked paradoxically by the interplay of dominant and counter-hegemonic discourses.

Riot Grrrls have also used cyberspace and the creation of e-zines as an alternative site for self-expression. In comparison to print zines, online zines have the advantage of limited production and distribution expenses after the initial investment of a computer, which is of course an expense out of the range of possibility for some. However, the material is accessible to anyone with a computer and modem and thus facilitates networking, community building, and dialog. The opportunity to post one's Web site without having to go through corporate, mainstream, commercial, official, and adult channels makes a difference for shifting the locus of political activism, as well as who can produce politicized cultural-technological objects. However, despite the opportunities opened up by using what has been a male-dominated Internet to communicate about feminist issues, it is important to recognize that this expansion of discursive space does not necessarily, nor easily, translate into shifts in dominant public discourse.

In the wake of the Riot Grrrls, numerous all-girl rock bands were born, among them the enormously popular Spice Girls from Britain, and the slogan "Girl Power" began to be bandied about. T-shirts with pro-girl sentiments like "Girls Rule" and Girls Kick Ass" started to show up at malls. The messages on these shirts bear a direct relationship to the words the Riot Grrrls wrote on their bodies. However, while T-shirts have a long history as conveyors of political slogans, it is important to remember that Riot Grrrl was deliberately against consumer culture. Writing on oneself with a marker is not only a political, feminist action (first, in choosing to "deface" the feminine body which is ideally a flawless object; second, in drawing attention to issues of women's oppression through the words) but also displays the classic do-it-yourself ethic of punk. Thus, in buying a trendy T-shirt, whether or not its slogan is meant to be ironic, any critique of capitalism is, by definition, lost in its (mass) production.

With the proliferation of the term, the meanings of "Girl Power" and what girls who embrace it could and should do with it did not remain static, nor did they get taken up with the same political and social intentions of Riot Grrrls by others who claimed it. For example, the following is a definition of "Girl Power" from a zine entitled *Supergirl*:

What girl power is:

feeling okay about being a girl—not left out or inferior

promoting girl love. It really is a good and wonderful kind of sisterhood-friendship. Don't talk to me about school sororities; I know a different kind of sorority and we don't tolerate any kind of "pledge week," thank you, and we don't set rules for each other or leave anyone out.

encouraging each other. Telling each other it's good to take risks to achieve our individual goals, and congratulating each other for taking risks.

teaching girls and boys and older/younger people about girl issues (equality, freedom or individuality in society, safety from victimization.) These are universal issues that often affect U.S. to a greater extent, especially for poor and minority women. When everyone understands these issues, they are almost solved.

learning to respect each other. How many times have you heard girls call each other a slut, or some other derogatory name? How many times have you called a girl/been called by a girl one of the many names that exist to put girls down? We can't divide ourselves into black/white rich/poor good/bad, cause we'll never really have power that way.

this of course comes from respecting yourself. Respect your mind and body. Respect yourself as a girl with an individual and beautiful combination of appearance, ideas, background, interests, strengths, etc etc etc.

being able to wear lots of lipstick or none at all, short skirts or loose jeans ... and still be simply a girl. It's not letting anyone judge you, because it's not about limitations! making noise sometimes!!!

GIRL POWER = GIRL LOVE = RESPECT = ENCOURAGMENT = STRONG SELF IMAGE = DESIRE TO TEAR DOWN THE RULES = GIRL POWER = GIRL POWER = OXOXOXOX = REVOLUTION

Coverage of Riot Grrrls quickly appeared in American mainstream magazines such as *Seventeen* (1992, 1993), *The New Yorker* (1992), *Newsweek* (1993), *Rolling Stone* (1993, 1994), and *Time* (1998). For the Riot Grrrls the coverage brought objectionable incursion. Not only was there a rush to categorize the movement whose members defied that there were strict definitions to be had, but the Girl Power message was also mutating and being rearticulated.

While the Riot Grrrls themselves clearly saw their movement as attached to a liberatory social and political agenda, the mainstream media opted to present a different message altogether. A *Rolling Stone* article concluded, for example: "Riot grrrls' unifying principle is that being feminist is inherently confusing and contradictory and that women have to find a way to be sexy,

angry, and powerful at the same time" (1993). Here, in a bizarre twist, it is feminism that is seen to complicate what is assumed would otherwise be an easy and straight-forward transition from girlhood to woman. *Newsweek* took a somewhat different stance to dismiss the seriousmindedness of the movements' politics. In doing so it drew on hegemonic discourses associating youth as a time when rebellion is expected but is also expected to be in most respects temporary. "There is no telling whether this enthusiasm or the Riot grrrls catchy passion for 'revolution girl style' will evaporate when it hits the adult real world. Most of the grrrls are still in the shelters of home or college—a far cry from what they'll face in the competitive job market or as they start to form their own families" (1993).

As soon as the coverage began, a nationwide "press block" was invoked in 1992–1993 by some movement participants to prevent the possibility of colluding with exploitation, misquoting, and such. The block was also meant to preserve the original intent of the movement. According to Kathleen Hanna, the lead singer of Bikini Kill, "We weren't doing what we did to gain fame, we were just trying to hook up with other freaks" (Greenblat, 1996, p. 26). The articles multiplied anyway, revealing more about their authors' lust to "uncover" a potential new trend than about the movement itself. The disruptive nature and threatening intent in the girls' voices and actions were ignored, while attention focused on their clothing and their appearances. One girl writes about her reaction to the way the mainstream press represented the movement in her zine *Function*:

So much stuff has been said about what riot grrrl is, actually what some misinformed people have said. I'm sick to death of defending riot grrrl every time I turn around. I don't even know why it should be defended. Riot Grrrl is NOT what Seventeen, Newsweek or the LA weekly make it out to be or any other media thing. The media attention has taken riot grrrl and twisted it and distorted the name to mean little if anything of importance.... Riot grrrl is about emotions, feelings, not fashion, or hating boys, it's about us, grrrls. It's real and a threat because it goes against the patriarchy as anything is a threat that goes against the patriarchy. Dawn, age 19, Seattle WA.

The antagonistic relations with the media and subsequent black-out response from some Riot Grrrls raises larger questions about the complicated relationships between subcultures and the politics of incorporation on the one hand and the politics of commodification and representation on the other. The dilemma the Riot Grrrl movement faced was one of reifying an opposition between preserving authenticity but risking elitism or reaching a wider audience but "selling out." The problem was that for a political movement that wanted to reach alienated girls, the media blackout strategy closed Riot Grrrls off to girls in smaller centers and risked defining Riot Grrrl as an exclusive, insular movement. The contradiction of the situation was not lost on some Riot Grrrls. As one girl wrote in her zine, "The mainstream media—what seemed like the best medium for communication, the best way to spread 'girl love'—had failed us" (Spirit 1995). Yet the author also recognized that this exposure inspired many more girls "to question, challenge, create, demand." This opposition between "authentic subculture" and "mainstream sell out" continues to shape the feminist Girl Power and Riot Grrrl debates.

See also Chat Rooms, Girls' Empowerment and; Feminism; Gender Differences in the Political Attitudes of Youth; New Media; Punk Rock Youth Subculture.

Recommended Reading

Chideya, F. (November 23, 1993). "Revolution Girl Style." *Newsweek*, 84–86.
Driscoll, C. (2002). *Girls: Feminine Adolescence in Popular Culture and Cultural Theory*. New York: Columbia University Press.
Ferris, M. (2001). "Resisting Mainstream Media: Girls and the Act of Making Zines." *Canadian Women Studies*, 20/21: 51–55.
France, A. (July 1993). "Grrrls at War." *Rolling Stone*, 8–22.

Garrison, E. K. (2000). "U.S. Feminism—Grrrl Style!: Youth (Sub)Cultures and the Technologies of the Third Wave." *Feminist Studies*, 26 (1): 141–170.
Godfrey, R. (1993). "Riot Girls in the Alternative Nation." *Alphabet City*, 3.
Green, K., and Taormino, T. (1997). *A Girl's Guide to Taking Over the World: Writings from the Girl Zine Revolution*. New York: St Martin's Griffin.
Greenblat, C. (December 1996). "Unwilling Icons: Riot Grrrls Meets the Press." *Border/ Lines*, 24–27.
Hamilton, S. (1999). "Subaltern Counterpublics: Feminist Interventions into the Digital Public Sphere." In *PopCan: Popular Culture in Canada*, edited by P. Walton and L. Van Luven. Toronto: Prentice-Hall, pp. 180–187.
Hebdige, D. (1979). *Subculture: The Meaning of Style*. London: Routledge.
Hesford, W. (1999). *Framing Identities: Autobiography and the Politics of Pedagogy*. Minneapolis: University of Minnesota Press.
Jacques, A. (2001). "You Can Run But You Can't Hide: The Incorporation of Riot Grrrl into Mainstream Culture." *Canadian Women Studies*, 20/21: 46–50.
Klein, M. (1997). "Duality and Redefinition: Young Feminism and the Alternative Music Community." In *Third Wave Agenda: Being Feminist, Doing Feminism*, edited by L. Heywood and J. Drake. Minneapolis: University of Minnesota Press.
Spirit (1995). What Is a Riot Grrrl Anyway? See http://www.columbia.edu/~rli3/music_html/ bikini_kill/girl.html.

Marnina Gonick

Russia, Youth Activism in. Russia's postcommunist transition has increased both the opportunities and the challenges for activism on the part of young people, as well as the ways in which activism can be expressed and enacted. In Soviet Russia "youth activism" was a highly ideologized and state-organized phenomenon. Young people were called upon to adopt "an active life position," which in practice meant that each individual should do the following:

• Actively participate in public life via the official (Pioneer and *Komsomol*) youth organizations.
• Show commitment to the ideals of the Soviet state expressed through patriotism and proletarian internationalism

as well as by prioritizing the interests of the "collective" over personal interests.

- Display high moral qualities including valuing spiritual over material values and having a strong sense of duty and responsibility.
- Be highly "cultured" (defined as having a thorough knowledge of Soviet literature and art as well as of the works of Lenin and key resolutions of the Communist Party of the Soviet Union).

"Activism" was thus a highly routinized process. Young people's level of social and political engagement, for example, was evaluated through exams—known as *Leninskie zachety*—which children took from their third year at school. At the same time genuinely spontaneous youthful activism was labeled "voluntarism" or youthful "extremism." Indeed, the attention paid by the state to organizing young people's social and political lives was driven to a large extent by the fear that young people's biological and social immaturity predisposed them toward such extremism. Extra-state activities—countercultural movements as well as passivity (nonparticipation in the *Komsomol*, pacifism, avoidance of conscription, etc.)—were considered to be antisocial or "deviant." So too was entrepreneurial "initiative." The petty trade in jeans, records, and other Western fashions and youth cultural artifacts undertaken by young people in order to overcome the constraints of the planned market, for example, was labeled anti-Soviet "speculation."

In post-Soviet Russia, by contrast, it is precisely this kind of independent and entrepreneurial activity that the Russian government is encouraging among young professional groups. Young people thus find themselves in the position of having to form themselves as citizens in the new Russia amid a massive shift in societal norms. Young people today may not have experienced the Soviet regime themselves, but their cultural knowledge remains steeped in the attitudes of the Soviet period as transmitted via the family, school, and university education systems. Yet, they have to manage this cultural heritage while shaping their own lives in quite different circumstances from their parents' generation; the world inhabited by today's young Russians is one of extreme social stratification and unequal life chances, of high youth unemployment, of unequal access to education and information technologies, and of the collapse of the mass youth organizations that previously ensured the integration of almost all, and the active participation of some, young people. Some sociologists have concluded that the combination of these factors has produced in Russia and other former Soviet republics a retreat by young people from public life as measured by membership and/or active participation in political, voluntary, recreational, and other organizations. They argue that youth have shifted into a private world characterized by civic passivity, low levels of civic-mindedness, and reliance on the family and informal economy for social and economic resources (Wallace 2003). Given the mass, and almost compulsory, nature of young people's organized activism in Soviet Russia, it is perhaps not surprising that in absolute terms there has been a rapid decline in membership of civic organizations among young Russians. However, the greater decline (relative to other postcommunist countries in Europe) and the comparatively lower rates of membership and active participation in civic organizations than those found in Western Europe requires further explanation—one that takes into account the meanings young people themselves attach to citizenship, civil society, and civic life.

Activism is associated with developed forms of citizenship and is premised on the understanding by individuals and social groups that they are fully empowered members of the civic community and on a shared perception of the need and purpose of civic activity. It is important to note here that the post-Soviet Russian state still has some ground to cover in fostering confidence among young people that they are full members of society. This is to some extent also a legacy of the Soviet period. Although youth were viewed within Soviet ideology as "constructors of Communism" (as well as "victims of bourgeois influence" when they went "wrong"), underpinning this ideological structure was a more deeply rooted positioning of young people as an economic, social, and political *resource* to be used to maximum effect. Although it is fair to say that post-Soviet Russian governments have made considerable progress in developing a new youth policy that moves away from this kind of exploitative paternalism and recognizes the full diversity of youth today, young people's energies remain constrained by their sense of continued subordination.

One illustration of this is that young people have a low sense of efficacy. Research among youth in the city of Ul'ianovsk in 2004 showed that the majority (54 percent) of young people feel vulnerable to and unprotected and pressurized by the state, especially where they envisage "the state" in the form of authority structures such as the police and military. Young citizens feel that first and foremost the state protects the interests of the elite (oligarchs and the new rich), criminal structures, and residents of the largest and most developed cities. Only 6.4 percent of respondents thought that young people were protected by the state, and the majority (54 percent) thought they were unable to influence state policy in any way. A second example of their insecurity in full citizenship status is that young people understand "civil society" not as a space for self-realization but as a protective mechanism (see http://www.region.ulsu.ru).

Separate research conducted in three regions of Russia in 2002 showed that only a small minority (10 percent) of young people think civil society already exists in Russia (see http://www.fesmos.ru/Green_society2.html). Perhaps more importantly, young people (64 percent of respondents) tend to understand civil society not as a space for self-organization but equate the term more or less with the principles of "the legal state." It is perhaps understandable in this context that by the mid-1990s, young people were citing participation in public life and politics last in a list of their values and when talking about their life plans demonstrated a desire to shut themselves off from Russian society, whose unpredictability was considered to be an obstacle to the realization of their personal plans. Thus, we might conclude that the ongoing and complex transformation processes in Russia to date have left the population without a commonly shared vision of how the civic sphere should be developed. This makes it difficult for young people to understand and decide for themselves what it means to be an "active citizen" in contemporary Russia.

While research based on measures of attitudes and values can highlight trends over time and assist in comparing levels of activism between different countries and communities, it would be misleading to paint a picture of post-Soviet Russia as a country of apathetic youth conditioned by a past in which political activity was compulsory, routinized, and thus meaningless, and by a present in which they seek to do little more than survive the turbulence of post-Socialist economic transformation. It is important to consider, in all its complexities and contradictions, the actual civic activity of young people and what this might mean in terms of understanding the quality as well as quantity of their "activism." Let us consider the following questions: Do young people participate in formal politics, and what does that say about their civic engagement? Do young people participate in key social movements and organizations in contemporary Russia? If not, why not? What kinds of other (cultural, lifestyle) activities afford space for young people's civic engagement? How actively do young people make use of this space?

There is a widely held view that contemporary Russian youth are apolitical or politically passive. This is largely based on the fact that young people in the former Soviet Union are much less likely to belong to political parties or labor unions than they were in the past and because of their relatively low rates of participation in elections. This, it is said, indicates that young people do not consider the interests of the state with the same seriousness they do their personal interests. Some support for this might be derived from the fact that events organized specifically to attract young Russians to the political process are treated pragmatically by young people for the leisure opportunities they offer while having virtually no impact on their voting patterns. Indeed, such attempts to seduce young people politically appear only to reinforce low levels of trust in state and political institutions. Research conducted in January 2004 by the Institute for Social and Political Research suggests that only 8.2 percent of Russian youth (fifteen- to twenty-nine-years-old) expressed trust in political parties, and just 15.8 percent trusted the democratically elected parliament. This survey painted a bleak picture of young Russians' confidence in their political institutions per se; only one-fifth trusted the police, and less than a quarter trusted the Russian government. Significant levels of trust existed only for President Vladimir Putin (57.7 percent) and the church (48.1 percent) (Popova 2004). This confirms earlier research from 1998 which found that two-thirds of eighteen- to twenty-nine-year-olds in Russia had a highly negative opinion of the key institutions of democratic governance.

However, putting this situation in various comparative contexts complicates the stereotype of Russian youth as politically disengaged. First, this low level of trust in political institutions is not a peculiar aspect of contemporary youth in Russia; sociologists have found a significant convergence of views across generations in contemporary Russia. Indeed on key markers like "intention to vote," Eurobarometer data show virtually no difference over the period 1995–1997 between Russian respondents aged eighteen to twenty-four (68 percent) and those over twenty-four (69 percent) when asked whether they intended to exercise their democratic right to vote (UNICEF 2000, 107). Second, while this intention is certainly not matched by actual voting behavior, lower turnouts among the youngest cohort of eligible voters are a clearly established pattern across Europe and in no way peculiar to Russia. Moreover, it is worth noting the dismal failure of parties and leaders across the political spectrum to attract young people by their ideas, policies, or political charisma. One exception to this rule is the flamboyant Vladimir Zhirinovskii whose theatrical image has successfully lodged him in young people's minds as the "the most fun" (samii prikol'nii) politician and earned him at times a disproportionately youthful vote. President Putin also has managed to establish himself as a strong and responsible figure among young people.

However, the readiness of young people to give their trust at this largely abstract national level is not repeated in local elections where more concrete and immediate responsiveness to the electorate's needs is demanded. But it is worth noting again that where a dissatisfaction with the political choice on offer is felt, young people do not just disengage from the political process but also register their disaffection. In the local elections for mayor of Nizhnii Novgorod in 2001 the highest proportion of the vote registered by the local electorate was for "none of the above" (27 percent compared to 17 percent for each of the two mayoral candidates). Of those opting to vote into office "nobody" rather than "anybody," young people constituted 18 percent (young people generally constitute 17 percent of the electorate). This, it might be argued, is evidence not that young people fail to treat the political sphere seriously but that the political system has failed as yet to treat the electorate (including young voters) with the seriousness it deserves.

There is no absolute rejection of civic engagement by young people; research among young people in Ul'ianovsk showed that eight out of ten young people were prepared to participate in social organizations and initiatives. However, young people are certainly selective about the content and context of such civic participation. The greatest enthusiasm was shown for participation in *youth* social organizations and for joining an existing organization rather than initiating their own. Moreover, there was a strong disinclination toward participating in organizations that were connected to overtly *political* activity. As an example of the ambivalence that young people in Russia have toward civic engagement, it is worth considering one of the most long-standing, well-developed, and "progressive" civic movements in Russia—the human-rights movement.

The human rights movement itself has multiple origins and driving forces. Young people in the movement have become involved as a result of a variety of experiences that have drawn them into spheres of life in which human-rights discourse features strongly: higher education—students on social-work programs, for example, constitute the main recruits for volunteer groups; participation in various "young leaders" schools and trainings; the process of military conscription (and its resistance); work on youth affairs or other regional government committees; membership of various social organizations, associations, and foundations; and membership of prodemocratic and right-wing political parties.

On the one hand young people active in the movement reflect the key strands of the movement as a whole. At the same time they develop initiatives around their own particular concerns. Take, for example, one of the most well-known organizations—the Charitable Foundation (*Sozidanie*), which literally translates as "constructive approach"—which devotes much of its efforts to supporting initiatives by young people seeking to develop civilian service projects as an alternative to military service. Other well-developed initiatives relating to youth concerns are the Committee for the Protec-

tion of Youth from Destructive Cults and the social organization Children's and Young People's Social Initiatives. Environmental movements and volunteer networks are also rapidly gaining strength.

Although the human-rights movement provides significant opportunity for young people to develop and implement their ideas, for the majority of youth this kind of activity remains directly associated with political (state) activity and is avoided for this reason. If the human-rights movement is to be more successful in recruiting young people to its cause, it will have to address a number of questions related to its image among young Russians. The movement enjoys an image—forged by former émigrés and the first Russian democrats alike—of being located at the political and social margins. While in some cases young people consider marginality to be "cool" (e.g., liking Russian rock rather than commercial pop), the marginality of the human-rights movement retains a predominantly negative image. Another damaging image is that of human-rights activists as either "scandalmongers" or career-seeking bureaucrats. The perceived level of infighting within the human-rights movement is also problematic, especially in relation to disputes between those who seek to defend absolute principles (fundamental rights to freedom of speech, movement, religion, etc.) and those who primarily respond to the daily problems of people who approach human-rights organizations. The widespread media-fueled image of human-rights activity as financed and controlled by the West via its charitable foundations or their Russian representatives is also perceived negatively by many young people who share "a new patriotic consciousness." If it is to attract young activists, the human-rights movement must also pay more attention to developing a youth-friendly interactive face. Although the movement has a well-developed network of Web sites, they are used primarily to house official documents, legislation, and speeches. While these may be useful resources for individuals seeking help, the form and content appears dry and unappealing to many youth.

Perhaps the single most difficult barrier to overcome, however, is not peculiar to the human-rights movement but relates to a wider lack of faith among young people in the possibility of resisting state power and achieving justice via this kind of activity. Indeed, one might go further to suggest that young people continue to view the majority of civic space as being linked to and complicit with state structures. This is hardly surprising given the continued efforts by the state to mobilize young people into "spontaneous" civic activity. The most vibrant illustration of this is the surrogate youth movement *Idushchie vmeste*, literally "marching together." This movement was founded in July 2000 and was registered as a national movement a year later. It claims to have around 100,000 members, 80 percent of whom are students. The movement, led by Vasilii Iakemenko, is a demonstrably national-patriotic, pro-Putin organization whose goals are the direct support of the president and his administration. Participation in events is encouraged by material rewards and new recruits are motivated often by financial interests. Indeed in July 2004 a mass meeting held in central Moscow to launch the movement's campaign to "rid Russia of those people who failed to support the president's policies" was boosted by the participation of teenagers bussed in especially from surrounding suburban towns in the Moscow region. Drawing on young people as a mass "ballast" marks continuity rather than rupture with the Soviet period and is likely in the long run to discourage young people's civic activism.

While there is widespread cynicism about this kind of "organized spontaneity," authentic youth activism continues to flourish in independent cultural spaces that are jealously guarded by young people not only from incursions of the state but to some extent also from civil society. Youth scenes today have developed rapidly from the first surge of "informal groups" (*nefor-*

maly) that were discussed at length in the press of the Gorbachev era. Indeed, so diverse and fluid are Russian urban youth cultural scenes today that not only would the majority of the adult population not be able to distinguish a "*roker*" (biker) from a "*roller*" (roller skater), but they would not feel the need to do so. At the same time and in contrast to those early days, however, many youth cultural groups now are officially registered and have some significant influence on the cultural life of the contemporary Russian city.

Some of these independent youth associations seek to make a positive contribution to society and in the major cities of European Russia the number of youth associations actively involved in developing the cultural infrastructure and leisure sphere for young people is growing. Perhaps more important is the fact that the projects pursued by young activists are genuinely original and dynamic in nature. One example is the Jerry Rubin Youth Club established by a twenty-five-year-old Muscovite, Svetlana El'chaninova, together with her hippie friends. This organization works with "alternative youth" (*neformaly*), putting on events such as exhibitions of youth style, avant-garde fashion shows and anarcho-youth theater shows. Another initiative—known as Cellar (*Podval*)—seeks to encourage students from schools in Moscow to get involved in volunteering. According to Anna Golovin, about 30 percent of the schoolchildren who attend Cellar seminars say they are willing to become volunteers in civic organizations.

Other organizations attract much greater publicity by engaging in mass activities such as Walk-2000—an event organized by young ecologists from the city of Tver to promote the cause of peace and nuclear disarmament. Another ecological group—Rainbow Saviors—employs nontraditional forms of protest to consciously attract press attention. Instead of standing with banners, they are more likely to be found blocking off a road or chaining themselves to railway lines. Young people also seem to be keen to be involved—on their own terms—in collective organizations akin to those of the Soviet era. Over the last two to three years alongside the direct inheritor of the Pioneer movement—the SPO-FDO (Union of Pioneer Organizations-Federation of Children's Organizations)—a number of other "Pioneer" organizations have emerged. The New Russian Pioneers, for example, undertake traditional Pioneer work steeped in general Christian principles rather than a particular ideological doctrine, while in Nizhnii Novgorod the mission of the newly emergent Cadet Corps suggests they are "Pioneers" in all but name.

Some spontaneous youth activism has a more national-patriotic tone and makes a more ambivalent social contribution, however. A key focus of such activity has been events in the former Yugoslavia. Following Western intervention in the region, anti-NATO demonstrations took place across the length and breadth of Russia during the spring of 2000. These events varied from a couple of dozen students waving banners saying "Yankees go home" in Ioshkar-Ole to the burning of American and British flags at a demonstration by around 400 young people in Voronezh. In April 2000 the Russian Union of Youth made an official declaration of protest at the military action by NATO countries.

Some of this activity is certainly exploited by organized political parties; we cannot underestimate the significance of a dominant discourse, which encourages Russians to reassert their national interest at the cost of ethnic "others." For example, at the meeting of *Idushchie vemeste* noted above, the movement's leaders advised the assembled participants that all those who "didn't agree" with current government policies should leave the country, and all those who hadn't yet made their minds up, should do so as a matter of priority. These calls were interpreted by the press as attempts to signal the need for a "political and ethnic cleansing" (*chistka*) of Moscow

and were apparently greeted positively by participants at the meeting despite the clear statement in the movement's founding "moral code" that the movement "does not tolerate nationalist and chauvinist ideologies." In July 2004 the organization launched a new campaign to expose "media lies." Newspapers and news agencies targeted for their mendacity included pillars of the independent press in post-Soviet Russia as well as international news agencies such as Reuters and the BBC.

While it would be an oversimplification to suggest that the current rise of national-patriotic consciousness is wholly orchestrated by political parties and unconnected to spontaneous youth activism, it remains important to distinguish between two quite distinct kinds of patriotism among Russian youth. The first—a kind of spontaneous patriotism—is widespread among young Russians today and is less an expression of a substantive national pride than the working through of a need to overcome a "national inferiority complex." This complex has formed in the context of fifteen years of broad and mass criticism of Soviet history, culture, and politics as well as of the state power structures of contemporary Russia. Alongside this criticism of the formal structures of politics and society, there has been a parallel romanticization of the criminal and semi-criminal world. For sections of Russian youth, for example, the television series *Brigada*—a kind of Russian variant of *The Godfather*—is iconic; the ratings for this series are so high that it has been showing constantly on one of the Russian TV channels for two years, while its theme music is the most popular telephone ring tone. The increasingly negative image of the United States, which became particularly evident with the election of George W. Bush to the American presidency, is another important reason for the consolidation of this kind of spontaneous patriotism.

The second form of national-patriotic consciousness is a more conscious patriotism and is characteristic of extreme right- and left-wing youth subcultural formations.

It is also associated with the newly emerging, rapidly growing, but politically informal skinhead movement, whose growing popularity among deprived provincial youth (*gopniki*), presents one of the key challenges for Russian society over the next few years. The emergence and development of informal, extremist groups should not surprise us given the rapid growth of risk in all spheres of life in post-Soviet Russia, the resultant turn to individualism as the basic strategy for survival and success, and the new significance of social resources such as lifestyles in this process. For those young people who see few of the benefits of globalization, territorially rooted, inward-looking collective responses are natural.

In the Soviet era the dominance of official structures and organizations made it easy to discern both the "mainstream" of youth activism as well as its deviant "other." The incorporation of young people into the institutions of politics, government, and society was routinized through official party and youth organizations. This produced high levels of civic integration although in practice active participation was confined to a few and was often motivated by career interests. In post-Soviet Russia both the opportunities and the challenges of youth activism are greater. At the regional level, especially, civically active young people are able to establish themselves quickly in nongovernmental organizations (NGOs), on regional youth affairs committees, and in regional political parties and voluntary organizations. On the other hand, the relative youth of such organizations themselves and the wider context of rapid transformations in the economic, social, and political spheres of Russian life, mean that commitment to active citizenship is more demanding than it might be within long-established and stable liberal-democratic states.

Not surprisingly, young people have responded to these challenges in a wide variety of ways. One response is essentially a conservative, conformist one consisting of strategies for inclusion and reproduction of

parental—or even older—traditional values. Such young people may become actively involved in religious organizations or other culturally and politically conservative movements such as the pro-Putin *Idushchie vmeste*. In contrast, other strategies might be best thought of as innovative or avant-garde in so much as they are taken up either by young people with Western lifestyles and the knowledge and skills necessary to succeed in a competitive society or by individuals looking to engage more directly in emergent, civic movements of a nonstate and nonpolitical kind. These young people are driven by a complex sense of responsibility not only for themselves but for the future of social groups and subgroups to which they belong or with whom they identify. Equally innovative, however, might be young people who have learned to live with the almost constant risk encountered in a rapidly transforming society and seek not to shape their future but to challenge negative political fatalism with the kind of laissez-faire ("all will turn out for the best") outlook on life.

In sharp contrast some young people position themselves within a spectrum of left-wing and right-wing "radical" positions. Such young people seek rapid and radical change and coalesce around either neo-Communist, national-patriotic, or proto-fascist organizations, movements, or gangs. Finally, there is a significant group among young people whose activism is mobilized by criminal and organized criminal structures for the purposes of financial and personal, rather than civic and communal, gain.

The life strategies and cultural practices of these groups vary enormously and it is not at all clear which, if any, will come to determine the "generational climate" of the current period. However, while the dangers of political apathy and the growth of national-patriotism should not be underplayed, there is an equal danger of jumping to hasty value judgments about young people's civic activism. In a rapidly changing society we need to be aware of the shifting background against which we seek to define

S

SAF. *See* Student Action with Farmworkers (SAF).

School Community and Youth Activism. *See* Just Community High Schools and Youth Activism.

School Engagement. There is general agreement that engagement is important for learning and achieving success in school. What exactly is engagement and how can it lead to success in school? As defined by a recent publication from the National Research Council (2004), engagement in schoolwork includes cognitive behaviors (such as paying attention in class, problem solving, using metacognitive strategies), observable behaviors (such as trying hard, persisting in the face of challenge, completing work, asking for help when needed), and emotions (such as enthusiasm, interest, and pride in one's accomplishments). Levels of cognitive, behavioral, or emotional engagement can vary from paying minimal attention (e.g., appearing attentive when actually thinking about last night's date) to actively processing information (e.g., making connections to previously learned material, critically analyzing new information), from dozing to dutifully doing the work, from being minimally interested to feeling excited and enthusiastic.

Students can also be socially engaged in school by participating in extracurricular activities or feeling a sense of loyalty to their schools. However, we are focusing on cognitive, behavioral, and emotional engagement rather than social engagement because students can be full participants in school sports, clubs, and other social activities without being academically involved in their learning.

An abundance of research indicates that higher levels of engagement in school are linked with positive outcomes such as improved academic performance. In fact, student engagement has been found to be one of the most robust predictors of student achievement and behavior in school—a conclusion that holds regardless of whether students come from families that are advantaged or disadvantaged economically or socially. Students who are engaged in school are more likely to earn higher grades and higher test scores and have lower dropout rates. In contrast, students with low levels of engagement are at risk for a wide range of long-term adverse consequences, including disruptive classroom behavior, absenteeism, and dropping out of school.

Students from disadvantaged backgrounds in high-poverty areas are particularly susceptible to the negative consequences associated with being disengaged from school. Compared to their more advantaged peers, these youth are less likely to graduate, dramatically increasing their risk of unemployment, poverty, poor health, and involvement in the criminal justice system.

While schools cannot control all of the social and economic factors affecting disadvantaged youth, they can provide more engaging educational environments with high expectations, skillful instruction, and the social support youth need to graduate and pursue postsecondary education or careers. Unfortunately, creating such environments has challenged educators for decades. Many studies show that students become more disengaged from school as they progress from elementary to middle and high school.

By high school as many as 40–60 percent of all students—urban, suburban, and rural—are chronically disengaged from school, not counting those who have already dropped out. There are, however, schools and districts that have managed to create more engaging educational environments for youth and ultimately increase the percentage of their students who graduate and go on to college.

The remainder of this entry will discuss the kinds of experiences that these successful schools and districts have created for their students including both the psychological precursors of engagement and the educational environments necessary to produce those precursors. We will conclude with a discussion of current education policies and how they hinder or support schools' abilities to create opportunities for their youth to become engaged in the learning process (National Research Council and the Institute of Medicine 2004).

Psychological Precursors of Engagement

There is an abundance of evidence that suggests that the relationship between students' experiences in school and their level of engagement is mediated by three sets of psychological variables: (1) beliefs about competence and control, (2) values and goals, and (3) a sense of social connectedness.

Competence and control. Students' beliefs about how "good" they are at school and how well they believe they can do in school have a direct effect on their engagement. These beliefs also lead to emotions that promote or interfere with engagement in schoolwork. The simple fact is that students enjoy academic tasks more and learn more when they feel competent and expect success. Feeling competent gives them a sense of personal control, which has been shown to be critical for enjoying

the learning process, exerting effort, and learning itself. In contrast, students who believe they are not competent and who don't expect to be successful are more anxious in learning situations and afraid of revealing their ignorance. These students are often reluctant to ask questions or offer opinions—even when confused or when they think they know the answer—because they anticipate embarrassment and humiliation. These students would rather not try at all than try and not succeed.

Values and goals. Even if students believe they *can* succeed in school, they won't exert effort unless they see some reason to do so. There are many reasons for doing academic work: enjoying learning, trying to get a good education, avoiding parental disapproval or punishment, or trying to stay eligible for the basketball team. Levels and qualities of engagement depend both on being motivated to do academic work and on what kind of motivation is involved. Internal sources of motivation—the work's intrinsic interest to the student and/or its importance to achieving goals important to the student—are more strongly associated with all three types of engagement (cognitive, emotional, and behavioral) than are external or extrinsic goals such as avoiding disapproval or receiving a material reward. These latter goals tend to dampen emotional and cognitive engagement in favor of compliance and getting the work over with. It is interesting to note that both feelings of competence and one's educational values and goals are intricately intertwined. A longitudinal study of children from grades 1–12 found that not only do students value academic work less as they progress through school but also that those declines can be accounted for by corresponding decreases in competence beliefs.

Social connectedness. Students who feel socially connected to school are more likely to be engaged. Being socially connected means that students feel that they are respected, that they and their opinions are valued, and that someone cares about them and how they do in school. Students who report such caring and supportive interpersonal relationships have more positive academic attitudes and values and are more satisfied with school. They are also more engaged in their academic work, attend school more, and learn more. Feeling psychologically connected to school is not sufficient for meaningful engagement in academic work, although students without such feelings may not stick around long enough to be successful. Youth who feel that nobody cares about them are much more likely to drop out.

Environmental Precursors of Competence, Values, and Belonging

Because a large percentage of adolescent's time is spent in school, a great deal of attention has been paid to the schooling environments that promote perceptions of competence and encourage positive values, goals, and feelings of social belonging. After all, knowing what psychological conditions promote engagement in school is only useful if we know what educational practices promote or undermine those conditions as well.

As mentioned above, students with caring and supportive teachers are more likely to feel connected to school. When teachers try to make class interesting, talk and listen to their students, show concern for them as individuals (e.g., making sure they understand what is being taught), and are honest and fair, students are more likely to reciprocate with good behavior in class. Students with caring teachers are more likely to feel a sense of responsibility toward those teachers by showing up and actively participating in class.

Providing choices within the context of clearly stated high expectations creates an environment that enhances student learning. Students are more likely to want to do schoolwork when they have some choice in the courses they take, the material they study, and the strategies they use to complete tasks. However, that autonomy must exist within a structure. Students still need

teachers to keep track of and care about whether they attend class, turn in homework, and understand the material. In contrast, students have been found to express a sense of dissatisfaction and disconnect from schools that have policies which discipline authoritatively and limit their academic options or freedom to make decisions. Students also tend to be disengaged from classes in which teachers are rigid and distrustful or do not encourage students to express their perspectives and opinions.

High expectations are also essential in promoting perceptions of competence and control over achievement outcomes. Academic tasks that are challenging though still achievable allow youth to develop confidence in their intellectual abilities. Schools with students who achieve high levels of performance have high expectations for student learning *and* hold all students to those high standards.

In addition to a supportive environment and high standards, students need to experience meaningful and engaging pedagogy and curriculum to be engaged in school. According to the National Council for Research (2004), the aspects of schooling that have been found to best engage students in their learning include the following:

Challenging work. Such work asks them to wrestle with new concepts, explain their reasoning, defend their conclusions, and explore alternative strategies and solutions.
Active involvement. Involvement in learning includes conducting experiments, participating in debate and role playing, or completing projects.
Collaborative work. Collaboration includes working in pairs or small groups on activities that require sharing and meaningful interactions. Students are also more receptive to challenging assignments when they can put their heads together rather than work in isolation.
Wide variety of activities.
Work that is meaningful to the world outside of school. Topics that are personally interesting and related to their lives make

learning more enjoyable and better enable students to integrate new information into their preexisting knowledge.

There is a general consensus in the literature that schools that provide high expectations, meaningful and engaging pedagogy and curriculum, and personalized learning environments are more likely to have students who are engaged in and connected to school. There is further agreement that schools need to develop a professional learning community among staff to ensure that teachers develop the skills they need to provide these conditions.

Is it realistic to believe that schools can create these conditions? Absolutely. Individual schools and districts across the country have embarked upon reform initiatives designed to improve student engagement and performance. In some cases, comprehensive school reform models such as the Coalition of Essential Schools, First Things First, Talent Development High School, and High Schools That Work have been utilized to help guide efforts of whole schools, and occasionally whole districts, to improve student learning.

Although they vary in approach, all comprehensive school reform models use a single school-wide vision as a focus for redesigning curriculum, student assessment, professional development, governance, management, and other key functions. These reform models are designed to raise expectations for student academic performance and ensure equity of opportunity to meet these higher standards; they provide organizational structures that offer ongoing assistance for implementation. Research suggests that when schools successfully implement these comprehensive models the results are positive, including increased levels of personalization, higher levels of attendance, improved test scores, increased persistence and graduation rates, and more parent involvement. There are also fewer disciplinary problems and lower dropout rates in these schools.

Policies Influencing Student Engagement

While it's clearly possible to create conditions to improve student engagement and learning, policies at the school, district, state, and federal levels are likely to undermine teachers' efforts to provide those conditions. The choices schools and districts make about how to organize students into learning groups, how long classes last, and whether to provide common planning time for staff impact how students and staff interact with each other. For instance, according to the National Research Council,

... tracking diminishes students' choices and the access of relatively low-skilled students to peers with positive academic values. Highly competitive school environments in which only high-performing students are recognized publicly undermine many students' sense of competence. Students are not likely to develop a sense of belonging in schools that are organized in ways that make it difficult for teachers to know and develop personal relationships with students, or in schools that tolerate racism or bullying. Schools that do not promote a sense of community and shared purpose among teachers are not likely to provide clear expectations and goals or to promote a sense of connectedness and belonging among students. If teachers spend all of their work day engaged directly with students, they will not have sufficient time to prepare appropriately challenging and culturally meaningful instruction and activities that involve collaboration and higher order thinking. Teaching that engages students takes much more time to plan than the repetitive textbook teaching that many teachers resort to because of the other demands on their time (2004, 36).

Other school policies can impact whether students feel supported and part of a community. Some schools have begun to provide additional help for students who are working below grade level such as after-school tutoring or an extra daily period of reading or math. Other schools match students with advisors/advocates who act as a bridge between students, parents, and community resources needed to meet the students' basic physical and psychological needs. Such efforts are likely to enhance students' feelings of belonging and help make school feel like a safe place in which to learn.

State and federal policies that promote higher levels of accountability may also influence student engagement in schools. Many states now require—or will soon require—that students pass an exit exam to graduate. A growing number of states now require students to pass an annual examination for grade promotion. Even more notable, a large proportion of states have begun to link certain privileges, such as the right to have a driver's license, to school attendance and performance.

In addition to these state-level accountability requirements, the federal No Child Left Behind Act (NCLB) requires states to test their students annually and expects a certain percentage of students to achieve proficiency each year. By 2014 every student in the United States, including minorities, low socioeconomic status (SES) students, special-education students, and English-language learners, is expected to demonstrate proficiency on state reading and math tests. Otherwise, schools and districts will face severe consequences.

Unfortunately, high-stakes tests have not been found to positively impact engagement in most students. The risk of being retained in grade or denied a high-school diploma may lead some students to exert more effort on schoolwork than they otherwise would. However, they will only exert such efforts if they believe they have the capacity to succeed. Simply asking students, especially low achieving students, to meet higher standards without providing them with the extra instructional resources they need to meet those standards is likely to be counterproductive. In fact, such experiences are more likely to encourage students to give up and even go so far as to drop out of school.

In conclusion, with the era of accountability showing no evidence of waning, it is of even greater importance that schools and districts work to provide the kind of educational environments that inspire all students—advantaged and disadvantaged alike—to delve into their education and strive to learn and perform at levels that guarantee success on high-stakes tests. More specifically, shouldn't we have high-stakes assessments of whether educational *systems* are providing engaging learning environments before we begin punishing individual students in those systems for not making the grade?

See also Character Education; Citizenship Education Policies in the States; Civic Virtue; Deliberative Democracy; Democratic Education; Diversity Education; Environmental Education (EE); IEA Civic Education Study; Just Community High Schools and Youth Activism; Kids Voting USA (KVUSA); National Alliance for Civic Education (NACE); Prosocial Behaviors; School Influences and Civic Engagement; Service Learning; Student Voices Project.

Recommended Reading

Connell, J. P., Halpern-Felsher, B., Clifford, E., Crichlow, W., and Usinger, P. (1995). "Hanging in There: Behavioral, Psychological, and Contextual Factors Affecting Whether African-American Adolescents Stay in School." *Journal of Adolescent Research*, 10 (1): 41–63.

Connell, J. P., Spencer, M. B., and Aber, J. L. (1994). "Educational Risk and Resilience in African American Youth: Context, Self, Action and Outcomes in School." *Child Development*, 65: 493–506.

Connell, J. P., and Wellborn, J. (1991). "Competence, Autonomy, and Relatedness: A Motivational and Analysis of Self-System Processes." In *Self Processes in Development: Minnesota Symposium on Child Psychology*, 23, edited by M. Gunnar and L. Sroufe. Hillsdale, NJ: Lawrence Erlbaum, pp. 43–77.

Marks, H. M. (2000). "Student Engagement in Instructional Activity: Patterns in the Elementary, Middle and High Schools Years." *American Educational Research Journal*, 37: 153–184.

National Research Council and the Institute of Medicine (2004). *Engaging Schools: Fostering High School Students' Motivation to Learn.* Committee on Increasing High School Students' Engagement and Motivation to Learn. Board on Children, Youth, and Families, Division of Behavioral and Social Science and Education. Washington, D.C.: National Academies Press.

Newmann, F. (1992). *Student Engagement and Achievement in American Secondary Schools*. New York: Teachers College Press.

Steinberg, A., and Almeida, C. (2004). *From the Margins to the Mainstream: Effective Learning Environments for Urban Youth*. Boston: Jobs for the Future.

Adena M. Klem and James P. Connell

School Influences and Civic Engagement. How do students' experiences in school relate to their becoming actively engaged citizens in their communities and the wider political world? That question has long interested researchers and educators and is the focus of this entry. In the United States it is generally assumed that a major purpose of schooling is to prepare people to become active participating citizens. Since the days of George Washington and Thomas Jefferson, numerous political leaders and educators have emphasized the need to educate people for their roles as citizens of a democracy. A recently published report, *The Civic Mission of Schools*, calls for renewed attention to the traditional role of schools in preparing youth to be engaged citizens of a democracy. Although in many other countries citizenship education has not been traditionally viewed as an important function of schools, today people in many parts of the world recognize that experiences in school are important to civic engagement. In recent years many countries began giving increased attention to the role of schools in preparing citizens. For example, in England, Scotland, Wales, and Northern Ireland there are new policies on citizenship education. In Australia major initiatives on citizenship/civics education in schools have been undertaken in recent years and in countries of Eastern and Central Europe there are new school-based programs to prepare youth for democratic citizenship. These are just a few examples of how widespread the belief is that schools can have an influence on the kind of citizens that students become.

Of course schools are not alone in fostering civic participation. Indeed, other entries in this volume demonstrate ways in which families, peer groups, media, and the wider culture contribute to civic engagement. Nevertheless, there are important ways in which schools can and do contribute to the civic engagement of youth and to their continued participation as adults. In this entry four types of school influences that can relate to youth engagement are discussed. The first set of influences is related to the school's curriculum. Curriculum includes both the intended curriculum (as it is outlined in curriculum standards and guidelines) and the enacted curriculum (as it is delivered in civic-related courses, such as social studies, civics or government, and history). The second school influence that is associated with civic engagement is classroom climate supportive of democratic discussions. The third school influence associated with engagement is school-level student participation, such as participation in student government and extracurricular activities. The fourth school influence is service learning in which students' experiences in community service are linked to the academic program of the school.

In this entry research that indicates the importance of these school influences is discussed. Before looking at the results from a variety of research studies, however, it is important to keep a few points in mind. First, readers should be aware that there are only a few longitudinal studies that follow the same individuals for several years and enable researchers to link school experiences with later adult participation. Additionally, most of the research that exists is based on correlational, not causal, analyses. That means that a researcher may find that students who belong to extracurricular activities are more likely than students who do not participate to say that they expect that when they are adults they will write letters to policymakers expressing their views. However, we cannot be certain that participation in activities is the cause of their expectation; possibly young people who are the most likely to express their views are the ones who join extracurricular activities to begin with. Even with these limitations, however, there is considerable research that links school experiences with civic knowledge and attitudes, and civic knowledge and attitudes appear to be important for later engagement. Another point to consider before we begin to examine research findings is that researchers know more about "conventional" political participation (such as voting, writing letters to decision-makers, and joining community and political groups) than about protest activities, perhaps because of the relatively small number of middle-school or high-school students who were involved in protest activities during the 1980s and 1990s. Finally, most of the research discussed in this entry—with the exception of one large-scale international study—is based on studies conducted in the United States. Similar research is beginning to accumulate in other countries.

The first school influence we explore is the one related to school curriculum. As part of the "accountability movement" that swept educational reform efforts in the United States from the 1980s onward (the years following the publication of the report entitled *A Nation at Risk*), groups of educators, citizens, and policymakers developed voluntary national standards for curriculum in civics and government, history, and social studies. Those documents recommend curriculum standards for teaching important concepts, themes, generalizations, and civic skills to students. Since the publication of the national standards documents in the 1990s, many states have adopted state testing programs, aligned with new state standards and frameworks, to determine if students are meeting standards of proficiency. Unfortunately, there is little information on the extent to which standards have been implemented and less on whether teaching to the standards is associated with civic engagement. Regardless, the standards movement has clearly influenced the environment in which the school curriculum is delivered.

Closely related to curriculum standards is the topic of assessment. In the United States, the National Assessment of Educational Progress (NAEP) regularly measures knowledge of representative samples of students in grades four, eight, and twelve. Over the years, NAEP studies in social studies, civics, and history have yielded information on what students in the United States learn about topics that are presumed to relate to civic engagement. For example, questions measure students' understanding of the U.S. Constitution and political institutions and processes. Researchers have analyzed results from NAEP assessments to identify levels of student knowledge or "proficiency," the topics that students study in school, and levels of engagement in civic-related experiences. Importantly, using results from NAEP, researchers have found that students who have had courses with civic-related content, such as civics, government, or social studies, do better on the NAEP test of civic knowledge than do students without such courses. The amount and recency of taking civics courses is also significant. The topics that eighth and twelfth graders report studying are the U.S. Constitution and Bill of Rights, Congress, political parties, elections and voting, and citizens' rights and responsibilities. The finding that students' having taken civic-related courses relates to civic knowledge is important because other researchers have found that adults who are most knowledgeable tend to be the most civically engaged. Furthermore, in one of the few longitudinal studies in this area, Miller found that students who had civic-related courses when they were in high school later became more civically engaged adults than their peers without such courses. Having had formal coursework in civics or government was especially important for minority students.

Other longitudinal data come from the National Education Longitudinal Study (NELS) of 1988. A nationally representative sample of 25,000 U.S. students, their parents, and teachers were initially assessed in 1988 when the students were in the eighth grade (approximately age thirteen). A subsample of 15,000 of the original sample was assessed six years later when the young people had been out of high school for two years. At that point, participants who had three or more social studies courses when they were in high school were more civically engaged; they were more likely to have registered to vote, to vote, and to do volunteer work than their peers with fewer social-studies courses.

Additional information on courses, students' level of civic knowledge, and predispositions to civic engagement come from the civic education studies of the International Association of the Evaluation of Educational Achievement, better known as the IEA (see also IEA Civic Education Study). Like the NAEP, the IEA studies use nationally representative samples of students, and they measure student knowledge, topics studied in school, and civic-related experiences. In addition, IEA studies reveal important information about student attitudes that may be important to later civic engagement.

In the 1999 IEA Civic Education Study, U.S. ninth graders who reported studying social studies everyday did better on a test of civic knowledge than did students who reported less frequent social studies instruction. Additionally, more that 75 percent of U.S. fourteen-year-olds reported studying about the U.S. Constitution, the presidency, Congress, and the courts sometime over the previous year; fewer had studied about other countries' governments or international organizations. Students who said they studied about the courts or the Congress had higher knowledge scores than students who did not study those topics.

Importantly, in the international analysis of over 90,000 students in twenty-eight countries, the IEA researchers found that civic knowledge was a predictor of expected likelihood of voting as an adult. That is, for fourteen-year-old students, both internationally and in the United States,

civic knowledge was positively correlated with students saying that they expected they would vote regularly in national elections when they become adults. In a later analysis of the IEA data from the United States, Colombia, Chile, and Portugal, civic knowledge was associated with a number of other expected conventional citizenship activities, as well as voting. Civic knowledge correlated with students' expectations that as adults they would seek information about candidates before voting in an election, write letters to a newspaper about a social or political concern, join a political party, and be a candidate for a local or city office. However, knowledge was not related to the expectation of volunteering in the community for students in the United States.

Another aspect of the enacted or delivered curriculum is whether or not students are deliberately taught about the importance of voting and the function of elections. In the IEA study in all of the twenty-eight participating countries students who reported that they learned in school about the importance of voting were more likely to expect to vote as adults than their peers who did not remember being taught about the importance of voting.

Providing courses and including particular content in the curriculum are important curricular influences but equally important is how the content is delivered. For example, on the NAEP, one predictor of twelfth graders' civic knowledge was whether or not students had participated in mock elections, mock trials, or simulations of legislatures.

Several researchers looked at the combination of civic content and active teaching methods used in particular curriculum projects. Researchers who studied the effects of projects that involved students with authentic content and tasks and encouraged peer discussion of alternatives found positive results. For example, evaluators of Kids Voting, a program that uses a variety of instructional activities to teach about elections, found that participating students communicated more with parents about politics, used political media such as newspapers in the home more, and had higher knowledge levels than comparable students who did not participate in the program. Similarly, evaluations of the programs We the People and Project Citizen, both of which use discussions and involving activities, have yielded promising results in terms of civic knowledge and attitudes. Project Citizen, a widely used program in the United States and a number of other countries, is particularly relevant to civic engagement. Middle-school-aged students participating in the program identify a problem in their community and research the problem. The students generate alternative solutions to the problem, weigh the evidence, and decide on a solution to propose to local decision-makers. Evaluators of the program found that students acquired knowledge of public policies and the policymaking process; developed research, communication, and group skills; and developed confidence in their ability to make a difference in their communities.

Evaluators of other curricular programs that engage students in discussion about civic issues have found that students develop attitudes that are important to civic engagement in today's world of diverse cultures and beliefs. For example, students who studied about civic tolerance (the willingness to extend rights to disliked groups) and who discussed the application of abstract principles of tolerance to specific case studies in the curriculum program called Tolerance for Diversity of Beliefs showed increased levels of civic tolerance.

Another program, the International Communication and Negotiations Project (ICONS), is a simulation exercise developed at the University of Maryland with participating students in the United States and other countries. Students play the roles of diplomats from a given country, and they engage in online computer discussions around such issues as immigration and international debt. Researchers found that students who participated in this highly involving program developed increased sophistication in their understanding of international problems such as debt in developing countries. Interestingly, many school-based programs that have a positive effect on student knowledge and attitudes require students to explore diverse views on social and political issues. This leads to the second important school influence that has been associated with civic engagement: the classroom climate for discussion.

In a series of studies researchers have repeatedly identified the importance of a classroom climate in which students are encouraged to explore diverse views and in which they feel comfortable expressing those views, even when they differ from those of the teacher and other students. In studies of high-school students in the United States and other Western democracies, researchers have found that student perceptions of an open classroom climate correlate with student levels of political interest, political efficacy, political trust, and political participation. However, the mere inclusion of controversial issues is insufficient. When such issues are touched upon in a "closed" climate in which only one view is presented and/or students do not feel comfortable expressing their views, then lower levels of political efficacy, participation, and sense of citizenship duty have been found.

In the IEA Civic Education Study, perceptions of an open classroom climate for discussion were predictors of both student civic knowledge and expectations of voting as adults. One researcher also found that discussion with teachers about national and international political issues and perceptions of an open classroom climate for discussion were significant predictors of expectations of engagement in conventional political activities, such as joining a political party and writing letters to newspapers about social and political concerns, and in social-movement activities, such as volunteering time to help people in the community and collecting money for a social cause, when the effects of gender and home literacy were statistically controlled.

Perceptions of an open classroom climate vary across and within countries. In the IEA study, U.S. students overall scored above the international mean on the classroom climate scale, and in another study of classroom climate for discussion students in the United States and Denmark reported that they experienced comparatively open classroom climates. Within the United States, differences have also been noted. For example, in one study researchers studied students in four purposefully selected communities—suburban, urban, rural, and immigrant. Students in the suburban and rural communities were more likely to report that they often experienced discussions of political issues in their classes than did students in the urban and immigrant communities. The researchers hypothesized that discussion in school develops skills and motivation for discussion in other settings, such as with families and peers. In addition, the researchers suspected that in urban and immigrant communities there might be less family encouragement for civic participation. Consequently, they argued, it is especially important for schools to provide opportunities for democratic discussion.

In planning instruction, it is important for teachers to give attention to three dimensions—content, pedagogy, and climate. Teachers need to include issues-centered content, such as historic and current issues over which citizens of the past or present disagree. With respect to pedagogy, teachers need to plan instructional approaches, such as open discussions, debates, and simulations that enable students to hear and express varied viewpoints on issues. Thirdly, teachers need to ensure that the climate for discussion is open and supportive of exploring diverse views. It appears to be the combination of issues-centered content, pedagogy, and climate that is the most promising for developing civic attitudes that support engagement.

Two possible school-related practices that can encompass issues-centered teaching in an open classroom climate are having students investigate local problems (as in the previously mentioned program, Project Citizen) and having students follow and discuss current events. Using data from the IEA study, researchers found that learning in school to solve problems in the community was a predictor of students' levels of anticipated society-related and conventional citizenship activities in the United States, Colombia, Chile, and Portugal. That is, students in those countries who recalled that in school they learned to solve community issues were the most likely to anticipate that as adults they would participate in society-related activities such as volunteering to help the elderly, collecting money for a social cause, collecting signatures for a petition, and participating in a nonviolent protest; they were also most likely to expect to engage in conventional citizenship activities, such as voting. Reading the newspaper—a practice that is encouraged in some schools and classrooms—was also a predictor of both expected society-related and conventional citizenship.

The third school influence related to engagement is participation in extracurricular activities and student governance. Much of the literature in civic education is based on the assumption that the most effective way to instill habits of democratic participation is to provide opportunities for student decision-making in school life. In a secondary analysis of data from four of the IEA countries, researchers found that students' confidence in school-level participation was a predictor of anticipated society-related citizenship activities. That is, students who believed that working together with their peers in solving school problems and believed that the student council made a difference in how the school functioned were the most likely to expect that they would undertake civic action in their communities. Participating in student government was also a predictor of

U.S. students' beliefs that they were likely to vote as adults.

Additionally, for the U.S. sample in the IEA study, students who reported participating in extracurricular activities had higher scores on civic knowledge than students without such participation. For the U.S. sample, it did not matter whether the participation was in student government or activities such as band or sports. In an earlier phase of the IEA study, students reported in focus groups that they learned about democracy and about diversity in society by participating in extracurricular activities.

Researchers who analyzed longitudinal datasets have found that participation in extracurricular activities in high school is associated with civic and political engagement in adulthood. Using data from the National Education Longitudinal Study (NELS), one researcher found that eighth graders' participation in extracurricular activities was a significant predictor of their level of civic and political participation six years later, when the sample was approximately nineteen years old. Other researchers who used longitudinal data from the National Center for Education Statistics (NCES) came to a similar conclusion. Students who had participated in high-school extracurricular activities, including honorary societies, student government, and sports, were more engaged in civic and political activities as adults than were their peers who had not participated in extracurricular activities; this was especially true for females. These findings corroborate research conducted earlier in which participation in extracurricular activities correlated with involvement in political and social activity in young adulthood. Despite the consistency of findings in different studies, it is important to keep in mind that participation in school-based extracurricular activities is associated with civic engagement; it does not necessarily cause the outcomes. It may be that students who are most interested in the political and civic arena to begin with are the ones who choose to participate in extracurricular activities. Nevertheless, it is likely that in the process of participating, they acquire skills and attitudes that will serve them well as adult participants.

The fourth school influence that may have an effect on civic engagement is service learning. Although other entries in this encyclopedia discuss service learning in depth, it is important to at least note here that service learning is one form of school-based program that may influence civic engagement (see also Service Learning and Service Learning and Citizenship Education). Most of the research on service-learning programs in which students' experiences in community service are linked to the academic program of the school examine outcomes such as student self-esteem and expressed desire to volunteer in the future, rather than to specific civic or political outcomes. However, a few researchers have found that school-based service-learning programs can foster outcomes related to civic engagement. For example, researchers found positive effects for service learning in the United States and England in one secondary analysis of the IEA Civic Education Study. The effects were considerably weaker in other countries.

The Civic Mission of Schools, mentioned earlier as calling for renewed attention to school-based civic education, concludes that the service-learning programs that are most effective for the purposes of civic education are ones that have the following characteristics: are designed explicitly for civic outcomes; encourage students to engage in meaningful work on serious public issues; give students an opportunity to choose and design their form of involvement; provide opportunities for students to reflect on their service work; and link service with school instruction, among other factors.

Finally although there are a variety of institutions that influence youth civic engagement, as *The Civic Mission of Schools* emphasizes: "schools are the only institutions with the capacity and mandate to reach virtually every young person in the country." In addition, the report adds, "Schools are the best equipped to address the cognitive aspects of good citizenship—civic and political knowledge and related skills such as critical thinking and deliberation." Clearly, schools can be an important element in preparing youth for active civic engagement through the curriculum, classroom climate for discussion, extracurricular activities, and service-learning programs.

See also Character Education; Citizenship Education Policies in the States; Civic Virtue; Democratic Education; Diversity Education; Environmental Education (EE); IEA Civic Education Study; Just Community High Schools and Youth Activism; Kids Voting USA (KVUSA); National Alliance for Civic Education (NACE); Prosocial Behaviors; School Engagement; Student Voices Project.

Recommended Reading

Baldi, S., Perie, M., Skidmore, D., Greenberg, E., and Hahn, C. (2001). What Democracy Means to Ninth-Graders: U.S. Results from the International IEA Civic Education Study. Washington, D.C.: National Center for Education Statistics, U.S. Department of Education.

Carnegie Corporation of New York and CIRCLE: The Center for Information and Research on Civic Learning and Engagement (2003). The Civic Mission of Schools. New York: Carnegie Corporation of New York.

Center for Civic Education (1994). National Standards for Civics and Government. Calabasas, CA: Center for Civic Education.

Hahn, C. L. (1998). Becoming Political: Comparative Perspectives on Citizenship Education. Albany, NY: State University of New York (SUNY) Press.

Hahn, C. L. (1999). "Challenges to Civic Education in the United States." In Civic Education Across Countries: Twenty-four National Case Studies From the IEA Civic Education Project, edited by J. Torney-Purta, J. Schwille, and J. A. Amadeo. Amsterdam: International Association for the Evaluation of Educational Achievement. ED 431 705, pp. 583–607.

Lutkus, A. D., Weiss, A. R., Campbell, J. R., Mazeo, J., and Lazer, S. (1999). The NAEP Civics Report Card for the Nation. Washington, D.C.: National Center for Education Statistics.

Niemi, R., and Junn, J. (1998). Civic Education: What Makes Students Learn. New Haven, CT: Yale University Press.

Torney-Purta, J., and Amadeo, J. A. (2004). Strengthening Democracy in the Americas through Civic Education: An Empirical Analysis Highlighting the Views of Students and Teachers. Washington, D.C.: Organization of American States.

Torney-Purta, J., Lehmann, R., Oswald, H., and Schulz, W. (2001). Citizenship and Education in Twenty-eight Countries: Civic Knowledge and Engagement at Age Fourteen. Amsterdam: International Association for the Evaluation of Educational Achievement.

Torney-Purta, J., Schwille, J., and Amadeo, J. A. (1999). Civic Education across Countries: Twenty-four National Case Studies from the IEA Civic Education Project. Amsterdam: International Association for the Evaluation of Educational Achievement.

Carole L. Hahn

Serbia, Youth Activism in (1990–2000). Rock and techno blasting over the radio, thousands of whistles blown in unison, impromptu theater after midnight, eggs thrown at government buildings, and dancing in the streets: these were the signs of young Serbian activists waging revolution in the 1990s. Throughout this decade young men and women across Serbia took to the streets to protest the oppressive policies of Serbian leader Slobodan Milošević. Known for their creativity, their political savvy, and their perseverance, Serbian activists fought ten years against a dictatorial regime and won.

These young men and women had come of age in the midst of high unemployment, a failing educational system, political despair, and rampant nationalism. They faced economic instability, isolation by the international community, and a hostile and violent political culture in which their needs were largely ignored. While other Socialist countries in Eastern Europe began to implement democratic political systems after the fall of the Berlin wall in 1989, Yugoslavia, the country of which Serbia was then a part, engaged in a series of terrible civil wars. The result of these wars was the breakup of Yugoslavia into five countries: Slovenia, Croatia, Bosnia, Macedonia, and

Serbia and Montenegro (which includes the still contested province of Kosovo). Many young men lived in fear of being drafted into military service and sent to fight a war they wanted nothing to do with. But despite all these difficulties, Serbian youth were the leading voices of political critique and social change in the country. They often played on the traditional social category of youth as the leaders of change and the vanguard of revolution, which had been a common perception in Socialist Yugoslavia. Youth activists built networks within Serbia and across Europe and used both protest and negotiation to achieve their goals. Student organizations were forged in protests and grew at the universities. Students took to the streets to call for better conditions at the university, a freer media, and democratic elections. They sought greater contact with young people from other countries, including their peers in the former Yugoslav lands. By the time of Milošević's ouster in 2000, the participation of young citizens had radically affected the nature of politics in Serbia, demonstrating that they were a significant force for change.

Much of the trouble began in 1990 when Milošević was elected to the presidency of Serbia on a campaign, which played on sentiments of fear and nationalism. From the beginning, Milošević used state television, radio, and newspapers to control the information to which people had access and to rally support for his nationalist policies. Naturally, anyone who had a different story to tell about the events in Serbia and the former Yugoslavia had no access to the Milošević-controlled media. The first major protest of the 1990s took place in March 1991, when, furious about this situation, students joined opposition leaders in Republic Square in the center of Belgrade, eventually marching on the Serbian parliament building. The demonstrations were met with military force, arrests, beatings, and national media coverage lambasting the demonstrators as unruly and violent traitors. Still the protests persisted. For ten

days students held the "Terazije Parliament," a massive, outdoor student parliament in central Belgrade from which students issued several antiregime demands. They wanted protestors who had been arrested to be freed; the minister of police to give his resignation; and greater freedom of the press, including the reopening of alternative music and news station B92, which the government had shut down. B92 was the heart of alternative media in Serbia through the 1990s, and this would not be their last tussle with the regime. While many of these protest demands were met, it was still the beginning of a long struggle between largely urban youth and the political leaders who held their country prisoner. By the following year the wars in the former Yugoslavia had begun, and Milošević, playing on the fear of his citizens, was more powerful than ever.

In 1991 Slovenia and Croatia declared independence from Yugoslavia, and the Yugoslav National Army (under Milošević's control) invaded. Fighting in Slovenia was short-lived, but the war in Croatia raged on, killing many and displacing hundreds of thousands. In reaction to Milošević's war policies just across the border and his squelching of democracy at home, as well as frustration at the introduction of international sanctions, students and opposition leaders took to the streets in June 1992. Again students mobilized through the universities in Belgrade, Niš, and Novi Sad (the largest cities in Serbia after Belgrade), calling for the disbanding of parliament, Milošević's resignation, and new elections. Students also protested the decreasing autonomy of the university, ending the protest in Belgrade with a symbolic burial of the "Freedom of the University" in front of the Serbian Parliament. Despite a university-wide petition, a new university law was passed shortly thereafter. The law increased state control of the university, increasing government representation in university bodies and government control in electing rectors and deans. The regime saw this crackdown on the university as a way to control a major source of resistance and protest. However, the struggle between antiregime students and professors and those who supported Milošević would continue throughout the decade.

Given the circumstances at the time, activism was often tempered by the struggle to survive. By late 1992 and into 1993 people in Serbia were tired and frustrated with the Milošević regime. Many felt hopeless. Beginning in the early 1990s young men and women, often urban and educated, left the country in astonishing numbers. Estimates indicate that as many as 300,000 of the country's best and brightest emigrated. The war in Croatia meant a flood of refugees swept into Serbia. The war in Bosnia began in April 1992. It would last until the signing of the Dayton agreement in 1995 and result in almost 2 million refugees and more than 200,000 dead. Meanwhile, Serbia was poor and getting poorer. The international sanctions meant not only economic but cultural and political isolation as well. And then things got even worse. In 1993 Serbia was hit by some of the worst hyperinflation Europe had ever seen. The Serbian dinar became worthless. Between November 2, 1993, and December 22, 1993, the price of a six-gram loaf of bread went from 12,500 to 4 billion dinars. The country was plagued with shortages and finding a market with food on the shelves could be a daily struggle. With the familiar dark humor of Serbia at that time, one radio station even offered a free toaster to the person who had the dinar bill with the most zeros on it.

Life for young men and women at this time was constantly insecure. Universities were severely overcrowded, more like holding pens for a generation rather than institutions of higher learning. In order to keep young people off the streets, the government had an almost open enrollment policy. With no jobs in sight and the sheer boredom of being poor and isolated in Serbia, many people saw no reason to graduate and leave the semisecurity of university behind. In addition, many young men

who would have otherwise been drafted for military service used student status to delay or avoid this fate. The problems at the university and Milošević's control over that key institution would be a sensitive issue throughout the 1990s and a source of many protest demands. At the same time, the university was also a training ground for young activists, a place where people could meet, plan, and eventually launch protests. By the end of Milošević's regime, some of the most clever protest strategies and influential protest leaders and organizations had emerged from the halls of Serbia's universities.

By 1995 the economy improved slightly, a tentative peace had been brokered in Bosnia, and people were ready to think about change. When Milošević called local elections in 1996 hope and anticipation were in the air. (Periodic elections helped maintain the appearance of a functioning democracy during Milošević's regime. This would be his final undoing in 2000.) For now, the challengers to Milošević's ruling party formed the *Zajedno* (Together) coalition, a wide umbrella organization of political parties. As the election results began to roll in on November 17, 1996, it became clear that Milošević's ruling party had been defeated in several major cities through Serbia. One by one, Belgrade, Niš, Novi Sad, and Kragujevac were taken by *Zajedno*.

Milošević, however, had different plans. With the votes still being counted, he announced the election had suffered from "voting irregularities" and the results were invalid. But this time, Milošević clearly underestimated how much citizens of Serbia cared about those results. Within days, tens of thousands—and soon hundreds of thousands—of people took to the streets in protest. Led on one side by a civic protest initiated by the democratic opposition and on the other by an independent student protest led by student activists, the protests lasted from November 17, 1996, until March 20, 1997. Despite the bitter cold, people filled city streets across the country every day for these three months, and the most famous pictures from this period are of columns of people snaking through the wide boulevards of central Belgrade. They carried signs, performed street theater, blasted music, and blew thousands and thousands of whistles in unison. The idea was to be as visible as possible, to stop hiding in homes, at the university, and in office buildings and factories. The protests were meant to publicly demonstrate once and for all that Serbian citizens cared about democratic elections. At various peak points, the number of protesters in Belgrade alone numbered between 200,000 and 500,000.

The student part of the protests was known, in particular, for its wit as well as its size. In Belgrade, students carried a huge banner declaring *Beograd je Svet* (Belgrade Is the World), and hundreds of people waved flags and logos from all over the world. The point was that young people were sick of the isolation that Milošević had brought on the country. In protest of his control of state media (which barely even covered the protests) students took to making as much noise as possible at 7:30 p.m. when the state news was on television. They blew whistles and banged pots and pans in a collective effort known as *Buka je u modi* (Noise Is in Fashion!).

The character of these protests was also expressed in the music people listened to during this time. What you listened to became an important symbol of affiliation with the resistance to the regime. It signaled openness to the world. Music could be creative, angry, and fun, as long as it was music that made you think, move, and resist. Music from around the world was juxtaposed with the syrupy new Serbian pop-folk music known as turbofolk associated with gangsters, nationalists, and war criminals. The turbofolk music scene was known for its connection to the regime and its lyrics that glorified the nation, romantic love, and images of macho men and scantily clad women, which often reinforced traditional gender roles. On the other hand,

Serbian bands, some of them with their roots in the rock, new wave, and punk scenes of Yugoslavia in the 1980s, provided underground musical alternatives. New bands like Darkwood Dub, Kanda Kodža i Nebojša, and Eyesburn wrote and sang what many young people wanted to hear or felt but were afraid to say. Songs like "*Proći Će I Njihovo*" (Their Time Too Will Pass) and "Fool Control" (Eyesburn) were anthems against the regime.

In the face of massive public dissent, Milošević caved, and in February he declared the election results valid. At this point the civic protests led by the opposition ended, but the students had more demands to make. In addition to the validation of the local election results, they wanted greater freedoms at the university and the resignation of key figures in the university administration who they felt were complicit with the regime. The student protests continued through March 20, 1997, when their demands were finally met.

The reinstatement of opposition election victories did not significantly hurt Milošević in the end, although the demonstrations did forge a new student leadership, teach the opposition some hard lessons about effective political organizing, and shake the regime's legitimacy at home and abroad. Ultimately, the *Zajedno* coalition fell apart, disappointing its supporters and strengthening the regime's political hold. However, many new youth initiatives sprang up out of the protests, and student and youth organizations began to flourish in Serbia. Two of the key organizations to emerge from these protests were the youth movement Otpor (Resistance) and the independent student organization Studentska Unija (Student Union).

Otpor, started by a group of friends from Belgrade University, was a well-directed organizational effort with the appearance of total spontaneity. This was the organization's strength. All across Serbia, anyone, especially youth, who was fed up with the Milošević regime had a new outlet. All of a sudden graffiti appeared all over Serbia displaying Otpor's characteristic black fist, raised against the regime and in solidarity with the youth of Serbia. Students began sporting Otpor T-shirts and badges, an offense that could mean arrest and even beating. Coverage of Otpor actions and messages and the regime's repressive response began to make its way into mainstream media.

Support for Otpor grew, such that an Otpor fist might pop up anywhere across the country at any time. Others began to get involved, especially parents. A member of Otpor could be the kid next door or the best student in your class. People began to ask themselves, how could we support a leader who allows police to beat and arrest our children?

In a related effort, many activists focused on freedoms at the university itself, and branches of Studentska Unija at faculties across the country multiplied, challenging the regime's control over the intellectual and social life of students. The student union, a grassroots organization which mobilized students to fight for their rights at the faculty, would eventually expand into a coordinated national effort. The student union became particularly important in and after 1998 with new crackdowns on freedom at the universities, including a new university law forcing professors to sign oaths of loyalty to the regime.

In 1998 in response to the rise of the Kosovo Liberation Army (KLA) in the majority Albanian province of Kosovo, Milošević sent massive numbers of troops into the region. The military crackdown by the Serbian army and violent confrontations with the KLA resulted in large numbers of murdered civilians and over half a million refugees. This spurred the North Atlantic Treaty Organization (NATO), a political and military coalition including the United States and many nations in Western Europe, to issue an ultimatum to Milošević: pull your troops out of Kosovo or we will bomb Serbia. When final negotiations broke down in March 1999, NATO made good on its promise. The first bombs began to fall on March 24, and they fell every day until June 9, 1999, seventy-seven days later.

NATO bombings made it impossible to publicly resist the regime in Serbia. Increased atomization of citizens and fear about the bombings made it unlikely that people would have questioned Milošević openly even if they could. People who had been protesting Milošević and his policies for years felt betrayed by the outside world, especially the United States, and anger grew as civilian casualties from the bombings increased. During this time all opposition effectively went underground, as people were frightened that regime violence, even murder, against the opposition would be easy to cover up in the chaos of the war. Sadly, another consequence of the war in Kosovo was that the bonds that Kosovar-Albanian and Serbian students had been able to maintain up to that point broke down almost completely. For many years youth activists in Kosovo and Serbia had struggled to maintain connections and open communication when politicians from the two regions had long since been hostile. But with the violence of the Serbian occupation and the brutal killing of civilians, young Kosovar-Albanians' anger, fear, and sense of betrayal made this dialog extremely difficult. On the other hand, the death of Serbian civilians in the war and the KLA's targeted destruction of Serbian historical and religious monuments in Kosovo fueled anger among young people in Serbia proper. Even as student groups became stronger in Serbia, their isolation from student groups elsewhere and the closing off of communication in the face of anger and fear was part of the story of youth activism in the 1990s.

Following the bombings, the Otpor resistance group made a key decision to regroup and begin again. They increased their activities and presence all over the country. When it looked like elections would be held in autumn of 2000 they initiated a massive "get out the vote" campaign, encouraging every young person and anyone who was sick of the Milošević regime to go to the polls. In the summer of 2000 joint efforts of student groups, including Studentska Unija and Otpor in Novi Sad gave birth to EXIT, a small music festival that started on the banks of the Danube and grew enormously. EXIT lasted one hundred days and led right up to the elections in September of 2000. Every day people gathered by the river across from the university in Novi Sad to listen to bands, watch movies and performances, and to be with other young people. After years of feeling alone, isolated, and hopeless, finally people could look around them and see a critical mass of other young men and women who were ready for a change and who wanted something more for themselves. Their mood was excited and hopeful and always a little scared of the next possible crackdown around the corner. The festival mantra, reflecting the central campaign of Otpor that summer and fall, was "*GOTOV JE*" ("He's Finished"). When elections finally came on September 26, young people came out to vote for the opposition candidate Vojislav Koštunica in unprecedented numbers. This massive youth support swept Koštunica to victory.

Milošević refused to honor the election results for almost two weeks until, finally, on October 5 hundreds of thousands of citizens from all parts of Serbia marched in Belgrade. They stormed the Serbian parliament and the headquarters of the state controlled media, Radio and Television Serbia. Instead of firing into the crowds, Milošević's massive police force stood quietly aside or joined the protest. By the end of the day Milošević had conceded defeat.

Serbia's youth activism is still alive and kicking in 2004 but with the disappearance of the central enemy, Milošević, young people have branched out and are experimenting with different ways to be citizens. In the 1990s the youth movement, and especially Otpor, was more an umbrella for people of many different backgrounds and with different political viewpoints united in the common goal of defeating Milošević. Groups, from antiglobalization anarchists

to the youth branches of democratic parties, have widely different goals and interests now. Some activists feel that the protests didn't do enough to address Serbia's responsibility for the wars in Croatia, Bosnia, and Kosovo, while others believe this position is a betrayal of their country. Some activists are focusing on new challenges in post-Milošević Serbia, such as the rights of women, minorities, gays and lesbians, and people with handicaps. Several youth and civic organizations are addressing the issue of Serbia's eventual integration into the European Union. All youth groups suffered a blow when Serbian Prime Minister Zoran Djindjić was assassinated in Belgrade on March 12, 2003. A former student leader himself, Djindjić was a pillar of support for student activism in the 1990s, and many young people had pinned their hopes for real democratic change on his leadership.

Many youth activists remain burned out and tired. If they want to organize at all, it is within professional organizations, sports teams, or cultural associations. Meanwhile, other activists have grown up and simply do not see themselves as part of a youth movement anymore. Otpor transformed from a student and youth movement to a new political party, agitating for democratic change from within, rather than from outside, the political system. Some youth activism has taken a negative turn and has embraced the nationalist policies of the 1990s, which has resulted in some direct conflict between activists who once found themselves on the same side of the Milošević issue. Other groups are building bridges with young men and women in Bosnia, Croatia, and in rare cases Kosovo, trying to reconnect ties of trust and common citizenship that were torn apart in the wars.

Alternative education programs, pulled together in the mid-1990s by students and professors dedicated to intellectual freedom and critical thinking, are also places where students have gathered. Many activists are trying to rebuild the university, which still suffers from overcrowding and underfunding, and to expand educational possibilities for Serbian students within the framework of European Union educational programs. Students in Serbia have joined efforts with other European student organizations such as ESIB, the organization of European student unions. Today, EXIT is still going on. It is one of the biggest music festivals in Southeast Europe, although it now lasts only four days. While it still has a civic education component, it is largely a festival where young people go to have fun, hear some bands, and meet new people. Such wide-ranging political positions cannot simply be reconciled in one movement. Whatever young activists are doing, however, they face a struggle to overcome the poverty, crime, and devastation of the last fifteen years. Yet young men and women remain hopeful. They keep moving and they stay active because if they want a better Serbia and a better future, they have no other choice.

See also Australia, Youth Activism in; Demographic Trends Affecting the World's Youth; Eastern Europe, Youth and Citizenship in; Europe, Comparing Youth Activism in; European Identity and Citizenship; Immigrant Youth in Europe—Turks in Germany; Immigrant Youth in the United States; India, Youth Activism in; Indonesia, Youth Activism in; Nigeria, Youth Activism in; Palestinian *Intifada*; Russia, Youth Activism in; Soweto Youth Activism (South Africa); State and Youth, The; Statute of the Child and Adolescent (Brazil); Tiananmen Square Massacre (1989); Transnational Identity; Transnational Youth Activism; Turkey, Youth Activism in; United Nations, Youth Activism and; Xenophobia; Zapatista Rebellion (Mexico); Zionist Youth Organizations.

Recommended Reading

Collin, Matthew (2001). *Guerrilla Radio: Rock 'n' Roll Radio and Serbia's Underground Resistance*. New York: Thunder's Mouth Press/ Nation Books.

Čolović, Ivan (2002). *Politics of Identity in Serbia*. New York: New York University Press.

Gordy, Eric (1999). *The Culture of Power in Serbia*. University Park, PA: Pennsylvania State University Press.

Halpern, Joel, and Kideckel, David, eds. (2000). *Neighbors at War*. University Park, PA: Pennsylvania State University Press.

Lazić, Mladen, ed. (1999). *Protest in Belgrade*. Budapest: Central European University Press.

Popov, Nebojša, ed. (2000). *The Road to War in Serbia*. Budapest: Central European University Press.

Woodward, Susan (1996). *Balkan Tragedy: Chaos and Dissolution after the Cold War*. Washington, D.C.: Brookings Institute.

Jessica Greenberg

Service Learning. Service learning is a method of teaching and learning whereby students learn important skills and gain academic knowledge while providing community service. The community service may address any authentic community need. For example, students may work on citizenship issues such as:

- Researching local voting procedures and facilitating a voter registration campaign
- Conducting a survey of political candidates to reflect their opinions on a variety of issues and analyzing similarities and differences, relating the issues to differences in political philosophy
- Engaging in a graffiti cleanup and mural painting activity to reflect the diversity of interests and people in the community and to reflect the values of the community
- Formulating criteria for model citizenship, interviewing candidates for a citizenship award, and conducting an award ceremony
- Researching native plants and developing public-service announcements (PSAs) or other information dissemination strategies for helping people see the importance of preservation and providing information on how to preserve areas
- Growing a community garden whose yield will feed the homeless, graphing the produce, and conducting a survey to

see how much of the produce was consumed

- Tutoring young children so that they learn to read and serving as positive role models for literacy and the value of education

The forms that service learning can take vary widely. The integrity of the concept is maintained as long as service learning meets real community needs; is integrated with curriculum; provides structured time for young people to think, talk, or write about what they experienced and learned; and has some sort of celebration or recognition for those involved. Service learning can take place during school hours, before or after school, or during the weekends. It can be integrated completely with curriculum and conducted on a school-wide basis or can be an elective course or club. It can be sponsored by various community groups, by school districts, or through nonprofit organizations.

School-based service learning requires that the learning be tied to curriculum and academic content standards, typically by ensuring that the tasks that take place in the community lead to learning of particular academic objectives, such as knowledge and skills covered in the areas of English/language arts, mathematics, or science. Service learning can involve young people of any age and nearly any type of meaningful service.

Service learning is currently in place in about a third of all public schools and half of all public high schools. However, it is practiced by only about 6.6 percent of teachers. Teachers who use service learning say that they do so because it has important benefits for young people particularly in the personal/social, civic, and academic realm. They also believe that because service learning involves planning, action, reflection, relating to others, and tangible results, service learning is a powerful motivator for learning.

Research has shown the benefits of service learning to its youth participants. The research points to the idea that service learning has benefits because it is more engaging for students than traditional instructional delivery for teaching and learning. Evidence is available to show that service learning is associated with students' cognitive (engaged in subject matter), affective (motivated to learn), and behavioral (willingness to complete tasks) engagement in schools. In pre- and postsurveys with comparison groups service-learning students were found to be more interested in subject matters (e.g., "I really pay attention to classwork" and "I find myself concentrating so hard that time passes quickly") and more likely to talk with others about their schoolwork. In some grades, participation in service learning was associated with higher test scores on state assessments, particularly in the areas of English/language arts, writing, and social studies, particularly on subtests that measured perspective taking and inquiry. On essays students show a strong increase in cognitive complexity over time.

Benefits also accrued beyond academic learning. In the personal/social realm, studies show increased student efficacy, stronger interpersonal skills, and better school attendance. Students also show increases in ethical and moral behaviors. Furco (2002) showed increased development of ethics among service-learning participants relative to nonparticipating peers, and Laird and Black showed that participation led to more social-moral awareness and social agency. In other studies Laird and Black (2002) and Melchior (2002) showed a statistically significant decline in the risk factors of young people who engaged in service learning, particularly those related to staying in school, unwanted pregnancies, and smoking and alcohol use.

In the area of civic engagement, recent studies have affirmed that students who engage in service learning are more likely to display leadership skills, are more connected to the community, and are more likely to develop social capital. These results typically only occur when service learning has sufficient quality, as indicated by strong curricular connections, meaningful tasks, and teacher-mediated reflection activities such that students understand how to connect their experiences with notions of how society works. Several studies show that lack of quality has no real impact on students. For example, a study of California service learning showed a significant change in civic engagement at some but not all sites. Differences were attributed to teaching quality and the intentional design of experiences to help students see the civic linkages. Henness (2001) also found statistically significant differences for participants and nonparticipants in development of social capital but no differences in civic knowledge and skills. Meyer, Billig, and Hofschire (2005) in a study of Michigan Learn and Serve sites also showed no impact for low-quality sites.

Several research studies were able to show a strong connection between participation in service learning and participation in other forms of civic engagement. For example, in a study of randomly selected students from three universities, Meyer, Billig, and Hofschire (2005) showed that participation in service learning was positively associated with following the news, boycotting goods for ethical reasons, discussing public issues with friends and family, attending lectures on public issues, and intentionality to vote. In that study service learning was perceived to be highly associated with civic engagement but less associated with politics. It was unclear, however, whether engaged students were motivated to participate in service learning or vice versa.

School-based service learning has limitations on the degree to which activism is fostered. School staff members often express reservations about nurturing activism in the form of expression of opinion that school personnel (especially school boards) may find offensive. Those who receive federal funding, in particular, are cognizant that those funds come with provisos limiting the types of activism allowed to be sponsored as part of their grants. Thus, many embrace the notion of participatory citizenry but are less likely to promote for example, justice-oriented citizenry in the sense of the Kahne and Westheimer model.

Other tensions that have recently emerged are the perceptions that service learning is competing with the stress put on academics by the No Child Left Behind Act of 2001. The act has served to narrow curriculum in many schools across the United States, and for those schools service learning is sometimes considered expendable. Those who resist curriculum narrowing often do so because they believe that schooling should address the whole child and/or that schools have a civic mission in addition to the educational one.

Other tensions inhibiting the implementation of service learning come in the form of a "soft" database of evidence of success (few experimental studies); concerns about transportation to sites and safety of children who are out of the school building; and the time it takes to plan a high-quality service-learning experience. The issues are also complicated by a general lack of understanding of the parameters of the service-learning approach and lack of school-wide adoption of the pedagogy. However, policies in support of service learning are currently in place in over twenty-seven states, so signs are that the concept will endure. Teachers who embrace service learning often find that they become passionate about its implementation and will not willingly abandon its practice.

See also Character Education; Citizenship Education Policies in the States; Civic Virtue; Democratic Education; Diversity Education; Environmental Education (EE); IEA Civic Education Study; Just Community High Schools and Youth Activism; National Alliance for Civic Education (NACE); Prosocial Behaviors; School Engagement; School Influences and Civic Engagement; Service Learning and Citizenship Education.

Recommended Reading

Berman, S. H. (2000). "Service as Systemic Reform." *School Administrator*, 57 (7): 20–24.

Billig, S. H. (May 2000). "Research on K–12 School-Based Service-Learning: The Evidence Builds." *Phi Delta Kappan*, (81) 9: 658–664.

Billig, S. H., Hofschire, L, and Meyer, S. J. (2004). *Civic Participation of College Youth, A Report for Campus Compact*. Denver, CO: RMC Research Corporation.

Billig, S. H., and Waterman, A. S., eds. (2003). *Studying Service-Learning: Innovations in Education Research and Methodology*. Mahwah, NJ: Lawrence Erlbaum Publishers.

Furco, A. (2002). "Is Service-Learning Really Better Than Community Service? A Study of High School Service." In *Advances in Service-Learning Research, Service-Learning: The Essence of the Pedagogy*, Vol. 1, edited by A. Furco and S. H. Billig. Greenwich, CT: Information Age Publishers, pp. 23–50.

Henness, S. A. (2001). *K–12 Service-Learning: A Strategy for Rural Community Renewal and Revitalization*. Washington, D.C.: Corporation for National Service. (ERIC NO. ED461466.) http://www.nationalserviceresources.org/file-manager/download/452/hennessbiblio.pdf .

Laird, M., and Black, S. (2002). *Report for U.S. Department of Education Expert Panel on Safe, Disciplined, and Drug-Free Schools*. Annapolis Junction, MD: Lions-Quest.

Melchior, A., and Bailis, L. N. (2002). "Impact of Service-Learning on Civic Attitudes and Behaviors of Middle and High School Youth: Findings from Three National Evaluations." In *Advances in Service-Learning Research, Service-Learning: The Essence of the Pedagogy*, Vol. 1, edited by A. Furco and S. H. Billig. Greenwich, CT: Information Age Publishers, pp. 201–222.

Meyer, S. J., Billig, S., and Hofschire, L. (2005) "The Impact of K-12 School-Based Service-Learning on Academic Achievement and Student Engagement." In M. Welch and S. H. Billig, eds. *New Perspectives in Service-Learning: Research to Advance the Field*. Greenwich, CT: Information Age Publishers, pp. 61–85.

National Commission on Service-Learning (2002). *Learning in Deed: The Power of Service-Learning for American Schools*. A report from the National Commission on Service-Learning, funded by the W. K. Kellogg Foundation in partnership with the John Glenn Institute for Public Service and Public Policy at Ohio State University.

Pritchard, F. F., and Whitehead, G. I. (2004). *Serve and Learn: Implementing and Evaluating Service-Learning in Middle and High Schools*. Mahwah, NJ: Lawrence Erlbaum Publishers.

Shelley Billig

Service Learning and Citizenship Education. As the name implies, service learning integrates community service into the classroom curriculum. It involves learning and using academic skills, performing needed service, reflecting on and learning from experiences, and producing real results that serve the student's own community.

In service learning: (1) young people are encouraged to take the lead at a level appropriate to their age and skills in responding to genuine needs in their school or community; (2) teachers are facilitators of a service experience that relates the academic subject to community life; (3) service opportunities are accompanied by regular, structured, and unstructured opportunities to reflect upon the meaning and significance of the service; (4) service learning is built on partnerships within the school or between the school and community.

Service learning has been found to help students develop intellectually, as well as into active principled citizens. When the community becomes the classroom and young people learn not just from books but also from their own experiences, they learn basic academic and critical-thinking skills in new and potentially powerful ways.

Educators and community leaders increasingly think involving young people in service-learning activities is a powerful strategy to improve achievement, support school improvement, and contribute to community renewal. In service learning, students relate their service experience directly to their school curriculum, while at the same time making a valued contribution to their schools, neighborhoods, and/or communities. Service learning:

Is grounded in how learning occurs. Service learning meets a criterion of school improvement that often is missed. While improvement efforts often focus on financial, political, or administrative solutions to educational problems, service learning is rooted in a sound understanding of education itself, taking its cue from how cognition and learning actually occur. Service learning embodies the belief that knowledge is not merely transmitted from teacher to learner but rather is gained by the learner through guided interaction with the environment.

Develops critical-thinking skills. Through service learning, students learn to reflect on their experiences and develop critical-thinking skills, such as the ability to bring disparate elements of experience together in meaningful ways, to analyze information for patterns and deeper meaning, and to make evaluations and judgments.

Benefits all students. Because it is an effective pedagogy and not specific to any one curriculum, service learning supports and deepens the existing curriculum and aligns with national and state standards already in place. No group gets singled out because every student can benefit.

Uses multiple intelligences. Service learning engages the multiple intelligences identified by Howard Gardner, a core idea in education improvement, especially in curriculum development efforts. Service activities and corresponding reflection can be organized to address multiple ways in which students learn. For example, students working with residents in a senior center can read aloud to the seniors, engage them in physical exercise, and/or discuss historical events. Student reflections can range from creating a portfolio or journal to writing a song or delivering a speech.

Makes real-world issues part of education. Service learning presents students with issues and problems that cannot be neatly defined or solved. Encouraging students to "think outside the box" fosters development of problem-solving skills.

Encourages interdisciplinary learning. Because service learning requires students to think across the boundaries of traditional academic disciplines, students become more adept at integrating and applying what they are learning.

Develops workplace skills. Service-learning experiences early and regularly in a student's education help to foster the development of important skills and positive attitudes toward work and the community. Research shows that students learn best when they use interdisciplinary concepts and processes to solve ill-defined problems; function as members of multiple groups; use documents and sources of information other than textbooks; create products others can use; relate the work of the classroom to the world outside the school; influence and shape the course of their own learning; and model their performance upon that of competent adults. High-quality service learning embodies these elements and provides students with rich and positive learning experiences that help prepare them for the world of work.

Promotes equity. By facilitating heterogeneous grouping, service learning allows students from a variety of backgrounds, ethnic groups, strengths, and abilities to work together on real problems that provide unity and purpose beyond the classroom. It also has been found to provide extrinsic motivation for at-risk students, help special-education students develop concrete skills and competencies which often enable them to work alongside their nondisabled peers, and provide a holistic approach that can help immigrant students learn English language and culture.

Fosters appreciation for cultural diversity. Service learning helps foster in students a greater understanding, appreciation of, and ability to relate to people from a wide range of backgrounds and life situations. It provides opportunities for youth not just to reach out to others but also to understand the value of differences among individuals and communities.

Promotes changes in school culture. Service learning can have a profound effect on the school culture because it creates new relationships between schools and communities. At the same time the community itself becomes a learning environment that benefits from the schools that its tax dollars support. Service learning can also create more collaborative relationships among teachers, administrators, and other school personnel. When all members of the school community gradually become participants in this new process of learning, they develop a personal and collective stake in making something positive happen beyond the walls of the school.

For example, students in a social-studies class who spend time in a homeless shelter tutoring younger children or serving meals develop an emotional and human connection with the course concepts. Homelessness is no longer just a vocabulary word; it is a complex issue with sounds, smells, and emotions as well as a lesson in history, geography, and economics. Service learning is not a form of simply "students doing good things in the community"; it involves learning and using real academic skills, performing needed service, and producing real results that command respect.

Strong evidence exists to show that service learning helps students develop intellectually and into good citizens. When community becomes the classroom and young people learn not just from books but also from their own experiences, they learn basic academic and higher-thinking skills in unexpectedly powerful ways. The motivation to learn is intensified, while opportunities to develop insight and judgment are multiplied. Social growth is advanced. Concern for the welfare of others and the ability to relate positively to a range of cultural backgrounds are encouraged as well.

Both teachers and researchers point out that service learning also contributes to young people's psychological and moral development. Through age and developmentally appropriate service experiences, youth can develop not only their sense of personal self-worth and competence but also the sense that they and their work have value in the community. They learn that their personal boundaries can span neighborhoods and take in other generations.

Service learning also provides positive ways for young people to make real contributions to their schools and communities. It helps students take risks on behalf of others, focuses their search for a personal value structure, and supports them as they accept responsibility, especially for their own learning and actions.

What impact does service learning have? According to Shelley Billig, service learning is a teaching strategy that links community-service experiences to classroom instruction. Recent research demonstrating the impacts of service learning on K–12 youth, public schools, and communities follows.

Prevalence of service learning. According to a 1999 survey conducted by the U.S. Department of Education, 64 percent of all public schools and 83 percent of all public high schools organize some form of community service for their students. Nearly a third of all schools and half of public high schools provide service-learning programs, where the service that is being provided is linked with the school curriculum.

Rationale for use in K–12 public schools. Educators are drawn to service learning because they believe it produces important educational results for students, schools, and communities. In individual interviews educators clearly articulate their observations of the effects. They give many examples of students becoming more altruistic and caring, growing more concerned about their communities and community issues, and learning more in specific content areas such as social studies or mathematics, or about specific subject matters such as the environment or the elderly.

Evidence of impact. The research in the field has not caught up with the certainty and passion that educators feel for service learning. What is available, though, begins to build a case for the impacts that practitioners believe to be true. This summary presents the past decade (1990–1999) of research on K–12 service learning, organized by area of potential impact. It does not include all research on the topic but rather is limited to those publications that have documented their results and have shown a positive impact. It is important to note that at the time of this writing, no research was identified with negative impacts and only a few studies showed no impact or no sustained impact over time.

I. The Impact on Student Personal and Social Development

Service learning has a positive effect on the personal development of public school youth.

Students who engaged in service learning ranked responsibility as a more important value and reported a higher sense of responsibility to their schools than comparison groups.

Middle- and high-school students who engaged in quality service-learning programs showed increases in measures of personal and social responsibility, communication, and sense of educational competence.

Students perceived themselves to be more socially competent after engaging in service learning.

Students who engaged in service learning were more likely to treat each other kindly, help each other, and care about doing their best.

Students who engaged in service learning were more likely to increase their sense of self-esteem and self-efficacy.

Middle-school male students reported increased self-esteem and fewer behavioral problems after engaging in service learning.

Service learning has a positive effect on students' interpersonal development and the ability to relate to culturally diverse groups.

Middle- and elementary-school students who participated in service learning were better able to trust and be trusted by others, be reliable, and accept responsibility.

High-school students who participated in high-quality service-learning programs were more likely to develop bonds with more adults, agreed that they could learn from and work with the elderly and disabled, and felt that they trusted others besides parents and teachers to whom they could turn for help.

Students who engaged in service learning showed greater empathy and cognitive complexity than comparison groups.

Students who engaged in quality service-learning programs reported greater acceptance of cultural diversity.

Students who engaged in service learning showed increases over time in their awareness of cultural differences and attitudes toward helping others.

Students who participated in service learning enjoyed helping others with projects, became more dependable for others, and felt more comfortable communicating with ethnically diverse groups.

Students who participate in service learning are less likely to engage in "risk" behaviors.

Students in elementary- and middle-school service-learning programs showed reduced levels of alienation and behavioral problems.

Students who engaged in service learning were less likely to be referred to the office for disciplinary measures.

High-school and middle-school students who were engaged in service learning were less likely to engage in behaviors that lead to pregnancy or arrest.

Middle-school students who engaged in service learning and experienced a structured health curriculum were less likely to engage in unprotected sexual activity or violent behavior.

II. The Impact on Civic Responsibility

Service learning helps to develop students' sense of civic and social responsibility and their citizenship skills.

Students who engaged in high-quality service-learning programs showed an increase in the degree to which they felt aware of community needs, believed that they could make a difference, and were committed to service now and later in life.

High-school students who participated in high-quality service-learning programs developed more sophisticated understandings of sociohistorical contexts, were likely to think about politics and morality in society, and were likely to consider how to effect social change.

Elementary- and middle-schools students who participated in service learning developed a greater sense of civic responsibility and ethic of service.

Students who engaged in service learning increased their understanding of how government works.

Service learning provides opportunities for students to become active, positive contributors to society.

High-school students from five states who participated in high-quality service-learning programs increased their political attentiveness, political knowledge, and desire to become more politically active.

High-school students who participated in service learning and service are more likely to be engaged in a community organization and to vote fifteen years after their participation in the program than those who did not participate.

Students who engage in service learning feel that they can "make a difference."

Over 80 percent of participants in high-quality service-learning programs felt that they had made a positive contribution to the community.

III. The Impact on Student Academic Learning

Service learning helps students acquire academic skills and knowledge.

Students in over half of the high-quality service-learning schools studied showed moderate to strong positive gains on student achievement tests in language arts and/or reading, engagement in school, sense of educational accomplishment, and homework completion.

Service-learning participation was associated with higher scores on the state test of basic skills and higher grades.

Eighty-three percent of schools with service-learning programs reported that grade-point averages of participating service-learning students improved 76 percent of the time.

Middle- and high-school students who participated in service-learning tutoring programs increased their grade-point

averages and test scores in reading/language arts and math and were less likely to drop out of school.

Elementary- and middle-school students who participated in service learning had improved problem-solving skills and increased interest in academics.

Students who participate in service learning are more engaged in their studies and more motivated to learn.

Students who participated in high-quality service-learning programs showed an increase in measures of school engagement and achievement in mathematics than control groups.

Students who engaged in service learning came to class on time more often, completed more classroom tasks, and took the initiative to ask questions more often.

Service learning is associated with increased student attendance.

Students engaged in service learning had higher attendance rates than control group peers.

Schools that sponsor service-learning programs reported that attendance increased every year over a three-year period.

IV. The Impact on Career Exploration and Aspirations

Service learning helps students to become more knowledgeable and realistic about careers.

Students who participated in service-learning reported gaining career skills, communication skills, and positive increases in career exploration knowledge.

Students who engaged in high-quality service-learning programs developed positive work orientation attitudes and skills.

Teachers believed that participation in service learning increases career awareness.

V. The Impact on Schools

Service learning results in greater mutual respect of teachers and students.

Teachers and students in schools with quality service-learning programs reported an increase in mutual respect.

Service learning builds cohesiveness and more positive peer relations among students, among teachers, and between students and teachers in a school.

Service learning improves the overall school climate.

Educators and students in schools with strong service-learning programs reported more positive school climates through a feeling of greater connectedness to the school, decreased teacher turnover, and increased teacher collegiality.

VI. The Impact on Communities

Service learning leads to more positive perceptions of schools and youth by community members.

Community members who participate in service learning as partners with the schools see youth as valued resources and positive contributors to the community.

VII. The Impact on Protective Factors

Another body of research corroborates the findings on youth voice and service-learning programs. Resiliency research, which examines ways in which people become healthy and competent adults in spite of significant childhood adversity, has identified a triad of "protective factors." These factors—which help to protect youth from the harmful impact of abuse, neglect, poverty, parental divorce, or illness and other problems—are caring relationships, high expectations, and opportunities for meaningful participation. According to research analyst Bonnie Benard, meaningful participation is characterized by "problem solving, decision-making, planning, goal-setting and helping others" (Burns 1994)—an apt description of service learning. And of course, effective service-learning programs incorporate the other two protective factors, caring relationships and high expectations. This research sheds additional light upon the capacity for service-learning programs to effect lasting and positive behavioral change in participants.

"Service-learning has to do with powerful purposes—getting kids into the world.

Jean Piaget says schooling isn't worth anything unless it creates for people the capacity to believe that when they leave school, they can change the world. If our kids don't believe they can change the world, then I think we ought to say that our education has not been powerful enough," said Vito Perrone, director of the Teacher Education Program at the Harvard Graduate School of Education at the 1992 Council of Chief State School Officers' Service Learning Conference in Racine, Wisconsin.

For the past ten years, states have been aggressively developing and implementing challenging content standards and curriculum frameworks. At the heart of all this work lies the goal of helping all students learn and achieve at high levels. Success in this endeavor, however, requires rethinking not only "what" students learn but also "how" they learn it.

Service learning also has to do with what Perrone calls "powerful purposes." It addresses the issue of academic relevance by connecting academic knowledge, skills, and concepts with accomplishing an "authentic purpose" in the school and community. In this context service learning is an integral part of school improvement.

How Does Service Learning Contribute to Civic Responsibility?

The foundation on which the United States was built is achieved only when all citizens are included in choice and decision-making. Yet many young people feel alienated from the communities in which they live and attend school. Richard Battistoni and William Hudson write in their introduction to *Experiencing Citizenship: Concepts and Models for Service-Learning in Political Science*, published by the American Association for Higher Education: "... service-learning in a democracy—whatever its particular connection to courses or the curriculum—must be seen as a crucial aspect of civic responsibility: a model of the relationship between rights-bearing citizens and the many communities to which they belong. To be a citizen is not merely to possess knowledge of government and its workings or to have legal rights; it is to take responsibility, to see our interests and ourselves as flourishing only as our community flourishes."

According to Jeremy Rifkin, broadening the mission of America's education to include a renewed commitment to the civic life of the country now needs to be given equal priority (to educating for professional skills) if we are to meet the growing challenges of the coming century.

Ernst Boyer states that "in the end, the goal is not only to prepare for careers, but to enable undergraduates to live lives of dignity and purpose ... not only to give knowledge to the student, but to channel knowledge to humane ends." The purpose of school, after all, is not merely to provide the next generation with the tools they need to make a living but also to help them discover the personal and collective means—that is, the perspectives, strength of character, and values—they will need to sustain our civilization. We need to help young people move toward a higher regard for democratic institutions and a greater willingness to be involved in them.

Proponents of free public education from Thomas Jefferson to Horace Mann have similarly argued that it is not enough simply to be born into a democracy; individuals must learn to engage in democratic action if they are to continue to govern themselves.

Thus, Americans believe that as the primary state institution to reach each successive generation, public schools have a particular responsibility to provide opportunities for young people to become civically engaged. For more than 150 years, public schools have been viewed as a primary means to prepare young Americans for that task.

Education reforms of the 1980s and 1990s have focused primarily on establishing and meeting educational standards and on making sure young people are well prepared for higher education or the workplace. But comparatively little attention has been paid to what it means to prepare young people to participate fully in our democracy—especially in those dimensions of participation that go beyond mere knowledge of government to include the development of skills, attitudes, and dispositions needed to sustain and continually renew our traditions of self-governance.

Teaching young people the specifics of civic engagement is, arguably, the crucial component of creating a democratic self and society. In creating a democratic self, young people need to learn how to bring their fellow citizens together around common concerns; how to give a (loud but articulate) voice to their ideas, support, and objections; how to persevere when faced with disagreement or opposition; and how to not lose heart when they have lost a battle.

Service learning also provides students with the opportunity to practice basic citizenship skills such as expressing opinion, speaking in public, organizing groups, and thinking critically about political issues.

Participating in high-quality service-learning activities can help develop many of the skills and competencies associated with good citizenship. Through service learning, students learn about their community and the people, processes, and institutions that are most effective in improving community conditions; develop the social, political, and analytical skills necessary to participate in the policymaking process at any level of political and community life; and foster within themselves and among their peers attitudes regarding the value of lifelong service for the common good.

In this age of educational accountability, the Education Commission of the States (ECS) National Center for Learning and Citizenship (NCLC) believes that the civic mission of schools should be given equal weight to the academic mission. The center's programs and projects emphasize the critical role of supportive policy, high-quality practice, and sufficient capacity to carry out the civic mission of schools.

The following four critical questions arise from an increased focus on citizenship education, and answers to these questions can direct education leaders to support, teachers to integrate, and communities to contribute to high-quality opportunities for all students to be active principled citizens.

1. How can we effectively frame the issues of civic education, citizenship, and civic engagement?

The NCLC (2000) report *Every Student a Citizen* articulates the critical need for schools to focus on their civic mission and suggests it can be accomplished by identifying student competencies, through effective teaching and learning strategies, corresponding school and community climates and cultures, and supportive policies and systems.

NCLC believes that citizenship education should be schoolwide and community-based to provide the highest quality opportunity for every student to acquire and enhance citizenship competencies. The report further suggests that these competencies include knowledge, values, skills, efficacy, and commitment to lifelong active principled citizenship.

2. How does service learning provide high-quality opportunities for students to acquire citizenship competencies?

Given these complementary citizenship competencies, Billig (2001) makes the case through her review of research that service learning helps to develop students' sense of civic and social responsibility and their citizenship skills.

The studies listed earlier show that elementary- and middle-school students who participated in service learning developed a greater sense of civic responsibility and ethic of service, and high-school students who participated in high-quality service-learning programs developed more sophisticated understandings of sociohistorical contexts, were likely to think about politics and morality in society, and were likely to consider how to effect social change.

Furthermore, service learning provides opportunities for students to become active, positive contributors to society. According to the Education Commission of the States,

Acquiring citizenship skills is not a matter of teaching techniques or routines or creating an education "program" that will deliver civic knowledge and skills as one would teach a chemistry student the procedures for conducting an experiment safely. Participating responsibly and effectively in the life of the community is more like a "craft," an art form that uses people's needs, rights and responsibilities as basic materials to create a common world. In this situation, the citizen becomes a co-creator of his or her own environment. The institutions and processes among which he or she lives can be re-envisioned as realities to be fashioned, rather than as givens to be accommodated. Education for citizenship leads to ownership—a stake. It is learned through practice, not out of a book (2000).

This demonstrates the positive association of service learning with student citizenship competencies.

3. What is already in place at the state level to assist education leaders, teachers, and other stakeholders to move citizenship education to the core of K–12 schools?

NCLC is currently conducting a fifty-state policy scan, tracking state legislation, surveying state leaders, examining state initiatives and programs, exploring citizenship-education collaborations, and reviewing news sources to establish a baseline of state support for citizenship education.

A full report is due to be released soon, but the following are initial examples of state efforts that encourage, support, and reward citizenship education: comprehensive set of citizenship rights and responsibilities in the social-studies standards (OH); increase number of civics courses (UT); statewide civics demonstration projects (AK and MI); citizenship as an essential component of state education reform (WA); state and district requirements for active student participation on state and district school boards (VT);

students able to work at the voting polls (AR, CA, CO, IL, and HI); citizenship is aligned with civics standards (MA, MN, NC, and ND); development of district-required courses on patriotism (NE); and establishment of internships for students to work in public offices for high-school credit (MI and TX).

Standards. Graduates must pass a social-studies graduation test and ninth-grade proficiency test in citizenship in Ohio. Fourteen states clearly include civics, citizenship, or social studies in statewide assessments; eleven include these assessments as part of a statewide school performance reporting system. And thirty-four states have statutes relating to civics, citizenship education, or social studies.

State leadership. State leaders encourage student engagement in critical decision-making in schools and civic arenas in the following ways: encouragement from chief state school officer to increase student civic participation in school decision-making (WI); support for service learning as a critical pedagogy to develop civic competencies (CA and SC); commitment from chief state school officer to increase civics courses (AZ); thirteen chief state school officers have written statements in support of citizenship education or civics (e.g., inaugural speech, statements of priority, etc.); and twelve state boards of education have issued supportive statements on citizenship. Also, Washington State has the following legislative statement of support: "The goal of the Basic Education Act for the schools of the state of Washington set forth shall be to provide students with the opportunity to become responsible citizens, to contribute to their own economic well-being and to that of their families and communities, and to enjoy productive and satisfying lives." And Terry Bergeson, Washington State's superintendent, has expressed her support for the civic mission of schools through her speeches and professional development workshops.

This initial review demonstrates that there are policies in place, programs oper-

ating, and demonstrable leadership that can be maximized to integrate citizenship education into the schools.

Statewide civic or citizenship education programs. The following have been created: a statewide consortium (P–16 North Carolina Civics Consortium) and a statewide infrastructure (Colorado Civics and Service-Learning Compact).

Pending legislation. There is pending legislation in Maine to lower the voting age to seventeen, and seventeen other states have civic or citizenship education legislation pending.

Programs. Examples of state programs include the Michigan Civics Institute (MI) and the Virginia Citizenship Institute (VA).

4. What are the most effective strategies to develop and sustain citizenship education in K–12 schools and communities?

NCLC designed and implemented a four-year *policy and practice demonstration project* in the W. K. Kellogg Foundation's Learning In Deed national initiative. The investment in five states, thirty-three districts and over one hundred schools identified a variety of *lessons learned* to develop and sustain education strategies and programs.

First, a focus on supportive policies, high-quality practice, and school/community infrastructure insures adequate system support, teacher competency, and capacity.

Second, a focus on aligning citizenship education with the following five educational issues moves it from the margins to the mainstream of K–12 schools: vision and leadership; curriculum, instruction and assessment; professional development; community partnerships; and continuous improvement.

Third, sustaining citizenship education is a developmental process that occurs during and after the implementation to become a way for an innovation to become an accepted way of educational practice.

Fourth, it is important to recognize that there are several obstacles to sustaining citizenship education, including a challenge to the status quo within schools and the community; paradigms about how students learn, how schools operate, and community roles in education; and weak relationships between schools and communities.

Fifth, identifying factors that promote sustaining citizenship education include: evidence of impact, powerful advocates/champions, perceived "fit" with local needs and culture, and "bottom-up" grassroots acceptance and practice.

Sixth, the initial steps to sustaining citizenship education include examining education policies and priorities to determine whether they inhibit or support service learning; making citizenship-education practice a central part of state, district, and school missions, standards, and priorities; and establishing a supportive infrastructure for citizenship education.

Seventh, the following questions should be asked and answered to sustain citizenship education: How are citizenship education goals integrated into school- and district-level *leadership* structures? What *instructional strategies* are most effective for citizenship education? How does *professional development* contribute to expanding support for and participation in citizenship? How are *school-community partnerships* providing a foundation for citizenship relationships among students, schools, parents, and community partners? Do opportunities exist to *review* citizenship education activities and determine how they contribute to the overall goals of a school or districts?

These seven *lessons learned* provide a set of steps to integrate citizenship education into K–12 schools and communities.

Summary

Service learning has been found to help students develop intellectually and become active, principled citizens. When young people learn not just from books but also from their own service experiences, they learn basic academic and critical-thinking skills in new and potentially powerful ways.

Educators and community leaders increasingly think involving young people in service learning activities is a powerful strategy to improve achievement, support school improvement, and contribute to community renewal. Research shows the positive impact service learning has on students' personal and social development, academic learning, civic responsibility, career exploration, and proactive factors.

The current interest expressed by political, education, and community leaders in civics, citizenship education, and civic engagement provides a platform for service-learning advocates to demonstrate the positive relationship between service learning and student citizenship competencies.

Defining these concepts as *citizenship education* aligns with the civic mission of American education and the rich and robust set of citizenship competencies (i.e., knowledge, values, experiences, efficacy, and commitment).

A focus on supportive state policies, high-quality pedagogy, and sufficient school and community infrastructure assists to develop and sustain high-quality citizenship education in K–12 schools and communities.

See also Character Education; Citizenship Education Policies in the States; Civic Virtue; Democratic Education; Diversity Education; Environmental Education (EE); IEA Civic Education Study; Just Community High Schools and Youth Activism; National Alliance for Civic Education (NACE); Prosocial Behaviors; School Engagement; School Influences and Civic Engagement; Service Learning.

Recommended Reading

Billig, S. (2002). "Adoption, Implementation, and Sustainability of K–12 Service-Learning Programs." In *Service-Learning: Essence of Pedagogy*, edited by S. H. Billig and A. Furco. Greenwich, CT: Information Age Publishers.

Corporation for National and Community Service, U.S. Department of Education, Points of Light Foundation, and USA Freedom Corps (2002). *Students in Service to America (SISTA): A Guidebook for Engaging America's*

Students in a Lifelong Habit of Service. See http://www.studentsinservicetoamerica.org.

Education Commission of the States (2001). *Service-Learning: An Administrator's Tool for Improving Schools and Connecting with the Community*. Denver, CO: Education Commission of the States.

Education Commission of the States (2003). *Building Community Through Service-Learning*. Denver, CO: Education Commission of the States.

Education Commission of the States (2004). *Involving Students in Governance*. Denver, CO: Education Commission of the States.

Education Commission of the States (2004). *Senior and Culminating Projects*. Denver, CO: Author.

Additional Web Sites

Civic Mission of Schools: http://www.civicyouth.org/research/areas/civicmissionofschools.htm

Every Student a Citizen: http://www.ecs.org/clearinghouse/16/77/1677.pdf

National Center for Learning and Citizenship: http://www.ecs.org/nclc

Terry Pickeral

Sexuality Activism. *See* Queer, Sexuality, and Gender Activism and Gay-Straight Alliances in Schools (GSAs).

Social-Emotional Learning Programs for Youth. Over the last quarter century various human-service providers such as psychologists, educators, and social workers have explored the utilization of youth programs that promote positive development in order to address widespread social and behavioral problems afflicting the nation. Incidence of youth violence, drug abuse, delinquency, gang involvement, political apathy, civic disengagement, and teen pregnancy have markedly increased over the last few decades. Whether due to family disruption, the effects of poverty, decay in the inner cities, or alienation in the suburbs, these problems persist and affect our society profoundly. Youth programs that specifically address these multifaceted issues are designed to foster prosocial, positive behaviors and skill sets that will best equip the nation's youth for navigating an often turbulent world. Youth prevention programs can be implemented through school systems, civic or religious organizations, summer camps, or community centers. Of these, programs that are enacted as schoolwide prevention efforts have had the greatest record of success. This entry will describe the theory and goals of positive youth development programs; explain the skill sets such programs cultivate, detail the components of successful programming; and elaborate on the program implementation process.

Youth positive development programs are most effective when they operate under an integrated and coordinated framework that targets key global skill sets and prosocial behaviors that the young individual requires to become successful in life and civically engaged in society. These global skills such as conflict resolution, prosocial methods of communication and cooperation, identifying feelings in self and others, and cultivating a sense of compassion and social responsibility are integrated in a cohesive fashion. Once the young individual attains mastery of these global skill sets, he or she will be better prepared to develop in a positive direction, avoid maladaptive and antisocial behaviors, and will be more likely to become civically or politically engaged by confronting pertinent social, economic, and environmental issues of the day. Prevention programs that work also operate from a fundamental position that all children have developmental rights. These rights include the right to gain knowledge, to develop into a responsible, caring, healthy, and peaceful individual; to gain global skills that will help the individual to become a productive, helpful, and positive force in the home, the workplace, and society at large; to acquire an education that will foster the student's critical thinking ability and political and civic interest; and to cultivate a sense of social responsibility that will lead the young individual down the path toward being an effective, democratically engaged citizen.

"Universal primary prevention" is a term applied to programs that seek to promote positive behavior, embrace the core developmental rights, and are implemented on a schoolwide scale for all children regardless of socioeconomic background, intellectual functioning, or academic and social performance. These programs are labeled universal because they do not discriminate between which child can or cannot benefit from effective service. The most effective, theoretically driven, and empirically supported example of a universal prevention program consists of the social-emotional learning (SEL) or character-building program model. Social-emotional learning programs are founded on the theory of emotional intelligence, which states that a child's ability to effectively monitor emotions, be aware of the emotions of others, and to utilize this knowledge to affect positive social outcomes is the most critical component to achieving success in life. Emotional intelligence and social competence enable the individual to pay attention in school, muster motivation to succeed, build healthy interpersonal relations, and to make wise decisions regarding his or her behaviors whether in class or outside the academic setting. The following are the five key global skill sets promoted through SEL programming:

1. *Self-awareness*: the ability to identify one's emotions and to understand the reasons and circumstances surrounding them.
2. *Self-regulation*: the ability to express emotions such as anger, frustration, depression, and anxiety and to find effective ways of coping when these feelings arise. Self-regulation also includes the ability to control one's impulses for antisocial behavior and to recognize and cultivate one's positive attributes and strengths (building self-esteem).
3. *Self-control and task performance*: the ability to concentrate and focus on accomplishing a goal or task, to control one's inclinations toward inattentiveness or restlessness in the classroom, to cultivate motivation and optimism toward attaining a goal, to work with others to achieve the best possible performance.
4. *Empathy*: the ability to take the perspective of the other person, essentially "walking in their shoes," and to show compassion, to be able to listen within interpersonal situations and to have sensitivity toward the feelings of others.
5. *Social skills*: the ability to navigate the social world effectively by working as a team, cooperating with others, being perceptive to social cues, building leadership skills, developing healthy assertiveness, and engaging in positive social problem solving behaviors.

Ideally, universal programs that promote positive youth development embrace and cultivate one or more of these essential global skill sets.

Positive youth development programs seek to prevent maladaptive, antisocial, and harmful behaviors through the promotion of psycho-social wellness and prosocial skill sets. Programs such as the ones based on the SEL model emphasize and focus on strengths. These strengths include the strengths and resources that reside within the individual, within the classroom, the school, and the community. Effective youth development programs take an ecological approach to problem solving and prevention. It is important to note that individuals do not develop in a vacuum, unaffected and unencumbered by other factors. The individual grows and develops within an ecological framework, which includes the family, peers, the school, and the community as well as society. Challenges are often presented on each level of ecological functioning. For instance, a child who experiences family discord or witnesses a parent abusing substances in the home will have a whole host of challenges that he or she may face regarding positive development. Communities rife with gang violence, substance abuse, and teen pregnancy present significant barriers to obtaining positive developmental outcomes. A society or culture that embraces materialism and fosters alienation and consumption over human relationships and connectivity will emerge as a powerful force for the development of antisocial and self-destructive behavior. Program implementers should take this ecological perspective when coordinating and organizing their efforts. By knowing the context in which our young people are developing, psychologists, educators, social workers, parents, and other program agents can address the specific challenges and threats to positive outcomes.

Conversely, program implementers would do well to conduct a thoughtful analysis of strengths and resources that may be available on an ecological level as well. For instance, in any given school district in America one will find engaging, caring, involved, and resourceful parents who provide a bountiful wealth of love and support to their children. These parents and family members should be identified and brought on board to any school- or community-based programming efforts. Parent-teacher organizations and extracurricular activities are ideal forums for meeting socially and academically engaged parents who are willing to act as a critical resource for the program implementation process. Likewise, communities have religious institutions and secular community-service organizations that are willing to be utilized as a force for positive social and community change. These groups can assist by providing opportunities for students to engage in community service and get involved in good works in coordination with helpful adults who can also act as positive role models. On the cultural, societal level, there are a host of resources that provide opportunities for positive growth. America has innumerable charitable organizations, national parks and recreation areas, educational museums, and libraries that help to promote a culture of service, knowledge, productivity, and healthy human connection. It is critical that program implementers view potential strengths and resources from this ecological perspective.

Program implementers must think critically when developing their strategies for success. This entry has already discussed the importance of operating from a position that promotes developmental rights and the necessity of taking an ecological-perspectives approach. The Collaborative for the Academic, Social and Emotional Learning (CASEL) has identified six other key characteristics for prevention program implementation that work:

1. Uses a research-based framework that involves families, peers, schools, and communities as partners to target multiple outcomes.
2. Takes a long-term and culturally sensitive approach for programs; quick fixes are not realistic.
3. Fosters development of individuals who are healthy and fully engaged through teaching them to apply social and emotional skills and ethical values in daily life. Program lessons that are taught in the school must be presented in a way that encourages students to utilize and apply the skill sets in their everyday activities.
4. Aims to establish policies, institutional practices, and environmental supports that nurture optimal development. In this respect implementers must work in tandem with school administrators and local government officials to ensure maximum coordination.
5. Selects, trains, and supports interpersonally skilled staff to implement programming effectively. Programming staff must be well equipped to not only implement positive development curriculum but also be able to address challenges and setbacks as they occur.
6. Incorporates and adapts evidence-based programming to meet local community needs through strategic planning, continuing evaluation, and dynamic improvement. As each community and school district varies in terms of the challenges they face, so positive youth programming should vary in terms of its scope and focus to meet local demands.

Finally, the last critical component for effective program implementation is evidence and accountability. Program administrators, whether researchers from the university or local members of the school board, should devise methods of testing and evaluation that ensure desired outcomes. Evidence must be gathered about how the program is working. This information will be necessary when modifications (which are inevitable) are being developed. Collecting data regarding progress is essential from a research perspective as well, since gaining continued funding is always tied to measures of demonstrable progress.

The last section of this entry will elaborate on the steps that are necessary during the program implementation process. There are ten essential steps needed to design, implement, and maintain an effective program that fosters positive youth development:

1. Conduct a needs assessment by surveying the target area and population. Interview educators, school administrators, parents, and community members to determine problematic aspects and challenges facing a particular locality.
2. Design a program curriculum based on proven measures and methods that work. This can be accomplished through research on the Web via sites such as http://www.casel.org or by consulting books and scholarly journal articles on the subject of positive youth development programs (for starters, consult the list of recommended readings below).
3. Write a comprehensive proposal outlining the target population: school district, age and grade level, and demographic factors. Describe what it is you intend to do, what curriculum will be used, who will implement the lesson planning, and how.
4. Train personnel, including teachers, administrators, parents, and community members. Design program packets and provide background literature so that the implementers can have substantial information to rely on during

the process. Personnel must be more than adequately familiar with the skill sets that the program seeks to foster.

5. Create guidelines: take steps to ensure that all program agents are familiar with the program's goals and philosophy so that all players are on the same page.
6. Starting the program: thoroughly brief the young people who will be participating in the program. Explain in clear terms the purpose of the program, the philosophy, and what outcomes you are seeking. This is the point in the process when preprogram data must be gathered regarding the target behaviors. For purposes of evaluation, program administrators will compare this "baseline" information with the data gathered after the curriculum has been fully implemented. Data comparisons should be made periodically.
7. Create a support system for program implementers. Conduct regular staff meetings to give implementers an opportunity to voice their concerns, discuss their experiences, and to share innovative ideas. It is important that all programming agents feel as though they are a part of a team.
8. Conduct periodic follow-ups and administer teacher/implementer evaluations in order to establish accountability and to assess the quality of implementation.
9. Conduct periodic data analysis, evaluate the program's effectiveness, write reports on program progress, and create thoughtful strategies for improving methods that appear to be stagnant. Create an honest assessment of program strengths and weaknesses.
10. Modify any aspect of the program that appears to be ineffective or counterproductive.

When attempting to create a prevention program that will affect positive change in the lives of young people and their communities, process is a fundamental aspect to successful implementation. In addition to the above "how to" steps of program implementation, it is also important to remember some common roadblocks to success. These include limited financial and human resources, poorly explained goals or theory, high turnover of educators or program implementers, loss of energy and innovation, poor organization or inconsistent implementation, and finally, resistance to the program from various program agents. A successful program will embrace both caution and innovation; it will take deliberate steps to be successful as outlined above; it will be cognizant of potential pitfalls at every step, and it will embody a spirit of persistent optimism. Positive youth development programs require enormous effort, fortitude, determination, and care. Although the effort on the part of educators, administrators, and other agents is tremendous, the payoff is unquantifiable. Programs that work can help to create compassionate, academically and socially successful, healthy, happy young people and further facilitate the growth of connected, productive, and civically engaged citizens within our society.

See also Character Education; Citizenship Education Policies in the States; Civic Virtue; Democratic Education; Diversity Education; Environmental Education (EE); IEA Civic Education Study; Just Community High Schools and Youth Activism; National Alliance for Civic Education (NACE); Prosocial Behaviors; School Engagement; School Influences and Civic Engagement; Service Learning.

Recommended Reading

Ciarrochi, J., Forgas, J. P., and Mayer, J. D., eds. (2001). *Emotional Intelligence in Everyday Life: A Scientific Inquiry.* Philadelphia: Psychology Press.

Collaborative for Academic, Social and Emotional Learning (CASEL) (2004). *Prevention for Children and Youth That Works: An Introduction.* See http://www.casel.org.

Elias, M. J., Zins, J. E., Graczyk, P. A., and Weissberg, R. P. (2003). "Implementation, Sustainability, and Scaling Up of Social-Emotional and Academic Innovations in Public Schools." *School Psychology Review,* 32 (3): 303–319.

Elias, M. J., Zins, J. E., Weissberg, R. P., Frey, K. S., Greenberg, M. T., Haynes, N. M., Kessler, R., Schwab-Stone, M. E., and Shriver, T. P.

(1997). *Promoting Social and Emotional Learning: Guidelines for Educators.* Alexandria, VA: Association for Supervision and Curriculum Development.

Goleman, D. (1995). *Emotional Intelligence.* New York: Bantam Books.

Greenberg, M. T., Weissberg, R. P., O'Brien, M. U., Zins, J. E., Fredericks, L., Resnick, H., and Elias, M. J. (2003). "Enhancing School-Based Prevention and Youth Development Through Coordinated Social, Emotional, and Academic Learning." *American Psychologist,* 10 (6/7): 466–474.

Lantieri, L. and Patti, J. (1996). *Waging Peace in our Schools.* Boston: Beacon Press.

Justin Robert Misurell

Social Justice. Justice is a highly abstract term that straddles considerations in religion, moral philosophy, legal theory, economics, and culture. Social justice combines equity, fairness, impartiality, and compassion in both social processes and outcomes. Despite its complex and abstract elements, it is as basic as the rules, norms, and expectations that govern everyday exchanges between children—just listen for the indignation that occurs when children dispute the distribution of candy among a group. A common thread through all considerations of justice is concern for the distribution of valued resources such as food, shelter, money, and education among individuals and groups. Another common concern has to do with access to these resources as mediated, for example, by transportation, rights, and sense of safety.

Thus, a meaningful distinction can be drawn between distributive and procedural aspects of justice. *Distributive justice* deals with the allocation of resources between individuals or groups while *procedural justice* deals with the means by which certain ends are achieved. For example, the gross economic inequality that exists across the world is a question of distributive justice. However, there are different ways to reduce such inequality. Stealing from the rich to give to the poor may be less just than taxation. Others may feel that using taxation in order to redistribute wealth is also unfair and that they should be free to decide for themselves how to allocate their money. Procedural justice also highlights the need to operate in ways that do not undermine the identity, pride, or needs of various groups. Many scholars and activists have therefore criticized the notion of charity because it can put people in a disempowering or shameful position as passive recipients. Recognizing the importance of procedural justice, Gandhi—the revolutionary who led India's anticolonial efforts—stated that "means and ends are convertible terms in my philosophy of life" (Kripalani 1972). To Gandhi, *how* you achieve something is as important as *what* you achieve.

Both distributive and procedural justice hinge on the concept of *fairness*. What is fair? Ancient religious and modern scholarly ideas about the topic do seem to agree that social justice requires a wise consideration of fairness. For example:

The Bible describes justice in the context of social class: "Do not pervert justice; do not show partiality to the poor or favoritism to the great, but judge your neighbor fairly" (Lev. 19:15, New International Version).

The Qur'an brings in the related concept of equity: "… be upright for Allah, bearers of witness with justice, and let not hatred of a people incite you not to act equitably; act equitably, that is nearer to piety …" (*The Dinner Table* 5:8).

Yet people perceive fairness in different ways. One of the most common principles underlying judgments of fairness or justice is the *equity* principle, which holds that people should receive resources proportionally to what they invest in effort and resources. Under the principle of equity, there will be and should be inequality between people and groups, because people vary in their abilities (innate or learned) and in how others in society view or value these abilities. An alternative principle of justice is that of *equality*, which holds that everyone should receive an equal portion of desired resources regardless of their effort or the value of their contribution. A third principle of justice is that of *need*, which holds that people should receive resources based on need rather than on their abilities or accomplishments. According to the need principle, distributions may be unequal because people's needs vary.

Societies differ in the extent to which they prefer each of these justice principles, and individuals may employ various principles depending on the situation. For example, a businessperson may favor the principle of equity in the business environment, yet operate on principles of equality or need in dealing his or her with family. In U.S. culture equity and need are the more popular principles of distributive justice, and fewer people believe that the equal distribution of resources is just. But equality can be more appealing when thinking about procedural justice. People in the United States are more likely to agree that everyone should be equal before the law or have equal access to government decision-making processes. In fact, competing versions of justice lie at the heart of the historic conflict between the political-economic systems of Communism, socialism, and capitalism, and between authoritarian and representative systems of government. That questions of justice are played out on an international and historical scale is a testament to how contentious and subjective they may be. Which principle of justice most resonates with your worldview or with your political work?

The last idea to consider in describing social justice is *oppression*, given that social justice can be defined as the elimination of institutionalized domination and oppression. Oppression refers to the unjust use of power by one group over another in a way that creates and sustains an inequitable distribution of resources and opportunities. Oppression is often maintained and spread through violence, restrictions on rights and mobility, and through social processes such as institutionalized racism, sexism, classism, heterosexism, and the like.

Typically advocates of social justice focus on the empowerment of disenfranchised groups, but more recently an analysis of *privilege* has been added to thinking on social justice. As a result, (1) the analysis of justice is not limited to poverty and to the lower end of the sociopolitical continuum, and (2) the responsibility for rectifying injustice does not rest solely on the shoulders of the oppressed. Oppression highlights what people have been denied in the absence of a just reason, whereas the notion of privilege highlights the advantages that some people possess without just cause. This perspective recognizes that power and privilege can be conferred on the basis of legacy, gender, race, age, physicality, and other attributes that are not a function of personal achievement. This perspective further suggests that the privileged will strive to maintain the status quo by publicly promoting and by privately internalizing principles of meritocracy. Meritocracy refers to the notion that people attain resources based solely on ability and effort—for example, that the rich are rich because they have greater skills and intelligence than the rest of society. If the majority believes that the privileged have fairly acquired and earned their resources and opportunities, it will assume that the privileged deserve their relative status. In other words the majority will assume that the society operates on commendable principles of meritocracy even though visible signs of inequality, oppression, and privilege prevail. As a result, the majority will abstain from challenging the practices or rights of the privileged few.

The analysis of privilege suggests that differentials in power and opportunities are often the result of unequal practices (e.g., discrimination) or the legacy of such practices (e.g., genocide or slavery). It thus follows that social justice cannot come about solely through the empowerment of underprivileged groups but through the engagement of privileged groups in a common cause. How the privileged are motivated to join efforts, however, remains a subject of debate. Some approaches work for some individuals but not others. The most common approaches consist of moral arguments of fairness and justice, personal

contact with the oppressed that shatter the individual's belief in their inferiority, and finally, challenging the logic that social injustice is ultimately to the benefit of the privileged. For example, it has been argued that as long as severe economic inequality exists, the rich will need to expend financial and psychological resources to secure their belongings and well-being. Thus, if the wealthy would help reduce the economic gap, they might reap a greater sense of security and ease.

Although we may, in theory, speak of a *state* of social justice, it is in reality a dynamic condition that requires ongoing monitoring, adjusting, and defense against perceived threats. Any one aspect of social justice is always merely one part of a larger puzzle. The racial integration of U.S. schools for example was a major goal of the civil rights movement. Although the most immediate objective consisted of overturning the legality of racial segregation (*Brown v. Board of Education*), this victory was but one component of the overarching goal: it required follow-up, such as the implementation of the court ruling, and a cultural shift toward multiculturalism pluralism among other things. Another example is that of decolonization. Anticolonial movements can be considered social justice movements because they stand for self-determination and fair treatment in the face of exploitation and oppression by foreign nations. Although formal independence has now been achieved by most colonized nations, thinkers such as Frantz Fanon have argued that "full" decolonization is not completed when statehood is achieved but also requires unlearning beliefs and attitudes that were acquired during the colonial period (e.g., reduced sense of pride as a developing-world person), reforming or creating institutions (e.g., reforming the colonial educational system that sought to repress critical thought and that was based on a different cultural framework), and more. In other words, decolonization is a continuous process that requires change on multiple levels, ranging from the psychological to the governmental and cultural realms.

The concept of social justice can inform two aspects of activism and political work: (1) *what* our vision is, that is, what conditions we seek to bring about and (2) *how* we go about it, that is, the process by which we work toward our goal of social justice.

Social justice is a dynamic outcome; it refers to the conditions or states of being that we seek to bring about and sustain. As an outcome it may be defined in a number of ways; each definition will in turn impact the choice of tactics and strategies. Following are some ways of thinking about social justice as an end goal. Keep in mind that when the goal is to challenge or eradicate oppression, it is much more easily and effectively done if an *alternative* is provided and effectively promoted!

Challenging oppressive belief systems. Injustice is often sustained by belief systems, whether or not they are explicitly acknowledged. The enslavement of black Africans was sustained by the belief that their lives and intellectual abilities were not as worthy as those of European and American whites, and violence against women (domestic violence, sexual harassment, rape) is built on the belief that men have the right to control women. Oppressive belief systems may stem from a variety of sources, including governmental policies, media, peer groups, culture, and family socialization. Challenges can be wielded on moral grounds (e.g., religious), functional grounds (e.g., injustice is bad for productivity), or empirical grounds (e.g., use of disconfirming statistics or research). Some oppressive belief systems affect youth as well. Educators and school administrators often see adolescents as being inherently irresponsible, rebellious, and/or apathetic. Clearly, some groups of people are always better placed to challenge a particular belief than others. In this case young people are best placed to promote an alternative belief system. Through their actions they can model the idea that young people can and do have valuable energy, insights, and skills to contribute to society.

Raising awareness. The purpose is to increase people's knowledge of and concern for a particular social issue such as child abuse or voting rights. Why is it that societies find it acceptable to make young people pay taxes before they have acquired the right to vote? Have young people thought about this instance of taxation without representation? A common youth-related issue is that of raising awareness among young people of the importance of taking part in the political process, be it through organizing, writing, campaigning, keeping informed, voting if the opportunity exists, and so forth. A more involved process involves *consciousness raising*, which does not limit itself to imparting knowledge but promotes people's ability to consider multiple levels of analysis and to tie their personal experiences to social and political phenomena. This process can either target victims of an issue (e.g., workers who are exploited by unjust labor practices), the privileged (e.g., corporate elite), or potential allies (e.g., university students who may organize in solidarity with the workers).

Challenging unjust practices. At times a state of injustice can be traced back to a widespread practice that is socially or culturally tolerated if not sanctioned. These practices might take place in any number of settings, including the family, school, and community. For example, women's advocates worldwide have argued that young women's genital mutilation/circumcision is a practice that must be stopped. The moral argument has been that it is an unjust practice that perpetuates women's oppression despite the fact that some justify it on cultural grounds, whereas the pragmatic argument has been that it is a dangerous practice that can seriously compromise a woman's health or livelihood. Another example is the common phenomenon of adults making or demanding physical contact with children—hugging, kissing, and so on—without first securing their consent.

One might argue that such a practice unjustly deprives children of their rights over their bodies.

Instituting new policies and laws. Whereas practices are informally maintained, policies are formally preserved by institutional forces; in other words, they are "on the books." Most formal institutions hold policies that they abide by, including hospitals, schools, NGOs, and governments. Although instituting a policy does not guarantee that it will be correctly implemented or enforced, policy is often a target of social justice work. For example many institutions (e.g., clinics and schools) hold policies that refuse to make condoms or sexual information available to youth. Such policies are being challenged worldwide on the basis that they are unjust to young people as well as counterproductive in the effort to curtail sexually transmitted infections and unintended pregnancies. France has recently implemented a policy that bans religious adornments from public school grounds. This practice has largely affected those female Muslim youth who wear head scarves or veils. Many of these youth found this to be an unjust policy and collectively protested it. Their argument was that the policy violated their right to religious freedom, whereas advocates of the policy argued that religious symbols in public schools violated the separation of religion from the state.

Creating new, alternative settings or institutions. Sometimes social justice calls for establishing new settings as alternatives to traditional ones. The intent might be to provide support to victims of injustice or to directly advance the cause of justice. An example of the former case is a crisis hotline for victims of rape, and an example of the latter is the United Nations. A sense of solidarity based on a shared social identity (e.g., gender or age) is an asset in creating alternative institutions. The shared, lived experience or worldview becomes the basis for a new set of priorities, policies, and practices. A group of youth might decide to create a youth-run newspaper as an alternative to adult-driven sources of information. The purpose of the newspaper might be to provide a venue for issues that are of direct concern to young people from a youth perspective.

Building capacity. Organizations, communities, and groups have varying levels of capacity—the potential to effectively recognize the need for changes and to produce them. Capacity is based on collective skills (e.g., fundraising, lobbying) and on collective power (e.g., knowledge, money, size). Capacity-building consists of building the readiness of collectives so that they are best able to pursue their goals, maintain the changes that they have achieved, and resist threats. Although capacity is often pursued in conjunction with a larger goal (e.g., policy change), it is also a legitimate goal in itself in that it may ease future struggles.

Organizing is a common strategy for building capacity. For example, tenant organizing entails building an infrastructure so that residents are not only able to advocate for immediate concerns but also are able to preserve their achievements. There is also a growing movement of youth organizing that combines youth development goals with the community organizing tradition. It assists and trains young people to bring about institutional change through community research, direct action, critical reflection, and leadership. For example, young student leaders in the United States in Portland, Oregon, Oakland, California, and Boston, Massachusetts, organized students, parents, and elected officials and persuaded transit authorities to provide free or discounted bus passes to public-school students. In so doing, they also built local youth's capacity to engage in future action.

These are all examples of outcomes that groups might work toward, depending on their particular social justice perspectives. Often the social justice projects people work on are called "campaigns" which, like political campaigns of all kinds, are based on one or more "issues." To be successful these issues must energize the group and motivate its members to do the necessary hard work.

Social justice is also a *process* that social justice efforts and organizations should abide by. It can inform how we conduct our collective political work. Do we communicate in nonviolent ways? Do we assign roles in ways that take into consideration each person's strengths and preferences? Have we set up a decision-making process (e.g., voting or consensus) that makes for a healthy balance between democratic principles and efficiency? Should we institute a cap on how much power any one person can hold? How do we keep each other accountable without becoming autocratic?

There are unfortunately many examples in history of efforts and organizations whose vision was one of social justice, but that operated in ways that actively perpetuated or passively turned a blind eye to oppression within their own ranks. The following are three examples of this.

Many anticolonial movements and racial justice efforts have been accused of excluding women from positions of leadership and/or of dismissing the issue of sexism in the name of national solidarity and cohesiveness.

Social-service agencies have been commonly criticized for operating in ways that treat the recipients of their services (e.g., the homeless or the unemployed) in ways that belittle them and undermine their sense of agency.

Most efforts and movements that have been aimed at addressing youth issues—be it by enacting policies and laws, improving services and education, or changing how youth are treated in society—have been defined and led by adults.

Process and outcome are interconnected: if we have an unjust process, then we might fail in promoting a socially just outcome because we did not solicit or include the voices of all members. Indeed, (1) our efforts might prove less relevant to the needs of the people whom we seek to represent,

(2) our strategies might prove less effective because we have missed out on valuable input and suggestions, or (3) our initiative's ability to secure the "buy-in" of our audience and allies might suffer.

But is the concept of social justice relevant to young people? It is because young people are developmentally "ready" to grapple with the abstract idea and vision and also because in many cases young people across the world suffer the consequences of oppressive policies, practices, and attitudes.

Youth is a ripe time for thinking about and acting on ideals of social justice (see also Emerging Adulthood). For one, it is in many cultures a time of transition to young adulthood and increasing *autonomy*. The level and kind of autonomy that this might involve partly depends on the prevailing cultural norms. For example, collectivist societies are not likely to consider independence from the family without interdependence a healthy or realistic development; whereas in more individualistic societies this might be more desirable. Nevertheless, the quest for greater autonomy than was the case in childhood is a relatively universal phenomenon, and it is particularly true of older adolescents and young adults.

Youth is also associated with *identity* formation and negotiation. In addition to personal identity young people are in the process of developing identities as community members, citizens, and members of social-identity groups that are based on ethnicity, sexual orientation, social class, and so forth. Finally, youth brings about increased attention to future *goals and achievements* with respect to educational, vocational, and relational pursuits. All of these developmental tasks make issues of justice, equality, liberation, and freedom directly relevant to young people's lives. Indeed, social justice issues affect a person's opportunities to establish autonomy and pursue his or her goals and brings into light questions of political, moral, and civic identity. For that matter, sometimes the right or the opportunity to explore these developmental tasks is itself a contentious issue of social justice. For example, homophobia, xenophobia, and community violence may hamper young people's ability to engage in the self-reflection and exploration that are typically associated with these years.

Youth also undergo changes in thinking or cognitive abilities that are potentially beneficial. Youth are often faulted for being naïve and idealistic. This perception partly results from the fact that they develop an ability to *envision alternative possibilities* and to think in *abstract* terms about such issues as democracy, justice, and fairness. Together, these changes confer upon young people the cognitive ability to envision a better and more just world and thus may increase their willingness to question the way that things are (the status quo). However, because these cognitive changes may be relatively new to young people, they may be more prone than more seasoned adults to downplay the difficulty or immediacy of the tasks that lie ahead of them. Youth's circumstances (e.g., political repression) can either promote or hamper the likelihood that they will cultivate these capacities. Nevertheless, these abilities can be fostered in any and all contexts—history after all has seen many bold and critical student movements that took on dictatorial governments, as in the case of the Indonesian student movements.

Youth also develop the ability to think in *multiple dimensions*, which allows them to critically evaluate statements, rules, values, and norms and to view them in *relative* rather than absolute terms. Such notions as truth, morality, justice, and evil may become more subjective; a society's policies or practices are subjected to reevaluation; and the shades of gray become more apparent and, for that matter, intriguing. Although these changes allow young people to analyze social problems from a more nuanced perspective, they also place them at a greater risk of feeling cynical or disempowered as they take on daunting social problems. Finally youth's ability to *self-reflect* is also an important developing skill: they are now able to consider their actions and responsibilities as community members, citizens, privileged persons, or youth. This development allows youth to engage in a systematic cycle of planning, research, action, and reflection, which is critical to the success of any initiative. However, this newly gained ability may also result in greater self-consciousness and undue concern with what others might think.

So what might social justice *for* youth look like? Each young person will need to define this for himself or herself, but one answer is suggested by the concept of adultism (see also Adultism). Adultism refers to a set of practices and belief systems that hurt young people psychologically and socially and that unfairly deprive them of a number of rights and resources. In that sense adultism may be viewed as a social justice issue as important as imperialism or white supremacy, for example. This form of injustice characterizes the experiences of many youth. As a result, social justice efforts that challenge adultist attitudes, practices, and institutions and that promote youth liberation are likely to enlist the enthusiasm and involvement of many young people who might not otherwise be interested in political work.

Adults are traditionally socialized by their culture to internalize and perpetuate adultist attitudes, behaviors, and policies. Even youth workers are customarily trained to operate in ways that undermine the autonomy of young people and assume that their adult insights and perspectives are inherently superior to those of "less experienced" and "naïve" youth. Thus, a procedural angle on social justice suggests that adults who want to be *allies* to young people in their work with or for young people must recognize and uproot deeply internalized beliefs and practices that negatively stereotype and disempower youth as a group. They can strive to be consultants to youth rather than leaders of youth.

On an institutional level adults would also be expected to engage in power sharing, as was done, for example, in Oakland, California, when a landmark ballot initiative was passed that set aside an additional $72 million over twelve years for youth development programs with the funds to be administered by a committee of adults as well as youth. Youth were thus not only involved in helping pass the resolution but were also formally assigned ongoing and significant roles in its administration and implementation. However, "youth-led" efforts have too often failed to enlist the buy in and involvement of young people. Sometimes this happens because the effort is adult-centric: issues are defined by adults and worked on in a way that undermines youth's opportunities for power and leadership. At other times it may be a matter of inadequate capacity: we tend to forget that youth-led work is more involved and demanding and therefore requires an extended period for building trust and for creating norms and an infrastructure. For reference, adults may also draw on alternative models of youth work and collaboration, such as that provided by the Funders Collaborative on Youth Organizing from a youth organizing perspective.

See also Catholic Education and the Ethic of Social Justice; Community Justice; Global Justice Activism; Juvenile Justice; Social Movements; Social Networks; Social Responsibility; Social Trust.

Recommended Reading

Fanon, F. (1963). *The Wretched of the Earth.* New York: Grove Press.
Freire, P. (1970). *Pedagogy of the Oppressed.* New York: Continuum Publishing Company.
Hooks, B. (1994). *Teaching to Transgress: Education as the Practice of Freedom.* New York: Routledge.
Horton, M., Kohl, J., Kohl, K., and Kohl, H. R. (1997). *The Long Haul: An Autobiography.* New York: Teachers College Press.
Kripalani, K. (1972). *All Men Are Brothers: Life and Thoughts of Mahatma Gandhi as Told in His Own Words.* Paris: World Without War Publications.
Ryan, W. (1971). *Blaming the Victim.* New York: Vintage.

Omar Guessous, Roderick J. Watts, and Adam Darnell

Social Justice Ethic. *See* Catholic Education and the Ethic of Social Justice.

Social Movements. Youth, like many other groups in society, face a variety of unique challenges in the twenty-first century. The educational system in America is becoming increasingly underfunded and therefore has failed many in the lower classes. Today, black youth as young as twelve are being adjudicated and sentenced as adults in the criminal justice system. Job prospects for college students today may be far worse than those twenty years ago. Not surprisingly, not only have youth actively mobilized social movements to address these issues, they have also made up significant portions of other movements, ranging from the recent antiglobalization protests to labor-union organizing through such programs as Union Summer. Recognizing the significant historical and contemporary role youth activism plays in social change, we focus here on addressing the particular challenges and opportunities young people face when engaging in social-movement activities. We detail both the obstacles youth face and the opportunities afforded to youth by their unique position in society. We then discuss particular movements in which youth have played a significant role.

Drawing upon most major social-movement perspectives, explaining why, how, and who engage in collective action, it initially appears that the potential for youth participation is slight. For example, in advanced postindustrial societies access to resources (financial and organizational) has become an increasingly important determinant of social-movement sustainability. Because most youth do not assume full-time employment beyond minimum wage until sometime in their late twenties, they lack access to important resources that are necessary for social-movement activity. Closely related to this is that given their age, youth have not had the time to develop extensive networks of relationships to important actors (e.g., foundations, other social movements) that could be potential supporters of youth activism. Because such actors are largely absent from youth networks, forming social movements is difficult for younger people.

In terms of political opportunities, youth also are often disadvantaged. Political opportunities can be described broadly as the institutional conditions and external environments which make movements more or less likely to emerge at a particular time. Those under the age of eighteen are denied access to the electoral sphere, the major institutionalized process for making their grievances heard by the state. Youth who are eligible to vote often fail to do so, limiting their importance in the political sphere, an important target for most social movements since the rise of the modern nation-state. Finally, given the supposed advantages youth currently enjoy in most Western societies, they face great difficulty framing issues that affect them in a manner that captures the imagination and support of the broader public. Related to the difficulties of youth in presenting their issues in a way in which they are taken seriously, the demographic category "youth" has not been as strong a source of collective identity compared to other groups, including race, gender, class, and religion. When taken together, the lack of resources, networks, and political and framing opportunities should be a major obstacle to youth activism.

However, despite these barriers, youth clearly do participate in social-movement activity at a very high rate. There are a number of reasons why this is the case and why social movements initiated by youth can be so successful. One of the most important explanations for the high level of youth participation in social-movement activity is the concept of biographic availability. Quite simply, because youth have few social obligations, such as a career and family, they are free to engage in other activities, including potentially high-risk protest. Ironically, not being employed full-time is in one way a hindrance to youth

activism but at the same time can be an asset.

There are other possible reasons, drawn from the theories discussed above, that also support increased levels of youth participation in social movements. First, although youth as a whole appear to lack access to important resources, one subcategory, students, often do not. Students, especially those in higher education, but also high-school students, have access to an infrastructure of clubs, organizations, and informal groups, many of which are supported by educational institutions. This environment is critical to the formation of social movements, as it serves as a "space" or a "micromoblization context" (McAdam, McCarthy, and Zald 1988), where resources and opportunities necessary for the construction of a social movement are readily available. This infrastructure has a variety of positive effects on the ability of youth to engage in social-movement activity, including the recruiting of like-minded individuals, opportunities for meetings, the development of leadership skills, and the networking between supportive groups. In addition to the important resources afforded students, the collective identity of student activists has played an important role in many social movements. Given the advantages students enjoy, it is no surprise that they tend to be the most socially active subcategory of youth.

Just as youth have access to unique resources, the political structure grants them opportunities not afforded to other groups. Like women of a century ago, youth under the age of eighteen lack the opportunity to influence what happens in a nation through the electoral process of voting. However, because youth represent the future of the country they have often been granted special treatment by the state. This symbolic representation can make them powerful leaders when they do enter the political arena. Given this history of paternalism, social movements that youth are involved in are often able to win support from the state on a variety of issues, including programs and assistance for problems facing youth, such as drug addiction, suicide, and education.

Finally, as mentioned above, because of the many advantages that society grants youth, it is often especially difficult to frame problems unique to youth. However, youth do hold certain advantages in framing their issues. First, there are some general beliefs in society about entitlements that youth should be granted. These include, first and foremost, access to quality education. When these entitlements are threatened youth are often able to successfully frame the issue to garner broad public sympathy. There is another particular advantage youth have in presenting issues in a convincing manner: the value placed on youth culture in our society. In nearly all public forums (notably mass media and advertising), youth culture is treated as something enormously valuable and desirable. Not only are youth the future leaders, they are also current and future consumers. Given this, if youth are able to link their particular issues to the broader appeal of youth culture (a process Snow and his colleagues refer to as "frame bridging"), they should enjoy wide support from society.

Therefore, despite the myriad of obstacles opposing youth activism, it is not surprising that young people have been heavily involved in some of the most important social movements of the past fifty years. Two of the most important include the civil rights and the student movements of the 1960s. While the student movement obviously depended almost exclusively on youth participants, young people were also important in the success of the civil rights movement as well. The sit-ins that sprung up across the South in the late 1950s and early 1960s were completely organized by students of historically black colleges and were vital in spurring more established civil rights organizations, such as the NAACP, in taking a more aggressive role in the movement. In addition, one of the most important civil rights organizations of the time, the Student Nonviolent Coordinating Committee, was also a youth organization. Finally, through programs like Freedom Summer, elite white students from the North also provided assistance to the movement. While biographical availability was clearly important for these white students, the success of young, black civil rights activists, notably those that organized the sit-ins, depended much more heavily on both existing group structures, such as student groups and churches, and networks between groups that were crucial both for solidarity and the diffusion of organizing "know-how."

A brief examination of the student movement of the 1960s also provides an insight into youth activism. College students from middle- and upper-class backgrounds who attended Eastern and Midwestern elite universities founded one of the most important student groups of the period, Students for a Democratic Society (SDS). These students, because of their social position, received support from the liberal elite, notably the League for Industrial Democracy, which sponsored the organization during much of its existence. As the organization began to grow, college students from working-class backgrounds who attended public universities began to struggle for control of SDS, pushing it in an increasingly radical direction. For example, these students sought stronger ties with the "Black Power" movement, became involved in the urban working class, and sought to mobilize high-school students. Ultimately, due to the combination of internal conflict and state repression, this important organization eventually splintered into a number of underground radical groups, such as the Weathermen.

The experience of SDS illustrates the particular challenges youth face when organizing. Given their lack of resources, the organizers of SDS were especially dependent on other groups (League for Industrial Democracy) for the resources necessary to sustain a viable social-movement organization. The radical political course taken by SDS was often in conflict with the goals of the league, yet SDS leaders were frequently successful in maintaining a working relationship between the two groups, although they did eventually split. Along with the importance of resources, it is also interesting to note the issues that SDS addressed. Early on it focused almost exclusively on a concern of central importance to students, how universities were administered. After achieving success in this area, which led to a larger membership base and increased resources, it began to focus on broader issues, notably the war in Vietnam. This shift in focus did not come without a great deal of debate among the largely student membership, however. In an effort to ensure continued support from its members, SDS sought to demonstrate how universities were often beneficiaries of the military-industrial complex. By linking the university reform frame to the Vietnam War issue, SDS was able to focus on new issues while maintaining its appearance as a primarily student organization. The formation and success of SDS exemplifies the potential and power of youth activism to reshape a nation and influence the world.

While college students have been among the most active youth historically, in recent times youth of various ages have chosen to become socially active. Two particular issues have been at the center of this activism. These include the educational and criminal justice systems. A number of organizations have formed to reform the educational system, primarily focusing K–12 education. In the United States education is largely controlled at the municipal and state levels of government. Therefore, many groups have chosen to create grassroots organizations that rely heavily on community participation, while maintaining ties with state and national organizations. Importantly, youth have often taken a central role in these organizations. An example of such a group is Good Schools of Pennsylvania, which was founded in 2001. Good Schools has a three-point mission. The first goal is to ensure adequate funding that is distributed on an equitable basis

to benefit all schoolchildren. The second goal is to implement more holistic methods of improving school outcomes, which include smaller class sizes, advanced technology, proven reading and math programs, health and social-service support, and quality school administrators and teachers. The third goal is to establish an accountability system for the academic achievement of students as an outcome of the work of the superintendent, principals, and teachers.

Although the organization was not founded by youth, Good Schools of Pennsylvania recognizes the critical role that they must play in school reform. The organization states, "Every civil rights movement depends on the enormous enthusiasm, commitment and courage that students bring to the work of creating greater social justice" (http://www.goodschoolspa.org). While the organization seeks support and participation from college students, Good Schools strongly encourages those seventeen and younger to assume active roles. The organization utilizes a number of strategies to generate youth activism. Speaking directly to high school students, Good Schools asks,

Are you getting the education you deserve and need? Maybe not, because 49 percent of Pennsylvania students graduate high school without the skills necessary to succeed in life. Why isn't anybody doing anything about it? Schools can improve, but they won't get better unless you are involved. If you don't help change things, then who will? You can make a difference. You need to take a stand. Join the Youth Action Network (http://www.goodschoolspa.org.)!

To encourage students to become well-informed on issues affecting the quality of their education, an essay contest has been established that actually provides resources for students to do research on specific topics. Not only do contestants receive prize money but also their winning essays are published in school and local newspapers. As students become more and more knowledgeable on issues, they are encouraged to educate their local communities as a means of empowering other individuals, particularly their peers, to join the movement for school reform.

To further cultivate leaders for the movement, Good Schools Pennsylvania has created a set of leadership training programs. The programs link youth to a network that includes older activists, high-school students, and college students. As youth leaders, they are asked to identify a set of actions they will take to achieve the organization's specified goals of school reforms. These actions include vigils, letter-writing campaigns, telephone campaigns, and rallies. Good Schools provides a number of resources to assist youth activists, such as prepared flyers, brochures, bumper stickers, research materials, money for transportation, and media contacts. As a result, youth in Pennsylvania have been able to have their voices clearly heard on the issue of school reform. Led by high-school students, youth have chosen to directly confront state politicians on the issue of school reform by staging rallies and marches at the Pennsylvania state capital in Harrisburg. Students from both rural and urban districts have united to request that legislators take decisive actions to distribute money more equitably among school districts. Youth of various ages and races leaving their classrooms to demand better education has been a powerful image that has forced political leaders to take the issue of school reform seriously.

School reform is clearly an issue that is currently sparking youth activism. Reform of the juvenile justice system is another issue that has attracted the attention of younger activists. Some of the first actions taken on the issue occurred in California in opposition to Proposition 21, which was drafted and passed to address youth crime. The proposition is an effort to be tougher on juvenile offenders. These provisions include allowing more children aged fourteen to seventeen to be tried in courts as adults; expanding the definition of a felony, such as graffiti damage of $400; and providing police with the authority to label gang members as any group of three or more in-dividuals who are dressed the same, share a common name, or are closely affiliated with one another. Outraged at Proposition 21 in California, similar measures in other states, as well as the federal crime bill of 1994, a number of groups have formed and mobilized with a strong youth presence to improve justice for juveniles. These organizations include Books Not Bars, Schools Not Jails, and the Prison Moratorium Project.

This emerging movement focuses on juvenile justice and reforming the criminal justice system. Not only does the movement draw upon the participation of youth, but it also speaks directly to youth culture through its creative methods of organizing. For example, Books Not Bars (BNB) has held an annual summer concert/rally entitled Not Down With the Lock Down that includes hip-hop and spoken-word artists along with activists. The event utilizes entertainment as a means to mobilizing opposition against the building of a "super-jail" in Alameda County in California. It is not simply a political event, but it is a concert as well. BNB keenly recognizes the power of youth culture in mobilizing activists for their movement. The art and culture arm of the group states, "We strive to appeal to the senses as well as the intellect with our work, using spray cans, music and dance" (http://www.booksnotbars.org). As evidence of their success, BNB was able to wage a successful two-year campaign to change the location and reduce the size of the proposed "super-jail." In attention to the rallies, the youth activists attended and sometimes disrupted public hearings, established alliances with juvenile justice advocates, and prepared an extensive report on the issue.

As stated, music is an important part of this youth movement for juvenile justice. Many groups recognize that music is a powerful part of youth culture. The Prison Moratorium Project (PMP), Schools Not Jails, and BNB have produced albums as a means of mobilizing youth participation and providing them with resources for activism.

Regarding the purpose of the albums, the PMP states, "They [albums] aim to bring art and activism together to educate and politicize young people most impacted by the PIC. These CDs contain embedded documents such as organizing manuals, fact sheets and other resource materials" http://www.nomoreprisons.org). Therefore, not only do the albums entertain youth, but they also empower them to take action on the issue of juvenile justice.

Attempting to create social change through collective action is a challenge for most anyone. Youth face a specific set of challenges, which include limited financial and organizational resources, underdeveloped networks, and restricted framing opportunities. However, youth have historically and continue in contemporary times to demonstrate that these challenges can be overcome. Student activism was the fuel of the civil rights movement, which reshaped American society, and youth of various ages continue to be an energizing force on a number of issues, such as the environment, drunk driving, mental health, sexism, and world peace. The current movements for school reform and juvenile justice are two examples which demonstrate that instead of waiting for tomorrow youth have decided to be leaders of today.

See also Global Justice Activism; Identity and Activism; Social Justice; Social Networks; Social Responsibility; Social Trust; Transnational Youth Activism.

Recommended Reading

Campbell, N., ed. (2000). *The Radiant Hour: Versions of Youth in American Culture*. Exeter: University of Exeter Press.
Carson, C. (1981). *In Struggle: SNCC and the Black Awakening of the 1960s*. Cambridge, MA: Harvard University Press.
Della Porta, D., and Diani, D. (1999). *Social Movements: An Introduction*. Malden, MA: Blackwell.
Epstein, J. S., ed. (1998). *Youth Culture: Identity in a Postmodern World*. Malden, MA: Blackwell.
McAdam, D. (1988). *Freedom Summer*. New York: Oxford University Press.
McAdam, D., McCarthy, J. D., and Zald, M. N. (1988). "Social Movements." In *The Handbook of Sociology*, edited by N. Smelser. Beverly Hills, CA: Sage, pp. 695–737.
Sale, K. (1973). *SDS*. New York: Vintage.

Andrew Martin and Assata Richards

Social Networks. The social ties that people have to others often pull them into or out of activism. Research on this topic is often called "micromobilization" because it tries to describe how individuals are mobilized to participate in unconventional political activity. The central principle that unites this work is that individuals participate in social activism because their structural location (i.e., their position in a network of social connections) makes them available to participate. Whether this effect occurs because they have ties to individuals already engaged in the activity or because they lack ties that keep them out of the activity, the idea is that network ties are critical determinants of social movement participation.

Network connections to other people are often characterized as *strong ties* or *weak ties* because these two types of relations have very different effects on people's voluntary activities. Strong ties are relationships that involve strong affect, frequent interaction, and many different kinds of connection, like kinship ties to immediate family or very close friends. Weak ties involve less frequent interaction and are less close; they often involve just one type of relationship, like co-worker, casual friend, or co-member on a sports team. Weak ties are usually more important than strong ties in pulling people into a new activity, primarily because we are more likely to have weak ties to people who are different from us. Because the weak ties are different they can bring us information to which we were not previously exposed. Strong ties are effective at keeping us engaged in an activity that we share with them but are less important to recruitment. Even more importantly, strong ties with those who are not involved with activism can compete with one's time and energy and make one less likely to participate. Since young people are at a life stage when they are moving away from strong ties based in family and neighborhood and are becoming increasingly embedded in a wider circle of more heterogeneous weak ties, it is not surprising that this age group shows an increase in activism, relative to younger children and older adults.

In general we can say that there are two mechanisms that can pull young people into activism. They may either have continuing strong (often family) ties to those who are activists and stay involved in those activities through the primary importance of these strong ties. Alternatively, they may be exposed to new activities as peer networks become more important; if strong ties and other weak ties do not compete sufficiently to impede activism, the new weak ties may engender new activism. Both activism and more conventional volunteering are much more likely to be motivated through face-to-face invitations, especially if the invitation comes from a person who knows something about the activity and its rewards. Extensive social networks, multiple organization memberships, and prior experience with activism or volunteering all help to predict further involvement. The fact that network resources and organization memberships are correlated with higher socioeconomic status, extroversion, intact family structures, and religiosity helps explain why these personal characteristics are correlated with activism, more conventional political involvement, and volunteering.

One of the primary mechanisms through which networks influence activism is through information. Youth learn about opportunities for voluntary action and about potential benefits that it may offer them through their interactions with others who participate. However, there are also other processes that flow through these networks. Some scholars have noted the critical role that *collective action frames* have in shaping potential activists' decisions about whether or not to participate in collective action. Mobilization depends on more than the existence of a social problem, the availability of resources to address it, and the openness of the political opportunity structure (the three major macro-level determinants of social-movement emergence); it also depends on the way these are all framed by movement leaders. Since we generally come to share the view of a political or social situation that is held by our associates, the framing of an issue can travel through social networks in ways that encourage (or inhibit) participation. If we see poverty as a problem that people bring on themselves, we are less likely to engage in antipoverty activism than if we believe that opportunities in the economy are unfairly distributed. Even conventional volunteering is associated with a cultural framing of citizenship as a set of responsibilities that is conveyed by parents and schools.

Finally, several scholars have noted the crucial role that *collective identities* play in social-movement emergence. A group's collective definition of an oppressive situation, coupled with its collective understanding of the meaning and purpose of the group, is critical to understanding how groups choose to mobilize and how they choose tactics and articulate their goals. Since youth develop collective identities through their membership in loosely connected cliques of similar others (often without having direct connections to all of the others in the clique), these processes also tend to emphasize the importance of weak ties. Both strong and weak ties, however, can reaffirm the positive connection between a youth's important self-identities and activism.

In addition to information, frames, and collective identity, some movement scholars have recently noted the crucial role of emotions in mobilizing youth toward activism. The fact that youth display more intense and quickly changing emotional states may induce them to be more likely to go to the streets, risking danger or arrest from opponents of their activism or from the forces of order. Being embedded in groups of similar others who are thinking about issues in the same way can evoke parallel emotions in a number of people, creating the motivational basis for unusual action.

See also Social Justice; Social Movements; Social Trust.

Recommended Reading

McAdam, D. (1988). *Freedom Summer: The Idealists Revisted.* Oxford: Oxford University Press.

McAdam, D., and Paulsen, R. (1993). "Specifying the Relationship Between Social Ties and Activism." *American Journal of Sociology*, 3: 640–667.

McPherson, M., Smith-Lovin, L., and Cook, J. (2001). "Birds of a Feather: Homophily in Social Networks." *Annual Review of Sociology*, 27: 415–444.

Wilson, J. (2000). "Volunteering." *Annual Review of Sociology*, 26: 215–240.

Miller McPherson and Lynn Smith-Lovin

Social Responsibility. In its most basic form social responsibility is the duty or obligation that an individual or group has to society. It is our concern for the welfare of others as well as ourselves and our willingness to take action based on that concern. Social responsibility is the foundation for the volunteerism and associations that form civil societies. This obligation often stems from a perception of having a privileged place in society and having the moral duty to help those who are less fortunate. Viewed as an orientation to help others even when there is nothing to be gained, it has an altruistic tone. Young people learn social responsibility through interaction with others: family, friends, peers, teachers, and strangers. An important part of social responsibility relates to the adolescents' feelings of agency and control, feeling that you have the ability to do something about what you are concerned about.

Social responsibility suggests an identification with and sense of obligation to a common good that includes the self but that stretches beyond one's own self interest. The socially responsible individual exhibits a high sense of duty, works for the good of the group rather than for self-gain, is loyal to friends, and can be trusted to pull his or her weight. He or she is a good teammate. Socially responsible individuals would be likely to be active in the civic affairs of their communities—by voting, joining voluntary associations, or contributing time and money to social or environmental causes. Socially responsible organizations take pride in addressing social and environmental issues.

Social responsibility is multidimensional. It exhibits different characteristics, depending on both the nature of the actor as well as the nature of the action. While generally thought of as a characteristic of individuals, a duty that the individual has to others and to society; it can also be conceived of as a characteristic of a group or organization. Corporate social responsibility is the obligation of the organization to "pay back" to society for the benefits it has received. Social responsibility can also be thought of as mutual responsibility, an acknowledgment of our connectedness to others and our need to work together to solve a problem. Social responsibility also contains elements of "generativity," one generation's obligation to ensure the welfare of future generations and the duty to make the world a better place.

Social responsibility is the foundation upon which youth activism is built. National surveys of Americans indicate that those who engage in protest overwhelmingly do so out of a sense of duty to the larger community. The common thread for those exhibiting these values is that they endorse public interest over self-interest goals as values by which to live. They identify with the common good and want to make the world a better place. On the other hand, they demonstrate their responsibility in different ways, sometimes as individuals, sometimes as groups, sometimes concerned about current conditions, and sometimes concerned about the future. In other words, social responsibility in youth activism exhibits all of the diversity characteristics of social responsibility itself.

Individual Social Responsibility

The class valedictorian is honored by her high school. She is a member of the National Honor Society, was president of her senior class, and maintained a 4.0 grade point average. In addition, she volunteers in her church soup kitchen on Sundays and tutors disadvantaged students during the week. Her activism is channeled into traditional settings. She participated in student government during the last two years and expects to be involved in civic organizations through the rest of her life. She will be attending college in the fall and sees a bright future ahead of herself. Biographies similar to hers are printed every spring in local newspapers across the country.

Barack Obama was born in Hawaii to a white Kansan mother and a black, Harvard-educated Kenyan father. He grew up in Indonesia and went to school at Columbia University. Later, he earned a law degree from Harvard, worked as a civil rights lawyer in Chicago, and served in the Illinois legislature. In 2004 he was elected to the U.S. Senate from Illinois as a Democrat. Upon graduation he could have opted for a lucrative career with any law firm in the country; instead he elected to dedicate himself to service for others and civic involvement.

Both the class valedictorian and Mr. Obama are examples of socially responsible individuals. They represent the traditional conceptualization of social responsibility. In this notion social responsibility is described as a characteristic of individuals rather than groups and is based on a sense of obligation or duty toward others who are dependent on us for their welfare—the greater the dependence, the greater the responsibility. These types of socially responsible youth tend to be comfortable members of their society, student leaders and activists from the middle class. They agree with its goals and values. They seek to promulgate these values by helping others in their community. They tend to be altruistic, helping others without seeking personal gain.

Socially responsible individuals are likely to be active in the civic affairs of their communities—by voting, joining voluntary associations, or contributing time and money to social or environmental causes. They are also more likely to be involved in political protests, whether they be progressive or conservative. The common thread for those exhibiting these values is that they endorse public interest over self-interest goals as values by which to live. They identify with the common good and want to make the world a better place for others. They also feel connected or identified in some way to the persons or group whose welfare concerns them. To a great extent volunteerism and civic action make it possible.

Corporate Social Responsibility

Across the country students in high schools and on college campuses are participating in antisweatshop campaigns to raise awareness of the plight of workers in third-world countries, pressure corporations and educational institutions to implement policies that reduce the exploitation of workers producing goods for sale in the United States, and boycott manufacturers and retailers that ignore their social responsibility to encourage humane working conditions. Students have organized antisweatshop networks across the country, been instrumental in forcing universities to adopt antisweatshop policies in the manufacture of clothing items, and even led to changes in state laws regarding ethical business practices.

In 2001 the Harvard University living-wage campaign ended a three-week sit-in of the president's office after concessions by the university that would lead to improvements in the situation of minimum wage employees. The students in the living-wage campaign had joined with organized labor in forcing the university to address the working conditions of its employees. The campaign lasted more than three years, resulted in developing a sense of community between workers and students, and sought to address the ethical and moral issues involved when the richest university in the world failed to meet its responsibilities to its employees.

In both these cases young people are engaged in efforts to encourage corporate social responsibility. Corporate social responsibility (CSR) is similar to individual social responsibility except that the group or organization is the actor. Usually, corporate social responsibility refers to private corporations and their obligations to society as a whole. Often, responsibility for the effects of corporate actions on the environment, the community, or its employees is of major concern. With increasing globalization the impact of corporate decisions on populations in developing societies is also a concern, as shown by the following quotations wherein CSR is defined as:

- "… the commitment of business to contribute to sustainable economic development, working with employees, their families, the local community and society at large to improve their quality of life" (World Business Council on Sustainable Development).
- "… operating a business in a manner that meets or exceeds the ethical, legal, commercial and public expectations that society has of business" (Business for Social Responsibility).
- "… a set of management practices that ensure the company minimizes the negative impacts of its operations on society while maximizing its positive impacts" (Canadian Centre for Philanthropy).

Corporate social responsibility tends to be more formal and less altruistic than other types. As a result, it also leads to more social activism. By definition it requires the organization of young people into groups that can confront and influence corporate actors to change their behavior.

Mutual Responsibility

A group of friends get together to talk about a party that they are going to attend. They know that there will be drinking, and they make their plans accordingly. They establish a rule that no woman will drink from an open container of alcohol. Women will only drink from containers that they open themselves, no drinking from glasses or cups. If they put a container down, then it is abandoned, there is no returning to an opened container. The friends agree to watch out for each other during the evening; no one will be allowed to get too drunk. One of the friends agrees to be the designated driver. He will not drink alcohol during the party and will be responsible for getting everyone home safely. In some cases the host of the party participates in the process and takes away the keys from each driver to make sure that only sober individuals attempt to drive home.

To some extent this scene is repeated among adolescents and young adults across the country every day. These young people are engaging in an exercise in social responsibility, looking out for each other and helping each other resolve social problems. They have exhibited solidarity with each other and have established social mechanisms to address problems that they could not resolve individually. This notion of social responsibility exhibits an element of "being in this together," an acknowledgment of connectedness, and an inability to solve problems individually. It is based on feelings of camaraderie among members of the group, that the problems of any one person could easily be the experience of any other. Any obligation felt by these friends is the obligation to look out for and help each other because it is easier to deal with the dangers together rather than alone.

This type of social responsibility is closely linked with social capital. Social capital is the asset derived from being a member of a group—a neighborhood, a community. It is the benefit that an individual receives from the associations that he or she has cultivated over his or her life. Social responsibility is the other side of social capital, the obligation associated with group membership that makes the accumulation of social capital possible. However, social responsibility is not an economic exchange, not the cost associated with some potential benefit. Nor is it a price that has to be paid in order to receive a reward. Rather it is based on the acknowledgment of the social bond, the fact that we are all in this together and that many social goods cannot be attained without working together.

This notion of social responsibility is quite different from the concept defined in the psychological literature. In the psychological notion social responsibility is a characteristic of individuals rather than groups and is based on a sense of obligation or duty toward others who are dependent on us for their welfare: the greater the dependence, the greater the responsibility. That type of social responsibility is akin to the idea of "noblesse oblige," the obligation of the aristocrat to help the less fortunate. Here, the emphasis is on membership, the feeling of inclusion and mattering to other members of the group.

Generativity

In another case a group of students organize a protest on Earth Day, focused on the problems of environmental degradation and global warming. They picket the offices of a major American power company because the company is burning high-sulfur fuels at its electric generating plants. Some activists vandalize the property because of their frustration with the slow pace of reform.

These students are also exhibiting social responsibility but of a slightly different kind. They believe that they have a responsibility to protect the present for the benefit of future generations. They are taking responsibility for the future of society and in some cases are risking their current welfare in the hope that their actions will benefit future generations.

This feeling of responsibility for the welfare of future generations is a powerful component of social responsibility. It is especially evident in environmental-action activities. Young people who participate in environmental action usually have this future orientation. They feel a responsibility not only for the present but also to the future.

Citizenship requires social responsibility, especially within a democracy in which the members of a polity rule themselves. For a successful democracy, individuals have to sacrifice their own immediate gratification in the longer-term interests of the group. They need to feel a sense of obligation to each other. Individuals in positions of power and privilege need to assist those who are less fortunate. Corporations and organizations need to be responsible for how their actions impact on the welfare of others. In some cases, individual action cannot solve a problem. Democracy requires working together for the benefit of all. Social responsibility is the foundation of democracy.

See also Democracy; Democratic Education; Social Justice; Social Movements; Social Networks; Social Trust.

Recommended Reading

Berkowitz, L., and Lutterman, K. G. (1968). "The Traditional Socially Responsible Personality." *Public Opinion Quarterly*, 32: 169–185.

Bierhoff, H. W. (2002). "Just World, Social Responsibility, and Helping Behavior." In *The Justice Motive In Everyday Life*, edited by M. Ross and D. T. Miller. New York: Cambridge University Press, pp. 189–203.

Flanagan, C. A., Elek-Fisk, E., and Gallay, L. S. (In Press). "Friends Don't Let Friends ... Or Do They? Developmental and Gender Differences in Intervening in Friends' ATOD Use." *Journal of Drug Education*.

Keyes, C. (2002). "Social Civility in the United States." *Sociological-Inquiry*, 72 (3): 393–408.

Marks, H. M., and Jones, S. R. (2004). "Community Service in Transition: Shifts and Continuities in Participation from High School to College." *The Journal of Higher Education*, 75 (3): 307–338.

Rossi, A. S., ed. (2001). *Caring and Doing for Others: Social Responsibility in the Domains of Family, Work, and Community*. Chicago: University of Chicago Press.

Leslie S. Gallay

Social Trust. Trust seems like such a simple thing to understand. We trust our families.

We trust our friends. Some people have treated us badly in the past, and we don't trust them. We don't know whether we should put faith in people we see on the street, so we neither trust nor mistrust them. Trust is based upon experience. Each day we learn something new about someone and this evidence helps us decide whom we trust and whom we distrust.

This is the usual way we think about trust. But it is not the only way to think about trust. Beyond trust based on experience is another type of trust, social trust or *moralistic* trust. Moralistic trust is the belief that *we ought to treat people as if they were trustworthy*. It is like the Golden Rule: you shouldn't treat people as they treat you ("an eye for an eye, a tooth for a tooth"). Instead, you should treat people *as you want them to treat you*. Moralistic trust rests on the belief that the world is a good place, is going to get better, and that you can help make it better. If we have a fundamentally upbeat view of the world, we quite naturally believe that "most people can be trusted." If we believe that the future looks bleak and that there are dark forces that are conspiring against us, we will believe that "you can't be too careful in dealing with people."

What is social about social trust? When we place faith in people through social trust, we accept them as part of our "moral community." We say that there are some common bonds among very different types of people. Even if others don't look like us or don't think like us, we have a shared fate with each other. We are responsible for the well-being of members of our "moral community." Everyone has someone they trust. Even criminals and terrorists have faith in their co-conspirators. Moralistic (social) trusters have faith in most people. This faith in others leads us to be more tolerant of people who are different from ourselves and to do good works such as volunteering time and giving to charity. Trust is in shorter supply than it was in the past and this means that we are doing fewer good deeds helping people different from ourselves.

The Roots of Social Trust

We don't count up good and bad experiences when we become moralistic trusters (or mistrusters). Moralistic trusters are essentially optimists, looking at the good side of life, and mistrusters are pessimists. Optimists and pessimists look at evidence in different ways. Trusters (optimists) see a glass as half full and mistrusters (pessimists) as half empty. Trusters look at disappointments as the exception to the rule. Mistrusters see letdowns as confirming their pessimism. Like Eyeore, they downplay the significance of good tidings.

We don't learn moralistic trust every day. But we do learn it early in life. The famous social psychologist Erik Erikson argued that we learn to trust at three years old. Perhaps some basic instincts are set in at this early age, but children—and even young adults—develop trusting sentiments somewhat later.

Where does social trust come from? Our early experiences matter. Most critically, we learn to be trusting or mistrusting from our parents. Young people whose parents have faith in others are likely to become trusters themselves. And a happy family life gives us a positive view of the larger world, including people we don't know. Kids are more likely to trust others when kids feel that their parents give them a say in family decisions, when they are free to choose their own friends, and when they feel that they can disagree with their parents. Teachers also matter: young people who feel that their teachers have treated them unfairly will be less likely to have faith in others. Kids who have friends of a different race will also be more likely to trust people who are different from themselves. And, of course, an upbeat view of the world matters: when you expect your future to be bright, you will take the risk of trusting people you don't know.

We often say that trust is easily broken. If someone lies to you or treats you badly, your faith in them will be shaken. This is certainly true for the day-to-day trust that *is* based on experience. It is not true for social trust. If one person or even a few people betray you, that won't shake your faith in human nature. Your early experiences shape trust throughout your life. High-school students and their parents were interviewed in 1965 and again when they were adults in 1982; 72 percent gave the same answer to the question, "Generally speaking, do you believe that most people can be trusted, or can't you be too careful in dealing with people?" in both surveys, eighteen years apart. How trusting your parents were in 1965 was one of the most important factors leading to trust as an adult. Good relations with your parents when you were in high school made you more likely to be trusting as an adult. And if you had positive views of people who are different from yourself when you were young, you will be more likely to trust strangers when you become an adult.

Why Trust Matters

Moralistic trust is the chicken soup of social life. It is *nice for us* that we trust our friends and family, but it is *good for society* when we believe that *most people can be trusted*. Trust matters because faith in others reflects a positive attitude. And this upbeat worldview makes us more tolerant of people who are different from ourselves, more committed to social action, and more likely to do good works.

Whites who believe that most people can be trusted have positive views of African Americans. They favor programs such as affirmative action to make up for past injustices against blacks. They don't believe that blacks can overcome these obstacles on their own. Trusters of all races are more likely to see immigrants as making positive contributions to society. They don't worry that people coming to America will take jobs away from people who are already here. And they believe that trading with other countries helps everyone.

Moralistic trusters also support equal rights for women. They strongly reject the argument that God has made women only to raise children and not to have their own careers. Trusters also support rights for gays and lesbians—to serve in the military, to teach in schools, and to adopt children. They are also less likely to hold negative stereotypes of other minorities, such as Jews.

Trusting people are more tolerant because they believe that we all suffer when some groups face discrimination. We have a shared fate; what happens to one group affects us all. And we share a common set of values that brings us together. In a 1993 survey 41 percent of people with faith in others agreed that "Americans are united and in agreement on the most important values," compared to 29 percent of mistrusters.

People with faith in others not only see one country, they see much in common between the United States and other countries. They are less prone to say that being an American is very important to them, that other countries should emulate the United States, and especially that the United States should go its own way in the world. Even after the events of September 11, people who trusted others were far less likely to see Saudi Arabia as an enemy of the United States. And they were much more reluctant to give the government power to restrict freedoms to protect against another terrorist attack.

Social trust does more than shape our values. Trusting people are more connected to other people. But which other people? The "social capital" explanation links trust and social connections. Trusting people are more likely to get involved in their communities. And when we get together with other folks, we learn to trust them and to work with them for some common purpose. We may get together with other people for purely social purposes: we join bowling leagues, play soccer, join bird-watching clubs and choral societies, or even go on picnics with each other. And, as the children's song goes, "the more we get together, the happier we'll be."

We don't take part in these activities to become better citizens, but our socializing will lead to greater trust. Trusting people get involved with others and social involvement leads to trust. As Robert Putnam, the leading advocate of the social-capital approach, argues, the connections between trust and engagement with others "are as tangled as well-tossed spaghetti" (Putnam 2000, 137). Stolle shows that trusting people are more likely to join more clubs. There is mixed evidence on whether joining clubs makes people more trusting. Some studies find support for the link among adults and young people, but others do not for both young people and adults.

Uslaner's study, perhaps the most elaborate, fails to find support for *either connection*: trusting people do not join groups more than mistrusters, nor does joining groups make you more trusting of strangers. Why? First, we spend little time in clubs and other community groups, perhaps a couple of hours a week. This is hardly enough to reshape basic values that we learned from our parents at an early age. Second, social trust is faith in people who may be different from us. But when we join groups or get together with friends for dinner or picnics, we hang out with people *very much like ourselves*. We go bowling with friends. Who joins choral societies? Single young people who like classical music. Choral societies seem to be dating clubs, not laboratories for producing better citizens. No matter how many times you get together with people like yourself, you won't learn to trust people who are different from you. Sometimes having a lot of contact with people of your own background might even lead to *less trust in strangers*. Not every group promotes tolerance (think of the Ku Klux Klan or many fundamentalist religions).

There is one area of participation where studies clearly show that trust matters: doing good works. People who trust others are far more likely than mistrusters to donate money to charity and to volunteer their time. These activities connect us to people who are different from ourselves. Indeed, trust matters for some forms of good works and not for others. Social trust *does not* make people more likely to donate money or volunteer time through their church, synagogue, or mosque. It is a powerful force, perhaps the major reason, behind giving money or time to causes such as homeless shelters and other causes for people who are less fortunate. You don't need social trust to make you feel an obligation to people of your own faith. You do need it to reach out and touch someone of a different background. And when we do good deeds, we become more trusting. Volunteering and charitable donations give us what economists call a "warm glow." Our good works make us feel good inside—and even more trusting.

The Decline of Trust

Americans are not as trusting as they used to be. In 1960, the first year a national survey asked about social trust, 58 percent of Americans agreed that "most people can be trusted." In 2002 only 37 percent agreed with that statement. Virtually every group in American society has become less trusting (except for early baby-boomers born between 1946 and 1955). The biggest drop has come among young people. In 1960, 61 percent of people twenty to thirty trusted others; by 1972 the trusting share of young people had fallen to 39 percent, and in 2002 barely more than a quarter of young adults had faith in other people. The drop in social trust over time has been just as sharp among high-school students, from 45 percent in 1977 to 30 percent in 1995.

Why have Americans become less trusting? Principally it is because they have become less optimistic for the future. Most Americans, and especially young people, no longer believe in the promise of the American dream—that life will be better for them than it was for their parents. More and more people say that success in life depends more on luck and connections than on hard work. And there was a sharp increase in the share of Americans (up to almost 70 percent by 1994) who agreed that "the lot of the average person is getting worse." People, especially young people, had a pessimistic view of their future and thought that their future was beyond their control. No wonder, then, that they became more concerned with how much they could make for themselves. Between 1977 and 1995 there was a sharp increase in the share of young people who believed that it was important to become wealthy. When the future does not look secure, people, especially young people, look out for themselves first. Concern for others comes a distant second.

Several major events shaped Americans' trust. In the 1960s the civil rights movement brought people together in a spirit of unity. Many Americans learned the lesson of the civil rights movement—we are one people even if we look different from each other—and became more trusting. In the 1970s, however, the Vietnam War tore the fabric of the country apart. Young protestors against the war chanted, "Don't trust anyone over thirty," and they meant it. Opponents of the war in the 1970s did not trust others then—or a decade later when they became adults. The social conflicts over the war split the country and weakened social trust.

Perhaps the most important reason why we have become less trusting is the growth in economic inequality in the United States from the 1960s to the present. When Americans argued that "the rich are getting richer and the poor are getting poorer," they were right, at least in part. The income gap between the rich and the poor has increased dramatically since the 1960s. The rise in income inequality is strongly related to the decline in social trust. As the income gap has increased, the level of optimism for the future—the belief that you can succeed—has fallen. Now more and more people say that the system is stacked against them. As the gap rises, there is less reason for people to believe that they share a common fate with others in society.

As Americans have become less trusting, they have become less committed to doing good deeds. Of course, Americans give more to charity now than they did in 1960. The United States is a much richer nation. However, we give a *much smaller share of our national wealth* to charity now than we did four decades ago. Our donations to religious institutions have not fallen as strongly as our gifts to secular causes, and the biggest drops have come for "human services" such as homeless shelters, food banks, vocational counseling, assistance to the handicapped, Meals on Wheels, disaster relief, summer camps for disadvantaged kids, Boys and Girls Clubs, and similar causes. The downward trends in human-services donations and social trust are strikingly similar. When we care less for other people, we are less disposed to help them. As we have become less trusting, we are less likely to volunteer for good causes such as the Red Cross or as volunteer firefighters.

The loss of trust has affected our government as well. Congress long depended upon an atmosphere of trust to reach compromises across party lines. As trust has fallen, each party has become more extreme. Democrats have become much more liberal, Republicans much more conservative. The two parties no longer see each other as partners in governing. Instead, compromise has become a dirty word, signifying giving in to the opposition. Parties now come together when they vote less often than at any other time since the late nineteenth century. It has become increasingly difficult for the two parties to find common ground to get bills passed in the House and the Senate.

Summary

Social trust leads us to reach out to others, to work with them rather than against them. It is an important moral resource in society that we gain from our parents early in life. We generally think of trust as based upon experience. This form of trust connects us to friends and family and warns us to be wary of people we don't know. But moralistic (or social) trust is largely based upon our early experiences. It is a key resource that helps us bridge different groups in society and makes our social and political life less conflictual. But it is in shorter supply now, especially among our young people. We are less optimistic for the future, and we do fewer good deeds than in the past.

Note: The research assistance of Mitchell Brown is greatly appreciated. I am also grateful to the Russell Sage Foundation and the Carnegie Foundation for a grant under the Russell Sage program on the Social Dimensions of Inequality (see http://www.russellsage.org/programs/proj_reviews/social-inequality.htm) and to the general research board of the Graduate School of the University of Maryland–College Park. Some of the data reported here come from the Inter-University Consortium for Political and Social Research (ICPSR), which is not responsible for any interpretations. I also appreciate the careful readings by Avery Uslaner and Deborah D. Uslaner.

See also Social Justice; Social Movements; Social Networks; Social Responsibility.

Recommended Reading

Brehm, J., and Rahn, W. (1997). "Individual Level Evidence for the Causes and Consequences of Social Capital." *American Journal of Political Science*, 41: 888–1023.

Erikson, E. (1968). *Identity: Youth and Crisis*. New York: W. W. Norton.

Flanagan, C. A. (2003). "Trust, Identity, and Civic Hope." *Applied Developmental Science*, 7 (3): 165–171.

Newton, K. (1997). "Social Capital and Democracy." *American Behavioral Scientist*, 40: 575–586.

Putnam, R. D. (1993). *Making Democracy Work: Civic Traditions in Modern Italy*. Princeton, NJ: Princeton University Press.

Putnam, R. D. (2000). *Bowling Alone*. New York: Simon and Schuster.

Rahn, W. M., and Transue, J. E. (1998). "Social Trust and Value Change: The Decline of Social Capital in American Youth, 1976–1995." *Political Psychology*, 19: 545–566.

Smith, E. (September 1999). "Youth Voluntary Association Participation and Political Attitudes: A Quasi-Experimental Analysis." Paper presented at the meeting of the American Political Science Association, Atlanta, GA.

Stolle, D. (1998). "Bowling Together, Bowling Alone: The Development of Generalized Trust in Voluntary Associations." *Political Psychology*, 19: 497–526.

Uslaner, E. M. (1999). "Democracy and Social Capital." In *Democracy and Trust*, edited by M. Warren. Cambridge: Cambridge University Press, pp. 121–150.

Uslaner, E. M. (2002). *The Moral Foundations of Trust*. New York: Cambridge University Press.

Yamigishi, T., and Yamigishi, M. (1994). "Trust and Commitment in the United States and Japan." *Motivation and Emotion*, 18: 129–166.

Eric M. Uslaner

South Africa. *See* AIDS Advocacy in South Africa; Soweto Youth Activism.

Soweto Youth Activism (South Africa). The Soweto riots represent a classic example of youth engagement in contentious political contexts. The date, June 16, is a constant reminder to all South Africans of the historic political events of 1976. On this day young people defying terror and death took matters into their own hands to make heroic sacrifices for the liberation of all South Africans. Now, June 16 is celebrated each year as a national holiday to commemorate the heroism of the Soweto youth.

On June 16, 1976, the schoolchildren of Soweto Township, protesting the introduction of Afrikaans as the medium of instruction in their schools, took to the streets in a massive, peaceful demonstration. Afrikaans was the language of the oppressor class, the class that was enforcing the system of apartheid in South Africa. Police reaction to the demonstration was brutal as they shot at the unarmed students. This was a miscalculated move, for the horrific attack created an uprising that spread to other parts of the country and beyond.

That day at least twenty-five people were killed. Twelve-year-old Hector Peterson, revered today as a martyr in South Africa's struggle against apartheid, was the first to fall. The violence precipitated a spontaneous uprising led by the students that spread rapidly to all parts of the country. By the end of the year it was estimated that 575 had died, and 2,389 people had been wounded in the fight against the apartheid state. The resolve of the activists to fight to death the injustice of apartheid strengthened in the face of state violence. To this day most activists cite the Soweto riots as a key event that shaped their civic identity. A wave of detentions and bannings were used by the state in an attempt to crush the revolt. Twenty-one thousand people were prosecuted for offenses related to the uprising.

Students and pupils of all ethnic groups responded to the liberation movement's underground calls to reject the fascist educational system that was being forced down their throats. Flyers distributed at the time by the African National Congress (ANC) proclaimed: "Whether you are subject to Bantu Education or Christian National Education, it is 3rd rate education designed to support an unjust system. Use the boycott weapon, raise your voices and demand a single, free, compulsory national education system, founded in a society which allows you to actually benefit from what you study."

From all corners of South Africa and countries beyond, the message was clear: "Everyone must be a freedom fighter! Our men, our women, our youth—the toilers in the town and countryside—the scholars and the professional groups. Amandla Ngawethu! Power to the people! The struggle continues! Victory is certain!"

And in the forefront of this struggle were the sons and daughters of the soil—some as young as twelve years old. There were tensions between the generations over these actions. Parents, teachers, and traditional adult caregivers were afraid of the youth's bold activism. The youth in turn felt that the older generations had complied too long with the oppressive treatment of the apartheid regime. They insisted that there was nothing left to lose, that active resistance was the only way.

Thousands left the country in the face of the repression by the state. They left to carry on the struggle from outside the country. Nineteen-year-old Solomon Kalushi Mahlangu was among them. He left his home in the night, not telling even his mother where he was going or if he would ever return. Determined to fight for change, he sought training as a soldier. A year later he returned home as a cadre of the armed wing of the African National Congress (ANC)—Umkhonto we Sizwe (MK), the Spear of the Nation.

Solomon returned to South Africa in 1977 on a mission to join student protests commemorating the Soweto massacre. He never made it to the protests. He and his team members, Monty Motloung and George "Lucky" Mahlangu, were accosted by police in Johannesburg, and in the gunfight that followed two white civilians were killed. George Mahlangu escaped. Solomon Mahlangu and Monty Motloung were captured. Monty was so brutally beaten during the course of his capture that he suffered severe brain damage, leaving him unfit to stand trial. Solomon had not fired a shot but was left to face the murder charges alone. The trial was started without his lawyers' knowledge, and it was inevitable that he was found guilty of murder.

On March 2, 1977, Solomon was sentenced to death by hanging. When he heard his sentence, he shouted, "Amandla!" (power). Indeed, his cause wielded power. For two years the international democratic community campaigned against his execution and called for the recognition of all South African freedom fighters as prisoners of war. But, despite international pressure, the apartheid government was not swayed.

On April 6, 1979, twenty-three-year-old Solomon Mahlangu faced the gallows, raised his hand in the ANC salute, and met his death at the hands of a racist regime. His final words are reputed to have been, "My blood will nourish the tree that will bear the fruits of freedom. Tell my people that I love them. They must continue the fight." Solomon's people did continue the fight. In honor of his courage and dedication to the cause of freedom, the ANC named a new school after him, the Solomon Mahlangu Freedom College.

There was a historical backdrop to the student uprising in Soweto. Young people first emerged as political stakeholders in the resistance movement in the 1940s. Although established in 1912, it was not until the 1940s that young people played a serious role within the structures of the African National Congress. The emergence of youth leaders in the ANC Youth League, under the leadership of people like Nelson Mandela and Oliver Tambo, injected a new sense of urgency into the ANC. It was this radicalism that was largely responsible for the momentum behind political protests in the 1950s. This was also a period of hardening attitudes on the part of the nationalist government, which was insistent on pursuing its apartheid ideology. Unwilling to entertain any notion of democracy, the white minority government responded with viciousness to all forms of protest. This was manifest most vividly in the Sharpeville massacre where the police shot into a crowd of 5,000 peaceful protesters killing sixty-nine and wounding 180.

It was around this period of resistance in 1961 when it became clear that only through armed struggle—no matter how long and bloody—could freedom be won. The national liberation movement, under the leadership of the ANC, formed a covert military structure named Umkhonto we Sizwe. This youth-led military structure provided the freedom fighters with the skills of modern warfare. Bomb blasts and sabotage actions rocked the country, instilling fear among the oppressors as well as in the parents of the very children involved in the struggle. Freedom radio broadcasts from Mozambique and Tanzania reiterated the call for the youth to join Umkhonto: "Our youth—African, Indian, and colored—must join Umkhonto in even bigger numbers and train to become skilled freedom fighters. Remember: to succeed in struggle it is essential to be disciplined, organized, and correctly identify the enemy.

You must be part of an organization, part of a revolutionary movement—the ANC with its allies and military wing Umkhonto we Sizwe will lead our people to victory!"

In response to the increasing momentum of the liberation movement, the apartheid government apprehended, prosecuted, and jailed many prominent leaders and forced many others into exile. With state violence, mass arrests, and the exodus of prominent leaders, the resistance movement was contained. Although underground activity continued to keep the movement alive, there was a lull in visible struggle activities, and the 1960s became known as the quiet decade. The apartheid system grew stronger and extended its control over all aspects of people's lives. But, despite the lull, people were not prepared to accept the hardships and oppression of apartheid.

Young people became impatient with the apparent lack of resistance to the increasingly oppressive policies in the labor force and in the schools. Thus, in the early 1970s workers and students fought back against the system. Their struggles changed the face of South Africa. Student-led organizations such as the South African Student Organization (SASO) under the leadership of Steve Biko, who was killed in detention in 1977, provided new outlets for the young people's social and political concerns. This period became the founding of the black-consciousness generation. The black-consciousness movement promoted the ideas of black power, black pride, and self-reliance. It instilled a new assertiveness and opened new channels for antiapartheid resistance. Many Soweto student leaders were influenced by the ideas of black consciousness. The South African Students Movement (SASM), one of the first organizations of black high-school students, played an important role in the 1976 Soweto uprising against Bantu education and the Afrikaans language as the medium of instruction.

In the repressive aftermath following the Soweto uprising, thousands of students escaped from the country to join the freedom fighters, enabling the initiation and development of a new phase of armed struggle. There were also small groups of student activists who were linked to old ANC members and the ANC underground. These underground structures issued pamphlets calling on the community to support students and linking the student struggle to the struggle for national liberation. Mass action by students in which almost a million students at all levels participated, contributed greatly to the transformation of African townships into fortresses of resistance. The apartheid regime felt obliged to send troops into African townships to intimidate students and force them to return to schools. Such state actions continued to fail in weakening the resolve of the student masses.

In retrospect, the student march in Soweto stands out as the definitive moment in the final push against apartheid and laid the basis for the evolution of a powerful political youth movement. It thrust the black-consciousness generation onto the political center stage at a scale never seen before in South Africa. Twenty-six years later, survivors of the black-consciousness generation are among the first generation of leaders of the democratic South Africa. They are our new cabinet ministers and members of parliament (MPs), human-rights commissioners and judges, police commissioners and army chief of staff, the reserve bank governor, and numerous other public faces of black economic empowerment.

The riots in Soweto started as a boycott of classes by the seventh-grade students of Morris Isaacson High School. They culminated in a titanic battle between the fascist minority regime and the younger generation who would ultimately lead a free and democratic South Africa.

See also AIDS Advocacy in South Africa; Australia, Youth Activism in; Demographic Trends Affecting the World's Youth; Eastern Europe, Youth and Citizenship in; Europe, Comparing Youth Activism in; European Identity and Citizenship; Immigrant Youth in Europe—Turks in Germany; Immigrant Youth in, the United States; India, Youth Activism in; Indonesia, Youth Activism in; Nigeria, Youth Activism in; Palestinian *Intifada*; Russia, Youth Activism in; Serbia, Youth Activism in (1990–2000); State and Youth, The; Statute of the Child and Adolescent (Brazil); Tiananmen Square Massacre (1989); Transnational Identity; Transnational Youth Activism; Turkey, Youth Activism in; United Nations, Youth Activism and; Xenophobia; Zapatista Rebellion (Mexico); Zionist Youth Organizations.

Recommended Reading

Febe, P. (2001). "Born Free and Proud of It." *Youth Development Journal*, 6: 4–11.

Glaser, C. (2000). *Bo-Tsotsi: The Youth Gangs of Soweto, 1935–1976.* Cape Town, South Africa: David Philip Publishers.

Mankayi, P. (2002). "In Conversation with Young Comrades at Morris Isaacson High School." *Youth Development Journal*, 6: 1–7.

Mannheim, K. (1952). "The Problem of Generations." In *Essays in the Sociology of Knowledge*, edited by P. Kecskemet. Boston: Routledge & Kegan Paul. (Original work published in 1927.)

Marx, A. W. (1992). *Lessons of Struggle: South African Internal Opposition, 1960–1990.* Cape Town, South Africa: Oxford University Press.

Mokwena, S. (June 2002). "Youth and Nation Building in South Africa: From Youth Struggles to Youth Development." *Youth Development Journal*, 5: 68–77.

Ngomane, T., and Flanagan, C. (2003). "The Road to Democracy in South Africa." *Peace Review*, 15 (3): 267–271.

Worden, N. (1994). *The Making of Modern South Africa: Conquest, Segregation and Apartheid.* Oxford, England: Blackwell.

Tsakani Ngomane

Spirituality. Within the social sciences spirituality refers to that which is considered divine, holy, or beyond the material. Additionally, it can be understood as a universal human capacity or a quality of a person's character, personality, or disposition. This quality or aspect of personhood is that which is aware of something beyond the self—whether that be God, absolute truth, all of humanity, or creation. Because spirituality involves the human capacity for self-transcendence, spirituality propels the search for connectedness, meaning, purpose, and contribution.

Spirituality, whether within or outside of religious traditions, beliefs, and practices, is often linked with civic engagement. Spirituality that takes shape within organized religion can lead to civic participation. Religiously active youth often report being more involved in volunteer service and anticipate high levels of civic activism than their less religious peers. Religious institutions (e.g., congregations, schools, faith-based organizations) often offer opportunities for involvement in volunteer service as well as provide a worldview that promotes the value of service and provides a meaningful framework within which to reflect on civic endeavors.

Spirituality can also lead to virtue, to a concern for others. Because transcendence provides a sense of connection with or awareness of a divine, human, or natural other, spirituality often promotes a heightened consciousness of others that triggers a sense of self that is intertwined and responsible to them. Consequently, spirituality usually relates to a manner of living that is carried out with the deep awareness of and concern for self, others, and the divine.

Thus spirituality has been recognized as a virtue or an emotional orientation that involves the transcendence of self that fuels or motivates the development of a commitment to contributing to others and institutions beyond self in time and place. Such an understanding of spirituality is beyond a feeling of transcendence but a motivational force that propels individuals to care for others and contribute to something greater than themselves. In this sense, spirituality provides the awareness of responsibility and the passion to initiate and sustain commitment to agency. Spirituality calls forth devotion and thus exerts ordering power on the rest of an individual's life. In summary, spirituality can lead to opportunities and provide motivation to engage civically with one's larger society.

See also Campus Crusade for Christ International (CCC); Catholic Education and the Ethic of Social Justice; Religiosity and American Youth; Religiosity and Civic Engagement in African American Youth.

Recommended Reading

Benson, P. L., Roehlkepartain, E. C., and Rude, S. P. (2003). "Spiritual Development in Childhood and Adolescence: Toward a Field of Inquiry." *Applied Developmental Sciences*, 7 (3): 204–212.

Donnelly, T. M., Atkins, R., and Hart, D. (In Press). "The Relationship Between Spiritual Development and Civic Engagement." In *The Handbook of Spiritual Development in Childhood and Adolescence*, edited by P. L. Benson, E. C. Roehlkepartain, P. E. King, and L. M. Wagener. Newbury Park, CA: Sage Publications.

Kerestes, M., Youniss, J., and Metz, E. (In Press). "Longitudinal Patterns of Religious Perspective and Civic Integration." *Applied Developmental Science*, 8 (1): 39–46.

King, P. E. (2003). "Religion and Identity: The Role of Ideological, Social, and Spiritual Contexts." *Applied Developmental Sciences*, 7 (3): 196–203.

Lerner, R. M. (2004). *Liberty: Thriving and Civic Engagement among America's Youth*. Thousand Oaks, CA: Sage Publications.

Miller, W. R., and Thoresen, C. E. (2003). "Spirituality, Religion, and Health: An Emerging Research Field." *American Psychologist*, 58: 24–35.

Youniss, J., McLellan, J. A., and Yates, M. (1999). "Religion, Community Service, and Identity in American Youth." *Journal of Adolescence*, 22 (2): 243–253.

Pamela Ebstyne King

Sports and Youth. *See* Athletic-Square Model of Youth Sport.

State and Youth, The. The influence of modern states looms large over the lives of the young. Perhaps more so than ever before, the terms of young people's lives, the dilemmas they face and the patterning of their choices are structured by the activities of government and the state. States actively construct the parameters of young people's lives, whether in terms of dependence upon the family, the enforcement of compulsory education, relationship to the labor market and other key institutions of civil society, or in establishing the framework for marriage and sexual conduct. States are also responsible for defining the terms upon which the young are integrated into social life. States foster certain models of the family; regulate closely the content of formal education; dictate young people's roles in the economy, business, and commerce; and place young people in specific relationships to the criminal justice system and public programs of welfare support. Most states, especially those in the industrialized world, now possess extensive administrative, legal, and political mechanisms that when taken together define much of the form and content of contemporary youth.

These state practices are usually organized around principles of chronological age. Eisenstadt, in *From Generation to Generation*, points out that age is a fundamental organizing principle for all societies, since "the function of differential age definitions is to enable the individual to learn and acquire new roles, to become adult, etc., and in this way to maintain social continuity" (1956, 29). Nevertheless, following industrialization, the political and bureaucratic significance given to age attained a new importance as states developed increasingly sophisticated and bureaucratic systems of administration explicitly directed at regulating the lives of the young. In postwar Western Europe and North America, the scale of this activity expanded and the influence of the state was taken deep into the lives of young people.

Why youth has come to assume such importance to states and to the activity of government is thus an important question. Answers to this have largely claimed that the industrialization process necessitated more elaborate transitional arrangements through which children brought up within the particularities of the family unit could be integrated into a complex social order. Today, this emphasis on youth's transitional significance remains, together with a more explicit focus on the implications for young people's civic engagement. As expressed by Jones and Wallace, "youth can be seen as that period during which the transition to citizenship, that is, to full participation in society, occurs" (1992, 18). Through an extensive and finely calibrated range of activities, states are judged to hold a determining influence in equipping young people with those technical, educational, moral, and emotional capacities necessary if they are to "grow up" socially and assume their rights and responsibilities as full adult members of society.

Following this, researchers place considerable importance on the prevailing models of citizenship that ultimately define the content of these transitional arrangements. Following World War II, for instance, the redefinition of citizenship to embrace a series of more expansive social entitlements is seen to have transformed the nature of youth. The consequence was the reshaping of youth through large-scale public investment in education, apprenticeship, and technical-training programs; the close regulation of the terms of young people's employment; greater access to programs of state welfare (as both dependents on families and as recipients in their own right), which in turn attracted more generous funding; and welfare-based measures to deal with the problem of young offenders. Formally speaking, these concessions were made available to all, regardless of their class, gender, or race.

Combined with the "relative affluence" of the times, some historians have identified these developments as partly responsible for the emergence of a genuinely self-conscious youth culture during the 1960s. With their new status as citizens-in-the making, the period of relative freedom between the cessation of childhood dependence and the assumption of full adult responsibilities widened. It is the expansion of this period of what Parsons' called "structured irresponsibility" that may also explain the subsequent turn to revolt. By the end of the 1960s, a youth counterculture infused with alternative and radical philosophies was questioning the very idea of citizenship that had, to some extent, been responsible for bringing it into existence.

By the end of the twentieth century, the basis of young people's relationship to the state had changed markedly. For all the energy and activism of youth during the 1960s and 1970s, the terms of this relationship were dictated from elsewhere. In the United States critics of the reforms associated with the "Great Society" (e.g., Mead 1986) attributed the economic malaise and deepening social tensions now spreading through the industrialized world to the uninhibited extension of social rights. Others similarly asserted that large parts of a once industrious and respectful youthful population are bereft of notions of civic obligation and have been turned into a criminal, indolent, and amoral "underclass" by a corrosive state paternalism.

Ideas like these were most forcibly advanced by the administrations of Ronald Reagan in the United States and by Margaret Thatcher in the United Kingdom. They were also keenly advocated by governments in Australia and New Zealand. More recently, similar themes have emerged in many of the programs and manifestos of governments throughout Western Europe.

The consequences have been immense. In the final quarter of the twentieth century, governments throughout much of the industrialized world have moved to redefine the relationship between young people and the state through a newfound emphasis on self-reliance, individualism, and obligation. The practical implications of this have been evident in rigid limits to the level of public resources made available for education and training and the curtailment of sources of public support for young people's aspirations to live independently. Paid employment's importance as a method of discipline and self-reliance has been reasserted through a thorough reregulation of the terms upon which the young can be employed, and public obligations to the large number of jobless young people have been reduced. In many countries principles of justice and punishment have progressively submerged considerations of welfare and care in the administration of young offenders.

The importance of youth to states and to the activity of government helps to counterbalance the customary concern with youth's subjective dimensions among youth researchers. While recognizing young people's agency, consciousness, and activity, a focus on the state also forces us to acknowledge how young people's lives are closely shaped by changes in broader political and administrative structures. Thinking about youth in this way leads to a consideration of why states relate to the young primarily on the basis of their age rather than, for instance, their gender, ethnicity, or class. The fortunes of young people are closely linked to those transactions characteristic of wider political processes, in which conflicts and struggles over the distribution of resources are key.

A number of questions nevertheless remain unanswered. When looking at the patterning of those rights and responsibilities that young people acquire through chronological age, it is often difficult to establish clear criteria for the transition that youth are seen as experiencing (or, more normatively, should be experiencing). Modern governments are regularly accused of fostering teenage confusion through the inconsistent, arbitrary, and sometimes conflicting ways in which they allocate the rights and responsibilities of full social membership. Often it is difficult to see much logic to the ordering of the ages at which young people are deemed to be criminally responsible; must undergo compulsory education; cease to be under the legal control of parents or guardians; have access to sources of welfare support in their own right; must pay taxes; are covered by workplace legislation; and can participate in the democratic process, engage in combat, or enter into consensual sexual relations. In many countries a situation exists in which a young person may be able to legally wed but not buy alcohol to celebrate; have sex but not watch a pornographic film; be liable for income taxes but exempt from minimum-wage legislation; vote but not stand for election; or open a bank account but be unable to access commercial credit. At best, young people's acquisition of the rights and responsibilities of full social membership may be said to operate in an ambiguous and sometimes contradictory fashion. At worst, the absence of clear transitional criteria may mean that the basis of young people's relationship to the state is located in the interests of powerful social and political actors rather than with young people themselves.

Thus, the degree of importance that governments themselves place on the notion of youth as a transitional phase or category should not be seen as an indication of their success (or even commitment) in fostering transitions to adulthood. What is certainly the case is that states do continue to exercise a defining influence over the lives of young people. This is an important point to emphasize since in recent times many administrations have extolled the need to get government "off the backs of the people." While this has usually been a prelude to significant changes to the nature of young people's relationship to the state, it does not necessarily mean that the influence of the state over the young has diminished. Indeed, states and governments continue to regulate closely the lives of the young, perhaps to a degree never recorded before. The terms upon which this relationship is conducted has, in recent times, been thoroughly transformed.

See also Deliberative Democracy; Democracy; Democratic Education; Generational Replacement; Minority Youth Voter Turnout; Rights of Participation of Children and Youth; Rights, Youth Perceptions of; Student Political Activism.

Recommended Reading

Coles, R., and Coles. B. (1995). *Youth and Social Policy: Youth, Citizenship and Young Careers.* London: UCL Press.

Eisenstadt, S. N. (1956). *From Generation to Generation: Age Groups and Social Structure.* New York: The Free Press.

Gillis, J. (1974). *Youth and History.* New York: Academic Press.

Helve, H. and Wallace, C. (2001). *Youth, Citizenship and Empowerment.* Aldershot: Ashgate.

Jones, G., and Wallace, C. (1992). *Youth, Family and Citizenship.* Milton Keynes: Open University Press.

Marwick, A. (1996). *The Sixties.* Cambridge: Cambridge University Press.

Mitterauer, M. (1992). *A History of Youth.* Oxford: Basil Blackwell.

Mizen, P. (2004). *The Changing State of Youth.* Basingstoke: Palgrave.

Parsons, T. (1942). "Age and Sex in the Social Structure of the United States." *American Sociological Review*, 7 (5): 604–616.

Wallace, C., and Kovatcheva, S. (1998). *Youth in Society.* Basingstoke: Macmillan.

Phillip Mizen

Statute of the Child and Adolescent (Brazil). Recognized by UNICEF as model legislation that could be beneficially applied in other national settings, Brazil's *Estatuto da Criança e Adolescente* (ECA, Statute of the Child and Adolescent) makes a unique contribution to both democratic political practices and youth legislation in the contemporary era. The ECA is a comprehensive piece of national legislation that seeks to define and protect the citizenship rights of persons under eighteen years of age. The ECA became law in 1990 as the culmination of a decade-long process of mobilization across several segments of the Brazilian population, including social workers, human-rights activists, journalists, the Catholic church, street children, and other groups. The ECA establishes the following:

- Citizenship rights of children (birth to eleven-years-old) and adolescents (twelve- to seventeen-years-old)
- Obligations of families, society, and the state for the protection and growth of people under eighteen years of age as "human beings in the process of development"
- New practices of juvenile justice
- Councils at the national, state, and municipal levels where representatives of the state and civil society meet to oversee and direct youth policy
- Locally elected *conselhos tutelares* (protection councils) that hear and accompany individual cases involving

child and adolescent rights through the appropriate state agencies

The ECA's incorporation of state-society participation in governance and legislative development makes the citizenship status of young people an important dimension of the transition to and consolidation of Brazilian democracy.

The immediate backdrop to the formation of the movement for children's rights in Brazil is the process of democratization that occurred as Brazil's military regime (1964–1985) began to lose its grip on power and seek ways to exit the political arena. In the 1970s, growing cross-class resistance to the regime's human rights abuses and the failure of its economic policies after the end of the economic "miracle" period (1967–1974) resulted in a cascade of new social movements that organized first around *opposition to military rule* and then emphasized *citizenship* once the regime's exit from power was all but assured by the early 1980s. A "new unions movement" rejuvenated organized labor as a new generation of workers came online after 1975. The current president of Brazil, Luis Inácio Lula da Silva (2003–2006), emerged in the new unions movement as a national labor leader and a founder of the Workers' Party, Brazil's largest left-of-center party, which from its inception challenged both the supporters of the military regime as well as the middle-class, democratically oriented opposition.

At the same time, community movements began to swell in the poor and working class neighborhoods of Brazilian cities. With the mandates of Vatican II (1962–1965) and the Latin American bishops' conference of Medellín (1968), the Brazilian Catholic church took a sharply progressive turn, influenced by the emergence of "liberation theology" in Latin America. The human-rights movement benefited from linkages to all these groups, growing along with the outcry against the regime's increasingly public abuse of its citizens (through imprisonment, torture, and assassination) during the most severe years of repression from 1967 to 1975. By 1983 the *Movimento Nacional de Meninos e Meninas de Rua* (MNMMR, National Movement for Street Children) placed issues of children's rights onto the national agenda within the context of human-rights abuses and began to develop a broader movement for the rights of children. Throughout its history, the street children's movement had built up ties to human-rights organizations, the Brazilian Bar Association, the Catholic church (whose Pastoral Programs for Youth had been an important training ground of many street children's activists), social workers, and other civil-society organizations and nongovernmental organizations (NGOs). In 1985 the military left power after congressional elections appointed Brazil's first civilian president since 1964; direct presidential elections followed in 1989 for the first time since 1960. Today, organizations associated with the children's rights movement exist in almost every city across the country, and they form a dense network in civil society that has ties across a variety of citizenship groups and NGOs.

The modern legal history of youth legislation in Brazil began in the 1890s, when legislators in the First Republic (1889–1930) passed the first laws regulating child labor, limiting the hours a child could work, the conditions, and a minimum age of beginning labor. At this time Brazil also created the first institutions devoted to social services for "invalid" (delinquent, at-risk, or without families) youth, which included a system of reform schools and social assistance for these young people. In October 1927, the *Código de Menores* (Code of Minors) was established and then revised in 1932 to consolidate all prior youth legislation from Brazil's colonial and postindependence (1822–) eras. The *Código de Menores* was particularly concerned with child labor and the treatment of delinquent youth, while the family was basically responsible for the treatment of children who were not industrial laborers or offenders.

The next major development was the establishment of the *Fundação Nacional do Bem-estar do Menor* (FUNABEM, National Foundation for the Welfare of Minors) in 1964, which was created by the new military government that had just taken power. FUNABEM was part of an overall attempt by the military to reformulate youth policy, bringing the protection of at-risk youth and treatment of youth offenders into a nationally consistent model of reform schools and other social assistance mechanisms. In the end, however, the FUNABEM schools were counterproductive for at-risk youths and became dead-end institutions that only exacerbated the problems they were charged with treating.

During the constitutional assembly of 1987–1988, movement organizations involved with children's rights were able to use an open petition process and the lobbying of sympathetic congressional representatives to influence the Constitution of 1988. Two articles laid the structure of a youth policy for minors that created universal citizenship rights for persons under age eighteen and mandated a role for the state not only in protecting or treating at-risk and offending youths but also in proactively protecting the citizenship rights of all persons under eighteen. The constitution defines the role of the family and the state and subordinates parents' interests to the interests of the child in accord with the United Nations (UN) Convention on the Rights of the Child (1989), which was under consideration at the time of the Brazilian constitutional assembly.

The ECA builds upon a growing body of international accords and conventions on children's rights, including the International Labor Organization's (ILO) original Minimum Age (Industry) Convention (1919), the UN's Universal Declaration of the Rights of Children (1959), the ILO's Minimum Age Convention (1973), and the UN's Convention on the Rights of the Child (CRC 1989). In Brazil the ECA, which was developed from the mid-1980s onward, concurrent with the CRC, was passed in 1990.

Article 15 of the ECA establishes the statute's constructive role by defining persons under eighteen as "human beings in the process of development," and the statute created the legal framework to enable both state and society to take a nurturing *and* protective role for these child-citizens. With this language, the movement for children's rights created *universal* citizenship rights for *all* persons under eighteen, rather than falling into the traditional Brazilian legal practice of defining citizenship rights through more specific categories (usually occupational) of persons. The statute's *protective* intent constructs child and adolescent citizenship both through the obligations of others as well as through the specific stipulation of rights. In this way, the ECA promotes the concept of "integral protection" (*proteção integral*), which the Brazilian children's rights movement offers as an alternative to "zero-tolerance" models that have emerged in the United States and Great Britain in the last twenty years.

Article 4 of the ECA reads, "It is the obligation of the family, the community, of society in general and of Public Authority to ensure, with absolute priority, the establishment of the rights which relate to life, health, nourishment, education, sport, leisure, job training, culture, dignity, respect, freedom and family and community life."

While children and adolescents, as "human beings in the process of development," benefit from the protection/obligation of the state and others to nurture their growth, persons under eighteen also enjoy the expressive citizenship rights of adults (a) to come and go from public places in accord with the law, (b) of opinion and expression, (c) of religious faith, (d) to play, practice sports, and enjoy oneself, (e) to participate in family and community without discrimination, (f) to participate in politics in accord with the law, and (g) to seek refuge and aid. All citizens have the "obligation" to "watch over and rescue" children and adolescents from "any inhuman, violent, terrorizing, abusive or coercive treatment." Parents and guardians are to guarantee, within their means, the sustenance of children, and the statute outlines the conditions and circumstances under which parents may be legally relieved of their authority over children, as well as the process by which children and adolescents may be relocated to another home.

The sections of the law that deal with the treatment of youth who break the law were written to address the traditional manner by which adults, parents, and public authorities have "disciplined" young people. Corporal punishment has been the norm for "minors," and in general, physical abuse by the police and parents has long been tolerated in daily life. The goal of the statute's policies toward youth offenders is to enable authorities to correct the misbehavior of young people but completely in keeping with article 18's prohibition of inhuman and abusive treatment. In a deeper sense these provisions of the statute are one attempt to address the violence of everyday life. The fact that about half of the statute's articles are devoted to dealing with youth offenders and the juvenile justice system is indicative of the scope of the problem.

The combination of endemic poverty and the lesser status of a "minor" has, for example, led to a general suspicion that poor kids steal and pickpocket passersby. A person who becomes aware of a missing wallet or purse may, without pausing to think, point a finger at nearby kids, who then become the target of police action. Traditionally, this action has included long detentions without explanation of the cause, as well as beatings or torture. The statute attempts to undermine such prejudice by preventing illegal detentions and providing that "no adolescent will be deprived of his freedom unless caught flagrantly in the act of infraction or by written order of the competent judicial authority." Furthermore, "minors under eighteen years old may not be attributed punitive responsibility, subject to the stipulations provided in this law," which provide that youth receive "socio-educational mea-sures" designed to reorient the youth's behavior and repair damages for any wrongs the youth has caused. "Socio-educational measures" include: (a) warning, (b) obligation to repair damages, (c) performance of community service, (d) freedom under the cognizance of others, (e) restricted freedom, (f) assignment to an educational institution, or (g) a number of more detailed regimes including removal from the family. The point of these detailed legal stipulations is that children and adolescents, as "human beings in the process of development," be given the guidance and supervision necessary to correct misbehavior and allow the youth the opportunity to mature in a way which would ameliorate and diminish the feelings of marginalization and discrimination that delinquent youths and gang members cite as reasons for entering "street life."

Finally, the law provides for the establishment of several layers of advisory and assistance councils involving the participation of both public officials and representatives of organizations in civil society that are devoted to youth issues. At the national, state, and local level, councils for the rights of children and adolescents (hereafter, rights councils) elaborate policies to secure the implementation and provision of the rights of children and adolescents as laid out in the ECA. One-half of the council members are state representatives, appointed by current executives (president, state governor, or mayor of the municipal district); the other half is made up of representatives from organizations in civil society, such as the bar association or other organizations associated with the movement for children's rights. Movement representatives on the councils are supplied by the movement organizations, who must meet in open forums to select their representatives. The NGOs or movement organizations that qualify to be part of the selection process vary according to policy needs and local conditions, but in general these organizations must be "entities devoted to infant/juvenile issues ... such as, for example, those that include among their institutional mission the direct servicing, research, promotion, or defense of the rights of children and adolescents."

These three levels of developing and implementing the ECA mirror Brazil's federal-state-local governmental structure. The fourth type of public participation in the statute's implementation is also at the local, *município* level, in *conselhos tutelares* (CTs). In territorial terms the *município* in Brazil is roughly equivalent to the county in the U.S. system; in structure and governance it operates like a U.S. municipality with a mayor (*prefeito*) and a municipal council. *Conselho tutelar* translates as "protection council," and we note again the law's intention to construct the child-citizen as a special category in need of "protection" from abuses by both the state and ordinary citizens. While the work of the rights councils involves the developing of policy, the CTs do actual casework that assists and accompanies claims of either the abuse of youth rights or the adjudication of youth offenders through the juvenile justice system. The ECA specifically delineates that the CTs must intervene where the rights of children and adolescents are violated (a) "by action or omission of the society or state," (b) "by the negligence, omission, or abuse of parents or guardians," and (c) "by reason of [the youth's] own conduct."

Each *município* is to have at least one CT with at least five councilors sitting on it; many *municípios* have more than one CT. Counselors are elected in small city districts and are from those districts, which ensures a familiarity with the context from which complaints emerge. They are frequently, but not always, movement activists, and sometimes candidates do emerge from "law-and-order" groups who oppose the ECA. All persons over sixteen are eligible to vote, but to do so they must register with the municipal rights council, which coordinates the election. CT members receive a small compensation for their work, generally much less than the salary a person earns in a regular job, and most CT members must keep their principal means of employment while serving on the CTs. In each *município* the mayor's office has an important role in providing the resources and political leadership that create favorable conditions for the implementation of the statute at the local level, and growth of the ECA's council structures is highly correlated with the political stance of a mayor or governor on the ECA. Those who support the ECA (mostly, but not always, from parties left-of-center) create more and more effective CTs and allow the rights councils greater say in the creation of policy; other governors and mayors can act to hamper the statute's implementation. As of 2001 all twenty-six states and the federal district (Brasília) had established state councils for the rights of the child and adolescent. Of 5,491 municipalities, 3,949 (about 72 percent) had established municipal rights councils, while 3,011 (about 55 percent) had established CTs. Some 1,383 municipalities (about 25 percent), mainly rural ones, have yet to establish either rights councils or CTs.

See also Australia, Youth Activism in; Demographic Trends Affecting the World's Youth; Eastern Europe, Youth and Citizenship in; Europe, Comparing Youth Activism in; European Identity and Citizenship; Global Youth Action Network (GYAN); Homies Unidos; Immigrant Youth in Europe—Turks in Germany; Immigrant Youth in the United States; India, Youth Activism in; Indonesia, Youth Activism in; Juvenile Justice; Nigeria, Youth Activism in; Palestinian *Intifada*; Rights of Participation of Children and Youth; Russia, Youth Activism in; Serbia, Youth Activism in (1990–2000); Soweto Youth Activism (South Africa); State and Youth, The; Tiananmen Square Massacre (1989); Transnational Identity; Transnational Youth Activism; Turkey, Youth Activism in; United Nations, Youth Activism and; Xenophobia; Zapatista Rebellion (Mexico); Zionist Youth Organizations.

Recommended Reading

Ahnen, Ronald (2001). "Civil Society's Push for Political Space: Child and Adolescent Rights Councils in Brazil." *International Journal of Children's Rights*, 9: 15–43.

da Silva, Roberto (January/February 2000). "Adolescentes: Punir ou Educar?" *Ciência Hoje*, 157: 63–67.

Dimenstein, Gilberto (1993). *O Cidadão de Papel: A Infância, A Adolescência e os Direitos Humanos no Brasil*. São Paulo: Editora Ática.

Guidry, John A. (2000). "The Useful State? Social Movements and the Citizenship of Children in Brazil." In *Globalizations and Social Movements: Power, Culture and the Transnational Public Sphere*, edited by J. A. Guidry, M. D. Kennedy, and M. N. Zald. Ann Arbor: University of Michigan Press, pp. 147–180.

Pontes Jr., Felício (1993). *Conselho de Direitos da Criança e do Adolescente*. São Paulo: Malheiros Editores.

Santos, Wanderley Guilherme dos (1979). *Cidadania e Justiça: A Política Social na Ordem Brasileira*. Rio de Janeiro: Editora Campus.

Sêda, Edson (1992). *ABC do Conselho Tutelar*. São Paulo: Centro Brasileiro da Infância e Adolescência.

Additional Web Sites (in Portuguese)

Escola Aprendiz, an internationally-known program of educational activities for youths in São Paulo, founded by youth rights activist and journalist Gilberto Dimenstein: http://www.uol.com.br/aprendiz/

Human Rights Net, a Brazilian organization dedicated to advancing human rights and compliance with national and international laws: http://www.dhnet.org.br/dhnet.htm (comprehensive, with articles, legislative history, and links)

Movimento República de Emaús, one of the leading children's rights organizations in Brazil, established in the city of Belém in 1970: http://www.emauscrianca.org.br

Service foundation of the Brazilian Association of Toy Manufacturers, dedicated to the implementation of the ECA, with history on the legislation and links to a variety of sites: http://www.fundabrinq.org.br

Special Secretary for Human Rights, an agency of the national executive (presidency): http://www.presidencia.gov.br/sedh/

UNICEF-Brazil: http://www.unicef.org.br

John A. Guidry

Student Action with Farmworkers (SAF).

The "with" in Student Action with Farmworkers' name is as important as "student," "action," or "farmworkers" in describing the organization's core goals. SAF, whose motto reads "solidarity since 1992," draws a distinction between working "with" people in a movement and working "for" them. In contrast to service learning, which often focuses on the positive effects of service without examining the ideological or political perspectives underlying it, Student Action with Farmworkers is very aware of the types of relationships that develop between students and those they serve. For example, serving food at a soup kitchen could easily lead to students perceiving themselves as "givers" and those being served as passive recipients. SAF offers an alternative model, one of solidarity, where everyone is active and accountable in the process. It is important for activists to explore the meaning of different types of service, contextualizing and questioning its value, implications, and outcomes and evaluating their role and the role of the community in which they want to work.

SAF is a nonprofit, nongovernmental organization that supports a variety of activities including documentation of human-rights violations, policy advocacy, migrant education, and labor organizing. Each year, their Into the Fields (ITF) summer internship and leadership-development program places thirty college students in farmworker agencies throughout North and South Carolina for an intensive ten-week summer immersion in activism. ITF has trained over 350 college students as farmworker advocates serving over 70,000 farmworkers. SAF was recently honored with Promising Practices and Defenders of Justice awards for its work in the area of grassroots empowerment and its ability to motivate and mobilize young people to work for social justice.

SAF originated on the Duke University campus in the 1960s and 1970s when Professor Bruce Payne and Dr. Robert Coles started teaching students in the public policy department about farmworkers in eastern North Carolina. An interns-in-conscience project in the department's leadership program continued to emphasize farmworker issues. After years of the program's summer-break delegations working with southern Florida farmworker agencies, Duke's Center for Documentary Studies was awarded a grant in 1990 by the U.S. Department of Education to fund college students as they documented the lives of migrant children. Inspired by these experiences, a group of students collaborated with farmworkers and their advocates in the community to incorporate SAF as a nonprofit in 1992.

SAF's Into the Fields internship begins with an intensive orientation structured as a systematic and critical inquiry of the many issues facing farmworkers. Students study demographics; read relevant legislation; and discuss working conditions, barriers to health care, and legal issues with an array of experts in each field, including farmworkers themselves. They explore the causes of a migratory workforce and the transnational forces, including legislation such as NAFTA, which impact the current climate. They also critically consider the ideologies surrounding immigration and labor. Workshops have themes such as "Being an Ally" and "Dismantling Oppression and Racism." At least half of each intern class is composed of students from farmworker families. The peer education that occurs between students from more privileged backgrounds and those from farmworker backgrounds offers a first opportunity of solidarity building and a chance to utilize different experiences in creating a diverse coalition. While some of the discussions are difficult and can take students out of their comfort zone, such a deep investigation is ultimately what fosters ideas and solutions that are far-reaching.

The ITF program is based on a critical approach to service. Whereas the soup kitchen model of doing "for" (rather than "with") focuses on charity and altruism as the highest ideals of civic engagement, the activist approach of ITF focuses on justice and systemic change. By taking such an approach, the hope is that the need

for such programs will eventually be eliminated because the problem/injustice will have been addressed at its roots. Charity and change are two conceptual models. Neither is mutually exclusive, and elements of both can be found in many service-oriented projects. Making the distinction between charity and change, however, is an important consideration for young activists. Solidarity is most closely associated with change work. As Libby Manly, a former SAF program director says, "Different than charity, solidarity calls on us to not just feed a hungry mouth but to ask why some people are hungry, to look at the systems that cause poverty, and to work together to change them, because to ignore them hurts us all."

While the charity model is usually done with good intentions, it has the possibility of condescension. The relationship of someone "helping" or "giving" to the "less fortunate" or "needy" creates a power dynamic that in many ways perpetuates the status of "otherness" of those receiving the help. The recipients of the service are often regarded as "clients" rather than as community members with a voice. Charity can also be a depoliticizing tool that deflects energy away from policy and its critique. By emphasizing altruism, the focus and onus is placed on individuals to ameliorate problems. This approach often neglects the systemic causes of a problem and ignores issues of oppression and discrimination. While temporary achievements are possible through charity, they tend to be ephemeral and do little to alleviate the problem in the long run.

Farmworkers have a long history of neglect in U.S. labor laws. The 1938 Fair Labor Standards Act (FLSA) which mandated employers pay at least a minimum wage excluded farmworkers in this protection until 1978, although today many still do not receive a minimum wage. FLSA also sets the minimum age for farmwork at twelve years old, making agriculture the only industry that allows children under the age of sixteen to work. Sixty percent of migrant children drop out of school to support their families. Seventy-five percent of farmworkers earn less than $10,000 a year and suffer from the highest rate of toxic chemical injuries of any workers in the United States. Since 85 percent of the fruits and vegetables consumed in the United States are handpicked by farmworkers, the simple act of buying food could be considered a political act. Getting ITF interns to think of themselves as consumers, workers, and young people helps them connect to each of these facts. They are able to see their own role in the agricultural system. SAF tries to internalize in students that they have collective power to change the system and that their actions have meaning and consequences. Becoming conscious as consumers and identifying the links between their own lives and the farmworkers with whom they will work helps pave the road toward establishing solidarity.

The critical thinking that begins at ITF's orientation continues throughout the internship experience. This continual critical reflection is essential to solidarity building. Students are required to write guided reports, each entry a response to a theme or question such as "Do you consider yourself an advocate?" or "What does being an advocate mean?" Some of these writings/reflections become letters to the editor of their local paper or jumping off points for further group discussion. Evaluation is key in determining whether the ITF model is effective or can be improved. This continual cycle of action and reflection allows students to think about the impact they are actually having on the community and vice versa.

Praxis is the intersection between action and thought. Once the students leave the orientation and spread out across North and South Carolina for their individual placements, they have the opportunity to act on all of the information sharing and reflection in which they have been participating. Since there is no one way to change entire systems or fight injustice, SAF uses a multifaceted approach in creating a farmworker justice movement. Internally, SAF makes the distinction between service and systemic change, believing both must happen simultaneously to create a sustainable social justice movement. Placements have interns engaged in everything, including conducting pesticide trainings, organizing union meetings, translating in health clinics, teaching ESL classes, and working with legal aid.

SAF also uses other activist tools, including protest theater and documentary projects, as avenues that encourage relationship building and serve as teaching/learning devices. Stemming from their connection to Duke University's Center for Documentary Studies, the documentary projects allow farmworkers to share aspects of their culture with students, as sharing and understanding are regarded as integral parts of establishing solidarity. Documenting particular folk traditions or cultural rituals allows students to learn from the community they are working with and view farmworkers as complex people rather than simply laborers. These projects not only personalize and humanize the plight of farmworkers, it also ensures that students are learning from them: in this way, students are not only the providers of service but also recipients of knowledge and information. Since solidarity at its core is the recognition of other people's humanity, and in the recognition lies a call to action to realize that this type of cultural exchange facilitates a relationship that moves beyond the simple and limiting dichotomy of those serving and those being served.

While it is important to keep sight of injustice and the need for change, it is also important to acknowledge the rich and varied backgrounds of people so they do not only become "the exploited" or "the oppressed." The documentary projects can be disseminated to larger audiences through publications and photographic exhibitions in order to spread awareness about culture and the obstacles farmworkers face.

The touring theater group, Project Levante ("rise up" in Spanish), takes its cue from El Teatro Campesino (The Farm-workers' Theater) that emerged in the 1960s as a troupe committed to supporting the organization United Farm Workers (UFW). Interns perform plays such as *No Saco Nada de La Escuela* (I Don't Get Anything Out of School) and *Gigantes En Los Campos* (Giants in the Fields) in order to initiate dialog. The plays are performed at parent-teacher nights, health fairs, and labor camps and are followed by discussion about the issues raised. The participatory format creates an environment for people to share their experiences. Students report that audience members have commented that the plays made them interested in finding out more about scholarships for migrant students, for example, or encouraged them to become active to change their working conditions.

In the summer of 2004 an ITF intern working with the Farm Labor Organizing Committee (FLOC) was arrested for trespassing while meeting with workers in a labor camp. Despite the workers' welcome to their visitors, the farmer called the police. Charges were ultimately dropped against him and another union organizer after one hundred supporters, including the entire ITF class, protested outside of the Nash County courthouse. On September 16, 2004, a five-and-a-half year nationwide boycott of the Mt. Olive Pickle Company was called off as the largest union contract in North Carolina's history was awarded to farmworkers. It is the first case of "guest" workers (workers from other countries brought to the United States legally) winning union representation and a contract in the United States. Many ITF interns worked with FLOC over nine years organizing workers and supporting the boycott campaign. Recently, a few students stayed after the internship finished in order to remain active in the effort. These are clear examples of solidarity in action and the power of sustained commitment.

Working for change and justice is a long process. Students are more apt to remain involved in the long run when they work in

solidarity—they see the common fellowship between themselves and others. Martin Luther King Jr. once said, "Injustice anywhere is a threat to justice everywhere." SAF's methodology creates not only farmworker advocates but students who are committed to social justice in general. A survey of SAF alumni who were interns between 1993 and 2002 showed that 76 percent agreed that participation in SAF affected their choice about working for social justice and that 64 percent were involved in activist organizations and activities after their Into The Fields internship. SAF maintains an alumni association and offers materials for ITF interns to organize and participate in Farmworker Awareness Week on their campuses or in their home communities after they have completed their internships. At the ITF final retreat students discuss ways in which to remain involved in the farmworker movement. The belief that everyone is better off when all of society's members are fully developed and treated fairly underlies the doctrine of solidarity. When students absorb this lesson, they remain activists long after they leave the fields.

See also Advocacy; Child Labor; Homies Unidos; Labor Movement.

Recommended Reading

Chomsky-Higgins, K., ed. (Fall/Winter 1999). "Focus on Protest Theater" [Theme Issue]. *From the Ground Up*, 7 (3).

Freire, A. M. A., and Macedo, D. (1998). *The Paolo Freire Reader*. New York: Continuum International.

Illich, I. (April 20, 1968). "To Hell with Good Intentions." Address to the Conference on InterAmerican Student Projects (CIASP) in Cuernavaca, Mexico. See http://www.bicyclingfish.com/illich.htm.

Kahne, J., and Westheimer, J. (May 1996). "In the Service of What? The Politics of Service Learning." *Phi Delta Kappan*, 593–599. See http://www.connectforkids.org/usr_doc/7759.pdf.

McIntosh, P. (July/August 1989). "White Privilege: Unpacking the Invisible Knapsack, Peace And Freedom," pp. 10–12. See http://www.campusaction.net/publications/Racism_Study_Circle/white_privilege.htm.

Student Action with Farmworkers (2004). See http://www.saf-unite.org.

United States Farmworker Fact Sheet (2004). See http://cds.aas.duke.edu/saf/pdfs/fwfact-sheet.pdf.

Sion Dayson

Student Political Activism. Student political activism is a worldwide phenomenon, at various times and in different countries overturning governments or stimulating university reform. It is important because of its potential to affect both the university and society. Activist organizations involve highly motivated students, some of whom become important in national politics. And activist movements tend to be among the best-organized groups, able to obtain very strong commitments from the students who are involved in them. It must be kept in mind, however, that student activist organizations are minority phenomena, involving a very small number of students in sustained organizational activity. Even when there are mass demonstrations on campus, those involved in them are generally a minority of the student body. This fact does not make student activist movements unimportant, but their scope and nature must be kept in careful perspective.

Activist movements are almost always oppositional in nature, challenging established governmental authority, university administrators, or others in authority. While most contemporary student movements are on the left in terms of their ideologies and politics, there are some counterexamples, such as student support for Islamic fundamentalism in Iran and elsewhere in the Muslim world and student opposition to the Communist authorities in Central and Eastern Europe prior to the collapse of the Soviet Union. Without question, student political movements are both complex and, at times, highly influential.

Student movements have a long history, and in many countries this historical tradition is part of the living memory of contemporary organizations. The involvement of students in the nationalist upsurge in Europe in the nineteenth century was very

Two teenagers take part in an anti-abortion rally, just one of the political causes that attracts youth participation in the contemporary United States. *Courtesy of Skjold Photographs.*

significant. Indeed, German nationalist ideas percolated in the universities before becoming a key political force in society. In the nationalist uprisings of 1848, both students and professors played a central role. Students were similarly active in the Italian nationalist movement and in both cases were important in social movements that resulted in significant change in Europe.

Nationalist ideas spread to student movements emerging in the colonial areas of Africa and Asia, and students emerged as key forces for independence in much of what is now the Third World. For example, students from the Dutch East Indies studying at universities in the Netherlands in the first several decades of the twentieth century were exposed to nationalist ideas and literally created the concept of an Indonesian nation. Former student leaders such as Sukarno and Hatta became the most important leaders of the nationalist movement that eventually drove the Dutch from Indonesia and created a new nation. Students were a central force in the Indian nationalist movement as well. Ideas of nationalism, Marxism, and secularism were part the Indian student experience while in England. Western-oriented universities in India also imparted nationalist orientations as well. Student movements emerged during the 1920s and were active in the struggle for independence, which culminated in the departure of the British in 1947. Significantly, Indian student organizations were always situated on the left of the nationalist movement, often in opposition to the tactics of Gandhi. The traditions of student activism established during the independence struggle both in Indonesia and India continued after independence and remain active.

Nationalist influences on European student movements turned some of them to the right during the period after World War I. In Germany the major student organizations supported the Nazis both before and after Hitler came to power. There were, of course, many student groups that opposed the Nazis as well. Similarly, in Italy the largest student groups supported Mussolini's Fascist movement. There was also strong student support in France for rightist nationalist movements during this period.

Another important historical example of student political activism is the powerful student movements that emerged in Latin America in the first decades of the twentieth century and which succeeded in transforming Latin American higher education by forcing the adoption of far-reaching reforms. The *reforma*, as it is known in Spanish, established student participation at all levels of the university from the election of the rector to important curricular decisions. It also enshrined the idea of the university as an autonomous institution which could claim not only the freedom to control academic decisions but whose campus could not be entered by civil authority without the formal permission of university officials. The *reforma* fundamentally changed Latin American higher education, and its impact has continued to the present, although in the past two decades severe political and economic pressures, military regimes, and the growth of private universities has weakened the power of the *reforma* ideals. The movement started in Argentina at the University of Cordoba and spread quickly throughout the continent, affecting the major institutions from Mexico in the north to Chile in the south.

Student movements are almost always sporadic—they seldom last for long periods of time. Even countries with high levels of activism exhibit considerable variation in the extent of involvement and in the strength of student movements. It is to some extent possible to chart international trends in student political activism. The volatile 1960s were clearly a time of worldwide activism, and while international influences were present, most national student movements were largely motivated by national concerns.

The historical development of the American student movement is an example of the episodic nature of student politics. While there was some campus unrest prior to the 1930s (including both antislavery and then antidraft agitation in the period of the Civil War), the first major American student movement emerged during the Great Depression of the 1930s, stimulated as much by foreign-policy concerns (such as the civil war in Spain and a desire to keep the United States out of World War II) as by the economic crisis of the period. There was very little activism between 1941 and 1960. However, it returned to campuses in the 1960s, stimulated both by the civil rights movement, which was sparked by black college students in the South, and growing opinion on campus against the cold-war-induced arms race and especially by nuclear weapons. American escalation of the war in Vietnam brought student activism to its highest level, culminating in nationwide campus disruptions and mass demonstrations in Washington, D.C., at the end of the decade. Once the war in Vietnam came to an end, campus activism declined to a very low level during the 1970s with a minor resurgence of political interest in the late l980s. Similar fluctuations can be seen in student movements in other industrialized nations, although the reasons and the timing of course vary according to national— or even local—political and academic circumstances.

Historical consciousness is also important because countries that have a strong tradition of activism tend to see campus movements as more legitimate political phenomena than countries that have relatively weak activist traditions. Where students played an important role in the shaping of national history, as in the Third World, activist movements are accepted as legitimate participants on the national political scene. In most Western countries, students have not been involved in key political events and, in part for this reason, are not generally accepted as actors on the political stage.

While most of the student activist movements of the post–World War II period have been to one degree or another on the left, contemporary student movements show a real and perhaps widening ideological range. The nationalist impulse, important historically, is difficult to characterize ideologically as left or right. Religion is also a powerful force, particularly when it is combined with nationalism. The growth of Muslim fundamentalism as a powerful political force in the universities of the Islamic world is one of the major developments in student politics worldwide in the past decade.

The extraordinarily important political role played by student activists in the political upheaval in Eastern Europe and to some extent in China in the late 1980s is equally complex. Students were the primary motivating force in the political movement that led up to the Tiananmen Square massacre in June 1989. Chinese students seem to have been motivated by a desire for better jobs, complaints about corruption, and by a demand for more democracy and freedom of expression rather than ideological opposition to the Communist regime. The role of students was critical in the successful upheavals in Eastern Europe at the end of the 1980s. In every country (except perhaps for Romania), university students and professors were among the first important groups to protest against the government. Students often articulated— and perhaps to an extent shaped—the discontent felt by large numbers of people in those countries. Students were in part motivated by nationalism—a desire to see their countries free of external (Soviet) influence. A desire for freedom of expression and representative government also played an important role. And the students were protesting against regimes that were unsuccessful in meeting the economic needs of the people. While these demands do not fall into a neat left-right dichotomy, they are certainly antiregime. The movements seem to be "antistatist" in terms of the control of the economy, but it is not at all clear that they are "procapitalist."

Islamic fundamentalism is now the most powerful force among students in most Muslim countries. In Iran, Egypt, Algeria, and Malaysia, student movements, which were at one time highly secularist and often leftist in orientation, are now mainly Islamic in orientation. The underlying reasons for this dramatic change are open to debate: the failure of secular-minded governments throughout the Islamic world to achieve their goals of modernization, the continuing challenge of the Arab-Israeli conflict, the breakdown of traditional values, and the absence of widely accepted new norms have all contributed to the rise of Islamic fundamentalism. In Iran students were a central force in overthrowing the shah and contributing to the installation of a theocratic regime. Several decades later, in 2002, students were at the forefront in demanding greater flexibility and freedom. Students, including those in high school, supported the Taliban (the term in fact means "student") revolution in Afghanistan.

Students have often exhibited a tendency to adhere to an all-encompassing ideology and to seek massive social change in an effort to create a utopian society. In the twentieth century students have tended to look to ideologies of the left to provide the path to a more perfect social order. The impact of Marxism and other Socialist ideas has been perhaps the most important influence on student movements around the world. During the volatile 1960s virtually all of the powerful student movements of the period identified with the left and very often with Marxism but without adherence to the Soviet Union or any other "official" Communist movement. There has been significant change since the 1960s, and the appeal of leftist alternatives has diminished, especially after the demise of the Soviet Union.

As the research literature on student political movements is limited and we know relatively little about the backgrounds and motivations of student activists in most countries, we can only speculate about the causes of student unrest. However, some sociological generalizations have been offered. While there are some counterexamples, the following generalizations reflect the realities of many countries in the contemporary period.

Student activists come largely from the social sciences and to some extent from the humanities. Fields such as sociology and political science produce a significant proportion of student leaders. The content of the curriculum in these fields may contribute to an interest in activism—the social sciences are, after all, concerned with the problems of society. There is no doubt a degree of self-selection involved as well, with students who have an interest in social issues gravitating to disciplines that focus on these questions. Furthermore, professors in these fields tend to be among the most liberal or radical in the university,

no doubt contributing to such attitudes and values among students. The intellectual atmosphere in the social sciences is more congenial to activism in both thought and action. At the other end of the activist spectrum, highly vocational fields such as management and agriculture tend to be much more conservative in terms of the attitudes of both faculty and students. The culture of such fields does not seem to promote either radical ideologies or a tendency to become involved in activist movements.

Activist students share other common characteristics. Not surprisingly, they are more politically conscious than the majority of students. They tend to come from families with a higher level of both income and education than the average student population. It must be kept in mind that students in most countries come from significantly more affluent families than the general population. The educational backgrounds of the parents tends to be much higher than average, and very often the political attitudes of the families of activists are to the left of the general population. Thus, activist students are very often from highly elite groups in their societies— groups that have benefited from existing societal arrangements. Activists tend to come from urban and cosmopolitan families— this is a key variable in developing countries where the majority of the population is rural and relatively uneducated. During the 1960s much was made of a perceived "generational conflict" between student activists and their families. However, research shows that, in general, there is relatively little conflict among activists and their families.

Dramatic differences exist between student activism in the Third World and the industrialized nations. Third World students have overthrown governments and have frequently had a direct political impact. This has not been the case in the industrialized nations where students only rarely have been at the forefront of political change.

Third World student activism is difficult to categorize. While students have been instrumental in overthrowing governments and precipitating political upheaval in many nations in the Third World, they have never been able to take power, and their efforts have often led to governments that have been highly unsympathetic to student goals. For example, in Indonesia, Korea, and Thailand, among other countries, student dissent caused the downfall of regimes but the military assumed political power rather than groups favored by the students. In Argentina student unrest led not to a leftist government but rather to right-wing repression of students and others. In Uruguay student-led activism was met with massive military repression.

In other cases, even while unable to seize power for themselves, students were nonetheless successful in precipitating political change that was generally in a direction that they favored. In 1987 student demonstrations in South Korea forced the government to call elections and the result was a significant move toward democracy. While student activists were dissatisfied with the degree of change, most Koreans saw it as highly significant. The pattern of student unrest in India and a few other Third World countries has focused on the universities themselves in an effort not only to express opposition to established policy but also to win improvements in difficult campus conditions and to address poor job prospects for graduates. Indian student "indiscipline" has frequently resulted in campus disruption. On occasion, Indian students have also demonstrated against political officials and have sometimes forced them to resign. Thus, the spectrum of Third World student dissent is very broad. Sophisticated ideological rhetoric characterizes some student movements, while others have no discernable perspective. Some movements aim at the overthrow of the government while others are concerned with poor conditions in the dormitories.

In comparing the relative success of Third World students in politics in relation to activist movements in the industrialized nations, it is worthwhile to point to some of the key factors.

Third World nations often lack the established political institutions and structures of the industrialized nations, and it is thus easier for any organized groups, such as the student movement, to have a direct impact on politics.

Students have in many cases been involved in independence movements and from the beginning of the state have been a recognized part of the political system. Thus, in contrast to the West, where activism is seen by most people to be an aberration and an illegitimate intrusion into politics, Third World students are expected to participate directly in politics and activism is seen as a legitimate part of the political system.

Third World university students constitute a kind of incipient elite and have, in many countries, a consciousness that they are somehow special. They are members of a tiny minority who have access to postsecondary education and their prospects for later success in careers are relatively strong. The advantages, real and imagined, accruing to those who have a university degree and the historical sense of elite status are a powerful combination.

The location of the major universities of the Third World contributes to the possibility of activism. Many are located in the capital cities, and a large proportion of the student population is within easy reach of the centers of power. This simple fact of geography makes demonstrations easier to organize and gives students a sense that they are at the center of power and have easy access to it.

Because Third World students, on the average, come from higher socioeconomic groups then their compeers in industrialized nations, they have an added impact. While there are important national differences and the situation is rapidly changing in terms of social-class background as higher education expands, a substantial portion of the student population in many Third World nations still comes from urban elite backgrounds, and they have, through their families, direct access to powerful segments of society.

These factors are a partial explanation for the relative effectiveness of student activist movements in the Third World in the past several decades. While students in the industrialized nations, particularly during the 1960s, had an impact on their societies, their role pales into insignificance when compared to the Third World student movements. Furthermore, Third World students have continued to be a force— they did not disappear at the end of the decade of the 1960s.

That decade was the period of greatest activism in the industrialized nations. It was followed by a period of quiet on campuses with activism at a low ebb. While it may appear that student movements emerged at the same time throughout the Western nations, in reality there were significant variations. In some countries there was little activism—Britain, for example, was relatively quiet during this period, and there were few changes in higher education and no significant threats to the government. In a few countries, notably France, activist movements threatened the stability of the state, while in some others, especially West Germany, student movements developed a concept for university reform and succeeded in forcing their partial implementation of those reforms. In the United States issues such as civil rights and a concern for campus reform stimulated a movement, which was greatly expanded when the war in Vietnam escalated.

In each case, there were specific motivating forces and the movement had characteristics determined by national circumstances. However, in all of these cases there was a general perception that established parliamentary processes were not functioning adequately, and students were seen as a kind of "conscience of the middle class." In France Charles de Gaulle's power was at its height, and the legislature was little more than a rubber stamp, leading many to feel

disenfranchised. In West Germany, the "Grand Coalition" of the two major political parties also left an oppositional vacuum, and the students emerged as the main force in what they called an "extra-parliamentary opposition." In the United States Lyndon Johnson was elected to the presidency with a pledge to end the Vietnam War, yet he escalated the conflict. With little outcry from the Congress, students spearheaded public opposition to the war.

Western academic systems were characterized by dramatic growth in this period. Expansion meant changes in the nature of the student population and also deteriorating conditions on campus, especially in France and West Germany. Students in many countries complained about inadequate facilities and overcrowding. Students demanded participation in academic decision-making and wanted to control some of the decisions being made that were negatively affecting their situation. The call for participation was especially powerful in Western Europe and resulted in significant change in France, Germany, the Netherlands, and Sweden. In each of these countries students were included in the governance process in higher education. In the United States, while students did not achieve significant institutional power, they did force the end of *in loco parentis* and also successfully pressed for the abolition of many parts of the traditional collegiate curriculum. Students also had an effect on the cultural norms of the period—in music, social attitudes, and in other ways.

Yet, the movement of the 1960s ended almost as quickly as it started. Students in many industrialized nations were struggling for fundamental change in both university and society and when this change did not occur, there was both impatience and frustration. Students, having achieved significant influence in higher education institutions, tired of the tedious process of academic governance and the compromises built into the system. Despite unprecedented societal impact, students also felt that they had failed in their basic goal—the downfall of the system. For a time student activists moved ever leftward, losing the support of the majority of students.

In North America and Western Europe the decade of the 1980s, while relatively peaceful, witnessed several notable episodes of activism. In the United States a flurry of activity protesting against the racial policies of the government of South Africa focused on a demand that American universities sell off their investments in corporations that had business in South Africa. These protests were nationwide and took place at several hundred universities; many institutions agreed to sell off their investments although a smaller number actually divested. These antiapartheid protests took place mainly during the 1984–1985 academic year. In France the Ministry of Education proposed a series of reforms in higher education, one of which imposed entrance examinations for the universities in addition to the traditional baccalaureate requirement. The response was massive student protests in Paris, and the government was forced to cancel reforms.

It is said that students learn as much outside the classroom as in it during their university years. Without question student organizational culture plays an extraordinarily important role in the collegiate experience of students. Student groups provide socialization; give students a sense of belonging in what can be a difficult and sometimes alienating environment; set up networks of support, which are important during the university years and often last throughout their lifetimes; and provide valuable skills.

The focus here has been on political organizations and movements because they tend to be the most visible and vocal and they have had the greatest direct impact on both university and society. Yet, in terms of the number of students involved or perhaps even in long-term effect on those involved in student organizations, activist movements are not necessarily the most important. The entire nexus of organizations and their different constituencies and functions are central to contemporary academic life.

See also Deliberative Democracy; Democracy; Democratic Education; Minority Youth Voter Turnout; MTV's Choose or Lose Campaign (1992–); New Media; Peer Influences on Political Development; Rights of Participation of Children and Youth; Rights, Youth Perceptions of; Social Movements; State and Youth, The; United Students Against Sweatshops (USAS).

Recommended Reading

Altbach, P. (1997). *Student Politics in America: A Historical Analysis*. New Brunswick, NJ: Transaction.

Altbach, P., ed. (1968). *Turmoil and Transition: Higher Education and Student Politics in India*. New York: Basic.

Altbach, P., ed. (1974). *University Reform*. Cambridge, MA: Schenkman.

Altbach, P., ed. (1989). *Student Political Activism: An International Reference Handbook*. Westport, CT: Greenwood.

Caute, D. (1988). *The Year of the Barricades: A Journey Through 1968*. New York: Harper and Row.

Emmerson, D., ed. (1998). *Students and Politics in Developing Nations*. New York: Praeger.

Feuer, L. (1969). *The Conflict of Generations: The Character and Significance of Student Movements*. New York: Basic Books.

Gitlin, T. (1987). *The Sixties: Years of Hope, Days of Rage*. New York: Bantam.

Keniston, K. (1971). *Youth and Dissent: The Rise of a New Opposition*. New York: Harcourt Brace Jovanovich.

Klineberg, O., Zavaloni, M., Louis-Guerin, L., Benbrika, J. (1979). *Students, Values and Politics: A Cross-Cultural Comparison*. New York: Free Press.

Kurlansky, M. (2004). *1968: The Year that Rocked the World*. New York: Ballantine.

Levitt, C. (1984). *Children of Privilege: Student Revolt in the Sixties*. Toronto: University of Toronto Press.

Lipset, S. M. (1976). *Rebellion in the University*. Chicago: University of Chicago Press.

Walter, R. J. (1968). *Student Politics in Argentina: The University Reform and Its Effects, 1918–1964*. New York: Basic Books.

Philip G. Altbach

Student Voices Project. Young voters were a hot commodity in the 2004 presidential election with millions of dollars poured into get-out-the-vote efforts and thousands of people working across the country to get young people to the polls. After years of declining voter turnout among eighteen- to twenty-four-year-olds, on Election Day 2004 young people responded by voting in numbers that had not been seen in more than a decade. Much was made of celebrities such as Sean "Puff Daddy" Combs and slick MTV advertising calling on young people to vote. But what is being done to develop up-and-coming teen voters for elections to come? How do we get them to participate in the political process in between presidential elections and learn about the government's impact on their daily lives?

In more than a dozen cities across the country during the past five years, the Student Voices Project has been trying to create the voters and engaged citizens of tomorrow by bringing the study of local government, policy issues, and political campaigns into high-school classrooms. The Student Voices Project of the Annenberg Public Policy Center at the University of Pennsylvania, which began in Philadelphia in 1999, gets students to think about the issues affecting their own lives and communities. The national project, which has been funded by the Annenberg Foundation and the Pew Charitable Trusts, also brings political candidates and community leaders into the classroom to try and break what has become a vicious cycle: young people say they do not vote or pay attention to politicians because politicians and candidates do not talk about issues youth care about, such as college costs and summer jobs. But many politicians do not talk about youth issues because young people do not vote. Think about all the political ads you see with candidates in nursing homes or talking about Social Security—the result of the fact that people sixty-five or older vote at much higher rates than eighteen- to twenty-four-year-olds. (The U.S. Census Bureau has found that in the 2000 presidential election eighteen- to twenty-four-year-old citizens were half as likely to vote as people aged sixty-five to seventy-four,

almost three-quarters of whom cast ballots in that election.)

While high-school classes on civics, government, and democracy once provided this education, today those classes have been reduced or dropped entirely thanks in part to the focus on the standardized testing of reading, math, and science. This means young people are spending less and less time studying civics and democracy in school. Even in places where students are required to take these classes, the focus is on learning historical facts rather than developing the skills and knowledge they need to become *active*, informed citizens. Through its efforts Student Voices has worked to fill this void and has given students the skills to increase their knowledge and understanding of local political processes and institutions and their ability to make their voices heard in city halls, their boards of education, or their state governments. As their teachers use the Student Voices curriculum and resources on their individualized, local Student Voices Web site, students also learn how to develop their citizenship skills—particularly, their ability to find information on an issue and make use of it in developing and articulating a point of view in the civic arena.

Their civic arena could be the SpeakOut! discussion board on every local Student Voices Web site, where students can read short stories that introduce them to an issue in their community and then post their own thoughts and ideas on the issues and see how they compare to those of their peers at other schools. The SpeakOut! topics students can comment on range from what can be done to get more young people to vote to whether there should be armed police officers in city schools, advertising on school buses, or smoking bans in public places.

The students' civic arena can also be the classroom or auditorium during a visit from the city's mayor or police chief, or it could be a candidate's forum, city council, or board of education meeting. In every case the Student Voices format allows students to raise issues that concern young people in their communities and their schools and to hear how those in government (or those who would be in government if elected) plan to address them. In the process young people gain the satisfaction of knowing that by raising their voices about issues, they may bring about positive changes in their governments and communities.

One example where a Student Voices class was able to make a difference in policy was in Seattle in early 2004. As part of their Student Voices class project, students at the Middle College High School at Northgate began researching the redevelopment of the mall and surrounding area where their school was located (yes, the school was IN the mall). The students ended up playing a part in the creation of the city's long-awaited plan to redevelop the Northgate area. Thanks to discussions the students had with the mayor's office while they were working on their project, a committee of stakeholders was created, and one of the students from the class was asked to serve on the committee and have a role in how the mall would be developed.

At Northeast High School in Philadelphia, a class project involved assessing the need for upgrading recreation centers in the city and, in particular, determining what kinds of activities centers might be added to attract more teens to their facilities. The class submitted the plan to the recreation commissioner, who was so impressed that he scheduled a visit to the school and asked the students to provide ongoing advice on how to improve the city's recreation centers.

In Chicago, Student Voices participants had the opportunity to question the man who would become Illinois' new senator in 2004, Barack Obama, as well as his opponent in the election, Alan Keyes, and were able to ask each candidate what they would do about urban education and gun violence. That same year students from Tulsa Student Voices were invited to participate

in a debate, moderated by the anchors of two Oklahoma television stations, with senatorial candidates Tom Coburn and Brad Carson. One student asked how each of the candidates would vote on an issue if his conscience contradicted his constituents' wishes.

Here are several other recent examples of the many instances in which the Student Voices Project has brought students together with leaders over the years, helping to raise issues that are often ignored in the public arena:

Denver: In April 2004 a Student Voices town-hall with Mayor John Hickenlooper drew one thousand students from the Denver public schools for a question-and-answer session in which the mayor responded to questions about his positions on homelessness, teen curfews, same-sex marriages, and arts education in Denver.

Philadelphia: At a March 2004 town-hall on youth voting with Pennsylvania Governor Edward G. Rendell and the state's highest elected official, Secretary of the Commonwealth Pedro Cortes, students shared their ideas on how to get more young people to vote from putting voting machines in malls for demonstrations, to replacing a single Election Day with a longer period for voting.

Seattle: The city's television station, the Seattle Channel, hosted a monthly program in 2004 called "Student Voices: Speak Out Seattle," in which city government leaders like Mayor Greg Nickels and Police Chief Gil Kerlikowske visited classrooms to respond to questions submitted by students from across the city to the Seattle Student Voices Web site.

Washington, D.C.: During an April 2004 D.C. Student Voices forum featuring Mayor Anthony Williams, Police Chief Charles Ramsey, and Housing Authority director Michael Kelly, seventy-five high-school students got to discuss education, housing, and public-safety issues.

It should not be understated that most of the high schoolers who have benefited from the Student Voices Project come from

America's urban centers, where the public-school populations are predominantly minorities and where poverty and lack of resources for education are a constant presence. Voting participation rates and civic knowledge are also often lower for minority youth compared to their white counterparts. Part of the problem is access and exposure, which Student Voices continues to try to overcome. For example, according to the National Assessment of Educational Progress' "The Nation's Report Card," students of color and students from low-education families were the least likely to report experiencing interactive classroom learning activities such as role-playing exercises, mock trials, visits from community members, or letter writing. The Student Voices curriculum incorporates these types of activities into daily classroom activities.

But Student Voices does not end where the suburbs and rural areas begin. During the 2004–2005 school year, more than 350 teachers from cities, suburbs, small towns, and rural areas in Pennsylvania used the Student Voices curriculum as part of a yearlong pilot program funded by the Carnegie Corporation of New York. Hundreds of students in more than 165 schools in forty-two Pennsylvania counties have been able to improve their understanding of local government and the electoral process thanks to Student Voices. Many Pennsylvania newspapers joined this effort to help young people make their voices heard by inviting students in their local high schools to write regular letters to the editor and op-ed essays about issues of concern to their communities.

High-school students involved with the Student Voices Project have demonstrated time and time again that, given the opportunity, they can rise up and be active and engaged citizens, whether it is in their schools, their neighborhoods, their cities or towns, or their country. At a time when the need for effective civics education is becoming recognized as vitally important to maintaining a strong democracy,

programs such as the Student Voices Project will be working to bring their innovative curricula to more students and teachers nationwide.

See also Communication and Youth Socialization; Deliberative Democracy; Democratic Education; KidSpeak; Kids Voting USA (KVUSA); Minority Youth Voter Turnout; MTV's Choose or Lose Campaign (1992–); New Media; Peer Influences on Political Development; Rights of Participation of Children and Youth; Rights, Youth Perceptions of; School Engagement; School Influences and Civic Engagement; Service Learning and Citizenship Education; State and Youth, The.

Recommended Reading

Carnegie Corporation of New York and CIRCLE: The Center for Information and Research on Civic Learning and Engagement (2003). *The Civic Mission of Schools.* New York: Carnegie Corporation of New York. See http://www.civicmissionofschools.org.

Jamieson, A., Shin, H. B., and Day, J. (2002). *Voting and Registration in the Election of November 2000: Population Characteristics.* Washington, D.C.: U.S. Census Bureau. See http://www.census.gov/prod/2002pubs/p20-542.pdf.

Student Voices Project. See http://www.student-voices.org.

U.S. Department of Education, Institute of Education Sciences, National Center for Education Statistics (1999). *National Assessment of Educational Progress (NAEP): Civics.* Washington, D.C.: U.S. Department of Education, Institute of Education Sciences, National Center for Education Statistics.

Phyllis Kaniss and Argelio Dumenigo

Sustainability. Sustainability crosses over environmental, economic, and social lines— yet in each system the theme is the same. Sustainability can be understood as humanity's capability to adapt to change. Political leaders speak of sustaining our economic growth; car manufacturers seek more sustainable designs; the food industry pursues sustainable farming practices; cities have developed sustainability indicators; and universities, high schools, and junior highs have created sustainability curricula. At the heart of this modern trend is the underlying need to define the current position of a rapidly changing world with finite resources.

Sustainability came about in the latter half of the twentieth century, spawned by the environmental activism movement of the mid-1960s and 1970s. Researchers began to take notice of the population growth that seemed to be developing at a near exponential rate. Two more lessons propelled the idea of sustainability: the increased realization that our seemingly endless natural resources—soil, water, fossil fuels, and clean air—are finite, and if we are not careful our consumption rate may exceed the regenerative capabilities of nonrenewable resources.

Youth and adults alike struggle to clarify the concept of sustainability because it is a way of thinking as much as something to think about. The current educational systems focus mostly on absorbing and restating information, not on the synthesis and integration of what we know and can know. Drawing together environmental, economic, and social systems is where educating about sustainability begins and becomes complex.

Higher education was the first to take on the challenge of weaving sustainability into a variety of curricula that cross the boundaries of engineering, business, health, agriculture, education, and art discourses. Centers for sustainability research and education have emerged at universities and as nonprofit organizations across the nation. Recently charter schools and project-based alternative schools have begun to add sustainability education to their teachings. The focus of their curriculum centers on the synthesis of information with hands-on learning as the central teaching tool, which allows students to draw their own connections between the systems that support life.

To help clarify sustainability thinking, five principles have been developed to serve as a guide. While each of these principles viewed separately will seem familiar, when taken together the interconnections between the systems that support our lives become the central theme. The five principles of sustainability are:

1. Respecting life and natural processes
2. Living within limits
3. Valuing the local
4. Accounting for full costs
5. Sharing resources

Sustainability commits us to respecting life and the natural processes that keep our world in balance. To do so reminds us that we must be conscious of the daily decisions we make in our lives and in the actions we take in our communities. Most places now have recycling programs for bottles, cans, paper, batteries, and oil. Many areas of the country now participate in composting programs that turn the leaves that drop in the fall into nutrient rich humus for the garden in springtime.

Living within our limits involves understanding that the resources on which all life depend—forests, topsoils, fisheries, pure water, fossil fuels, and clean air—are finite. Although these endowments are capable of regenerating they are nonrenewable because most require several lifetimes to replenish on their own and only a short amount of time for humanity to consume. Limited natural resources must be used carefully and at a rate equal to their ability to regenerate.

Valuing the local commits us to show respect for the natural components of our neighborhoods and bioregions. This principle focuses on preserving, restoring, and making use of local knowledge. Local knowledge of the place ones lives is often found in members of the community who have spent a lifetime working the land, observing the seasons, and recognizing the change created by development of chain businesses that can afford to charge less for products than small, specialized merchants.

Accounting for full costs requires that we become aware of the true price we pay for the products that support our lives. This means tracing the production process back to the extraction of the fossil fuel used to create and produce goods, and then forward again to the shelf where the item is purchased. The environmental and social impact must also be taken into account when accounting for the full cost of the products that support our lives.

Sharing power demands that we recognize that we are all interconnected—humans, the environment, and the elements. Problems are solved by each individual assuming a share of the responsibility. Even the smallest decision, such as turning off the lights when you leave the room or installing low-flow showerheads can affect the community in which one lives.

One can gauge the commitment level to sustainability by using metrics like the *ecological footprint calculator.* Researchers have developed the ecological footprint to help measure individual/national consumption of natural resources. The footprint can be compared with nature's ability to renew these resources. An individual's footprint is the total area required to produce the food, fiber, and water that one consumes, absorb the waste from their energy consumption, and provide space for infrastructure. People consume resources and ecological services from all over the world, so their footprint is the sum of these areas, wherever they are on the planet.

The space each of us is entitled to is known as the *fare earth share.* The fare earth share is calculated by dividing the total amount of usable land and sea on the planet (30 billion acres) by the global population (roughly 6.5 billion), providing each of us with 4.5 acres per person. This number does not account for animals and other creatures and the space they require to live. To support the current lifestyle of an average American, this requires twenty-five acres of land per person. It would take nearly five earths for all humans to live the American lifestyle. In contrast, the average footprint of an African is 2.5 acres.

Current research in sustainability is happening on all fronts because efficiency is not only environmentally responsible but profitable these days as well. For example, McDonald's saved $350,000 a year when they switched from Styrofoam packaging for their products to recycled paper. Government-funded incentive programs offer consumers money back to purchase hybrid vehicles in many states, which in turn helps to motivate car manufacturers to produce more energy efficient and cleaner-running vehicles. Advanced methods of farming known as biointensive practices and permaculture allow one to grow more food in smaller spaces, but more importantly they allow them to focus on rebuilding depleted topsoil and returning native plants to one's bioregion.

Sustainability is everywhere. Take the government-backed Energy Star program, which most of us our familiar with. The Energy Star insignia can be found on a variety of appliances, computer technologies, and lights. Energy Star is helping businesses and individuals protect the environment through superior energy efficiency while creating a more conscious society of resource consumers.

Most importantly, sustainability brings hope and inspiration to the future. It is the most ambitious, creative, elegant, innovative, out-of-the-box, exhilarating, difficult, frustrating, comprehensive, enlightening, rewarding, holistic, ego-boosting, and humbling work there is to do. Those who have been provoked to learn and educate for sustainability would not miss it for the world.

See also Civic Environmentalism; Earth Force; Environmental Education (EE).

Recommended Reading

Brower, M., and Leon, W. (1999). *The Consumer's Guide to Effective Environmental Choices.* New York: Three Rivers Press.

Brown, L. (2001). *Ecoeconomy.* New York: W. W. Norton.

Lovelock, J. (1979). *Gaia: A New Look at Life.* Oxford: Oxford University Press.

Orr, D. (1994). *Earth in Mind.* Washington, D.C.: Island Press.

Uhl, C. (2004). *Path to a Sustainable World: Developing Ecological Consciousness.* New York: Rowan and Littlefield.

Vanmatre, S. (1990). *Earth Education.* Greenville, WV: Institute for Earth Education.

Wheeler, K., and Bijur, A. (2000). *Education for a Sustainable Future: A Paradigm of Hope for the Twenty-first Century.* New York: Kluwer Academic/Plenum.

David A. Lettero

T

Terrorism, Youth Activism Responses to.
The September 11, 2001, hijackings and subsequent attacks on the World Trade Center towers in New York, on the Pentagon outside Washington, D.C., and crash of the plane in Pennsylvania, represented most Americans' first introduction to international terrorism within the United States itself. Although there are sharp differences on definitions (see discussions in Moghaddam and Marsella 2004), terrorism can be described as "the use of force or violence by individuals or groups that is directed toward civilian populations and intended to instill fear as a means of coercing individuals or groups to change their political or social positions" (Marsella 2004, 16).

Among concerns that youth would react to the terrorist attacks with posttraumatic stress symptoms, pessimism about the future, hostile attributions about others, or increased risk-taking behavior, there was also a hope that youth would rise to the occasion with increased activism and volunteerism. Indeed, many public observers saw the events of September 11 as an opportunity, following years of low levels of youth civic engagement, to encourage or perhaps even require youth engagement in civic activities and community service.

Although a surge in youth activism may not be expected in response to most natural disasters, the nature of the events of September 11, namely terrorist-group attacks on both civilians (at the Word Trade Center and on the hijacked commercial airlines) and noncombat military personnel (at the Pentagon), were seen as attacks on the country as a whole and thus sparked heightened feelings of patriotism and of a desire to help those affected. We know from media accounts that Americans responded overwhelmingly to the events of September 11 with patriotism and volunteerism (Danieli, Engdahl, and Schlenger 2004), yet very little research has documented the increase in these behaviors either by youth or adults.

The uniqueness of the events of September 11 have made it difficult for social scientists to forecast how youth would respond; specifically, should the literature on disasters, on exposure to war, or on trauma in general be best used as guides for studying the impact of the events (Gershoff and Aber 2004; Smelser and Mitchell 2002)? Ultimately, lessons from each of these types of literature have helped frame the events and their aftermath. A typical reaction observed in response to disasters or traumatic events is a "social solidarity," exemplified by increases in trust in other individuals and authorities as well as in altruistic behavior, effects that were evident in the days and weeks following September 11. This is in accord with social-psychological research on intergroup relations suggesting that group cohesion increases in the face of an external threat, as do outgroup stereotyping and discrimination.

Even with such types of literature as a guide, very little is known about the effects of traumatic events on youth activism. Whereas the psychological responses of children and youth to traumatic events such as disasters and other acts of terrorism have been well documented—with posttraumatic stress disorder, anxiety, and

Like many young people touched by the tragedy of September 11th, this fourteen-year-old girl participates in a local memorial service. *Courtesy of Skjold Photographs.*

depression being primary responses (Vogel and Vernberg 1993)—much less is known about the impact terrorism can have on youth activism.

Drawing from previous literature on exposure to terrorism, natural disasters, or war, several key factors are thought to determine how youth respond to terrorism:

• Amount and extent of exposure (particularly whether youth had direct, indirect/media, or family exposure to the events)
• Previous exposure to trauma
• Previous levels of mental health (particularly depression and anxiety)
• Social support (such as from family, friends, or religion) and coping skills
• Age, gender, and race-ethnicity

This entry summarizes what is known to date on the impact of exposure to terrorism

on youth activism. As more surveys regarding the reactions to September 11 were conducted with adults than with youth, findings with adults are used as reference points for the little that is known about youth reactions to terrorist events such as September 11.

After the attacks of September 11, many were worried that Americans, particularly young Americans, would respond with prejudice toward individuals of Arab descent or with more anger toward others and assumptions of hostile intent. A longitudinal study of over 700 New York City youth examined the associations between exposure to September 11, prejudiced beliefs about immigrants concerning their contributions and costs to society, and general mistrust of others (e.g., that others may take advantage of them) (Aber, Gershoff, Ware, and Kotler 2004). With middle childhood mental-health symptoms, gender, race-ethnicity, age, and immigrant status controlled, family exposure to the events of September 11 was associated with greater mistrust of others generally, but also with less prejudice toward immigrants. Direct exposure was also associated with greater mistrust of others.

A phone survey found that, in line with the social solidarity thesis as well as with social-psychological research on group cohesiveness following a threat, adults surveyed after September 11 were more likely to believe that people are fair (63 percent), helpful (67 percent), and trustworthy (41 percent) than adults surveyed in years before September 11. However, young adults (aged eighteen- to twenty-nine-years-old) were much less likely to endorse these beliefs in others, with 51 percent believing that others are fair, 49 percent that others are helpful, and only 19 percent that others are trustworthy (Smith, Rasinski, and Toce 2004). The percent of young adults holding negative perceptions of people in general remained unchanged at a follow-up one year after September 11, whereas such views among adults declined over the year (Rasinski, Berktold, Smith, and Albertson 2002).

In unpublished data Aber, Gershoff, Ware, and Kotler (2004) found that the more youth reported direct exposure to the attack (through seeing it with their own eyes, being in the cloud of smoke after the towers fell, and so forth), media exposure, or family exposure (a family member was in the towers), the *more* optimism they reported. This is contrary to what many expected. It may be that the outpouring of patriotism, concern, and assistance present throughout the country renewed the faith of these youth in others and as a result their optimism about the future. Further evidence from this study that showed that youth who experienced direct or media exposure to the attacks were also more likely to engage in volunteer work as a way to "help the way [they] felt about the WTC attack" may also be relevant to these findings. Optimism and volunteer activity may mutually reinforce each other.

These studies suggest that, at least in the relatively short term, youth have responded to September 11 with increases in social mistrust toward others in general but that, contrary to prediction, youth did not evidence increased prejudice toward immigrants or decreased optimism.

Although rates of volunteerism and donations were up around the country after September 11, there is some indication that youth were more likely to respond in these altruistic ways than adults. In one national study two-thirds of young adults (aged eighteen to twenty-nine years) reported donating money, clothing, or blood and/or doing extra volunteer work in the week following September 11, compared with 59 percent of the full adult population sampled (Smith, Rasinski, and Toce 2002). Among a sample of young adults (aged eighteen to twenty years) in New York City two to three months after the attacks, 47 percent reported donating money, 45 percent donating blood, 31 percent donating their time, 72 percent participating in a vigil or other service, and 76 percent displaying a flag (Sherrod, Quiñones, and Davila 2004). Such rates of youth volun-

teerism and donation are also substantially higher than those reported in a separate survey of adults: immediately after September 11, one-third of adults reported that they had participated in a vigil recognizing the attacks and 36 percent reported having donated blood or money or having done volunteer work (Schuster, Stein, Jaycox, Collins et al. 2001). However, engagement in such altruistic activities dropped off significantly among all adults sampled one year later (Rasinski, Bertold, Smith, and Albertson 2002).

A sample of adolescents in a suburb of Boston reported increased interest in politics from pre– to post–September 11, although they did not report changes in their intended civic engagement in activities such as demonstrations or volunteer work (Metz and Youniss 2003). However, 85 percent of the adolescents in this sample engaged in one or more form of civic engagement in response to the terrorist attacks, such as attending vigils, donating money, clothes, or blood, and performing community-service activities. Over the next seven months youth who engaged in community service showed increases in their likelihood to engage in future civic activities, while those who attended vigils showed increases in their political interest.

Another area thought to be affected by September 11 and its aftermath is trust in the government. A comparison of adolescent cohorts interviewed before and after September 11 determined that after September 11 all youth were more likely to trust the federal, state, and local governments; male youth interviewed after September 11 were more likely to report religion as an important influence in their lives and to donate blood (Ford, Udry, Gleiter, and Chantala 2003). These findings are similar to those found with adults: adults surveyed a year before September 11 and one month after September 11 reported a large increase in their trust in the national government (44 percent increase) and modest growth in interest in politics

(14 percent increase) and in behaviors such as volunteering and giving blood (7 percent increase each) (Putnam 2002). Other studies of adults have found similarly small increases in volunteering, due largely to increases in the amount of time individuals volunteered (rather than an increase in the number of volunteers) in the months after September 11 (Traugott, Brader, Corla, Curtin et al. 2002; see also http://www.isr.umich.edu/cps/har/index.htm).

Links between youth experiences of and reactions to the September 11 attacks and their political attitudes have also been found. The extent to which youth were worried about future terrorist attacks was positively correlated with their concern about economic inequality, their concerns with defense and the economy, and their support of a conservative morality. The extent to which youth emphasized retaliation against those who perpetrated the attacks was associated with less concern for economic inequality, availability of quality of life services for all citizens, or social causes and instead with more concern for self-preservation in government policy (Sherrod, Quiñones, and Davila 2004).

Given that youth responded to September 11 with increased volunteerism and donations, it is important to know if these behaviors helped youth cope with the terrorist attacks and their aftermath. In a study of adolescents and youth geographically distant from the terrorist attacks of September 11, participants were asked whether they had engaged in a range of coping activities, both public and private, and how helpful each activity was in making them feel better. The most helpful activities, as self-reported by the youth, were fundraising, attending a religious service, donating items, and flying a flag (Wadsworth, Gudmundsen, Raviv, Ahlkvist et al. 2004), suggesting that engagement in public activities was perceived to be more helpful in dealing with the events of September 11 than engagement in private activities (such as writing in a journal or talking with parents, friends, or a therapist).

In a study of fourth through sixth graders in Washington, D.C., over a quarter of the children reported donating goods or money or volunteering time to relief efforts or memorializing the event. The children were not asked if they found these activities helpful; however, those who engaged in more of these constructive activities reported greater, not reduced, feelings of shaken safety than their peers who engaged in fewer such activities. This finding may indicate that more distressed children sought out such activities as a form of coping or that in this age group these activities exacerbate fearful reactions.

These two studies relied on concurrent, self-reported data of both engagement/volunteerism and coping. Without independent and longitudinal assessments, we cannot definitively say whether and to what extent such activities aid in coping with terrorist events. These data do suggest that volunteerism and displays of patriotism may be ways in which youth can actively cope with terrorist events.

The potential for exposure to extreme acts, such as terrorism, to affect youth activism, volunteerism, and engagement as documented here is an important "silver lining" to otherwise destructive and traumatic events. Especially important is the potential for such activities to help youth cope with such an event and its aftermath.

It is important to note that these studies primarily have examined the short-term (i.e., up to two years) impact of September 11 on youth activism. The long-term impact of this tragic event on youth is still unfolding and awaits future studies.

The short-term impact results summarized here suggest that schools and youth programs would do well to include such activities in their disaster preparations as ways to help youth channel their complementary feelings of anger, fear, optimism, and patriotism into constructive activities that can benefit the community at large.

See also Antiwar Activism; Arab Americans.

Recommended Reading

Aber, J. L., Gershoff, E. T., Ware, A., and Kotler, J. A. (2004). "Estimating the Effects of September 11th and Other Forms of Violence on the Mental Health and Social Development of New York City's Youth: A Matter of Context." *Applied Developmental Science*, 8 (3): 111–129.

Danieli, Y., Engdahl, B., and Schlenger, W. E. (2004). "The Psychosocial Aftermath of Terrorism." In *Understanding Terrorism*, edited by F. J. Moghaddam and A. J. Marsella. Washington, D.C.: American Psychological Association, pp. 223–246.

Ford, C. A., Udry, R., Gleiter, K., and Chantala, K. (2003). "Reactions of Young Adults to September 11, 2001." *Archives of Pediatrics and Adolescent Medicine*, 157: 572–578.

Gershoff, E. T., and Aber, J. L. (2004). "Editors' Introduction: Assessing the Impact of September 11th, 2001, on Children, Youth and Families: Methodological Challenges to Research on Terrorism and Other Non-Normative Events." *Applied Developmental Science*, 8 (3): 106–110.

Marsella, A. J. (2004). "Reflections on International Terrorism: Issues, Concepts, and Directions. *Understanding Terrorism*, edited by F. J. Moghaddam and A. J. Marsella. Washington, D.C.: American Psychological Association, pp. 11–47.

Metz, E., and Youniss, J. (2003). "September 11 and Service: A Longitudinal Study of High School Students' Views and Responses." *Applied Developmental Science*, 7: 148–155.

Moghaddam, F. M., and Marsella, A. J., eds. (2004). *Understanding Terrorism: Psychological Roots, Consequences, and Interventions*. Washington, D.C.: American Psychological Association Press.

Phillips, D., Prince, S., and Schiebelhut, L. (2004). "Elementary School Children's Responses Three Months after the September 11 Terrorist Attacks: A Study in Washington, DC." *American Journal of Orthopsychiatry*, 74: 509–528.

Putnam, R. D. (February 11, 2002). "Bowling Together." *The American Prospect*, 13, 20–22.

Rasinski, K. A., Berktold, J., Smith, T. W., and Albertson, B. L. (August 7, 2002). *America recovers: A follow-up to a national study of public response to the September 11th terrorist attacks*. Chicago: NORC, University of Chicago.

Schuster, M. A., Stein, B. D., Jaycox, L. H., Collins, R. L., Marshall, G. N., Elliott, M. N., Zhou, A. J., Kanouse, D. E., Morrison, J. L., and Berry, S. H. (2001). "A National Survey of Stress Reactions after the September 11, 2001, Terrorist Attacks." *New England Journal of Medicine*, 345: 1507–1512.

Sherrod, L. R., Quiñones, O., and Davila, C. (2004). "Youth's Political Views and Their Experience of September 11, 2001." *Journal of Applied Developmental Psychology*, 25: 149–170.

Smelser, N. J., and Mitchell, F., eds. (2002). *Terrorism: Perspectives from the Behavioral and Social Sciences*. Panel on Behavioral Social and Institutional Issues, Committee on Science and Technology for Countering Terrorism. Washington, D.C.: National Research Council, Division of Behavioral and Social Sciences and Education, National Academies Press.

Smith, T. W., Rasinksi, K. A., and Toce, M. (October 25, 2002). *American Rebounds: A National Study of Public Response to the September 11th Terrorist Attacks: Preliminary Findings*. Chicago: NORC, University of Chicago.

Traugott, M., Brader, T., Coral, D., Curtin, R., Featherman, D., and Groves, R. (2002). "How Americans Responded: A Study of public Reactions to 9/11/01." *Political Science and Politics*, 35, 511–516.

Vogel, J. M., and Vernberg, E. M. (1993). "Children's Psychological Responses to Disaster." *Journal of Clinical Child Psychology*, 22: 464–484.

Wadsworth, M. E., Gudmundsen, G. R., Raviv, T., Ahlkvist, J. A., McIntosh, D. N., Kline, G., Rea, J., and Burwell, R. A. (2004). "Coping with Terrorism: Age and Gender Differences in Effortful and Involuntary Responses to September 11th." *Applied Developmental Science*, 8: 143–157.

Deborah Phillips and Elizabeth T. Gershoff

Tiananmen Square Massacre (1989). On the evening of June 3 and early morning of June 4, 1989, troops of the People's Liberation Army surged into the streets of Beijing in China under orders to clear Tiananmen Square of the student protesters who had occupied it for six weeks. To get to the square the soldiers chose to violently disperse the thousands of Beijing citizens who had turned out to protect the students. With tanks and assault rifles the troops brutally ended the complex dance of defiance, diplomacy, and drama that had transfixed the world. Ironically, China's modernization and relative openness to the world, ambitiously pursued by the reigning Communist Party, permitted images of the prolonged stalemate and bloody crackdown to be broadcast beyond China's

Youth protestors in Beijing's Tiananmen Square in May 1989, just before the People's Army bloodily dispersed the demonstrators. *Copyright Peter Turnley/Corbis.*

borders. Some of these images—the home-made "goddess of liberty" confronting the official portrait of Mao Zedong, a lone man in street clothes blocking the advance of a line of tanks, a student in pajamas with an oxygen bag lecturing stern Communist cadres in Mao suits, and the broken bodies of the dead draped over crumpled bicycles—have become icons of the movement itself.

Western observers have interpreted the confrontation in light of their own assumptions and past experiences. Calling it a "student movement" drew attention to the student movements that had wracked Western Europe and the United States in the 1960s; where the latter movements had largely been repudiated, the Chinese student movement could be lauded as a positive use of student power. Others labeled the movement a "pro-democracy movement," linking it to the anti-Communist upheavals in Eastern Europe and suggesting that Western-style, multiparty democracy was both the desired goal of all the world's peoples and the inevitable end of history. The ruthlessness of the Chinese government's response to the movement confirmed both the superiority of Western governments (whose use of force against their own students did not constitute

massacres) and the futility of Communist efforts to halt the advance of democracy.

The Chinese, however, call the event the "Tiananmen Square Massacre," or simply the "June 4 Incident." While some of the actions of student protesters deliberately played to a Western audience (like the creation of the goddess of liberty or signs—in English—demanding democracy), the massacre is in fact deeply rooted in Chinese culture and history. Calling it a "student movement" or a "pro-democracy movement" obscures its Chinese roots.

To begin with, Chinese students play a fundamentally different role in their society than do their counterparts in the West. While attending college is nearly a basic right in much of Europe and the United States, it is still a cherished privilege in China. Few Chinese have the opportunity to attend school beyond the secondary level. Moreover, while Western societies adulate youth but tend to discount college students as serious players in the political realm, in China things are reversed. Age is more admired than youth, but students and intellectuals are highly regarded. Because student protests against government corruption and malfeasance have such a long history in China, dating back to the sixth century BCE, there is a cultural expectation that Chinese students will dare to "speak truth to power" and pay the penalty, if need be.

Second, while student protesters improvised brilliantly in their use of modern communications technology and manipulation of symbols that were easily read around the world, the forms their protests took contained deep resonances of earlier protests and of Chinese cultural traditions. The very space in which the confrontation took place—Tiananmen Square in the capital of Beijing—attested to the magnitude of the struggle. There is no single place in Europe or the United States that can match Tiananmen Square's evocation of both governmental power and the weight of history.

Finally, although the protesters did aim to open up and reform the Chinese government in ways that can be described as "democratic," they never suggested that other political parties should contest with the Communist Party or that popular elections should replace internal party management or even that they wanted a representative government. The reforms they sought had little to do with their understanding of how other democratic governments work; instead they focused on what they believed was possible and desirable under a Socialist system.

The contest between students and government began with the death of Communist leader Hu Yaobang on April 15, 1989. As had happened more than a decade earlier with the death of Premier Zhou Enlai, students seized the opportunity of mourning Hu's death as a way to express their dissatisfaction with the current regime. While Zhou Enlai had the reputation of being a humane leader who personally intervened to save some individuals from the extremism of the Cultural Revolution, Hu was revered by students for his apparent toleration of a "prodemocracy movement" led by students in 1986. However, while the demonstrations following Zhou's death appear to have

been largely spontaneous, some of the students who marched to Tiananmen Square on April 18, 1989, had already participated in a "democracy salon," organized by history students at Beijing University.

Several days of marches and demonstrations followed, with some students clashing with Beijing police. On April 22, three students knelt outside the Great Hall of the People, where the Communist government transacts its business, with a petition they hoped to present to their leaders. The image of students kneeling in supplication with the petition outstretched in their hands evoked for the thousands of watching demonstrators the cultural memory of honest and upright government officials of bygone years rebuking a corrupt and wayward emperor. To no one's surprise no official came out to receive the petition.

In the days that followed, however, the government made some efforts to conciliate the students and revealed schisms within the leadership over how to handle the growing demonstrations. An editorial in the *People's Daily* condemned the movement as disruptive, strongly warning them and showing which way the government leaned; however, when students, joined by their teachers, journalists (who were demanding a freer press), and citizens of Beijing came out to protest the next day, the government withheld an attack. A peaceful solution still seemed possible, but concessions to students (mostly in the form of government representatives agreeing to meet and talk with student leaders) and the growing size of supportive crowds emboldened the dissidents to believe that the government would not crackdown, while simultaneously each concession firmed the conviction of hardliners within the government that only force could end the confrontation.

The anniversary of May 4 came and went with little change in the standoff. The date was significant, for in 1919 thousands of students and citizens of Beijing had massed in Tiananmen Square to protest what they perceived as the "sell-out" of their country by their leaders at the Versailles Peace Conference at the end of World War I. This demonstration, which was broken up by police, spawned a cultural and nationalist ferment that shaped a generation of Chinese leaders—including the older members of the ruling Communist elite. By this time students were groping toward a greater unity. Students from other cities made their way to Beijing to lend their support. Others organized parallel demonstrations in their own towns. Students formed new organizations that distanced themselves from officially sponsored student groups. Although the government attempted to block news of the protests from the national media, students communicated through fax machines (available in posh tourist hotels) and some established campus radio stations.

The students then escalated the confrontation by declaring a hunger strike on May 13. This was theater rather than an absolute determination to starve themselves (some apparently fasted while in the square but then took breaks in which they ate), but it was inspired. By fasting, students cast themselves not as disruptors of a stable society, but as martyrs to an ideal. In a land historically plagued by hunger, it was an electrifying protest.

International affairs also helped shape events. The presence of foreign media may have both restrained and inflamed the government. The Soviet leader Mikhail Gorbachev had scheduled a summit with Chinese leaders, none of whom were pleased that this historic rapprochement was overshadowed by the actions of student dissidents. Moreover, it was already clear that Gorbachev was presiding over a weakening Soviet bloc; Chinese officials warned ominously that there would be no replay of the events transpiring in Poland, where the Communist government tamely agreed in February to let the opposition Solidarity Party participate in elections.

The movement grew. Over a million demonstrators now milled in and about Tiananmen Square. Students, workers, intellectuals and residents all formed "autonomous unions." On May 19, leaders Li Peng and Yang Shangkun declared martial law, signifying the victory of the hardliners within the government. But still no attack came. Determined Beijing citizens peacefully turned back 50,000 hesitant troops outside the city. On May 30 students unveiled a statue of the "goddess of liberty."

In response, the government called in veteran troops and ordered them to clear the square. On June 4, they did. After a tense standoff with PLA soldiers, students who were still occupying the square were allowed to leave; some may have been crushed by tanks as they were in retreat. Elsewhere in Beijing, the massacre had begun. Soldiers fired at places where crowds had gathered, at bold protesters who threw stones, and at random. Some fired into buildings.

Afterward, no one was sure how many had died—hundreds, certainly, possibly thousands. The government claimed the incident was the work of counterrevolutionaries and that the majority of victims were soldiers. Some soldiers were killed, attacked by furious crowds, but there is no doubt that the majority of the dead were civilians. Show trials and a few executions followed, but the most famous of the student leaders were allowed to escape. Foreign governments condemned the violence but imposed no sanctions. Government workers cleaned up the debris in the square and hosed away the bloodstains.

See also Australia, Youth Activism in; Demographic Trends Affecting the World's Youth; Eastern Europe, Youth and Citizenship in; Europe, Comparing Youth Activism in; European Identity and Citizenship; Immigrant Youth in Europe—Turks in Germany; Immigrant Youth in the United States; India, Youth Activism in; Indonesia, Youth Activism in; Nigeria, Youth Activism in; Palestinian *Intifada*; Russia, Youth Activism in; Serbia, Youth Activism in (1990–2000); Soweto Youth Activism (South Africa); State and Youth, The; Statute of the Child and Adolescent

(Brazil); Transnational Identity; Transnational Youth Activism; Turkey, Youth Activism in; United Nations, Youth Activism and; Xenophobia; Zapatista Rebellion (Mexico); Zionist Youth Organizations.

Recommended Reading

Brook, Timothy (1992). *Quelling the People: The Military Suppression of the Beijing Democracy Movement.* New York and Oxford: Oxford University Press.

Calhoun, Craig (1994). *Neither Gods nor Emperors: Students and the Struggle for Democracy in China.* Berkeley: University of California Press.

Feigon, Lee (1990). *China Rising: The Meaning of Tiananmen.* Chicago: Ivan R. Dee.

Oksenberg, Michel, Sullivan, Lawrence R., and Lambert, Marc, eds. (1990). *Beijing Spring, 1989: Confrontation and Conflict, the Basic Documents.* Armonk, NY: M. E. Sharpe.

Spence, Jonathan D. (1999). *The Search for Modern China.* New York: W. W. Norton.

Gael Graham

Tinker v. Des Moines Independent School District **(1969).** The Supreme Court decision in the 1969 case, *Tinker v. Des Moines Independent School District* was a landmark victory for the First Amendment rights of children. The decision is still considered "good law" and has been often cited in other legal opinions; nevertheless, both the facts of the case and the language of the opinion reveal much about how American society regards youth, both in school and before the law. Indeed, *Tinker* has worked to limit students' rights as much as to expand them.

By the end of 1965, America's war in Vietnam was heating up and so was the nascent antiwar movement. In December of that year John Tinker and Christopher Eckhardt, both high-school students in Des Moines, Iowa, wore black armbands to school as a symbol of mourning the dead in Vietnam. John's sister Mary Beth Tinker also wore a black armband to her junior-high school. Their actions violated a hastily contrived rule against wearing black armbands to school, which the principals of the Des Moines schools had passed after hearing about the planned demonstration.

All three children were suspended and told they could not return to school unless they came without armbands. With the aid of the Iowa Civil Liberties Union, the state branch of the American Civil Liberties Union (ACLU), the Tinker and Eckhardt families sued.

The legal case centered on the First Amendment rights of children on the one hand and the need for schools to maintain an atmosphere conducive to education on the other. At the same time lawyers for the administration tried to persuade the Court that the children's action had not truly been an expression of their own opinion, that their parents or Students for a Democratic Society (SDS), the college antiwar group, had put them up to it. In later years both John and Mary Beth Tinker insisted that although their parents also opposed the war in Vietnam, the young people had acted independently in carrying out their symbolic protest.

The Tinkers and Eckhardt lost in the district court and appealed. The Eighth Circuit Court of Appeals sat *en banc* to hear the appeal. When the appellate court split four to four in its decision, the students appealed to the U.S. Supreme Court. It was now 1968, and the social, political, and military context had all altered dramatically. Both the war and the antiwar movement had escalated, although neither was making much headway. In addition, the rights revolution was in full swing as numerous social groups—including youth younger than eighteen—pressed for greater freedoms under the law. The Supreme Court, led by Chief Justice Earl Warren, played an important role in expanding the rights of citizens and in limiting the powers of various governmental agencies. Thus, it is not surprising that the Court ruled in favor of the Tinkers and Eckhardt. In February of 1969 the Supreme Court handed down its decision with seven justices joining in the majority opinion and two dissenting.

The Court's opinion, written by Justice Abe Fortas, affirmed the First Amendment rights of children in ringing tones. "It can hardly be argued," Fortas wrote, "that either students or teachers shed their constitutional rights to freedom of speech or expression at the schoolhouse gate." Moreover, "state-operated schools may not be enclaves of totalitarianism" (*Tinker v. Des Moines* 1969). Having thus highlighted the rights of schoolchildren, however, the majority opinion proceeded to pare down the rights of youth and to hedge them with qualifications, leaving a fuzzy rather than clear-cut definition of those rights.

For example, the Court emphasized that in the *Tinker* case school officials acted not because of any actual disruption of school but only because they feared that such disruption might take place. Citing a decision by the Fifth Circuit Court of Appeals to uphold school rules banning African American students from wearing "freedom" buttons in school (*Blackwell v. Issaquena County Board of Education* 1966), the Court in *Tinker* upheld administrators' right to quell student expression that interfered with the orderly operation of the schools. In addition, the Court held that armbands were "akin to 'pure speech,'" unlike hair or mere apparel. Students' choice of hairstyle or dress, the Court implied, were not constitutionally protected. By these statements the opinion stressed the "special characteristics" of the school that permitted some students' rights to be curtailed in the name of education (*Tinker v. Des Moines* 1969).

Despite these limitations, other justices believed that Fortas' opinion erred by granting too much to minor children. Justice Potter Stewart, concurring specially, noted that he could not "share the Court's uncritical assumption that, school discipline aside, the First Amendment rights of children are co-extensive with those of adults." Justice Hugo Black dissented from the majority opinion on the grounds that the Supreme Court had no business telling school administrators how to run their schools. Firmly upholding the authority of adults, Black wrote scathingly: ". . . if the time has

come when pupils of state-supported schools, kindergartens, grammar schools, or high schools, can defy and flout orders of school officials to keep their minds on their own schoolwork, it is the beginning of a new revolutionary era of permissiveness in this country fostered by the judiciary." Mockingly he suggested that perhaps it was unconstitutional to bar youth from voting or serving on school boards of education (*Tinker v. Des Moines* 1969).

For judges in the lower courts, swamped by lawsuits from youth seeking redress of grievances or a clearer delineation of their rights, the *Tinker* case offered grist for many a mill. For example, in the more than one hundred cases concerning male hair length heard by the Federal Circuit Courts of Appeals in the late 1960s and early 1970s, half the circuits upheld the rights of school administrators to regulate haircuts, citing *Tinker's* dismissal of hair length and apparel as meaningful, protected forms of expression. The other half defended students' right to wear their hair as they wished, again relying on *Tinker* to support their ruling. Although appealed to half a dozen times, the U.S. Supreme Court refused to rule on whether hairstyles are constitutionally protected.

For other forms of youth expression, *Tinker* has proved more of a boon to students than to school officials, but even here student rights have eroded over time and courts continue to point to *Tinker* to justify diminishing these rights. Student freedom of the press, for example, involves "pure speech" issues parallel to those raised in *Tinker*, and thus initially expanded in the late 1960s and early 1970s. In general, the courts put the onus on school officials to justify any censorship of student publications, gave free rein to the writing and distribution of underground student papers, and permitted students to pass out "outside" literature on campus (American Civil Liberties Union 1971). In 1988, however, the Supreme Court substantially narrowed the scope of youth press freedom by arguing that since students received academic credit for contributing to a school-sponsored student newspaper, the newspaper was a classroom activity, not a public forum. In that case the justices ruled that the *Tinker* standard need not apply in "determining when a school may refuse to lend its name and resources to the dissemination of student expression." Three justices dissented, arguing that a course in journalism ought to impart lessons about student "rights and responsibilities under the First Amendment," but in the more conservative Court of the era, their views did not prevail (*Hazelwood v. Kuhlmeier* 1988).

Two years before the *Hazelwood* decision, the Supreme Court had already shrunk the limits of acceptable student speech in *Bethel School District v. Fraser*. In this case the Court upheld the suspension of a student for lewd and sexually suggestive comments in a speech to a school assembly. Again referring to *Tinker*, the Court ruled that "the use of an offensive form of expression may not be prohibited to adults making what the speaker considers a political point, but it does not follow that the same latitude must be permitted to children in a public school." In a wry dissent Justice John Paul Stevens pointed out that he and his colleagues on the bench, "at least two generations and 3,000 miles away from the scene of the crime," were probably not the best situated to determine whether or not the student had in fact offended his audience (*Bethel v. Fraser* 1986). Nevertheless, the Supreme Court once again upheld the diminution of students' First Amendment rights on the grounds of their youth. While the *Tinker* decision did expand the Constitutional rights of minors with regard to expression, the fact that it defined students as "persons" under the Constitution (rather than "citizens") and marked schools as special arenas in which students' rights could sometimes be circumscribed has allowed school officials to chip away at the foundation of students' right to free speech and press.

According to legal scholar William S. Geimer, courts and American society as a whole continue to assume that youth are immature and incapable of thinking for themselves; these assumptions justify "age-discriminatory laws." Some of these laws seek to protect youth from situations believed to be solely appropriate for adults (sex, wage labor, political representation), while others purport to protect youth from themselves. The fact that most youth depend on parents and guardians for their physical support, undergo mandatory education, and "are largely without the power to acquire property" limits their ability to claim an independent legal status and assert their rights. Geimer finds the Supreme Court's claim that the Bill of Rights applies to young people a "mystery," in light of numerous rulings that privilege adult interests over children's rights (Geimer 1988). However, the "soaring rhetoric" of the *Tinker* ruling may yet nudge open the door to greater First Amendment rights for the young. It would not be the first time in history that the rhetoric of freedom has preceded the reality.

There is evidence that the *Tinker* case continues to inspire young people today. In February of 2003, as the United States was poised to invade Iraq, school officials in Dearborn, Michigan, sent home Bretton Barber, a junior in high school, for wearing a T-shirt that proclaimed George W. Bush an "international terrorist." Convinced that he had the right to wear the shirt, Barber first attempted to contact the ACLU and then revisited the *Tinker* case on the Internet. Thus armed, he was not taken in when his high-school principal quoted from the dissenting opinion in *Tinker* and tried to convince him that students had lost the case. Backed by the ACLU, Barber took his school to court and in October a federal judge granted him a preliminary injunction. In his opinion Judge Patrick Duggan relied heavily upon the *Tinker* case—with all of its ambiguities (ACLU 2003; *Barber v. Dearborn Public Schools* 2003).

See also High-School Student' Rights Movement of the 1960s; Juvenile Justice;

Rights of Participation of Children and Youth; Rights, Youth Perceptions of.

Recommended Reading

American Civil Liberties Union (1971). *Academic Freedom in the Secondary Schools*. Originally printed Sept. 1968; reprinted Dec. 1969, May 1971.

American Civil Liberties Union. See http://www.aclu.org/StudentsRights/StudentsRightslist.cfm?c=156.

Barber v. Dearborn Public Schools. See http://www.mied.uscourts.gov/_opinions/duggan.htm.

Bethel School District No. 403 et al., v. Fraser, a Minor, et al. (1986). 478 U.S. 675; 106 S. Ct. 3159.

Geimer, William S. (1988). "Juvenileness: A Single-Edged Constitutional Sword." 22 Ga. L. Rev. 949.

Hazelwood School District v. Kuhlmeier (1988). 484 U.S. 260; 108 s. Ct. 562.

Johnson, John W. (1997). *The Struggle for Student Rights*: Tinker v. Des Moines *and the 1960s*. Lawrence: University Press of Kansas.

Lewin, Tamar (February 26, 2003). "High School Tells Student to Remove Antiwar Shirt." *New York Times*. See http://www.commondreams.org/headlines03/0226-04.htm.

Shelton, David E. (1980). "The Legal Aspects of Male Students' Hair Grooming Policies in the Public Schools of the United States." PhD diss., University of North Carolina at Greensboro.

Tinker et al., v. Des Moines Independent Community School District et al. (1969). 393 U.S. 503; 89 S. Ct. 733.

Gael Graham

Transnational Identity. Transnational identities are a way of understanding one's place in an increasingly interconnected international context and refer to a sense of belonging that is not confined to the geographical boundaries of the nation-state. Youth today experience this interconnection intensely. New communication technologies like the Internet allow young people on opposite sides of the globe to interact. International news media present stories and pictures of life in other societies. Our communities are becoming much more diverse as international immigration means multiculturalism is not just a policy stance but the reality in many places in the world.

The concept of transnational identity can be understood in three different ways.

First, it can refer to ethnic or cultural groups that live in one or more countries other than the one traditionally defined as their "homeland," such as the Jewish diaspora or Latino identity in North America (*diasporic transnational identity*). A second definition extends the "homeland" to include a larger continuous geographic and cultural area beyond the nation-state (*supranational transnational identity*). This is reflected in French men and women who also define themselves as European or Ethiopians who ascribe to a larger pan-African identity. Both of these definitions mirror traditional national identities in combining a sense of place with a cultural community. However, the idea of place changes to refer either to a homeland in which one no longer lives or to a group of countries that are thought to have a shared cultural heritage.

Lastly, transnational identities can also refer to feelings of belonging not tied to a geographic cultural space (*global transnational identity*). Such belonging can be tied to common experiences or a sense of shared humanity, reflected in identity-based new social movements that mobilize individuals in different national settings for a common cause, such as demonstrations against free trade or peace rallies (see also Global Justice Activism).

What these three definitions share is an emphasis on forms of identity that transcend traditional nation-states. All three types of identities are becoming more relevant in an increasingly globalized world. Globalization is defined by David Held (1998) as "a shift in the spatial form of human organization and activity to transcontinental or interregional patterns of activity, interaction, and the exercise of power. It involves a stretching and deepening of social relations and institutions across space and time such that, on the one hand, day-to-day activities are increasingly influenced by events happening on the other side of the globe and, on the other, the practices and decisions of local groups or communities can have significant global reverberations." Globalization is especially relevant for youth. Economic restructuring has led to extremely high youth unemployment in many industrialized countries. At the same time the younger members of society are often the most adept at mastering the new communication technologies that connect them to the rest of the world. In many respects youth are living experiences distinct from their predecessors and are more similar to other young people around the world.

Transnational identities are thus very relevant to the present global order, and youth—as they come of age in this environment—may be particularly prone to express themselves through such identities. As mentioned, transnational identities can be categorized into three types: diasporic, supranational, and global. How are youth affected by and, at the same time, shaping such transnational identities?

In terms of transnational identities associated with diasporas, youth are in a unique position. Children of immigrants face difficult choices about their identity. While their parents may try to reinforce the identity and associated practices of the homeland, youth are also faced with the identity of the dominant culture and subcultures in which they find themselves. Mary Waters, in a study on Afro-Caribbean immigrants in New York City, finds that young people are likely to shift between a number of different identities, differentiating themselves from African and European Americans by carving out a specific Afro-Caribbean identity that does not exist in their homelands. This identity ties them to their parents' country of origin but at the same time reconstructs it for their new environment. As international immigration intensifies with globalization and continued contact with the country of origin is increasingly common, second-generation immigrants are in a unique position to construct a transnational identity that reflects both their country of origin and their new host country experiences. Youth are particularly likely to experiment with such combinations as adolescence is a period when young people begin to form their own identities.

While the immigrant experience is one conduit to the formation of transnational identities among youth, globalization also presents other opportunities for the creation of supranational identities. With the increase of cross-border contacts in established nation-states as well as the creation of regional organizations, individuals are becoming more likely to identify with individuals in neighboring countries. Contemporary Europe provides an interesting example. The creation of shared institutions such as the European Union (EU) and the Council of Europe has solidified people's sense of community within Europe and, at least in Western Europe, has led to an increasing number of individuals who identify as European. The young and the educated are particularly likely to embrace this identity. The European Union has focused efforts on promoting this identity, as evidenced in its recent white paper on European youth and an increasing emphasis on education-related initiatives. Regional integration is a second route to transnational identity formation (see also European Identity and Citizenship).

As globalization renders national boundaries less important, it facilitates the expression of identities that lack a geographic dimension. Youth, as a social category, is itself a transnational identity in many ways. While adolescence has traditionally been conceived as a transitional phase between childhood and adulthood, research is beginning to recognize youth as an identity with its own cultures and systems of meaning. Youth identity thus has the potential to link young people across national boundaries. Increased communication and the globalization of cultural practices means that punk culture, grunge, and other expressions of youth identity provide a shared cultural repertoire on which young people from different countries can interact and understand one another. As such, youth as an identity itself can be thought of in some instances as a transnational identity.

Youth identity is not the only way in which young people identify with a larger, transnational community not defined by geography. Perhaps the best example is the concept of global citizenship, which is gaining currency among many youth activists and organizations targeting youth. The idea is simply that people form a community based on their shared humanity. This is the foundation of the human-rights discourse and movements that have gained such prominence in world politics. Activism in areas such as the environment is making clear that one country's practices can have global implications. The creation of international organizations to deal with this recognition has similarly been followed by calls for their functioning to be more democratic since these organizations increasingly represent interests that cross national boundaries. Young people have proven open to claims based on such an identity. The prominence of young people in the antiglobalization movement provides one example. Recent antiwar protests also have taken on a transnational character. The protests on March 5, 2003, illustrate this point. Tens of thousands of college and high-school students in the United States, Europe, and other parts of the world participated in walk-outs, teach-ins, and other forms of protest against the impending military intervention in Iraq. This coordinated, transnational protest by young people shows both the presence and the power of the interconnection felt among many youth.

In conclusion, transnational identities can take many forms, but all of them are accentuated by the processes of globalization. Young people react to these processes and embrace different transnational identities in a variety of ways that reflect their shared experiences with other young people in other countries. The development of such identities has important implications in terms of youth activism as well. How individuals define themselves has always been important in terms of the expectations they hold and the demands they make on society. As young people take on new definitions, they are likely to modify old forms of activism and create new ones in an effort to express their interests in a rapidly changing world.

See also Civic Identity; Ethnic Identity; European Identity and Citizenship; Identity and Activism; Identity and Organizing in Older Youth; National Identity and Youth; Transnational Youth Activism.

Recommended Reading

Bradford Brown, B., Larson, R., and Saraswathi, T. S., eds. (2002). *The World's Youth: Adolescence in Eight Regions of the Globe.* Cambridge: Cambridge University Press.

European Commission (2001). *A New Impetus for Youth.* See http://www.europa.eu.int/comm/youth/whitepaper/download/whitepaper_en.pdf.

Heaven, C., and Tubridy, M. (2003). "Global Youth Culture and Youth Identity." In *Highly Affected, Rarely Considered: The International Youth Parliament Commission's Report on the Impacts of Globalization on Young People*, edited by J. Arvanitakis. Fitzroy, Australia: Oxfam Community Aid Abroad.

Held, D. (1998). "Democracy and Globalization." In *Re-Imagining Political Community: Studies in Cosmopolitan Democracy*, edited by D. Archibugi, D. Held, and M. Köhler. Stanford, CA: Stanford University Press.

Kahane, R. (1997). *The Origins of Postmodern Youth: Informal Youth Movements in Comparative Perspective.* New York: de Gruyter.

Keane, J. (2003). *Global Civil Society.* Cambridge: Cambridge University Press.

Nayak, A. (2003). *Race, Place and Globalization: Youth Cultures in a Changing World.* New York: Oberg.

Waters, M. (1999). *Black Identities: West Indian Immigrant Dreams and American Realities.* Cambridge, MA: Harvard University Press.

Yeoh, B., Charney, M., Kiong, T. C. (2003). *Approaching Transnationalisms: Studies on Transnational Societies, Multicultural Contacts, and Imaginings of Home.* Boston: Kluwer.

Allison Harell

Transnational Youth Activism. Transnational youth activism is activism in which young people work consciously with members in two or more countries to solve social problems. Such activism is one of the most striking current examples of globalization's human networks. Increasing numbers of young people work in transnational activism networks that involve activists outside, as well as inside, the organizers' nations of origin. Many such young people hope quite literally to "change the world" through the creation and political use of transnational human and technological networks. These networks often have young people analyzing social problems and inequality structures as orders created through transnational processes—and thus best solved through transnational cooperation.

Such political activity—in which people often literally labeling themselves as "youth" engage in activism in collaboration with peers in other nations—may indeed be an exploding worldwide phenomenon. Yet the scope and forms of such activity has yet to be systematically investigated. "Transnational advocacy networks," whose members link up both inside and outside their nations of origin to solve social problems, have so far been examined most thoroughly in political science. Such networks are increasingly of interest to disproportionately sociology-based "social movement" theorists and to a lesser but growing extent to anthropologists and other social scientists analyzing globalization. However, too little scholarship has yet investigated how young people may be disproportionate participants in many current forms of self-consciously transnational activism, which capitalizes particularly on the available time, mobility, communication savvy, and excitement about things "global" that characterize the population of people increasingly labeled "youth" worldwide.

"Youth" actors have primarily been framed in anthropological scholarship as the world's most spectacularly "global" citizens due to the increasingly global circulation and consumption of "youth" products and (desired) lifestyles. Youth indeed seem particularly excited to think and act "globally" about fashion or leisure

activity, but youth are also increasingly central participants in transnational circulations of analyses, information, and strategies for addressing a broad range of social problems. Rather than solely tracking the global circulation of youth products, then, scholarship must increasingly work to track a global circulation to and by diverse youth of analyses of injustice—keeping open for investigation the question of *which* youth are most likely to think and act "globally" to solve social problems.

Too little scholarship yet exists on youth inside or outside the United States acting as global activists—that is, as people using transnational networks to accomplish political goals or as people analyzing social issues as phenomena produced through globalized processes. Instead, the overwhelming majority of academic literature on youth activism eschews global analysis—and most makes youth participation in "politics" synonymous with nation-bound voting, adult-run political party work, or local community service. Yet any search for actual transnational youth networks will quickly unearth young activists within the United States and worldwide who are thinking and acting transnationally when framing and solving social problems. Some activists literally move their bodies transnationally to participate in activism with peers, while others stay put and facilitate the global transfer of knowledge, social analyses, or strategies via the Internet or written paper text. Some activists are based in the "First World" and others in the "developing" world. Some focus on literally global problems (e.g., AIDS), while others focus on local instances of economic formations created through transnational processes (e.g., sweatshops); still others focus on using transnational ideas to improve local communities. Examples of activism include U.S. low-income youth of color who travel to Mexican villages to get ideas for community development that they take back home; Brazilian youth activists who share rights logic from home via e-mail with transnational peers; South

African township youth who travel to U.S. cities to help build an international environmental-activism network; youth from across the world who converge in Palestine to try to end the Israeli-Palestinian conflict nonviolently through demonstrations and human-rights assistance; and Internet "hubs" based in the United States, Canada, Australia, the United Kingdom, and Nigeria connecting young people worldwide to share ideas on employment or sexual health. Amassing more such examples, it becomes possible to identify key models of young activists engaging in political action that involve transnational peers in addressing specified social concerns. This population of young people appears to be both an unstudied and a crucial generational cohort and a fundamental example of humans networking for transformational change.

Examining this topic requires drawing upon multiple bodies of scholarly work and filling an intellectual void at their intersection. For one, social scientists studying globalization and transnationalism are framing youth as key actors in global networks. Yet scholarship on globalized youth largely ignores activism, primarily theorizing global youth as a population tied together by transnational leisure activities. In turn, developmental theorists are working to study youth activists as particularly important exemplars of moral and political development. Still, most scholarship on the moral-political development of adolescents addresses no unit larger than the nation, focusing on young people developing politically within the confines of nation-states or local communities. Furthermore, social-movement theory, helpful in theorizing the organization of political activity, has done little to update theories on youth action developed in the 1960s. Finally, existing scholarship on global advocacy networks typically overlooks youth-dominated activity. Thus, current scholarship is producing too little systematic knowledge about how young adults are now creating and utilizing global networks to solve social problems. Scholars and activists working together must seek, classify, and examine existing social movements that are youth-led, transnational, and political.

It is essential to first understand and classify the full range of ways in which youth are currently organizing transnationally, so that other analysts can investigate developmental and process-oriented questions of *why* and *how* youth are coming to analyze and address social problems in transnational ways—that is, how today's youth are coming to think and organize globally. We need far more detailed investigation into such questions of how youth in various places in the world are coming to think transnationally about social problems, how youth are ending up connecting transnationally to solve social problems, and why so many young activists today are organizing *as* "youth" in social movements. Yet the basic knowledge necessary to help scholars pursue such process-oriented (and comparative) research is simply not yet available.

A concept central to understanding transnational youth activism is that young activists today are themselves analyzing globalization to an unprecedented extent, rather than simply experiencing it. That is, youth are conceptualizing the very networks necessary for getting things done within a globalizing world system. When young activists figure out a strategy for getting toilets in their local Ghanaian community by sketching out a "power map" of necessary transnational actors that includes World Bank officials, the CEOs of transnational corporations, NGOs in Washington, D.C., human-rights workers, and local politicians, they are themselves *theorizing globalization*. In figuring out how to accomplish specified political goals through the use of transnational networks, youth activists are using (and, often, creating) the global communication networks made possible by globalization itself. And by connecting to transnational players through the Internet, letters, phone calls, or face-to-face contact, today's youth activists are devising and communicating strategies derived from their own analyses of global social formations and social problems.

Transnational youth activism invites debate on the very definition of contemporary "activism" for transnational youth activism now ranges from physical demonstrations to Web-based action, art and musical performance, letter-writing campaigns, Internet fundraising, and youth-led lecture tours. Youth activists trying to think and act globally today are not just marching and meeting but also building new computer infrastructures for Web-based activism or physically moving their bodies to sites for coordinated work. Consolidating, debating, and updating known versions of "youth activism" globally are thus necessary. Two basic questions can be posed:

1. What forms does youth activism take today? What "counts" as youth activism?

2. What forms does *transnational* youth activism take today? What might "count" as *transnational* youth activism?

Currently, it seems that today's transnational activism involving young participants might be classified generally along four "axes" in which activists *analyze* a diverse range of problems, *address* those problems through diverse strategies, *link* themselves spatially in diverse manners, and *organize* themselves through diverse organizational structures that exhibit varying levels of adult influence. First, as indicated above, transnational activists analyze different social problems, framing some problems literally as concerns threatening the entire world (like the environment or, for some, the Israeli-Palestinian conflict) and others as local problems created through global flows of funding or political/corporate influence (like the demise of one region's farming economy or the troubles of specific Palestinian villages under U.S.-supported Israeli occupation). Some youth activists organize around a generational consciousness *as* "youth," while others organize around other social identifications or organize intergenerationally around specific social problems.

Second, young transnational activists often share, transnationally, a variety of ideas for activist activities for *addressing* these social problems. Spectacular antiglobalization protests are only one form of today's transnational youth activism: some young people write e-mails or post to blogs to act transnationally, while others raise money and still others share artistic performance. For example, young people in the International Solidarity Movement (ISM), who travel to Palestine for nonviolent demonstrations in collaboration with nonviolent Palestinian communities, self-consciously model nonviolent tactics from India, South Africa, and the United States (such as marching and sit-ins) and intertwine these tactics with ongoing Palestinian tactics of nonviolent resistance (picking olives and camping upon farmlands slated for takeover). Back at home, ISMers raise money, publish reports, and recruit new "delegates" to Palestine to continue their efforts to end the occupation.

Third, activists link themselves transnationally in different spatial manners. Some transnational activists (like ISMers) attempt literally to link the entire "globe," while others attempt to link just two or more nations. Some activists move their bodies to single sites to participate in activism with peers, while other activists travel to fixed or changing sites for conferences, and still others stay put and facilitate the transnational transfer of knowledge via the Internet or telephone.

Finally, some activist communities involving young people exist as more formal youth-run "organizations," or even as corporate or government-sanctioned spin-offs of adult-run organizations designed for "youth participation." Other transnational youth activism is self-consciously informal and antihierarchical, demonstrating more porous, loose, intergenerational communities of activists who circulate information relatively freely and make consensus-based decisions. Every activist community varies in ideologies, tactics, and internal cohesion.

Much transnational youth activism suggests that young activists may also now be key circulators of self-consciously *nonviolent* problem-solving tactics all too rarely explored by researchers. Youth have already been shown to play key roles in violent transnational political activity; young people from all social backgrounds (although especially the poor) are disproportionately recruited or forced by adults to participate in militias, armies, or guerrilla movements fighting across the borders of nations or proto-nations. Youth of all classes and social groups also seem to get the most attention from police *and* from researchers when they break windows or hurl homemade explosives in demonstrations. Yet equating young "global justice" activists with violence risks analytically overlooking trends of self-consciously *antiviolent* transnational activism among the world's youth.

Furthermore, many transnational activists also prove that the notion of "globalization" should not presume the demise of the concept of nations; transnational political activism often utilizes nation-based organizations. Yet many transnational activists also frame their activism self-consciously as "*global*"—not just because they are linking transnational actors but also because they are often claiming particular social problems as a world responsibility.

Finally, young Americans and Europeans are perhaps disproportionately more able than youth elsewhere to *be seen* conducting transnational activism—that is, to play spectacular roles that are publicly recognized in "the West." While political *ideas* about transnational responsibility for social problems might flow multidirectionally to and from "the West," the political power to *be seen* coordinating transnationally to solve a social problem may not often be equally distributed. That ISM "internationals," for example, transport themselves physically to Palestine to place themselves in front of bulldozers and tanks suggests a level of "global" political commitment dwarfing that of young people who write letters or raise money or march at home to solve social problems at home or abroad. But of course the young Americans and Europeans who dominate the ISM's ranks are also disproportionately endowed with the travel funds and mobility to conduct spectacular transnational campaigns that, like the ISM, require temporary physical movement. They are also more likely than Palestinians to be recognized for their nonviolent work. Young "Westerners" are also far more likely than their peers worldwide to be connected to the Internet, even while many young transnational activists worldwide demonstrate that the Internet is by no means a medium utilized *only* by the economically "privileged." Indeed, in the ISM's case, the first e-mail calls for "international solidarity" in Palestine emanated from Palestinian computers, and "ISM's" nonviolent strategy built upon preexisting Palestinian nonviolent activism.

In sum, while researchers work to classify the diversity of the global youth activism community (considering each youth activist group's *problem analysis*; *strategies* for solving said problems; *spatial model of transnationalism*; and *organizational structure*), more specific analysis of trends in transnational youth activism should also be solicited from global activist networks. Scholars and activists can also begin formulating research questions to pursue more process-oriented and developmental understanding of *how* and *why* youth are currently organizing along transnational lines. Others will then be able to undertake investigations designed to illuminate how and why young citizens of the world are identifying, analyzing, and addressing social problems as dilemmas that must be solved in collaboration with citizens outside their nations. Transnational youth activists and scholars can collaborate to help build the foundation for a research agenda that would not only extend current knowledge of youth activism beyond its current nation- and locale-bound confines but also open up for study a core phenomenon of contemporary global human networking. Transnational youth activists are not only using the analytic, communication, and travel networks made possible by globalization, they also are actively conceptualizing and creating the networks necessary for solving social problems within a globalizing world system. By coming to analyze and address shared social problems, many transnational youth activists are capitalizing upon a "think globally, act globally" mentality of globalization, rather than promoting the insular ethnocentrisms that are also often globalization's result.

See also Australia, Youth Activism in; Demographic Trends Affecting the World's Youth; Eastern Europe, Youth and Citizenship in; Europe, Comparing Youth Activism in; European Identity and Citizenship; Global Justice Activism; Immigrant Youth in Europe—Turks in Germany; Immigrant Youth in the United States; India, Youth Activism in; Indonesia, Youth Activism in; Nigeria, Youth Activism in; Palestinian *Intifada*; Russia, Youth Activism in; Serbia, Youth Activism in (1990–2000); Soweto Youth Activism (South Africa); State and Youth, The; Statute of the Child and Adolescent (Brazil); Tiananmen Square Massacre (1989); Transnational Identity; Turkey, Youth Activism in; United Nations, Youth Activism and; Xenophobia; Zapatista Rebellion (Mexico); Zionist Youth Organizations.

Recommended Reading

Appadurai, Arjun (2000). "Grassroots Globalization and the Research Imagination." *Public Culture*, 12 (1): 1–19.
Appadurai, Arjun (1996). *Modernity at Large: Cultural Dimensions of Globalization.* Minneapolis, MN: University of Minnesota Press.
Cunningham, Hilary (1999). "The Ethnography of Transnational Social Activism: Understanding the Global as Local Practice." *American Ethnologist*, 26 (3): 583–604.
Edelman, Marc (2001). "Social Movements: Changing Paradigms and Forms of Politics." *Annual Review of Anthropology*, 30: 285–317.
Juris, Jeffrey S. (2004). "Networked Social Movements: Global Movements for Global Justice." In *The Network Society: A Global Perspective*, edited by Manuel Castells. London: Edward Elgar.
Keck, Margaret, and Sikkink, Kathryn (1998). *Activists beyond Borders: Advocacy Networks in International Politics.* Ithaca, NY: Cornell University Press.
Klein, Naomi (2002). *Fences and Windows: Dispatches from the Front Lines of the Globalization Debate.* New York: Picador.
Maira, Sunaina, and Soep, Elizabeth, eds. (2004). *Youthscapes: Popular Cultures, National Ideologies, Global Markets.* Philadelphia: University of Pennsylvania Press.
Pollock, Mica (Spring 2005). "Using and Disputing Privilege: U.S. Youth and Palestinians Wielding 'International Privilege' to End the Israeli-Palestinian Conflict Nonviolently." Center for Public Leadership Working Papers Series, Kennedy School of Government, Harvard University.
Stohlman, Nancy, and Aladin, Laurieann, eds. (2003). *Live from Palestine: International and Palestinian Direct Action against the Israeli Occupation.* Boston: South End Press.
Wittkamper, Jonah. "A Snapshot of the Global Youth Movement." See http://www.youthmovements.org/guide/globalguide.html.

Mica Pollock

Turkey, Youth Activism in. The period of westernizing reforms in the nineteenth century ushered in a new conception of youth in Ottoman society. In Turkish society the term *delikanli*, which translates roughly as "the one with wild blood," is commonly used to refer to young men (and sometimes young women). Although this term suggests the marking of a period known as youth in Turkish society, it was the process of modernization which set off new meanings and new roles for youth. Thus, it is no coincidence that the main social movements of the late Ottoman period were known as the "young" Ottoman movement and the "young" Turk movement. At this time new Western-style schools were established, including a military school, a medical school, and a school to train public servants. The first official student associations were paramilitary groups, which served the joint purpose of mobilizing young people for war and inculcating Turkish nationalism. The students of these new schools would eventually challenge the empire they were educated to protect and maintain, paving the way for modern Turkey. It is from such a group of Western-educated young army officers that Mustafa Kemal Atatürk, the first president of the Turkish Republic, would emerge.

The role of youth in modern Turkish society can be understood in terms of three stages: 1923–1950, 1950–1980, and 1980 to the present. In the first period (1923–1950) youth—and educated youth in particular—came to embody the new nation. The creation of modern Turkey involved an attempt to construct a modern nation-state and a national consciousness upon the remains of a multireligious, multiethnic, multilingual empire.

Education played a central role in the Turkish social-engineering project aimed at creating a new type of person. The main instrument in this civilizational process, based on a localized version of Enlightenment ideas, was educated youth. This culminated in the 1920s in a veritable cult of youth. Young men and women were the main images through which the Turkish Republic was represented. A "youth and sports holiday" was established and celebrated with great shows of gymnastics.

The term "the children of the Republic" (or "Atatürk's children") refers to the new Republican youth. At the end of the long speech to the Second Congress of the Republican People's Party on October 15–20, 1927, Atatürk directly addressed Turkish youth. The famous lines from this speech, known by heart by every Turkish student, include the following: "Turkish youth! Your first duty is to maintain and protect Turkish independence and the Turkish Republic forever. This is the primary basis of your existence and of your future. This constitutes your most valuable treasure. The child of Turkey's future! Your duty is to save Turkish independence and the Republic. You will find the strength that you need to achieve this in the noble blood that flows in your veins!"

The oath recited by Turkish schoolchildren every morning, written by a former minister of education, goes as follows: "I am a Turk, upright, diligent. My law is to respect my elders, protect those younger than myself, and to love my country and nation more than my own self. My ideal is to rise up and go forward. Let my being be sacrificed for the sake of Turkish existence!" This oath shows the degree to which individuals were expected to conform to what was viewed as the good of the collective.

The second period (1950–1980) corresponds to the change from single-party to multiparty rule in Turkey. The liberal constitution of 1960 allowed more room for the expression of alternative political views, and a legal party emerged on the left for the first time. University students, spurred on by local developments as well as by the events of May 1968 in Europe, rapidly began to organize. Initially calling for an improvement in the conditions of universities, they soon began to support other mass movements, such as those of teachers, workers, and peasants. This period was characterized by the widespread politicization of youth, particularly university students, who were increasingly divided into the two opposed camps of "rightists" and "leftists."

From 1968 onward, increasingly disillusioned with the status quo, influenced by parallel movements in Europe, Latin America, and elsewhere, and spurred on by various forces with much to gain from the rise of extremism, the student movement gradually moved outside the legal terrain. It culminated in increased violence, followed by brutal repression subsequent to the military coup of 1971 (and again in 1980).

During this period youth were portrayed in public discourse as a "threat" to the national interest. On the other hand, many young people claimed that it was the government itself that was illegitimate, perceiving themselves as acting in the name of "the people" to build a just society. While ideologically opposed, the political movements on the left and on the right shared significant features. These were modernist, nationalist, anti-imperialist, and corporatist political movements, whose rhetoric underscored the independence of the Turkish nation-state and the "duty" of youth to dedicate their lives to the construction of a future society.

Autobiographical accounts repeatedly underscore how activists felt the need to repress their individual desires and emphasize their belief in the necessity of living for the future and their sense of having been chosen to play a special, unique role in history. Individuals tended to pride themselves in dressing exactly like members of their own group: a "leftist" or a "rightist" male could be distinguished, for example, on the basis of his moustache or beard. In these two periods, despite a change in discourse on youth, educated youth largely identified with the mission assigned to them of transforming society from above.

The third and current period (post-1980) constitutes the first serious rupture with modernist models of youth in Turkey. The 1980 military coup was an important watershed in Turkish politics. Even though civilian rule was quickly established, a new constitution was put into effect, which restricted civil liberties. Young people born in the 1970s and after were raised in a relatively depoliticized environment coinciding with the liberalization of the economy and its incorporation into global markets. With privatization, the rise of a consumer society, and the influx of new communication technologies, the media became a major player in Turkish society.

The political repression of the 1980s was accompanied by increased freedom of expression on the cultural and personal front. In the 1980s and 1990s, a variety of organizations and subcultures including environmentalists, human-rights activists, feminists, gays, rockers, and others entered the public sphere. Social movements in which young people played an active role included Kurdish nationalism and Islamism.

Today, one-half of Turkish society is under the age of twenty-five; these young people are increasingly urban. In the 1990s new urban spaces emerged, particularly in the global city of Istanbul, as well as exclusive suburbs. These sites became the basis for the emergence of new identities centered on new age or youth subcultures and new localized social categories such as street children. The rise in educational attendance and age of marriage, coupled with high unemployment, have led to the extension of youth as a life stage—without, however, reducing the economic dependence of young people on the older generation. Growing economic inequalities threaten to disenfranchise an increasingly urban and youthful population from the rights of citizenship. The Turkish state is increasingly unable to provide health and educational services or employment. The development of a more participatory public sphere in the long term is predicated upon the restructuring of a gerontocratic political system—most leaders of political parties in Turkey are in their seventies, while the majority of the population is below the age of twenty-five.

Although the family (and local and ethnic-religious networks) remains a central node of personal identity and social mobility, there is evidence of increased generational and familial conflict. Members of the generation known as the "post-1980 generation" tend to be represented in the media as selfish, individualistic consumers. This perceived individualism of young people seems to be about their hesitancy in linking their identities and lifestyles to an overarching national project. Young people, particularly high-school and university students, tend to be increasingly represented in new social movements and alternative (including virtual) forms of political mobilization based on identity politics.

One example of the growing individualization of Turkish youth is the disproportionate participation of youth in new communication technologies. Internet cafés, found not only in large cities such as Istanbul and Ankara but also in other Turkish towns, make it possible for Turkish youth to communicate with one another as well as with other young people around the world. The Web site http://www.sozluk.sourtimes.org is an example of a forum in the form of a dictionary through which young people communicate with one another about current events.

A major event that showed that young people in Turkey were able to politically mobilize in new ways was the devastating earthquake of 1999. Following this earthquake in which thousands of people died, new civil organizations were created and manned by young people to help save lives and care for stricken families. This example suggests that young people in Turkey remain committed to notions of community, although these communities are multiple and diverse. Understanding Turkish youth at present necessitates attention to identity politics and transnational youth movements, possibly resulting in new definitions of youth and of youth activism.

See also Australia, Youth Activism in; Demographic Trends Affecting the World's Youth; Eastern Europe, Youth and Citizenship in; Europe, Comparing Youth Activism in; European Identity and Citizenship; Immigrant Youth in Europe—Turks in Germany; Immigrant Youth in the United States; India, Youth Activism in; Indonesia, Youth Activism in; Nigeria, Youth Activism in; Palestinian *Intifada*; Russia, Youth Activism in; Serbia, Youth Activism in (1990–2000); Soweto Youth Activism (South Africa); the State and Youth; Statute of the Child and Adolescent (Brazil); Tiananmen Square Massacre (1989); Transnational Identity; Transnational Youth Activism; United Nations, Youth Activism and; Xenophobia; Zapatista Rebellion (Mexico); Zionist Youth Organizations.

Recommended Reading

Arat, Yeşim (1997). "The Project of Modernity and Women in Turkey." In *Rethinking Modernity and National Identity in Turkey*, edited by Sibel Bozdoğan and Reşat Kasaba. Seattle: University of Washington Press, pp. 95–112.

Bozdoğan, Sibel, and Kasaba, Reşat, eds. (1997). *Rethinking Modernity and National Identity in Turkey*. Seattle: University of Washington Press.

Kaya, Ayhan (2000). "Ethnic Group Discourses and German-Turkish Youth." In *Redefining the Nation State and Citizen*, edited by Günay Göksu Özdoğan and Gül Tokay. Istanbul: Eren Press, pp. 233–251.

Mardin, Şerif (1988). "The Mobilization of Youth: Western and Eastern." In *Perspectives on Contemporary Youth*, edited by S. Kcuzynski, S. Eisenstadt, L., Boubakar, and L. Sarkar. Tokyo: United Nations University, pp. 235–248.

Mardin, Şerif (1977). "Youth and Violence in Turkey." *International Journal of Social Science*, 29 (2): 251–289.

Neyzi, Leyla (August 2001). "Object or Subject? The Paradox of 'Youth' in Turkey." *International Journal of Middle East Studies*, 33 (3): 411–432.

Leyla Neyzi

Turkish Immigrants in Germany. *See* Immigrant Youth in Europe—Turks in Germany.

U

United Nations, Youth Activism and. Youth activism at the United Nations can be defined as concerted efforts by youth organizations, formal networks, and informal structures that intend to influence the decision-making process involving youth policy at the United Nations. For many years the United Nations (UN) has regarded young people as an important group in any country's social and economic development. It has generally recognized that young people can be instrumental in bringing about peaceful change, peace, security, and development, issues at the heart of the mandate of the United Nations from its very establishment. It should be noted that to avoid confusion on the term the United Nations General Assembly agreed to define the term "youth" as all persons between fifteen and twenty-four years of age, although it was also recognized that many UN member-states have their own national definitions based on the cultural, economic, religious, and social backgrounds of each country. The main purpose of this agreement was to make optimum use of existing demographic data that had been used by the United Nations since the 1960s. This definition would provide an easy common ground for comparative work to be done internationally.

For present purposes "youth" and "young people" are used interchangeably. To avoid further complications, terms often used in UN deliberations—especially "children" (defined in the UN Convention of the Rights of the Child as those below eighteen years of age) but also "adolescents" (those between ten and nineteen) or "young adults" (nineteen and above, sometimes up to age thirty)—will not be used.

Decision-making at the United Nations happens almost exclusively through the General Assembly, which has the ultimate authority over important issues, such as the appointment of the Secretary-General, the composition and election of members of the Security Council, and other matters. The General Assembly consists exclusively of the member-states of the United Nations. The role of nongovernmental organizations (NGOs) and thus of youth organizations, while being increasingly promoted in efforts to reform the decision-making processes at the United Nations, is therefore limited. The General Assembly also sets, through various subsidiary commissions, committees, and other bodies, many other decisions that affect the daily operational work of the United Nations in the areas of peacekeeping, peacemaking, and economic and social development. It is in this latter field that youth activism has been most influential, although youth groupings and caucuses have had influence in some of the UN conferences on sustainable development (Rio de Janeiro 1992 and Johannesburg 2002), racism (Durban 2001), and information and communication technology (Geneva 2004).

Many historic episodes demonstrate that young people have played instrumental and crucial roles in the establishment of spontaneous and informal movements that have brought about regime change, quite often as part of decolonization movements in the 1950s and 1960s, and possibly also in the dissolution of the former Soviet Union. Thus, youth form an important part of increasingly globalized social movements, which make international claims on the basis of national or local concerns.

Youth activism has existed throughout history. Young people have stood at the forefront of many political and religious movements and revolutions. The rights of students to education, freedom of thought, speech, association, assembly, and travel were formally recognized and spread throughout Europe during the medieval period. During the latter half of the nineteenth century and the beginning of the twentieth century, many national, regional, and international student movements were formed to both promote and protect the rights of students. The first international student organizations stem from that period. This is also the time when the more youth-service-oriented organizations, such as the YMCA, YWCA, and scout movement, were established. Together with political and religion-oriented youth organizations, these groups were present at the first World Youth Congress, organized in 1936 in Geneva to involve youth in the work of the League of Nations, the predecessor of the current United Nations.

The traditional youth-service organizations, including the Red Cross and Red Crescent societies, are still present at United Nations meetings today, representing youth from all parts of the world. These organizations became progressively less youth driven and youth led as compared to newer organizations of a more activist and political nature, which were active in the 1960s and 1970s. Prominent organizations in this period were the World Federation of Democratic Youth (WFDY), established in 1945 and supported actively by Communist regimes, and the Western-oriented World Assembly of Youth (WAY), established in 1948. Other groups included the International Union of Students (IUS) and the International Union of Socialist Youth (IUSY). The end of the cold war resulted in an erosion of the number and membership of those organizations in the early 1990s and subsequently, their influence on policymaking at the United Nations.

Since then, a new grouping of regional clusters of national youth and student organizations has emerged in almost all parts of the world. Examples include the European Youth Forum, a grouping of some one hundred national youth councils and international NGOs based in Europe, heavily sponsored by the Council of Europe and the European Union, as well as the Federation of Latin American Youth (known as FLAJ per its Spanish acronym) and other groups. The current group of international youth organizations that are involved with the work of the United Nations represents a mix of organizations with diverse ideological and developmental objectives. The only commonality with the older and more established organizations appears to be their ability to adjust their objectives to the political climate and changing needs of their constituents (i.e., young people).

Although the influence of nongovernmental organizations has increased over time, and youth participation is nowadays one of the core principles of the United Nations, young people very often feel frustrated by their limited capacity to exert real influence in decision-making processes. Many reasons can be cited to explain this sentiment—some from within the youth movement itself, others caused by the cultures and structures of the United Nations and by the lack of support from other stakeholders.

First, young people are one of the many voices within the United Nations where, due to a coming together of all different world opinions, decisions are difficult to reach and are often avoided. Influencing these processes is extremely difficult and requires a strong, unified voice. Second, young people are not a homogenous group with necessarily common interests, compared to other groups like the women's movement and movements of people with disabilities. The diverse landscape of problems, opinions, interests, and beliefs hampers the emergence of a strong, unified voice among young people and a global youth movement. A lack of decisiveness, caused by internal conflicts about the envisaged outcomes, often frustrates the success of youth caucuses at international meetings.

Third, although youth participation is widely accepted, young people are not always taken seriously by adult parties, nor is a mechanism always in place to incorporate their findings. There are many levels of youth participation on a scale between tokenism and being equal partners in decision-making. With the scale tipping to tokenism in many initiatives, one can question the motives of some institutions in involving youth.

Fourth, participation within the UN system requires that youth delegates represent a certain number of young people. They have to represent an organization with ample grassroots support to be granted consultative status in international meetings. With a decrease in membership-based youth organizations in many parts of the world, this is increasingly difficult. Also, not all governments support the establishment of large and opinionated youth organizations in their countries.

Fifth, the culture of many intergovernmental meetings at the United Nations is one of extensive documents in difficult prose, long meetings, and complicated decision-making structures with a highly political and diplomatic character. It takes time and skills to become able to contribute and actively take part in the negotiation processes, even when access to this process has been provided. Indeed, despite the fact that many youth organizations have obtained the consultative status required for participation in UN meetings, very few actually make use of that right. Leaders of youth organizations normally only serve their organizations for short periods, and not many have the chance to become sufficiently familiar with the UN system and its workings. Thus, many opportunities for participation in some of the events at the United Nations pass by.

Finally, participation on an international level requires access to resources, such as money, computer facilities, and visas to enter other countries. Not all governments are able or willing to support young people with these resources. This may be one of the reasons that the international youth activist scene has historically been dominated by the European and North American youth and their organizations.

Although youth advocacy within the United Nations has certainly made a positive impact, the involvement of youth organizations in the conferences and events of the United Nations has been mixed. While some conferences had facilitated a voice for youth through the provision of youth-specific or youth-only caucuses or forums, other events have been marked by the absence of participation by young people, either as a result of a lack of awareness among youth or as a result of a lack of perceived benefit from the respective youth organization.

The United Nations' purposes of peace, development, and democracy, set forth in its charter, have always laid the foundation for discussions on youth-related topics within the UN context. While in the decades of the cold war, peace was the most discussed theme connected to youth policy, since the 1980s participation and development have become increasingly important themes.

The first resolution of the General Assembly on youth dates from 1960 and encourages the education of young people about the United Nations' ideals of peace, mutual respect, and understanding. In 1965 the first youth declaration emphasized these ideals. Neither the resolution and declaration mention youth participation, but they see young people and their organizations as beneficiaries of United Nations' policies and as the messengers and implementers of its policy: "National and international associations of young people should be encouraged to promote the purposes of the United Nations."

Influenced by the worldwide student riots in the late 1960s, the General Assembly shifted its focus toward a more developmental perspective on youth issues. A small unit in the UN Secretariat, called the "youth unit" (currently Programme on Youth), was established to assist the Secretary-General in developing these policies. New subjects related to youth development were discussed, such as housing, health, drug abuse, social services, employment, and participation in national development and international cooperation. Governments were encouraged to design national youth policy plans and to include youth and youth organizations in their preparation and implementation. In 1972 the General Assembly adopted a resolution on channels of communication with youth and international youth organizations. It requested the Secretary-General evaluate the existing United Nations' programs and projects in order to enable youth to participate fully at appropriate levels of policy formulation and in the implementation and evaluation of projects.

A key goal of the youth movement in the 1960s and 1970s was ultimately achieved in 1990 with the adoption of the Convention for the Rights of the Child. This convention, now ratified by almost all countries in the world, states in its Article 12 that each child has the right to express his opinion on matters concerning him. Another result was achieved somewhat earlier in 1985 with the celebration of International Youth Year around the themes of participation, development, and peace. The International Youth Year of 1985, proclaimed by the United Nations, laid the foundation for social and political thinking on youth matters, resulting in the development of a global youth policy drafted as the "World Programme of Action for Youth to the Year 2000 and Beyond" (WPAY), which was adopted by the General Assembly in 1995. The WPAY described ten priority areas for youth development, of which participation in decision-making was one (the others are poverty, education, employment, health, environment, drugs, juvenile delinquency, leisure, and gender). Youth were regarded not only as the subjects of development but as very important assets in

achieving development. Within a changing world, the issues young people deal with change as well.

In 2003 five new emerging topics were added to this agenda by the UN Secretariat, including globalization, information and communication technologies, HIV/AIDS, youth in armed conflict, and intergenerational relations. The fifteen priority areas are due to be reviewed by the General Assembly in 2005.

The General Assembly has not been the only UN platform to adopt resolutions on youth rights and responsibilities. Various UN bodies and agencies—the UN Commission on Human Rights (UNHCR); International Labor Organization (ILO); UN Educational, Scientific, and Cultural Organization (UNESCO); World Health Organization (WHO); the various UN regional commissions; and others—adopted a diverse range of international instruments and resolutions on youth-related topics. Increasingly, youth participation is incorporated as a reference point in all bodies and agencies from UNICEF to the World Bank. Via Web sites, interactive forums, panels, and global meetings and as youth delegates in official meetings, young people are involved in the formulation, implementation, and review of youth development policy.

The most direct form of youth participation at the United Nations has been through the inclusion of youth representatives in a country's official delegation to the United Nations General Assembly. The General Assembly has recommended since 1981 that member-states include a youth representative in their delegations.

Youth representatives usually participate at General Assembly meetings in New York, which are held for at least two weeks around mid-September through the first half of November. The role of a youth representative varies depending on priorities of member-state delegations. Many youth representatives are responsible for delivering a statement to the Third Committee, a subsidiary of the General Assembly that deals with social, humanitarian, and cultural issues. Not many countries have included a youth delegate, and the contribution that he or she makes varies, depending on the preparation of the delegate and the support by his or her diplomatic mission to the United Nations.

To obtain recognition as a nongovernmental organization with the United Nations a subsidiary body, the Economic and Social Council (ECOSOC), needs to accord an official consultative status. Consultative status with ECOSOC for NGOs is based upon the recommendation of an intergovernmental committee on nongovernmental organizations that is composed of nineteen member-states and meets annually. International, regional, and national youth and student organizations in consultative status with the United Nations (ECOSOC) are able to make oral statements and submit written statements on items on the agenda of each session. Organizations such as the International Union of Students (IUS) and World Student Christian Federation (WSCF) have often used such opportunities to contribute directly to such discussions at meetings of the Commission on Human Rights and its subcommission on the prevention of discrimination and protection of minorities.

ECOSOC is the only UN body that has a continuing mechanism to accredit NGOs with consultative status. ECOSOC status does not result in recognition by the General Assembly, since the latter only consists of member-states. However, other UN bodies or international meetings that facilitate NGO participation often make use of the list of accredited NGOs by ECOSOC to determine eligibility for participation.

Another format has been the organization of specific youth-related events at or around major conferences of the United Nations. In 1970 the World Youth Assembly gathered as part of the celebration of the twenty-fifth anniversary of the United Nations to discuss the world's ills. Participants under twenty-five years of age were selected by the UN member-states and international youth and student organizations to discuss world

peace, development, education, and the environment. The International Planning Committee incorporated thirteen international youth and student organizations. Over 650 participants attended. Their message called, among other things, for peace, protection of human rights, and recognition of the right of young people to have an active role in the activities of the United Nations. They also proposed to convene a world youth assembly biennially and on a more democratic basis. Their message was noted but not adopted by the General Assembly. In 1971 a UN Symposium on the Participation of Youth in the Second Development Decade was held in Geneva. The purpose of the meeting was to outline practical means for involving youth in the solution of development problems at the local, national, and international levels and to provide guidelines for procedures whereby young people can be involved with development activities.

On various occasions youth's NGOs expressed their dissatisfaction with the organization of these events as not being democratic enough and not being representative of all regions of the world. They expressed disappointment that the outcome document was not accepted by the General Assembly. Four sessions of the World Youth Forum of the UN system (in 1991 and 1996 in Vienna, Austria; in 1998 in Braga, Portugal; and in 2001 in Dakar, Senegal) suffered to some extent from the same pitfalls. In an evaluation of the fourth session of the World Youth Forum, the United Nations Secretariat recommended to the General Assembly that, to address those concerns, future World Youth Forums should only be held if explicitly requested by the General Assembly. In this way, the concerns of young people expressed at these events would take on more weight in the official deliberations of the United Nations. Despite this issue, many large-scale forums for youth organizations have been held around many large UN conferences in the 1990s.

On the basis of the difficult experiences encountered to make youth participation in the decision-making processes of the United Nations a reality, most recently an attempt has been made to involve young people in the evaluation of national youth policies that stem from, or relate to, internationally agreed upon targets. Since resolutions and declarations of the General Assembly are not binding, advocacy for youth issues on a national level is critical. The United Nations Programme on Youth developed a toolkit, called "Making Commitments Matter, a Toolkit to Evaluate National Youth Policy." The booklet intends to support young people in the evaluation of their national youth policy along the standards agreed upon in the World Programme of Action for Youth to the Year 2000 and Beyond (WPAY). The aims are to make the goals of the WPAY known among young people, to support their efforts at the government level to achieve those goals, and to gather input for the two General Assembly meetings in 2005 when the WPAY will be reviewed. It is hoped that their involvement at the national level, which could be more effective than at the international level, will result in increased opportunities for youth to create the very policies that affect them.

At the national level various efforts are being made to include young people in decisions related to UN activities. One recent example of work involving young people directly in the design and implementation of development projects is the effort to combat the spread of HIV/AIDS, which has rapidly become a very pressing youth problem with an estimated 6,000 infections among young people occurring every day. In the area of youth employment, UN country teams, lead by the ILO, have involved youth groups in many countries by seeking their input into addressing school-to-work transitions, youth entrepreneurship, and equal opportunities for young women and men in the labor market.

In many cases UN country offices have set up consultative groups of youth organizations that are given an opportunity to comment and take part in the program planning of the UN country teams. The World Bank in 2004 set up an ambitious program—Youth Voices @ the Bank—that aims to involve young people in the daily operations of the institution and give a fresh perspective on its operations and interventions aimed at poverty alleviation. These efforts, while certainly beneficial for the quality of the UN interventions for and with young people, are somewhat distinct from activism. These country-level efforts tend to focus on youth participation through joint project implementation rather than youth activism that aims to change the policies of the national government.

See also Australia, Youth Activism in; Child Labor; Child Soldiers; Demographic Trends Affecting the World's Youth; Eastern Europe, Youth and Citizenship in; Europe, Comparing Youth Activism in; European Identity and Citizenship; Immigrant Youth in Europe—Turks in Germany; Immigrant Youth in the United States; India, Youth Activism in; Indonesia, Youth Activism in; Nigeria, Youth Activism in; Palestinian *Intifada*; Rights of Participation of Children and Youth; Russia, Youth Activism in; Serbia, Youth Activism in (1990–2000); Soweto Youth Activism (South Africa); State and Youth, The; Statute of the Child and Adolescent (Brazil); Tiananmen Square Massacre (1989); Transnational Identity; Transnational Youth Activism; Turkey, Youth Activism in; Xenophobia; Zapatista Rebellion (Mexico); Zionist Youth Organizations.

Recommended Reading

Angel, William D. (1995). *The International Law of Youth Rights*. Dordrecht: Martinus Nijhoff Publishers.

United Nations (2003). *World Youth Report 2003*. New York: United Nations, DESA.

United Nations Programme on Youth. *Navigating International Meetings: A Pocketbook Guide to Effective Youth Participation*. See http://www.un.org/esa/socdev/unyin/library/index.html.

Charlotte van Hees and Joop Theunissen

United Students Against Sweatshops (USAS). The United Students Against Sweatshops (USAS) was formed in 1997 to protest the conditions under which college-logo apparel was being produced. Very simply stated, students in the United States devised a plan to turn their college bookstores into "conscientious consumers." Starting in the mid-1990s student activists at scores of campuses picked out a few representative samples from the T-shirts and hats on offer at their bookstores and asked school officials what they knew about the conditions under which those articles of clothing were being produced. Whereas this was not on the radar screen of many college presidents, it was an issue that the students knew and cared about. Soon, student newspaper reporters were tapping into the vast literature available from "sweatshop-research" NGOs and tracking down the reports about the Dominican Republic, Indonesia, or other countries identified on the labels of clothes sold at their college bookstores. It should be noted that the Federal Trade Commission (FTC) requires that apparel be labeled with the country of origin where the items were produced.

In less than a decade college students in the United States have cobbled together the most formidable challenge to businesses operating in the international sportswear-producing industry. Using a combination of patient goal-setting, Internet organizing, old-fashioned protest tactics, and shrewd negotiating skills, they have begun to exercise influence over an industry that has maximized profits by minimizing the wages and benefits of garment workers, particularly those in developing countries. In 2002 the Worker Rights Consortium (WRC) was launched by USAS to conduct original research and devise solidarity strategies with garment workers around the globe. The WRC has undertaken in-depth studies in countries where labor-rights campaigning has proven to be quite dangerous.

While labor practices monitoring reports are the stock-in-trade of a plethora of new "corporate social responsibility" consultants, the WRC's reports have actually led to collective bargaining gains in several factories producing for the collegiate-licensed market. The story behind the students' dedication and perseverance is inspiring. But more importantly, the strategies used may be replicable, as groups all over the globe seek to campaign in partnerships that cross borders.

Starting in the mid-1980s, the great majority of antisweatshop campaigners *outside* the student community had rejected the traditional pressure technique of boycotting target companies, due to a boycott's deleterious impact on workers—most of whom were in the developing world and desperate for any type of employment. With this in mind the students decided to agitate for their school administrators to adopt codes of acceptable working conditions in factories producing college-logo apparel—a $2.5 billion segment of the clothing industry. After negotiations—often lasting over a year—many universities concluded agreements with USAS chapters. Then the activists shrewdly upped the ante by mounting campaigns for the disclosure of factory locations.

When university administrators asked bookstore managers to pass this demand on to suppliers, they met with resistance. In less than a year, however, major producers of college-logo products had acceded, and the USAS database contained over 4,000 factory names and addresses. This was the point at which USAS activists decided that they needed to get people into the field in order to measure compliance with the agreed-upon codes of conduct. In the yearlong process of consensus-building prior to launching the Worker Rights Consortium, students held fast to a key principle of rejecting apparel-company (i.e., the corporations themselves) participation in the WRC. Knowing that many schools' administrators would refuse to sign on without businesses being represented did not sway the overwhelming majority of activists.

Throughout the late 1990s, the USAS organizers learned important tactical and organizing skills. They also lent meaningful support to other progressive campus groups. For example, many USAS chapters became deeply involved in collective bargaining battles for campus clerical staff, food-service personnel, and janitors. In the broader U.S. community, too, USAS members and leaders had an impact on campaigns to reform practices of the international financial institutions (i.e., the World Bank and International Monetary Fund) and for fairer trade agreements. Recently, student activists campaigning for responsible disposal of computers with toxic components and for responsible endowment investments (in February 2004 at the University of Arizona and Duke University, respectively) cited USAS activism as inspiring them.

It is in the global civil-society-development arena, however, where the USAS has had the most significant impact. In countries such as Indonesia, the Dominican Republic, and Bangladesh, independent trade unions are calling for more pluralistic political structures willing to defend workers against rapacious garment contractors. Nobel laureate Joseph Stiglitz, while he was still chief economist at the World Bank, delivered a speech outlining the importance of independent trade unions in fighting corruption and the concentration of power in authoritarian developing countries.

Other economists have argued that collective bargaining and demands for higher minimum wages could hurt workers since apparel jobs would just move to other low-wage countries if bosses were forced to comply with codes of conduct and pay higher wages. This prediction must be assessed in light of what took place in Indonesia. Due to the pressure generated by local strikes and international media attention, the Indonesian minimum wage for factory workers went up over 300 percent (from $.86 to $2.47 a day in the main export zone) during the period 1989–1996. During the same period the number of workers producing Nike footwear and apparel in Indonesian contract factories increased from 18,000 to over 100,000.

The issue of jobs that pay a living wage is a particular problem in poor countries but also one that is ideally suited for educating those in the developed world about global capital and the role consumers can play in holding multinational corporations accountable. Labor laws, even those outlined in the International Labor Organization (ILO) conventions, often are not enforced in developing countries. In large measure this is due to the fact that poor countries are desperate for foreign investments.

Poor countries want to be as hospitable as possible to foreign investment and granting workers meaningful trade-union rights and enforcing factory health and safety regulations are known to keep investors away. It is not uncommon for multinationals to pull out of a particular country and relocate elsewhere because they disapprove of the political- or industrial-relations conditions. Even in developed countries like Italy and the United States, a large proportion of apparel production is allowed to operate with almost no government oversight. This leads to the recruitment of illegal workers, more readily exploited than resident workers.

The USAS is battling what Joseph Nye, former dean of Harvard University's Kennedy School of Government, has called the "de facto governance" of transnational corporations and offshore fund managers operating in developing countries. The Worker Rights Consortium has leverage because of the buying power of the college bookstores; when student-led research detects genuine, independent trade-union action being subverted by garment contractors, real pressure is brought to bear. This leverage is what is missing from other "code of conduct" and monitoring schemes, such as the United Nations' Global Compact, the Nike- and GAP-funded Global Alliance, or the Fair Labor Association (FLA).

In 2001, for example, the Global Alliance released a report based on a survey of 4,000 contract workers producing Nike shoes and apparel in Indonesia. While hundreds of young women complained to surveyors about sexual harassment, nothing was paid in compensation by Nike or the company's contractors. Contrast this with (far fewer) Mitsubishi workers voicing similar complaints in a factory near Chicago: the Japanese firm was made to pay $9.5 million to the women who suffered the harassment and $34 million to the U.S. Equal Employment Opportunity Commission (EEOC). The FLA, for its part, has a skimpy track record to assess, despite the fact that its precursor organization, the Apparel Industry Partnership, began planning for monitoring operations over seven years ago. The first field report from the FLA in spring 2003 met with harsh criticism. Since over 170 colleges and universities have been paying dues to the FLA, student activists have a deep-seated interest in whether the FLA methodology provides apparel companies with a credible fair-labor-practices certification.

Another disturbing aspect of the proliferation of new schemes for "issue networks" or dubious code/monitoring operations is that they relieve governments of the responsibility for protecting workers' right to organize and independent unions' right to collectively bargain. This is a failure of the richest nations, as well as those poor nations that presently attract the most rapacious contractors. Some people contend that the problem of sweatshops would go away if nations would join with nongovernmental groups such as the International Labor Organization because the ILO's conventions specify practices that protect workers' rights. However, since the ILO is a tripartite organization (business, trade unions, and governments), it is a fair assessment that the world's powerful governments place an extremely low priority on protecting workers' rights. Rich nations are too busy pursuing business, security, and political agendas with authoritarian regimes, thus subverting the ILO's workers' rights rule-enforcing authority.

Even after progressive forces in the United States won the legislative battle for getting workers' rights protections into the U.S. trade law (the generalized system of preferences, known as the GSP), successive administrations refused to punish recalcitrant nations. A representative example of the fecklessness of U.S. trade authorities was the widely reported pledge by the Suharto government in Indonesia to stop military and police units from breaking up strikes—responding to the threat of losing GSP benefits in 1995. According to the Jakarta-based Legal Aid Institute, protesting workers experienced no change whatsoever. Further, the military-dominated government jailed prominent independent union activists shortly after signing the accord with Clinton administration officials. It is left to groups like the USAS, then, to press ahead with what Andrew Hurrell calls "norm creation": "... either as lobbyists within individual states or as participants directly within international regimes and institutions."

Where some see norm creation, others assail the students as no more than shock troops in a union-led assault on free trade. The students, however, came upon this workers' rights activism largely on their own. The AFL-CIO did begin the Union Summer program in 1996 as an educational internship to develop skills useful for union organizing drives and other campaigns for workers' rights and social justice, but this activity took the place of what had been a larger financial commitment to student/labor cooperation that was operated along the lines of a youth auxiliary with lines of authority running to the AFL-CIO's department of organization and field services at the federation headquarters. The Union Summer program has attracted over 3,000 young people, not all college activists, and generally assigns the interns to ongoing organizing campaigns or educational activities in a dozen locations. More recently, the U.S. unions' international arm, the American Center for International Labor Solidarity (ACILS), has begun an internship that sends several students abroad each summer to work with trade-union training programs in developing countries.

An examination of the students' methodology shows that their skills in civic-engagement techniques are both somewhat ad hoc and also rather sophisticated. To understand more clearly we must look at the news media, that is, the "new" news media, which is not corporate-controlled. The students' development of an "alternative news center" holds the key to furthering the gains made recently by the USAS (through the WRC) and may help like-minded groups achieve similar victories. For example, some communities have recently enacted "selective purchase" laws to force an examination into the production practices behind public workers' uniforms and other apparel bought with taxpayer dollars.

For student activists the media that matters the most are the e-mail Listservs (also called discussion lists). Through the various USAS Listservs—some have a light volume while others may be tailored to specific interests—activists stay connected with struggles at other schools, learn about the WRC's research, and get information from other groups in the antisweatshop movement. The Listserv is also very important as a consensus-building mechanism. Within the USAS, democratic decision-making is almost a fetish—plodding and somewhat painful to experience firsthand. But I believe it is one of the keys to the group's effective projection of power in the global economy. This type of decision-making is also rather unique in the community of NGOs, whose leaders, more often than not, press ahead with the "vision" of one dominant person, rarely delving into introspection any deeper than that which analyzes tactics.

The creation of a communication network and alternative center for news in the area of sweatshop garment production became extremely important for the students' campaign, due to the public relations blitz undertaken by the key target firms, such as Nike. The shoemaker hired political consultants—a so-called "corporate responsibility" team to provide university administrators with voluminous reports that were often used to rebut students' allegations of continuing worker abuse, their veracity later challenged in court with lawsuits ultimately settled out of court.

The USAS, demanding real change, has not been satisfied with mere pledges of reform, accompanied—as they usually are—by thick, slick, "corporate responsibility" reports. They are well aware that the task before them includes a lot of "grunt work"—out there in the trenches in industrial areas from Chittagong, Bangladesh, to Buffalo, New York. They know that without an awareness of the problem, it will just get worse.

The greatest challenge facing activists of the USAS, then, is to fight the usual apathy and poor media on campus. In so doing they bring international affairs to the attention of the campus community. In a broader sense the students have found a way to popularize a form of global citizenship through attention to the purchasing practices of the college or university. This is an important contribution, particularly when the United States finds itself with such a huge influence in world affairs but is becoming ever more unilateralist. Only through informed engagement of the type that the USAS practices can Americans demand that elected leaders be more proactive in building a better world.

Sometimes protest movements are harbingers of a new kind of political involvement. This can be observed in the antislavery campaign in nineteenth-century England where what Niall Ferguson called "a new generation of grassroots activists" mounted "one of the first great extra-Parliamentary agitations." Using the tactics of antislavery lapel badges, high-profile campaign endorsers and mass petition-signing, activists got the trade abolished in 1807. Similarly, the antiapartheid movement devised a strategy whereby corporations would be directly confronted with the demand to cut ties with the odious South African regime. While but a few corporations actually complied, the publicity generated by protestors' demands had a snowball effect: thousands of small groups—a great number being campus-based, examining the shareholdings of college endowments—joined the struggle. The United Students Against Sweatshops is a contemporary example of young activists drawing public attention to the connections between university-logo apparel and the working conditions of the people whose labor goes into producing that apparel. By drawing those connections it enables students and alumni of universities to insist that their alma maters live up to the values they believe in and insist that the corporations who manufacture university apparel guarantee decent wages and working conditions to their employees.

See also Advocacy; Child Labor; Global Justice Activism; Labor Movement; Political Consumerism; Student Action with Farmworkers (SAF); Student Political Activism; Transnational Youth Activism.

Recommended Reading

Featherstone, L. (2002). *Students Against Sweatshops.* New York: Verso.
Hurrell, A. (2001). "Global Inequality and International Institutions." In *Global Justice*, edited by T. Pogge Malden, MA: Blackwell.
Keck, M. E., and Sikkink, K. (1999). *Activists beyond Borders: Advocacy Networks in International Politics.* Ithaca, NY: Cornell University Press.
Lantigua, J. (2003). "Where Was Your Cap Made?" New York: Progressive Media Project. See http://www.nosweat.org.uk/article.php?sid=496.
Miller, J. (2003). "Why Economists Are Wrong about Sweatshops and the Antisweatshop Movement." *Challenge*, 46 (1): 93–122.
Ross, A. (2004). *Low Pay, High Profile: The Global Push for Fair Labor.* New York: New Press.

Jeff Ballinger

Urban Communities, Youth Programming in. Urban youth programs are typically envisioned as those extracurricular activities within inner-city communities that provide opportunities for youth out of school. While these venues serve a major purpose in youth development, they often lack the total structure needed for young people to reach their full potential. This entry describes essentials necessary for youth programs in urban areas to achieve positive youth development. The author addresses the societal issues often encountered by urban youth and the challenges urban programs face when attempting to provide high-quality academic, civic, and social opportunities that aid in personal and professional growth.

As with all localities, urban communities have a need for thriving youth programs. Although rural areas also face crime, poverty, and various other issues that are detrimental to young people, urban neighborhoods have experienced such obstacles at a much higher rate. The threat of negative community factors generates problems that place local youth at risk, leading to engagement in undesirable behaviors. Research has shown that young people with access to local resources, including structured out-of-school time, can and will engage in lower levels of negative behaviors, thus enhancing positive development. Now is the time to implement programs that will provide urban youth with alternatives that perpetuate positive development and reduce conditions that encourage high-risk behavior.

Although it is apparent that successful youth programs can thrive within schools during regular school hours, many occur after four p.m. or during summer months. Communities around the country have invested time and money in promoting a structured out-of-school agenda for youth. Much of the enthusiasm has emerged due to recent funding opportunities, which in turn stem from an extensive amount of research on the benefits of after-school programs. Studies on resiliency have also presented approaches and models that provide intervention strategies for decreasing risk factors among youth, often noting that resources such as quality youth program, can offset the negative effects of adversity often associated with neglected urban communities. Ensuring accessibility to safe, youth-friendly places throughout the day helps to expose those young people who would be vulnerable to negative behavior to more consistent, productive forms of youth engagement.

Today's youth are not to be placed on "autopilot" and allowed to grow up as best they know how. Ironically, this seems to be the norm for some who believe that young people are to experience pitfalls that will enable them to learn from grave mistakes. This imposes a false sense that youth must encounter hardships as a prerequisite to adulthood. Many urban communities are often plagued with what has been described as "new urban poverty." These communities with higher concentrations of poor families and joblessness tend to isolate young people from acquiring the opportunities that are necessary for success. Researchers have reported that urban areas often lack economic, social, and political factors, as well as the quality and variety of programs that are frequently found among their suburban neighbors. Due to fewer opportunities (other than school activities such as sports) for urban youth, many pursue their own options, which oftentimes are not as productive.

Adolescents in particular are at a point of self-actualization, where they strongly desire independence. Moreover, it is at this critical stage where they are in most need of positive experiences through community connectedness (or strong ties among residents) and with adult allies in order to experience a smooth transition into adulthood. In addition to teachers and parents, youth require relationships with other adults who can serve as positive role models. Young people partnering with adults in communities can also serve as a source for building social networks as a means not only to experience positive levels of growth but also to allow youth to be fully engaged in their own developmental process. Like many of the young people in

rural and suburban areas who are often afforded a chance to partake in hands-on approaches to community involvement, urban youth must also encounter opportunities to participate as contributors in their neighborhoods. Crafting this ideal environment (or notion of community youth development) in which these relationships may naturally occur begins within local youth programs where caring adults can assist youth in developing critical life skills.

Most urban areas are endowed with a number of youth organizations that offer a host of activities and projects. However, a majority are geared toward athletic programs that are often unmonitored with minimum evidence of strong outcomes. Many of the larger urban programs take on a narrow, single-outcome focus, such as a concentration on sports or academics. Although these programs serve a meaningful purpose, a vast majority lack the financial resources needed to make a lasting impact through a broader range of activities. With budgets being trimmed, funding remains an issue for most programs that are already operating with limited capital. Youth program directors in urban settings must possess the ability not only to provide quality opportunities but be creative in obtaining adequate funding. A measure of success for urban programs should not only focus on program content but also be able to demonstrate self-sufficiency.

As more nonprofit and government agencies are seeking grant funding, there is also an increase in competition between similar programs. As a result, youth-serving organizations in urban communities face difficulty in promoting projects where several schools and community-based organizations are developing programs with the same objectives. Despite the challenge of striving to be recognized for a unique role in serving youth, one strategy for urban programs should include focusing on achieving goals that meet the needs of all young people in communities. Organizations are often found competing with other groups for funding to assist the same target audience. It is not ideal to make exhaustive and often hasty efforts to outperform other local groups. No one organization can be all things to all people. If one youth program is succeeding at mobilizing youth in one neighborhood, there should also be similar opportunities available to high-risk youth in adjacent communities. Only when programming efforts take on an all-inclusive approach to positively affecting young lives is the impact of community youth development maximized. Communities are often strengthened through collaborations, which in turn can offer experiences that are advantageous for all children, youth, and their families.

Many rural and suburban areas often have a strong sense of community connectedness that produces willingness for residents to want to volunteer. These close ties associated with small neighborhoods are often absent in large metropolitan areas. Because of the number of adults with more demanding lifestyles (e.g., work, professional responsibilities, family obligations) urban youth programs are faced with the difficulty of recruiting committed people. One reason, in part, may be due to so many programs competing for the same volunteers, as well as the same participants. Smaller communities have historically been able to garner support because of more close-knit neighborhoods where "everybody knows everybody." Since most rural and suburban residents are familiar and connected with many of the existing local programs and activities, they are more flexible and willing to serve in various capacities (to volunteer as mentors, tutors, coaches, facilitators). Urban programs, although often focusing primarily on physical and academic-skill development, are plentiful yet scattered, forcing adult volunteers to pick and choose between only a few activities. Most often they become involved with those that are closest to their homes and supported by those organizations and institutions with which they are affiliated (local clubs, churches, schools).

At times their choices may neglect those programs "across town" where youth with far fewer resources are in even more need of adult role models. Volunteers must be recruited from every source, for positive interactions with adults are by far one of the most important factors in a young person's life.

Urban programs should also capitalize on the fact that young people want to be associated with extracurricular activities that are enjoyed by their friends. Solidarity among peers has been proven to have a major influence on the lives of other youth. If energy is channeled to raise the levels of positive behavior among a small group of young people, then the possibility of creating a domino effect transpires. Creating programs that offer peer groups an opportunity for direct involvement in social, constructive activities increases the likelihood of positive, community youth development on a more extensive scale. Older adolescents often possess the skills needed to serve as very competent volunteers. While assisting younger youth, teens are also afforded the chance to experience the importance of giving back through civic engagement.

Youth programs have changed dramatically over the years. With so many diverse young people living in urban areas, now is the time to develop strategies that foster successful programs. Youth-service providers must execute action plans that focus on impacting the lives of urban youth by seeking out funding sources that are willing to invest in urban youth and form short- and long-term partnerships with other organizations. Several long-standing traditional youth organizations (4-H, for example) are collaborating and even revamping to address urban issues that affect youth. Scholars in the allied youth fields must conduct research studies that test the effectiveness of various types of programs. There must also be more evidence presented on concepts such as youth-adult partnerships to more closely examine the pros and cons of these efforts and the impact on communities. Many assumptions are evolving around the relevance of strengthening the social networks between youth and adults, but very few discoveries have been proclaimed. More research is also needed in these areas to assist youth workers with creating programs that are sustainable and effectively improving the lives of young people within cities—block by block.

See also 4-H.

Recommended Reading

Eccles, J., and Gootman, J. A., eds. (2002). *Community Programs to Promote Youth Development*. Washington, D.C.: National Academy Press.

Flanagan, C., Bowes, J., Jonsson, B., Csapo, B., and Sheblanova, E. (1998). "Ties That Bind: Correlates of Male and Female Adolescents' Civic Commitments in Seven Countries." *Journal of Social Issues*, 54 (3): 457–475.

Kempfer, K. L. (1999). "Factors and Processes Contributing to Resilience: The Resilience Framework." In *Resiliency and Development: Positive Life Adaptations*, edited by M. D. Glantz and J. L. Johnson. New York: Kluwer Academic, pp. 179–224.

Knop, N., Tannehill, D., and O'Sullivan, M. (September 2001). "Making a Difference for Urban Youth." *Journal of Physical Education, Research and Dance*, 72 (7): 39–44.

Littell, J., and Wynn, J. (1989). *The Availability and Use of Community Resources for Young Adolescents in an Inner-City and a Suburban Community*. Chicago: Chapin Hall Center for Children at the University of Chicago.

Masten, A. S. (March 2001). "Ordinary Magic: Resilience Processes in Development." *American Psychologist*, 56 (3): 227–238.

O'Donoghue, J. L., and Strobel, K. R. (November 2003). "Directivity and Freedom: The Role of Adults in Youth Civic Engagement." Research paper presented at the International Conference on Civic Education, New Orleans, LA.

Perkins, D. F., and Borden, L. M. (2003). "Positive Behaviors, Problem Behaviors and Resiliency in Adolescence." In *Handbook of Psychology*, Vol. 6, *Developmental Psychology*, volume edited by R. M. Lerner, M. A. Easterbrooks, and J. Mistry. New York: John Wiley and Sons, pp. 373–394.

Scales, P. C., Benson, P. L., Leffert, N., and Blyth, D. A. (2000). "Contribution of Developmental Assets to the Prediction of Thriving Among Adolescents." In *Applied Developmental Science*, edited by R. M. Lerner, C. B. Fisher, and R. A. Weinberg, 4 (1): 27–46.

Tolman, J., Pittman, K., Yohalem, N., Thomases, J., and Trammel, M. (2002). *Moving an Out-of-School Agenda: Lessons and Challenges Across Cities*. A publication of the Greater Resources for After-School Programming (GRASP) Project. Washington, D.C.: Forum for Youth Investment.

Werner, E., and Smith, R. (1992). *Overcoming the Odds: High Risk Children from Birth To Adulthood*. Ithaca, NY: Cornell University.

Wilson, W. J. (1997). *When Work Disappears: The World of the New Urban Poor*. New York: Knopf.

Kenneth R. Jones

USAS. *See* United Students Against Sweatshops (USAS).

V

Video. *See* Film/Video as a Tool for Youth Activism.

VISTA. *See* AmeriCorps.

Voice. It has become increasingly fashionable to link the idea of "voice" with terms such as "working from the bottom-up," "partnership," and "participation" to describe different forms of collaboration between young people and adults. As voice is reinterpreted in these different collaborative relationships and applied to an increasing range of issues, there is a danger that it becomes a "bandwagon" approach that loses much of its usefulness. Voice is now being used in a wide variety of projects and policies from advocacy to consumer rights and citizenship education. Work claiming to use the voice of young people is part of a general move toward social inclusion. In the United Kingdom it has become an established element of central and local government rhetoric, but as it gains in popular usage it becomes increasingly open to question and criticism. This is particularly so over the issue of whether the focus of working with the voice of young people should be on supporting young people to articulate their voice or directed at getting adults and professionals to listen and respond. Inevitably, at the heart of this debate are the questions relating to issues of power and how power intersects with and emerges through positions of age, social class, ethnicity, and gender, for example. The converse of having a voice is being silenced. This can happen in different ways. Sometimes another more powerful voice is positioned by others to speak for you. An example here would be the voice of the white researcher speaking on behalf of a minority community to which the researcher does not belong. Young people are silenced in this way and in many other ways, from being ignored to being stereotyped in such a way as to invalidate what they say. A key part of the discussions around voice is to examine and challenge the processes "silencing" different groups of young people.

The problem with voice is that it has become such a broadly used term that it is losing much of its specific meaning, particularly as it becomes disconnected from the different theoretical sources and critical praxis from which it originated. There are four common themes running through much of the literature about voice. The first theme is that it privileges experience over theory or training as the basis of the understanding of an individual or an issue or activity and the meaning given to it. This privileging of experience fundamentally relies on an "interior authenticity" which is hard to demonstrate. The second theme is that it favors excluded, silenced, or subordinate voices over dominant voices to initiate and guide change. This raises concern over the appropriateness of existing mechanisms to facilitate the voice of those already marginalized and ignored. The third theme is that voice is an inclusive idea that recognizes the proliferation of voices and the increasingly fragmented nature of people's experiences and hence their understanding. It is culturally specific with its validity arising from who is speaking, rather than the sanction of those listening. The fourth and last theme is that voice is linked to issues of activism, participation, and empowerment. Voice is often drawn into the debates around the level of participation of young people and how and if they are really empowered by the process.

Over recent years there has been a movement in communities, schools, young people's services, and universities to involve young people in carrying out their own research to influence the policies and practices that affect them. As there are numerous forms of research, so there are different types of voice. For some it is synonymous with people simply expressing their point of view on a subject. For others it is a much more involved act of participation in which people engage with the organizations, structures, services, and communities that shape their lives. To understand these links a crude typology of voice can be created although typologies such as this come with several health warnings to do with the consequences of categorization and labeling. On the positive side the usefulness of this typology is that it helps to make choices about the nature of the action young people wish to get involved in.

The first type of voice can be classified as the *authoritative voice*. At its best those listening take a voice to be authoritative because it is an honest, loud, clear, and inclusive voice. At its worst it is cynically given authority because it can be used to justify the decisions already made by those listening because it fits in with their agendas. This is a voice that its audience can often choose to use in the way it wants, mainly because of how it is presented. An example of this type of voice would be the consultations carried out by organizations with young people to get their views on a variety of issues. In the United Kingdom the "Real Deal Consultation" produced a powerful portrait of fourteen- to twenty-four-year-olds living at the "sharp end" of 1990s Britain by asking homeless and otherwise excluded youth about their views on governmental policies, youth issues, democracy, and social exclusion.

The second type of voice is a *critical voice*. A critical voice does not try to provide a clear basis for professional actions or decisions. Instead it attempts to challenge the existing basis and is often expressed by young people through "actions" and "words" as they try to influence the power relationships with adults, practitioners, and their peers. It is a persistent voice that develops through dialog and interaction. Action-research projects working with young people or conducted by young people often use this type of voice. An example here is a project carried out in the United Kingdom with a group of fourteen young men, called Seen But Not Heard, who had self-excluded or been excluded from school. These young men set out to change their school's approach to dealing with pupils like themselves at risk of exclusion. The young men worked as co-researchers with a university-based team, their teachers, and their youth workers to make a video targeted at the school management to tell them what it felt like to be excluded from their school. They felt their teachers found it easier for them not to be in school. They wanted to show their teachers that at times their teachers were as disrespectful to them as they were to their teachers, and they wanted to open up a dialog by showing it at a staff meeting. By doing this they felt it would help other younger students at the school.

The third type of voice is a *therapeutic voice*. This type of voice arises from an individual's own difficult experiences. Voicing these difficulties has a cathartic effect on the speaker and gives him or her the chance to support others through validating their experiences and showing ways of coping with the problems they face. Mentoring projects use this type of voice. There are several examples here, but one such project in the United Kingdom was set up by a small group of young people who had experienced different periods of homelessness throughout their lives. This group worked with a local social-services team to carry out a reconnaissance on the needs of care leavers. Having done this they used this information to make presentations and applications to funding bodies to set up a "drop-in" center with a peer-mentoring scheme. These bids were successful and they now run a "drop-in" center with continuing support from social workers. Through the mentoring approaches they have developed they provide ongoing support to other young people who are experiencing similar problems to themselves.

Each type of voice reflects a different process of articulation and intended outcome so this typology is useful when working with young people because it helps them to make decisions about what kind or kinds of their voice they want to articulate. It also gives them an understanding of the sorts of activities they could be drawn into and most importantly, the types of voice that may help them achieve the changes they desire. It also draws attention to the criticisms they will expose themselves to as they set out to influence others. With each type of voice comes a set of assumptions that can be broadly discussed in four main areas. If each of these assumptions is looked at more critically, alternative arguments and perspectives reveal how these assumptions can be challenged, and this is key to the debate about the worth of voice as a concept.

The first assumption is that young people are in the best position to talk about being young. The assumption is that the views of young people are significant because of the immediacy of their experiences. This assumption is probably the most fundamental assumption made about the voice of young people. We should listen to it because it is the voice of experience. Only young people can really know how it is to be a young person at this particular time, in a particular community, as a member of a youth club, as a pupil in a school, or within the family. It is a combination of unique experiences, beliefs, and opinions and their general outlook, which makes it so worthwhile to listen to young people.

The core challenge to this assumption has its roots in how society views young people. The opinions of professionals on the relative maturity of young people are shaped by these social norms and the theories used to justify them. Those who see the voice of young people as immature because they have not developed the cognitive skills and understandings to make "real" sense of the world will treat it with a degree of suspicion—suspicions that in some cases have led to young people being ignored when they should have been listened to. The more extreme versions of this view have become increasingly discredited, sometimes due to the tragic consequences of ignoring young people. Professionals are left to struggle with the tension between recognizing that young people may hold certain views because of a lack of experience or maturity, as well as because they have unique insights.

The second criticism of this assumption asks to what extent the views of young people are indeed their own and to what extent their views are influenced by the opinions and agendas of other people. It touches on debates about how "independent" are the opinions we get from young people and raises questions about the power of others to shape their perceptions. Like adults, young people form their opinions partly on the basis of the social norms and values that surround them, as well as from experience. They can be seen though as particularly susceptible to certain forms of manipulation because of the power relationships in which they are caught up. The issue here is the extent to which young people have the opportunity to critically define their own perspectives in the process of articulating their views.

The second key assumption is that the voice of young people is based on their experiences, but to tell adults and professional adults about their experiences in a way that is meaningful they need help to articulate their views effectively. Young people are asked to voice their views not only because it is seen as beneficial to them personally but also because people believe they can learn from what they are saying. The arguments here are not so much that young people will or will not make sense but rather what kind of meaning they set out to create. The phenomenon of professionals being told what they want or expect to hear is widely recognized. Of course this is not restricted to young people, and neither is it a one-way process. Those working with young people are influenced by a wide range of factors that affect what they are told, and this inevitably influences what they encourage young people to say and what they treat as important.

An important challenge to this assumption is that young people only appear to need help to find their voice because others fail to recognize how they are already expressing themselves. We have to question whether we undervalue the way young people express themselves through their behavior, clothes, music, apathy, loyalty, and just as importantly, their silence. Do adults attach too much importance to certain forms of expression? Research and policy development tends to fall back on those who are verbally articulate and self-confident. Young people who are less articulate or confident can be stereotyped as not having developed the capacity to express their voice in the way required of citizens with rights.

The lives of young people and their experiences are at least as diverse as others. In listening to the voice of young people it should be recognized that being young is only part of what creates their perspective. They are also young men and women, and they come from different ethnic and social-class backgrounds, have different ranges of abilities, live in different family structures, and come from a range of communities. This links back to the first assumption about the primacy of their experiences and the specific insights they have.

The third assumption is that there is a particular "young person's" perspective on many issues and problems, but professionals have few opportunities to hear it.

Behind this is the idea that professionals will listen to the voice of young people, but young people require their own structures and specific processes to help them make an impact. The growing interest in voice is partially premised on the assumption that professionals are distanced from certain groups of young people. This may be because they have limited contact with this group, or the kind of contact they do have means there is little opportunity for them to listen to their honest views and opinions. With this come further assumptions about the kind of voice professionals and in some cases politicians prefer to listen to and the need for specific innovations to support them. Do people need more and better training about how to consult others? How well are professionals coping with a more fragmented and diverse society? Or is it the case that the voice of young people often gets drowned out by other dominant voices that professionals have to listen to? Professionals are bombarded with surveys, reports, and research, which they often have little time to absorb or which they cannot easily relate to their own practice. Young people need to understand the audience of their voice if they want to have an impact. By becoming more knowledgeable about their audiences, young people are in a position to strike a better balance between being listened to and challenging professionals sufficiently to change their practice. To a degree what constitutes a "considered" argument is determined by the audience and reflects their preferences and biases, whether it is a belief in "hard" statistics in a glossy report or a preference to hear it "straight from the horse's mouth" at a public meeting.

Possibly the biggest criticism of this assumption is that in practice there is no one kind of voice most likely to get a reaction. Rather, it is a question of knowing when to put forward one's views, how best to put them forward, and doing so with confidence and persistence. Some of the assumptions already discussed have led people to argue for the need for particular techniques and processes when working with young people. Developing approaches, which are attractive to young people so they get involved, is seen as particularly important because of their alienation from existing structures. There are problems though with the extent to which the perspectives and issues of young people are framed by what and how they are asked, leading to a tension between foregrounding the voice of young people and compartmentalizing their issues.

The fourth assumption is that young people can get things changed by getting their concerns and issues heard, but there are only certain issues on which young people need to be consulted, and young people are particularly effective at influencing other young people. Although there are numerous personal benefits claimed for young people involved in voicing their views and experiences, this is not generally their sole motivation. Generally, young people want things to change, something to happen, somebody to take note. They want to have an impact and think, even if many adults do not, that they can get things changed by getting their voices heard. For all the effort and time put into the numerous projects that have tried to get the voices of young people heard, their widespread impact on the wider policy concerns of local authorities and service providers such as schools is debatable. As adults we need to ask ourselves why this should be so, and this means asking the question concerning the difference between being heard and being listened to.

Increasingly young people are being asked to take part in a wide range of initiatives considered by adults to be of relevance to them. Partly this is because of increasing expectations placed on practitioners that they show evidence of working with a broad range of groups in terms of race-ethnicity, gender, disability, sexuality, and age. This drive toward more inclusive and "bottom-up" approaches that reach out to the most excluded of young people is responsible for the popularity of many of the new consultation techniques and structures. However, there is a danger that all this activity at the "bottom" does not result in better or more innovative decision-making. A failure to change the culture within many organizations and services about who actually has the power to make decisions means that too often nothing is devolved downward to young people.

Just as there are issues where young people are seen as having a certain expertise, there are also groups that they are considered to be more effective at influencing. The most obvious group is other young people. Combining these areas of expertise and influence has led to the popularity of peer-education projects dealing with issues such as sexual health and drugs for which professionals have struggled to have an impact. Combining empathy and understanding with the ability to relate to other young people in a similar situation to themselves is what makes these projects effective. Approaches such as peer mentoring come with several "health warnings." There is the issue of defining groups by the problems they have experienced. There is a danger that placing people into crude categories of experience and matching them up with "similar" young people can become a very subtle form of silencing. For example, becoming homeless is a devastating event but one that is experienced very differently by young people. Becoming homeless after leaving care, through drug addiction, or because one has broken the moral codes of one's community are all very different experiences. Bringing together young people to voice about being homeless can paradoxically fail to articulate the general issues that affect young people while failing to grasp the uniqueness of their individual experiences.

There are always voices that are silenced within any area of activity. The utility of using voice as a concept is that it should be about how voice gets heard throughout the process. The difficulty is in how different voices are honored alongside each other throughout the activity. In setting out to do any activity in which the voice of young people is important, the issue is not their lack of expertise but the unwillingness of others to listen and respond to them, particularly when they are being critical. This is a particularly crucial consideration for any approach committed to inclusiveness and working "with" young people and not "on" them. It raises questions about how we work with young people and give due consideration to the legitimacy of their voice. This is increasingly important when their voice is only one among many other and more dominant voices. We need to take a step back and think about the silencing of certain voices by different, dominant voices within the process of any piece of activism. For adults working with young people there are four key questions they should critically ask themselves in their efforts to improve their own policies and practices. First, how are they using the voice of young people in what they are doing? Second, what sort of voice is it? Third, what is the involvement of all voices throughout the project, and what effects are they having? Fourth, what is the difference between hearing young people and listening to them, and what can be done about it?

See also Deliberative Democracy; Democracy; Democratic Education; KidSpeak; Kids Voting USA (KVUSA); MTV's Choose or Lose Campaign (1992–); New Media; Peer Influences on Political Development; Rights of Participation of Children and Youth; Rights, Youth Perceptions of; State and Youth, The; Student Political Activism; Student Voices Project.

Recommended Reading

Bentley, T., and Oakley, K. (1999). *The Real Deal: What Young People Really Think About Government Politics and Social Exclusion.* London: Demos.

Hadfield, M., and Haw, K. F. *The "Voice" of Young People: Hearing, Listening, Responding.* See www.nottingham.ac.uk/education/centre/uprg.

Hart, R. (1997). *Children's Participation.* London: Earthscan.

Haw, K. F. (1998). *Educating Muslim Girls: Shifting Discourses.* Philadelphia: Open University Press.

Weis, L., and Fine, M. (1994). *Beyond Silenced Voices: Class, Race, and Gender in United States Schools.* Albany: Albany State University of New York Press.

Willow, C. (2002). *Participation in Practice: Children and Young People as Partners in Change.* London: Children's Society

Kaye Haw

Volunteerism. Volunteerism or volunteer community service is defined as a freely given action that directly or indirectly benefits a recipient, whether a person, a cause, an organization, or society in general. (For a more thorough discussion see the article "Volunteering" by Wilson, listed in the recommended reading section below.)

In schools, neighborhoods, and cities across the United States youth volunteerism is burgeoning. Figures indicate that about one-third to one-half of fifteen- to twenty-five-year-olds perform voluntary community service with trends showing that today's youth are volunteering at higher rates than past generations. What are youth volunteers doing? High-school students are traveling to impoverished communities to build houses during their school vacations and are visiting elderly in nursing homes. College students are tutoring in inner-city schools and organizing volunteer projects on campuses, and recent college graduates are mentoring teenagers from disadvantaged backgrounds and enlisting in full-time national programs providing stipends such as AmeriCorps, Jesuit Volunteer Corps, and Teach for America. All told, these are just a few of the many types of service in which youth are involved today.

The benefits of youth volunteerism are, in principle, widespread. Recipients benefit from youth's energy and enthusiasm, and organizations profit from free services that may not have been possible otherwise. Society benefits when citizens work together for peace and social justice. And, youth benefit from volunteering by acquiring new skills, developing self-esteem, and gaining the feeling of a job well done. Many volunteer activities can also foster active citizenship by exposing

Youthful volunteers fill sand bags to help control flooding on the St. Croix River. *Courtesy of Skjold Photographs.*

youth to broader systemic issues and prompt them to become agents for social change. With such potential, volunteer service has become increasingly institutionalized through school-based and national programs with the belief that service can enhance youth's understandings of the rights and responsibilities of democratic citizenship. The purpose of this entry is to describe some of the facets of youth volunteerism by defining youth volunteerism, discussing trends and benefits of youth volunteerism, assessing youth volunteerism as a form of activism, and concluding with a brief discussion that looks at the past and future of youth volunteerism.

While similar to and often used interchangeably with other prosocial behaviors and actions, such as helping or altruism, group membership, and other forms of service such as service learning, volunteerism distinguishes itself for several reasons:

Volunteering is proactive rather than reactive and entails more of a formal time commitment than incidental helping or altruistic acts (Wilson 2000). Thus, helping an elderly person or a child across the street is a kind act but would not be considered volunteerism unless done regularly or with a commitment (e.g., volunteering as a crossing guard).

The action component distinguishes volunteering from membership in a group or an organization. Thus, a teen could be a member of a youth group or a school club but still not be a volunteer if the group does not partake in prosocial helping activities.

Free choice distinguishes volunteerism from some other forms of community service, such as required community service. While identical in most regards, when service is required by a school or is court-mandated it is no longer freely given and cannot be considered volunteerism.

Volunteering is similar to service learning and forms of experiential education, yet volunteerism is not formally structured or embedded within an academic curriculum and is not done for academic credit.

Volunteering is an activity that all young people can do regardless of background or educational status. Because there are literally hundreds of unique service types, there are opportunities that suit a range of young persons' interests. Research shows that the most common types of volunteer service that middle- and high-school students perform include: (1) visiting the elderly at nursing homes, (2) teaching, coaching, and mentoring peers at school, (3) property maintenance in the community, (4) property maintenance at school, and (5) serving and assisting persons in need in the community.

Each type of volunteerism shares the feature of providing youth with the practical experience of serving for a purpose and contributing to a local community and society. At the same time there is wide variability from one type to the next. Serving at a homeless shelter may expose a young person to complex systemic problems such as unemployment, alcoholism, and mental illness. Tutoring a peer may provide a volunteer with appreciation and understanding for the difficulties of teaching. Picking up garbage may give a volunteer a good feeling for having beautified a highway. There are other factors that come into play when determining a young person's volunteer experience, such as the amount of time volunteered, the training and support offered to the volunteer, and how challenging the service is for the young person.

Pinning down an exact rate of youth volunteerism is tricky, as the numbers vary significantly from study to study depending on factors such as how volunteer service is defined and who is being assessed. For example, when volunteerism is defined broadly to include other forms of community service (such as service learning or school-based service), about 50 percent of teenagers report serving (Kleiner and Chapman 1999). Rates can be even higher when the study sample is comprised of a specific group of young people that may be more predisposed to volunteerism. For example, a study of incoming college freshman reported that about 75 percent had volunteered during their final year of high school. On the flip side, rates of youth volunteerism tend to be lower (20 to 30 percent) when a more stringent definition of volunteerism is used.

There are also important distinctions in how often young people volunteer depending on individual and demographic factors. Studies consistently show that female teens volunteer more than their male counterparts, although gender differences even out in their early twenties. High-school students are more likely to volunteer than younger middle–school-age students as well as older college-age students. Students with higher grade-point averages (GPAs) and those who are more involved in extracurricular activities are more likely to volunteer. Youth whose parents have a high level of education are more likely to volunteer. Youth who are more involved in their community through religious or civic organizations are more likely to volunteer. Studies also show that if a parent or friend volunteers, a young person is also more likely to volunteer (see Child Trends 2004).

Overall, rates of youth volunteerism were relatively stable from the 1970s to the mid-1990s. Recent trends indicate that young people today volunteer at a higher rate than youth in previous generations. Why? There are no indications that the average young person today is more altruistic or deeply concerned about the common good than youth in the past. Rather, one explanation for the increased rates is that youth have more service opportunities than in the past. Research shows that when given opportunities or an invitation young people are more likely to volunteer and to stay involved into adulthood.

In recent years opportunities for youth volunteerism have become more structured and institutionalized. Schools and higher-education institutions have created community-service programs with placement offices and volunteer coordinators to provide ready-made opportunities for students to serve at school and in community-based organizations. More and more private and public schools are making community service a part of the academic curriculum through requirements. For example, Washington, D.C., the state of Maryland, and cities such as Detroit and Chicago all have requirements for students to complete a specific number of service hours as a prerequisite for graduation.

The institutionalization of volunteerism and service at the national level is another likely reason for the increase in rates in volunteerism. Full-time volunteer programs such as the Peace Corps, Teach for America, and the Jesuit Volunteer Corps have become more prevalent and provide an attractive option for recent college graduates. Programs such as Campus Compact involve college students in volunteerism at some 850 colleges and universities. And nationwide events such as National Volunteer Week, Clean-Up America Day, and Global Youth Service Day all provide opportunities for young people to get involved in their communities.

Information technology is another probable reason for the increased opportunities and rates of volunteerism. Visit any K–12 school or college Web site, and there is sure to be a link to many volunteer opportunities in the local and world community. Most full-time volunteer programs now have Web sites that young people can browse and explore. Specialized service Web sites such as SERVEnet (http://www.servenet.org) and WorldVolunteerWeb.org (http://www.worldvolunteerweb.org) advertise opportunities for volunteer projects and mobilize youth to become active participants. In just five or ten years, the Internet has become an irreplaceable resource that fuels the youth-service movement. Of course, there are other plausible reasons why youth volunteerism has increased in recent years. For example, many volunteers meet like-minded individuals when serving and make long-lasting friendships. Many invite their friends and family to serve with them as well. And many view volunteering as an important part of their résumé to improve the chances of getting into college or securing professional employment.

Volunteerism receives acclaim because of potential benefits to recipients, organizations, society at large, *and* to the youth server. *Recipients* are the most obvious beneficiaries of volunteerism. For instance, elderly people in nursing homes enjoy visits from enthusiastic middle-school students, and the environment benefits when high-school students pick up trash and beautify a highway by planting flowers. *Organizations* benefit from youth volunteerism, especially nonprofit and religious organizations that depend on youth's efforts to complete projects that likely could not exist at the same level or at all. Young volunteers often provide the manpower to carry out food drives and to make environmental campaigns and clean-air days successful in local communities. *Schools* benefit when their students clean or paint the grounds. *Society* also can benefit from youth volunteerism. Youth volunteers often lead public-health campaigns such as those to prevent drunk driving and smoking. Youth volunteerism can foster democratic values and peace in society. For example, programs such as City Year promote greater tolerance, trust, and understanding by bringing youth together from distinct socioeconomic and ethnic backgrounds.

Young people themselves also benefit from volunteering. A meaningful volunteer experience can foster youth's sense of who they are and the kind of adult they wish to become. For example, a teenager can gain a sense of efficacy and confidence by making a presentation in front of a town board or by coaching a Little League team. Volunteerism can provide youth with marketable and practical skills not normally provided within educational settings. For instance, serving in a business office or volunteering to build houses can expose and teach youth new trades. Volunteering allows young people to try out potential future careers, such as working at a hospital as a candy striper or in a school setting as a teacher's aide, and looks good on young people's résumés. Volunteerism has also been shown to keep young people away from trouble. Studies show that adolescents who volunteer are less likely to become pregnant, use drugs or alcohol, or drop out of high school (see Child Trends 2004).

Volunteerism can also enhance character development and provide opportunities for young people to make a difference by contributing to the betterment of society. For example, young people can practice and gain important virtues of empathy and kindness when they help others in need. By running a Students Against Drunk Driving (SADD) campaign or a clothing drive or serving in a soup kitchen, young people can make a real difference in peoples lives. In this sense, during the time of life when young people are forming their attitudes and beliefs and deciding what they are going to with their lives, volunteerism can shape how youth view the world and themselves in relation to it. Furthermore, as the period when people begin to understand themselves as citizens, volunteerism can teach young people about their own responsibility in sustaining democracy (see Flanagan and Faison 2001).

Of course, not all volunteer experiences benefit the server, recipient, or organization. A successful volunteer experience may depend on any number of factors from the type of service, to the level of challenge that a young person feels, to the service involving direct interaction with a recipient, to the support and training the server receives, and so on. For example, picking up trash or filing papers seem less likely benefit a young person than other more service-oriented types of activities that have face-to-face interaction with a recipient, like tutoring a child or serving at a soup kitchen, or youth volunteers placed in challenging positions, such as building houses or answering phone lines at a crisis clinic, who likely need ample training and frequent supervision to ensure that the services are rendered properly. If a young person is bored by his or her role or task or an organization does not support a youth volunteer, the recipient of the service also would be less likely to have a beneficial experience.

Many forms of youth volunteerism are also forms of youth activism, be it for political, social, or environmental causes. This is the case when the action of solving problems (volunteering) is *combined with* a broader purpose of affecting change for the betterment of society (activism). Historically, *youth volunteer activists* were partly responsible for bringing about sweeping social and political change in the United States. Examples of volunteer political activism in the 1960s and 1970s include young people's participation in the civil rights and antiwar movements by organizing and partaking in demonstrations and protests. This activism brought praise from some as youth were interested in matters of justice more than in self-gain, but it also brought concern because much of the activism threatened American traditions and the governmental and educational institutions that supported them.

Young people today continue to combine volunteerism with activist causes. Some common examples include youth volunteer activists who:

- Led discussions on the importance of civil liberties and who organized candlelight vigils and memorial services after the September 11 terrorist attacks on the United States
- Serve as youth representatives on school and organizational boards
- Take initiative for causes such as environmental protection, school reform, or minimum-wage laws
- Run campaigns to prevent sexual assault, organize events such as Take Back

the Night marches, and raise awareness of the dangers of drunk driving through groups such as SADD

- Mobilize others by organizing demonstrations for or against the government's position on issues such as the war in Iraq or the World Trade Organization's stance on free trade

While these are clear examples of youth volunteer activists, questions remain about whether service actually promotes certain forms of activism, such as political interest and political behaviors such as voting. The answer is not clear. For any study that reports positive gains for youth volunteers, there is another study that fails to find a relationship. One possible reason for the lack of connection between volunteerism and forms of political activism may be due to an "apple-and-oranges" problem. That is, for some young people volunteering consists of raking lawns or cleaning courtyards at school, for others it involves tutoring classmates, and for still others it entails weekly stints at soup kitchens or environmental conservation projects. It is not hard to see that such varied experiences doubtfully lead to the same outcomes when assessing measures such as political interest and voting.

In this regard, the answer may be that some types of volunteerism are more likely to promote activism than others, especially ones that prompt youth to reflect on the political basis of social problems such as poverty, homelessness, disparity in distribution of wealth, racism, the environment, and so on. For instance, a young person volunteering at a homeless shelter would probably be more likely to ask broad questions about the government's role in reducing poverty than a young person who was painting a classroom during his summer vacation.

Another question that remains in the literature is whether volunteer activism during youth promotes longer-term civic and political involvement into adulthood. There happens to be solid data from the civil rights era that speaks to this question. For example, Fendrich (1993) and McAdam (1988) report longitudinal findings from adults who participated in the civil rights movement in the American South in their youth, risking their safety to help the cause of racial integration. When these activists had reached middle age, they differed from their peers with similar backgrounds but who did not partake in the movement during their youth. Jennings (2002) has reported parallel results in his longitudinal study of antiwar activists. Civil rights and antiwar activists matured into adult citizens who were more likely to vote, to belong to voluntary associations, and to be involved in organizing their communities. It is worth noting that these longitudinal results are supported as well by retrospective studies in which recalled activism versus nonactivism differentiated mid-life adults on these same civic measures. Such studies support speculation that certain forms of volunteer activism may provide the basis of an identity in which individuals come to understand themselves as participatory citizens (see Youniss, McLellan, and Yates 1997 for a discussion).

Youth volunteerism in the United States has a rich and storied history. At the start of the twentieth century influential thinkers such as William James, John Dewey, and Arthur Dunn extolled youth volunteer service as a means to instill social responsibility and promote social cohesion among diverse persons within our democratic society. For the last century religious and public organizations such as the scouts, 4-H, and the YMCA have pioneered volunteer programs to help the needy and improve society. On a national policy level U.S. presidents have stressed the importance of service to country and have sought to institutionalize volunteerism. Examples include President Franklin D. Roosevelt's creation of the Civilian Conservation Corps (CCC), President John F. Kennedy's creation of the Peace Corps for the purpose of nation building, President George H. W. Bush's creation of the Points of Light Foundation, President Bill Clinton's creation of the Corporation for National Service, and President George W. Bush's support of AmeriCorps and creation of the Freedom Corps.

The recent climate for youth volunteer community service appears promising and the benefits of national service appear clear, as policies and programs provide youth an active role in their communities and are an effective strategy for development. Rather than providing programs that deliver services "to" young people, structured volunteer programs empower young people to address critical issues in their communities and allow them to develop transferable skills and competencies in the process. In what is often described as a growing era of consumerism, individualism, and competition to get into college and to get the highest paying job, volunteerism provides young people the opportunity to serve and work for the public good. In many forms youth volunteerism challenges portrayals of youth as problems in society and highlights young people's efforts as competent citizens who actively participate and contribute to the betterment of society.

See also AmeriCorps; Civilian Conservation Corps (CCC); Community Service; 4-H; National and Community Service; Prosocial Behaviors; Service Learning; Service Learning and Citizenship Education.

Recommended Reading

Astin, A., and Sax, L. J. (1999). "The American Freshman: National Norms for 1999." See http://www.gseis.ucla.edu/heri/norms_pr_99.html.

Bass, M. (2003). "National Service: The Enduring Panacea." See http://www.cato.org/cgi-bin/scripts/printtech.cgi/pubs/pas/pa130.html.

Bureau of Labor Statistics (2003). "Volunteering in the United States." See http://www.bls.gov/news.release/volun.nr0.htm.

Carnegie Corporation (2003). *The Civic Mission of Schools*. Report released by CIRCLE, the Center for Information and Research on Civic Learning and Engagement.

Child Trends (2004). "Volunteering." See http://www.childtrendsdatabank.org/indicators/20Volunteering.cfm.

Corporation for National Service. See http://www.nationalservice.org.

Egan, H. (2002). *Volunteering: An Easy, Smart Guide to Volunteering*. New York: Silver Lining Books.

Flanagan, C., and Faison, N. (2001). "Youth Civic Development: Implications of Research for Social Policy and Implementation of Programs." *Social Policy Report*, 15. See http://www.srcd.org/sprv15n1.pdf.

Independent Sector (2002). "Giving and Volunteering among American Youth." See http://www.independentsector.org/GandV/s_volu.htm.

Kleiner, B., and Chapman, C. (1999). *Youth Service-Learning and Community Service among Sixth- through Twelfth-Grade Students in the United States*. United States Department of Education. See http://nces.ed.gov/pubs2000/20000028.pdf.

McAdam, D. (1988). *Freedom Summer*. New York: Oxford University Press.

Wilson, J. (2000). "Volunteering." *Annual Review of Sociology*, 26: 215–240. See http://arjournals.annualreviews.org/doi/full/10.1146/annurev.soc.26.1.215.

Youniss, J., McLellan, J., and Yates, M. (1997). "What We Know about Engendering Civic Identity." *American Behavioral Scientist*, 40: 620–631.

Edward Metz

X

Xenophobia. Xenophobia refers to negative and hostile attitudes and behaviors toward people who are defined as members of outgroups or "aliens." When taking a closer look at youth activism and xenophobia it is important to distinguish between two aspects: xenophobic youth activism and antixenophobic youth activism. Whereas the first is part of right-wing extremism and fascism, the latter aims at equality, tolerance, and the prevention of xenophobia, although there are also extremist tendencies in parts of the antixenophobia movement.

Several youth researchers point out that in contrast to the progressive activism of the 1960s and 1970s, some of today's youth activism has strong xenophobic tendencies that express hostility toward outsiders. Following the German sociologist-philosopher Georg Simmel, an "alien" is a person tied to a certain location from which this person did not originate. Xenophobia is an expression of ethnocentrism. American sociologist William G. Sumner sees ethnocentrism as the technical term for a worldview in which one's own group is the center of everything, and all others are measured and judged with reference to it. Each group nourishes its own pride and vanity, boasts of its superiority, exalts its own divinities, and looks with contempt on outsiders. The term "ethnocentrism" has evolved to apply not only to relations between ethnic groups but to all sorts of intergroup relations (e.g., between football fans, groups with differing sexual orientations). Usually, the term "xenophobia" is used as a synonym for ethnocentrism but with a stronger emphasis on the "other" in the form of an ethnic group. Objects of xenophobia are not "natural" outsiders but outsiders socially constructed as such by those who show xenophobic attitudes or behaviors. People use so-called biological or cultural ethnic markers (e.g., skin color, clothing) to distinguish between ingroups and outgroups.

Xenophobia is always an ingredient of right-wing extremism, but right-wing extremism is defined by more elements than merely xenophobia. In addition to xenophobic patterns, right-wing extremist ideologies contain an active and aggressive rejection of the principles of equality, an acceptance of violence, and a tendency to use violent force.

Xenophobia is expressed in attitudes and behaviors. According to attitude-behavior theories and ample empirical evidence, xenophobic attitudes—widely spread in most societies—provide a base for xenophobic behavior. Behavioral patterns of xenophobia range from everyday conduct to crime. Subtle xenophobia—exhibited by large numbers of people—includes preference for members of the ingroup and discrimination against foreigners or other outsiders at the workplace, in schools, or on the street. For instance, to refuse to help a foreigner who asks for assistance in finding a certain street for reasons of his or her foreign appearance is xenophobic behavior. A more serious pattern is that of aggressive behavior toward foreigners, including verbal attacks (e.g., xenophobic shouts at foreigners or xenophobic slogans on walls) and physical violence (e.g., attacking foreigners, burning houses of immigrants). More serious types of xenophobic behavior have recently been subsumed under the rubric of "hate crimes."

Xenophobia is often seen as a problem of young people. However, what distinguishes different age-groups is mainly behavior. Most xenophobic crimes are committed by people under age twenty-five, whereas xenophobic attitudes are found in all age-groups. Looking, for example, at Germany, between 10 and 20 percent of all Germans (depending on the exact study) exhibit strong negative attitudes toward minority groups, approximately another 30 percent are ambivalent. This means that almost one-half of the population is not immune to xenophobia. According to the most recent comprehensive study of ethnocentrism in Europe, the European Social Survey, German percentages are the European average, while Scandinavian countries (Sweden, Finland, Norway) report lower percentages, and countries like Hungary, the Czech Republic, and Greece, in particular, exhibit even higher percentages of xenophobic orientations. Adolescents and older people generally show somewhat higher levels of xenophobia than middle-aged adults.

A deeper analysis makes it obvious that xenophobia is not just a youth problem. Many social theorists point out that the roots of xenophobia may be found in the core features of society. Structural inequalities, competitiveness, and insecurities among young people who are going through a critical phase of life lead to xenophobia and right-wing extremism under certain circumstances. Such processes are supported by a xenophobic structural context often implied in laws or administration practices and by politicians who promote xenophobic slogans, particularly during election campaigns.

A look at xenophobic youth activism reveals a variety of formal and informal youth groups and organizations. Most youth who participate in xenophobic hate crimes or political violence belong to ingroups, ranging from informal subcultural groups (e.g., Nazi skinheads) to formal xenophobic and right-wing groups (e.g., White Aryan Front) to youth divisions of right-wing extremist parties (e.g., American Nazi Party). Racism, nationalism, and xenophobia are core elements of the ideology of such right-wing groups. Although evidence suggests that many members of xenophobic and right-wing organizations are young people, the thinkers and organizers of such groups are mainly of an older age. These extremist intellectuals provide the ideology that leads to the xenophobic crimes of younger people. Most committed crimes are so-called propaganda offenses like wearing of Nazi symbols (outlawed in Germany and other European countries) or distributing xenophobic fliers. However, violence is a key element of xenophobic groups. In attacking people who are different from the "mainstream" citizen, group members commit crimes like assault, arson, and attempted homicide. Their actions range from demonstrations and music festivals to the defiling of tombs and monuments and bomb attacks. Young people are attracted to such groups through a specific type of group community spirit and aggressive music, which plays an important role for youth group coherence, particularly among skinhead groups.

Xenophobic groups and right-wing extremist parties increasingly use the Internet to promote their aims, to agitate against foreigners and other minorities, and to recruit new members. Many right-wing extremist parties have their own youth groups. Although relations between xenophobic groups and parties tend to be difficult, as competitiveness and distinction are highly valued among them, there are many national and international links. Often right-wing groups invite international speakers and representatives of other right-wing groups to their conferences. The Internet makes global relationships possible and provides a virtual global xenophobic network. An example is the "Stormfront–White Nationalist Resource Page," founded by a U.S. citizen. This Web site provides information, a forum, and links to American, Euro-American, British, and German xenophobic extremist groups and parties. As right-wing extremists are not as severely persecuted in the United States as in Europe, some European xenophobic extremists have moved to the United States or are at least launching their campaigns from U.S. Web sites.

Xenophobic offenses and xenophobic violence are collective forms of action and are typically committed within a group context. However, group acts of violence against foreigners or "aliens" are not always caused by xenophobic ideologies, since informal groups without strong right-wing attitudinal patterns are also involved in violent xenophobic acts. Research suggests that alcohol, music, and impoverished living conditions as situational factors play an important role in the occurrence of xenophobic violence. Groups—whether xenophobic or not—provide young people with a network of friends and help compensate for experiences of familial or economic deprivation. Young people who want to satisfy specific needs and compensate for specific shortcomings may encounter highly ideological opinion leaders in a xenophobic group context, internalize xenophobic attitudes, and eventually become tools of these group authorities. Social identity theory postulates that individuals tend to aim for a satisfactory self-image as a matter of principle. Parts of this self-image are highly dependent upon integration into groups. To gain a positive self-image an individual needs to have a positive perception of his or her own group (ingroup). Such a positive image can be derived from a comparison with other groups and the defamation and devaluation of other groups (outgroups). Therefore an individual perceives outgroups in a negative way, whereas the ingroup is seen uncritically. Xenophobia thus appears to be a necessary element of group and individual identity and therefore rather "natural." This view neglects situational factors and in particular evidence that xenophobia is not a universal phenomenon but varies between groups and individuals.

From a more social-psychological perspective, xenophobia is seen as a tool that helps individuals to cope with experiences of deprivation and familial or economic disintegration. In these approaches the importance of societal value systems and individual value dispositions are often highlighted. The occurrence of xenophobic tendencies, some argue, is more likely in materialistic and hierarchical cultures. Modern industrial societies that tend to be highly competitive and strongly tied to the logic of free-market capitalism are centered on a pattern of dominance ideologies. Dominance ideologies contain the notion that success in all areas of life means to "perform better than others." On the individual level Hagan and colleagues see such ideologies as expressed in the value syndrome of "hierarchic self-interest" (HSI). The more individuals feel deprived and have no other resources to compensate for this situation, the more they will act according to the values of HSI. These values suggest xenophobia as a solution to individual problems of deprivation. However, a differing view is held by Sidanius and Pratto, who postulate that groups of a higher status tend to be more dominance-oriented and therefore more racist than lower-status groups because higher-status groups are more interested in maintaining social hierarchy and their relatively powerful position. While this assumption is challenged quite frequently, the main assumption of social-dominance theory—the link between social-dominance orientation and xenophobia as a legitimizing myth for discrimination—is backed by evidence.

Xenophobia and right-wing extremism tend to be characterized by a substantial gender gap. Whereas the gender difference in xenophobic attitudes is low, and the difference in voting for xenophobic parties is of intermediate extent, xenophobic behavior and participation in right-wing extremist organizations is mainly a male phenomenon. The reason for this gap lies in gender-specific socialization processes and only to a lesser extent in biological differences. According to the power-control theory of Hagan and colleagues, the difference in the position and authority of the parents in the sphere of work (fathers work more and in higher positions than mothers) leads to a gender-specific parental style in the family (i.e., girls are more subject to parental control than boys). Being less controlled, boys show a higher risk preference and eventually more deviant behaviors and attitudes. While structural gender differences (e.g., participation of women and men in the labor market) have declined over the last decades, ideological patterns of patriarchy like traditional gender roles and the gender gap in market-oriented values—hierarchic self-interest—remain important for socialization processes.

Youth activism opposing right-wing tendencies, that is, antixenophobic and antifascist groups often engage in spontaneous and organized responses to xenophobic crime. Examples of such action are letter-writing campaigns, fundraising drives, demonstrations (e.g., against the introduction of ethnocentric laws), or candlelight vigils to protest against xenophobic contents of education (http://www.youthactivism.com). More formal and structured groups are so-called "antifa" (short for antifascist) action groups such as SOS Racisme in France and youth organizations of (mainly left-wing) parties. These organizations have more opportunities to launch campaigns, to organize antiracist camps and to form local, nationwide, or even global networks. However, violent tendencies can occasionally also be found in parts of the "antifa" movement. A smaller number of extremists commit crimes like bodily harm and disturbing the peace in their attempts to fight xenophobic groups and their actions. They throw stones during demonstrations and carry out violent attacks on the premises of xenophobic groups.

The relationship between xenophobic and antixenophobic youth activism becomes most complex in light of the so-called antiglobalization movement. Interestingly, fighting globalization is an objective of both xenophobic and antixenophobic youth. The former fight globalization because it is seen as bringing in "foreign" elements to an unbearable degree, while the latter fight globalization as an imperialist attack on human rights and human dignity. It remains to be seen to what degree cooperation between xenophobic and antixenophobic youth will emerge.

See also Australia, Youth Activism in; Demographic Trends Affecting the World's Youth; Eastern Europe, Youth and Citizenship in; Europe, Comparing Youth Activism in; European Identity and Citizenship; Immigrant Youth in Europe—Turks in Germany; Immigrant Youth in the United States; India, Youth Activism in; Indonesia, Youth Activism in; Nigeria, Youth Activism in; Palestinian *Intifada*; Queer, Sexuality, and Gender Activism; Racial and Ethnic Inequality; Russia, Youth Activism in; Serbia, Youth Activism in (1990–2000); Soweto Youth Activism (South Africa); State and Youth, The; Statute of the Child and Adolescent (Brazil); Tiananmen Square Massacre (1989); Transnational Identity; Transnational Youth Activism; Turkey, Youth Activism in; United Nations, Youth Activism and; Zapatista Rebellion (Mexico); Zionist Youth Organizations.

Recommended Reading

Altemeyer, R. (1981). *Right-Wing Authoritarianism*. Winnipeg: University of Manitoba Press.

Boehnke, K., Hagan, J., and Hefler, G. (1998). "On the Development of Xenophobia in Germany: The Adolescent Years." *Journal of Social Issues*, 54: 585–602.

Hagan, J., Boehnke, K., and Merkens, H. (2004). "Gender Differences in Capitalization Processes and the Delinquency of Siblings in Toronto and Berlin." *British Journal of Criminology*, 44: 659–676.

Hagan, J., Hefler, G., Classen, G., Boehnke, K., and Merkens, H. (1998). "Subterranean Sources of Subcultural Delinquency Beyond the American Dream." *Criminology*, 36: 309–342.

Heitmeyer, W. (1993). "Hostility and Violence Towards Foreigners in Germany." In *Racist Violence in Europe*, edited by T. Bjorgo and R. Witte. Basingstoke: Macmillan, pp. 17–28.

Sidanius, J., and Pratto, F. (1999). *Social Dominance. An Intergroup Theory of Social Hierarchy and Oppression*. Cambridge: Cambridge University Press.

Tajfel, H., and Turner, J. C. (1986). "The Social Identity Theory of Intergroup Behavior." In *Psychology of Intergroup Relations*, edited by S. Worchel and W. G. Austin. Chicago: Nelson-Hall, pp. 7–24.

Klaus Boehnke and Andreas Hadjar

Y

YLDI. *See* Youth Leadership for Development Initiative.

Youth Bulge. Youth bulge refers to a population of youth in a society that is large relative to the population of adults. One definition refers to the fraction of nonadults in a population. For example, according to data from the United Nations (Fukuda-Parr 2002), many countries at the beginning of the twenty-first century have very youthful populations. More than half of the population of Yemen is under the age of fifteen, and there are at least forty countries worldwide in which youth younger than fifteen constitute 40 percent or more of the population. In contrast, in the United States the percentage of the population is only half as large (22 percent), and in some other countries such as Japan and Italy youth under the age of fifteen constitute less than 15 percent of the total population. The former countries (Yemen) are usually characterized as having youth bulges while the latter (United States) are not.

Some analysts have suggested restricting the term youth bulge to populations in which youth—those between the ages of fifteen and twenty-four—are relatively numerous in comparison to the population of adults. Urdal (2002) has argued this narrower connotation of the term has many advantages, including greater clarity of the individuals to which it refers and greater explanatory power in empirical research. Because the notion of a youth bulge seems to have its most important applications in understanding warfare, activism, and revolution, all of which frequently involve youth but infrequently involve young children,

we believe that there are good reasons to restrict the term youth bulge to those in the ages of fifteen to twenty-four.

The explosion of interest in youth bulges in recent years (an Internet search returned nearly 50,000 hits) is largely a product of claims that these demographic phenomena are linked to warfare, revolution, and political and religious activism. The relation of youth bulges to warfare has received the most attention. Analysts in the United States believe that youth bulges are an important ingredient in political transformations. For example, John Helgerson, a former deputy director of intelligence for the U.S. Central Intelligence Agency (CIA), has claimed that "the inability of states to adequately integrate youth populations is likely to perpetuate the cycle of political instability, ethnic wars, revolutions, and antigovernment activities that already affects many countries" (2002, 4). Huntington (1996), Wiley (2000), and Cordesman (1998) have made similar claims concerning the relation of youth bulges to political instability.

There is good research to support such claims. Urdal (2002) examined the relationship between youth bulges and warfare, using historical data for the last half of the twentieth century. Urdal reported that "youth bulges increase the risk that a country will experience armed conflict" (30). Similarly, Mesquida and Wiener found in their analyses that the "relative abundance of young men is associated with occurrence of coalitional aggression and the severity of conflicts as measured by reported casualties." Not all of the research is supportive of this relationship, however. For example, Goldstone and colleagues (2003) report that in their analyses the relation of youth bulges to political instability is minor or insignificant. There are formidable statistical problems involved in identifying a relationship between youth bulges and warfare (Goldstone et al. 2003), and definitional differences between research groups prevent an easy synthesis of the various studies. However, the findings to date suggest that the link of warfare to youth bulges is worthy of future research.

There is also considerable speculation that youth bulges are linked to political and religious activism. Moller (1968) has linked youth bulges to the Protestant Reformation and to revolutions in eighteenth-century France and twentieth-century Indonesia, and Huntington (1996) has suggested that youth are generally more attracted to such movements than are adults. Goldstone (1999) pointed out that youth may be less invested in the existing social and religious structures—they are less likely than adults to be married, have children, occupy prestigious positions in their communities and churches, and so on—and that as a consequence youth may be more open to movements which seek to overthrow or revise existing orthodoxies. Although there is a great deal of fascinating writing on the relation of youth bulges to the emergence of powerful social and religious movements (Moller 1968 is particularly thoughtful), there is as yet a dearth of systematic research of the type found in the study of youth bulges and welfare.

Why are youth bulges possibly associated with warfare, revolution, and activism? The following three broad answers have been offered:

Economic prospects. One explanation for activism, revolution, and warfare accompanying the maturation of a youth bulge focuses on the dismal economic conditions that may confront those entering the job market. Young adults in a maturing youth bulge are members of a large cohort seeking jobs, and there are likely to be too few opportunities in the existing workforce to accommodate the unusually large number of young adults. Inevitably, there is a collision between career expectations and the realities of an economy with too few openings for all young adults seeking jobs; many young adults are unable to obtain jobs, and those that do find employment may be paid poorly. The consequence for a young adult of the sharp contrast between expectation and reality is disillusionment in prospects for the future. For example, Wiley, a security analyst for the U.S. CIA, examined demographic trends in the Middle Eastern countries and concluded that "job markets in these countries are already severely challenged to create openings for the large mass of young people entering the labor force each year."

This disillusionment may be the emotional fuel for lines of action that are associated with activism, revolution, and reform. For example, disillusioned youth may join political movements that aim to reform society. Sayre has analyzed economic and historical data concerning the frequency of Palestinian suicide bombings and has concluded that these tragic events are most likely to occur when unemployment is high. If economists (e.g., Easterlin 1987) are correct in concluding that job prospects are poorer for those in youth bulges than for youth in smaller cohorts, then Sayre's research is consistent with claims that the economic conditions associated with youth bulges may lead to extreme forms of political activism. The economic explanation is undoubtedly the most popular, although not all studies find confirming evidence for it (e.g., Urdal 2002).

Sociobiological explanation. Mesquida and Wiener have suggested a sociobiological account for the relation of youth bulges to warfare. According to their theory, young men are particularly prone to violence, a propensity due to qualities selected in evolution for the successful competition of mates. Warfare is the societal consequence of the biologically-based tendency for young men to fight. Accordingly, whenever there are large groups of young men in a society, warfare ought to be more common than when the fraction of the population constituted of young men is relatively small. Mesquida and Wiener (1996, 1999) analyze several different sets of historical data and generate results consonant with their theory. The sociobiological theory for the association of youth bulges with warfare has not gained many adherents, and it probably cannot be used at all to explain the influence of youth bulges on the emergence of social, political, and religious movements, if such an influence exists. Moreover, many wars are initiated by the leaders of states, and these leaders are often old men, not the young men central to the sociobiological accounts.

Socialization. Hart, Atkins, Markey, and Youniss have offered a third explanation for the relation of youth bulges to warfare and activism. These authors suggest that both the economic and sociobiological theories neglect the consequences of growing up from birth to adolescence in large cohorts of similarly aged individuals. Hart and colleagues suggest that those who grow up in communities and societies with large cohorts of children (*child-saturated contexts*) are less influenced by adults than are children who develop in communities and societies in which adults constitute large majorities (*adult-saturated contexts*). They hypothesized that growing up in adult-saturated contexts results in the transmission from adults to children of knowledge of and respect for the culture and society. This transmission is possible because in adult-saturated contexts many of a child's interactions will naturally involve adults, who typically possess knowledge about society and culture. In contrast, in child-saturated contexts children interact frequently with other children, and less transmission of cultural information can take place because children typically have little information about their societies. Hart and colleagues demonstrated that children living in child-saturated communities in the United States have less civic

knowledge than do children living in adult-saturated communities and showed as well that children in child-saturated countries possess less civic knowledge than do children in adult-saturated countries. Hart et al. suggested but have not proved that those who possess little civic knowledge are more likely to become involved in radical political and social activism than are those who possess more civic knowledge. In summary, Hart et al., argue that members of youth bulges have less civic knowledge than youth of the same age who were not socialized in large cohorts of children and that a deficit in civic knowledge can lead to participation in extremist political activities.

Because the socialization theory posits only that those maturing in youth bulges are more likely to be influenced by other youth than those who develop in adult-saturated environments, it is possible that in eras in which youth have *more* knowledge than adults that child-saturated contexts can better facilitate the transmission of ideas than adult-saturated ones. It might be argued, for instance, that the widespread activism of U.S. youth in the 1960s, associated with a nationwide youth bulge (Moller 1968), reflected the influence of knowledgeable, authority-challenging youth on each other.

In conclusion, blending demographic factors such as youth bulges into accounts of political movements, revolutions, and warfare offers the potential for genuinely synthetic, interdisciplinary accounts of important, enormously complicated human events. The research evidence to date concerning this particular synthesis of demography, history, and political science is promising but not conclusive. However, it is sufficiently promising that further investigation is warranted.

See also Child Soldiers; Demographic Trends Affecting the World's Youth.

Recommended Reading

Cordesman, A. H. (1998). *Demographics and the Coming Youth Explosion in the Gulf*. See the Center for Strategic and International Studies

Web site at http://www.csis.org/stratassessment/reports/demograp.pdf.

Easterlin, R. A. (1987). *Birth and Fortune: The Impact of Numbers on Personal Welfare.* Chicago: University of Chicago Press.

Fukuda-Parr, S. (2002). *Human Development Report, 2002.* See the United Nations Development Programme Web site at http://www.undp.org/hdr2002/complete.pdf.

Goldstone, J. A. (2001). "Toward a Fourth Generation of Revolutionary Theory." *Annual Review of Political Science*, 4: 139–187.

Goldstone, J. A. (2002). "Population and Security: How Demographic Change Can Lead to Violent Conflict." *Journal of International Affairs*, 56: 3–21.

Goldstone, J. A., Gurr, T. R., Harff, B., Levy, M. A., Marshall, M. G., Bates, R. H., Epstein, D. L, Kahl, C. H., Surko, P. T., Ulfelder, J. C., and Unger, A. N. (2000). *State Failure Task Force Report: Phase III Findings.* See the State Failure Task Force Web site at http://www.cidcm.umd.edu/inscr/stfail/SFTF%20Phase%20III%20Report%20Final.pdf.

Helgerson, J. L. (April 30, 2002). *The National Security Implications of Global Demographic Change.* Proposed remarks to the Denver World Affairs Council and the Better World Campaign, Denver, CO. See the U.S. Central Intelligence Agency Web site at http://www.cia.gov/nic/graphics/Denverspeech.pdf.

Moller, H. (1968). "Youth as a Force in the Modern World." *Comparative Studies in Sociology and History*, 10: 238–260.

Urdal, H. (March 2002). *The Devil in the Demographics: How Youth Bulges Influence the Risk of Domestic Armed Conflict.* Paper presented at the International Studies Association Annual Convention, New Orleans, LA. See http://www.prio.no/publications/papers/YouthBulgesUrdal.pdf.

U.S. Central Intelligence Agency (2002). *The World Factbook 2002.* See http://www.cia.gov/cia/publications/factbook/.

Wiley, W. P. (2000). *Agenda 2001: Middle East Policy Planning for a New Administration: Keynote Address.* See http://www.ciaonet.org/conf/wiw01/.

Daniel Hart, Robert Atkins, Patrick Markey, and James Youniss

Youth Commissions.

The scene is the city council chamber of a medium-sized, racially mixed city in the Southeast on April 22, 2002. Sitting in the councilor seats are twenty-two youth commissioners, who meet here in open session every month and in a planning session again once each month. This night the chambers are packed to standing room only. One hundred and fifty-seven high-school students from the city's seven public and private high schools, along with various adult mentors and officials, have come together to consider how to develop joint strategies with the Citizens Unity Commission (CUC) on supporting diversity—especially racial diversity—in the city. An African American high-school senior, who is one of the "youth planners" hired by the city to work with the youth commission, coordinates breakout sessions with perfect poise. Groups of thirty or so move off to different rooms and corners of the chamber to deliberate about racial dynamics in classes, the role of teachers and other adults, the merits of neighborhood schools versus racial redistricting, and other issues. They are serious in their analyses and recommendations for further action, yet they laugh and give spontaneous high-fives even as they disagree about sensitive issues. Neither black nor white students take stereotypical positions on any issue or proposed remedy.

The city in this scene is Hampton, Virginia, which has one of the most ambitious citywide systems to support youth civic engagement of any municipality in the United States. But San Francisco also has a youth commission that is energetically engaged in a broad range of policy discussions and formal recommendations to the city's board of supervisors and mobilizes hundreds and sometimes several thousand young people to pressure for change. Likewise, Boston has a mayor's youth council that advises the mayor and various agencies on policies affecting youth and convenes more than one thousand youth at its annual youth summits and forums designed to share and celebrate best practices of youth empowerment, community health, and violence prevention. These three cities now have nearly a decade of experience with these innovations. And youth commissions and councils in other cities across the country are developing their own models for youth representation and policy development or youth philanthropy where youth commissioners play an active role in

Youth commissioners in Hampton, Virginia, debate the merits of their new project, which will identify and recognize "youth-friendly" businesses and organizations. *Courtesy of Coalition for Youth and Hampton Youth Commission.*

making grants to young people who have creative projects for community service, service learning, and social change. The National League of Cities has been encouraging youth participation at its own national meetings, as well as youth commissions and councils among its member cities.

Youth commissions and councils are organizations recognized by the city (or in some cases the state) as an official representative of young people. They are constituted in various ways. In Hampton, the twenty-four commissioners are selected from the four public and three private high schools in the city. They are chosen by a team of current commissioners, working with adult staff from Alternatives, Inc., the local youth development agency, through a process of broad outreach to community centers, schools, and other youth groups and organizations. Some individuals are encouraged to apply based on their demonstrated leadership and community service in previous years, thus enabling structured pathways from simpler to more complex and sustained forms of engagement and community problem solving. Thus, a youth commissioner might previously have been involved in a local environmental project; then she might have served in her school on the principal's advisory group or on her neighborhood's youth advisory board, then on the citywide superintendent's advisory group, and finally on the youth commission itself.

In San Francisco young people between twelve and twenty three years old can apply to the commission. The staff selects an initial group and then submits these names to the mayor and supervisors. Each of the eleven supervisors has final say over one youth commissioner, whom it can appoint at the staff's recommendation or first invite to an interview. The mayor has one choice but also approves five additional commissioners to assure diversity. This gives the mayor more than one-third of the choices, although he or she generally approves the recommendations of the commission staff. Commissioners come from an array of other organizations where they have displayed leadership. These include public and private high schools (class president, student-council president, sports team captain), student advisory councils (San Francisco Unified School District; Lesbian, Gay, Bisexual, and Transgender Advisory Council), youth advocacy groups (Youth Making a Change, Youth in Action, LYRIC), neighborhood and Beacon centers (Western Addition, Bernal Heights), community and service groups (San Francisco Promise, Chinatown Youth Art Program), and universities (San Francisco State University).

The mayor's youth council in Boston is composed of thirty-four high-school juniors and seniors from the sixteen major neighborhoods in the city. They meet twice per month in a citywide meeting, often with the mayor. They also conduct neighborhood meetings, as well as participate in a variety of focus groups to provide advice to agencies. Applications for the youth commission are distributed widely throughout high schools, youth agencies, community centers, and among community leaders. In 1999, 600 institutions received them. Training focuses primarily on team building, running meetings, making presentations, surveying local agencies, and outreach. In the summer following initial selection or reappointment for a second year, youth councilors are enjoined to visit and build a relationship with every youth-service agency in their neighborhood. This usually involves meeting with an adult youth worker. It can also involve meeting peer leaders from that agency. The Boston Youth Connection Program, which

is a citywide youth development and peer leadership program that is part of the forty-three-member network of Boston community centers, provides a basis for relationship building that is quite extensive. Nearly every center has an adult youth worker and three paid peer leaders, aged fifteen- to eighteen-years-old, who work ten hours per week in addition to two hours of community service. Peer leaders are empowered to generate positive activities and recruit teens into their programs. Some 3,000 teens are engaged in the Youth Connection Program in a given year. Eight community centers also offer the girls' program, which has leadership development and empowerment as part of its goals. The Boston Youth Connection also co-sponsors the annual Mayor's Youth Summit.

Youth commissions and councils have certain advantages as a form of engagement. First, they can play an official role in policy development. In Hampton they report regularly to the city council and have multiple avenues of access to other agencies. Youth planners who serve as staff to the youth commission are part-time employees with offices in the planning department and receive support from adult planners in various technical matters that enable them to do participatory planning with young people across the city. They helped design and got approval for a large, new multipurpose teen center serving all areas of the city. They reviewed transportation and got changes in bus routes serving schools and a new bikeways system. In San Francisco the board of supervisors is required by charter to consult the youth commission on any changes in policy regarding children and youth—a requirement that was passed by referendum in a vigorous campaign by the city's youth movement. The youth commission holds public hearings on a broad range of issues: juvenile justice, youth homelessness, educational budgets, violence against girls and young women, agency policies on gay, lesbian, bisexual, and transgendered youth. In Michigan the Grand Rapids mayor's youth council has co-sponsored several annual KidSpeak town meetings where youth provide testimony on various issues. In attendance have been city commissioners, staff from the offices of both U.S. senators, as well as the school superintendent and other school officials. The 2001 event was televised on a major television station.

A second advantage of youth commissions and councils is that they can help develop broad and complementary forms of civic engagement and youth leadership. The San Francisco commission has sponsored several youth empowerment conferences that have drawn young people from many different kinds of organizations that are loosely part of the city's youth movement. Like Hampton, it has been very intentional about developing leadership through these linked networks. Hampton is especially intentional in this regard, which is made possible by staff members who provide continual training, mentoring, and relationship building. The city itself has several staff in the Coalition for Youth who facilitate such leadership development, but it also contracts with the nonprofit agency Alternatives, whose staff—some of whom were once youth commissioners themselves—mentor the commissioners as well as the many other young people who work on the youth advisory boards in schools, neighborhoods, and with the superintendent of schools. Youth leadership is well developed both within and across these different institutions because the city has chosen to invest significantly in developing it.

A third advantage of youth commissions or councils is that they can become an important pivot for changing the culture of the various institutional systems that affect young people. For young people to become empowered takes more than just having a voice in formal settings, like public hearings or youth commissions. It requires that institutional systems—and the adults who manage them—begin to view youth as resources for problem solving and community betterment rather than as bundles of deficits in constant need of professional "fixing." To make this shift requires allies within schools, youth-service agencies, juvenile justice and police departments, and much more. Thus, the San Francisco youth commission has worked with the California Department of Children, Youth, and Their Families to help evaluate agency programs, which fund over 140 community-based organizations and city departments. The Hampton youth commission is but one link in a citywide strategy to change the culture and practices of the police department, parks and recreation, planning department, and schools so that the professionals in these agencies work with young people as partners who have real contributions to make and not simply as clients to be served, problems to be controlled, or citizens in waiting. Culture change seeks to treat youth as citizens who have real things to contribute today. And change first began in the early 1990s when young people gathered to tell the city's leaders that this is how they expected to be treated. They were not just making more claims on behalf of youth. They wanted opportunities to make real contributions to the community, to produce things of genuine public value.

Thus, when there was a spike in juvenile crime in two neighborhoods a few years ago, instead of imposing curfews and assigning more police, the chief sought to build upon the culture of collaboration that had emerged within the department—"developing relationships with young people … as part of an overall community policing strategy," as he put it. Young people were engaged at all levels, and both youth and police were trained to build relationships and focus on assets. A school resource officer program now places officers in schools where they build relationships and trust, provide mentoring, and teach modules in classes on law. Youth and police together wrote a curriculum for the police academy to train new officers in relationship-building strategies with young people. And juvenile crime in those two neighborhoods fell by half.

From what we know of citywide systems of neighborhood representation for adults, a good institutional design can enable citizens to have real and sustained impacts on local planning, public safety, recreation, and the creative uses of public space. They can help catalyze many others forms of civic action and can give voice to previously marginalized groups. Youth commissions and councils—if well designed and staffed to provide systematic leadership development for young people and if part of culture change strategies within city agencies and school systems—promise to have similar impacts. We now have some good models from which youth, as well as city officials open to innovation, can learn. And any robust vision of a democratic city of the twenty-first century must make room for such innovation.

See also Identity and Organizing in Older Youth; KidSpeak; Political Participation and Youth Councils.

Recommended Reading

Carlson, C. (In Press). "The Hampton Experience: Creating a Model and a Context for Youth Civic Engagement." *Journal of Community Practice.*

Carlson, C., and Sykes, E. (2001). *Shaping the Future: Working Together, Changing Communities: A Manual on How to Start or Improve Your Own Youth Commission.* Hampton, VA: Hampton Coalition for Youth.

Checkoway, B., Tanene, A., and Montoya, C. (2004). "Youth Participation in Public Policy at the Municipal Level: The Case of the San Francisco Youth Commission." Unpublished Draft.

Sirianni, C. (In Press). "Civic Innovation and Youth Engagement: The Hampton Model of Systems Change and Culture Change." In *Critical Studies in Organization and Bureaucracy,* 3rd ed., edited by F. Fischer, C. Sirianni, and M. Geppert. Philadelphia: Temple University Press.

Sirianni, C. (2001/2002). *Interviews, Field Observations, and Case Analyses: Hampton, San Francisco, Boston.* Waltham, MA: Brandeis University, Center for Youth and Communities.

Sirianni, C., and Friedland, L. (2001). *Civic Innovation in America: Community Empowerment, Public Policy, and the Movement for Civic Renewal.* Berkeley: University of California Press.

Zeldin, S., Kusgen McDaniel, A., Topitzes, D., and Calvert, M. (2000). *Youth in Decision Making: A Study on the Impacts of Youth on Adults and Organizations.* Chevy Chase, MD: National 4-H Council/Innovation Center for Community and Youth Development.

Carmen Sirianni

Youth Councils. *See* Political Participation and Youth Councils.

Youth Leadership for Development Initiative (YLDI). In 1999 the Ford Foundation and the Innovation Center for Community and Youth Development set out to explore how young people benefit from involvement in civic activism and to discover new strategies and practices that youth development organizations can learn from the field of youth activism. From this powerful vision the Youth Leadership for Development Initiative (YLDI) was born. The Ford Foundation funded twelve U.S. community organizations to be part of a three-year learning collaborative. The Innovation Center for Community and Youth Development managed the initiative, selected sites with the Ford Foundation, offered technical assistance, and convened learning events with grantees.

The twelve organizations chosen to participate in YLDI reflect the diversity of the United States. They represent a broad spectrum of youth constituencies, including African American, Latino and Latina, Native American, Asian Pacific American, low-income white suburban, young women, gay, lesbian, bisexual, transgender and questioning, faith-involved, and low-income Asian immigrant women and children. Their selection was based on several factors, including the following: maintaining a focus on addressing community and social issues; having been established or run by young adults; and recognizing the relationship among youth leadership development, civic activism, and positive youth development.

The Ford Foundation also funded four international fellows from Kenya and South Africa to participate in YLDI learning.

These fellows shared perspectives on youth development and activism from their countries and took new ideas and practices with them when they returned home.

Throughout the three years the Innovation Center facilitated annual learning group meetings for the grantees. The Innovation Center also conducted annual site visits to provide individualized technical assistance on organizational development. A multiyear evaluation process conducted by social-policy research associates explored civic activism as an approach to youth development and assessed the needs and practices of youth development organizations (Lessons in Leadership 2003).

A summary of evaluation results, including lessons learned through this initiative, can be found in the full text of *Lessons in Leadership: How Young People Change Their Communities and Themselves* (2003), the executive summary of findings from the Youth Leadership for Development Initiative (YLDI). *Lessons in Leadership* summarizes the end result of the initiative; what follows here is some of its story. In truth, hundreds of stories could be told from the three years of YLDI, from the young people who participated at twelve grassroots civic activist organizations in the United States, from the four international fellows who shared their strategies and successes, and from the youth and adult staff members who attended annual gatherings of YLDI organizations. Each story is just one example of the ways young people changed themselves and their communities during this initiative and learned to continue the work and pass it on.

At Leadership Excellence Camp Akili sixty-five African American young people are led in a guided visualization of voice, music, and other sounds. The visualization begins in Africa with peaceful music, a sense of connection and freedom. It moves through the middle passage with the sound of chains, screaming, and moaning. Continuing through history, young people hear the sounds of black on black violence, gun shots, degrading music, and calls of "nigger" and "bitch" in the street. Afterward in small circles led by young adult counselors, some cry quietly, some are silent, all recognize a pain as deep as time is long.

This is the start of an educational process that begins with a connection to what Nedra Ginwright, co-founder of Leadership Excellence in Oakland, California, calls the "legacy of pain" and results in what a rough English translation of the Swahili word *akili* means (excellent minds—free minds, strategic minds, determined and empowered minds). Having experienced Camp Akili, a summer program, young people move into a yearlong experience of Stand 4 Somethin', which offers training and experience in community activism. During their participation in YLDI, the youth and adult leaders of Leadership Excellence solidified their belief that activism beyond service was a key to the kind of development they sought for young people. Nedra Ginwright sums up the difference in this way, "It's the difference between [saying], 'The park is dirty. Let's clean it up,' and 'The park is dirty. Why is the park dirty only in this low-income neighborhood? And what are we going to do about that why?'" Young leaders learn to ask those questions and to address the answers with organizing and action. As they do, says Shawn Ginwright, Leadership Excellence co-founder and assistant professor of sociology and ethnic studies at Santa Clara University, they also address the issues described by Alvin Poussaint (2001) and others as posttraumatic slavery syndrome: hopelessness, shame, despair, and disconnection from humanity. "Our work," says Nedra Ginwright, "creates healthy, socially conscious young people who have the tools and commitment to create social change" (2001).

Like Leadership Excellence, young people involved in Youth Ministries for Peace and Justice (YMPJ) in the Bronx, New York, work out of an understanding of the sociopolitical context in which they live. YMPJ youth organizers and community educators work with young people as young as seven years old to understand the culture and history of their community. Older youth engage in a program called Arts and Activism and move on to Education for Liberation. Both of these action/education programs prepare teens to participate in community service and action organized by young people engaged in a fourth program, in which they receive stipends to take on real responsibilities in community assessment and organizing social justice campaigns. During their participation in YLDI, YMPJ youth addressed environmental justice through river cleanups and organizing for green space. One youth activist, a high-school senior at the time of this writing, described the process of understanding his role in this work in the following way. On a ride through wealthy Westchester County, north of the Bronx, he and his friends saw, "A green walking park with geese, turtles, and other wildlife." Their part of the river was filled with old cars and tires, bordered by factories and roads. "We were asking ourselves, 'Why can't we have this?' The answer was, 'We can. We just have to organize.'" They did—with rallies, information campaigns, lobbying, and work projects. Their successful campaign resulted in a park where a road and a cement plant were to have been. "I grew up here," the same youth activists says, "I feel safe here. I'll stay here. I see things in the future, how they can be. I don't want a cement plant. I want a park for my children. This is my community. Nothing gets done here without my permission."

At Tohono O'odham Community Action (TOCA) on the Tohono O'odham reservation outside of Tucson, Arizona, young people also connect to a strong sense of community. In fact their work is almost exclusively about strengthening that community through revitalizing traditional culture. TOCA youth learn about traditional culture—basket weaving, farming, and so forth—from elders and pass that on to younger people. At TOCA, as in other indigenous cultures, young activists are not defined so much by their leadership as by their engagement in the work of strengthening community resources and connection.

While organizations like Leadership Excellence, YMPJ, and TOCA are organized as youth-adult collaboratives, Youth United for Community Action (YUCA) in East Palo Alto and Los Angeles, California, is entirely youth-led with staff and volunteers from their early twenties and younger. Executive director Oscar Flores speaks to one major underpinning of the organization when he says, "We trust that youth have the capacity to do their own work" (in *Youth Activism and Civic Engagement* 2001). Like other YLDI organizations, YUCA begins with education and training. YUCA youth learn how to analyze a situation, come up with a plan, and implement it. YUCA brings together youth of color to identify and address issues in their home communities. Young people prepare for this work through programs like Organizing 101 and a statewide internship program called FIRE (Fighting Injustice and Regulating Equality). At the time of this writing YUCA youth in Los Angeles were organizing around school reform; in East Palo Alto, they were addressing environmental justice.

Other YLDI organizations focused their attention on developing youth-driven activist work within larger organizations, such as was the case with Mi Casa Resource Center for Women in Denver, Colorado, or on community education, rather than organizing. At OUTRIGHT in Portland, Maine, for example, young people developed presentation skills and went in teams to schools, civic organizations, and government offices and hearings to educate and advocate around issues of concern to gay, lesbian, bisexual, transgender, and questioning young people. The Coalition for Asian and Pacific American Youth (CAPAY) in Boston, Massachusetts, created a youth-led cultural education workshop series for young people. In both OUTRIGHT and CAPAY, YLDI activities focus as well on assuring the genuine participation of young people on governing boards and in senior staff positions.

In all of the YLDI organizations young people responded to issues that directly affected their own communities. Young people at AIWA (Asian Immigrant Women Advocates) in Oakland, California, responded to the issues their parents faced in the workplace with organizing around sweatshop labor. The Young Women's Project in Washington, D.C., addressed foster care and harassment policies in the D.C. school system. The four organizations affiliated with the National Youth Advocacy Coalition's Racial and Economic Justice Initiative changed their own organizations so that they would be more inclusive of poor and of-color GLTBQ youth.

Each YLDI organization attended to preparing young people for civic and social justice activism through training and education, and all addressed organizational capacity issues, such as the training and organizational development efforts already described. In addition, many created manuals and curricula to address sustainability of their efforts. Young people at C-Beyond in Concord, California, created forms, meeting formats, and a policy and protocol manual, for example, that highlights an increasing understanding of the importance of accountability in successful community activism.

YLDI fellows in South Africa and Kenya, facing vastly different cultural and historical contexts, nonetheless addressed many of the same issues as did their colleagues in the United States. Young people and young adult activists in four different organizations—the Joint Enrichment Project and Youth Development Network in Marshalltown, South Africa, and the Kiberia Community Self Help Programme and Slums Information Development and Resource Centres in Nairobi, Kenya—organized around HIV prevention and other health issues, economic opportunities, and education. Their participation in annual learning-group meetings with other YLDI organizations led to an exchange between youth and young adult leaders of skills, ideas, organizational development initiatives, and organizing methods that enriched both U.S. and African efforts.

The Youth Leadership for Development Initiative succeeded in supporting the efforts of the youth activists involved, but more importantly, it increased their capacity for the work through technical assistance, training, information exchange, evaluation assistance, and organizational development. YLDI also sought to contribute to the knowledge base around youth activism such that other organizations could learn from the work of the YLDI participants. A thorough discussion of the lessons and stories from YLDI can be found in several Innovation Center publications, including the aforementioned *Lessons in Leadership: How Young People Change Their Communities and Themselves* and *Extending the Reach of Youth Development through Civic Activism*, as well as *Youth Activism and Civic Engagement: Lessons and Stories from Sixteen Communities*. Practical applications of the lessons of YLDI can be found in *Evaluating Civic Activism: A Curriculum for Community and Youth-Serving Organizations* and *Learning and Leading: A Tool Kit for Youth Development and Civic Activism*, both developed by the Innovation Center for Community and Youth Development. These publications and others that demonstrate, study, and support fresh ideas and strategies to engage young people and their communities are available through the Innovation Center at http://www.theinnovationcenter.org or by calling 301-270-1700.

See also Participatory Action Research (PAR) by Youth; Youth-Led Action Research, Evaluation, and Planning.

Recommended Reading

Poussaint, Alvin (2001). *Lay My Burdens Down: Suicide and the Mental Health Crisis among African Americans*. Boston: Beacon Press.

Lucinda J. Garthwaite

Youth-Led Action Research, Evaluation, and Planning. If knowledge is a form of power, then to lack knowledge is to lack power, and to build knowledge is to build power. Adding a new dimension to theories and practices that embody this understanding—participatory action research, community-based research, popular education, and empowerment evaluation—is youth-led action research, evaluation, and planning.

Youth-led action research, evaluation, and planning expands the social critique of monopolies on power/knowledge to include age-based inequities, along with (and in relationship to) inequities based on race, ethnicity, class, gender, sexuality, and other markers of difference. It seeks to build the power and capacity of young people, who are often at the margins of society, to examine, define, and ultimately shape their worlds according to their needs, visions, and values.

Breaking down the term youth-led action research, evaluation, and planning (youth REP) into its constituent parts helps build a useful definition. First, "youth-led" refers to processes in which youth make key decisions in the design and implementation of a given project. The term "action" signifies that the activities of organizing knowledge to answer questions (research), comparing performance of a system against a predetermined set of benchmarks (evaluation), and the ordering of actions to achieve specified goals (planning) are conducted in a way to produce some kind of social change. Therefore, youth REP is a process in which youth direct the development, implementation, and application of efforts to critically assess and improve the issues, institutions, and communities that affect their lives. Youth REP helps young people and their adult allies grapple with pressing social issues and formulate well-researched strategies for action or advocacy on their own behalf.

Youth REP can be understood as the convergence of two broad streams of theory and practice. One stream derives from the field of positive youth development and represents an extension of youth development principles into the realms of research, evaluation, and planning. This stream incorporates the notion of youth as resources and works in progress (as opposed to problems or risks), a value on youth leadership, the notion of creating contexts with enabling supports and opportunities, youth action, civic engagement, and more recently through youth organizing and attention to youth as "agents of social change" in communities and institutions such as schools.

The other stream arises from the fields of research and evaluation and represents an extension of their participatory-oriented dimensions to include youth as researchers/evaluators. Such practices are based on an epistemology of intimacy, of local knowledge, and the closeness of the researcher to the research subjects, as opposed to the notion of truth arising only at an objective distance. In this ethnographic perspective research about youth could have no better researchers than youth themselves. Principal inspirations in participatory research include the action research of Miles Horton and the Highlander Center, popular education, and the notion of *conscienceiçao* (developing a critical awareness and agency) from Brazilian educator Paulo Freire, ethnography as participatory-action research, and feminist critiques of the power inherent in the act of research. These foundational sources have been applied to the practices of youth ethnographers. Notions of indigenous and decolonized research, empowerment evaluation, and participatory-health assessment are defining a new branch of the evaluation field that focuses on the participant and the community from which he or she comes, as a means in realizing social change and self-determination, as opposed to merely producing data. More recent work has focused explicitly on youth-led research and evaluation.

Together these two streams define a region of theory and practice that values both the insights from the informational *products* of the inquiry by engaging youth in critical inquiry and the empowerment *processes* experienced by its participants directly, and the larger community as a whole as a result of developing and applying new analytical and communication skills. When combined the products and processes of youth REP provide a critical component of progressive social change.

The constituent terms of youth REP— research, evaluation, and planning—can be thought of as distinct yet interrelated elements of a cycle of praxis, that is, action/ reflection. Considering these elements as a whole is important for reasons relating to both effectiveness and equity. Planning mechanisms that utilize research and evaluation to guide and critique social action are necessary to ensure a social-learning process and to avoid a fragmentation between the thinkers and doers, so prevalent in class-stratified societies. While affecting most disenfranchised classes, such fragmentation often serves as a special barrier to youth engagement in decisions that affect their lives. Youth are typically objects of study but not the authors of these research or evaluation studies; they are typically the subjects of policies but not the policymakers. Even when youth do have opportunities to participate in research and evaluation, their involvement typically ends with the production of the final

report, with the action steps occurring in forums reserved (implicitly or explicitly) for adults. Alternatively, when youth are granted a policy voice—as in the case of youth councils—they are rarely able to generate independent data sources to inform or assess their policy recommendations. To truly serve a progressive role in youth activism, youth-led research, evaluation, and planning must be part of an ongoing process in which the production of knowledge and the organization of action are mutually informative.

The term youth-led research, evaluation, and planning raises the question of what it means to be "youth-led." As it turns out, there is no one answer to this question, and instead there is wide variation in approaches to youth leadership within research, evaluation, and planning. The model below consists of four quadrants characterized by differing mixes of youth leadership roles in a project. The two major dimensions are *authority* or extent and depth of their decision-making and *inclusion* or the quantity and frequency of their involvement.

As one moves from the origin point along the horizontal axis, youth are included in more phases of the project. Projects in the higher inclusion quadrant will tend to involve youth in both the earlier stages

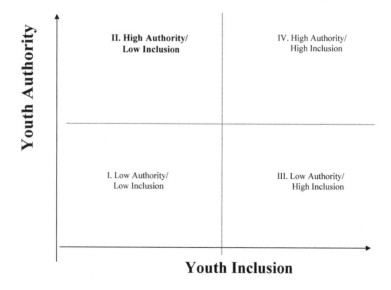

(project initiation and conceptualization) and later stages (analysis, writing, presentation, and implementation). Projects in which youth are involved in only the data collection, to take a typical example, would be characterized as being low in inclusion. As one moves upward on the vertical axis, youth have greater authority within the project, that is, they exert greater degrees of decision-making leadership over the phases in which they are included. For example, projects in which youth carry out research and evaluate designs produced by adults or play only an advisory role would be characterized by a low degree of authority. In contrast, projects in which youth have equal or even superior decision-making authority to that of adults—such as youth having veto power over research-design decisions—would be considered high youth authority projects.

This model raises the question of what kinds of institutional resources are needed to support meaningful and sustainable youth involvement in a given project. Different locations in the matrix will require organizational supports, resources, and training. For example, projects with high levels of youth authority will need staff with strong facilitative leadership capacities as well as an organizational culture and structure that can at least accommodate if not embrace youth leadership. Projects with high levels of inclusion will need a planning process that brings in youth early and has the capacity to maintain this youth involvement throughout the project. Of course, projects that are high in both youth authority and inclusion will require organizational capacities to respond to both dimensions. In sum, it is critical that youth-led research, evaluation, and planning projects ensure an alignment between their goals, organizational capacities, and levels of youth inclusion and authority.

One example of a youth REP project that was successful in its alignment of these factors was a youth-led neighborhood needs assessment conducted in the South of Market neighborhood of San Francisco, California.

Once a vibrant low-income neighborhood populated largely by a range of immigrants and merchant marines, South of Market (SOMA) in San Francisco has been the site of heated conflicts over its redevelopment and gentrification. Concerned that youth voice was missing from the debates and decisions over future planning in the neighborhood, a collaborative of local youth-serving organizations called SOYAC (Serving Our Youth and Community) secured funding from the San Francisco Redevelopment Authority for a youth-led community needs assessment. Ly Nguyen, then co-director of Oasis, one of the member organizations of SOYAC, described the purpose of the project by noting, "I have worked in the neighborhood for almost five years and found it difficult to find any documentation of current youth needs and trends in the South of Market neighborhood. I knew that it was crucial that the youth voice and needs be documented so that the rest of the city would finally believe that there are children and youth in SOMA who demand a higher quality of life."

Youth In Focus, a nonprofit organization that trains underrepresented youth and adult allies in youth-led action research, evaluation, and planning, provided technical assistance for the project. Over the course of four months a seven-member team of high-school students calling itself the Social Investigators designed, administered, analyzed, and reported on the results of a survey on youth experiences and aspirations for the SOMA neighborhood. Based on their data, the SOYAC Social Investigators produced a detailed written report and video called *Realism*.

Because of the youth team's control over most of the decisions associated with the research design and implementation and its involvement from the beginning to the action phases of the project, the SOYAC project can be considered to be located in the high-inclusion/high-authority quadrant.

Many of the youth team's recommendations speak to the connections between youth development and social change that their action-research project uncovered. For example, the youth's research provided a critical update in a city-sponsored study of the neighborhood done a decade ago. SOYAC stated:

One of the major issues identified during the 1992 assessment was the lack of a large neighborhood park. This need still has not been fulfilled by the city. [Our data show] that out of the 194 youth surveyed, one hundred stated that they would like to see a new park.... The need for a neighborhood park is essential in the South of Market neighborhood since 53 percent of the youth stated that their housing lacks a play area.... South of Market youth and families are forced to travel outside the neighborhood to find a space for outdoor family functions. It is essential that there be a green or open space for the well-being of the neighborhood (SOYAC Youth Collective, 2002).

The team used these products to advocate for SOMA youth neighborhood development and investment priorities with the San Francisco board of supervisors, the redevelopment agency, neighborhood networks, and funders. For its efforts the project received a special commendation from the San Francisco board of supervisors. Through its research, evaluation, and creative final products, the SOYAC Youth Collective was able to give voice to perspectives of young people in a neighborhood that has historically been shaped by outside commercial and civic forces. For example, SOYAC used the youth-led needs assessment as a basis for a collaborative campaign to pressure the local movie theater to offer low-priced youth tickets as a way to create more accessible youth spaces in the neighborhood. One youth activist described this as an effort to push the movie theater to "stop displacing youth of color" through high prices and aggressive antiloitering practices. The youth also screened their *Realism* video for the San Francisco Department of Parks and Recreation to inform the design of a new neighborhood park.

Ly Nguyen affirmed the value of youth REP as a resource for youth and community activism, saying, "It can make a huge impact on an entire community. For us, the process impacted SOYAC and our members along with the community. One of the community impacts is that it gives a reason for organizations to lend their resources to a youth-led process. In a sense it is safe to say that the youth REP process can be completed not only by an organization but also by a neighborhood network" (Youth in Focus 2002).

Youth REP has shown itself to be a potent approach to organizing knowledge for social action. However, there are a number of questions and challenges that face the developing field of youth-led action research, evaluation, and planning. Many of these questions relate ways that youth REP can be structured and implemented to respond to varying organizational and community contexts. For example, under what circumstances and in response to what sets of goals should a youth REP project be located within the above-described youth leadership quadrants? What are the tradeoffs between varying levels of youth leadership and youth authority in the quality of the product and the developmental impacts of the youth REP process? And finally, how do the variables of youth authority and youth inclusion affect the ability of a youth REP project to catalyze social change? These are clearly empirical questions and will require careful research to understand—research ideally undertaken in partnership with youth researchers themselves.

See also Innovations in Civic Participation (ICP); Participatory Action Research (PAR) by Youth; Youth Leadership for Development Initiative (YLDI).

Recommended Reading

Checkoway, B., and Goodyear, L., eds. (Spring 2003). "Youth Engagement in Community Evaluation Research" [Special issue]. *Community Youth Development Journal*, 4 (1).

Fetterman, D. M. (2001). *Foundations of Empowerment Evaluation*. Thousand Oaks, CA: Sage Publications.

Freire, P. (1970). *Pedagogy of the Oppressed*. New York: Seabrook Press.

Irby, M., Ferber, T., and Pittman, K. with Tolman, J., and Yohalem, N. (2001). "Youth Action: Youth Contributing to Communities, Communities Supporting Youth." *Community and Youth Development Series*, vol. 6. Takoma Park, MD: Forum for Youth Investment, International Youth Foundation.

London, J., and Chabran, M. (Spring 2004). "Action Research and Social Justice: Exploring the Connections." [Special issue]. *Practicing Anthropology*, 28 (2): 45–50.

Rubin, B., and Silva, E., eds. (2003). *Critical Voices in School Reform: Students Living through Changes*. London: Routledge.

SOYAC Youth Collective (2002). *Youth Led Needs Assessment for the South of Market*. San Francisco: SOYAC Youth Collective.

Youth in Focus (2002). *Youth REP Step by Step: An Introduction to Youth-Led Research and Evaluation*. Oakland, CA: Youth in Focus.

Jonathan London

Z

Zapatista Rebellion (Mexico). In Mexico young people have a history of resistance against corrupt hierarchal power structures. The most well-known of these student movements are those of the 1960s, 1970s, and 1990s, in which mainly urban, middle- and working-class students from ages thirteen to mid-twenties rallied the nation against the corruption and abuse of the Institutional Revolutionary Party (PRI), the political party that had monopolized Mexican government since the 1920s. Less obvious is the participation of youth in one of the most visible of contemporary rebellions, that of the Zapatista insurgents of Chiapas, Mexico.

The role of youth is well known in movements in Argentina and Brazil through such groups as H.I:J:O:S., a coalition of the children of those who were "disappeared" during their countries' so-called dirty wars. In contrast, the presence of the youth activists in indigenous movements is less noticeable, as they do not form groups apart from the main insurgency or movement, but rather they comprise the majority of the movement. In other words, the youth in Chiapas *are* the Zapatistas. This is due in part to the fact that indigenous societies are communal and the lines between generations are not marked in the same way as their European-influenced mestizo counterparts.

Furthermore, in general Mexico is a country of youth who constitute more than 32 percent of the population. Due to cultural tradition and infant mortality, indigenous women begin childbearing as early as thirteen or fourteen. In the recent community consultations held throughout the Zapatista-held municipalities, the voices of all community members twelve years old or older were heard. In fact, many positions of authority within the communities are held by young members, a significant number of them young, single women. And while in general youth activists have shaped public discourse and acted as catalysts for social change, young indigenous women of the Zapatista movement have set the stage for changes in women's position in Mexico's rigid, patriarchal society, transformations that have profoundly impacted women throughout the country.

Youth and Social Change: The 1960s

Students in Mexico rose up against authority in the 1960s, as did their counterparts around the world. They, too, experienced the violent backlash of those in power. In their struggle against the Institutional Revolutionary Party (PRI), which had then been ruling for forty years, the Mexican student movement of the 1960s galvanized for the first time in that country's history a broad coalition of civic grassroots organizations and workers' unions that cut across class lines. They protested at and occupied their schools and university campuses. Just before the 1968 Olympics in Mexico City they took to the streets, angering and embarrassing Mexican President Díaz Ordaz just as the cameras of the international press, on site for the Olympics, transmitted the unrest to the world.

President Ordaz, however, was unwilling to forego the opportunity to showcase a "modern" Mexico. To eliminate any distraction the President ordered the army to shoot to kill during a peaceful, jubilant

In this 1994 photo, young members of the Zapatista National Liberation Army guard the entrance to the secret Zapatista camp. *Copyright Keith Dannemiller/Corbis.*

student protest. He also had on hand sharp-shooters who, positioned on rooftops, were directed to shoot at the army (killing an estimated forty members) to provide the president with an alibi to justify this horrific act. In other words, he would claim that the students were armed and had shot first. That day more than 300 students were gunned down in the Plaza of the Three Cultures in what became known as the Massacre of Tlatelolco. Many were cornered in the plaza and then chased and shot as they tried to escape, and more than 1,000 others were arrested and jailed.

In sad irony this blatant violence against unarmed youth so shocked the nation that the massacre became a watershed in Mexican history. Through these youth civil society gained a face and a voice as they laid bare for the world and their fellow Mexicans the corruption and impunity of their government. The students had openly challenged the ruling elites over funda-

mental issues, including constitutionally guaranteed free higher education; freedom of speech and assembly; police brutality and the harassment and torture not only of students but also of independent journalists, human-rights monitors, environmentalists, workers, peasants, and indigenous peoples; electoral fraud; and the widening income gap, lack of jobs, and a growing generalized hopelessness among the swelling ranks of the poor.

The students would rise up several times more during the last decades of the twentieth century. They would protest peacefully and again be targeted by a corrupt government and a repressive police force that would brutalize and disappear the protestors with impunity. The students' installations on university campuses were ransacked; many students were unjustifiably arrested or hunted down and beaten by government-paid paramilitary squads of reactionary youth. The students' strength of purpose rallied and emboldened broad sectors of society. In these and subsequent struggles young Mexican activists risked brutal retaliation as they inserted themselves on the public stage as they fought for social justice and transformation for all Mexicans.

But Mexico is a divided country in which indigenous people comprise approximately 30 percent of the population (60 percent are mestizos, people of mixed European and indigenous ancestry) and are estimated to number 10–20 million (5 million of whom speak one of more than fifty surviving indigenous languages). Despite their large numbers, indigenous Mexicans have remained, since the Spanish conquest 500 years ago, marginalized, devalued, invisible, or worse, abused, and oppressed. In light of their long history of marginalization and abuse, the emergence of an indigenous insurgency in 1994 should not have been surprising. That indigenous insurgency sent waves of hope, not felt since the 1960 Marxist socialist revolutions that swept Latin America, across the national and international landscape. The story of these later revolutionaries also reveals the cultural differences between the indigenous and mestizo cultures of Mexico. It shows clearly that indigenous resistance today is not a folkloric, nostalgic glance back to the past but a vibrant movement in which youth, notably young women, play a major role. Some basic historic information will help those of us on the outside to understand the indigenous peoples and insurgency from their point of view.

In 1521 the Spanish conquered the Aztecs in central Mexico, a developed civilization known for its architecture, science, medicine, art, poetry, and rich culture. That brutal defeat ushered in 300 years of colonization and annihilation of tens of millions of Indians in Mexico alone. From the conquest to the present day, disenfranchised and denied the most basic human rights, the indigenous peoples of Mexico have labored on the lands of the wealthy or served as maids and nannies in their homes.

Long after the colonial period, in the modern democratic Republic of Mexico, indigenous Mexicans continue to have their lands stolen; their cultural identity, languages, and traditions suppressed; and their wisdom and knowledge devalued and ignored—at least until those things become profitable, as has been the case of indigenous herbal medicine. Many indigenous groups have fought against this abuse and for dignity and recognition of their rights as Mexican citizens and for their autonomy, only to be further suppressed, murdered, disappeared, and violated. Racism and discrimination against the indigenous in Mexico has continued almost unabated since the conquest and has indeed flourished over the last century. Their fertile lands along the Pacific Coast (once the breadbasket of the indigenous world) were stolen from them. They were pushed onto the thin, rocky soil of the highlands. As if that weren't enough, the discovery of oil and other investment-attracting resources in this part of Mexico has enticed Mexican and foreign elites to once again push into indigenous lands. The result has been struggles and violence among communities competing for the same poor lands and the highest level of poverty and desperation in Mexico occurring in Chiapas and the neighboring state of Oaxaca, as these government statistics comparing Chiapas with the rest of the country indicate. The literacy rate in Mexico is 87 percent, 69 percent in Chiapas (90 percent do not have even a primary education). The percentage of households with running water is 79 percent in Mexico, 58 percent in Chiapas. The percentage of households with access to electricity is 88 percent in Mexico, 67 percent in Chiapas (95 percent living in houses with dirt floors) (*Anuario Estadstico de los Estados Unidos Mexicanos* 1991).

This situation has been exacerbated over the last fifteen years, particularly since the conceptualization and implementation of the North American Free Trade Agreement (NAFTA). Mexico needs to create 19.2 million jobs in order to keep up with the demands of its labor force. As a country of youth, job growth will lag behind the number of job seekers. But more devastating to the economy and to Mexican youth have been the job losses across the country in all sectors, attributable to NAFTA. Like other developing nations, Mexico, a nation of microbusinesses and agriculture, cannot compete with the United States and its "unfree" trade practices such as agricultural subsidies. Consequently, through the 1990s the disparity between the rich and the poor has become very severe. Fifty million people sank into poverty, while twenty-four new billionaires topped Forbes' list of the wealthiest people in the world. As if that were not already enough, the conditions faced by most people, especially the poor, have worsened substantially during the past ten years as the government has implemented structural adjustment and free trade policies that have eroded 40 percent of the purchasing power of the Mexican poor. Mexican President Carlos Salinas' controversial antipoverty program, ironically called *Solidarity*, never reached the Lacandon area to any significant extent. Eight to ten people continue to sleep together in one-room structures, and most water supplies are polluted by human waste. Lack of health care means children readily die of diarrhea and dehydration, of tuberculosis, or of some other preventable or curable disease; rates of malnutrition, infant mortality, and morbidity are the highest in the country.

So, like their ethnic brothers and sisters of Central America did in earlier decades, the inhabitants of the southeastern region of Mexico decided they would take no more, and Chiapas became an incubator of armed resistance. One of the most recent and perhaps the most well-known rebellion is that of the Zapatista National Liberation Army (EZLN). EZLN, which is located in the southeastern Mexican state of Chiapas and is led by subcommandant Marcos (a young urban college professor), sprang onto the national scene on January 1, 1994. In this new manifestation of a centuries-old battle women and youth have played a significant role in bringing revolution not only to the "outside"—to nonindigenous Mexican society but also to the "inside," forging revolutionary change in the structures of Indian society and culture.

The Rebirth of the Zapatistas

On New Year's Eve 1993 the Zapatista army rose up in the highlands of Chiapas and took control of the government offices in six municipalities. The Mexican army, already with a strong presence, attacked and violence raged for twelve days until both sides agreed upon a ceasefire. Their personal identities erased behind ski masks, in 1993 the Zapatistas declared in the EZLN Declaration of the Lacandon Jungle: "We have nothing to lose, absolutely nothing, no decent roof over our heads, no land, no work, poor health, no food, no education, no right to freely and democratically choose our leaders, no independence from foreign interests, and no justice for ourselves or our children. But we say enough is enough! We are the descendants of those who truly built this nation, we are the millions of dispossessed, and we call upon all of our brethren to join our crusade, the only option to avoid dying of starvation!"

The EZLN takes its name in honor of Emiliano Zapata, hero of the landless peasants of the south during the 1910 Mexican Revolution. The Zapatista movement is composed primarily of Tzeltal, Tzotzil, Ch'ol, and Tojolabal Maya Indians. Unlike similar guerrilla armies in Central America, the Zapatistas' rank and file is filled with large numbers of teenagers and young adults. Decades after the 1910 revolution, these new Zapatista peasant rebels are still fighting for justice, democracy, liberty, and dignity for all Mexicans.

The young generation is fighting to maintain its cultures, languages, and dignity, even as these youth seek twenty-first-century methods for a sustainable economy and improvement of the misery that has been theirs for centuries. They are not opposed to taking advantage of alternative methods to better their lives and livelihoods, including modern farm machinery and production technologies. However, they strongly condemn neo-liberal capitalist globalization that has even further dehumanized and exploited the people who are already the poorest in the world. Thus, they chose January 1, 1994, to "come out," the day the North American Free Trade Agreement (NAFTA) went into effect. The Zapatistas were demanding a voice in the national arena, the right to self-representation, and autonomy.

The Zapatistas are not stuck in a romantic notion of their indigenous culture or past. In fact, from the beginning they have utilized technology to get their message out, a tactic that has helped them avoid total annihilation at the hands of the Mexican army, the fate of indigenous uprisings throughout Mexico's history. The Zapatistas, by transmitting through phones, faxes, cell phones, and computers, quickly gained sympathizers in the United States, Eastern and Western Europe, South America, Asia, Africa, and Australia. Their model of nonviolent self-determination and self-governance has become a model for numerous movements of marginalized and minoritized peoples worldwide. The Zapatistas have also generated hundreds of groups, many made up of youth activists, which have organized and taken up their fight worldwide. Young people from around the world have joined the youth of the Zapatista movement in the international struggle against corporate greed and environmental degradation and for dignity for all humans.

Zapatismo has become a worldwide popular movement of youth who infuse into music, art, dance, and theater their expressions of unrest and noncompliance. Graffiti artists from around the country and world join young Zapatista artists who, like the Mexican muralist of the postrevolutionary period, create visual histories of indigenous peoples' struggles, which cover public walls throughout the Zapatista municipalities. These murals serve as an important educational and motivational tool, especially in the largely illiterate communities.

In 2004 at the ten-year anniversary of the uprising it appeared that peace efforts had stalled. This was a period marked by the invasion of some 60,000 army troops in indigenous territories and unfulfilled promises of the San Andrés Peace Accord. Thus the Zapatistas inaugurated a new initiative, Committees for Good Government, which seeks to cultivate local governance in autonomous communities. Young Zapatistas are at the forefront of this effort to create for indigenous people alternative, sustainable ways of living. From its inception the EZLN was a movement of young rebels. Five men and one woman first organized in the mountains of the Lacandon jungle of Chiapas in 1983. By 1993 the movement's membership had grown to approximately 4,500 combatants and 2,000 reserves, the majority of whom were teenagers and young adults under the age of twenty-five. While they were integrated into all levels of the organization, they did form subgroups, such as the Youth Rebels, who met weekly to read, participate in sports, dance, and socialize. And by 1994, 40 percent of them were women.

Women on the Front Lines

Many of the women Zapatistas joined as young teenagers, all to join the fight for indigenous rights. Other motivations gave these young women the strength to face off with their traditions. In those traditions women are viewed as the property of males, subject to their desires, violence, and abuse and to a life of servitude that includes sixteen- to eighteen-hour workdays with little or no control over their bodies or lives. They have been denied education and could be given away in marriage, as early as age thirteen. Rape is common, even among family members, and being raped leaves a woman a social outcast. By custom and lack of availability women have been barred from using birth control. Consequently they may give birth to five to ten children, sometimes beginning as a young teen. Indigenous women occupy the lowest rung of the social ladder and, consequently, are the most vulnerable to poverty.

These examples of women's devalued position in indigenous society explain why so many have been willing to leave home for the harsh mountainous jungles to fight for social change. They ran away without permission from their families or communities, and if caught, they could be subjected to beatings and other violent punishments. But they continue to take the risk. They do so for the ideals of the Zapatistas as well as in self-defense against the physical and psychological abuse imposed upon them by patriarchal society. More than 30 percent of those who have joined the Zapatista movement denounce having children in order to dedicate themselves to the struggle.

Captain Maribel of the Insurgent Infantry is Tzeltal and was not yet fifteen years old when she joined the insurgency in the mountains. She says, "The toughest moment in those nine years was when I had to climb the first hill, called "the hill from hell"; after that everything else was easy" (http://www.actlab.utexas.edu/~geneve/ zapwomen/enter.html). Ana Maria, a twenty-six-year-old infantry major tells that since she was eight years old she has participated in peaceful protests, marches, and meetings. She says, "I am an insurgent. I have dedicated my whole life and all my time to the cause. My family is committed to the struggle and has always been organizing in order to have a life with dignity, but we never achieved it in that way.... I was fourteen when I joined the struggle. At first there were only two of us women among the eight or ten people who began the movement over ten years ago. Many of the women who have joined the EZLN have come without telling their families" (http://www.actlab.utexas.edu/~geneve/ zapwomen/enter.html). Major Ana Maria led the commando that occupied San Cristobal de las Casas at dawn on January 1, 1994.

A most significant contribution of the young Zapatista women, however, has been the revolution inside the movement. Early in the insurgency's history the women realized that the sexism that shaped their miserable existence outside the movement did not disappear once they joined. Men resisted women combatants, expected the women to take care of the "domestic" tasks, such as preparing food, laundry, and so on. The women, however, would not accept inferior positions in a movement supposedly dedicated to democratic reform. They took their complaints to the EZLN leaders, particularly subcommandant Marcos, and eventually won parity with their male counterparts. All members of the army would rotate jobs in the camps; all would fight side by side, and both women and men could work their way up the chain of command. This was a coup, considering that in earlier Marxist movements and in the student and Latino/Chicano movements of the 1960s women did not gain such equality and had to form feminist groups to fight generalized sexism.

Old habits do not disappear overnight, but nonetheless, Zapatista women, many in their teens and early twenties, have achieved status and respect within the movement and their communities. They have worked inside and outside the rebel areas to create a national forum for changes in laws and traditions that begin to safeguard women from the violence perpetrated upon them at all levels and in all socioeconomic groups in Mexican society. Through conventions and meetings these young Zapatista women have shaped the discourse on gender and democracy in a way that serves as a model for women around the world. They are like their counterparts of the 1910 Mexican Revolution, the *Soldaderas*, some of whom became leaders, even generals, when they were mere teenagers. They have served on the front lines. Unlike their predecessors, though, they have gotten their story out, inspiring women across Mexico and around the world.

Final Thoughts

The youth of Mexico have placed their bodies and spirits at the service of social change. We think of the urban student movements of 1968 and the decades to follow. But one of the most important revolutions of the twentieth century, the Zapatista rebellion in Chiapas, Mexico, has provided a model for disenfranchised and oppressed groups around the world. Although not generally known as a youth movement, it nonetheless was conceived of and carried out by indigenous youth. And young women, with perhaps the most to gain from true democratic reform, continue to serve on the front lines of the armed and cultural battles.

See also Australia, Youth Activism in; Demographic Trends Affecting the World's Youth; Eastern Europe, Youth and Citizenship in; Europe, Comparing Youth Activism in; European Identity and Citizenship; Global Justice Activism; Homies Unidos; Immigrant Youth in Europe—Turks in Germany; Immigrant Youth in the United States; India, Youth Activism in; Indonesia, Youth Activism in; Nigeria, Youth Activism in; Palestinian *Intifada*; Russia, Youth Activism in; Serbia, Youth Activism in (1990–2000); Soweto Youth Activism (South Africa); State and Youth, The; Statute of the Child and Adolescent (Brazil); Tiananmen Square Massacre (1989); Transnational Identity; Transnational Youth Activism; Turkey, Youth Activism in; United Nations, Youth Activism and; Xenophobia; Zionist Youth Organizations.

Recommended Reading

Anuario Estadstico de los Estados Unidos Mexicanos (1991). Mexico City: Instituto Naconal de Estadistica, Geografia E Informatica.

Ecker, R. L. (January 2005). *The Tlatelolco Massacre in Mexico*. See http://www.hobrad.com/massacre.htm.

Katzenberger, E. (1995). *First World, Ha, Ha, Ha: The Zapatista Challenge*. San Francisco: City Lights Books.

Rojas, R., ed. (1994). *And the Women?* Mexico: Editiones La Correa Feminista. Centro de Investigacion y Capacitacion de la Mujer A.C.

Selected readings available at http://www.eco.utexas.edu/Homepages/Faculty/Cleaver/begin.html.

Rosset, P., and Cunningham, S. *Understanding Chiapas*. See http://www.apostate.com/politics/understanding-chiapas.html.

Stephen, L. (2002). *¡Zapata Lives¡ Histories and Cultural Politics in Southern Mexico*. Los Angeles: University of California Press.

University of Texas. See Web site at http://www.actlab.utexas.edu/~geneve/zapwomen/enter.html.

Women and the Zapatista Movement. See http://www.actlab.utexas.edu/~geneve/zapwomen/enter.html.

Zapatista National Liberation Army (EZLN) Declaration of the Lacandon Jungle (1993). In *Understanding Chiapas* by Peter Rosset and Shea Cunningham. See http://retanet.unm.edu.

Roselyn Costantino

Zionist Youth Organizations. A famous sage, Rabbi Hillel, once said, "If I am not for myself, then who will be for me? But if I am only for myself, what am I? And if not now, when?" (Pirkei Avot 1:14). In a time when declining social interaction and low political engagement abound, more citizens appear to be for themselves than for their communities or countries. Zionist youth organizations attempt to change this pattern by engaging Jewish youth in civic-minded peer groups. Like many other youth organizations, Zionist youth organizations get youth more civically and politically engaged. They encourage participants to support Israel, as well as their own countries and communities, through volunteerism, social justice, leadership, political engagement, and environmentalism. Before evaluating how they achieve such goals it is important to define the term Zionism.

In 1893 when the term was first used Zionism described an international movement that sought the official establishment of a Jewish national or religious homeland in Palestine, the Jewish people's historical and biblical native soil. Today, though, the word denotes an international movement that supports the existing state of Israel. Such support is executed in many ways, including: (1) fiscal aid, including monetary donations, visits to Israel, and the

In this 1925 photo, members of a Zionist youth group prepare to march through Jerusalem. *Library of Congress.*

purchase of Israeli goods; (2) educational programming on topics like Israeli history, Jewish holiday events, and learning Hebrew; and, (3) promoting activism in the form of social justice and leadership.

Despite the claims of some, Zionist ideology is not inherently equivalent to racism, especially from a Jewish point of view; it simply encourages a sense of nationalistic pride in the state of Israel. As both an ideology and a movement, Zionism was, in fact, born as a response to anti-Semitism. The very notion of Zionism as racism was one of the biggest slogans in German propaganda encouraging anti-Semitism and justification for the Holocaust. There is a fine line between feelings of nationalism and thoughts of xenophobia or racism, but the separation is there; it is up to individuals to ensure that the line does not blur. Zionist youth organizations tend to do just that.

In fact, some specifically promote intergroup relations. In at least one Israeli Zionist youth organization, Ha'Noar Ha'Oved V'HaLomed, there are groups made up partially of Arab and Druze members. Another organization, Habonim Dror, has sponsored events that teach Jewish youth about Muslim culture and beliefs in an attempt to increase acceptance between the groups. This type of pluralistic activity is inconsistent with a racist ideology. Even Martin Luther King Jr. supported the Zionist cause. In a 1967 letter he wrote, "What is anti-Zionist? It is the denial of the Jewish people of a fundamental right that we justly claim for the people of Africa and freely accord all other nations of the globe" (Schneier 1999). This right is the basis of Zionist philosophy and the collective tie that binds various Zionist youth groups together into a larger movement.

The Zionist youth movement began in the early 1900s after a group of educated Belarusian teenagers read Dr. Theodor Ze'ev Herzl's (1896) book called *The Jewish*

State. In Russia these young people had faced anti-Semitism demonstrated through violent or fatal acts committed by the ruling Cossacks. Thus, they longed for a safe place for themselves and their families. The momentum spread internationally, and the Zionist movement was created. The commitment of the youth members helped revive the then dormant language of Hebrew. These youth also raised money for the cause, created activist communities, and spread their dream of statehood. They were so dedicated, in fact, that members of these groups comprised many of the first and most influential settlers in the land of Israel. They established agricultural settlements (*moshavot*) and voluntary communal villages (*kibbutzim*), many of which still exist today.

Today the Zionist youth movement includes Jews of multiple ethnic and national origins, political perspectives, and levels of religiosity (and secularism), and some non-Jews as well. The more than thirty existing organizations serve millions of youth, some as young as seven years of age and others as old as thirty-five. According to the World Zionist Organization, youth group organizations exist in more than forty countries, including some large ones like Canada and the United States, as well as other smaller countries like Estonia, Macedonia, and Slovakia.

Although the groups that exist in the movement are as diverse in their perspectives as in their membership, they share certain goals. An examination of thirty organizations' mission statements revealed their commitment to the promotion of community service; good communal, national, and international citizenship; interest in domestic and international politics; fighting anti-Semitism; developing Zionist values and a Jewish identity; promoting intergroup relations; and in the case of some, preserving the environment. Different organizations, though, carry out these objectives in different ways. Religious groups tend to examine these issues through the lens of biblical and holy texts,

while secular ones may not; some groups are completely led by youth members, while others utilize paid adult staff. Many groups offer older members a trip to Israel, where, in addition to sightseeing, political debates, education, history, and service are generally part of the itinerary. Some groups also have affiliated summer camps, which are either completely youth run (even the director is a member younger than twenty-five years of age) or utilize a combination of older youth and adult leadership.

Despite their activist nature and the size of their membership, very little research has been done on Zionist youth organizations. What little research does exist suggests that youth who participate in these organizations feel that it intensifies their religious commitments, sense of Jewish identity, connection to Israel, civic engagement, and participation in social action.

See also Australia, Youth Activism in; Demographic Trends Affecting the World's Youth; Eastern Europe, Youth and Citizenship in; Europe, Comparing Youth Activism in; European Identity and Citizenship; Immigrant Youth in Europe—Turks in Germany; Immigrant Youth in the United States; India, Youth Activism in; Indonesia, Youth Activism in; Nigeria, Youth Activism in; Palestinian *Intifada*; Russia, Youth Activism in; Serbia, Youth Activism in (1990–2000); Soweto Youth Activism (South Africa); State and Youth, The; Statute of the Child and Adolescent (Brazil); Tiananmen Square Massacre (1989); Transnational Identity; Transnational Youth Activism; Turkey, Youth Activism in; United Nations, Youth Activism and; Xenophobia; Zapatista Rebellion (Mexico).

Recommended Reading

Bernstein, D. (1992). *Pioneers and Homemakers: Jewish Women in Pre-State Israel*. Albany: State University of New York.

Dean, K. C., and Yost, P. R. (1990). "A Synthesis of the Research and a Descriptive Overview of Protestant, Catholic, and Jewish Religious Youth Programs in the United States." Paper commissioned by the Carnegie Task Force on Youth Development and Community

Programs. Washington, D.C.: Carnegie Council on Adolescent Development.

Flanagan, C. (2001). "Volunteerism, Leadership, Political Socialization, and Civic Engagement." In *Handbook of Adolescent Psychology*, edited by R. M. Lerner and L. Steinberg. New York: Wiley.

King Jr., M. L. (1999). "Letter to an Anti-Zionist Friend." In *Shared Dreams: Martin Luther King, Jr. and the Jewish Community*, edited by M. Schneier. New York: Jewish Lights. (Original work published 1967.)

Neuberger, N. (n.d.). Binyamin Ze'ev Herzl: Father of Zionism 1860–1904. See http://www.mfa.gov.il/MFA/History/Modern%20History/Centenary%20of%20Zionism/Binyamin%20Ze-ev%20Herzl-%Father%20of%2020 Zionism.

Putnam, R. (1995). "Bowling Alone." *Journal of Democracy*, 6: 65–78.

Weill, B. (n.d.). "Zionist Glossary." See http://www.jafi.org.il/education/100/gloss/#z.

Lisa Chauveron

List of Useful Organizations

Academy for Educational Development (AED) Center for Youth Development and Policy Research
AED Headquarters
1825 Connecticut Avenue, NW
Washington, D.C. 20009-5721
Tel: 202-884-8000
Fax: 202-884-8400

New York Office
100 5th Avenue
New York, NY 10011
Tel: 212-243-1110
Fax: 212-627-0407

The center's mission is to create and strengthen the infrastructures that support positive development for all youth in America. Activities include public education, research, policy formulation, and technical assistance aimed at U.S. communities that seek to expand opportunities and support systems for disadvantaged young people.

Applied Research Center
3781 Broadway
Oakland, CA 94611
Tel: 510-653-3415
Fax: 510-653-3427
E-mail: arc@arc.org

The Applied Research Center is a public policy, educational, and research institute whose work emphasizes issues of race and social change.

Australian Clearinghouse for Youth Studies (ACYS)
Private Bag 64
Hobart Tasmania 7001
Australia
Tel: 61-3-6226-2591
Fax: 61-3-6226-2578
E-mail: ACYS@educ.utas.edu.au

ACYS provides information products and services for those working in the youth field and for anyone with an interest in youth. This includes practitioners in areas such as health and education, researchers, policymakers, youth workers, and youth-service providers, as well as students and parents.

Australian Youth Research Centre
Education Faculty Office
The University of Melbourne
Victoria 3010
Australia
Tel: 61-3-8344-8285
Fax: 61-3-8344-8529
E-mail: education-enquiries@unimelb.edu.au

The Australian Youth Research Center is located in the Department of Educational Policy and Management, Faculty of Education, at the University of Melbourne. It was established in 1988 in response to a recognized need by the youth affairs sector for relevant and up-to-date research on the issues facing young people today.

Board on Children, Youth, and Families, the National Academies
The National Academies
500 5th Street, NW
Washington, DC 20001
Tel: 202-334-1935
Fax: 202-334-3584
E-mail: bocyf@nas.edu

The Board on Children, Youth, and Families (BCYF) brings the multidisciplinary knowledge and analytic tools of the behavioral, health, and social sciences to bear on the development of policies, programs, and services for children, youth, and families.

Campaign for Young Voters
111 5th Avenue
New York, NY 10001
Tel: 312-260-4778
Fax: 312-260-4779

A program of the Center for Democracy and Citizenship at the Council for Excellence in Government, the campaign has produced a free online toolkit to guide candidates on reaching out to young voters.

Campus Compact
Brown University
Box 1975
Providence, RI 02912

Tel: 401-867-3950
E-mail: campus@compact.org

The Campus Compact provides information and resources on civic engagement and service learning in higher education. It also offers activism resources for students.

Carmel Institute for Social Studies

5 Kadesh Street
PO Box 97
30900 Zichron Ya'akov
Israel
Tel: 972-4-6396818
Fax: 972-4-6397085
E-mail: carmel@carmelinstitute.org.il

Independent, interdisciplinary institution dedicated to research, policy design, and advocacy on societal and national issues.

Carnegie Foundation for the Advancement of Teaching

51 Vista Lane
Stanford, CA 94305
Tel: 650-566-5100
Fax: 650-326-0278

The foundation is a major center for research and policy studies about teaching.

Center for Child and Youth Policy, University of California–Berkeley

16 Haviland Hall
Berkeley, CA 94720-7400
Tel: 510-643-7026
Fax: 510-642-1895
Web site: http://www.ccyp.berkeley.edu

The center conducts a variety of activities all of which focus on interdisciplinary child and youth policy research and dissemination.

Center for Civic Education

5145 Douglas Fir Road
Calabasas, CA 91302-1440
Tel: 818-591-9321
Fax: 818-591-9330
E-mail: cce@civiced.org

The center offers civic education curriculum at both the high-school and middle-school levels. Visit its We the People program site for more information.

Center for Communication and Civic Engagement, University of Washington

Department of Communication, Rm. 125
Box 353740
Seattle, WA 98195
Tel: 206-685-1504
E-mail: ccce@u.washington.edu

The Center for Communication and Civic Engagement is dedicated to research, the creation of citizen resources, and student-designed learning experiences that develop new areas of positive citizen involvement in politics and social life. The primary focus is to understand how new information technologies can supplement more traditional forms of communication to facilitate civic engagement.

Center for Democracy and Citizenship

Humphrey Institute of Public Affairs
301 19th Ave. South
Minneapolis, MN 55455
Tel: 612-625-0142
Fax: 612-625-3513
E-mail: ajadin@hhh.umn.edu

Based at the Council for Excellence in Government, the center identifies and implements ways to improve the performance of America's representative democracy.

Center for Information and Research on Civic Learning and Engagement (CIRCLE)

University of Maryland
School of Public Policy
College Park, MD 20742
Tel: 301-405-2790

CIRCLE promotes research on the civic and political engagement of Americans between the ages of fifteen and twenty-five. Although CIRCLE conducts and funds research, not practice, the projects that it supports have practical implications for those who work to increase young people's engagement in politics and civic life. CIRCLE is also a clearinghouse for relevant information and scholarship.

Center for Liberal Education and Civic Engagement

Association of American Colleges and Universities
1818 R Street, NW
Washington, DC 20009
Tel: 202-387-3760

The center is a partnership between the Association of American Colleges and Universities (AAC&U), the foremost leader of liberal education, and Campus Compact, the nationally known organization promoting service learning. Acting as a catalyst and incubator of new ideas, campus-based innovations, research, and collaborations, the center seeks to deepen understandings of the relation of liberal education to service and civic responsibilities. In so doing, the center links this new understanding to actions that address complex, urgent social problems.

Center for Social Development, Washington University
Campus Box 11961
Brookings Drive
St. Louis, MO 63130-4899
Tel: 314-935-7433
Fax: 314-935-8661
E-mail: csd@gwbmail.wustl.edu
This research center within the GWB School of Social Work at Washington University focuses on social-development issues, defined as the developing and building capacities of individuals, families, and communities.

Center for Social Justice Research, Teaching, and Service, Georgetown University
Poulton Hall, Suite 130
1421 37th Street, NW
Washington, DC 20057
Tel: 202-687-5330
Fax: 202-687-8980
E-mail: csj@georgetown.edu
In order to advance justice and the common good the center promotes and integrates community-based research, teaching, and service by collaborating with diverse partners and communities.

The Center for Youth and Communities (CYC), Brandeis University
Heller School for Social Policy and Management
60 Turner Street
Waltham, MA 02453
Tel: 781-736-3770
Fax: 781-736-3773
E-mail: cyc@brandeis.edu
Since its inception in 1983, the center has established a national reputation as one of the nation's leading research centers and professional development and policy organizations in youth and community development. CYC is part of the Heller School for Social Policy and Management at Brandeis University.

The Center for Youth as Resources
1000 Connecticut Avenue, NW, Suite 1300
Washington, DC 20036
Tel: 202-261-4131
E-mail: yar@cyar.org
The center is the umbrella organization for Youth as Resources (YAR) programs. YARs are governed by boards composed of youth and adults and provide grants for youth-initiated, youth-led community projects.

The Center on Congress at Indiana University– Civic Participation E-Learning Module
SPEA 320
Bloomington, IN 47405
Tel: 812-856-4706
Fax: 812-856-4703
E-mail: congress@indiana.edu
http://congress.indiana.edu
The center has produced a series of interactive e-learning activities designed to enhance high-school and college civics curricula, as well as be of interest to the general public.

Centre for Children and Young People (CCYP), Southern Cross University
B Block
PO Box 157, Lismore, NSW 2480
New South Wales, Australia
Tel: 02-66203613
Fax: 02-66221833
E-mail: ccyp@scu.edu.au
The center was established at Southern Cross University to provide an interdisciplinary approach to research, education, and advocacy linked to children and young people.

Changemakers
188/3/1A Prince Anwar Shah Rd.
Calcutta 700045
India
Tel: 91-33-2483-8031 or 91-33-2417-2587
This initiative of Ashoka: Innovators for the Public provides inspiration, resources, and opportunities for those interested in social change throughout the world.

Chapin Hall Center for Children, The University of Chicago
1313 East 60th Street
Chicago, IL 60637
Tel: 773-753-5900
Fax: 773-753-5940
Building knowledge to serve children is the mission of the center. Located at the University of Chicago, Chapin Hall is a research and development center that brings the highest standards of scholarship and the intellectual resources of one of the world's great research universities to the real-world challenges of policymakers and service providers struggling to ensure that children grow, thrive, and take their place in a formidable world.

Children, Youth and Environments (CYE)
University of Colorado
Campus Box 314
Boulder, CO 80309-0314
Tel: 303-492-1319
Fax: 303-492-6163
CYE is a refereed journal and multidisciplinary, international network dedicated to improving the lives of young people. The journal targets

researchers, policymakers, and professionals and is guided by a distinguished editorial advisory board.

Childwatch International Research Network
Childwatch International
PO Box 1132
Blindern, N-0317
Oslo
Norway
Tel: 47-22-85-43-50
Fax: 47-22-85-50-28
E-mail: childwatch@uio.no
Childwatch International is a nonprofit, nongovernmental network of institutions engaged in research for children. The network seeks to strengthen child-centered research to contribute to real improvement in children's well-being.

Civic Practices Network (CPN)
Center for Human Resources
Heller School for Advanced Studies in Social Welfare
Brandeis University
60 Turner Street
Waltham, MA 02154
Tel: 617-736-4890
Fax: 617-736-4891
E-mail: cpn@cpn.org
CPN is a collaborative and nonpartisan project bringing together a diverse array of organizations to bring practical methods for public problem solving into every community.

Constitutional Rights Foundation
601 South Kingsley Dr.
Los Angeles, CA 90005
Tel: 213-487-5590
Fax: 213-386-0459
The foundation seeks to instill in our nation's youth a deeper understanding of citizenship through values expressed in our Constitution and its Bill of Rights and educate them to become active and responsible participants in our society. Its Web site includes online lesson plans, teaching resources, and a service-learning minigrant competition.

Data Center/Impact Research for Social Justice
1904 Franklin St., Ste. 900
Oakland, CA 94612-2912
Tel: 510-835-4692 or 800-735-3741
Fax: 510-835-3017
E-mail: datacenter@datacenter.org
The center's mission is to provide social justice advocates, especially for the poor and people of color, access to strategic information, analysis, and research skills that will help them conduct more effective campaigns.

Declare Yourself
http://www.declareyourself.com
A one-year nonpartisan campaign committed to registering and empowering young voters.

Do Something
24–32 Union Square East, 4th Floor South
New York, NY 10003
http://www.dosomething.org
This organization helps youth get involved in their communities and has a special educator Web site.

The Eagleton Institute's Civic Engagement and Political Participation Program
Eagleton Institute of Politics
Rutgers, The State University of New Jersey
191 Ryders Lane
New Brunswick, NJ 08901-8557
Tel: 732-932-9384
Fax: 732-932-6778
The program oversees several projects aimed at increasing voter turnout, political participation, and Americans' involvement in civic life.

Economic and Social Research Council (ESRC)
Polaris House
North Star Avenue
Swindon SN2 1UJ
United Kingdom
Tel: 01-793-413000
Fax: 01-793-413001
The Economic and Social Research Council is the United Kingdom's leading research funding and training agency addressing economic and social concerns.

European Centre for Social Welfare Policy and Research
Berggasse 17
A–1090 Vienna
Austria
Tel: 43-1-319-4505-0
Fax: 43-1-319-4505-19
E-mail: ec@euro.centre.org
The European Centre is an international center for social research, policy, information, and training. It is an intergovernmental organization focused on social welfare, affiliated with the United Nations.

Forum for Youth Investment
The Cady-Lee House
7064 Eastern Avenue, NW

Washington, DC 20012
Tel: 202-207-3333
Fax: 202-207-3329
E-mail: youth@forumforyouthinvestment.org
This forum works to increase the quality and quantity of youth investment and youth involvement by building connections, increasing capacity, and tackling persistent challenges across the allied youth fields.

Freedom's Answer
1233 20th Street, NW, 206
Washington DC 20036
A movement led by high school students to encourage voting.

Global Program on Youth, University of Michigan
School of Social Work, Room 4728
1080 South University
Ann Arbor, MI 48109-1106
Tel: 734-764-5347
Fax: 734-764-9954
E-mail: ssw.global@umich.edu
The Global Program on Youth is establishing broad-based groups of scholars, policymakers, and service providers who are working together to address critical and timely issues related to children and youth. This innovative program is addressing the translation from research to practice in an effort to make research more accessible and applicable to policymakers and practitioners.

Highlander Research and Education Center
1959 Highlander Way
New Market, TN 37820
Tel: 865-933-3443
Fax: 865-933-3424
E-mail: hrec@highlandercenter.org
The Highlander center is a residential popular education and research organization. It sponsors educational programs and research into community problems, as well as a residential workshop center for social-change organizations and workers active in the South and internationally. Generations of activists have come to Highlander to learn, teach, and prepare to participate in struggles for justice. The center runs the Young and the Restless program and the Children's Justice Camp in addition to its adult programs.

Hip-Hop Summit Action Network
E-mail: info@hsan.org
The network is dedicated to engaging the hip-hop community in community development and sponsors hip-hop summits around the country.

Innovation Center for Community and Youth Development
6930 Carroll Avenue
Suite 502
Takoma Park, MD 20912
Tel: 301-270-1700
Fax: 301-270-5900
E-mail: info@theinnovationcenter.org
The center connects thinkers and leaders of all ages to develop fresh ideas, forge new partnerships, and design strategies that engage young people and their communities.

Innovations in Civic Participation (ICP)
1776 Massachusetts Avenue, NW, Suite 201
Washington, DC 20036
Tel: 202-775-0290
Fax: 202-833-8581
Founded in 2001, ICP is a nonprofit social change organization that provides expertise, ideas, information, research, and advocacy support in the United States and around the world to develop and strengthen policies and programs that promote civic engagement through service.

The Institute for Community Research (ICR)
Two Hartford Square West, Suite 100
Hartford, CT 06106-5128
Tel: 860-278-2044
Fax 860-278-2141
E-mail: info@icrweb.org
ICR uses the tools of research to build community capacity and foster collaborative community-based partnerships. By gathering information in partnership with residents, we are helping communities locally and globally to ask better questions and get better answers about the complex problems they face.

Institute for Volunteering Research
Regent's Wharf
8 All Saints Street
London N1 9RL
United Kingdom
Tel: 44-0-20-7520-8900
Fax: 44-0-20-7520-8910
E-mail: instvolres@aol.com
This initiative of Volunteering England and the Centre for Institutional Studies at the University of East London develops knowledge and understanding of volunteering with particular relevance to policy and practice. It produces the journal Voluntary Action.

International Consortium for Higher Education, Civic Responsibility and Democracy
221 Stiteler Hall
208 S. 37th Street

Philadelphia, PA 19104-6215
E-mail: fplantan@sas.upenn.edu
http://www.upenn.edu/ccp/programs/
consortium/index.shtml

The consortium has a page of online resources for civic education.

International Institute for Child Rights and Development (IICRD), University of Victoria
Centre for Global Studies
PO Box 1700
Victoria, BC
V8V 2Y2
Canada
Tel: 250-472-4762
Fax: 250-472-4830
E-mail: iicrd@uvic.ca

The institute works in partnership with a multi-disciplinary team of academics, frontline workers, community members, policymakers, and professionals from universities, professional associations, NGOs, government agencies, and UN organizations.

International Sociological Association (ISA), Research Committee on Sociology of Youth, RC 34
Web site for newsletter: http://www.alli.fi/
youth/research/ibyr/index.htm

The aim of RC 34 is to contribute to the development of theory and practice of youth sociology and youth research on an international level, uniting the professional knowledge, scientific consciousness, and social commitment of its members to work on problems and issues of youth on a local, regional, and international level.

John W. Gardner Center for Youth and Their Communities, Stanford University
School of Education
CERAS Building, 4th Floor
520 Galvez Mall
Stanford, CA 94305-3084
Tel: 650-723-1137
Fax: 650-736-2296
E-mail: gardnercenter@lists.stanford.edu

The key strategies employed by the center are bridging research and practice, supporting community action, and sharing what works.

Kids Voting USA (KVUSA)
Superstition Office Plaza
3933 South McClintock Drive
Suite 505
Tempe, AZ 85282
Tel: 480-921-3727 or 1-866-500-VOTE (toll-free)

Fax: 480-921-4008
E-mail: kidsvotingusa@kidsvotingusa.org

KVUSA works with schools and communities to enhance civics education and provide youth with an authentic voting experience. Participating students visit official polling sites on Election Day and cast ballots similar in content to the official ballot.

LISTEN, Inc.
413 A Eighth Street SE
Washington, DC 20003
Tel: 202-544-5520
Fax: 202-544-5992

This group identifies, convenes, trains, and supports urban youth aged fourteen to twenty-nine to serve as assets in transforming their communities and solving urban problems.

Moving Ideas Network
2000 L Street, NW
Suite 717
Washington, DC 20036
Tel: 202-776-0730
Fax: 202-776-0740
E-mail: movingideas@movingideas.org

A project of the American Prospect, this network is dedicated to explaining and popularizing complex policy ideas with a broader audience.

MTV's Choose or Lose Campaign
http://www.mtv.com/chooseorlose

This campaign provides online voter registration, information on candidates, and youth issues polls.

National Alliance for Civic Education (NACE)
Institute for Philosophy and Public Policy
Maryland School of Public Affairs
3111 Van Munching
College Park, MD 20742

The alliance is a network of about 150 people and organizations dedicated to promoting civic education.

National Center for Learning and Citizenship
700 Broadway, Suite 1200
Denver, CO 80203-3460
Tel: 303-299-3606
Fax: 303-296-8332
E-mail: arautio@ecs.org

The center works on several interrelated fronts: leadership and service learning, citizenship and civic education, and policy. It provides resources to help teachers, administrators, policymakers, and leaders use and promote service learning and citizenship education.

National Council of La Raza-Center for Emerging Latino Leadership
Raul Yzaguirre Building
1126 16th Street, NW
Washington, DC 20036
Tel: 202-785-1670

The center is designed to increase the number, skills, and influence of young Latino leaders in the United States by building a national network that supports and strengthens programs and organizations that develop Latino youth.

National 4-H Council
7100 Connecticut Avenue
Chevy Chase, MD 20815
Tel: 301-961-2800

The council provides grants, establishes programs/initiatives, designs and publishes curriculum and reference materials, and creates linkages fostering innovation and shared learning to advance the 4-H youth development movement, building a world in which youth and adults learn, grow, and work together as catalysts for positive change.

New Millennium Young Voters Project
National Association of Secretaries of State
Hall of the States
444 N. Capitol Street, NW, Suite 401
Washington, DC 20001
Tel: 202-624-3525

A national youth voter campaign by the National Association of Secretaries of State designed to encourage political and civic participation in young people aged eighteen to twenty-four.

Nordic Youth Research Information (NYRI)
E-mail: NYRI@alli.fi

NYRI is the general organization of a range of networking activities and information systems for youth research in the Nordic countries (Denmark, Finland, Iceland, Norway, and Sweden).

Observatory of Youth and Society
490, rue de la Couronne, 6e étage
Quebec G1K 9A9
Canada
Tel: 418-687-6429
Fax: 418-687-6425
Web site: http://www.obsjeunes.qc.ca/default.asp?p=ANGL (mostly in French, with some information in English and Spanish, http://www.obsjeunes.qc.ca).

The Observatory of Youth and Society, based at the University of Quebec, collects and analyzes information on young people and distributes the results.

Partnership for Trust in Government
Council for Excellence in Government
1301 K Street, NW, Suite 450 West
Washington, DC 20005
Tel: 202-728-0418
Fax: 202-728-0422
E-mail: partners@excelgov.org

A project of the Council for Excellence in Government and the Ford Foundation, the partnership is a diverse alliance of nongovernmental organizations working to improve and sustain government's place in the understanding and esteem of the American people.

Rock the Vote
RTV LA
10635 Santa Monica Blvd., Suite 150
Los Angeles, CA 90025
Tel: 310-234-0665
Fax: 310-234-0666

RTV DC
1313 L Street, NW, 1st Fl.
Washington, DC 20005
Tel: 202-962-9710
Fax: 202-962-9715

Rock the Vote engages youth in the political process by incorporating the entertainment community and youth culture into its activities.

Search Institute
The Banks Building
615 First Avenue NE, Suite 125
Minneapolis, MN 55413
Tel: 612-376-8955 or 800-888-7828 (toll-free)

The institute provides leadership, knowledge, and resources to promote healthy children, youth, and communities.

Social Policy Research Associates (SPR)
1330 Broadway, Suite 1426
Oakland, CA 94612
Tel: 510-763-1499
Fax: 510-763-1599

Founded in 1991, SPR is a nationally recognized research, evaluation, and technical assistance firm located in Oakland, California. The firm specializes in providing rigorous and responsive services related to employment assistance, job training, education, youth programs, and comprehensive social services.

Society for Research on Adolescence (SRA)
3131 South State Street, Suite 302
Ann Arbor, MI 48108-1623
Tel: 734-998-6567
Fax: 734-998-9586
E-mail: socresadol@umich.edu

SRA is a dynamic, multidisciplinary, international organization dedicated to understanding adolescence through research and its dissemination.

Stanford Center on Adolescence, Stanford University
Cypress Hall C
Stanford, CA 94305-4145
Tel: 650-725-8205
Fax: 650-725-8207
E-mail: taru@stanford.edu

Third Millennium Foundation Harvard Research Project
650 Madison Avenue, 18th Floor
New York, NY 10022
Tel: 212-421-5244
Fax: 212-421-5243
E-mail: tmf.usa@verizon.net

The aim of the Harvard Research Consortium is to strengthen common themes. One common goal is to study the linkages between cultural forms of tolerance and prejudice that are experienced by children and youth growing up and the forms of positive or negative orientations to others that develop later in life.

Trust for the Study of Adolescence (TSA), Ltd.
23 New Road
Brighton BN1 1WZ
E. Sussex
United Kingdom
Tel: 44-0-1273-693311
Fax: 44-0-1273-679907
E-mail: info@tsa.uk.com

TSA was founded in 1989 to help improve the lives of young people and families. TSA's work is derived from the belief that there is a lack of knowledge and understanding about adolescence and young adulthood.

What Kids Can Do Inc.
PO Box 603252
Providence, RI 02906
Tel: 401-247-7665
E-mail: info@whatkidscando.org

This group offers a feature, Kids on the Trail, with writings and essays by youth active in politics, along with resources on voting and activism for youth. It provides examples of how young people have worked with adults on projects that combine powerful learning with public purpose.

YMCA Civic Engagement Initiative
Spencer Bonnie, IMPACTPLUS project coordinator/director of civic engagement

YMCA of the USA
235 North Jefferson St.
Green Bay, WI 54301-5181
Tel: 800-872-9622, ext. 3836; 312-419-3836 (direct)
Fax: 920-436-9663
E-mail: spencer.bonnie@ymca.net

This initiative promotes the development of civic-engagement attitudes, skills, and behaviors in young people.

Youth Action Research Group (YARG)
Center for Social Justice Research, Teaching, and Service
Georgetown University
Poulton Hall, Suite 130
1421 37th Street, NW
Washington, DC 20057
Tel: 202-687-5330
Fax: 202-687-8980
E-mail: csj@georgetown.edu

YARG involves community residents in defining, researching, and critically analyzing the challenges facing their neighborhoods. The young people in YARG learn participatory action research (PAR) methods and ethnographic techniques to better understand their surrounding communities for the purpose of addressing pressing social issues.

Youth Action Research Institute (YARI)
The Institute for Community Research
2 Hartford Square West, Suite 100
Hartford, CT 06106-5128
Tel: 860-278-2044
Fax: 860-278-2141
E-mail: info@icrweb.org

YARI (formerly the National Teen Action Research Center) of the Institute for Community Research was formed in 1996 based on nearly a decade of work on youth-led action research for development, risk prevention, and social change. YARI promotes the use of action research for personal, group, and community development. Participants include children, preadolescents, and youth of diverse ethnic backgrounds as well as sexual minority youth.

Youth in Focus
Melissa Chabran, Public Education Improvement Initiative
Tel: 510-251-9800, ext. 304
Fax: 510-251-9810
E-mail: melissa@youthinfocus.net

Central Valley Office
1930 East 8th Street, #300
Davis, CA 95616

Tel: 530-758-3688

Since 1990 Youth in Focus has developed and field-tested youth REP (youth-led action research, evaluation, and planning), a powerful technique for bringing young people's energy and information to bear upon social and organizational challenges.

Youth Noise
2000 M Street, NW, Suite 500
Washington, DC 20036

The Web site www.youthnoise.com links young people around the country with news and nonprofit partners to spark youth action and youth voice.

Youth on Board
58 Day Street
Somerville, MA 02144
Tel: 617-623-9900, ext. 1242

Fax: 617-623-4359
E-mail: info@youthonboard.org

Youth on Board strives to revolutionize the role of young people in society by preparing youth to be leaders and decision-makers in all aspects of their lives and ensuring that policies, practices, and laws reflect young people's role as full and valued members of their communities.

Youth Service America
1101 15th St., Ste. 200
Washington, DC 20005
Tel: 202-296-2992
Fax: 202-296-4030

This resource center partners with thousands of organizations committed to increasing the quality and quantity of volunteer opportunities for young people in America. It also sponsors a database of volunteer opportunities at http://www.servenet.org.

Bibliography

Books and Articles

Barber, B. K. (2005). *One Heart, So Many Stories: The Story of the Palestinian Youth.* New York: Palgrave.

———, ed. (2005). *Adolescents and War: How Youth Deal with Political Violence.* New York: Oxford University Press.

Bell, B., Gaventa, J., and Peters, J. (1990). *We Make the Road by Walking: Conversations on Education and Social Change, Myles Horton and Paulo Freire.* Philadelphia: Temple University Press.

Deroche, E. F., and Williams, M. W. (1998). *Educating Hearts and Minds: A Comprehensive Character Education Framework.* Thousand Oaks, CA: Corwin Press.

Downs, J., and Manion, J., eds. (2004). *Taking Back the Academy! History of Activism, History as Activism.* New York: Routledge.

Eisenstadt, S. N. (1956, 2002). *From Generation to Generation.* 2nd ed. New Brunswick, NJ: Transaction Books.

Erikson, E. H. (1968). *Identity: Youth and Crisis.* New York: W. W. Norton.

Everatt, D. (2002). "From Urban Warrior to Market Segment? Youth in SA 1990–2000 in Development Update." *Quarterly Journal of South African National NGO Coalition and INTERFUND: The Dead Decade? Youth in Post-Apartheid South Africa,* 3 (2): 1–39.

Flanagan, C. A. (2004). "Volunteerism, Leadership, Political Socialization, and Civic Engagement." In *Handbook of Adolescent Psychology,* edited by R. M. Lerner and L. Steinberg. New York: Wiley, pp. 721–746.

Gitlin, T. (2003). *Letters to a Young Activist.* New York: Basic Books.

Keniston, K. (1968). *Young Radicals: Notes on Committed Youth.* New York: Harcourt, Brace, and World.

McAdam, D. (1988). *Freedom Summer.* New York: Oxford University Press.

Miller, J. (1987). *"Democracy Is in the Streets": From Port Huron to the Siege of Chicago.* New York: Simon and Schuster.

Sherrod, L., Flanagan, C., and Youniss, J., eds. (2002). "Dimensions of Citizenship and Opportunities for Youth Development: The What, Why, When, Where and Who of Citizenship Development." *Applied Developmental Science,* 6 (4): 1–14.

Urban, H. (2003). *Life's Greatest Lessons: Twenty Things That Matter.* New York: Fireside Press.

Welton, N., and Wolf, L. (2001). *Global Uprising: Confronting the Tyrannies of the Twenty-first Century.* Gabriola Island, British Columbia, Canada: New Society Publishers.

Relevant Web Sites

Advocates for Youth
http://www.advocatesforyouth.org/about/index.htm
Dedicated to helping young adults make informed decisions regarding sexual health.

Afterschool
http://afterschool.gov
Provides information about federal resources that are available to agencies running afterschool programs.

America's Promise
http://www.americaspromise.org/
   A collaborative network that aims to provide community support for children based upon five fundamental promises: caring adults, safe places, a healthy (nutritious) start, marketable skills, and opportunities to serve.

American Civil Liberties Union
http://www.aclu.org
   Dedicated to preserving the rights guaranteed to America's citizens in the Constitution and to extending these rights to segments of the population who have traditionally been excluded.

American Political Science Association
http://www.apsanet.org/CENnet/
   Offers resources for teaching civic engagement and responsive government, including links to online political science textbooks, core history documents, and teaching resources such as college-level service-learning syllabuses.

Amnesty International
http://www.amnesty.org
   A worldwide movement of individuals who campaign for international human rights.

Better Together
http://www.bettertogether.org/
   A program, initially an initiative of the Saguaro Seminar: Civic Engagement in America at Harvard University, calling for a national effort to cease civic apathy.

Bread for the World
http://www.bread.org/
   A Christian citizens' movement dedicated to feeding poorer people by lobbying the nation's policymakers.

Carnegie Corporation
http://www.carnegie.org/
   A program aimed at the advancement of knowledge in four main areas: education, international peace and security, international development, and strengthening U.S. democracy.

Check Your Head (CYH)
http://www.checkyourhead.org/
   A youth-driven organization located in Vancouver, educating young people on global issues by looking at the connection between global events and issues and local realities.

Children, Youth, and Families Education and Research Network
http://www.cyfernet.org/
   Provides comprehensive information on children, family, and youth from all of the public land-grant universities in the country with a Web site offering many resources, including tools for working with children, family, and youth, providing resources and information for program evaluation, and helping people locate experts on the aforementioned groups.

Citizenship Foundation
http://www.citizenshipfoundation.org.uk/main/page.php?6
   Aims to empower individuals to engage in the wider community through education about the law, democracy, and society, focusing particularly on developing young people's citizenship skills, knowledge, and understanding.

Democracy Matters
http://www.democracymatters.org/
   A collaborative and nonpartisan network whose aim is to bring tools for public problem solving into institutional and community settings across the country, providing case studies, training manuals, and evaluative tools to educate people on public work.

Do Something
http://www.dosomething.org/
   A program whose founding mission was to make service common and appealing for American youth, accomplishing this by providing community building, health, and environmental

programs, having specially trained and recruited certified educators, and honoring young people through their BRICK awards honors.

e.thePeople
http://www.e-thepeople.org/
   A public forum for discussion about democracy and politics, hosting discussions and conducting surveys to open up dialogue, and aiming to use the Internet as a means of increasing civic participation.

Educators for Social Responsibility (ESR)
http://www.esrnational.org
   An educational advocacy group that promotes education for social engagement and responsibility with a Web site offering many resources, most notably information on the Resolving Conflict Creatively Program, a comprehensive school-reform model for promoting character and reducing violence, as well as many excellent publications.

Fabulous Independent Educated Radicals for Community Empowerment (FIERCE)
http://www.fiercenyc.org/
   Dedicated to providing support and strength to Transgender, Lesbian, Gay, Bisexual, Two Spirit, Queer, and Questioning (TLGBTSQQ) youth of color in New York City, fighting institutions that promote bias through activism, political education, and leadership development.

Facing History and Ourselves
http://www.facing.org/facing/fhao2.nsf
   Begun as a high-school social studies curriculum on the Nazi holocaust but now evolved into a broader set of curricula on genocide and hatred.

Family and Youth Resiliency
http://resiliency.cas.psu.edu/
   Provides resources for professionals on family and youth resiliency and useful information for parents regarding these issues.

First Amendment Center
http://www.firstamendmentcenter.org
   A program of the Gannett Corporation's Freedom Forum, sponsoring the First Amendment Schools program.

Free the Children
http://www.freethechildren.org
   An international network of children helping children at a local, national, and international level through representation, leadership, and action with a primary goal to not only free children from poverty and exploitation but to also free children and young people from the idea that they are powerless to bring about positive social change and to improve the lives of their peers; this organization by, of, and for children fully embodies the notion that children and young people themselves can be leaders of today in creating a more just, equitable, and sustainable world.

Freechild Project
http://www.freechild.org/
   Promotes social change among young people around the world by connecting with organizations that support these individuals.

Freedom's Answer
http://www.freedomsanswer.org/
   A voter turnout program, led by the nation's youth, which seeks to gain pledges for the servicemen stationed overseas.

Global Kids
http://www.globalkids.org/
   An organization that prepares urban youth to become global citizens and community leaders with methods including leadership development, peer education, and teacher training.

Global Youth Action Network (GYAN)
http://www.youthlink.org

One of the largest networks of youth organizations in the world, focused on networking and democracy.

Grassroots Innovative Policy Program (GRIPP)
http://www.arc.org/gripp/index.html
Works with communities to obtain local policy change in writing through GRIPP's eight nationwide groups that provide training, research, and support to bring about social change.

Hazen Foundation
http://www.hazenfoundation.org/
Seeks to assist young people, particularly those belonging to minority groups or who are disadvantaged, to achieve their potential and become active participants in society.

Homies Unidos
http://www.homiesunidos.org/
A nonprofit gang violence prevention and intervention organization with projects in San Salvador, El Salvador, and Los Angeles, California; founded in 1996 in San Salvador, the organization formally began organizing in the United States in 1997.

Human Rights for Workers (HRFW)
http://www.senser.com/
Focuses on how globalization affects working men and women and on how it creates the need to incorporate the human rights of workers into global rules and practices at the national, regional, and international levels through governmental, quasi-governmental, private business, labor union, and other nongovernmental channels with a Web site replete with links to groups that address this agenda.

Institute for Applied Research in Youth Development
http://ase.tufts.edu/adsi/
Promotes positive development among children through research projects, outreach programs, scholarly resources, practitioner tools, and collaborative connections.

Inter-American Foundation
http://www.iaf.gov/
Provides grants to community-based organizations in Latin America and the Caribbean for innovative, sustainable, and participatory self-help programs.

International Council for National Youth Policy (ICNYP)
http://www.icnyp.net
Seeks to follow up the World Conference of Ministers Responsible for Youth in Lisbon, Portugal, by bringing together representatives of governmental ministries responsible for youth from all UN member-states and of world and regional nongovernmental youth organizations in a biennial International Conference on National Youth Policy.

International Labor Rights Fund (ILRF)
http://www.laborrights.org/
An advocacy organization dedicated to achieving just and humane treatment for workers worldwide, serving a unique role among human-rights organizations as advocates for and with working poor around the world; ILRF believes that all workers have the right to a safe working environment where they are treated with dignity and respect and where they can organize freely to defend and promote their rights and interests.

International Sociological Association
http://www.ucm.es/info/isa/
See Research Committee 34 "Sociology of Youth"

Journal of Youth Studies
http://www.tandf.co.uk/journals/titles/13676261.asp
An international scholarly journal devoted to a theoretical and empirical understanding of young people's experiences and life contexts.

Kids as Self-Advocates (KASA)
http://www.fvkasa.org/
A national grassroots network of children that seeks to increase their peers' knowledge of a variety of topics, including education, employment, and health-care issues.

Learn and Serve
http://www.learnandserve.org/
Supports service-learning programs nationwide that help children meet community needs while they improve their academics and learn to become good citizens.

Maquila Solidarity Network (MSN)
http://www.maquilasolidarity.org/
A Canadian network promoting solidarity with groups in Mexico, Central America, Africa, and Asia.

National Center for Learning and Citizenship (NCLC) at the Education Commission of the States (ECS)
http://www.ecs.org/nclc
Providing information about service learning and citizen education and organizing meetings to share information about effective service learning and use of school volunteers.

National Civic League
http://www.ncl.org/
A nonprofit, nonpartisan membership organization dedicated to strengthening citizen democracy, fostering political reform, and bringing together all sectors of society to build a successful democracy.

National Coalition for Promoting Physical Activity
http://www.ncppa.org/
Consists of a national group of organizations, including the American Cancer Society, the American Heart Association, and the YMCA of the USA, that aim to inspire Americans to lead more active lifestyles.

National Youth Development Information Center
http://www.nydic.org/nydic/
A Web site designed for youth workers with a variety of interests, including funding, programming, and research.

National Youth and Student Peace Coalition (NYSPC)
http://www.nyspc.net/
Formed shortly after the tragic events of September 11, 2001, to organize and mobilize the youth and student response to the so-called "war on terror," this broad-based youth and student-led coalition works to build strategic, long-term opposition of youth and students to the war, both at home and abroad.

Organizers' Collaborative
http://www.organizenow.net/index.html
A membership organization for activists and technology consultants that provides social-change groups with easy-to-use technology and needs-specific support.

Pew Partnership
http://www.pew-partnership.org/
A civic-research organization that helps communities, governments, foundations, and non-profit agencies to initiate community-building strategies.

Positive Psychology Center
http://www.positivepsychology.org/
Promotes the research, teaching, and dissemination of positive psychology.

Public Allies
http://www.publicallies.org/
Identifies talented young adults from diverse backgrounds and advances their leadership through a ten-month program of full-time, paid apprenticeships in nonprofit organizations, weekly leadership trainings, and team service projects with the goal of strengthening communities, nonprofits, and civic participation.

Rural School and Community Trust
http://www.ruraledu.org/
Aimed at strengthening the quality of education, community life, and state policies in rural schools and communities.

Search Institute
http://www.search-institute.org
A research organization that has generated the "forty developmental assets" model and has expanded its research agenda to include educational implementation, offering an assessment package and many other resources valuable to character educators with a Web site detailing its theory, programs, and resources.

SERVEnet
http://www.servenet.org/
A service and volunteering Web site that matches users' interests, skills, and locations with nearby organizations; the largest Web site of its kind in the world with over 6,000 registered non-profit organizations, more than 35,000 service projects, and over 52 million volunteer opportunities available.

Society for Research on Adolescence
http://www.s-r-a.org
Aims to promote the understanding of adolescence through research and dissemination and focuses on the theoretical, empirical, and policy research of adolescence.

Society for Research in Child Development
http://www.srcd.org
Promotes multidisciplinary research in human development to foster communication between professionals of various disciplines with current ventures including having the Committee on Ethical Conduct in Child Development, the Committees on Ethnic and Racial Issues, the Policy Fellowship Program in Child Development, and a biennial meeting for researchers and scientists.

Sports 4 Kids
http://www.sports4kids.org/
An organization that works with elementary schools to provide sports programming for children during and after school, emphasizing skill-based, rather than competitive, sports to build children's self-esteem while increasing their body awareness and physical health.

Student Environmental Action Coalition
http://www.seac.org
A grassroots environmental coalition in which thousands of youth have transformed their concerns about the environment into action by, among other things, sharing resources and building allegiances.

Student Global AIDS Campaign (SGAC)
http://www.fightglobalaids.org/
A national movement with more than eighty-five chapters at high schools, colleges, and universities across the United States committed to bringing an end to AIDS in the United States and around the world through education, informed advocacy, media work, and direct action.

Study Circles
http://www.studycircles.org/
Dedicated to creating dialogue among diverse participants on critical social and political issues, providing communities with the resources to organize dialogue, recruit participants, and work for change.

Sweatshop Watch
http://www.sweatshopwatch.org/
A coalition of over thirty labor, community, civil rights, immigrant rights, women's, religious, and student organizations, and many individuals committed to eliminating the exploitation that occurs in sweatshops, serving low-wage workers nationally and globally since its founding in 1995 with a focus on garment workers in California.

TakingITGlobal
http://www.takingitglobal.org
The largest community of youth activism on the Internet.

Teaching Tolerance
http://www.teachingtolerance.org

The educational arm of the Southern Poverty Law Center, promoting tolerance and fighting oppression, hatred, and bigotry, publishing a journal titled Teaching Tolerance, which is distributed free, and disseminating curricula on toleration.

Thai Labour Campaign
http://www.thailabour.org/
A Thai-run nonprofit, nongovernmental organization committed to promoting workers' rights in Thailand and increasing awareness.

Third Wave Foundation
http://www.thirdwavefoundation.org/
Helps to support the leadership of young women by providing resources, education, and relationship-building opportunities.

Tolerance
http://www.tolerance.org/
An online organization dedicated to replacing bigotry with diverse values.

US/LEAP
http://www.usleap.org/
An independent, nonprofit organization that supports economic justice and basic rights for workers in Central America, Colombia, the Dominican Republic, Ecuador, and Mexico, focusing especially on the struggles of workers who are employed directly or indirectly by U.S. companies such as Starbucks (coffee), Chiquita (bananas), and Gap (clothing).

Voices of Youth
http://www.unicef.org/voy
A site collecting contributions from children and young people on issues that are of concern to them.

Wiretap
http://www.alternet.org/wiretap/
An independent Internet information source that emphasizes workable solutions to aggravating problems, publishing grassroots success stories and inspirational narratives alongside critiques of policies, investigative reports, and expert analysis.

YES!
http://www.yesworld.org
A nonprofit organization that connects, inspires, and empowers young change makers to join forces for a thriving, just, and sustainable way of life for all.

Youth Action Net (YAN)
http://www.youthactionnet.org/
A dynamic Web site created by and for young people, spotlighting the vital role that youth play in leading positive change around the world; launched in 2001 by the International Youth Foundation (IYF) and Nokia, YAN serves as a virtual gathering place for young people looking to connect with each other—and with ideas for how to make a difference in their communities.

Youth Action for Peace (YAP)
http://www.yap.org
An international movement that aims for societies of justice, peace, and human solidarity; it struggles against the different forms of violence, exploitation, injustice, and exclusion; against networks of ideological, religious, sexist, political, cultural, and economic oppression and imbalance of natural surroundings; and supports all those, women or men, who want to take their destiny into their own hands so as to organize collectively a responsible and liberating society.

Youth Activism Project
http://www.youthactivism.com/
Encourages youth to participate in finding solutions to problems that they are passionate about; among its goals are training adults on how to collaborate with young people, providing advice, promoting activism in youth, and sharing best practices and resources with nonprofit and government agencies.

Youth Leadership Institute (YLI)
http://www.yli.org/

Building communities where young people and their adult allies come together to create positive social change; designing and implementing community-based programs that provide youth with leadership skills in the areas of drug- and alcohol-abuse prevention, philanthropy, and civic engagement; building on these real-world program experiences, by creating curricula and training programs that enable people to foster social-change efforts across the nation, all while promoting best practices in the field of youth development.

YouthAction
http://www.youthaction.net/

An organization working primarily with minority groups that provides training, events, technical assistance, and networking opportunities to strengthen youth organizing and create change for local communities.

YouthBuild
http://www.youthbuild.org

A national nonprofit organization that works with low-income youth to rebuild their communities and lives by providing them with leadership opportunities, conducting research to find the best practices, and obtaining loans and grants for its affiliates.

YouthNoise
http://www.youthnoise.com/

An international group of youth that works with adults to provide information from more than 300 nonprofit partners that will spark youth action and voice; goals are to inspire, connect, and empower youths worldwide to create positive change.

Index

About the Editors and Contributors

Editors

LONNIE R. SHERROD is Professor of Psychology and Director of the Applied Developmental Psychology Program at Fordham University. He has a long history of research and policy work in youth development, including youth political development.

CONSTANCE A. FLANAGAN is Professor Youth Civic Development, College of Agricultural Sciences at Pennsylvania State University, University Park. She is a pioneer in research on youth civic engagement, including activism.

RON KASSIMIR is Associate Dean of the New School for Social Research and Associate Professor in the Department of Political Science. Until September 2005, Kassimir was a Program Director at the Social Science Research Council where, among other things, he organized a collaborative research network on Youth and Globalization.

AMY K. SYVERTSEN is a PhD student at Penn State University. Her scholarly interests include youth civic development and political activism and peer loyalty and social responsibility.

Contributors

Amy Adamczyk
Wayne State University
Detroit, MI

Wale Adebanwi
University of Cambridge
Cambridge, England,
   United Kingdom

Suzanne E. Agha
The Pennsylvania State
   University
University Park, PA

Myesha Alberts
University of Nebraska–
   Lincoln
Lincoln, NE

Brett Alessi
Innovations in Civic
   Participation
Washington, DC

Philip G. Altbach
Boston College
Chestnut Hill, MA

Jeffrey Jensen Arnett
Journal of Research on
   Adolescence
University Park, MD

Robert Atkins
Temple University
Philadelphia, PA

Gokhan Balaban
Century Foundation
Somerset Home for
   Displaced Youth
John Hopkins University
Baltimore, MD

Jeff Ballinger
McMaster University
Hamilton, Canada

Teo Ballvé
North American Congress
   on Latin America
   (NACLA)
New York, NY

Brian K. Barber
University of Tennessee–
   Knoxville
Knoxville, TN

Jason J. Barr
Monmouth University
West Long Branch,
   New Jersey

Lauren Baskir
Fordham University
Bronx, NY

Melissa Bass
University of Puget Sound
Tacoma, WA

Gordon Bazemore
Florida Atlantic
    University
Fort Lauderdale, FL

Merav Ben-Nun
New York University
New York, NY

Marvin Berkowitz
University of Missouri–
    St. Louis
St. Louis, MO

Shelley Billig
RMC Research Corporation
Denver, CO

Susan Blank
The After-School
    Corporation
New York, NY

Klaus Boehnke
International
    University
Breman, Germany

Kimber Bogard
Fordham University
Bronx, NY

Margaret M. Braungart
SUNY Upstate Medical
    University
Syracuse, NY

Richard G. Braungart
Syracuse University
Syracuse, NY

Eric Braxton
Philadelphia Student Union
Philadelphia, PA

Jeanne Brooks-Gunn
National Center for Children
    and Families
New York, NY

Robert Bussel
Labor Education and
    Research Center
University of Oregon
Eugene, OR

Linda Camino
University of Wisconsin–
    Madison
Madison, WI

Gustavo Carlo
University of Nebraska–
    Lincoln
Lincoln, NE

Elizabeth Cauffman
Western Psychiatric
    Institute and Clinic
University of Pittsburgh
Pittsburgh, PA

John Cecero
Fordham University
Bronx, NY

Lisa Chauveron
JESNA's Berman Center
    for Research and
    Evaluation
New York, NY

Matan Chorev
Tufts University
Medford, MA

Robin L. Clausen
The Pennsylvania State
    University
University Park, PA

Allanise Cloete
Human Sciences Research
    Council
Cape Town,
    South Africa

Cathy J. Cohen
University of
    Chicago
Chicago, IL

Jeremy Cohen
The Pennsylvania State
    University
University Park, PA

Kara-Kaye Colley
Innovations in Civic
    Participation
Washington, DC

James P. Connell
Institute for Research and
    Reform in Education
New York, NY

Catherine Corrigall-Brown
University of California,
    Irvine
Irvine, CA

Roselyn Costantino
The Pennsylvania State
    University
Altoona, PA

Kevin S. Cramer
Corporation for National
    and Community Service
Washington, DC

Mihaly Csikszentmihalyi
Quality of Life Research
    Center
Claremont Graduate
    School
Claremont, CA

Ann Michelle Daniels
South Dakota State
    University
Brookings, SD

Adam Darnell
Georgia State University
Atlanta, GA

Luis Davila
Global Youth Action
    Network
New York, NY

Kalisha Davis
The Forum for Youth
    Investment
Washington, DC

Sion Dayson
Social Science Research
    Council
New York, NY

Maria R. T. de Guzman
University of Nebraska–
    Lincoln
Lincoln, NE

Michael X. Delli Carpini
Annenberg School for
   Communication
University of Pennsylvania
Philadelphia, PA

Adam Desrosiers
Innovations in Civic
   Participation
Washington, DC

Thomas M. Donnelly
Camden College of Arts
   and Sciences
Rutgers University
Camden, NJ

Kate Dube
University of New
   Hampshire
Durham, NH

Argelio Dumenigo
Annenberg Public Policy
   Center
Philadelphia, PA

Jacquelynne Eccles
Institute for Research on
   Women and Gender
University of Michigan
Ann Arbor, MI

Abigail Falik
NetAid
New York, NY

Jessica Fields
San Francisco State
   University
San Francisco, CA

Michelle Fine
The CUNY Graduate Center
New York, NY

Constance A. Flanagan
The Pennsylvania State
   University
University Park, PA

Eric Freedman
University of Wisconsin–
   Madison
Madison, WI

Elizabeth Fussell
Tulane University
New Orleans, LA

Erin Gallay
Earth Force
Ann Arbor, MI

Leslie S. Gallay
The Pennsylvania State
   University
University Park, PA

Lucinda J. Garthwaite
Goddard College
Plainfield, VT

Elizabeth T. Gershoff
National Center for Children
   in Poverty
Columbia University
New York, NY

Melinda D. Gilmore
Kettering Foundation
Dayton, OH

Shawn Ginwright
Santa Clara University
Santa Clara, CA

Marnina Gonick
The Pennsylvania State
   University
University Park, PA

Kristin A. Goss
Duke University
Durham, NC

Julia A. Graber
University of Florida
Gainesville, FL

Gael Graham
Western Carolina
   University
Asheville, NC

Jessica Greenberg
University of Chicago
Chicago, IL

Margaret E. Greene
Population Action
   International
Washington, DC

Meredith J. Greif
The Pennsylvania State
   University
University Park, PA

Robert T. Grimm Jr.
Corporation for National
   and Community Service
Washington, DC

Sue Grundy
University of Edinburgh
Edinburgh, Scotland,
   United Kingdom

Omar Guessous
Georgia State University
Atlanta, GA

John A. Guidry
New York Academy of
   Medicine
New York, NY

Andreas Hadjar
University of Bern
Bern, Switzerland

John M. Hagedorn
University of Illinois at
   Chicago
Chicago, IL

Carole L. Hahn
Emory University
Atlanta, GA

Carmen M. Hamilton
The Pennsylvania State
   University
University Park, PA

Marci Hansen
People for the Ethical
   Treatment of Animals
   (PETA)
Norfolk, VA

Sam Hardy
University of Nebraska–
   Lincoln
Lincoln, NE

Allison Harell
McGill University
Montreal, Canada

Daniel Hart
Camden College of Arts and
 Sciences
Rutgers University
Camden, NJ

Roger A. Hart
Center for Human
 Environments
The CUNY Graduate Center
New York, NY

Kaye Haw
The University of
 Nottingham
Nottingham, England,
 United Kingdom

Kristina Hebner
Mental Health
 Association of
 New York
New York, NY

Donald J. Hernandez
State University of New
 York, Albany
Albany, NY

Sarah M. Hertzog
Applied Developmental
 Science Institute
Tufts University
Medford, MA

Diana Hess
University of Wisconsin–
 Madison
Madison, WI

Ann Higgins-D'Alessandro
Fordham University
Bronx, NY

Kyle Hodges
University of Chicago
Chicago, IL

Grace Hollister
Innovations in Civic
 Participation
Washington, DC

Gary A. Homana
University of Maryland
College Park, MD

Patreese Ingram
The Pennsylvania State
 University
University Park, PA

Merita Irby
The Forum for Youth
 Investment
Washington, DC

Heather M. Jones
The Pennsylvania State
 University
University Park, PA

Kenneth R. Jones
University of Kentucky
Lexington, KY

Jeffrey S. Juris
Annenberg Research
 Network on Globalization
 and Communication
Annenberg School for
 Communication
University of Southern
 California
Los Angeles, CA

Ariel Kalil
University of Chicago
Chicago, IL

Phyllis Kaniss
Annenberg Public Policy
 Center
University of Pennsylvania
Philadelphia, PA

Matthew Kaplan
The Pennsylvania State
 University
University Park, PA

Abby Kiesa
Campus Compact
Brown University
Providence, RI

Pamela Ebstyne King
Fuller Theological Seminary
Pasadena, CA

Adena M. Klem
Institute for Research and
 Reform in Education
New York, NY

Siyka Kovacheva
The Paissii Hilendarski
 University of Plovdiv
Plovdiv, Bulgaria

Reed Larson
University of Illinois
Urbana, IL

Abigail Lawrence-Jacobson
University of Michigan
Ann Arbor, MI

Richard M. Lerner
Tufts University
Medford, MA

David A. Lettero
The Pennsylvania State
 University
University Park, PA

Peter Levine
University of Maryland
College Park, MD

Shenita Lewis
Search Institute
Minneapolis, MN

Heather Lewis-Charp
Social Policy Research
 Associates
Oakland, CA

Jonathan London
Youth in Focus
Davis, CA

Mark Hugo Lopez
Center for Information and
 Research on Civic
 Learning and Engagement
 (CIRCLE)
University of Maryland
College Park, MD

Nancy S. Love
The Pennsylvania State
 University
University Park, PA

Anna M. Malsch
Claremont Graduate
 University
Claremont, CA

Marc Mannes
Search Institute
Minneapolis, MN

Patrick Markey
Villanova University
Villanova, PA

Andrew Martin
The Ohio State University
Columbus, OH

Shanetta Martin
Forum for Youth
    Investment
Washington, DC

Marlene Matarese
Technical Assistance
    Partnership for Child
    and Family Mental
    Health
Washington, DC

David Mathews
Kettering Foundation
Dayton, OH

Michael McDevitt
University of Colorado
Boulder, CO

Jack M. McLeod
University of Wisconsin–
    Madison
Madison, WI

Miller McPherson
University of Arizona
Tucson, AZ and
Duke University
Durham, NC

Edward Metz
The Life Cycle Institute
The Catholic University
    of America
Washington, DC

Michele Micheletti
Stockholm University
Stockholm, Sweden

Jeffery J. Miller
Leading Now Consulting
Denver, CO

Cynthia Miller-Idriss
New York
University
New York, NY

Andrew J. Milson
Baylor University
Waco, TX

Claudia Mincemoyer
The Pennsylvania State
    University
University Park, PA

Justin Robert Misurell
Fordham University
Bronx, NY

Phillip Mizen
University of Warwick
Coventry, England, United
    Kingdom

Anna Muraco
University of Michigan
Ann Arbor, MI

Sophie Naudeau
Tufts University
Medford, MA

Leyla Neyzi
Sabanci University
Istanbul, Turkey

Tsakani Ngomane
Ministry of Agriculture
Limpopo Province, South
    Africa

Olga Nieuwenhuys
Amsterdam Research School
    on Global Issues and
    Development Studies
University of Amsterdam
Amsterdam,
The Netherlands

Pam Nilan
The University of Newcastle
Callaghan, New South
    Wales, Australia

Sandra O'Brien
Florida Gulf Coast
    University
Fort Myers, FL

Elena Omel'chenko
Interdisciplinary Research
    Centre
Ul'ianovsk State University
Ul'ianovsk, Russia

Allen M. Omoto
Claremont Graduate
    University
Claremont, CA

Laura M. Padilla-Walker
University of Nebraska–
    Lincoln
Lincoln, NE

Nansook Park
University of Rhode Island
Kingston, RI

Daniel F. Perkins
The Pennsylvania State
    University
University Park, PA

Christopher Peterson
University of Michigan
Ann Arbor, MI

Michele Peterson-Badali
Ontario Institute for Studies
    in Education
University of Toronto
Toronto, Canada

Deborah Phillips
Georgetown University
Washington, DC

Jean S. Phinney
California State University,
    Los Angeles
Los Angeles, CA

Terry Pickeral
National Center for
    Learning and
    Citizenship
Education Commission
    of the States
Denver, CO

Natalia Pilato
The Pennsylvania State
    University
University Park, PA

Hilary Pilkington
The University of
   Birmingham
Birmingham, England,
   United Kingdom

Karen Pittman
The Forum for Youth
   Investment
Washington, DC

Mica Pollock
Harvard Graduate School of
   Education
Harvard University
Cambridge, MA

Leslie Pope
MTV
New York, NY

Jennifer S. Pratt-Hyatt
Michigan State University
East Lansing, MI

David A. Reingold
Indiana University
Bloomington, IN

Pamela Reynolds
Johns Hopkins
   University
Baltimore, MD

Assata Richards
University of Pittsburgh
Pittsburgh, PA

Scott Richardson
Earth Force
Alexandria, VA

Howard Rodstein
Scarsdale Alternative High
   School
Scarsdale, NY

Jodie Roth
Teachers College
Columbia University
New York, NY

Ian V. Rowe
MTV
New York, NY

Martin D. Ruck
The CUNY Graduate Center
New York, NY

Stephen T. Russell
University of Arizona
Tucson, AZ

Christopher Scheitle
The Pennsylvania State
   University
University Park, PA

Julie A. Scheve
The Pennsylvania State
   University
University Park, PA

Eva Schmitt-Rodermund
Friedrich-Schiller University
   of Jena
Jena, Germany

Isis H. Settles
Michigan State
   University
East Lansing, MI

Dhavan V. Shah
University of Wisconsin–
   Madison
Madison, WI

Robert Sherman
Surdna Foundation
New York, NY

Leickness Chisamu Simbayi
Human Sciences Research
   Council
Cape Town, South Africa

Kathinka Sinha-Kerkhoff
Asian Development
   Research Institute
Ranchi, Jharkhand, India

Carmen Sirianni
Brandeis University
Waltham, MA

Pamela R. Smith
Institute for Children, Youth,
   and Families
Michigan State University
East Lansing, MI

Lynn Smith-Lovin
Duke University
Durham, NC

Sengsouvanh Soukamneuth
Social Policy Research
   Associates
Oakland, CA

Levent Soysal
Kadir Has University
Istanbul, Turkey

Adam G. Stein
Mental Health Association
   of New York
New York, NY

Laurence Steinberg
Temple University
Philadelphia, PA

Jason Steinman
Tufts University
Medford, MA

Dietlind Stolle
McGill University
Montreal, Canada

Susan Stroud
Innovations in Civic
   Participation
Washington, DC

Aarti Subramaniam
University of California,
   Davis
Davis, CA

Amy K. Syvertsen
The Pennsylvania State
   University
University Park, PA

Carl S. Taylor
Institute for Children, Youth,
   and Families
Michigan State University
East Lansing, MI

Marylee C. Taylor
The Pennsylvania State
   University
University Park, PA

Virgil A. Taylor
Institute for Children, Youth,
    and Families
Michigan State University
East Lansing, MI

Janice Templeton
Institute for Research on
    Women and Gender
University of Michigan
Ann Arbor, MI

Joop Theunissen
Division for Social Policy
    and Development (DESA)
United Nations
New York, NY

Peter F. Titzmann
Friedrich-Schiller
University of Jena
Jena, Germany

Joel Tolman
The Forum for Youth
    Investment
Washington, DC

Judith Torney-Purta
University of Maryland
College Park, MD

María Elena Torre
The CUNY
Graduate Center
New York, NY

Eric M. Uslaner
University of Maryland
College Park, MD

Ron Van Cleef
State University of
    New York, Stony Brook
Stony Brook, NY

Justin van Fleet
NetAid
New York, NY

Charlotte van Hees
Division for Social Policy
    and Development (DESA)
United Nations
New York, NY

Joshua L. Vermette
The Pennsylvania State
    University
University Park, PA

Natalia Waechter
Austrian Institute for Youth
    Research
Vienna, Austria

Claire Wallace
Institute for Advanced
    Studies
Vienna, Austria

Roderick J. Watts
Georgia State University
Atlanta, GA

Nicole Webster
The Pennsylvania
University
University Park, PA

Michael Wessells
Randolph-Macon College
Ashland, VA

Rob White
University of Tasmania
Hobart, Tasmania, Australia

Jonah Wittkamper
Global Youth Action Network
New York, NY

Dustin Wood
University of Illinois
Urbana, IL

Ariel Wyckoff
Innovations in Civic
    Participation
Washington, DC

Michael Wyness
University of Northampton
Northampton, England,
    United Kingdom

So-Hyang Yoon
Annenberg School for
    Communication
University of Southern
    California
Los Angeles, CA

James Youniss
The Life Cycle Institute
The Catholic University of
    America
Washington, DC

Hanh Cao Yu
Social Policy Research
    Associates
Oakland, CA

Shepherd Zeldin
University of Wisconsin–
    Madison
Madison, WI